HIDDEN®
Tahiti

HIDDEN®
Tahiti

Robert F. Kay

Ulysses Press®
BERKELEY, CALIFORNIA

Published by:
ULYSSES PRESS
P.O. Box 3440
Berkeley, CA 94703-3440

Library of Congress Catalog Card Number 96-60710

ISBN 1-56975-063-7

Printed in Canada by Best Book Manufacturers

10 9 8 7 6 5 4 3 2

EDITOR: A. Smithee
MANAGING EDITOR: Claire Chun
EDITORIAL ASSOCIATES: Lily Chou, Deema Khorsheed,
    Jennifer Wilkoff
TYPESETTER: Kenya Ratcliff
CARTOGRAPHY: Kelly Babbit, Stellar Cartography,
    (Lawrence, Kansas)
COVER DESIGN: Sara Glaser and Sarah Levin
INDEXER: Sayre Van Young
COVER PHOTOGRAPHY: Front: Douglas Peebles
    Circle and back: Ron Dahlquist
    Back: Rob Kay
    Color insert: Andi Martin
ILLUSTRATOR: Glenn Kim

Distributed in the United States by Publishers
Group West, in Canada by Raincoast Books,
and in Great Britain and Europe by World
Leisure Marketing

To the memory of Rebecca Bruns
and my loyal friends,
Philippe and Rosalie Guesdon, of Papeete

Acknowledgments

There are a number of friends and colleagues who have assisted me in the long and sometimes arduous preparation of *Hidden Tahiti*. First the academics: These include Dr. Mimi Kahn of the Burke Museum (University of Washington); Dick Taylor of Seattle, Washington; and Dr. Yoshi Sinoto of the Bishop Museum in Honolulu, Hawaii. I am most deeply indebted to Dr. Bob Suggs of Alexandria, Virginia—perhaps the foremost expert on the Marquesas Islands—who was always generous with his time and knowledge.

A special thanks goes to Allegra Marshall of Bondi, Australia, who generously provided encouragement and first-class excellent research.

The other folks I would like to acknowledge are Heidi Baumgartner of Papeete, Anne and Michele Condesse of Bora Bora, Butch and Andi Martin of New York City, Claude McCarter and Pascale Siu (both of San Francisco) and Reed Glenn of Boulder, Colorado.

Finally, I would like to acknowledge the assistance offered by Kurt Stewart, interpreter and traveling companion extraordinaire, of Porto, Portugal.

What's Hidden?

At different points throughout this book, you'll find special listings marked with a hidden symbol:

◄ HIDDEN

This means that you have come upon a place off the beaten tourist track, a spot that will carry you a step closer to the local people and natural environment of Tahiti.

The goal of this guide is to lead you beyond the realm of everyday tourist facilities. While we include traditional sightseeing listings and popular attractions, we also offer alternative sights and adventure activities. Instead of filling this guide with reviews of standard hotels and chain restaurants, we concentrate on one-of-a-kind places and locally owned establishments.

Our authors seek out locales that are popular with residents but usually overlooked by visitors. Some are more hidden than others (and are marked accordingly), but all the listings in this book are intended to help you discover the true nature of Tahiti and put you on the path of adventure.

Write to us!

If in your travels you discover a spot that captures the spirit of Tahiti, or if you live in the region and have a favorite place to share, or if you just feel like expressing your views, write to us and we'll pass your note along to the author.

We can't guarantee that the author will add your personal find to the next edition, but if the writer does use the suggestion, we'll acknowledge you in the credits and send you a free autographed copy of the new edition.

ULYSSES PRESS
3286 Adeline Street, Suite 1
Berkeley, CA 94703
E-mail: ulypress@aol.com

You may also contact the author directly. His E-mail address is rkay@htdc.org.

Contents

3 THE LAND AND OUTDOOR ADVENTURES 77

Maps

Special Features

OUTDOOR ADVENTURE SYMBOLS

The following symbols accompany beach and park descriptions throughout the text.

 Swimming

 Snorkeling or Scuba Diving

 Surfing

 Waterskiing

 Windsurfing

Canoeing or Kayaking

Foreword

Tahiti is not easy to describe because there are, in fact, many Tahitis: the ancient Tahiti, still visible in the overgrown ruins which dot the coastal plains and valleys; the historical Tahiti, which emerges in all its sensual brilliance and violence from the journals of Captain Cook and other early voyagers; the modern Tahiti, embodied by bustling, traffic-choked Papeete, deluxe tourist hotels and the dazzling *Heiva* festival, and the Tahiti of the remote quiet "districts," where life goes on as it did nearly 50 years ago.

In this *tour de force*, veteran South Pacific travel author Rob Kay has provided a remarkably comprehensive, objective and utilitarian guide to the many-faceted realities of what must still be considered the world's most alluring island. He does not limit himself to Tahiti or even to the Society Islands alone. Instead, he applies his acute powers of observation and his wealth of background knowledge to guide the more adventuresome tourist far off the beaten pathways of tourism, to the exotic "outer islands" of the Tuamotu, Austral and Gambier archipelagos, and even the still mysterious Marquesas. Rob's coverage of this vast area is truly amazing: for example, few Americans have ever heard of the Mata Iva, a small atoll at the northwest end of the Tuamotu chain. Rob has not only been there, he's seen more of this fascinating spot than I have and gives a very balanced view of its tourist potential, a service he performs for many other islands in the Tuamotus and other archipelagos.

Hidden Tahiti is much more than a tourist guide, however; it's actually a good introductory text to the natural history, archeology, history, sociology and politics of the entire area. Within one set of covers, it provides answers to a host of questions commonly asked by visitors on a wide variety of subjects. Rob deftly summarizes all the major events in Eastern Polynesian geologic, prehistoric and historic time, from the geological origins of the Pacific island world to the recent anti-nuclear demonstrations and their aftermath. He combines this breadth and depth of coverage with insightful and practical notes about such highly diverse matters as the pervasive Tahitian *fiu* attitude (a national characteristic which has probably hurt French Polynesian tourist revenues), negative local attitudes toward European surfers, the transsexual population of Tahiti and its history, the hazards of tattooing and many other current topics. This is no small achievement! For each island or island group, material on archeology, history, etc., is neatly meshed with carefully arranged descriptions of tourist accommodations, restaurants, recreational opportunities, nightlife and transportation—aimed at the full range of pocketbooks—and all well-seasoned with good tips and warnings. There are good biographical summaries for leading South Pacific authors and artists such as Herman Melville, Jack London, Somerset Maugham and the perennial Paul Gauguin, the not-so-noble savage of Tahiti, as well as an annotated bibliography which will prove quite useful.

Rob has demonstrated his familiarity with tourists' needs by assembling information which is difficult to obtain but nonetheless absolutely necessary for efficient travel in these far-flung outposts of France. He includes an excellent guide to French Polynesia's colorful but strangely assorted interisland transportation industry (with often pungent evaluations of the quality of service and accommodations), as well as explains the so-called PK mailing address system. He also presents lists of normal store hours, banking procedures and legal holidays.

Finally, as one who might be called an "old Polynesian hand," it was a pleasure to find so many old friends and acquaintances and familiar places so accurately portrayed in Rob's book. For me, this volume is more than a reminder of bright days of the past: it is an essential guide to equally bright days of the future under the tropical sun. I hope that it will be the same for you!

Robert C. Suggs, Ph.D.
Alexandria, Virginia
September, 1996

ONE

History and Culture

The origins of the Polynesians are shrouded in mystery. Despite advances in technology and recent archeological discoveries, we know very little of the roots of the Polynesian race, much less how they discovered and populated some of the most remote islands on the planet. The most widely accepted theory is that the Polynesians are a blend of peoples originally from various parts of Asia. Indications are that this amalgamation took place in the area extending from the Malay Peninsula through the islands of Indonesia. After an undetermined length of time, these people journeyed across the Pacific, possibly between 3000 and 1000 B.C.

Archeologists tell us that the ancient history of Tahiti and its neighboring islands dates back about 2000 years to when the Marquesas Islands were first settled by migrating Polynesians from the Samoan and Tongan regions. From the Marquesas, ancient Polynesian mariners continued their migration, settling in New Zealand, the Society Islands (to which Tahiti belongs), Hawaii, and Easter Island.

Perhaps the most well-known alternative theory, expounded by the adventurer Thor Heyerdahl, is that Polynesians may have migrated from South America. His theory was given at least some credence by the successful crossing of his *Kon Tiki* expedition from Peru to French Polynesia in 1947.

Wherever they came from, there's no disputing the Polynesians were among the finest sailors in the world. They used the sun, stars, currents, wave motion and flight patterns of birds to navigate the vast reaches of the Pacific. When for some reason, whether it was tribal warfare or overpopulation, Polynesians chose to settle elsewhere, they put their families, worldly goods, plant cuttings, animals and several months' supply of food into their huge, double-hulled canoes and set sail to find new homes.

POLYNESIAN ARRIVAL   According to the most widely held beliefs, the people of Southern China and Taiwan began to migrate south and east some 6000 years ago. Their languages, culture and genes can be found in the Polynesians of today.

The first archeological evidence of any migration is from the Lapita culture, so named for a pottery called Lapita ware discovered in New Caledonia. The "Lapita people" established themselves in Melanesia about 1600 B.C., and during the next 600 years began the migration eastward to Fiji, Tonga and Samoa.

The latest theory suggests the Marquesas were settled in a subsequent migration, at about 500 B.C., as was Mangaia in the Cook Islands. The proximity of Mangaia to the Society Islands gives fuel to speculation that Tahiti was settled much earlier than empirical evidence indicates.

Using radiocarbon dating techniques and comparative studies of artifacts, scientists have pinpointed the earliest settlement of Tahiti and its neighboring islands at around 850 A.D. The most intensive research in this area is being undertaken by Dr. Y. H. Sinoto of the Bishop Museum in Honolulu, Hawaii. In 1973, Dr. Sinoto began excavation of the Vaito'otia/Fa'ahia site (on the grounds of the Bali Hai Hotel) on Huahine and found it to be the oldest settlement yet discovered in the Society Islands. The implements that were excavated closely match those found in the Marquesas Islands, strengthening the theory that the Society Islands were settled by Polynesians migrating from the Marquesas.

> The most important *marae* is Taputapuatea on Raiatea, which was the most prominent political and religious center in the Society Islands.

Why were the journeys undertaken? No one knows for sure, but war, banishment and overcrowding may have been factors. It may also be that the distant ancestors of Polynesians were forced to migrate because of a change in sea level caused by the earth's emergence from the last ice age. (It appears the sea level rose fastest between 12,000 and 5000 years ago, which corresponds to patterns of migration to the islands.)

While some scientists subscribe to the rise-in-sea-level theory, there is no conclusive evidence to buttress this hypothesis. The reason is obvious. Former Fiji Museum Director Fergus Clunie points out that evidence for migrations during this period would most likely be found underwater. Retrieving artifacts and other proof to confirm the early migrations would be difficult.

Pre-contact religion remains an enigma to archeologists. It is known that Polynesians believed that the human race descended from gods and spirits. There was no distinction between the world humans inhabited and the supernatural universe. Because spirits and humans occupied the same turf, parts of that world were *tapu* or restricted. It is thus from Polynesia that we get the concept of taboo.

Ancient Polynesia was a hierarchical society and chiefs, the nearest thing to gods on earth, were afforded the privilege of declaring things *tapu*. Naturally, they used this concept to their advantage by restricting consumption of anything they deemed valuable—pigs, fruit, water or any other item necessary for survival. A *tapu* that was disobeyed meant swift and sometimes deadly consequences. In this manner, the ancestral spirits, through their divine offspring, ran society. However, everyone—regardless of their rank—lived in fear of spiritual retribution.

SURVIVAL OF THE FITTEST The navigational talents of the ancient Polynesians are legendary, but one must admire their superb survival skills as well. How were the first colonizers of Polynesia able to survive in their new island homes? After enduring a bluewater crossing to settle a new island, Polynesian voyagers arrived on their canoes like South Pacific Noahs, fully provisioned with breeding stocks of pigs, chickens and dogs, as well as stowaway rats, lizards and, no doubt, insects. In addition to animals, seeds, and vegetable cuttings, cultivated plants were taken onboard. They also brought along tools such as lines made from coconut fiber and seashell hooks to catch fish. These tools and the precious cargo of animals, vegetables and plants were essential for sustaining life. Of the indigenous flora that already grew on or near the islands, there were only a few varieties such as seaweed, pandanus nuts and coconuts that could provide any real sustenance.

Although wild coconuts were waiting for them in abundance on the new islands, the settlers would most certainly have brought them along on the voyage. And with good reason. It's almost impossible to imagine how life on an island could be supported without this humble nut. Of all the tropical plants found on the islands, no other had a wider number of applications than the coconut. The timber was used to construct homes; coconut fiber was plaited into cord or sandals; the leaves were woven into baskets, thatch and walls; and the shells were used as cups or containers. Coconut milk was drunk when there was no fresh water. The flesh was eaten raw, grated and strained for cream, or dried and its oil extracted for use as *monoi* or salve. The sap derived from cutting the spathe was fermented and used as an alcoholic beverage or boiled down to a syrup that when dried and rolled in grated coconut flesh was made into a nutritious candy.

Other plants carried onboard included breadfruit, bananas, taro, yams, arrowroot, sugarcane and a woody-stemmed lily known as *ti*. Rich in sugar, *ti* was used to make candy, and is still used by modern-day Polynesians to wrap food in underground ovens for cooking.

The mythic vision of the noble savage living in harmony with the environment has some validity. However, like all humans, Polynesians forever changed the face of the land they inhabited. As an island was populated, varieties of indigenous plants and animals declined or disappeared altogether. For example, several species of

Text continued on page 6.

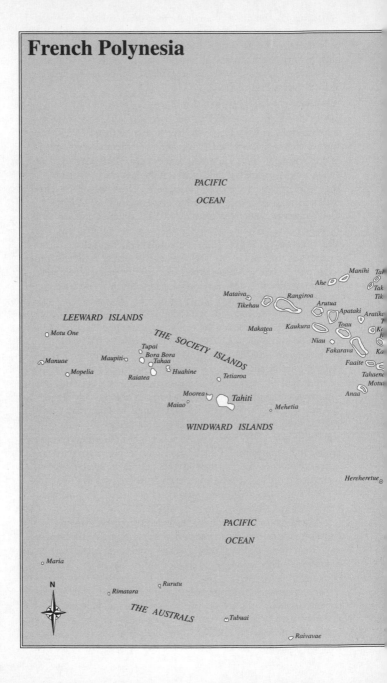

French Polynesia

PACIFIC

OCEAN

Manihi   Tai

Ahe   Tak

Tik

Mataiva   Rangiroa

Tikehau   Arutua

Apataki   Aratika

LEEWARD ISLANDS   Makatea   Kaukura   Toau

Motu One   THE SOCIETY ISLANDS   Niau   Ka

Tupai   Fakarava   Ka

Manuae   Maupiti   Bora Bora   Faaite

Mopelia   Tahaa   Tahaeno

Raiatea   Huahine   Tetiaroa   Motu

Anaa

Moorea   Tahiti

Maiao   Mehetia

WINDWARD ISLANDS

PACIFIC

OCEAN

Hereheretue

Maria

N   Rurutu

Rimatara

THE AUSTRALS   Tubuai

Raivavae

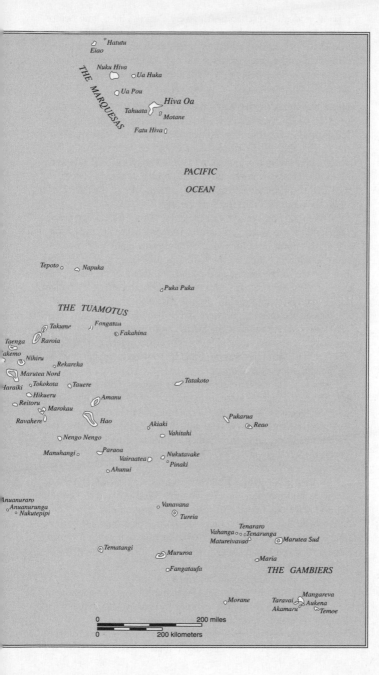

Hatutu
Eiao
Nuku Hiva
Ua Huka
THE MARQUESAS
Ua Pou
Hiva Oa
Tahuata
Motane
Fatu Hiva

PACIFIC

OCEAN

Tepoto
Napuka

Puka Puka

THE TUAMOTUS

Takume
Fangatau
Taenga
Raroia
Fakahina
akemo
Nihiru
Rekareka
Marutea Nord
Tokokota
Tauere
Tatakoto
Haraiki
Hikueru
Reitoru
Amanu
Marokau
Ravahere
Hao
Pukarua
Akiaki
Reao
Nengo Nengo
Vahitahi
Manuhangi
Paraoa
Vairaatea
Nukutavake
Pinaki
Ahunui

Anuanuraro
Anuanurunga
Nukutepipi
Vanavana
Tureia
Tenararo
Vahanga
Tenarunga
Matureivavao
Marutea Sud
Tematangi
Mururoa
Maria
Fangataufa
THE GAMBIERS

Morane
Taravai
Mangareva
Aukena
Akamaru
Temoe

0   200 miles

0   200 kilometers

pigeons and rails reached nearly every Pacific island long before man. However, today there is only a fraction of the bird population that once existed and many are threatened with extinction. Other rail and pigeon species were part of the pre-contact Polynesian cuisine and were no doubt hunted to oblivion. So much for the environmentally correct "noble savage."

FIRST EUROPEAN CONTACT—BIRTH OF "THE MYTH"   It would be close to 250 years after Ferdinand Magellan sailed to the East Indies, and after more than 20 explorers sailed the vast waters of the Pacific, that the first Europeans would set foot on Tahiti. But as the islands were few and far between and navigational aids were often inaccurate, explorers often had no idea where they were. In 1767, British Captain Samuel Wallis, commander of the HMS *Dolphin*, lay claim to Tahiti for King George III.

The initial contact between the crew of the HMS *Dolphin* and the Tahitians was of a mixed nature. The crew bartered beads, looking glasses and knives for food and sex. Nails quickly became the most sought-after item by the Tahitians, who used them to make fish hooks. To the horror of those responsible for the seaworthiness of the *Dolphin*, nails became the chief medium of exchange for sexual favors and rapidly disappeared from the vessel.

Not all the meetings between the British and Polynesians were amicable. On one occasion the English were pelted with stones and in savage reprisal the *Dolphin* opened fire with cannon and muskets. The Tahitians set about making amends by giving lavish gifts, which included the favors of women.

Although Captain Samuel Wallis and his crew "discovered" Tahiti, the first English explorers learned very little about the Tahitians. Wallis, who was ill most of the time, never had the opportunity to investigate the new land and, although the crew found the natives hospitable and carefree, they learned little about the island's government, religion or laws. These remained for later explorers to uncover.

In April 1768, while Wallis was on his way back to England, Louis de Bougainville, commanding the *Boudeuse* and the *Etoile*, found his way to Tahiti. Not realizing the English had beaten him to the task, Bougainville took possession of the island for France. The Frenchman was met by a flotilla of canoes bearing bananas, coconuts, green boughs and fowl as gifts. In return Bougainville gave them nails and earrings.

This is how Bougainville described the scene:

"They pressed us to choose a woman and come on shore with her; and their gestures, which were not ambiguous, denoted in what manner we should form an acquaintance with her."

Once ashore the French were treated with kindness and quickly learned the obvious qualities about their guests—the Tahitians

The Tahitian Temple

Ancient Polynesians worshiped their gods in open-air sanctuaries known as *marae*. These rock formations were a place of worship consecrated to a particular god, as well as a meeting place tied to a family organization.

The size of the *marae* marked the importance and social rank of the owner, and the social implications were of more importance than the god associated with the *marae*. Thus, a man's position was linked to where he would sit within the enclosure. His position in society was determined by the genealogies chanted during the religious ceremonies.

What little that is known about the ancient religion was compiled by Teuria Henry, the daughter of one of the first missionaries to Tahiti. Her book, *Ancient Tahiti*, is considered a classic on the subject. Henry tells us that there were several categories of *marae*, ranging from a simple cluster of stones a few square feet in area to elaborate structures covering hundreds of thousands of square feet. The most simple *marae* were known as *marae tupuna* or "*marae* of the ancestor." Here the ordinary Tahitian would fulfill his (they were strictly for men) religious duties.

The *marae* consisted of a paved area surrounded by a small wall that had a stone platform or *ahu*. Inside the confines of the structure was a wooden platform, *fata tupap'au*, protected by a roof of leaves. (This is where the dead lay in state before their burial.) Various sacred objects such as consecrated feathers or relics belonging to the ancestors were placed in a box hidden under a paving stone. Close to the *marae* a pit was dug to hide cult objects, fingernail clippings, hair clippings, the umbilical cord of the newly born and anything else that could be considered dangerous for the family if some evildoer were to confiscate it and use it for black magic. (Personal objects and effects could be used to place a hex or spell on the individual by enemies or mischief makers.)

were friendly, generous, sexually uninhibited—and they stole. To their credit, the French were philosophical about the latter characteristic, realizing that the islanders simply did not have the same sense of private property that Europeans did. Bougainville, unlike his English counterpart, was a distinguished scholar and perhaps a better observer. Because of his good health during the visit, he had the opportunity to mix more freely with the Tahitians. In just a few days the French captain had acquired a skeletal working knowledge of the island's government and customs. But Bougainville's stay was cut short by anchorage problems among the dangerous coral heads.

CAPTAIN COOK   In 1769, Captain James Cook, perhaps the greatest English navigator who ever lived, arrived in Tahiti on the HMS *Endeavour*. The purpose of his visit had relatively little to do with Tahiti or its residents. Cook had come to study the transit of Venus across the sun, which would enable scientists to precisely measure the distance between the sun and the earth. This determination would be an invaluable navigational aid for future explorers. For the voyage, an impressive group of scientists, scholars and artists was assembled to study Tahiti as well as the transit. However, their 18th-century instruments weren't accurate enough to gather the data needed, and in terms of observing the transit, the voyage was a failure.

On the other hand, Cook's three-month Tahitian sojourn did provide a wealth of information about the island and its people. His experience was generally a good one, but there were problems. Cook was a tolerant man but he simply could not deal with one aspect of Tahitian character—their thievery. Tahitians found it amusing to confound their visitors by devising ways of relieving them of their property. For the natives it was a game to outwit the English, and they usually gave back what was taken. For Cook the matter was deadly serious. At one point he impounded Tahitian canoes in order to get equipment back. In another instance he unfairly imprisoned five chiefs and held them for ransom until two of his sailors (who had deserted ship to be with their Tahitian girlfriends) were returned to his custody.

Cook cared about his crew and their behavior toward the Tahitians. He was particularly bothered by a shooting incident that left a Tahitian dead. He was also concerned about the spread of venereal disease (which the English later blamed on the French), and about the internment of the chiefs. Two days before the *Endeavour* lifted anchor he wrote, "We are likely to leave these people in disgust at our behavior." Perhaps Cook was too sensitive because one of the Tahitians' greatest qualities was their forgiving nature. When Cook left, the Tahitians genuinely wept. He was to return to Tahiti two more times before his death in Hawaii.

BLIGH AND THE BOUNTY   The year 1788 marked the arrival of the HMS *Bounty*, a name forever associated with legendary Tahiti. It also marked the end of the era of exploration and the beginning of exploitation.

The Bounty's mission was to retrieve breadfruit plants needed as a cheap source of food for the numerous slaves working on West Indies plantations. The voyage was led by Captain William Bligh, a former sailing master who had accompanied Cook on a previous visit to Tahiti. Bligh, who may have been unfairly maligned in the annals of history because of his reputation as a ruthless taskmaster, spent six months in Tahiti supervising his crew's transplanting of the valuable plants onto a makeshift greenhouse aboard the ship.

The crew made the most of their time here, befriending the fun-loving Tahitians and living like sultans. Not surprisingly, some of the crew did not wish to depart when it was time to set sail. Three weeks after leaving Tahiti, a mutinous band of men led by Fletcher Christian coldly turned Bligh and 18 other crew members adrift in a 23-foot cutter with minimal provisions. Bligh and his followers faced what seemed like certain death through uncharted waters, tempestuous weather and islands teeming with savage cannibals. Miraculously, they survived 41 days in an open craft, traveling 3609 miles to the Dutch-held island of Timor in Indonesia.

Meanwhile, under orders from Christian, who wished to avoid returning to Tahiti, the *Bounty* sailed for the island of Tubuai in the Austral Group, where the mutineers briefly attempted to settle. Finding the natives unfriendly, Christian returned to Tahiti to pick up pigs for food and female consorts for companionship on Tubuai. Not all of his crew wished to return with him to the forlorn island, so Christian allowed seven loyalists and nine mutineers to remain behind on Tahiti.

◆◆◆

A MATTER OF DEBATE

The cause of the celebrated mutiny on the *Bounty* is still a matter of debate. Some historians believe that the real reason for the uprising may have been the sailors' longing to return to their Tahitian *vahines* rather than Captain Bligh's cruelty. For the most part, novels and films have portrayed Bligh as a monster, when in fact the real villain may have been the unstable and perhaps emotionally disturbed Fletcher Christian. In his book *Pitcairn: Children of Mutiny*, Australian journalist Ian M. Ball tells us that if anything, Bligh, a former officer under the legendary Captain Cook, was a tolerant man who treated his men better than did the average English captain of his day. After the *Bounty* affair was over, Bligh was promoted to admiral and eventually became the governor of New South Wales in Australia.

The attempt to establish a community on Tubuai soon failed. The Polynesians were hostile to the Europeans. The *Bounty's* final destination was lonely Pitcairn Island, where Fletcher Christian and his men soon quarreled with their erstwhile Tahitian comrades. Only one European survived the butchering that ensued during the following months. (The mutinous crew's descendants still live on Pitcairn Island today and are quite proud of their English/Polynesian roots.)

The Polynesians culti-
vated 16 different
varieties of coconuts
and gave them
names dependent
on their uses.

After recovering from his mutiny, Bligh returned to Tahiti for the breadfruit—this time with a contingent of 19 marines aboard. He did not want to take chances on another uprising. In the interim, the survivors of the crew that Christian had left behind on Tahiti had been rounded up by another British ship, the *Pandora*, put in shackles and taken back to England to stand trial before Bligh returned.

A MISSION FROM GOD   As always, in the wake of explorers came the men of the cloth. In 1797, 30 members of the London Missionary Society arrived in Tahiti. Although previous visitors had been appalled by many of the local customs (such as human sacrifice), the Society seemed more distraught over the overt sexual proclivities of Tahitians. They attempted to dissuade the population from this "immoral" behavior by converting the king to Christianity.

Anthropologist Bengt Danielsson writes that they also persuaded the natives to drink tea, eat with a knife and fork, wear bonnets and coats, sleep in beds, sit on chairs and live in stone houses—in short, to emulate the English lower middle-class manner of Society members. Within a few years, the missionaries succeeded in converting the entire population and managed to rid them of such customs as infanticide and human sacrifice. However, they never quite convinced the natives to give up their hedonistic ways. (Even after his conversion to Christianity, Tahitian King Pomare II continued his relationship with his two sisters—one of whom he was married to—and eventually died from the effects of alcoholism.)

THE FRENCH   In 1836, a French naval vessel under the command of Admiral Dupetit-Thouars arrived in Papeete and demanded indemnity for a previous expulsion of Catholic missionaries from Tahiti. Queen Pomare IV, the current ruler, paid the money under threat of naval bombardment and later was forced to sign an agreement that would allow French missionaries to spread Catholicism.

Admiral Dupetit-Thouars returned to Polynesia in 1842 and annexed the Marquesas Islands with the idea of turning them into a penal colony. In the process of procuring land, he decided to annex Tahiti as well. This move outraged the London Missionary Society and almost whipped up enough anti-French sentiment in England to send the two nations to war. In 1843, the French returned to

Tahiti with three ships to take formal possession of the island. This marked the beginning of European colonization in the South Pacific.

After the Tahitians realized the French were there to stay, they took up arms (bush knives and a few muzzle-loaders) and waged a three-year guerrilla war on French garrisons, settlements and missionary stations. In the end, the Tahitians were crushed and Queen Pomare came out of hiding to become a rubber-stamp monarch. Likewise, the Missionary Society, seeing the futility of resisting French influence, ceded their holdings to a French Protestant group and headed for greener pastures.

The colonial period marked the gradual erosion of the Tahitian culture. By the time Paul Gauguin arrived in the late 19th century, what remained of pre-contact Tahitian society and religion were gone. The colony of Tahiti was a quiet, unassuming place and the lack of natural resources meant there was little to plunder or extract from the earth. There was no inducement for change or ferment, and for many years French Polynesia remained a distant outpost in the empire. It wasn't until the mid-20th century that life would be drastically transformed for the Tahitians.

MID-20TH CENTURY POLYNESIA French Polynesia remained a backwater colony until the 1960s, when three events triggered drastic changes in the island chain. These were the building of an international airport in Tahiti, the beginning of nuclear weapons testing in the nearby Tuamotu Islands and the making of the MGM film *Mutiny on the Bounty* starring Marlon Brando and Trevor Howard. As tourists—lured no doubt by Hollywood's version of the islands—and military personnel flooded Tahiti in increasing numbers, the character of the once-sleepy island changed dramatically. Money was pumped into the economy, new businesses sprang up to accommodate the influx of arrivals, and thousands of Polynesians left their far-flung island homes to look for work in Papeete. Suddenly, Tahiti found itself very much in the 20th century.

The topics of the day were dissent over nuclear testing, brawls between soldiers and Tahitians, inflation and a shift from a subsistence economy to one based completely on money.

The increased French presence was not without its positive effects: new roads, schools, hospitals, agriculture and aquaculture projects, many new airstrips and eventually the highest standard of living in the South Pacific. Accompanying economic growth was a greater political awareness and a demand by the Polynesians for more voice in the government, which was controlled more or less by France. In 1977, French Polynesia was finally granted a much greater degree of autonomy under the auspices of a new constitution. The new arrangement provided Polynesians with a larger voice in internal affairs, which included managing their own budget.

In 1984, a statute passed by the French parliament in Paris created yet another incarnation of the French Polynesian constitution, giving Tahiti even more autonomy. For the first time, the legislative body was allowed to elect the Territorial government's own president. (Prior to this, the highest position a Tahitian could hold was Vice-President of the Territorial Government Council.) Thus, instead of sharing power with the Paris-appointed High Commissioner, which the vice-president had to do, the president was given the power to run the Council of Ministers alone.

The 1984 statute did not create complete autonomy for Tahiti's local government. However, in areas that remain in the hands of the French, such as defense or foreign affairs, the Tahitian government has been granted the right to participate in negotiations regarding matters that may have a bearing on French Polynesia's future.

French Polynesia Today

GEOGRAPHY

French Polynesia lies in the South Pacific, halfway between Australia and California, and approximately halfway between Japan and Chile. The term *French Polynesia* refers to the five archipelagoes that comprise this entity, each of them being culturally, ethnically and climatically distinct. They include the Marquesas, the Tuamotus, the Society Islands, the Australs and the Gambiers. Although French Polynesia is spread over an expanse of water the size of Western Europe (2,000,000 square miles or approximately 5,000,000 square kilometers), the total land mass of its 130 islands only adds up to about 1544 square miles (4000 square kilometers).

Tahiti is the largest and best known of the Society Islands. The Society Islands are divided into the Windwards or *Iles du Vent* (Tahiti, Moorea, Maiao and Tetiaroa) and the Leeward Islands or *Iles sous le Vent* (Bora Bora, Maupiti, Huahine and Raiatea). The Leeward Islands lie 100 miles (160 kilometers) to the northwest of Tahiti and are so named because of their position in relation to the prevailing wind.

For the most part, the Society Group consists of high islands—volcanic peaks surrounded by a fringing coral reef that protects from the full force of the pounding surf. All have similar terrain and vegetation.

Tetiaroa, an atoll that lies 26 miles (42 kilometers) north of Tahiti, is classified geographically as part of the Windward Islands, but is geologically much older than Tahiti and the other members of the Society Group. It consists of 12 small islets grouped in a circular configuration surrounding a lagoon about 4.3 miles (7 kilometers) in diameter. This circular or oblong contour is characteristic of an atoll or low island.

The other member of the Society Group that does not conform to the typical high island classification is Maiao, located 43 miles

(70 kilometers) southwest of Moorea. It is also a low-lying coral island, but with the unusual characteristic of having a 154-yard-high hill at its center, flanked on two sides by a brackish lake. Inhabited by about 250 individuals, this island is infested with mosquitoes and is rarely visited by outsiders.

This is in sharp contrast to Bora Bora, which has been inundated with visitors since the 1960s and is best known as the seductive Bali Hai of the Broadway musical *South Pacific*. Bora Bora derives its natural beauty from the erosion of a volcano that erupted at least three million years ago. Since then, its central core has split and eroded, leaving sheared peaks created by volcanic chimneys. The surrounding lagoon, which is proportionally much larger than the core of the island, is vast.

> The current population of French Polynesia numbers around 225,000, half of whom are under 20 years of age. Approximately 75 percent of the population of French Polynesia live on the island of Tahiti.

The Tuamotu Archipelago, a giant arc of coral atolls located between the Society and Marquesas islands, consists of two parallel island chains 740 miles (1200 kilometers) long. It is the largest collection of atolls in the world. One of the islands in the Tuamotu Group, Rangiroa, is the second-largest atoll in the world. Indeed, it is so large, the lagoon could accommodate the entire island of Tahiti within its perimeter. The island is so wide—17.5 miles (28 kilometers)—that a sea-level–based observer looking across the lagoon would be unable to see the opposite side of the atoll.

Though atolls are what readers of *Robinson Crusoe* may consider paradise, they are actually not well suited for sustaining life, whether it be plant, animal or human. The absence of precipitous peaks shrouded by clouds means there is less rainfall and almost perennially dry soil. Not only is the soil arid, it is primarily derived from coral (which created the atoll) and thus lacks many of the nutrients otherwise found on a more biologically diverse high island. Consequently, it's very difficult, if not impossible, to grow such crops as taro, bananas and the like. What does sustain the inhabitants are the nearby reef systems, which are rich in sea life.

At the far eastern end of the Tuamotu Archipelago, almost on the Tropic of Capricorn, are the Gambier Islands, located 1031 miles (1650 kilometers) southeast of Tahiti. Often linked geographically with the Tuamotus because they appear to be the eastern terminus of the archipelago, the Gambiers are in reality a different class of islands. The Gambiers are a cluster of ten rocky islands surrounded by a barrier reef on three sides. The largest and most northerly is Mangareva.

The Australs are the southernmost island chain in French Polynesia and are geologically related to the Cook Islands. Lying 375 miles (600 kilometers) south of Tahiti, they are actually an extension of the same submerged mountain chain as the southern Cooks, and share similar geologic aspects. For example, Rurutu in the Australs and Mangaia in the Cooks are both upthrust islands, with extremely rugged terrain and numerous limestone caves.

PEOPLE

The population of French Polynesia is an amalgam of Polynesians (75 percent), Chinese (10 percent) and Europeans (15 percent). Among these racial categories exists every conceivable mixture. It would not be unusual for a Tahitian named Pierre Jamison to have Chinese, American, Polynesian and French ancestors.

The social structure of French Polynesia is a complicated study in politics, economics and intermarriage. Economically, the Chinese are the most powerful group, while *demis* (half-castes) of Polynesian and Caucasian blood make up a class of Europeanized Tahitians that controls the political sphere. The *demi* population maintains an interesting mixture of Tahitian and European values. While some have adopted French culture and eschew speaking Tahitian, others identify with both cultures. The majority of the population—those whose ancestry is primarily Polynesian (with perhaps a splash of Chinese or European blood)—are known as *kaina* (pronounced kai-na) and are at the lowest rung of the socioeconomic ladder.

Due to their lack of economic clout, the Polynesians have the least amount of political power, even though they are the majority of the population. They make up the blue-collar segment of society—the dock workers, the laborers, etc. Not surprisingly, it is the *kaina* who harbor a particular discontent with the status quo, especially in the sometimes harsh, urban setting of Papeete. And who can blame them? They have the smallest share of the economic pie.

The Chinese first came to Tahiti as plantation workers during the 1860s, the time of the U.S. Civil War. They were the labor force in a scheme hatched by two Scottish businessmen to produce cotton, then unavailable in the northern U.S. When the Civil War ended, the venture went bankrupt but the Chinese indentured laborers remained in Tahiti. Through the years, Chinese have continued to migrate to Tahiti, while keeping their culture. Many have married Polynesians or Europeans. Through hard work and their mercantile tradition, the Chinese gained prominence as merchants and traders to become the wealthiest class in Tahitian Society.

**GOVERN-
MENT**

Today, French Polynesia is governed by a 34-member Territorial Assembly, elected by popular vote every five years. The members select ten among them to form a Council of Ministers *(Conseil des Ministres)*, the most powerful ruling body. The assembly also elects the president.

French Polynesia's official status is "Overseas Territory of France," which roughly means it is a semiautonomous colony, much like the

Nuclear Fallout

In 1995, Tahiti made international headlines as protests mounted over France's plans to resume nuclear testing in the region. Riots broke out on September 5 in Papeete and lasted 36 hours. During the rampage, which involved hundreds of participants, the International Airport in Faa'a was severely damaged. The airport was closed from September 5 to September 8. During this period, several buildings in Papeete were burned, storefront windows at the Vaima Center and another tony shopping area nearby were smashed and, in some instances, looted. The rioting was brought to a halt when Foreign Legionnaires and paramilitary troops arrived.

So, what caused the riots? The resumption of nuclear testing on Mururoa clearly was the catalyst for the riot. But there were other issues as well. A pro-independence, Tahitian-language radio station was allegedly urging Tahitians to take to the streets and wreak havoc. Reports were that many of the rioters were disenfranchised Tahitians venting their rage.

After all, nuclear tests are nothing new to French Polynesia. Since 1960, there have been 45 atmospheric and 134 underground tests. However, in this case, the countdown in Tahiti to the September 5th detonation was a media circus. The presence of Greenpeace off Mururoa was highly publicized by a gaggle of international journalists in Papeete, reporting to news bureaus in New York, Sydney, Paris, Auckland and around the world. From the French point of view, the media whipped up a frenzy of propaganda aimed at Paris. While many Tahitians were never big fans of nuclear testing, many had good-paying jobs related to the experiments. The resulting drop in tourism meant the loss of a great deal of revenue by small hoteliers, not to mention job cuts for Tahitian hotel workers. Ironically, many of the Papeete area hotels were kept afloat during the time of the tests by the 800 gendarmes brought in from France. Due to a shortage of housing, virtually all of the visiting policemen were billeted at local hotels until the tests ended in March 1996.

The airport has been repaired and things are calm once again, but the tourism fallout of the experiments is still very much a concern in Tahiti.

U.S. territories of Puerto Rico and Guam. However, unlike the residents of the United States territories, French Polynesians are permitted to vote in national elections and elect representatives (two deputies and a senator) to the metropolitan French National Assembly and Senate in Paris.

The metropolitan French government runs French Polynesia's foreign affairs, defense, police, justice system and secondary education. In addition to local rule, a French High Commissioner is charged with administrative duties, especially regarding the observance of French law.

ECONOMY   Although French Polynesians cling to traditional values, the face of Tahiti has changed considerably in the past 30 years. The influx of money from both tourism and a large military presence has transformed the region's economy from agriculturally based subsistence level to that of a modern consumer society. Money, not essential to an islander years ago, is now necessary for buying outboard motors, stereos, color televisions, video decks, cars, motorcycles, gasoline and—when one can afford them—the latest fashions. The younger generation has become enamored with the things money can buy and their ability to consume is tempered only by the high price of imported goods.

Lured by the promise of a better life, French Polynesians from the outer islands have moved to Tahiti in ever greater numbers. Life in Papeete, however, often is not easy for those who have left their outlying homes. In the capital the cost of living is high, and life for the new inhabitants is fraught with such basic problems as finding housing and employment. In Papeete, it is simply not possible to fish for an evening meal or gather fruits and vegetables from the land. Thus, for those who have migrated, traditional life has been exchanged for an urban existence and all its woes. To counter this trend, the Tahitian government has been promoting economic development of the outer islands. Through aquaculture, tourism and commercial pearl ventures, the authorities hope to encourage the rural population to stay put.

The two main sources of hard currency for French Polynesia are tourism and the moneys generated by the metropolitan French government.

Indeed, agriculture still plays an important role in supporting the rural population. The leading product is copra (dried coconut), produced by drying coconut meat in the sun, after which it is processed into oil for copra cakes (cattle feed), soap, cosmetics, margarine and other items. Processed coconut oil known as *monoi* is scented with flower blossoms and used locally for skin care. Copra is a vital source of income to families on remote islands where a shortage of resources and/or lack of accessibility to distant markets make it difficult to eke out a living. The government buys the dried coconut at inflated prices to subsidize French Polynesians caught in this situation. Other agricultural and aquacultural products include vanilla, coffee, fruit, cultured black pearls, pearl shell, fish, shrimp and oysters.

The black pearl industry remains one of the few bright spots in the Tahitian economy. Black pearl cultivation and its related activities now take place on approximately 30 islands in the Tuamotu Group and have largely replaced copra and commercial fishing as a source of revenue. Prior to the commercial exploitation of pearl shell in French Polynesia (where mother-of-pearl was used primarily in buttons) early in the 19th century, locals used it for religious and decorative ornamentation and for implements such as fishhooks and lures.

Harvesting oysters for pearls gained importance in the Tuamotu Islands during the 1850s, but it wasn't until the early 1960s that scientists began cultivation experiments with the indigenous black pearl oyster *Pinctada margaritifera*. Today the pearls are cultivated in the Gambier and Tuamotu islands.

In recent years pearl cultivation has become an increasingly important source of income for French Polynesia, particularly as consumers in the international marketplace have become more aware of the black pearl.

Making pearls is an intriguing process: three- to five-year-old oysters are collected by divers and selected for pearl cultivation. A nucleus, or tiny mother-of-pearl sphere fashioned from the shell of a Mississippi River mussel (or similar species), is then attached to a graft of tissue from the oyster and placed inside the animal's gonad. If all goes well, the tiny graft grows around the nucleus and acts as an irritant, which causes the slow formation of layer upon layer of black pearl. After a donor nucleus has been added to each oyster, they are placed inside cages to protect them from predators. Under ideal growing conditions, they are left to recuperate from the operation for 18 months to three years before harvesting. During that time, the shells are repeatedly inspected and hauled to the surface for cleaning. Water conditions are scrupulously checked for salinity, temperature and possible pollutants.

Only 20 percent of the oysters implanted with a nucleus ever bear salable pearls, and only 5 percent of the crop harvested bear perfect pearls—specimens that meet exacting industry standards. Value is determined by size, luster, sheen, color and lack of defects such as bumps, dents or scratches. The price for a perfect pearl is about US$1200. Prices may range from US$50 to US$2500 for an individual pearl.

LANGUAGE

The official languages of French Polynesia are Tahitian and French, but numerous other tongues are spoken as well. Paumotu (the language of the Tuamotu Islands), Mangarevan (spoken in the Gambiers) and Marquesan (the language of the Marquesas Islands) are all native tongues. These languages belong to the great Austrone-sian or Malayo-European language family. This widely scattered fa-mily includes the languages of Micronesia and Melanesia as well as Bahasa Malay (the language of Malaysia and Indonesia), Mala-gasy (the language of Madagascar) and the original languages of Taiwan. The origins of the Tahitian languages date back some 5000 years to the ancient languages of Indonesia, which later spread to Fiji, then to Samoa and Tonga.

The first explorers to set foot on Tahiti thought the Tahitian lan-guage childishly simple. Cook recorded 157 words and Bougain-ville estimated the entire vocabulary to be approximately 500 words. Tahiti was chosen as a fertile ground for evangelical groups such as the London Missionary Society in part because the Tahitian lan-guage appeared easy to learn. As the missionaries were soon to dis-cover, however, their assumption was wrong. As each day passed, they encountered baffling subtleties, foreign idioms and confusing sounds. The slightest change in pronunciation, barely discernible to an untrained ear, could impart a very different meaning. There were no words to express Western ideas about the arts, sciences or busi-ness, but there were words describing the natural environment such as the weather, the ocean, the stars, animal behavior, and the like. The Europeans could not even begin to understand these nuances because their powers of observation were not attuned to Tahitian sensibilities.

Another reason Tahitian was so difficult for early visitors to grasp was that it was a language of oral record. People were ex-pected to know their genealogies and could recite them seemingly forever back into time. Thus they knew intimately the details of their forebears' lives and sometimes the origins of property claims. When no written language existed, memory alone was relied upon.

Once exclusively the language of Tahiti and its neighbors, Ta-hitian is now spoken on about 100 islands of French Polynesia. The language gained prominence because Tahiti was the most populous island and the primary island chosen for missionary work. As the written word and Christianity were spread by native pastors, the printed Tahitian word more or less superseded other local dialects and languages.

Like all languages, Tahitian was influenced by foreigners, most-ly early missionaries and seafarers who mingled with the local pop-ulation. Many languages, including Hebrew, Greek, Latin, English and French, contributed words that have become part of modern-day Tahitian. The translation of the Bible into Tahitian introduced such words as *Sabati* (Sabbath); but the English connection provided many loan words such as baby, butter, money, tea, pineapple and frying pan, which became *pepe, pata, moni, ti, painapo* and *farai-pani* in Tahitian.

Why Is Life So Expensive in Tahiti?

There are several reasons for the high prices in Tahiti. Perhaps the pivotal one is the high tariffs the government tacks on to almost everything that is imported. Only certain foodstuffs such as sugar, rice and flour are exempt from import duties. When you combine high tariffs, the price of transporting goods to Tahiti and the added profit (often a large margin) that merchants tack on, it's easy to see why prices are so high.

Despite the high tariffs, the revenue raised by these duties covers only 70 percent or so of the government's operating budget. A yearly infusion of capital from France covers the deficit. France's largess probably encourages a "France-will-take-care-of-it" attitude.

To complicate things even more, the tremendous outflow of capital overseas to pay for exports goes against every sane economic tenet. After all, the classic definition of a solvent economy is one that exports more than it imports—not the other way around. However, if a government depends almost totally on import duties for its revenue, it will have difficulty surviving without encouraging spending on imported goods. And spending money on imported goods is something Tahitians do a lot of.

Papeete is a wonderland of tropical consumerism. Walking through the capital it's almost impossible not to notice that many of the people drive late model cars, sport flashy watches, drip with jewelry and wear the latest Paris fashions. Often the most humble Tahitian shack will have a stereo, VCR and TV—all costing double what you would pay in a developed country.

Even those high in government acknowledge that there are some serious problems for a nation that spends a lot on imports. There is little, however, that can be done to alleviate Tahiti's economic woes and high prices. Though French Polynesia is beginning to export fruit juice, pineapples, black pearls and fish, the islands have practically no export crops or minerals to provide substantial amounts of hard currency. No one in Tahiti knows what the future will bring given these circumstances. No one in Tahiti likes to think about it.

The problem is that the French metropolitan government, which previously was ready to finance Tahiti's deficit spending, is not keen to continue this practice. One government official told me that back in Paris, few people were even aware how much Tahiti was costing the taxpayers. That is no longer the case. However, unless you are a French citizen, these are not your worries. Just remember to pack all the suntan lotion, film, medicine and tennis balls you need—otherwise you will pay double for it in Tahiti.

PRONUNCIATION

There are five vowels in Tahitian:

a as in "far"
e as in "day"
i as in "machine"
o as in "gold"
u as in "flute"

There are eight consonant sounds in Tahitian:

f as in "fried"
h as in "house"; pronounced "sh" as in "shark" when preceded by "i" and followed by o, as in *iho* (only, just)
m as in "man"
n as in "noted"
p as in "spark"—shorter than the "p" of "pan"
r as in "run"—sometimes trilled like a Scottish "r"
t as in "stark"—softer than the "t" of "tar"
v as in "victory"

Aside from the eight consonants, a glottal stop is used in many words. For example, the word for "pig" is *pua'a;* "person" is *ta'ata;* "beer" is *pia* and "coconut" is *ha'ari.* A U.S. English equivalent, as D. T. Tryon points out in his excellent Tahitian primer *Say it in Tahitian,* is "co'n" for "cotton."

Although English is spoken by many shopkeepers, hotel personnel and students, it would help to have some command of French. If you really want to talk with the people and acquire knowledge of the culture, learn Tahitian.

PLACE NAMES

Ahe (Ah-hay)
Faa'a (Fah-ah-ah)
Gambier (Gahm-bee-aye)
Huahine (Who-ah-hee-nay)
Mangareva (Mahng-ah-rave-ah)
Manihi (Mahn-nee-hee)
Maupiti (Mau-pee-tee)
Nuku Hiva (New-kew-hee-vah)
Papeete (Pa-pee-ay-tay)
Raiatea (Rye-ah-tay-ah)
Rangiroa (Rang-ghee-row-ah)
Tahaa (Tah-ha-ah)
Tuamotu (Too-ah-mow-too)
Tubuai (Toop-oo-eye)

SOME USEFUL WORDS AND PHRASES

Those who spend any time in the islands are sure to run into catch phrases containing important concepts that are useful in trying to understand the Tahitian character.

Fiu is an expression that encompasses varying shades of boredom, despair, hopelessness and frustration. Put yourself in the place of a person who has spent his or her life on a small island, perhaps only a bit of coral in the midst of a blue expanse of ocean. The only stimuli are the ceaseless trade winds, the sound of the waves crashing on the reef, the sight of the sun bleaching the coral white and the sweltering heat. You can always go fishing or turn on Radio Tahiti, but this can get boring after a while. Life can be an endless monotone, and when someone mutters, "I'm *fiu*" with husband or with job, very little explanation is necessary. The essence of *fiu* is in the languorous tropical air.

The word *taboo* is derived from the Tahitian word *tapu*.

Aita pe'ape'a' is another often-used expression; it translates literally as "no problem." It means take things the way they are and don't worry about them. It is basically the Tahitian equivalent of *mañana*. At best, it implies a fatalistic and easy-going acceptance of the here and now. At worst, it is a kind of intellectual lethargy and lack of concern.

Following is an abbreviated vocabulary list with Tahitian and French translations:

American—*marite* mah-ree-tay (*Américain*)
ancient temple—*marae* marah-ayee (*marae*)
Cheers! Down the hatch—*manuia* mahn-wee-ah (*a votre santé*)
crazy—*taravana* tar-ah-vah-nah (*fou, folle*)
finish, finished—*oti* woh-tee (*fini*)
friend—*e hoa* ay-oh-ah (*ami, amie*)
good—*maita'i* my-tye (*bon*)
goodbye—*nana* nah-nah (*au revoir*)
good morning; good day—*ia ora na* your-rah-nah (*bonjour*)
house—*fare* fah-ray (*maison*)
I'm bored; disgusted—*fiu* phew (*Je suis dégoûté*)
man—*tane* tah-nay (*homme*)
no—*aita* eye-tah (*non*)
no good—*aita maita'i* eye-tah-my-tye (*pas bien*)
no problem; don't worry—*aita pe'ape'a* eye-tah-pay-ah-pay-ah (*pas de problème*)
pretty, beautiful—*nehenehe* nay-he-nay-he (*joli, jolie*)
thank you—*mauru'uru* mah-rhu-rhu (*merci*)
traditional dance—*tamurei* tah-mu-ray (*danse traditionelle*)
very good—*maita'i roa* my-tye-row-ah (*très bien*)
woman—*vahine* vah-hee-nay (*femme*)

CUISINE

The blend of Polynesian and French cultures has proved a fertile environment for cuisine. There is a wide array of excellent food available in Tahiti ranging from traditional Tahitian fare to fine French cuisine. One can also find any number of Italian, Vietnamese and Chinese restaurants of various price categories and quality. Fast-food–starved Americans will find outlets serving steak and fries, hamburgers and other similar fare throughout Papeete and on some of the outer islands. Although food in French Polynesia is generally expensive, one need not pay a king's ransom for a tasty meal. The price of a decent, inexpensive meal starts as low as US$10.

Tahitian fare is more or less the same as in the rest of Polynesia—fish, shellfish, breadfruit, taro, cassava (manioc), pork, yams, chicken, rice and coconut. Beef, very popular, is rare on most of the outer islands. Vegetables such as tomatoes and onions are grown on Tahiti and some of the outer islands, but are nonexistent on the atolls. On most of the high islands, tubers such as manioc and taro are staples for the locals. Visitors soon find them bland and heavy. In the Tuamotus, where taro and manioc cannot be grown, rice, breadfruit and white bread are the main starches.

The dish most likely to grace a French Polynesian table is *poisson cru*. This consists of chunks of raw fish marinated in lime juice or vinegar and salt and is usually topped with coconut cream, oil and onions. When prepared properly, the bite-sized pieces of fish melt in your mouth.

Chevrettes, found on most high islands, are freshwater shrimp. *Salade russe* is a potato salad with tiny pieces of beet. Manioc and taro are usually boiled and eaten as the main starch. Taro, which is served in large slices, contains significant quantities of fluoride and keeps teeth healthy. Young taro leaves, boiled and topped with coconut cream, resemble and taste like spinach. Finally, poi is a heavy, sweet pudding usually made with taro, bananas or papayas. It is served warm and topped with coconut milk. (Those who have sampled Hawaiian poi will find the Tahitian variety entirely different.)

A local fruit that no visitor should miss is the *pamplemousse*, a huge variety of grapefruit, which was most likely brought from Asia. Unusually sweet and tasty, the *pamplemousse* is available fresh in markets or you can buy the juice in liter-sized cartons. Occasionally, you can find it fresh-squeezed in restaurants or cafés. Likewise the *rambutan*, a soft, spiny, red fruit (also from Asia) related to the lychee, can be found at roadside stands or in local markets in season. Don't leave Tahiti without trying both of them.

EAT ON THE CHEAP

Sandwiches are a food bargain in French Polynesia. They typically cost 125 to 175 CFP in snack bars or takeaways, 250 to 300 CFP in small eateries where you can sit down to enjoy them. The tasty local bread (made from subsidized flour) makes a fine sandwich or *casse-croûte*. Note that snacks (as snack bars are known locally) are ubiquitous in the communities of French Polynesia. Many are small grocery stores or shops with a counter, usually with a handful of stools at a bar.

The Polynesians who originally settled the islands brought with them bananas, breadfruit, taro, yams and, strangely enough, the South American sweet potato. How the Polynesians got this last item is a mystery, but Dr. Y. H. Sinoto of the Bishop Museum conjectures that Polynesian mariners traveled to South America, perhaps traded with the locals and made their way back to Polynesia with the sweet potato.

The missionaries later introduced sugarcane, cotton, corn, limes, oranges, guavas, pineapple, coffee and numerous other fruits and vegetables.

Depending on their degree of assimilation, many Tahitians have adopted French cuisine, including coffee, French bread, butter and canned goods. Unfortunately, it is a sign of the times to see them opening cans of Japanese tuna instead of fishing for the real thing.

Shoppers will discover that the best bargain in the store is French bread, which sells for about 40 CFP per loaf or *baguette*. Note that on the larger islands it is delivered daily in boxes along the roadside where one might think mail would be placed. Fruit is the next least expensive food in the islands, with the exception of watermelons—which cost 1000 CFP and up.

Art and Culture

Upper-class Tahitians have adopted Western pop culture with a vengeance. French Polynesians wear the most chic fashions, listen to the latest pop music and, if they can afford it, drive the latest German cars and Japanese motorcycles. Yet they still have their own language and customs despite 200 years of foreign influence.

Tahiti has captured the imagination of European intellectuals and artists since Rousseau waxed about the "Noble Savage" and Melville penned *Typee*, the first novel about a romance between a white man and a Polynesian native. However, perhaps the most famous and influential artist to ever set foot on Tahiti's shores was Paul Gauguin. (See "Tahiti's Literati" at the end of the book.)

MUSIC, DANCE & THEATER

Perhaps the most resilient aspects of Polynesian culture are music and dance. To hear the thunder of their drumming for the first time is a stirring experience. Traditional percussionists, who always accompany dance troupes, offer one of the purest expressions of Polynesian music and are as much a part of the music scene today as are electric guitarists. Traditional music is performed both for the entertainment of visitors and local audiences. Drumming, unless part of the reenactment of a religious ceremony, is never performed without accompaniment of dancers.

As in all cultures, modern Tahitian music and dance owe quite a bit to outside influences. Popular Tahitian music (as opposed to the chants and traditional songs performed during a *tamure*) is an admixture of various derivations. This includes melodies and rhythms acquired from American pop or rock and roll, reggae, French *chansons* and even hymns borrowed from the missionaries. Like musicians anywhere else in the world, Tahitian bands equipped with the most modern Fender guitars and Yamaha amplifiers crank out endless songs about love, romance and betrayal.

Perhaps the most familiar aspect of Tahitian culture is its dance, in particular the hip-shaking and often erotic *tamure*, a step that every Tahitian is taught at an early age. The *tamure* resembles the Hawaiian hula from the waist down, but is more forceful, suggestive and sometimes more violent than the Hawaiian dance. Tahitian dancers have amazingly flexible and controlled hip movements— an art that has to be seen to be appreciated.

The modern *tamure* is a bastardized form of the traditional dance performed by troupes acting out a legend or event depicting warriors, kings, fishermen, heroes, priests—a far cry from today's slick, often showbiz-style productions.

CRAFTS   Traditional mat or basket weaving and carving have all but disappeared in Tahiti, Bora Bora and Moorea, the most visited islands. For example, I have never seen a French Polynesian woman of any age (young or old) weave a mat, a skill that is ubiquitous in other parts of the Pacific. That is not to say it is not done anymore.

In the more remote areas, such as the Marquesas, Tuamotu and Austral islands, traditional crafts are still practiced. The Australs, in particular, are famous for the quality of mats and hats woven from pandanus, a tree that grows throughout the South Pacific. Carving or wood sculpture is strictly a product of artisans in the Marquesas Islands. The most popular items are reproductions of tiki, exquisite bowls and coconut shells with intricately etched Marquesan motifs.

FLOWERS IN THEIR HAIR

You will never see a race of people so enamored with putting flowers in their hair as the French Polynesians. Fresh *tiare* or hibiscus blossoms are always worn behind the ear or braided with palm fronds and other greenery into floral crowns. Tradition has it that if a woman or man tucks the flower behind the left ear she or he is taken; a flower placed behind the right ear means the person is available. Tahitians joke that if someone waves a flower behind their head it means "follow me." I have never witnessed this but will report the outcome of such an invitation if fortunate enough to experience it.

Hats, mats, weavings and wood sculpture can be purchased at the municipal market in Papeete, and at several private shops or boutiques. It's also possible to buy art directly from the artisans in the outer islands. On some of the outer islands, such as Huahine, it is also possible to purchase *tifaifai* (Tahitian quilting). A traditional skill that is still very much in vogue throughout French Polynesia is the weaving of flowered leis (*hei*), crowns (*hei upo'o*) and shell necklaces (*hei pupu*). Several different varieties of flowers are used in making leis, including *pitate* (the national flower), hibiscus and frangipani.

TATTOOS

Polynesia is the birthplace of the tattoo, where it has been an integral part of the culture since ancient times. During the current era of Polynesian cultural revivalism, the tattoo has experienced a resurgence. And if you haven't noticed, this ancient art form is undergoing a renaissance in North America and Europe. In fact, it's difficult to walk down a busy street in Papeete or a quiet country lane in Moorea without seeing men or women with tattoos on any body part where there is skin.

The word tattoo is derived from the Tahitian term *tatau* and was first recorded by Captain James Cook in 1769, who described in great detail how it was done and what type of designs were used.

Although in former times all adult men and women were tattooed, the design and area decorated were restricted by social, political and economic factors. Certain motifs were suitable only for the chiefly class. Since the artists were paid with mats, pigs and other goods, wealthier men were the only people extensively tattooed. Unfortunately, there are gaps of knowledge of the ancient art of tattooing. Since the canvas used had a limited life expectancy and few photos of this art were ever taken, little is known. The practice was abandoned at an early date because the missionaries (naturally) condemned it as, in Bengt Danielsson's words, "a morally dangerous glorification of the sinful body."

The missionaries no doubt understood that Polynesians found tattoos to be erotic. People who were not tattooed were less desired by the opposite sex. This explains why so many European sailors and beachcombers gladly submitted to the excruciating experience of getting a tattoo.

At the turn of the century, when British anthropologist H. Ling Roth proposed a study of tattooing, there were no living specimens in the Society Islands. However, he was fortunate enough to find a preserved specimen close at hand, that of a Tahitian who had signed on as a sailor on a European ship and died in England in 1816. Prior to burial, a doctor who admired the tattoo skinned the sailor and donated the specimen to the Royal College of Surgeons. Using the preserved skin along with observations of early explorers and missionaries, Roth determined that women had fewer tattoos than men, but for both sexes the bare minimum was having one's thighs, hands and feet adorned. In general, geometric designs were the most popular motifs, along with plants, leaves, fish and birds. Some of the designs were particular to geographic areas so that one could tell if an individual was from the Australs, Tuamotus or elsewhere.

Nowhere was the art of tattooing as developed as in the Marquesas, where both men and women covered their faces and bodies with intricate geometric designs. When German anthropologist Von Steinen arrived in 1897 he found a number of fully decorated men and women. His photos were reproduced in the first volume of his classic work *Die Markesaner und Ihre Kunst* (*The Marquesans and Their Art*). Twenty-three years later, when American anthropologist Willowdean Handy visited the same islands, she found only 125 partially tattooed men and women. In 1951 when Bengt Danielsson did an acculturation study on Hiva Oa, he found only one man with traditional tattooing.

Today young Tahitians are reinventing their ancestors' artistry, freed from the constraints of the missionaries. Aside from these neo-traditional tattoos, this ancient art form can still be found if you go far enough afield to Polynesian outliers in the Solomon Islands.

CULTURAL RENAIS-SANCE

As with other Third World peoples, Tahitians experienced a cultural blossoming and reawakening in the 1970s, manifested through the *Maohi* or neo-Polynesian artistic movement. Artists explored traditional Polynesian motifs, while writers and playwrights went digging into their own mythology for themes. According to the late Bobby Holcomb, a respected Hawaiian artist who lived in Tahiti until his death in 1991, neo-Polynesian painters like himself use the Polynesian color scale (earthy browns, reds, yellows) in traditional Polynesian historical and mythical themes. Neo-Polynesian art is often more abstract than traditional Pacific art and may incorporate eroticism, sensuality, local flora and fauna, as well as the classic Polynesian geometric patterns as displayed in tattoos and tapa cloth.

Politically, the movement produced nationalist stirrings, calling for greater autonomy and even independence from France. Today, the nationalist maelstrom and a "back-to-the-roots" sentiment have taken hold over a greater portion of society. Teaching the Tahitian language in schools, once illegal, is now part of the curriculum. Politicians of every stripe espouse traditional Tahitian culture, and artists enjoy the support of the state. In the last few years, the French Polynesian government has nurtured the talents of young artists by displaying their works in exhibitions and providing cash prizes. Displays of Tahitian art and re-enactments of ancient ceremonies—such as the crowning of a king—can readily be seen during *Heiva*, which takes place in July as part of Bastille Day celebrations.

One of the most novel groups to appear on the cultural scene is *Pupu Arioi*, a small but dedicated organization that specializes in teaching children about their Polynesian heritage. Named for an ancient Polynesian society that allowed members to criticize their leaders and rise in an otherwise rigid social structure, *Pupu Arioi* began in 1977 as a theater troupe. Later, the group's emphasis shifted to education. Members now travel from school to school, teaching teachers and pupils relaxation techniques, which calm children and put them into a receptive state, and then introduce them to theater, dance, music and costuming. Children are not pushed, but nudged into thinking about their culture and traditions. *Pupu Arioi* members also discuss Polynesian mythology and philosophy with the idea of educating children in the oral traditions that were once the backbone of Tahitian culture. Perhaps they will be successful in re-infusing values into a society that for many reasons has lost a number of its old traditions.

"There is a scale in dissolute sensuality, which these people have ascended, and which no imagination could possibly conceive."
—Captain Cook

SEX & THE TAHITIAN MYTH

When discussing Tahiti, inevitably the beauty and (the real or imagined) sexual proclivities of the natives arise. Since the time of Wallis and Cook, the myth of Tahiti as the "Isle of Love" has flourished—and is still used as a major selling point by the travel industry. As a result of books such as *Typee* and *The Marriage of Loti* and movies such as *Mutiny on the Bounty*, countless men have traveled to Tahiti's shores in search of its beguilements.

From the earliest accounts, Tahitian women genuinely relished lovemaking, and sailors arriving in the islands were greeted by boatloads of willing maidens. According to those narratives, the arrival of a ship was like a circus visiting a small town. Days and nights were filled with wild abandon, rum drinking and the comic sight of pale white men in strange costume. Amorous flings had the benefit of material rewards as well, usually a trinket of some sort. In Cook's day, nails were often given as gifts. This sometimes reached a hazardous stage as eager sailors began to wrench nails from the very ships themselves.

Today, things are quite different. Tahitians have by no means lost their gay abandon, but male visitors are mistaken if they think Tahitian women are just waiting to fulfill their fantasies. Male tourists are advised not to adopt the attitude that they are God's gift to *vahines*. More often than not, they will feel that they are on the outside, looking into a totally different world.

And what a different world it is. I for one do not profess to understand much about the psycho-sexual nature of the Tahitian. One can only assume that Tahitian customs and traditions, which are so foreign to the Judeo-Christian ethic, existed long before the white visitor appeared on the scene. I also think it is wrong to assume that Tahitians are totally uninhibited and free from neuroses. As with people everywhere, they have their share of hang-ups and sexual difficulties.

For those going to Tahiti seeking pleasures of the flesh, some final words on the subject: for those lucky in love, Tahiti will be just like anywhere else, only warmer.

TAHITI'S THIRD SEX

Homosexuality has been a culturally accepted lifestyle in Polynesia for centuries. When the Europeans came they were shocked and puzzled at the behavior of male transvestites who did striptease acts for the crews and unabashedly had sexual relations with other men. Commenting on this behavior, Captain Bligh said:

"It is strange that in so prolific a country as this men should be led into such sensual and beastly acts of gratification, but perhaps no place in the world are they so common or extraordinary as in this island."

In the years that followed, the brethren from the London Missionary Society did their best to convert the Tahitians into upright Protestants, but with little success. The cultural heritage of the *mahu* (transvestites or men that take on female roles) continues to play an important role in Polynesian culture. According to anthropologist Bengt Danielsson, the *mahu* is "a popular and honored member of every village throughout the Society Islands."

Anthropologist Robert I. Levy writes that one becomes a *mahu* by choice or by being coaxed into the role, or both, at an early age. The boy associates primarily with females and learns to perform the traditionally feminine household tasks. After puberty, the *mahu* may assume a woman's role by cooking, cleaning, looking after children and wearing feminine clothing. He may dance what are normally the women's parts during festivals, often with greater skill than the women around him. Despite their proclivity to take on female roles, *mahus* are not necessarily homosexual in their preferences. In the villages he may work as a maid, and in Papeete can often find employment as a waiter, bartender or professional dancer. (Some male visitors may find out belatedly that the attractive Tahitian dancer who had been looking their way, is actually a man.)

Although Tahitians may poke fun at *mahus* there is none of the deep-seated hostility that exists towards homosexuals in the West. Young adolescents may seek out *mahus* for sexual favors, but generally only if there are no girls available. If a young man does have sex with a *mahu*, there is little stigma attached to the act. *Mahus* are accepted as human beings, not aberrations. In Papeete there are several nightclubs that feature male striptease acts and cater to a varied sexual spectrum.

Anthropologist Danielsson fears that the *mahu* tradition is in danger of disappearing because of what he calls the "brutal modernization process." He has already noticed the trend of *mahus* turning to Western-style homosexual prostitution as a way of making a living in a modern society incompatible with the traditional *mahu* way of life.

Though we shall never fully understand the religious beliefs of the ancient Tahitians, it is known that the creator was *Te Atua*, who was rarely seen on earth. A pantheon of lesser gods, however, were often encountered in one manifestation or another. These included *Ta'aroa* (god of the sea), *Oro* (god of war), *Rongo* (god of agriculture) and *Tane* (god of sex and procreation). Spirits were forever intruding in the lives of man and communicated with people in a number of ways. Trees were often a medium and the rustling of the wind was a sure sign that the gods were present. Tiki figures, carved of wood or stone, were a medium through which spirits or gods interacted with mortals.

MYTH & LOCAL BELIEFS

Although Christianity has spread throughout the islands, there is still a strong belief in vestiges of Polynesia's pre-Christian religion. In the outlying areas especially, myths of gods, giants and supernatural creatures are spoken of as fact and it is not unusual for a person to have had encounters with *tupa'pau* (ghosts).

One man in Maupiti matter-of-factly described to me the occasion on which he had seen a dozen ghosts floating down a moonlit road outside his village. These ghosts, he said, were the spirits of passengers who had perished in a shipwreck several weeks earlier. The spirits were those of native Maupitans, returning home as the dead always do.

Accepting the locals' belief that the supernatural is a normal part of life often makes Westerners question their own beliefs. In the Tuamotus, I met a young Frenchman by the name of Patrick who had spent several years living on the atoll of Ahe. He said that one

RELIGION

The church is an important institution throughout the Pacific island nations and French Polynesia is no exception. On the outer islands the local priest or minister often wields a powerful hand in community affairs. In most areas, church attendance is high. Most French Polynesians (about 55 percent) are Protestants, followed by Roman Catholics (30 percent), Mormons (6 percent) and Seventh-Day Adventists (2 percent). Buddhists and Confucianists make up about 2 percent of the population.

evening he and an old villager were fishing in a skiff inside the atoll's lagoon. The Frenchman spotted an object resembling a ball of fire which rose from a spit of land on the lagoon's far edge and floated in the direction of the village. Awe-struck by the sight, he pointed it out to the old man who sat contentedly fishing. The Tahitian glanced at the luminous ball and nonchalantly remarked that it was only the spirits returning to the village and really nothing to get excited about.

TWO

Traveling in French Polynesia

Choosing where to go in French Polynesia is akin to perusing the menu at a five-star restaurant. There are so many places to visit, it's really a tough call. Each of the five major island groups has its own distinctive attractions. The main thing is to get *out* of Papeete and either spend time in one of Tahiti's outer districts or visit one of the outer islands. Only in Tahiti's countryside or on an outer island are you likely to experience the pace and hospitality of genuine French Polynesia.

My personal favorites in the Society Group (which includes the Windward and Leeward Islands) are Moorea, Huahine and Maupiti. If you can, you should also make a point of visiting at least one island in the Tuamotu Group so that you can experience an atoll, which is entirely different from a high island. Among these islands you might consider one of the lesser visited atolls such as Tikehau, Takaroa, Mataiva or Fakarava. If you have the time and the budget, at least one of the Marquesas Islands should also be on your itinerary. Remote and seldom visited by tourists, their precipitous terrain is absolutely spectacular. I like Nuku Hiva, but any island in the Marquesas Group is worth seeing.

SOCIETY GROUP **Tahiti,** French Polynesia's largest and most populous island, is home to the international airport and the capital, Papeete. Papeete has a charming waterfront, fine restaurants and the *marché* (public market), but the capital is only one part of the equation. To really get a handle on Tahiti it's best to get out of town. I would suggest renting an car and spending at least one day exploring the countryside, or *district*, as the locals call it. Outside Papeete's urban jungle, people are friendlier, and chances are you'll see a glimpse of old Tahiti. My favorite corner of Tahiti is *Tahiti Iti* or (Little Tahiti), the smaller appendage of the island connected to the main body by the Isthmus of Taravao. There are some restaurants in the tiny hamlet of Taravao and a multitude of stunning vistas. The Tautira Village area in particular has a spooky edge-of-the world feeling about it that stays with you. Here the coastal road traces the steep terrain. The mountains are thick with foliage and rise precipitously into the mist. On Tahiti Iti one senses that progress has yet to encroach on this corner of French Polynesia.

Because of its proximity to Tahiti, **Moorea** has become a "suburb" of Papeete. The island is dramatically beautiful, with sharp serrated peaks that command deep cleft valleys. The pace is slower than Tahiti, it's less congested with cars, and it has an abundance of good beaches—many more than Tahiti. Tourism development on the island has increased considerably over the past few years—more than I'd like to see—but the island still retains its charm and friendliness. It's very easy to get to Moorea from Tahiti (I suggest that you take a ferry, the way the locals do it). I'd consider staying at one of the smaller pensions rather than a large hotel. You'll find the service more personal and the feeling more intimate. Once there, rent a car and take the time to drive around the island. Be sure to visit the interior for the vistas and the archeological sites. The jeep tours are a terrific way to see hidden Moorea.

When James Michener called **Bora Bora** the most beautiful island in the world, he may have been right. Once a sleepy outpost, the island is dominated by two towering volcanic peaks that overlook a stunning translucent blue lagoon. There are terrific white-sand beaches and wonderful places to eat. The luxury hotels along the Matira Beach are world class. The island also offers scuba divers some once-in-a-lifetime opportunities such as swimming with giant manta rays. My personal feelings about the island are, however, ambivalent. Though the name Bora Bora evokes magic, its fame has brought in multitudes of visitors. It has become too popular, too crowded and out of the range of mid-range and budget visitors. That's the bad news. The good news is, a fair number of reasonably priced restaurants and lodgings have sprung up like mushrooms in the past few months. If you do plan to visit and don't have a king's ransom to pay, there is hope!

Huahine is a diamond in the rough, and a stronghold of Polynesian culture. One of the most picturesque and geographically diverse islands in the Society Group, the tourism market has not yet discovered this verdant isle. There are numerous white-sand beaches, the best and most consistent surfing in all of French Polynesia, and a variety of lodging for every budget. Restaurants in Fare, the main community, are diverse and reasonably priced. Those who come to Huahine for cultural tourism will not be disappointed. Huahine's resilient people prefer to speak Tahitian rather than French and regard their traditions as sacred. There are also more ancient temples (many of which have been reconstructed) per square foot than anywhere else in the South Pacific. The only thing it doesn't have are swarms of visitors—one of the best reasons to come here.

The sister islands of **Raiatea** and **Tahaa** are unreservedly off the beaten track. Uturoa, the main community of Raiatea, is a government administrative center, while Tahaa is still an undeveloped backwater. Both islands have recommended budget and mid-range accommodations. There is also one superb *motu* resort, Vahine Island, located off Tahaa, that ranks as one of the best in French Polynesia. There are a number of good restaurants in the Uturoa area. Those with an interest in archeology will want to visit Raiatea, which has the largest and most important Polynesian temple in the South Pacific—Marae Taputapuatea. There are no beach resorts on either island, but you can find them on the offshore *motus.* Diving is first rate in the lagoon shared by Raiatea and Tahaa. Like Huahine, few visitors find their way to Raiatea and fewer yet to Tahaa.

The smallest of the Society Islands, **Maupiti** is the hidden gem of the group. Mountainous and verdant, it's so small you can walk around it in several hours. There is also a superb white-sand beach and lovely beaches on the *motus,* as well. Locals have spurned the advances of major hoteliers so there are no major resorts or hotels here. In terms of tourism it is perhaps the least developed of any in the Society Group, but has a fine selection of pensionstyle accommodations in the main village and on the offshore *motus.* Despite Maupiti's location (it's the most far-flung of the Society Islands), there is daily air service. Visitors who want a taste of traditional Polynesia would do well to visit this stunning island.

TUAMOTU GROUP   The Tuamotus (also known as the Paumotu Islands) differ from the Society Islands both geographically and culturally. Unlike the high islands that characterize most of French Polynesia, the Tuamotus are each a flat ring of coral surrounding a

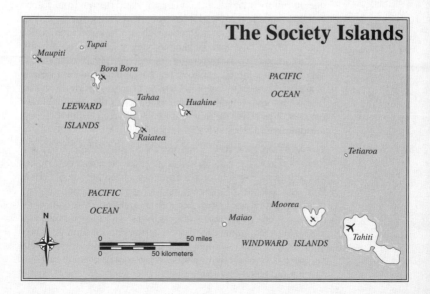

lagoon. Culturally and linguistically, they are also distinct from the rest of French Polynesia. If you believe, as I do, that geography influences human behavior, you will agree that the Tuamotu experience is unique. It is my belief that anyone who takes the time and effort to explore French Polynesia should spend several days on an atoll. Why? Unlike a high island, there is no place to hide (physically or psychologically) on an atoll. You naturally turn inward on a flat island surrounded by only a few square yards of soil and an endless ocean. You are laid bare before the elements—the hot sun, the pounding surf and unceasing trade winds that whistle through the palm fronds. Don't expect the lap of luxury in the Tuamotus. With the exception of Rangiroa or Manihi, the accommodations are modest. Lodging is pension-style and there are no restaurants, no stores, no amenities. However, you will be cared for. Tuamotu hospitality is unforgettable. The Tuamotus generally have excellent beaches and diving. And the traditional Paumotu music is hauntingly beautiful.

MARQUESAS ISLANDS Physically, the Marquesas Islands are nothing short of phenomenal. Volcanic in origin, they have few reefs and rise like jagged spires from the sea. Rocky and precipitous, these isolated outposts have deep, lush trench-like valleys and remote beaches. Of the six that are inhabited—Nuku Hiva, Ua Huka, Ua Pou, Hiva Oa, Tahuata and Fatu Hiva—three are accessible by air, the others by sea. All the Marquesas Islands have pension-style or mid-range accommodations—none have luxurious lodging. Marquesan culture (quite distinct in language and custom from Tahiti) and breathtaking scenery are the draws here. There are numerous archeological sites, and an otherworldly ambience straight out of *Raiders of the Lost Ark*. Unlike the Society Group, you can still find traditional woodcarvers and craftspeople plying their trades. Visitors to the Marquesas Group need to be independent travelers, patient and be able to rough it. Overland travel is nearly always by four-wheel-drive vehicle (or via horseback) as the roads are horrendous. If you have the time and money, I would strongly recommend a sojourn to these isolated rocks.

THE AUSTRAL ISLANDS The Australs seldom get outside visitors. Perhaps that is the best reason to go there. You can be virtually guaranteed there will be few, if any, guests from outside of French Polynesia. Like the Marquesas, they are quite remote and very expensive to get to. The latitude here offers a milder climate than you'll find in the other Polynesian island groups. There are few beaches in the Australs. Tubuai, the largest of the Austral Group, is best known for the way its people sing—their purposefully atonal sound is perhaps one of the last vestiges of pre-contact religion and culture left in French Polynesia.

THE GAMBIER GROUP The Gambier Islands are another remote and seldom-visited island group. Like the Australs, their southerly latitude makes them slightly cooler than the Society Group. The largest and most accessible of the inhabited islands is Mangareva. Rikitea, the main community in Mangareva, has a number of ruins from its days as a missionary center. The mostly tumble-down ruins have an eerie, dark feel about them. The main industry in the island group is black pearl cultivation. There are few beaches here, but there are several excellent pensions on Mangareva—but no other amenities.

When to Go

SEASONS

November through May are the warm and humid months, while June through October brings a cooler and drier climate. It may rain any time of the year, and tropical downpours can be quite heavy. In June, July and sometimes August a gusty trade wind called the *mara'amu* bears down on the islands, bringing wind, rain and sometimes nasty weather from the south. If your resort is located on a southern coast of the Society Islands, chances are you will experience the *mara'amu*. Nothing to worry about, just don't forget to bring an extra windbreaker. If you are a diver, for visibility you're better off going in the drier months.

If you are interested in dance and music, the best time to visit is during July when the country is in the midst of *Tiurai*, the month-long Tahitian holiday that melds into traditional French Bastille Day celebrations. Unfortunately, that is the time most other visitors come to French Polynesia as well. If you choose to go at this time of year, book early.

Another seasonal wild card that affects the visitor, especially the budget traveler who needs low-cost pensions or hotel rooms, is the timing of local school holidays. It may be a good idea to orchestrate your vacation around school holidays so that you don't end up fighting for a bed with a Tahitian student. If you think this may be an issue, check with the Tahiti Tourist Board.

CALENDAR OF EVENTS

JANUARY

January 1 New Year's Day is a time for friends and families to gather for merrymaking. The long-standing tradition is to spend New Year's Day driving around visiting friends and relatives. Children's games are held in town halls on most islands.

Late January to early February Chinese New Year is celebrated on Tahiti during a four-day *fête* that includes dances, martial arts demonstrations, calligraphy, painting and fireworks.

FEBRUARY

Mid-February The International Marathon is held on Moorea. This is a 26-mile (42 kilometer) marathon starting in Maatea on the island's south coast and finishing in Paopao on the northern coast. A traditional feast is held that evening in Tiki Village.

Late February to early March   The **Polynesian Cultural Fair** is held at the Place Vaiete, a public square adjacent to the Port of Papeete on Tahiti. The fair showcases ancient cultural traditions such as tattooing, basket weaving and Ra'au Tahiti—traditional medicine.

MARCH

March 5   Protestant parishes throughout the islands celebrate the **Arrival of the First Missionaries** (Arrivée de l'Evangile) in 1797. The celebrations feature re-enactments of the missionaries' arrival. Many of the activities are held at the Willy Bambridge Stadium complex in Papeete, Tahiti, and on Afareaitu in Moorea.

Early March   The **International Billfish Tournament**, a deep-sea fishing contest (held every other year) takes place in Tahiti.

March 26   **International Day of the Woman** is celebrated in Tahiti. Visitors are welcome to join the many discussion groups that examine the role of women in French Polynesia.

APRIL

Mid-April   The **Miss Bora Bora Beauty Contest** is held in one of the hotels followed by a Tahitian feast and dance on Bora Bora.

Late April   On Tahiti, the **Polynesian Sports Festival** features traditional activities such as javelin throwing, outrigger canoe racing and fruit carrying races.

MAY

Mid-May   **Miss Tahiti** is selected to represent the country in international beauty pageants at a Tahiti venue. **Miss Heiva i Tahiti** is also chosen to reign over the Bastille Day celebrations or Heiva. A contest for Miss Moorea is held on Moorea also. Not forgetting the other half of the human race, contests for **Mr. Muscles, Mr. Heiva i Tahiti** and **Mr. Tahiti** are held on Tahiti.

JUNE

Late June   In Papeete, the **Day of the Tahitian Fern** (Maire) is held at a local hotel. The festival includes an exhibition of the many varieties of ferns found in Tahiti and demonstrations of crowns made from them. The celebration ends with a feast and ball decorated, naturally, with ferns.

JULY

July 1–21   Centered around France's **Bastille Day** (July 14), *La Fête*, known as *Tiurai* or *Heiva* in Tahitian, is French Polynesia's biggest celebration. The festivities last around three weeks and begin at the tail end of June or the start of July. They are celebrated with dance competitions, singing, *pirogue* races and other sporting events.

Late July   The annual **pro-am surfing competition** held in Tahiti features some of the best amateurs and pros from around the world. The **Tahiti International Golf Open**, held in Papeete, is a pro-am event that attracts some of the less than stellar pros from the South

Pacific, Hawaii and Australia. The **Te Aito Marathon Outrigger Canoe Races** held in Tahiti are one of the more important competitions for both men and women in the islands.

Late August Local musicians compete in Papeete's **Night of the Guitar and Ute** performing *ute*, which are satirical improvisational songs as old as the Tahitian culture.

AUGUST

Late September **World Tourism Day** is celebrated by employees of travel-related industries donning festive clothing. The Public Market in Papeete is the venue for singing and dancing.

SEPTEMBER

Early October In Papeete, the **Tipanier Ball**, organized by the Women's Liberation Council of Tahiti, is a traditional dinner dance where prizes are awarded for the loveliest woven floral crowns.
Late October The **stone-fishing ceremony** held on the island of Tahaa in late October or early November features traditional activities include copra-cutting contests, canoe racing, and a firewalking ceremony. The stone-fishing ceremony is held on the last day and is followed by a Tahitian feast.

OCTOBER

November 1 On **All Saints Day** families throughout the islands visit cemeteries and illuminate the graves with candles. In the evening hymns are sung in memory of the dead.
Mid-November The annual **Hawaiki Nui Canoe Race** between Huahine, Raiatea, Tahaa and Bora Bora is held over a three-day period.

NOVEMBER

Early December Tahitians pay homage to the Tiare Tahiti by celebrating **National Flower Day**. Post office bureaus, banks and other businesses compete for the best floral decorations and Tiare Tahiti blossoms are handed out throughout the town.
December 25 **Christmas Day** in Tahiti is a time for families and friends to congregate.

DECEMBER

All incoming international flights to French Polynesia touch down at the Faa'a Airport near Papeete, Tahiti. Tahiti is generally a stopover destination between Australia or New Zealand and the United States. There are also connections between Tahiti and Chile via Easter Island, as well as connections from other Pacific islands.

▼▼▼▼▼▼▼▼▼
How to Go

AIR

Airlines that fly into Tahiti include Air France, Air New Zealand, AOM French Airlines, Corsair, Hawaiian Airlines, Lan Chile, Polynesian Airlines and Qantas. Needless to say, the best fares can be found by calling several travel agents and checking out the ads in newspaper travel sections for discounted air tickets.

Text continued on page 40.

Heiva—
Bacchanal
in the Islands

Heiva or *Tiurai* combines France's Bastille Day (which commemorates the storming of the Bastille Prison during the French Revolution) with traditional Tahitian festivities. It begins on or around June 29, and lasts for approximately three to four weeks. During this period business grinds to a halt and is replaced by an orgy of food, drink and dance. It is the islands' most important festivity—a combination of Mardi Gras, 4th of July and Walpurgis Night rolled into one.

Many island communities put on their own *fête* consisting of traditional dance competitions, rock-and-roll bands, foot and canoe races, javelin throwing, spearfishing and other sports activities. The largest celebration occurs in Papeete, where the waterfront is turned into a fairground crowded with hastily constructed booths, makeshift bars and restaurants, a ferris wheel and a grandstand for viewing the all-important dance competitions.

Though the biggest celebration takes place in Papeete, there are other *Heiva* activities going on simultaneously at various locales around the country.

Along with dance competition, the most interesting event is the "Crowning of the King" re-enactment at the Marae Arahurahu, held 22.5 kilometers outside of Papeete. A gala outdoor theatrical event that re-creates the glory of Tahiti's pagan heritage, it is taken very seriously by locals who observe the celebration in hushed tones. If you have the opportunity, the festival is well worth seeing.

The event in Papeete opens with a parade featuring beauty contestants, sports association members, folkloric and *tamure* groups, and flower-studded floats. On Bastille Day (July 14) there is a military parade that begins with a salvo of canons, followed by a sea of uniforms, brass bands playing military marches, and baton-twirling troupes of majorettes. The grand finale in the evening is the Ball held at the mayor's residence.

The three weeks of celebration are also crowded with numerous activities such as horse races, speedboat races, bicycle races, parachuting displays, motorcycle competition, an international golf tournament and waterskiing. There is even room for the traditional Polynesian sports of fruit-carrying races and archery contests, as well as displays of tattoos, basket weaving, tapa cloth, copra cutting and Polynesian arts and crafts.

During this period French Polynesians converge on Tahiti to watch the dancing and partake in the good times. It is not unusual for Tahitians to stay up all night and frolic, sleep through the day, start chugalugging Hinano beer and begin the cycle again. *Tiurai* is above all a time to socialize, forget your troubles, and perhaps mend fences with a neighbor.

One criticism that long-time residents of Papeete have about *Tiurai* is that it has become too commercialized. During the holiday, prices shoot up and merchants make windfall profits. Commercialized or not, *Tiurai* in Papeete is packed shoulder-to-shoulder with people shoving their way along the carnival row. In one section, a crowd gathers in front of madly gesticulating Chinese shills, who spin the wheels of fortune in their gambling booths and attempt to out-bark each other on bullhorns. Meanwhile, locals try their luck at the shooting galleries, vendors hawk kewpie dolls and cowboy hats, and young children tug their parents' arms in the direction of the merry-go-round. The temporary outdoor cafés selling beer, barbecued chicken and steak swell with inebriated tourists and Tahitians alike.

Outside the grandstand entrance, the scene is a mob of performers and gawkers. Troupes of tasseled, straw-skirted dancers mill around on the grass awaiting their turn to go on stage. They are the *crème de la crème* of French Polynesian dancers. The air is thick with nervous energy and the scent of *Tiare Tahiti* blossoms. Nearly everyone is adorned with a crown of flowers or a single blossom behind the ear.

Tiurai is more than a carnival. For local entrepreneurs of the smaller island communities the festival is economically important. Not only is it a big affair for the established merchants but ordinary families set up small concessions and sell food and liquor as well. The celebration also performs an important educational function. It provides French Polynesian youth with an outlet for traditional cultural expression, which is in increasing danger of being lost due to the encroaching influence of Western culture.

FROM THE U.S. Los Angeles is the only city in the continental U.S. that offers nonstop flights to Tahiti. Carriers servicing this route include Air France, Air New Zealand, AOM French Airlines and Qantas, as well as Corsair, a charter service. During the low season, December 25 to June 15, Corsair offers the least expensive fare. It's a good idea to call around, as some airlines, such as AOM, may offer lower fares on a seasonal basis.

Hawaiian Airlines also services Tahiti out of Los Angeles, San Francisco and Seattle with a stopover in Hawaii.

Discounted round-trip tickets to Tahiti can be found from consolidators—but you must be prepared to shop around. The *New York Times*, the *Los Angeles Times*, the *Chicago Tribune* and the *San Francisco Examiner* all produce Sunday travel sections where you'll find a number of advertisements. Council Travel and STA Travel, companies specializing in inexpensive tickets, have offices in major cities nationwide.

The magazine *Travel Unlimited* publishes details of the cheapest air fares and courier possibilities for worldwide destinations from the United States. ~ P.O. Box 1058, Allston, MA 02134.

There are also other options available, such as the circle-Pacific fares to New Zealand or to Australia, that can be routed via Tahiti.

FROM AUSTRALIA AND NEW ZEALAND Despite Australia's and New Zealand's relative short distance from French Polynesia, there are no significant discounts on direct flights to Tahiti. In fact, you could probably get a return ticket to Los Angeles via Tahiti for the same price as a return ticket to Tahiti only (unless you used a package plan that would most likely include accommodations in the price). Keep in mind that there are three pricing seasons for flights out of Australia—low, shoulder and high. Shop around: prices vary enormously. From New Zealand, Air France and Air New Zealand sell 45-day round-trip tickets from Auckland to Papeete.

FINDING A GOOD TRAVEL CONSULTANT

A competent travel agent should be able to tailor an itinerary around your special interests, such as golf or snorkeling. In most cases South Pacific specialists have toll-free phone numbers and can advise you of the current air fare bargains and seasonal discounts. They should also have fares for interisland travel. Most importantly, a reputable agency can save you money. For U.S. residents, I recommend **Manuia Tours** in San Francisco. It is owned by a Tahitian family, and they know their destination. They offer a variety of package tours that cater to divers, sailors, honeymooners, cruises and those interested in condo rentals or home stays. ~ 74 New Montgomery Street, San Francisco, CA 94105; 415-495-4500, 800-532-3000, fax 415-495-2000.

Another option is to make Tahiti a stopover on a Round-the-World (RTW) ticket. The available combinations on an RTW ticket are almost endless. You can fly via Tahiti to the United States or Canada, for example, then to Europe, and the same on return, or come back via Asia. Continental/KLM offer a one-year RTW ticket with unlimited stops, returning via Asia.

FROM THE UK AND EUROPEAN CONTINENT   Few travelers fly all the way to the South Pacific just to visit Tahiti. Tahiti can, however, be easily visited en route to Australia or on a RTW ticket. Airline ticket discounters (bucket shops) in London offer RTW tickets that include Tahiti in their itinerary.

A typical round-the-world route from London is Los Angeles, Tahiti, Sydney, Fiji, Rarotonga, then back to London via Los Angeles. Or, you could fly to Bangkok, Cairns, Sydney, Tahiti, and once again back to London via Los Angeles. As with flights out of Asia, Air France is generally the airline carrier servicing Tahiti, though Air New Zealand flights may also be used from London (via Los Angeles).

Trailfinders in west London produces a lavishly illustrated brochure that includes air-fare details. STA Travel also has branches in the United Kingdom. Look in magazines such as *Time Out*, the Sunday papers, and *Exchange & Mart* for ads.

Most British travel agents are registered with the ABTA (Association of British Travel Agents). If you have paid for your flight to an ABTA-registered agent that then goes out of business, ABTA will guarantee a refund or an alternative. Unregistered bucket shops are sometimes cheaper, but are also riskier.

Getting to and from French Polynesia from the Continent is straightforward. You go through Paris on Air France, AOM or Corsair, all via Los Angeles. (Note: 95 percent of European travelers go to Tahiti with package deals.)

FROM OTHER PACIFIC ISLANDS   There are surprisingly few connections between Tahiti and other Pacific islands. The ones that exist are not inexpensive. Air France flies between Noumea (New Caledonia) and Tahiti. They also have a connection from Fiji, via Noumea, to Tahiti using Air Caledonie.

There are also various excursion fares that span the South Pacific. For example, Air New Zealand has a fare from Los Angeles to New Zealand (with three stopovers) that takes you to Tahiti, Fiji and the Cook Islands. A similar ticket is available to Australia. If you want to stop in more than in three places along the route, the price goes up accordingly.

FROM ASIA   At the time of publication tourism from Japan has largely disappeared. There are still direct flights, however, from Narita to Papeete on Air France.

FROM SOUTH AMERICA   Lan Chile connects Tahiti with Santiago, Chile via Easter Island.

SEA

Unfortunately, the romantic days of catching a tramp steamer and working your way across the Pacific no longer exist. Unless money is no object, the prohibitive cost of taking ships long distances makes it much more inviting to fly. However, once you are in the islands it is still possible (although difficult) to take freighters from one South Seas port to another.

Booking passage on a freighter between French Polynesia and other Pacific Islands entails going down to the dock and talking the vessel's skipper into giving you a berth. If there is room aboard, and the captain likes you, you are in luck. (On U.S.-registered ships, hitching a ride is impossible unless you have sailor's papers.) The schedule of international cargo vessels coming into Papeete is posted at the waterfront branch of the immigration police adjacent to the tourist office.

YACHTS   For people with time on their hands and adventure in their hearts, traveling to Tahiti by yacht can be a reality. To become a crew member, go to Honolulu or one of the larger ports on the West Coast—preferably Los Angeles, San Diego or San Francisco—which are departure points for most Tahiti-bound yachts.

To find the boats headed to the South Pacific you must do some sleuthing down on the docks of the local yacht club. Usually notices are placed on yacht-club bulletin boards by skippers needing crew members, or by potential sailors looking for a yacht. The best thing to do is ask around the docks or marine supply shops. Naturally, someone who has previous sailing experience, or is a gourmet chef or a doctor, will have a better chance to get on as a crew member. The six-week sailing season starts during the last half of September, with a secondary window opening in January and continuing through March.

If you are serious about getting on a yacht, it's best to start doing your research at least six months ahead of time. Get to know the people you are going to sail with and help them rig the boat. Sailing time from the West Coast of the U.S. to French Polynesia takes about a month, with nowhere to get off in the middle of the Pacific. Papeete is one of the major transit points for yachts in the South Pacific, and once there it is generally no problem for an experienced sailor to hitch a ride from Papeete to any point east or west.

ENTRY PERMITS—YACHTS   The captain and crew must have valid passports and previously secured tourist visas. A five-day transit visa is also desirable. If coming from a country that does not have a French consulate, the visitor must, after five days, secure a valid visa from the Immigration Service—good for three months for all of French Polynesia.

Along with the visa, each crew member must have a deposit in a special account at a local bank or at the Trésorerie Générale equal to the fare from Tahiti back to the country of origin. During the yacht's stay in French Polynesia the crew list must correspond with the list of passengers made at the time of arrival. Any changes must be accounted for with the Chief of Immigration. Crew changes can only be made in harbors or anchorages where there are *gendarmes* (police). Disembarkation of crew members can only be authorized if the person in question has an airline ticket with a confirmed reservation. Yachts may not stay longer than one year. There is a branch of the Immigration Office near the *Fare Manihini* (Visitors' Bureau) directly on the waterfront.

TRAVEL BETWEEN ISLANDS

Traveling between the islands of French Polynesia served by Air Tahiti or scheduled ferry service is not usually a difficult affair. Thanks to French largess the transportation infrastructure is quite sophisticated. There are modern airstrips, well-paved highways, numerous boats and ferries, and a bus system that works. Visitors will find that most transportation is reasonably priced, and despite the general *mañana* attitude, things generally run on time.

The two means of transportation to the outer islands are by air and interisland vessels. Traveling by air is the fastest and most efficient method, but not necessarily the most economical. Although the local carrier, Air Tahiti, flies to quite a few destinations, it does not go to all the islands.

Interisland vessels, on the other hand, do go to every inhabited island but take more time, and overall are a much cheaper form of transportation than planes. On shorter routes they can be a great bargain and, at the same time, give you the chance to meet some locals.

A third possibility is to combine air and sea transportation. For example, if you want to visit Ahe, which has no air service, it is possible to book a flight to Manihi and then catch a speedboat from there to Ahe.

LOCAL AIR SERVICES   The major interisland carrier, Air Tahiti, provides service to every island group. The island hoppers are well-maintained first class ATR equipment. However, Air Tahiti's virtual monopoly means fares are high and service is inconsistent. Air Tahiti reservations agents tend to be very professional in Papeete, but not necessarily on the outer islands. Changing plans on the outer islands means reservations are apt to disappear. Discounted fares on Air Tahiti are not advertised but are available if you apply for family or student rates. The catch is that applications for discounts can *only* be made in French Polynesia and it may take several days to a week to process. My suggestion is to look into this immediately after arrival in Papeete. ~ Papeete; 86-42-42.

In some cases, flights to and from the outer islands are direct, while in others they are routed via Papeete. For example, you can fly directly from Huahine to Raiatea but to fly from Huahine to Rangiroa you must pass through Faa'a Airport in Papeete. The type of aircraft used on most flights is the ATR 42 (hi-tech, twin prop, 46-seat). Nineteen-seat Twin Otters and smaller Britten-Norman Islanders are used on shorter routes. Air Tahiti has five different passes, good for 28 days, allowing one stopover for each island on a circular route. The five options, which have sub-options that are reminiscent of a Chinese menu, are:

1. The Leeward/Windward Islands (Moorea/Huahine/Raiatea/Bora Bora).

2. The Leeward/Windward Islands (Moorea/Huahine/Raiatea/Bora Bora) plus Rangiroa/Manihi or Manihi/Rangiroa/Tikehau.

3. The Leeward/Windward Islands (Moorea/Huahine/Raiatea/Bora Bora) plus Rangiroa/Manihi or Manihi/Rangiroa/Tikehau.

4. The Leeward/Windward Islands (Moorea/Huahine/Raiatea/Bora Bora) plus the Austral Islands (Rurutu/Tubuai).

5. The Leeward/Windward Islands (Moorea/Huahine/Raiatea/Bora Bora) plus Rangiroa and the Marquesas Islands (Atuona/Nuku Hiva).

The difference between options number two and number three is that the lesser fare means swinging through the islands in one direction, starting in the Society Islands and finishing in the Tuamotus, whereas the more expensive fare allows you to start in either direction. Thus, with option number two you can begin your journey from the Tuamotus or the Society Group. The fourth option also allows you to start from the Australs and continue through the Society Group. Likewise, the fifth option allows the traveler to begin the journey from the Marquesas or the Society Group.

For information on Air Tahiti in the U.S. contact Tahiti Vacations. ~ 800-553-3477.

A new upstart charter carrier called **Air Alizé**, based in Raiatea, has a small fleet of nine-passenger Piper Chieftain aircraft that fly throughout the Society islands, although with much less frequency than Air Tahiti. Most flights originate out of Raiatea. Air Alizé also has discount programs for families and students. Again, they must be applied for in French Polynesia and may take up to a week to process. ~ Uturoa; 66-00-00, fax 66-10-01.

Several other small airlines charter planes or helicopters for visitors. If flights are full, standby service is often available. Baggage allowance on interisland flights is only 22 pounds (10 kilograms). Airlines will charge you without hesitation if your baggage is overweight.

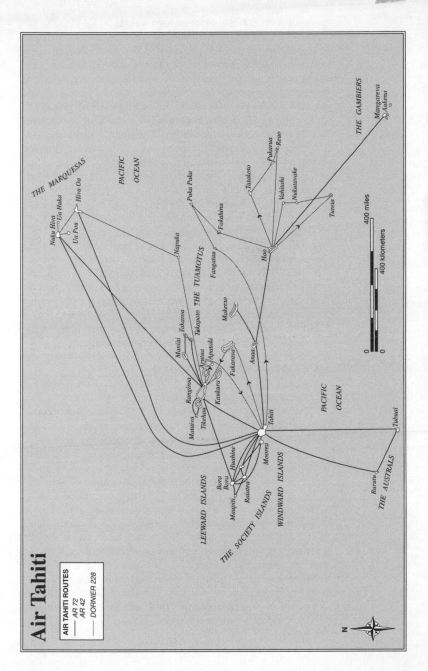

Air Tahiti

AIR TAHITI ROUTES
— AR 72
— AR 42
—— DORNIER 228

THE GAMBIERS

Mangareva
Aukena

PACIFIC OCEAN

THE MARQUESAS

Nuku Hiva
Ua Huka
Ua Pou
Hiva Oa

Pukarua
Reao
Tatakoto
Vahitahi
Nukutavake
Tureia
Puka Puka

Napuka

Fakahina

Fangatau

THE TUAMOTUS

Takapoto

Hao

Makemo

Maniiai
Tokaroa
Aratua
Apataki
Fakarava
Kaukura
Rangiroa
Mataiva
Tikehau

Anaa

PACIFIC OCEAN

Tahiti

Bora Bora
Maupiti
Huahine
Raiatea
Moorea

LEEWARD ISLANDS

WINDWARD ISLANDS

THE SOCIETY ISLANDS

Tubuai

Rurutu

THE AUSTRALS

400 miles

400 kilometers

N

FERRIES AND OTHER INTERISLAND VESSELS Despite the increase in air transportation, interisland vessels remain a vital transportation link for travelers and cargo to the outer islands. In many instances, interisland steamers or much smaller skiffs are the only way to reach isolated communities. If you don't mind roughing it, interisland boats are a wonderful way to travel and meet local people. Make sure you allow plenty of time for this type of voyaging. Trips may range from a few hours to a few weeks. They are also usually inexpensive. Check the itineraries carefully before setting sail.

If you decide to travel by a conventional interisland boat, the best reported conditions were on the *Vaieanu,* which is the cleanest, and has marginally better accommodations. You will, however, not confuse it with the *QE II*.

Unlike the interisland boats, the ferries to Moorea generally leave on the hour, and you can purchase a ticket literally minutes before the boat departs. In sharp contrast to the old-style ferries that crawl like tortoises, a speedy new type of catamaran ferry should be in operation by the time this book is published. Called the *Tamahine II B,* this 380-passenger vessel will race across the channel in 12 minutes on an air cushion powered by a waterjet propulsion system. Not to be outdone by the competition, the other major transportation company is slated to launch a 500-passenger ferry capable of carrying 120 autos. (When the ferry is anchored in Papeete each night it will double as a seafood restaurant.)

All of the Moorea-bound ferries depart from the dock opposite the Royal Papeete Hotel. They include:

Aremiti Channel Express ~ 42-88-88

Tamahine Moorea, Tamarii Moorea II B ~ 56-13-92

The following is a description of ferry itineraries and operator addresses for ferries serving each of the island groups.

Society Islands   There are five vessels serving these islands.

Taporo VI is one of the larger interisland boats, but it only takes 12 passengers because it is a freighter. During the day, when the tickets are purchased at the wharf, the 12-passenger rule is strictly enforced. In the evening, when the ticketing becomes the responsibility of the captain, the rule is stretched, especially if the boat is not on its way to Papeete where an official may check the number of passengers on arrival. The vessel has fewer passenger amenities than ferries and is not as clean or comfortable. When the seas are rough, the *Taporo VI* is *the* vessel of choice if you are prone to seasickness because it is doesn't pitch and roll as much as a smaller vessel. *Taporo VI* departs Monday, Wednesday and Friday at 4 p.m. ~ *Compagnie Francaise Maritime de Tahiti Maritime de Tahiti,* BP 368, Papeete (Fare Ute), Tahiti, 42-63-93, 43-79-72, fax 42-06-17.

Interisland Vessel Booking

To book passage on an interisland vessel, walk down to where the boats are moored (past the naval yard in Fare Ute in Papeete) and see which ones are in port. You can also obtain a list of all the copra boats and their destinations at the government tourist office. Chat with the skippers on the dock, double-check the current prices and determine where they are going and when they are departing.

Boat schedules are not reliable. Like so many things in the South Pacific, they are subject to change. Departure and arrival times listed are only approximate. If you absolutely, positively *must* catch a vessel, especially on a remote island where communication is minimal, take a tip from the locals and camp on or near the dock.

You often have the option of either bringing your own food for the journey or eating the ship's fare—the difference in price can be substantial. Sometimes only deck passage is available, which means just that—sleeping, eating and drinking on deck with others who have chosen this economical route.

It is recommended that you purchase tickets at least a half-day before the scheduled departure date. In the outer islands tickets can be bought on the dock. Although old-fashioned ferries are a cheap alternative to air transportation to the outer islands, they are by no means comfortable. The toilet facilities are usually appalling. Despite their seafaring ancestry, Polynesians (not to mention all the rest of us) are apt to vomit at the first hint of rough weather. If you add the odor of fresh vomit to the acrid smell of diesel fumes you begin to get the true flavor of ferry travel in the romantic South Seas (at least during foul weather). If you're not willing to put up with these inconveniences, I suggest you book a ticket on Air Tahiti.

Keep in mind that a round-trip voyage may last a month or more, so jumping ship on an island that has no air service may turn out to be a long-term commitment—at least until another ship comes along.

A sea cruise on a copra boat is appealing as long as you can contend with the occasional storm, seasickness, diesel fumes, engine noise, claustrophobia and cockroaches. The camaraderie, adventure, salt air, guitar playing and drinking of Hinano beer by moonlight, on the other hand, are hard to beat.

Taporo IV Route	Voyage time
Papeete/Huahine	9 hours
Huahine/Raiatea	2½ hours
Raiatea/Bora Bora	3 hours
Bora Bora/Tahaa	2½ hours
Tahaa/Raiatea	1 hour

The *Ono Ono* is a sleek, new generation of high-speed ferry that could give Air Tahiti a serious run for its money. Traveling time to the destinations, although slower than by air, is one-third the time it currently takes on a conventional ferry. For example, traveling time on the *Raromatai* is 9 hours between Huahine and Papeete and only 2 hours and 50 minutes on the *Ono Ono*. There are no sleeping areas on the deck nor are there cabins. A 66-pound (30-kilogram) allowance is made for baggage. Because of the speed, I would seriously consider the *Ono Ono* for convenience sake, even though it is much more expensive than a conventional vessel. The one-way tariff ranges from 4300 CFP from Papeete to Huahine to 5800 CFP from Papeete to Bora Bora. Price for infants under the age of two years is 350 CFP when accompanied by an adult. ~ Papeete, 45-35-35, fax 43-83-45.

The *Ono Ono* leaves Papeete on Monday and Wednesday, returning on Tuesday and Thursday. The Friday departure from Papeete returns Sunday evening, with interisland service on Saturday.

ONO ONO DEPARTURE AND ARRIVAL TIMES

Monday and Wednesday

Departs	at	Arrives	at
Papeete	9:00 a.m.	Huahine	12:30 p.m.
Huahine	12:45 p.m.	Raiatea	1:30 p.m.
Raiatea	1:45 p.m.	Bora Bora	4:15 p.m.

Tuesday and Thursday

Departs	at	Arrives	at
Bora Bora	7:00 a.m.	Raiatea	9:15 a.m.
Raiatea	9:30 a.m.	Huahine	10:30 a.m.
Huahine	10:45 a.m.	Papeete	2:15 p.m.

Friday

Departs	at	Arrives	at
Papeete	4:30 p.m.	Huahine	7:45 p.m.
Huahine	8:45 p.m.	Raiatea	9:00 p.m.
Raiatea	9:15 p.m.	Bora Bora	11:00 p.m.

Saturday

Departs	at	Arrives	at
Bora Bora	8:00 a.m.	Raiatea	10:15 a.m.
Raiatea	10:30 a.m.	Huahine	11:30 a.m.
Huahine	3:00 p.m.	Raiatea	4:00 p.m.
Raiatea	4:15 p.m.	Bora Bora	6:15 p.m.

Sunday

Departs	at	Arrives	at
Bora Bora	12 noon	Raiatea	2:15 p.m.
Raiatea	2:30 p.m.	Huahine	3:30 p.m.
Huahine	3:45 p.m.	Papeete	7:15 p.m.

The *Temehani II* carries 116 passengers, including 27 in cabins. The prices for Deck/Cabin berths are 1650/3300 CFP for Papeete/All Leeward Island destinations. ~ *Société de Navigation Temehani*, BP 9015, Papeete (Motu Uta), Tahiti, 42-98-83.

Temehani II Route	Voyage time
Papeete/Huahine	8½ hours
Huahine/Raiatea	2 hours
Raiatea/Bora Bora	2½ hours
Bora Bora/Tahaa	2 hours
Tahaa/Raiatea	1 hour

Raromatai is a passenger and vehicle ferry that travels between Papeete, Huahine, Raiatea, Tahaa and Bora Bora. It is most comfortable for traveling short distances, such as those between the Leeward Islands, because there are benches for sitting and taking in the South Seas vistas. In addition to the benches on the outer decks, there is an air-conditioned lounge inside (with television) that has comfortable seats, most of which are filled with travelers from Papeete who stretch out on them to sleep. Although the seating is comfortable on the vessel, at times the toilets (both men's and women's) can be vile. The ship has recently been overhauled and perhaps this problem has been ameliorated.

Raromatai Options	Rates
1 berth with 2 bunks	8500 CFP/trip
1 berth with 4 bunks	6000 CFP/trip
Deck passage	3200 CFP/trip
Interisland passage (between 2 islands)	1000 CFP

Don't forget to BYO toilet paper. The *Raromatai* has two sailings, rotating every week. The first sailing departs Papeete for Huahine on Monday at 6 p.m. After visiting Huahine, Raiatea, Tahaa and Bora Bora it returns to the capital on Thursday at 9:30 p.m. The second sailing departs Papeete on Friday at 4:30 p.m. and arrives back on Monday at 5:30 a.m.

If you're still interested, tickets for the ferry can be purchased on the boat. Note that there are two ticket tables, one for passengers and the other for motor vehicle or bicycles. This means you must line up twice if you are taking a vehicle with you. A snack bar is open on board all the time and there is a restaurant that is open only between Papeete and Huahine. The ferry's capacity is approximately 300. ~ BP 50712, Pirae, Tahiti; 43-19-88, fax 43-19-99.

Vaieanu is my favorite of the boats because it is filled with Tahitians who cover the decks and the vessel's huge hold wall-to-wall with their sleeping mats. For the long, overnight trip from an outer island to Papeete sleeping on the deck covered with mats and pillows is quite comfortable and lots of fun. Inexpensive mats can be purchased at any Chinese store in any town. There is no snack bar so BYO food. The bathrooms on this ship are relatively good. Tickets can be purchased ahead of time at the wharf. The fare is 700 CFP between any of the islands. The vessel departs Monday, Wednesday and Friday at 5 p.m. ~ *Société Coopérative Ouvriere de Production IHITI NUI*, BP 9062 (Motu Uta) Papeete; 41-25-35, fax 41-24-34.

Vaieanu Options (one way)	Rates
Berth "A" class	6000 CFP
Cabin "A" class	12,000 CFP
Berth "B" class	4500 CFP
Cabin "B" class	9000 CFP
Berth "C" class	4000 CFP
Deck "C" class	1600 CFP

Tuamotu Islands   The *Cobia II* operates between Papeete/Kaukura/Arutua/Apataki/Tikehau/Aratika/Toau. No meals are served and no cabins are available. There is one voyage weekly, which departs from Papeete on Monday and returns to Papeete on Thursday. Contact Ms. Mehiti Degage to reserve a berth. The cost is 3000 CFP per person. ~ *SNC Degage & Cie*, BP 9274; Papeete, Tahiti; 42-88-88.

The *Manava II* has three routes, which include the far-flung islands of Makatea, Tikehau, Mataiva, Kaukura, Rangiroa, Arutua, Apataki, Toau, Ahe, Manihi, Takapoto, Takaroa, Fakarava, Aratika, Raraka, Taiaro and Kauehi. The voyage length is about ten days for each route. No scheduled days or times are available. No cabins are available—deck passage only. Prices (one-way) for Route 1: 2100 CFP, Route 2: 2800 CFP and Route 3:3900 CFP. Round-trip is 7800 CFP for deck passage plus 1800 CFP per day for meals. ~ *TMI (Sociéteé des Transports Maritimes des Îles), Simeon & William Richmond*, BP 1816, Papeete, Tahiti; 43-83-84.

The *Manga Nui* has an irregular schedule that visits Takapoto/Takaroa/Fakarava/Aratika out of Papeete on a monthly basis. (No schedule is available.) The voyage length is 30 to 40 days. Deck space is limited, and no meals are available. Phone reservations are not accepted. This vessel is for the truly adventurous. ~ Mr. Jimmy Culina Vicei, *Manga Pacifique*, BP 136913, Papeete, Tahiti; 42-69-69.

The *Ruahatu* visits Papeete, Hereheretua, Tematangi, Nukutavake, Tureia, Nukutepipi, NengoNengo, Pinaki, Vanavana, Vairaatea, Takapoto, Reiao, Pukarua, Vahitahi. The voyage length: 20 to 22 days. (There is no set schedule.) Tariff ranges from 7000 CFP for deck passage to approximately 12,000 CFP for cabins. deck. Meals are available for 2800 CFP per day. All prices quoted are for one-way fares. ~ *Cie de Developpement des Tuamotu* BP 1291, Papeete, Tahiti; 43-32-65.

The *Saint-Xavier Maris Stella* has six routes that visit the Tuamotus, and which also include Rangiroa, Ahe, Manihi, Takaroa, Arutua, Apataki, Kaukura, Niau, Kauehi, Raraka, Tikehau and Mataiva. The average length of a voyage is eight days—two voyages per month. (There is no set schedule.) Round-trip fare is about 20,000 CFP for deck passage, including three meals per day. ~ *Société de Navigation des Tuamotu SARL*, BP 11366, Mahina, Tahiti; 42-23-58.

Marquesas Islands The *Aranui*, French Polynesia's largest interisland freighter, was completely revamped in 1984 to accommodate 40 passengers for regularly scheduled service to the Marquesas Islands. This is the only vessel specifically outfitted for passenger traffic. The 262-foot *Aranui* offers three classes of air-conditioned cabins as well as deck passage. First-class cabins include private shower and toilet facilities; second- and third-class cabins share communal showers. The only real difference between second- and third-class accommodation is a wash basin in the second-class cabins. Refurbished for tourists, the rooms are large considering that the boat was never designed as a passenger vessel.

Mattresses on the deck, two toilets and two showers are provided for deck class. The public rooms are a small lounge with a modest library and selection of games, and a bar area on the upper deck.

The itinerary consists of three days in the Tuamotu Islands (Rangiroa, Takapoto and Arutua) and a ten-day swing through the Marquesas Islands (Nuku Hiva, Ua Pou, Ua Huka, Hiva Oa, Tahuata and Fatu Hiva). Activities include fishing, a visit to a pearl farm, land tours and horseback riding. The *Aranui* is still a working cargo boat and offers you an opportunity to visit the islands in comfort while seeing a slice of outerisland life. The ship has a French chef and the menu includes plenty of fresh fish, lobster and shrimp. The cuisine is Tahitian, French and Chinese. The length of the voyage is 16 days. The schedule varies each month. Call for information. The price includes three meals a day and excursions. ~ For more information in the U.S. call 415-574-3560 in San Francisco. Locally, *Compagnie Polynesienne de Transport Maritime* can be reached at 42-62-40.

Austral Islands The *Tuhaa Pae II* is reportedly unreliable, changing its schedule rather often, which makes it impossible to plan a visit if one has a scheduled return flight home. The trip to the Australs is rather rough but the islands, especially incredibly remote Rapa, are worth a visit. The route includes Tubuai, Rurutu, Rimatara, Raivavae, Rapa and takes about 15 days. ~ *Société Anonyme d'Economie Mixte de Navigation des Australes*, BP 1890, Papeete, Tahiti; 42-93-67.

Gambier Group The *Manava III* plies a route that includes Hao, Vairaatea, Nukutavake, Marutea Sud, Puka Puka, Reao, Takapoto, Vaitahu, Amanu, Eastern Tuamotus, Gambier Group. The voyage length is 20 days. ~ *Compagnie de Développement Maritime des Tuamotu*, Richmond Bene, BP 1291, Papeete, Tahiti; 43-32-65.

CRUISES For those who like the idea of exploring the islands by sea and don't want to rough it, there is one passenger vessel that plies French Polynesian waters—the 440-foot motor sailor *Windsong*.

Cruising the islands has a distinct advantage for travelers who want to be taken care of *and* desire a "structured" tour package. The disadvantage is that you are at the mercy of the ship's schedule.

The 150-passenger *Windsong* is a four-masted luxury motor sailor catering to a well-heeled crowd. Though reminiscent of an old-fashioned yacht, there is nothing anachronistic about this boat. One of the main advantages is its shallow draft, which allows it to enter small coves and secluded beaches. Its sails are operated by computer (eliminating the need for a crew), and VCRs and color TVs are found in every room. Inside, the vessel is exquisitely detailed and crafted, using hardwoods such as teak. It's a class act, but then, you are paying for it.

There's also a comprehensive recreation program. Sports equipment and instruction are available for waterskiing, using Zodiac inflatable motor launches, and there are windsurfing, sailing, deepsea fishing, scuba diving and snorkeling excursions available. A Tahitian dive master is on board to provide scuba assistance, but passengers must be certified divers to use the diving gear. Other on-board recreational facilities abound. ~ Call Windstar Sail Cruises at 800-258-7245 in the United States.

▼▼▼▼▼▼▼▼▼▼▼▼
Before You Go

PASSPORTS & VISAS

Visitors need passports. Citizens of the U.S., Canada and Japan can stay for up to 30 days without a visa. Guests from EC countries have even greater latitude—they can visit for three months or less without a visa. If you are from the United States, Canada, Japan, New Zealand, South Korea or most European nations, it is *not* necessary to obtain a visa.

Australian citizens must have a visa before going to French Polynesia or they will not be granted permission to enter. Visitors from a host of nations from South America, Africa and Asia are also obligated to apply for their visa before entering, but don't need the approval of the local French High Commissioner. However, visitors from some nations need the approval of the French High Commissioner before visiting the country.

Get to the airport early! There is no departure tax charged to visitors leaving French Polynesia, but there *can* be an inordinate amount of time waiting at the airport in order to pass through airport security, immigration and the like.

In most cases, visitors will automatically be granted visas of up to three months without the High Commissioner's approval. Upon expiration, tourist visas may be extended for another three months, with a possibility of renewal for an additional six months. No foreigner can stay for more than a year with a tourist visa.

For visitors who wish to extend their stays in French Polynesia beyond the normal 30-day limit and wish to apply for a visa, the best bet is to go back to the airport immigration office and make your arrangements there, instead of going to the government offices in town. (The immigration people in Papeete will eventually send you to the airport anyway.) After filling out the necessary forms, the airport people will then send you to the post office to purchase a 3000 CFP stamp. To avoid the hassle and spending the 3000 CFP, if you know before leaving for Tahiti that you will stay for more than 30 days, it's much better to arrange things with the nearest French consulate.

Overseas addresses of the Tahiti Tourist Board are:

TOURIST BOARDS

AUSTRALIA Tahiti Tourism Promotion Board ~ Suite 301/620 Street, Kilda Road, Melbourne 3004, Victoria; (613) 521-3877, fax (613) 521-3867.

CHILE Tahiti Tourism Board ~ Ave 11 de Septiembre 2214, OF 116, Box 16057, Stgo. 9, Santiago; (562) 261-28-26, fax (562) 261-28-26.

FRANCE Office du Tourisme de Tahiti et ses Îles ~ 28, Boulevard Saint Germain, 75005 Paris; (46) 34-50-59, fax (43) 25-41-65.

GERMANY Tahiti Tourisme ~ Haingasse 22, D-61348 Bad Hamburg; (49) 6172-21021, fax (49) 6172-690-488.

HONG KONG Tahiti Tourist Promotion Board ~ c/o Pacific Leisure Group, Tung Ming Building, 10th floor, 40, Des Voeux Road, Central Hong Kong; (5) 241-361, fax (5) 253-290.

INDONESIA Tahiti Tourist Promotion Board ~ c/o Aviamas, Chase Plaza, Surdirman Kav 21, Jakarta 12910; (021) 558-185/588-195/588/550, fax (021) 570-3439.

JAPAN Tahiti Tourist Promotion Board ~ Sankyo Building (No 20), Room 802, 3-11-5 Iidabashi, Chiyoda-Ku, Tokyo; (03) 265-0468, fax (03) 265-0581.

SOUTH KOREA Tahiti Tourist Promotion Board ~ c/o Bando Air Agencies Ltd, 15th floor, Ankuk Insurance Building, 87, 1-ka, Ul-chi-Ro, Chund-ku, Seoul; (027) 761-039, fax (027) 522-970.

MALAYSIA Tahiti Tourist Promotion Board ~ 2-5-2-6 Raya Building, Angkasa, Jalan Ampang, Kuala Lumpur; (032) 480-644, fax (032) 613-630.

NEW ZEALAND Tahiti Tourist Promotion Board ~ 172 Wellesley Street, P.O. Box 5, Auckland, New Zealand; (649) 373-2649, fax (649) 373-2415.

SINGAPORE Tahiti Tourist Promotion Board ~ 11 Craig Road, Tanjong Pagar, Singapore 0208; (0065) 221-1747, fax (0065) 221-1747.

TAIWAN Tahiti Tourist Promotion Board ~ 98 Nanking Road, Section 2, 6th floor, Taipei 10048; (02) 252-1393/252-3520, fax (02) 253-5159/254-1271.

UNITED STATES Tahiti Tourist Promotion Board ~ 300 North Continental Boulevard, Suite 180, El Segundo, CA 90245; (310) 414-8484, fax (310) 414-8490

SHOTS Tahiti is malaria-free and inoculations are not required except for those arriving from an area infected with smallpox, cholera or yellow fever, which exempts 99.9 percent of visitors. (For more information on the general topic of health, please see the "Medical Info" section later in this chapter.)

INSURANCE You might consider purchasing a travel insurance policy to cover theft, loss and medical problems. There are a number of policies

WORKING IN PARADISE

Who hasn't thought about chucking it all and moving to paradise? But the cold facts run contrary to the dreams. To live and work in Tahiti is not easy for nonresidents. A work permit is tied to a residence permit and is issued two months following the request for a work contract. The permit is issued care of the employer, who is responsible for the employee's return to his or her homeland. A local is always given priority in filling a job so you have to be able to provide a special skill not found in Tahiti. U.S. citizens skilled in the hotel/restaurant business may have the best chance because some of the hotels in Tahiti are owned or operated by Americans.

available and your travel agent will have recommendations. Check the small print. Some policies specifically exclude "dangerous activities," which can include scuba diving, motorcycling or even trekking. You may prefer a policy that pays doctors or hospitals for claims later rather than you paying on the spot. If you have a claim make sure you keep all documentation. Some policies ask you to call back (reverse charges) to a center in your home country where your problem can immediately be assessed. Be sure to check if the policy covers ambulances or an emergency flight home. If you have to stretch out you will need two seats and somebody has to pay for them! Emergency Evacuation Insurance may be a good idea if you are planning to visit a very remote area such as the Marquesas or the Tuamotu Group.

PACKING

Dress in Tahiti is almost always casual and because of the warm climate it is easy to subscribe to the adage "travel light." Unless you are planning to travel to the outer fringes of French Polynesia, such as the Austral Islands, you can be certain it will be warm, even at night. Clothing should be lightweight. Bathing suit and shorts (for both men and women) are always practical and fashionable. Cotton shirts and dresses are also necessary, as are sandals, a light plastic raincoat or windbreaker for the odd tropical downpour, a light sweater, a hat to shield you from the intense rays of the sun, sunscreen, insect repellent, a first-aid kit, and perhaps some small souvenirs or toys for Tahitian children. If you plan to walk on the reef, reef shoes are an absolute necessity. Nike makes a good model and Speedo's brand also works. Keep in mind that virtually everything is frightfully expensive here so purchase film, sun block and other such items before you leave home (see the "Medical Information" section later in this chapter for suggestions). You'll thank yourself later for being so clever.

CUSTOMS

In addition to personal effects, the following are allowed into Tahiti duty-free: 200 cigarettes or 100 cigarillos or 50 cigars or 250 grams of smoking tobacco, 50 grams of perfume, .25 liter of lotion, 55 grams of coffee, 40 grams of tea and 2 liters of spirits.

MONEY MATTERS

Costs   French Polynesia is not a budget holiday spot. While some of the pensions, particularly on the outer islands, are reasonably priced, nothing is inexpensive. You should not even consider visiting French Polynesia without realizing that "sticker shock" will be your constant companion. Expect to spend more money than you planned on food, accommodation, film, liquor and virtually everything else—except bread.

Currency   The currency used in French Polynesia is the French Pacific franc or CFP. Notes come in denominations of 500, 1000, 5000 and 10,000, and coins in denominations of 1, 2, 5, 10, 20, 50 and 100. The CFP is on parity with the French franc—(1 CFP = 0.055 French francs).

Banks Major banks include Westpac Bank, Banque de Polynesie, Banque Socredo, Banque de Tahiti and Banque Paribas Polynesie.

Credit Cards and ATMs Visa credit cards are accepted (banks will give you a cash advance), as are American Express and, in some places, MasterCard. (On many of the smaller islands, credit cards are not accepted.) ATMs are rapidly making inroads in Tahiti but don't assume that American ATM cards will work here. Though I've read that some American ATM cards may work at an ATM machine in Paris, I did not find this to be the case in Tahiti when I tried to withdraw money from my American bank account. An Australian or a New Zealander who banks with Westpac might have better luck.

Traveler's Checks While seemingly old-fashioned, traveler's checks are easily cashed at banks and hotels. Traveler's checks combined with a major credit card are the best way to travel in French Polynesia. All banks charge a 350 to 400 CFP commission on a traveler's check transaction, particularly if you are changing from one currency to another.

Tipping Tipping is discouraged by the tourism office but Tahitians have been introduced to this practice and are not averse to receiving tips. Though some "experts" discourage tipping, I believe it should be done at your discretion.

LODGING Room prices for conventional hotels in Papeete and in much of the rest of French Polynesia fall into two general categories—expensive and very expensive. Aside from air-conditioning, beach frontage, discos, restaurants and bars, upscale resorts may provide swimming pools, tennis courts, bicycles and free snorkeling gear. Prices for this type of hotel range from US$150 to US$250 for double occupancy.

On the other end of the scale is lodging for the budget-minded traveler. Your choices may include older hotels that lost their luster when the more modern resorts opened up, smaller family-operated pensions, or boarding arrangements with families. Some resorts also offer campgrounds or dorm facilities with spartan accommodations (usually small bunks, primitive kitchen areas and shared bathroom facilities). Somewhat better and in the budget-to-moderate spectrum are local-style *fares,* or thatched-roof bungalows. Indigenous to French Polynesia, these units offer modest but comfortable lodging that usually includes a kitchenette, one or two bedrooms, and a sitting area. Depending on the tariff, it may or may not have hot water, but it will always sport overhead fans instead of air-conditioning. Budget accommodations may not afford all the luxuries, but nevertheless many people find them acceptable. Prices range from US$50 to US$100 for a double.

Throughout this book, hotels are described according to price category. *Budget* hotels have rooms starting from US$50 to US$100 per night for two people. *Moderate* facilities begin between US$100 and US$150. The smaller, budget-to-moderate hotels may have air-conditioning, a pool and not much else in the way of extras. *Deluxe* hotels offer rates starting from US$150 to US$200. *Ultra-deluxe* establishments rent rooms at prices above US$200.

These prices do not include an 8 percent room tax and—like all things in this world—are subject to change.

DINING

Eating out in French Polynesia generally requires copious amounts of cash. However, an important step in reducing hotel food costs was implemented by the local government, which reduced import tariffs on liquor and encouraged hoteliers to lower prices on food. This dramatically reduced prices on MAP (Modified American Plan—three meals per day) and AP (American Plan—breakfast and dinner) plans at various hotels as well as tabs at hotel bars. Although it varies from hotel to hotel, the law has resulted in a 15 to 40 percent reduction in food bills. Though the government has made a valiant attempt to bring prices down by slashing import duties on liquor, these reduced prices apply only to special tourist menus featured at some hotels and some restaurants that have volunteered to go along with the revised pricing scheme. Most à la carte items retain their normal (usually expensive) price. The government is encouraging all restaurants to provide discounts in the future.

If you are interested in staying in a pension contact Patty Lussan at Tekura Travel in Papeete. ~ 43-12-00, fax 43-84-60.

If the high price of restaurants has you spooked, there are plenty of modern grocery stores and supermarkets on the islands with major population centers. The selection of cheese, produce, wine and meat is first class, as you might expect of a French colony. Naturally, the stores and fine restaurants are frequented by Polynesians who have adopted the French science of appreciating fine food. This very civilized quality separates even the most humble French Polynesians from their island neighbors, and, from most North Americans. You may not know a good Bordeaux from a bad Burgundy but middle-class Tahitians will. What this also means is that stores are incredibly well stocked with every conceivable cheese, wine, olive oil and fresh produce. Rest assured that people who like to cook for themselves will not want for quality food.

A few guidelines will help you chart a course through French Polynesia's restaurants. Within each chapter, restaurants are placed geographically and categorized as budget, moderate, deluxe or ultra-deluxe in price. Dinner entrées at *budget* restaurants cost US$12 or less. The ambience is informal café style and the crowd is often a local one. *Moderately* priced restaurants range between US$12 and US$20 for dinner entrées and offer pleasant surroundings, a more varied menu and a slower pace. *Deluxe* establishments tab their entrées around US$20 to US$30, featuring a more sophisticated cuisine, and more personalized service. *Ultra-deluxe* are entrées priced above US$30.

Breakfast and lunch menus vary less in price from restaurant to restaurant. Even deluxe-priced kitchens usually offer light breakfasts and lunch sandwiches, which place them within a few dollars of their budget-minded competitors. These early meals can be a good time to test expensive restaurants.

Beyond the bright lights of Papeete and other large population centers dining is an entirely different proposition. The outer islands frequented regularly by visitors (such as Moorea, Bora Bora and Huahine) offer a good selection of restaurants and *roulottes* (vans that sell simple meals) as well as supermarkets where ample and varied food supplies may be obtained. However, the remote areas of the Tuamotu Group, the Australs and the Gambiers are generally devoid of restaurants and large markets. Visitors must rely on their pension or hotel to provide food. Incidentally, virtually all the islands have small mom-and-pop stores, but these establishments sell only a limited selection of canned goods (such as sardines or tinned beef) and other staples. The availability of food and manufactured goods on the remote islands is almost always dependent upon when the last interisland boat visited.

NIGHTLIFE   French Polynesia offers a variety of nightlife ranging from tony private clubs, dance halls, casinos and discos to seedy bars. Papeete, one of the genuine fleshpots of the South Pacific, is where the nightlife is centered. However, most urban areas on the outer islands also have nightclubs or offer entertainment at hotels.

In Papeete, the clubs that are situated along the waterfront or in the Vaima Center area don't open up until 9 p.m., and the action doesn't start until 11 p.m. Closing time is usually 2 or 3 a.m. (or later), and most of the nightclubs are closed on Sunday. Expect to pay a 1000 CFP to 1500 CFP cover charge, which also includes the first drink. Beer is around 500 CFP and mixed drinks range from 1000 CFP to 1500 CFP.

"Making the scene" at the clubs is a big thing for locals, as there just isn't much else to do on a weekend, especially on the outer islands. Another cultural observation is that everyone in Tahiti dances, sings, plays guitar or does it all. Thus going to a club to dance, especially for young single people, is part of growing up in the islands. Those who want to experience an important part of local culture would miss a great deal by not at least spending one evening at a nightclub that features a traditional Tahitian band. But, be prepared to spend money. Being tightfisted won't get you too far with the locals.

In many ways, French Polynesia is an ideal place to take young-sters—the warm sea, friendly inhabitants and the excitement of new, exotic surroundings stir their imaginations. Polynesians in general are terrific with kids, and anthropologists tell us that in many ways they care for them better than so-called developed societies. A visit to the islands gives a child a great opportunity to meet young-sters from other countries and to glimpse how other cultures live.

TRAVELING WITH CHILDREN

Use a travel agent to help with arrangements; they can reserve spacious bulkhead seats on airlines and determine which flights are least crowded. They can also seek out the best deals on inexpensive lodging, saving you money on both room and board.

Planning the trip with your kids stimulates their imagination. Books about travel, airplane rides, beaches, and Polynesian culture help prepare even a two-year-old for an adventure. This preparation makes the "getting there" part of the trip more exciting for children of all ages.

And "getting there" means a long-distance flight. Plan to bring everything you need on board the plane—diapers, food, toys, books and extra clothing for kids and parents alike.

Allow extra time to get places. Book reservations in advance and make sure that the hotel or pension has the extra crib, cot or bed you require. And when reserving a rental car, inquire to see if they provide car seats and if there is an added charge.

Besides the car seat you may have to bring along, also pack shorts and T-shirts, a sweater, swimsuit, waterproof sandals, and a sun hat. A stroller with sunshade for little ones helps on sightsee-ing sojourns; a shovel and pail are essential for sandcastle building. Most importantly, remember to bring a good sunblock. The quick-est way to ruin a family vacation is with a bad sunburn. Also plan to bring indoor activities such as books and games for evenings and rainy days.

Many supermarkets carry diapers, food and other essentials—though at very steep prices. If your child is very young, to econo-mize you might consider bringing a separate suitcase with diapers, wipes, food, toys and the like.

Among the basics you should pack are a first-aid kit. Check also with your physician about taking along a treatment for diar-rhea.

If your child becomes sick or injured in Tahiti, first-class med-ical care is available from French doctors. In Papeete, both the **Pao-fai Clinic** (43-02-02) and the **Cardella Clinic** (42-81-92) have pe-diatricians on staff. On Bora Bora there is also good quality care available. **Dr. Juen** speaks English and can be found next to Chez Roger, a store adjacent to the boutique/studio Patine. ~ 67-70-62. **Dr. Martina Roussanaly** is around the corner from the post office in Vaitape. ~ 67-70-92. **Dr. Duval** at the government-run medical center in Vaitape, is said to be very good, but chances are visitors will not have access to this clinic unless it is a dire emergency. ~ 67-70-77. (In the case of an extreme emergency, visitors are airlifted to Papeete).

Medical assistance can be obtained on **Huahine** ~ 68-88-33; **Raiatea** ~ 66-34-55; and **Tahaa** ~ 65-60-60.

The only caveat about taking children is that it might prevent you from staying in some of the luxury hotels. Many have "no children" policies. However, hotels that welcome kids generally have no problem arranging babysitters.

WOMEN TRAVELING ALONE

It is a sad commentary on life today, but women traveling alone must take precautions.

Rape in French Polynesia is common among the local population, but as far as I know it is a rare occurrence for visitors. I know of only one instance of an attempted rape at a campground in Bora Bora. In this case, the attempted rape was by a local. If you are by yourself late at night in downtown Papeete, be extra cautious. In Tahiti, when a man asks you out, chances are he expects more than a good night kiss—even on the first date. Likewise, an invitation to a midnight stroll on the beach implies more than gazing at the stars and holding hands. Dating in the Pacific tends to mean sex may be in the offing or expected sooner than later. This is especially true for Northern Europeans or North Americans, who, for better or worse, are perceived as sexually liberated in the eyes of locals.

It's unwise to hitchhike alone. At night, even in rural areas, if you are alone keep the doors and windows shut. There are many uninvited lotharios attempting the classic climb-through-the-window-at-midnight routine. I say classic because this seems to be rather a common practice in the Pacific.

Should a woman traveling solo accept an invitation from a family to stay with them? Absolutely. That is, if you feel good about the invitation. More often than not it will be a great experience, espe-

THE "PK" SYSTEM

On larger islands like Tahiti and Moorea, you can pinpoint your position on the map from the red-topped "PK" (kilometer) markers along the inland, or mountain side, of the road. Thus to find someone's home you must rely on the PK system, which means watching the kilometerage and knowing what side of the road (ocean or mountain) you are headed. Thus a PK address in Tahiti might be PK 3.3 *cote mer* (ocean side) in Arue (the district). There are no street names on the majority of the islands and most people receive mail at a P.O. Box.

cially in an outer island setting with a traditional family. Being invited to spend time in a local home has become a rarity in French Polynesia when compared to other South Pacific destinations, so count yourself lucky if you have been invited.

Finally, I've had letters from several women, including a Peace Corps volunteer with years of experience, who suggest that I bring up the subject of "Peeping Toms." My Peace Corps reader tells me that this behavior is relatively common throughout the South Pacific. Without probing the sociocultural aspects of this practice or judging whether or not it is innocuous, just be forewarned that "they" are out there and visitors are fair game.

SENIOR TRAVELERS

French Polynesia gets more than its share of well-heeled older travelers. Given the expensive nature of travel in this area, it takes a great deal of disposable income to afford a first-class vacation in this part of the world. Unfortunately, I am not aware of any senior discounts in French Polynesia.

The **American Association of Retired Persons** (AARP) offers membership to anyone over 50. AARP's benefits include travel discounts with a number of firms. ~ 3200 Carson Street, Lakewood, CA 90712; 310-496-2277.

Those with fragile health should take into consideration the intense tropical heat and humidity when planning a trip to the tropics. Visitors who have never experienced this type of climate should not overextend themselves. Fortunately, first-rate doctors and health care facilities are available in Tahiti. While the other islands have less sophisticated amenities, excellent health practitioners are available. Consider carrying a medical record with you—including your medical history and current medical status as well as your doctor's name, phone number and address. Make sure your insurance covers you while you are away from home.

GAY & LESBIAN TRAVELERS

The good news for gay and lesbian travelers is that people in French Polynesia do not discriminate against homosexuals. French society has traditionally been tolerant toward same sex relationships, and Polynesians are even more tolerant. Another way to state this is that in French Polynesia one's sexual preferences are not an issue. Two people of the same gender booking a room will scarcely evoke a second thought, much less a second glance. Gays are treated with respect, or disrespect, like other tourists. Due, perhaps, to the lack of discrimination, gay-exclusive facilities do not tend to form. The closest thing to gay gathering places I could find are the bars in Papeete that feature female impersonators. (See the "Nightlife" section for Papeete in Chapter Four.)

DISABLED TRAVELERS

Tahiti is not very accessible to travelers with disabilities. Unlike the United States and other more enlightened destinations, French Polynesia has no laws that stipulate wheelchair access to public buildings or similar policies that consider the needs of persons with disabilities. Hotel facilities in the more remote areas of French Polynesia have marginal infrastructure with regard to this issue. Some hotels and facilities are more helpful than others. If there is a question about your particular situation, be sure and check in advance.

The **Society for the Advancement of Travel for the Handicapped** offers information for travelers with disabilities. ~ 347 5th Avenue, #610, New York, NY 10016; 212-447-7284.

Travelin' Talk, a network organizations, also offers assistance. ~ P.O. Box 3534, Clarksville, TN 37043; 615-552-6670.

Once You Arrive

VISITORS CENTERS

The headquarters for the Tahiti Tourist Board (known as *GIE Tahiti Animation*), which is also the main information center, is on the quay nearly opposite the Vaima Shopping Center. It is situated in a cluster of brown buildings constructed to resemble traditional Tahitian dwellings (*fares*). It is known as the *Fare Manihini*, which translates as "guest house." Inside you will likely find several Tahitian women who are there to provide you information in English. ~ Fare Manihini, Boulevard Pomare, BP 65, Papeete, Tahiti, French Polynesia; 42-96-26.

Some of the outer islands do have tourist offices and information centers but they are run by the local government and are not part of the national administration. Hours and availability of the locally run tourism bureaus vary a great deal. In some locales, professionalism is very high, while on other islands you're lucky if a staff member is actually in the office.

On some of the outer islands the tourist board information office is also a tour booking office. Despite this seeming conflict of interest, I found the information to be quite accurate.

FOREIGN CONSULS

AUSTRIA Honorary Consul Paul Maetz ~ BP 4560, Papeete; 43-91-14, home 43-21-22.

BELGIUM Honorary Consul Pierre Soufflet ~ BP 1602, Papeete; 41-70-36, home 53-27-20, fax 42-33-76.

CHILE Honorary Consul Pasquelatta Daniela ~ Immeuble Norman Hall, Rue du General de Gaulle, BP 952. Papeete; 43-89-19, home 43-25-67.

FINLAND Honorary Consul Janine Laguesse ~ BP 2870, Papeete; 42-57-63, home 42-97-39.

GERMANY Honorary Consul Claude Eliane Weinmann ~ BP 452, Rue Le Bihan-Fautaua, Papeete; 42-99-94, home 42-80-84, fax 42-96-89.

GHANA Honorary Consul Inike Bandar-Chimbe ~ BP 343, Papeete; 43-98-66.

ITALY   Honorary Consul Augusto Confalonieri ~ BP 420, Papeete; c/o Tikichimic, Fare Ute, Papeete; 58-20-29, home 43-91-70, fax 58-21-95.

KOREA   Honorary Consul Bernard Baudry ~ BP 2061, Papeete; 43-04-47, home 43-76-22, fax 42-3140.

MONACO   Honorary Consul Paul Emile Victor ~ BP 33, Papeete; 42-53-29.

NEW ZEALAND   Honorary Consul Christian Destrieux ~ BP 73, Papeete; 43-88-29, home 43-40-59, fax 42-45-44.

NORWAY   Honorary Consul Victor Siu ~ BP 306, Papeete; c/o Services Mobil, Fare Ute Papeete; 43-79-72, home 42-05-62.

Canadian and U.S. residents should note that there are no honorary consuls to represent them.

NETHERLANDS   Honorary Consul Jan Den Freejen Engelbertus ~ BP 2804, Papeete; c/o Immeuble Wong Liao, Building d'Alsace, Papeete; 42-49-37, home 43-58-74.

SWAZILAND   Honorary Consul Francois Imbewe ~ BP 1969, Papeete; 43-11-77.

SWEDEN   Honorary Consul Michel Solari ~ BP 2, Papeete; c/o Ets Soari, Impasse Cardella; 42-73-93, home 42-47-60, fax 43-49-03.

UNITED KINGDOM   Honorary Consul Charles Vienot Sr. ~ BP 1064, Papeete; c/o Avis Rent A Car; 42-86-88, fax 42-43-55.

TIME

French Polynesia is ten hours behind Greenwich mean time (GMT), two hours behind U.S. Pacific standard time and twenty hours behind Australian eastern standard time. Thus, when it is noon Sunday in Tahiti, it is 2 p.m. Sunday in Los Angeles, 5 p.m. Sunday in New York, 10 p.m. Sunday in London, 11 p.m. Sunday in Paris, and 8 a.m. Monday in Sydney. The Marquesas Islands are half an hour ahead of the rest of French Polynesia, so when it's noon in Tahiti, it's 12:30 p.m. in the Marquesas.

BUSINESS HOURS

Most businesses open their doors between 8 and 10 a.m. on weekdays and close at 5 p.m. Some larger stores stay open until 7 p.m.; small, family-run corner stores may not close until 10 p.m. There is usually a very long lunch hour (12 noon to 2 p.m.), but most banks are open at this time. On Saturdays, shops close for the day at 11 a.m.

Legal Holidays   Legal holidays, where government services are shut down, include New Year's Day, *Arrivée de l'Evangile* (March 5), Good Friday, Easter, Easter Monday, May Day (May 1), Victory Day 1945 (May 8), Ascension (the last Thursday in May), Pentecost and Pentecost Monday (the first Sunday and Monday in June), Internal Autonomy Day (June 29), Bastille Day (July 14),

Assumption (August 15), All Saints Day (November 1), Armistice Day (November 11) and Christmas Day.

Government employees are off on these days, but the observance by store owners varies.

Banking Hours   Regular banking hours vary slightly. The Bank of Tahiti opens for business at 7:45 a.m. and closes for lunch from 11:45 a.m. to 2 p.m. It re-opens at 2 p.m. and closes at 4 p.m. The Bank of Polynesia has the same hours, except that it opens at 7:30 a.m. The Westpac Bank and the Bank of Socredo are open from 7:30 a.m. to 3:30 p.m. Some banks (e.g., the Bank of Tahiti) are open from 7:45 to 11:30 a.m. on Saturday mornings.

If you need to get to a bank on Saturday, your hotel can tell you where the nearest open one is. Exchange counters are available at Faa'a International Airport at arrival and departure times.

WEIGHTS & MEASURES   Whether you're getting gas, checking the thermometer or looking at road signs, you'll notice the difference: everything is metric. French Polynesia is on the metric system, which measures temperature in degrees Celsius, distances in meters, and most substances in liters, kilos and grams.

To convert from Celsius to Fahrenheit, multiply by 9, divide by 5 and add 32. For example, 23°C equals [(23 x 9)/5] + 32, or (207/5) + 32, or 41.4 + 32, or about 73°F. If you don't have a pocket calculator along (but you probably should), just remember that 0°C is 32°F and that each Celsius degree is roughly two Fahrenheit degrees. Here are other useful conversion equations:

1 mile = 1.6 kilometers	1 kilometer = $^{3}/_{5}$ mile
1 foot = 0.3 meter	1 meter = $3^{1}/_{3}$ feet
1 pound = 0.45 kilo	1 kilo = $2^{1}/_{5}$ pounds
1 gallon = 3.8 liters	1 liter = ¼ gallon, (about a quart)

ELECTRIC VOLTAGE   The current is 220 volts AC in the more modern hotels and 110 volts in the older facilities. All modern units have power outlets for electric shavers, hair dryers and other appliances. If you have any doubts, don't plug in a thing until you check with the facility. You may want to examine the light bulbs for any hints of what voltage is utilized. Many hotels also have converters for appliances. If you use a computer or any other appliance that utilizes a three-pronged plug, you may have to purchase a two-pronged adapter at a local hardware store for several hundred CFP. (Or bring one with you!)

DRIVING   Those interested in renting a car may use a driver's license from their own country (or state) or an international license.

The roads that follow the perimeters of Tahiti, Bora Bora and Moorea are almost fully paved. This is not the case with the more remote communities where auto traffic is less frequent or, as in the

Tuamotus, virtually nonexistent. The roads that do exist, especially in more populated areas, are modern and well maintained.

Car and Motorcycle Rentals For the visitor spending any appreciable time in Tahiti, or someone wishing to do an around-the-island tour solo, renting a car, motorcycle or scooter is a necessity. Aside from the big names like Budget, Hertz and Avis, there are small, locally-owned, good-quality rentals—but consumers should be wary. Scrutinize the vehicle before you drive it away, lest you find nonexistent brakes or flat tires. Allow plenty of time when collecting and returning your car; this may happen on island time. Depending on your choice of model, prices range from US$60 to US$120 per day or more. Rates are generally based on time plus distance and there is an insurance charge of 600 to 1500 CFP. Gasoline (petrol) is not included and it isn't cheap—figure on paying around 110 CFP per liter!

Once in French Polynesia you will realize that locals have their own concept of time, usually one to two hours behind what you had planned.

Bicycle Rentals Bicycle rentals are available on most islands, generally at hotels. If the traffic is not too congested, a bike is a great way to get around an island. I don't recommend bicycles for Tahiti because of the sheer numbers of automobiles on that island. Bora Bora used to be a great place to explore by bicycle but growing numbers of vehicles make it more precarious. Expect to pay at least 1500 CFP per day for a rental. One reader mentioned that he consistently rented vehicles for half a day and inevitably brought them back late without being charged extra. While I don't encourage this, Tahitians may allow for "Tahitian time" in regards to rentals. Then again, they may not.

HITCHING

With the exception of Tahiti, Moorea and Bora Bora, hitchhiking is fairly easy. As a rule, the less populated the island, the easier it is to hitchhike. Hitching is fairly safe in French Polynesia but always exercise common sense. Travelers may find it easier to get rides if they are not perceived as being French. The lesson here is, leave your berets at home.

PUBLIC TRANSIT

On most of the Leeward islands there is a marvelous bus system consisting of owner-operators driving jitney-like vehicles known as *Le Truck*—a triumph of small-scale entrepreneurship. Many French Polynesians cannot afford cars, so *Le Truck* transports the majority of the population, especially on Tahiti where commuting to work in Papeete from the rural areas has become a way of life.

On the outer islands, where commuting is not as big a factor and the population density is much smaller, buses are less frequent. On these islands (such as Bora Bora, Huahine or Moorea) it definitely behooves you to rent a car, motorcycle or bicycle for the day's sightseeing rather than depend on public transportation. Taxis can be found everywhere, but tend to be very expensive.

I find Tahitian motorists uncommonly courteous compared with American or Continental drivers, but they do have their own rules of the road, so when in doubt, drive defensively. Watch out for motorists who may insist on passing on blind curves, tailgating and turning without signaling. Beware also of children playing on the street, pedestrians who seem oblivious to traffic, dogs, and on the weekends, drunks—both in automobiles and on foot.

PHONES   The phone service in Tahiti is quite good, and a number of public phones are appearing on the streets of Papeete and villages around French Polynesia—even in the most remote Tuamotu atolls. In addition to coin-operated public phones, card-operated ones have been installed as well.

One rule of thumb is to never, absolutely ever, make a long distance phone call from a hotel unless you use a telephone card from your home country. Rates in French Polynesia are astronomical enough and a hotel-placed call is likely to be double the rate of the local Office de Postes & Telecommunications—Polynesie Française. If you don't have a calling card, a few of the phone booths are still coin operated. A local phone call starts at around 50 CFP.

You might want to take advantage of the new "call back" services available from U.S. vendors. These services get around the outrageous rates charged in French Polynesia. You call the vendor in the U.S., who in turn calls the user back and connects them with the number you wish to call. This takes advantage of much lower U.S. telephone rates and saves a lot of money. If you are not enrolled in a "call back" service and have an AT&T, MCI or similar

WRAPAROUND WEAR

If you stay long enough in the islands you will undoubtedly adopt the local article of clothing called a pareu (par-ay-you), a rectangular piece of cloth about five to six feet long. This practical item is a brightly colored wraparound cotton cloth worn by men and women and is sold in every store. It makes a terrific and inexpensive gift. It can be tied a number of ways but is usually wrapped skirt-like around the waist and worn with a T-shirt. Although Western men might at first cringe at the idea of wearing a skirt, they soon find that in Tahiti's often sweltering climate, a pareu is a practical item of clothing to wear around the hotel. Get hooked and you will find yourself bringing a few pareus back home. They come in a variety of colors and patterns, as well as several grades of quality.

long-distance calling card, you can still save money by using these long-distance carriers. To do so, you must go through the French Polynesian operator, who will process and verify your card through the AT&T or MCI operator. Try not to use the hotel phone to call overseas. Rates from hotels differ, but sometimes calls can be inflated as much as 200 percent from the already outrageous French Polynesian rates.

To make a direct overseas call, dial the country code, the area code and the phone number. International codes are as follows: (0054) Argentina, (0043) Austria, (0061) Australia, (0032) Belgium, (0055) Brazil, (001) Canada, (0056) Chile, (0044) England, (16) France, (0049) Germany, (00852) Hong Kong, (0039) Italy, (0081) Japan, (0052) Mexico, (0064) New Zealand, (0063) Philippines, (0065) Singapore, (0034) Spain, (0046) Sweden, (0041) Switzerland, (0031) Netherlands and (001) U.S.

Telephone Calling Cards Calling cards are worth looking into and can be purchased at any post office or other retail outlets such as newspaper stands or shops with phone booths nearby.

There are three denominations of cards that purchase corresponding "call units"—5000 CFP, 2000 CFP and 1000 CFP. If you do plan to make a long-distance call, it's a good idea to pick up a 5000 CFP card and keep it with you.

MAIL

The French Polynesian postal system is generally very efficient. Due to the numerous flights in and out of Papeete, delivery time from the islands to the U.S., Australia and Europe is usually no longer than a week. The main post office in Papeete is a gleaming modern wonder.

In addition to the main post office on Boulevard Pomare, there is a branch at Faa'a Airport that is open weekdays from 5 to 9 a.m. and 6:30 p.m. to 10:30 p.m. On Saturdays, the hours are 6 to 10 a.m. You can make international phone calls from this small office as well as purchase stamps.

Most postal addresses given in this book include a BP (*boîte postale*), or post office box number. A lodging accommodation may have a BP number or address that's different from the actual location. For example, a pension in Moorea may be located in Haapiti but may have a mailing address in Pao Pao. It can be confusing.

Stamps from Polynesie Française are gorgeous and sought after by collectors. Sets are available in special philatelic windows. Postcard correspondents should note that stamps from French Polynesia are so large that it's wise to put them on the postcard first and then try to squeeze the address and message in afterward.

Sending and Receiving Mail Foreigners wishing to receive mail may do so by asking at the *poste restante* (general delivery) window. Holders of American Express cards and/or traveler's checks may re-

ceive mail at the American Express office at Tahiti Tours, Rue Jeanne
d'Arc. Telegrams, telexes and a fax service are also available at the
post office. Hours are 7:30 a.m. to 5:00 p.m. on weekdays and 7:30
to 11:30 a.m. on Saturdays.

Postal Rates Postal rates are as follows: letters up to 10 grams:
84 CFP; Europe except France letters up to 10 grams: 84 CFP; France:
60 CFP. Aerograms, good for anywhere in the world, are 76 CFP.

Mail	to	Cost
letters up to 10g	Africa	84 CFP
letters up to 10g	North America	76 CFP
letters up to 10g	Asia	80 CFP
letters up to 10g	Australia/New Zealand	72 CFP
Large postcards	Europe (except France)	84 CFP
Large postcards	France	60 CFP
Large postcards	Africa	84 CFP
Large postcards	Asia	80 CFP
Large postcards	North America	76 CFP
Large postcards	Australia/New Zealand	72 CFP
Small postcards	Europe (except France)/Africa	64 CFP
Small postcards	France	42 CFP
Small postcards	North America	56 CFP
Small postcards	Asia	60 CFP
Small postcards	Australia/New Zealand	52 CFP

Faxes The following is a chart showing the rates for sending one-
page faxes from the post office:

One page on	to	Cost
post office form	North America	1760 CFP
own paper	North America	2600 CFP
post office form	Australia/New Zealand	980 CFP
own paper	Australia/New Zealand	1400 CFP
post office form	France	1200 CFP
own paper	France	1820 CFP

MEDIA

Newspapers Kiosks and bookshops selling the *International Herald Tribune* (flown in regularly from Paris) and the Pacific edition
of *Time* and *Newsweek* are scattered throughout Papeete. Other European publications are also available. (The kiosk at the Vaima
Shopping Center on the waterfront is a convenient place to browse.)
French Polynesia is served by two daily French-language newspapers, *Les Nouvelles* and *Le Dépêche de Tahiti*. French-language
weeklies include *L' Echo de Tahiti,* which examines local politics;
Tahiti Pacifique Magazine, which covers economics, politics and
the environment; and *La Tribune*, a general interest publication.
Of special interest to tourists is an English-language weekly, *Tahiti*

Beach Press, which covers the local scene extensively (often better than the French press), and has excellent travel information on hotels, airlines and tourism in general. The paper also has news on museums and special events. This tabloid-style weekly is given away free at most hotels in French Polynesia. English-language papers such as the *International Herald Tribune*, as well as magazines from the U.S. and Australia, are available at the larger bookstores or at the kiosk at Vaima Center.

A local French-language general-interest magazine is *Tahitirama*, which also has the TV scheduling. Three English-language magazines circulating throughout the Pacific are *Pacific Islands Monthly* (PIM), *Pacific* and *Islands Business*. PIM, published in Fiji, is an excellent regional publication and a venerable institution in the Pacific, oriented mostly toward the old Anglo colonies. *Pacific*, published in Honolulu, is a younger upstart that also covers the Pacific basin, but has better coverage of former U.S. Trust Territories and current U.S. dependencies than its rival. *Islands Business* is a Fiji-based monthly magazine that attempts to cover business and political developments in the Pacific.

Radio and Television   The local radio station, France Region 3, also known as Radio Tahiti, broadcasts in French and Tahitian. Along with local news and international news from the national French network, it features a pop-music format with selections by French, U.S. and Tahitian artists. There are also privately owned radio stations, including Radio Tiare, which broadcasts in French and has mostly a pop-music format, as well as two smaller district stations in Papara and Papenoo.

There are several television channels (some originating in France) that broadcast drama, quiz shows, highbrow French programs and interviews. A local TV station broadcasts news and footage from international correspondents in Tahitian and French. CNN is not available in most hotels, but can be seen in private homes with cable.

TRAVEL ETIQUETTE

Avoiding offense involves common sense and sensitivity to cultural nuance more than anything else. For example, if you are about to enter someone's home and you note that everyone takes off their shoes before they enter, it's probably a good idea to do the same. Some occasions, such as a *tamara'a* (a feast usually held outdoors), call for eating without utensils, so in this instance, you are expected to eat with your fingers as well.

Though French Polynesians as a whole seem to be a raucous lot, their table manners are impeccable. Unless you wish to be classified as a barbarian, adopting good manners is a must.

You will also notice that friends greet each other or say goodbye with a peck on each cheek—French style. If you feel familiar enough with someone, it's okay to do the same. If you are an American, you may wish to hug them, but resist. It's not really done in this society unless you are on an intimate basis.

PHOTOS   Film and photographic accessories are readily available in Papeete's modern shops, but they will probably be 25 percent to 50 percent more expensive than you will be accustomed to. Color prints can be developed from Kodacolor in one hour at QSS in Papeete's Vaima Shopping Center. Always take twice as much film as you think you'll need.

Keep in mind that daylight is very intense in the tropics. When in doubt, underexpose. That is, if you really want that photo, shoot according to what your normal meter reading dictates and then shoot another at a third to one full stop under. It's always best to take photos at dawn or dusk for optimal lighting conditions.

Always keep film dry and cool, and have your camera cleaned when you get home if it has been exposed to the elements—the humidity and salt air can ruin sensitive photo equipment in no time. If you plan to go through airport security frequently, it's advisable to buy a laminated lead pouch for film, available at most camera shops.

When taking photos of local people, smile and then ask permission. Most of the time people will be glad to let you photograph them, but some locals may not want to be part of your slide show.

BARGAIN SHOPPING   A word on shopping. Unlike Asiatic countries, one does not haggle or bargain when shopping in the public marketplaces in Tahiti. More often than not, the price you see is the price you get. Tahitians, though perhaps not the Chinese merchants, might find it rude to haggle over prices. If you try to dicker with a Polynesian, more than likely the seller will get angry and either inflate the price even more or decide not to deal with you altogether. The only exception in the "bargaining rule" is when you are making a large purchase of black pearl jewelry. The margins on these items are very high and a merchant might well consider knocking off a percentage in order to make a sale.

DRESS   Dress in French Polynesia is as varied it is in Europe or North America. Contemporary, informal garb for both sexes is a pareu with a T-shirt or variations thereof. In town, perhaps because of the long-standing French influence, people are expected to dress with flair. Tahitian women take a great pride in their dress and always exhibit impeccable grooming. On a night on the town or even an average workday, you will often see women wearing the latest Paris fashions, and they look drop-dead stunning.

Many local designers have taken a cue from the cultural renaissance and have created a neo-Polynesian style. A great deal of influence in dress comes from Hawaii and California as well as France, and colorful surf wear, tank tops, spandex and athletic-style bikini tops are definitely in vogue.

Bikini tops and lots of exposed skin are not taboo in Tahiti, although unusual in town. Tahitians tend to be the least modest of all Pacific Islanders and can often be seen sunbathing topless on the beaches. Given the local standards, the female visitor has a great deal more latitude in dress here when compared to the rest of the Pacific Island nations.

Are you a man doing business in French Polynesia? I advise you to wear a nice pair of slacks and a good short-sleeve shirt if you expect the locals to take you seriously. One can usually tell the difference between tourists and locals a mile away because of their appearance. (That is not meant to be a compliment!)

SAFETY

Papeete is very safe by U.S. big-city standards, but there are still occasional reports of robberies. Some Tahitians are very poor and occasionally youths may resort to crime. Even though this is rare, you are urged to keep an eye on your valuables, just as you would anywhere else in the world. Depositing jewelry or cash in a hotel safe is a good idea. Outside Papeete and on the outer islands, there are fewer problems—the worst you may encounter is petty theft and the perpetrator may well be another tourist rather than a local! It's also a good idea not to leave cameras or other items of value unattended at the beach. There's a chance they will have disappeared when you return.

MEDICAL INFO

Tahiti is malaria-free and inoculations are not required, except for those arriving from an area infected with cholera or yellow fever. The water is generally safe and plentiful in most areas, but for the skittish, there is always bottled water, canned or bottled soda or beer. To date, I have never had problems with the drinking water anywhere in French Polynesia, but I have heard reports of visitors acquiring waterborne parasites in the outer islands. When in doubt, it might be prudent to drink the local bottled water.

There are modern clinics and hospitals in Tahiti, and many of the outer islands also have hospitals. These include: Moorea, Huahine, Raiatea, Bora Bora, Maupiti, Rangiroa, Tubuai, Hiva Oa, Ua Huka and Nuku Hiva. If there is no hospital on an island, there will at least be a clinic or a pharmacy.

If you must seek medical assistance, hospitals in Tahiti are open 24 hours a day. On the outer islands dispensaries are open from 7:30 a.m. to noon and 2 to 5:30 p.m. during the week. Saturday hours are 7:30 to 11:30 a.m.

The extreme changes in humidity, exotic food and other foreign conditions may tax your system. The best advice is to take it easy for the first few days until you have acclimatized. You would do well to be prepared and bring sunscreen, an ice bag, cornstarch powder, antacids, cold tablets and cough syrup. Here are some other useful items to pack:

- Antibiotics. You may want to take along your own antibiotics, especially if you are going to be on the outer islands where there is little in the way of medical care. They must be prescribed and you should carry the prescription with you. An antibiotic ointment such as Neosporin is also handy to have along.
- Antihistamine (such as Benadryl). These can be used as a decongestant for allergies and colds, though some may make you tired. Antihistamines also relieve the itch from insect bites or stings.
- Antiseptics such as Bactine. Bring antiseptics in swabs or ointment form for cuts and bites.
- Aspirin, Advil or Tylenol or a similar pain reliever.
- Bandages and Band-aids.
- Calamine lotion or Benadryl ointment. These relieve the discomfort from bites or stings.
- Medications for diarrhea such as Pepto-Bismol or Imodium AD. You might want to get a prescription for something stronger, such as Lomotil, if you are prone to digestive problems while traveling. It might be advisable to bring along a rehydration mixture as well for treatment of severe diarrhea. This is particularly important if you are traveling with children.
- Scissors, tweezers and a thermometer.
- Water purification tablets.

Butch Martin, a colleague from New York City, recommends two products that he picked up at a local health food store. The first is "PB8," a pro-biotic acidophilus in capsule form that can be taken daily to promote a healthy balance of intestinal flora. The second is called "Pro Seed," an extract of grapefruit, an effective treatment for intestinal disorders. The latter has a bitter taste but is palatable in tea.

Food   There is an old saying: "If you can cook it, boil it or peel it, you can eat it—otherwise forget it." Salads and fruit should be washed with purified water or peeled where possible. Ice cream is usually okay if it is a reputable brand name, but beware of ice cream that has melted and been refrozen. Thoroughly cooked food is the safest, but not if it has been left to cool or if it has been reheated. Shellfish such as mussels, oysters and clams should be avoided— steaming does not make shellfish safe for eating. Undercooked meat can also be a problem.

If a place looks clean and well run and if the vendor also looks clean and healthy, then the food is probably safe. In general, places that are packed with travelers or locals will be fine, while empty restaurants are questionable. Busy restaurants mean the food is being cooked and eaten quite quickly with little standing around and is probably not being reheated.

Sunburn No matter how cool it feels on a given day in the tropics, the sun's ultraviolet rays are less filtered by the atmosphere than in other latitudes. Damage can be done to your skin and eyes, so be careful. Use a sunscreen with at least 25 SPF—you'll still get a tan with sunscreen, it just takes longer. A hat provides added protection, and you should also use a barrier cream, such as zinc, for your nose and lips. Don't forget to put sunscreen on your feet. The skin on the top of your feet are very susceptible to burning! Calamine lotion is good for mild sunburn. A bad sunburn can ruin a vacation and a severe burn requires medical attention. A minor burn can be treated with a cool bath or cold compresses, soothing cream or steroids. If your skin "bubbles" don't peel it away because it may become infected. An aspirin two or three times a day will help to ease the pain. Some people are allergic to ultraviolet light, and the result is redness, itching and pinpoint-sized blisters. Clothing is the only answer for them. Fair-skinned people have to be very careful in the tropics!

Diarrhea A change of water, food or climate can cause an upset bowel; diarrhea caused by contaminated food or water is more serious. Despite all your precautions, you may still have a bout of mild diarrhea, but a few rushed trips to the toilet with no other symptoms does not indicate a serious problem. Moderate diarrhea, involving a half-dozen loose movements in a day, is more of a nuisance. Lomotil or Imodium can be used to relieve the symptoms,

MONOI OIL

Another locally grown product to bring back that is considerably less expensive than black pearls is *monoi* (mohn-oy) oil, soap, shampoo, body cream and other items derived from this indigenous product. Monoi is a blend of the extracts of two plants—the Nucifera coconut and the fragrant *tiare* flower *Gardenia Tahitensis*. Tahitians (and other Pacific Islanders) have used the oil for centuries as a salve or moisturizer. The homemade version of the oil is readily available in the public markets. You can find the amber or olive-oil colored liquid in refilled gin bottles or medicine flasks. What may be more appealing to the folks back home are the fine, commercially developed Monoi de Tahiti products that are available in shops. The best place to purchase the commercial products are at the large discount stores (see the section on markets North and South of Papeete in Chapter Four).

but they do not cure the problem. For children, Imodium is preferable, but fluid replacement is important to avoid dehydration.

Sexually Transmitted Diseases   As in many other Pacific nations, there are a multitude of sexually transmitted diseases in French Polynesia. AIDS has been reported in Tahiti, but statistics on its prevalence are hard to come by. Given the sexual proclivities of Tahitians, the large bisexual population and the numbers of visitors from every corner of the globe, the presence of AIDS should not come as a surprise. Needless to say, it's a good idea to practice safe sex and use condoms. As my good friend, Dr. Jim Mielke, an AIDS researcher, advises male travelers, "wrap it up" when having sexual relations.

Insect-borne Diseases   Health authorities have expressed concern about filariasis, an insect-borne disease that attacks the lymphatic system. Short-term visitors have little to be concerned about, but doctors advise you to avoid mosquito bites.

Outbreaks of dengue fever also appear from time to time. There is no prophylactic available for this mosquito-spread disease; the main preventive measure is to avoid mosquito bites. A sudden onset of fever, headaches and severe joint and muscle pains are the first signs of dengue fever. Then a rash starts on the trunk of the body and spreads to the limbs and face. The fever usually subsides after several days. Recovery time varies.

Here is how to avoid mosquito and *nono* (sandfly) bites:
- wear light-colored clothing
- wear light-weight long pants and long-sleeved shirts
- use mosquito repellents containing the compound DEET on exposed areas
- avoid scented perfumes or aftershave lotion
- use a mosquito net—it may be worth taking your own

Cuts, Bites and Stings   Skin wounds can easily become infected in hot climates. Be certain to treat any cut with an antiseptic or antibiotic cream such as Neosporin. Avoid bandages that keep wounds wet. Coral cuts are extremely slow to heal because coral injects a weak venom into the wound. Avoid coral cuts by wearing reef shoes and clean any cut thoroughly with peroxide or an antiseptic.

Centipede stings are notoriously painful. They are are usually found in damp areas, under rocks, and in buildings constructed from palm fronds. Centipedes often find quarters in shoes or clothing. If you are in an area where centipedes are found, always shake out your shoes and clothing before putting them on.

Ciguatera   A word of warning about ciguatera, a form of poisoning from eating infected fish. It has been reported in French Polynesia and other areas such as Hawaii, Papua New Guinea and northern Australia, and was known to have infected Captain Cook's crew in 1774. The toxin that causes the poisoning is released by a microscopic marine organism living on or near coral reefs, particularly reefs that have been disturbed (for example by development). When fish eat the organism, the toxin becomes concentrated in the head, organs and roe of the fish. Symptoms of ciguatera include: diarrhea; muscle pain; joint aches; numbness and tingling around the mouth, hands and feet; reversal of temperature sensation (cold objects feel hot and vice versa); nausea; vomiting; chills; itching; headache; sweating and dizziness. If you experience any of these symptoms after eating fish, contact a doctor immediately.

According to Dr. Yoshitsugi Hokama, a recognized ciguatera expert from the University of Hawaii, fish caught in the open sea, particularly large pelagics such as tuna, are safe. However, reef fish, particularly groupers, jacks, and snappers from the *Letjnus* genus, commonly known as *Bohar*, should be avoided, even in restaurants. Barracuda should also be avoided. (In addition to ciguatera, barracuda also tend to have worms.) Dr. Hokama notes that yachties or others who plan to fish for their food should be on the lookout in the near future for a commercial ciguatera test kit.

In general, eating seafood in the restaurants in French Polynesia is as safe a proposition as anywhere in the world, but it is definitely a good idea to avoid reef fish such as snappers and the other species mentioned above. If you catch your own fish, be sure and check with the local people before you cook it (cooking doesn't eliminate toxins). Don't eat fish that have come from a disturbed environment. Also, avoid eating the head, gonads, liver and viscera of fish.

Swimming and Snorkeling   Divers are likely to run into underwater hazards such as fire coral, sea anenomes, crown-of-thorns starfish, scorpion fish and sharks. Shore-bound visitors may meet up with rays on a sandy beach or eels on the reef at low tide. Beware: never stick your hand in a crevice or cavity in the reef! I've seen eels in shallow water on the reef.

**OCEAN
SAFETY**

Avoid swimming, walking barefoot or collecting seafood from beaches or lagoons directly in front of settlements. Raw sewage is often dumped or piped into the nearest convenient outlet—i.e., the beach that forms the villagers' front yard. When bathing, watch where the locals go—that's where it's most likely safe to swim.

Swimming in the lagoons and rivers is a safe practice—shark attacks are rare. A few commonsense precautions are in order: don't swim in the ocean at night; don't wear bright jewelry when swimming or snorkeling; and don't swim in an area where fish have just been cleaned or fish remains have been thrown into the sea.

Aside from the (minimal) threat of sharks, every year there are tragic drownings. Always be aware of the currents in the area where you are swimming. As a general rule, if the locals are swimming in a particular area, it's probably safe for you.

When snorkeling, avoid contact with sea urchins. In case you weren't aware, their long black spines can inflict a painful wound.

(If you come into contact with a sea urchin, a local remedy is to urinate on the wound.) Sea urchins are plentiful—I've seen them near beaches in Moorea.

Fire coral should also be avoided. You can recognize it by its relatively smooth, almost velvet-like surface and fawn color. Bathing a coral scrape with lime juice is a good treatment or applying the outermost bark of *Tiari* (candlenut) is also effective.

Swimmers or snorkelers may also run into jellyfish at certain times of the year. Local advice on swimming conditions is the best way of avoiding contact with these sea creatures with their stinging tentacles. The Medusa jellyfish (related to the Portuguese Man-of-War) is sometimes found in the waters of French Polynesia but fortunately is not common. The stings from most jellyfish vary from being simply painful to causing shock or even loss of consciousness. Dousing in vinegar will deactivate any stingers which have not "fired." Calamine lotion, antihistamines and analgesics may reduce the reaction and relieve the pain.

Up on the Reef   Rule number one around the reef is to always wear reef shoes! Certain cone shells found in French Polynesia sting and the venom is dangerous or even fatal. However, one will generally get hurt only by picking them up. Chances are you're not going to step on a nasty seashell. The stonefish, which resembles its namesake, is an insidious creature (about six inches long) that is found in shallow water. Their natural camouflage makes them almost impossible to see. Surfers, because of the nature of their sport, tend to be the unfortunate recipients of their venom.

THREE

The Land and Outdoor Adventures

Tahiti and the five archipelagos lie at the very center of the Polynesian Triangle. The three points of the triangle—Hawaii to the north, New Zealand to the southwest and Easter Island to the southeast—are nearly equidistant from Tahiti. Not only is Tahiti separated from the rest of Polynesia but she is far from the nearest continents and cut off from the biotic mainstream. Tahiti's isolated location has everything to do with its natural history.

GEOLOGY More than 25 million years ago a fissure opened along the Pacific floor. Beneath tons of seawater molten lava poured from the rift. This liquid basalt, oozing from a hot spot in the earth's center, created a crater along the ocean bottom. As the tectonic plate that comprises the ocean floor drifted over the hot spot, numerous other craters appeared. Slowly, in the seemingly endless procession of geologic time, a chain of volcanic islands, stretching almost 2000 miles, emerged from the sea.

On the continents it was also a period of terrible upheaval. The Himalayas, Alps, and Andes were rising, but these great chains would reach their peaks long before the Pacific mountains even touched sea level. Not until a few million years ago did these underwater volcanoes break the surface and become islands. By then, present-day plants and animals inhabited the earth, and apes were rapidly evolving into a new species.

For many millennia, the mountains continued to grow. The forces of erosion cut into them, creating knife-edged cliffs and deep valleys. Then plants began germinating: mosses and ferns, springing from windblown spores, were probably first, followed by seed plants carried by migrating birds and ocean currents. The steep-walled valleys provided natural greenhouses in which unique species evolved, while transoceanic winds swept insects and other life from the continents.

Tahiti is actually very young when compared to her sister islands of Polynesia. For instance, the Tuamotus, the oldest Polynesian islands, are coral atolls that date back 50 million years. Some of the Hawaiian islands date back 40 million years, and New Zealand, once part of an ancient continent, has been an island group for at least 135 million years. Just a glance at the sharp, cone-shaped profile of Tahiti offers a clue to her volcanic origins and the fact that the island is so young. (A geologically older island would be worn and rounded by the elements.)

Of High and Low Lands   We can divide the islands of French Polynesia geologically into two basic categories: atolls (or low islands) and high islands.

High islands can be either volcanic in origin or the result of an upheaval from the ocean floor. Their terrain can be smooth, rocky and barren, or incredibly steep and covered with lush rainforest. Unlike atolls, where drinking water must be collected in cisterns and a limited range of crops can be grown, high islands often have an abundance of water and have the soil to support a variety of fruits and vegetables. Examples of high islands are Tahiti or Nuku Hiva, which are precipitous, craggy and quite young in geological terms.

Atolls are what Daniel Defoe had in mind when he wrote *Robinson Crusoe*—flat strips of coral with little more than scrub growth and coconut palms adhering to the thin soil. There is little diversity in the flora and fauna, in part because the flat terrain discourages the development of diverse ecosystems. The soil found on atolls is usually poor in nutrients, which also hinders biotic diversity. This is generally accompanied by a chronic shortage of water. In relative geological terms, atolls are much older than high islands—they are in fact the final cycle in an island's evolutionary process.

But let's start at the beginning. The life of a volcanic island begins in the depths of the sea with a mound or rise created on the bottom of the ocean by magma forcing its way upward from the bowels of the earth. Eventually, the magma breaks free through the earth's crust and becomes lava as it erupts from the mouth of a volcano. As long as the lava flows, the island grows. When it stops, the dynamic of wind, water and wave action fashion the surface of the island and eventually help to create a topsoil from which plant and animal life can gain hold. Simultaneously in tropical environments, coral communities begin to take shape on the periphery of the island and the growth of reef systems begins. As the island sinks and the mountains erode and subside, the growth of the reef system keeps pace with the submergence of the land mass. This results in the formation of nearly vertical coral walls on the island's fringes, often creating lagoons.

Geologists actually order Pacific islands into six different classifications that pertain to the specific evolutionary stages from a high island into an atoll.

The culmination of the volcanic island's erosion and submergence, combined with the full development of the coral reef is the atoll. The sinking of the volcano leaves only the coral, which then surrounds a lagoon. Some atolls contain a circular or oblong reef, which may entirely enclose a lagoon, while other atolls have lagoons that are enclosed by segmented islets separated by passes. From a bird's eye view, these atolls appear to be a lush green series of segments in a necklace of islands punctuated by narrow slits of blue water. The long, thin islands or *motus* as they are called, may vary in length from several hundred yards to several miles long. Though narrow, utterly flat and proscribed by the confines of the sea, the dazzling intensity of an atoll can overwhelm the senses.

Primal colors abound. The lagoon radiates with primitive blues and greens—lapis lazuli, cobalt and turquoise. The ceaseless trade winds stir the palm fronds overhead but do little to quell the fierce heat of the tropical sun. The ocean laps or pounds interminably on the blinding white coral shore. Though strikingly beautiful from afar, most people find atolls difficult if not impossible to live on for any length of time.

▼▼▼▼▼▼▼▼▼▼▼▼
Coral Reefs

Reefs in French Polynesia are classified into two general categories: the fringing reefs that border shores and the flat-topped platform reefs or "patch" reefs enclosed within a lagoon. Reefs may be hundreds of thousands of years old with new coral growth constantly occurring. The old and dead coral is cemented together with coralline algae and can be compressed by the massive weight above to form a kind of limestone. Some coral atolls are formed over undersea volcanic mountains that are slowly sinking. If the coral growth matches the rate of submergence, coral limestone hundreds of yards deep may accumulate. Charles Darwin was the first to come up with this theory and, with slight modification, it has withstood the test of time and modern scientific inquiry.

The reef itself is created by the combined efforts of billions of tiny marine organisms ranging from algae and protozoa to coral animals known as *coelenterates*. Many of the organisms remove calcium carbonates from the water and build calcareous structures that we collectively call coral. The coral you may pick up from the beach or purchase at the souvenir stand represents only the skeleton of a once thriving colony of sea-anenome-like creatures known as polyps.

The polyps live in small depressions in the coral and generally feed at night by extending tentacles—exactly like their biological cousins, the sea anemones. The tentacles contain stinging cells that inject poison into small animal prey. The victim is then transferred to the mouth by the tentacles and into the organism's digestive cavity. Most coral stings are too weak to be felt by humans although some species, such as fire corals, have a nasty sting.

Interestingly enough, scientists find that theoretically there is not enough food in a reef ecosystem to keep these billions of animals fed. However, coral communities continue to expand despite what scientific logic dictates. How can this be so? Most corals contain algal cells, known as *zooxanthellae*, embedded in their tissues. Scientists tell us that photosynthesis by *zooxanthellae* during the day provides the coral with energy. The coral in return provides a home for the *zooxanthellae* and so both benefit.

As with all plants, the *zooxanthellae* require light for photosynthesis and this restricts coral to a depth of no more than 200 feet. Below this level there is insufficient light for the *zooxanthellae* and not enough food for the polyp. Temperature also effects coral distribution; reef-forming corals flourish between temperatures of 68°F (20°C) and 86°F (30°C).

The coral reef ecosystem is one of the most diverse on the planet, and its high productivity is matched only by the tropical rainforest. Despite the robust appearance of a coral reef, it is quite fragile. A careless snorkeler can destroy 20 years' growth just by kicking corals or breaking them off with his fins.

REEF LIFE

The creatures of the shore and coral reef are accessible to just about everyone. Some of the more common species you are likely to contact in or around the reef are mollusks, echinoderms and a crustacean or two. Mollusks include clams, sea slugs, octopus, bivalves and the most common mollusk of the reef, the gastropod. Gastropods (many of which produce what are commonly known as seashells) generally possess a single spiraled shell. Nearly all have an obvious head, with eyes and tentacles. Gastropods feed on a wide spectrum of organisms ranging from algae to small fish. If you find a live gastropod on the reef, such as a cowry, it's tempting to pick it up and stick it in your pocket. Remember that this creature may look like it will make a great souvenir, but like all living things it will die and begin to deteriorate immediately. If you place it in this state in your suitcase, it will indeed leave an acute odiferous imprint upon your belongings.

Some mollusks, especially cone shells, are best left on the reef. For example, the *conus textile*, so named because of its textile-like pattern analogous to cloth, are downright venomous. This species and others have developed a harpoon-like radula that is meant to immobilize or kill prey. The lesson here is that it's not a good practice to touch live cone shells. If you are a shell collector, your best bet is to collect shells whose host organisms have gone on to another world. If you do find a shell on the beach that appears to be dead, double-check to make sure it's not inhabited by a hermit crab.

Bivalves such as oysters and other clams are also common on the reef and their shells are often seen in profusion on the beach. Bivalves lack a head, although they may have eyes. They are usually filter feeders, taking water into the body with an inhalant siphon.

Crustaceans make up a varied class of creatures including crayfish, shrimp, prawns, crabs, barnacles, fish lice, water fleas and woodlice. Shrimp and prawn include a variety of forms living both in freshwater and saltwater. Large freshwater prawns provided an important source of protein in times past and are still a popular item in Tahitian cuisine. Crayfish, which will only be seen by divers, are a much sought-after delicacy and are found in great numbers in the Marquesas Islands. Unfortunately, they have become so desired as cuisine for tourists that there is an imminent danger of overfishing this resource.

The largest members of the *Coenobitadae* family are the coconut crabs, which resemble lobsters. They have extremely powerful chelae (pincers) that are capable of opening up, yes, a coconut. Evidently this creature will actually climb a tree, cut off the nut at the spathe, descend and eat the nut. Anyone who has tried to husk a coconut will no doubt be amazed by this feat. Although rare on Tahiti, they may be found in the Tuamotus and are a great delicacy.

In addition to the various crabs found on the reefs and boulders that line the shore, there are a variety of terrestrial crabs, or *tupa* as they are called by Tahitians. Land crabs can be found in great profusion in low-lying coastal areas. They often can be seen crossing roads at night in search of food—they eat just about anything organic they can scavenge. During the day they stay close to their lairs, ready to disappear down their chutes at the first vibration or shadow. Male fiddler crabs, characterized by their enormously enlarged chelae (which are used to attract females), are small and are found by the thousands in swampy ground. Ghost crabs can be seen on the beach running so fast they appear to glide along the sand.

Coral bleaching, another way of describing the massive dying off of coral communities, was first discovered in 1980 on Australia's Great Barrier Reef. Since then, this phenomenon has been observed in the reefs of Hawaii, the Maldives, East Africa, Indonesia and French Polynesia.

CORAL BLEACHING

The bleaching process occurs when the coral expels *zooxanthellae*. Without the algae living in symbiosis with the coral, it does not receive enough energy to survive. Corals expel the algae when under stress caused by excessive sunlight, temperatures outside the normal range or extreme changes in salinity. Only a few degrees above the optimum temperature range of 80 to 86°F (27 to 30°C) can cause problems. Some scientists believe the culprit in this worldwide phenomenon may be global warming.

STROLLING SEASHELLS

One of the stranger sights for the first-time island visitor is finding a seashell "strolling" down the beach. Upon closer inspection, you'll note that the shell is inhabited by a crab, a hermit crab to be specific. Hermit crabs can be found near the shore or on land rustling through the underbrush (though I once found one creeping along the floor of a Catholic Church!). Hermit crabs take up residence in empty shells to protect their vulnerable soft abdomens. They have developed a tail fan that grips the inside of the shell and an oversized pincer to block the shell's opening, lest they be easily extracted from their adopted homes. As the crab grows in size, it must look for a larger shell to find refuge. More at home on the ground, they return to the sea to find new shells or to reproduce.

In *The Snorkeller's Guide to the Coral Reef*, Paddy Ryan quotes Thomas Goreau, the president of the Global Coral Reef Alliance, who notes that "Coral reefs now appear to be the first major eco-system seriously disrupted by climate change." While it's difficult to pin the blame of bleaching solely on global warming, it is certainly implicated. Goreau reported that every documented case of bleach-ing correlated to the highest water temperatures on record at the various study sites in Puerto Rico, Jamaica, Cayman, Cozumel, Flori-da and the Bahamas.

Given that the rise in temperature correlates with coral bleach-ing, a counterargument to global warming as the cause is that there is no hard evidence that the rise in water temperatures is caused by global warming. A shift in currents may be the cause of bleaching in certain instances. For example, several years ago in Tetiaroa, the manager of the resort showed me a portion of the reef that had been bleached. According to his data, the reason for the bleaching was El Niño, the mysterious current that has been blamed for a num-ber of weather-related problems.

▼▼▼▼▼▼▼▼▼▼▼▼
Flora and Fauna

The flora and fauna of the tropical Pacific were, with few exceptions, unknown to the Western world until Cap-tain James Cook and others of his ilk explored the Paci-fic in the late 18th and early 19th centuries. When Cook's ship, the *Endeavour*, ventured to Tahiti and other islands, he found an en-tirely new universe of plants and animals. These included mollusks such as the golden cowry, fish such as the butterfly fish, birds such as honey-creepers and cultivated plants such as taro and breadfruit. Illustrating documentation of the "new" species was done by Sir Joseph Banks and Daniel Solander. Along with the illustrations, spec-imens of shells, preserved fish, bird skins and pressed plants were collected by seamen and naturalists. Bearing the label *Otaheite*, ma-ny of these items were placed in museums and herbaria. Others were sold as objects of curiosity to well-heeled Londoners. It wasn't until the mid-19th century that Tahiti and the Pacific islands were rec-ognized as having their own distinct biota.

A MYSTERY   How flora and fauna reached the distant islands of French Polynesia and the other Pacific isles) is one of the world's great mysteries. Modern scientists are torn between two opposing views. One theory has it that the Pacific's distant islands were pop-ulated from seed and birds brought by wind and sea currents—dis-persing by chance. The majority of plants and animals in the South Pacific are closely related to species in Southeast Asia. However, the prevailing currents and winds that may have aided in their disper-sal flow from the opposite direction, from the Americas. If the Dis-persal Theory is valid, why then are there so few species in the Paci-fic from the Americas?

The second view, the "Vicariance Theory" postulates that flora and fauna populated islands across (now submerged) land bridges, or simply stayed put while the land moved under them. In other words, the present position of the islands of Oceania are not where they were millions of years ago. Thus, it would have been possible for groups of plants and animals to travel great distances simply by remaining where they were. Another factor in this equation is that the sea level has varied greatly over the years. A lower sea level would have exposed more land, making it possible to cross land bridges with ease.

This brings us to the most important point to consider regarding the evolution of French Polynesia's natural history—its distance from Australasia, the main source of its flora and fauna. Being so far away from everything has put the islands out of the natural reach of most of the plants and animals that would otherwise have populated it. This is especially true with the Society Islands whose rich volcanic soil would be an ideal medium to support a variety of species. Compared to Asia or South America, French Polynesia's natural diversity is impoverished.

The paucity of bird life is a good example. Most of the Pacific's ancestral birds came from New Guinea. Even the most distant islands such as Pitcairn and Hawaii have birds originating from there. Their colonizing route across the Pacific appears to have taken them from New Guinea to the Bismarck Archipelago, on to the Solomons, Vanuatu and New Caledonia, to Fiji, Samoa, east to the Society Islands and lastly north to the Tuamotus and the Marquesas Group. The megapodes, cuckoo shrikes, fruit pigeons, kingfishers, weaver finches, white-eyes and honey eaters all followed this route. As one would expect, their numbers dwindled as they flew eastward. In Tahiti, there are just 12 species of land birds, while an island of similar size in the Solomons or Vanuatu supports perhaps 40 species.

The male ghost and fiddler crabs are among the few crustacea that use sound to attract females. They create noise by vibrating their big claw or by tapping the ground with their legs.

In a similar distance-makes-all-the-difference theme, there are no native land mammals in French Polynesia. There are no amphibians and only four species of reptiles. Only insects and spiders, which can be carried great distances by the wind, are represented. Likewise, there are several families of flora which bear windblown seeds, and plant species such as the coconut, which can travel enormous distances over the water.

Yet another issue to consider regarding the distribution patterns of organisms in French Polynesia is island type. Differences of development both in marine and terrestrial flora and fauna are dependent upon whether the island is a high island or atoll. A rule of thumb is that atolls and other low-lying islands will have less diverse fauna compared to high islands. Atolls tend to have few species, and those they do have are widely distributed.

HUMAN INTRODUCTIONS   When the original settlers of French Polynesia first arrived, the variety of vegetation was limited to the seeds and spores borne by wind, sea and the birds that happened to find their way to the islands. To provide food and materials for shelter, the Polynesians brought with them a variety of plants, such as taro, yams, coconuts, bananas and breadfruit.

To the bafflement of scientists, they also cultivated the South American sweet potato—a plant that does not exist in Asia. How the sweet potato, a native of the Andes, got there is still a mystery. It may be that the seeds were dispersed naturally, rafting on coconuts or other organic material or perhaps assisted by birds. According to Thor Heyerdhal's theory, which he attempted to prove with his voyage on the *Kon Tiki*, Polynesians may have had contact with South America.

Long after the Polynesians settled, the missionaries came and introduced corn, cotton, sugarcane, citrus fruits, figs, pineapples, guavas, tamarinds, coffee and other vegetables.

Tahiti also owes quite a bit of its present-day flora to Edouard Raoul, a pharmacist-botanist who in 1887 brought a cargo of 1500 varieties of plants to the islands and experimented with the cultivation of hundreds of types of fruit trees. He also brought *kauri* (from New Zealand), red cedar, eucalyptus, rubber, gum and jack. Ten years after his arrival, Raoul's plentiful gardens were donating about 150 species of plants to farmers to improve their stock.

In 1919 Harrison Smith, an American professor turned botanist, purchased 340 acres in Papeari and settled down to cultivate hundreds of plant varieties that he had imported from tropical regions throughout the world. Like Raoul, he helped local farmers by giving them seeds and cuttings to better their crops. (For more information on Smith, see Chapter Four.)

There can be a price to pay for bringing in new species. Indeed, the introduction of alien flora and fauna often represents a real threat to the ecological balance. An interesting case in point can be made from the lowly *Partula*, a bean-sized snail native to the Society Islands. The *Partula* of Moorea evolved into different species, originally separated by the valleys and serrated ridges of this emerald isle. The *Partula* makes excellent fodder for scientific inquiry into evolution for a number of reasons. It lived on isolated islands, it didn't travel far, it had a relatively short life cycle (about 17 years) and it could be easily bred. Genetically, they were extraordinarily varied. They were in fact the perfect subject for observation of speciation, as noted in 1932 by H. E. Crampton, the great mollusk collector of the South Pacific.

The Islanders'
Staff of Life

The coconut palm has been the staff of life for islanders for thousands of years and continues to provide a source of income to those in French Polynesia who harvest copra—the flesh of the dried nut. The coconut husk, which acts as a cushion to protect the inner nut from its rapid descent to the ground as well as acting as a life raft at sea, is also extremely useful. In the old days, islanders used sennit (braided twine or rope made from coconut husk fibers) to make sandals that protected them while walking on the sharp reefs. On at least one island, Bora Bora, locals have found a unique use for the discarded husk—using it as a fuel to power an electrical generator.

A coconut takes about a year to mature from flower to ripe nut. After reaching full size, but long before ripening, the green or yellow nut is at the drinking stage. It is easily whacked open with a machete and its liquid contents consumed. The pint or so of clear coconut milk can be almost effervescent and is wonderfully refreshing, especially when cold. In the islands vendors of cold drinking nuts are very popular.

During the green or "drinking nut" phase of maturation, a thin translucent layer forms inside the shell and is quite tasty. The soft, whitish pulp can be scraped from the inside of the shell with a spoon or, lacking any utensil, your fingers. When finished drinking the juice, simply crack open the shell on a rock and start eating. As the nut ripens, the soft pulp turns hard and the sweet juice loses its taste. The raw flesh of the nut is still good to eat at this stage and is sometimes roasted, shaved and used as an appetizer. Locals use it in cooking with fish, vegetables and in desserts. The raw meat is grated, squeezed through a cloth and the result is a white, rich liquid. The final eating stage of the nut is prior to germination. At this point the meat has become spongy in texture and has totally absorbed the juice. The soft flesh still makes good eating and is worth trying.

For modern-day Polynesians the coconut's value is as copra, a vital source of income for rural islanders. Copra production entails harvesting the nuts, cracking them open and letting them dry in the hot tropical sun or in special dryers made from corrugated zinc sheets. The dried meat turns yellowish-brown, shrinks from the nut casing and is removed by hand. It is then placed in burlap bags for shipment. The rancid, pungent smell of copra is unforgettable and you will very likely see bags of copra being weighed on the dock. The processed copra provides an oil that has many uses as an ingredient in soaps, vegetable oil, margarine and even nitroglycerine.

Note that the past tense is used. The snail no longer exists on Moorea. The history of its decline began in 1803. At that time the Governor of Reunion wanted to please his mistress, who had a fondness for Madagascan snail soup. In that year he imported some very large snails from that island and they promptly escaped from his garden. The creatures became a sort of slimly locust destroying the island's crops. By 1847, the giant African Land Snail (as it is now known) reached the Indian subcontinent and by the 1930s made its way to the South Pacific where it was introduced as a gastronomical treat, *l'escargot*. Although Polynesians showed little appreciation for the huge snail, the snail was greatly enamored with local fruit crops and multiplied with gusto.

The colonial authorities had to find some way to control this new pest and by the 1970s they were in a desperate state. A biological control perhaps was in order. Why not introduce another alien creature to combat the current plague?

In Moorea farmers had learned of a predatory snail from the southeastern United States that had been used elsewhere in the Pacific with success. In 1977 *Euglandina rosea* was introduced to Moorea. The effect was dramatic. *Euglandina* can sniff the chemical scent of its prey like a bloodhound. Unfortunately, the local *Partula* snails were much easier to catch than the introduced African Land Snail. The result was that the *Partula* were being gobbled up as *Euglandina* spread like wildfire throughout the forests of Moorea. By 1987 a survey determined that the native mollusk was extinct on the island.

Fortunately for the *Partula*, scientists rescued some specimens from the wild and bred them in captivity. One day it may be possible to introduce them to Moorea, but not for the foreseeable future.

▼▼▼▼▼▼▼▼▼▼▼▼▼▼
Outdoor Adventures

French Polynesia offers a wide array of outdoor and sporting activities for the visitor including snorkeling, scuba diving, surfing, windsurfing, hiking and horseback riding. The venues for these activities are listed in each island chapter. *Pirogue* (outrigger canoe) racing is the closest thing to a national sport in French Polynesia. The best time to see both regional and international competition is during the *Heiva* festival in July.

Visitors may join the locals, many of whom are sports fanatics, in more recreational activities such as golf, bicycle racing, tennis, basketball, track and field, soccer and swimming. It should be noted that in 1995 French Polynesia hosted the South Pacific Games, a regional, Olympics-like event featuring only South Pacific athletes.

OUTRIGGER CANOEING

If one could zero in on a specific sport that indisputably captures the spirit of Tahitian society, it would have to be outrigger canoe or *pirogue* racing.

Racing *pirogues* or *va'a* are long, slender canoes around 25 feet (7 meters) long. All have one outrigger and are manned by six or more individuals. Racing canoes that partake in international class competition weigh no more than 400 pounds (181 kilos) and are made of fiberglass. There are also traditional canoes constructed from local hardwood. In the late afternoon, it's not unusual to see teams of paddlers practicing or racing against other teams in lagoons throughout French Polynesia.

Tahitians take great pride in the Polynesian tradition of canoeing and were shocked in 1981 when for the first time, the visiting American club from Hawaii trounced the leading Tahitian team in a major race.

Paddling clubs are not solely the domain of men. There are also women's and children's divisions. Races between different islands and clubs are highly charged and extremely competitive affairs. Canoe teams train rigorously throughout the year for races held during the *Tiurai* celebrations, the highlight of the racing season. Another important race is the Hawaiki Nui Va'a marathon contest, which is held over a three-day period among four of the Leeward Islands. Once a year at least one Tahitian team travels to Hawaii (where the sport is also popular) to compete in the 41-mile Oahu to Molokai race with clubs from Hawaii, other Pacific islands and the mainland U.S.

SAILING

Who has not visualized dropping anchor in the calm waters of a lagoon and falling asleep to the gentle sound of trade winds rustling through palm fronds? The romantic idea of setting sail for the palm-tree-studded shores of French Polynesia is perhaps a universal dream. Fortunately, the dream can become reality.

Ideal weather (both winter and summer), steady trade winds and an abundance of anchorages make French Polynesia one of the great cruising destinations of the seven seas. And there is no better way to explore the islands than by yacht. In fact, the scarcity of roads and airstrips on the more remote islands make sailing the only way to see them. Navigation is generally easy throughout the archipelagos.

Although French Polynesia is expensive, groceries and supplies can generally be procured on all but the most remote islands. In addition, excellent charts of the area are available and telecommunications are first rate compared to other South Pacific destinations. (See Chapter Two for Entry Permit information and island chapters for anchorage information.)

DIVING

Most of the islands of French Polynesia are bounded by reefs where tropical fish of every color and description thrive. Snorkeling, easily learned, is safe and leads you to fascinating underwater worlds. Mask and fins (flippers) are readily available at most hotels. The best snorkeling is found on the outer islands, where marine resources have been less affected by humans.

Snorkelers are apt to see oysters, or *pahua,* a large white clam that is often marinated in lime juice and eaten. In addition to having edible fish, *pahua* shells make nifty soap dishes and you may see them in your hotel room.

Echinoderms may not sound like a household term, but you will undoubtedly see them while snorkeling or on a reef walk. Some of the familiar or recognizable echinoderms are sea cucumbers, sea urchins, starfish, brittle stars and feather-stars. Most are plankton feeding, and the sea cucumbers, which appear to just lie on the sand all day, actually perform a very important function to the lagoon community. By feeding on organic matter in the sand they plough up the sea bottom and are vital to the health of the ecosystem.

One echinoderm you do not want to get to know intimately is the sea urchin. Most are algal grazers and this important task allows corals to flourish. They do, however, have spines that can be very painful if stepped on, and some species have spines that are coated with toxin. They are often found on reefs and some grow in sandy-bottomed lagoons where swimmers might congregate. The only place I've seen this is on Temae Beach on Moorea. Keep on eye on where the locals swim, or better yet, bring your snorkel mask to check out the lagoon for yourself.

DIVE SIGHTS   The undersea attractions of French Polynesia vary a great deal from archipelago to archipelago. The coral growth on the fringing reef of the Windward Islands (Tahiti and Moorea) is dense, according to scuba diving savant Carl Roessler, but "not terribly interesting."

Corals are low growing and do not reach much more than several feet in height above the reef mass. This lack of development may be explained by excessive freshwater runoff. Another possible explanation is that by remaining squat, the corals may be responding environmentally by protecting themselves from violent wave action during storms. It is also possible that the land masses themselves block nutrient-bearing currents from reaching the coral colonies.

The most complex coral colonies in the Society Group, and hence those best for viewing, are found in the quiet sheltered lagoons of Raiatea and Huahine, where the fragile coral communities are protected from the pounding surf.

The Tuamotu Group, which consists almost solely of atolls, offers a much different environment for coral, and is in fact better for coral viewing. There are no mountains and no freshwater runoff to limit coral development. The reef corals, while still low growing, are far more massive and geologically older communities. Here one finds huge tabular structures two to four yards in diameter. The squat coral growth is a response to intermittent wave action, but food and nutrient supply is very rich, resulting in branching corals found in the quiet protection of the lagoons.

Unlike the high islands, fish life is generally more dense in the Tuamotu reef systems. The low-growing coral offers good protection against predators and multitudes of soldierfish, masked butterfly fish, Achilles tangs and parrot fish dart through the waters. Some of the schools of tangs seem so nonchalant that they flock around divers as if tame.

The reef shallows in the Tuamotus are often narrow. From the fringing *motus* or islets to the outer reef's dropoff may be only 30 feet. Being extremely close to deep water, these marine gardens are exposed to pelagics such as gray sharks or manta rays that often suddenly appear from the depths and, just as unexpectedly, disappear.

Undoubtedly the most popular island to dive is Rangiroa. Its most famous marine features are its two passes. A diver exploring the passes will witness the daily movement of a tremendous amount of tidal water. The deep channels are barren, with the exception of a few coral heads, and marine life tends to congregate on the shallower side walls of the passages.

Divers tend to visit "Rangi," as it's called, for one major reason—sharks. Large numbers tend to dwell in the passes. One survey estimated at least 1500 gray sharks inhabit this area at any given time. The creatures align themselves against the sides of the channel facing the current and hold their positions much like aqueous hawks holding stationary, waiting for the right moment to attack from on high. Divers who sweep through the channels at the same speed as the current are ignored by the sharks. This blasé attitude changes rapidly if a diver anchors himself to one of the scattered coral heads and spears a fish. At that point up to ten gray sharks might charge the diver, posing a very real threat.

Bring along your PADI (or equivalent) open-water certificate if you are an experienced diver. If you are a novice, you may need a certificate from a doctor or a local exam.

In addition to sharks and reef fish, divers in French Polynesia are apt to run into manta rays, moray eels, barracuda and other pelagics such as tuna.

You will see a flying fish or two when traveling any distance on a boat. If you are lucky you may also observe some dolphins at play, and if you're really lucky, a sea turtle, although they are still actively hunted by locals and are harder to spot.

SURFING

Tahiti has good surf but it's not in the same category as the awesome rideable waves that Hawaii offers because fringe reefs buffer Tahiti's shores. Big waves hit the barrier reefs with such force that they dissipate, or there isn't time for a takeoff before they hit the reef and pitch over. Nonetheless, surfing has become ever more popular in French Polynesia, specifically in Tahiti, Moorea, Raiatea and, particularly with Americans, in Huahine.

There are two surf seasons: summer (from November to March) and winter (from April to October). The summer swells come from the north. That means if there are 15-foot waves breaking in Hawaii, chances are there will be eight-foot waves on the north coasts of the Society Islands a few days later. Moorea's north coast, with its reef breaks, is considered better than Tahiti's north coast, which has almost exclusively beach breaks. The northeast trade winds intensify after mid-morning during this season so it's best to surf early in the day. The best time for quality surf is actually in the winter, as the big winter storms from Antarctica and New Zealand provide plenty of swells to the Society Islands' southern shores. When the swells come out of deep water and break along the reefs, the result can be very powerful, hollow waves. Most of the breaks tend to be passes in the reef system and a long paddle is usually obligatory.

The main hazard for surfers is getting bashed up on the reefs. There have also been problems with stonefish and, to a lesser extent with sharks, crown-of-thorns starfish and sea urchins. Stonefish are exceptionally nasty, and I've heard several reports of encounters with these less-than-cuddly creatures. The best way to avoid them is to shuffle your feet instead of high stepping it across the water. Walking on one would seriously spoil your surfing holiday.

Tahitian surfers have traditionally been friendly to *popa'a* foreign) surfers, but this has changed, perhaps due to the influence of some visiting Hawaiians who sport a serious anti-*haole* (white) attitude. Local surfing etiquette calls for shaking hands with your Tahitian colleagues when you first paddle out to a lineup (even if you don't know any of them).

According to the *Surf Report* (Vol. 6, #4), use any board that works well in hollow waves up to eight feet—the best surf is in the six- to eight-foot range. It is recommended that you bring remov-

WHERE ARE THE NATURAL RESERVES?

Given the worldwide destruction of the natural environment and the specific threats imposed by development in French Polynesia, one might expect local government to have instituted a coherent environmental policy. This is not the case. Throughout the years there have been ad hoc environmental protections, but no cohesive plan has been implemented. Furthermore, there are no terrestrial reserves in the Society Islands. Moorea, the Marquesas Group and Rapa are all at risk for environmental degradation. The Marquesas do have four, albeit inadequate, reserves on Ei'ao, Hatutu, Ilot de Sable and Mohotani.

able fins and spares as well as an extra leash. A wetsuit might be useful to prevent tit rash and to save your skin should you encounter the reef.

Shop Tahiti in Vaima Center sells boards and accessories and has four locations on the island of Tahiti. Like everything else here, repairs and gear are expensive. ~ Papeete; 43-74-94.

For more detailed information on where to surf in French Polynesia, I recommend that you get a copy of *The Surf Report*, Vol. 6, #4. Send US$6 to P.O. Box 1028, Dana Point, CA 92629, USA; 714-496-7849.

WIND-SURFING

Windsurfing or sailboarding has become very popular in Tahiti over the last decade. There's no lack of warm water and gentle breezes in French Polynesia, so it is an excellent place to windsurf for experts—neophytes may be another matter. Many of the hotels advertise windsurfing as an activity, but you may find the equipment dilapidated or green with algae from lack of use. Coral heads in shallower areas of the lagoons may present a hazard for beginners who are not able to traverse deeper waters.

FISHING

Deep-sea fishing has been a popular recreational activity for visitors to French Polynesia for generations. By my reckoning there are over 30 charter fishing boats in the islands. Gamefishing was a favorite pastime of American pulp western writer Zane Grey, who had his own fishing camp in Tahiti in the 1930s. Game fish include marlin, sailfish, barracuda and other pelagics. If you plan to eat the fish you catch, stick with pelagics—deep water fish. (Some reef fish carry *Ciguatera,* a rather unpleasant disease.)

For visitors interested in booking a charter, the best thing to do is call Tahiti Sportfishing & Adventure, a government nonprofit company located at the Taina Marina in Punaauia. They will book one of 12 fishing boats represented by the organization. This is the only way for you to book a vessel on the spur-of-the-moment. All boats are manned by an English-speaking captain. Prices for booking a half-day charter start at US$400, or US$650 for a full day on a 29-foot vessel. The price usually includes drinks and food served onboard. ~ Punaauia; 41-02-25, fax 45-27-58.

RIDING STABLES

There is no shortage of horseback riding opportunities on Tahiti, Moorea, Raiatea and in the Marquesas Islands. The horses are usually of Marquesan stock. Information on riding is provided island by island in this book. Figure on spending about 2000 CFP per hour.

HIKING

Hiking has become a popular activity in French Polynesia; however, it's primarily favored by visitors or French residents rather than locals. There are a few professionals who lead day trips on Tahiti, Moorea and Bora Bora, all of whom are listed in the "Hiking" sections found in the area chapters. Trails are numerous on all the islands, but are often not clearly marked, and some may be dangerous. It's not a smart idea to take off into the rainforest unless you have a reasonably accurate idea of where to go. Though the likelihood of being confronted by wild beasts is nil, every year a trekker or two gets lost.

BIKING I don't recommend bringing your bike to Tahiti unless you plan to spend most of your time on the more remote islands that are not overrun by automobiles. Riding a bicycle in Tahiti or Bora Bora can be hazardous. There have been some serious accidents with travelers. Despite the dangers, getting around on rental bicycles is a handy way to explore a smaller island. Just be careful.

Note that many of the larger hotels used to provide their guests free bikes but now rent them at exorbitant prices.

GOLF Tahiti's only golf course is Olivier Breaud International Golf Course, a par 72 located at Atimaono in the Papara district. The area was formerly a cotton plantation established during the American Civil War to provide Europe with the fiber that was in short supply. The course was designed by Bob Baldock & Son, a Costa Mesa, California, firm that has designed links throughout the U.S. and Mexico. It features expansive fairways, two artificial lakes and lush greens planted with hybrid Bermuda grass brought in from Hawaii.

Olivier Breaud Gold Course is a 45-minute drive from Papeete. The course is open daily from 7 a.m. to 6 p.m. year-round. It has recently undergone a 100 million CFP renovation, which includes a new clubhouse, restaurant, pro shop, pool, tennis courts and driving range. Green fees are 3000 CFP. Clubs can be rented for around 2500 CFP per day. To get there call Hui Popo, a tour company that caters to golfers and they will pick you up at your hotel Monday to Saturday. ~ Papara; 57-40-32.

CAMPING Camping in French Polynesia is restricted to a few campgrounds on Tahiti, Moorea, Bora Bora, Huahine and Raiatea. These campgrounds are always private; there are no facilities in parks or areas such as wildlife refuges. The habitués of campgrounds are typically backpackers or students looking to save a few francs rather than Audubon Society members in search of rare birds. For those interested in spending time camping in the wilderness, there are guides on Tahiti that will take visitors on camping trips.

FOUR

Tahiti

It has been two hundred years since Captain James Cook first anchored off its shores, yet the island of Tahiti still evokes a sense of the idyllic South Seas. The jasmine scent of the *tiare* blossoms, the swaying palm trees silhouetted by the tropical moon and all the other clichés that Hollywood and a thousand novels have foisted upon us, come to mind.

So what is Tahiti really like?

An island in French Polynesia, there are grains of truth in the romantic silver screen and pulp fiction portrayals of Tahiti. Though sometimes Tahiti is invoked to mean French Polynesia in its entirety, technically, this is incorrect.

Tahiti is actually the largest island in French Polynesia, with an area of 402 square miles (1041 square kilometers), and can best be visualized as a figure eight on its side. The larger section of the island (Tahiti Nui) is connected to the smaller section (Tahiti Iti) by the narrow Isthmus of Taravao. The island's rugged terrain, marked by numerous rivers and deep valleys, is dotted with precipitous green peaks. The highest points are Mt. Orohena at 7334 feet (2236 meters) and Mt. Aorai at 6783 feet (2068 meters). Both peaks are often obscured by wispy clouds. Given Tahiti's mountainous interior, it's no surprise that the vast majority of the population live on the coastal plain or fringes of the island's perimeter.

Tahiti is surrounded by a barrier reef on nearly all sides, creating a tranquil lagoon protected from the pounding surf. The coastline that encircles the island is about 95 nautical miles. The average year-round temperature is a mild 78°F (25.9°C) and it can be humid—up to 98 percent to be precise.

One main road makes a 73-mile (118-kilometer) circuit of the larger section of the island (Tahiti Nui), and comes to a dead end in the outer reaches of the smaller part of the island (Tahiti Iti). PK (Point Kilométrique) markers start at zero in Papeete and progress around the island clockwise and counterclockwise. Resembling miniature tombstones, they are painted a two-tone red and white, and are easily recognized on the roadside. When circumnavigating the island, it's a good idea to pay attention to them. There are few street signs outside of Papeete so residents use mileage (or kilometrage in this case) to pinpoint their location.

Upon reaching the opposite side of the island (PK 60) at the Isthmus of Taravao, motorists may either complete the circle or explore one of three dead-end roads in Tahiti Iti. The main road around Tahiti Nui, which follows the perimeter of the island, is well maintained but tends to be narrow and overcrowded, particularly during commute hours (8 a.m. and 5 p.m.).

For the reader interested in an in-depth overview of the historical sights around Tahiti, Bengt Danielsson's *Tahiti Circle Island Tour Guide* is the definitive book on the subject and is available at most bookstores in Papeete.

Before there were books to consult, Tahitian mythology dictated that the island came into being as a giant fish pulled out of the sea by Maui, one of the most powerful gods in the Polynesian pantheon. In this vision of creation, Tahiti Nui was the body of the fish and Mt. Orohena, the highest peak, was the dorsal fin. The tail lay in Punaauia, just south of Papeete, and the head of the fish was the smaller section of the island, Tahiti Iti, to the east.

Tahiti has a rich cover of volcanic soil that nourishes a verdant tropical rainforest. From the air the island appears to be carpeted with a luxuriant layer of vegetation. However, biologically, the island is impoverished compared to biotically diverse islands such as Papua New Guinea, the Solomon Islands or even Fiji. Why impoverished? Tahiti is far from Australasia, the main source of its flora and fauna. Simply put, Tahiti's location at the center of the Polynesian Triangle, far from the Asian landmass, made it a difficult journey for most plants and animals and out of the natural reach of most of the flora and fauna that would otherwise have populated the island.

The coconut palm, perhaps the one species of flora most associated with the tropics, is very prominent on the landscape, growing wild from the shoreline to all but the very highest mountains. Other trees such as kapok, *pandanus, mape* (Tahitian chestnut), ironwood and giant bamboo are also present—some wild and some planted in yards and villages throughout the island. There are numerous plants and trees introduced by Polynesians or Europeans, including mango, breadfruit, papaya, avocado, orange, lime passion fruit and *pamplemousse,* a delicious species of grapefruit. Flowering plants are everywhere, either growing wild or in the gardens of private homes and hotels. Some of the more common species include gardenia, hibiscus, oleander, frangipani, bird of paradise, poinsettia, bougainvillea and ginger. Only two of the more widespread flowers, the *tiare* (Gardenia tahitiensis), which seems to be tucked behind the ear of every Tahitian, and the *pua,* are native to Tahiti.

Land fauna is scant. The ubiquitous rat was first brought to Tahiti by Polynesians, as were dogs and pigs. Other than the insects and lizards, birds represent the most numerous species of fauna. Though there are some birds native to the island such as herons, kingfishers and flycatchers, many of the indigenous varieties were hunted to extinction or pushed out of their niches by introduced species such as the myna bird.

In pre-contact times (prior to European influence) Raiatea and Huahine were the most important islands in Eastern Polynesia. It was only after the Europeans arrived that Tahiti became the center of missionary activity and trade, and eventually the focus for colonization. This is probably why the name *Tahiti* translates as "far removed" or "at the periphery." Most likely, Tahiti was settled after Raiatea and may

Tahiti

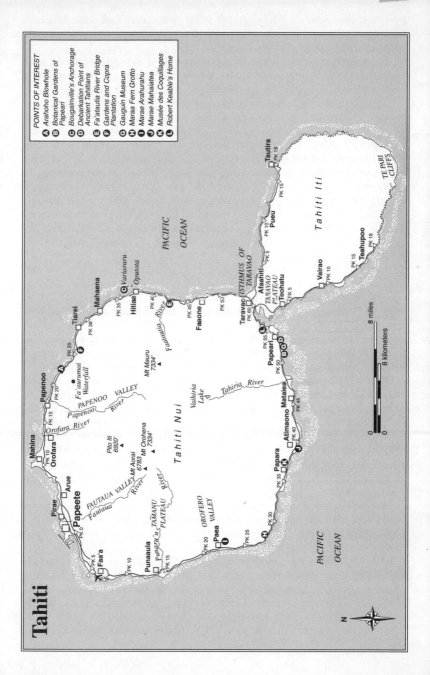

PACIFIC OCEAN

Tautira
PK 18

Te Pari Cliffs

Tahiti Iti

PK 15

Pueu
PK 10

Teahupoo
PK 18

Ataahiti
PK 5
Teohatu
PK 5

Vairao
PK 10

PK 15

ISTHMUS OF TARAVAO

Taravao PK 60
TARAVAO PLATEAU

Variaraau
Oputota

Mahaena
PK 35

Hitiaa
PK 40

Fa'atautia River

PK 45

Faaone

PK 50

Papeari
PK 55
PK 50

Tiarei
PK 30

PK 25

Papenoo
PK 20

Fa'aruumai Waterfall

Mt Mauru 7334'

PAPENOO VALLEY

Papenoo River

Vaihiria Lake

Tahiria River

Matalea
PK 45

Atimaono
PK 40

Papara
PK 35

Orofara River

Orofara
PK 15

Mahina
PK 10

Arue

Pirae

Papeete
PK 0

FAUTAUA VALLEY

Fautaua River

Mt Aorai 6783

Pito Iti 6920'

Mt Orohena 7334'

Tahiti Nui

TAMANU PLATEAU

OROFERO VALLEY

Punaauia
PK 15

Puurau

PK 30

Paea
PK 25

PK 20

Faa'a
PK 5

PK 10

PACIFIC OCEAN

N

0   8 miles

0   8 kilometers

have been considered an outer province. Today, ironically, Tahiti is hardly a province—indeed, it is the most densely populated and the most developed island in all of French Polynesia.

According to the latest archeological evidence, Tahiti was settled sometime after 900 A.D. (after the Marquesas and Cook Islands). There is speculation that it may have been populated earlier but solid evidence has not yet been found.

Though Samuel Wallis was the first European to arrive (in 1767) it was the three voyages made by Captain James Cook from 1769–77 that really put Tahiti on the map. Cook was the first to launch a full-fledged scientific expedition to Tahiti, complete with a botanist, astronomer and illustrator. The missionaries came on the heels of the explorers and Tahiti fell under the influence of both the Catholic and Protestant churches. Within decades, much of the native population was converted to one form of Christianity or another. Meanwhile, the French, who had been slowly consolidating their influence over the islands from the late 18th century, declared Tahiti their protectorate in 1842. By the time Paul Gauguin, Tahiti's most famous visitor, arrived in 1891 with the idea of creating art and seeing, in his words, "no one but savages," much of the pre-European religion and the cultural fabric of Polynesian life had been lost forever.

Life in modern-day Tahiti centers around its capital, Papeete, but it is only one of 20 municipalities or districts on the island. Still, of Tahiti's approximately 100,000 residents, most live in or around the capital. A bustling city with a preponderance of smoke-belching trucks, cars and rush-hour traffic, nothing could be further from the languid, storybook South Seas image of Tahiti than this mini-metropolis. Everything you could possibly want is here—discos, restaurants, travel agencies, baguettes, Beaujolais and a sophisticated late 20th-century populace eager to consume whatever pop culture from North America or Europe washes up on the beach.

Although traditional culture no longer sustains the population of contemporary French Polynesia, there are still glimmers of the old Polynesian ways, even on this seemingly tarnished isle of love. Take a rental car for an hour's drive down to Tautira on the easternmost edge of Tahiti Iti and you will enter a world far removed from the clogged streets of Papeete. The distant sounds of pounding surf on the barrier reef and the spectacle of towering green mountains are unchanged since Captain Cook's arrival. Here fishing nets dangle gently from sturdy racks on the water's edge and the tranquility is interrupted only by the hollow thud of a coconut that occasionally crashes to earth.

As one long-time resident of Tahiti told me, "This island has the best and worst of all things. It will take some persistence, but smart travelers with good will and some time on their hands can discover its secrets."

▼▼▼▼▼▼▼▼

Papeete

The translation of Papeete is "water (from a) basket," which most likely means that it was once a place where Tahitians came to fetch water. Indeed, at the time of captains Wallis and Cook, Papeete was a marshland with a few scattered residents. The town didn't attract too much foreign attention until 1818 when Reverend Crook of the London Missionary Society settled in Papeete with his family.

Papeete began to grow in earnest when Queen Pomare made it her capital in the 1820s and sailing ships began to use the protected harbor, which was a much safer anchorage than Matavai Bay to the east. By the 1830s, it had become a regular port of call for New England whalers. A number of stores, billiard halls and makeshift bars appeared on the waterfront to handle the business. When the French made Tahiti a protectorate in 1842–43, the military came on the scene and in their footsteps came French Catholic priests and nuns.

In 1884, a fire destroyed almost half of Papeete, which resulted in an ordinance prohibiting the use of native building materials. Not much of consequence happened until 1906, when huge waves, the result of a cyclone, wiped out a number of homes and businesses. In 1914, two German men-of-war bombarded Papeete, sinking the only French naval vessel in the harbor.

Today, the population of greater Papeete is around 90,000. It is French Polynesia's capital and only real city, and continues to be a major South Pacific port of call for freighters, ocean liners and yachts. Papeete is *the* center of commerce and government. It is the site of the French High Commissioner's residence, the Territorial Assembly, the tourist bureau, the post office and telecommunications center, the banks, travel agencies, airlines, hospitals, and every other conceivable service.

Since the early 1960s, Papeete has undergone a construction boom necessary to support its rising population (about 20,000 immigrants from France and 15,000 from the outer islands of French Polynesia). Although growth was inevitable, much of it can be attributed to the growth of tourism infrastructure and France's nuclear testing program.

The expansion has been at the expense of some of Papeete's beauty but despite new apartments and offices, the town still has the provincial charm of a French colonial capital. There are whitewashed houses, buildings of painted wood with large verandas and corrugated tin roofs, narrow streets, parks, street vendors, an outdoor market and a profusion of odors ranging from pungent copra

JAILHOUSE BLUES

Church was not where you would find Herman Melville during his 19th-century sojourn to Tahiti. Long a foe of missionaries, **Melville's Calabooza Beretani** was the jail where Herman Melville was imprisoned in 1842. Long since destroyed, it was located on Boulevard Pomare, two blocks south of the Temple de Paofai. During his time here Melville gathered the grist for his second book, *Omoo*, and accurately described life during the early French colonial period.

(dried coconut meat) to the aroma of frying steaks. When the breeze blows from the mountains you can catch the sweet fragrance of the *Tiare Tahiti*, the national flower.

Papeete is designed for walking. The sidewalks and avenues bordering the public market are lined with vendors selling shell necklaces, straw hats, sandwiches, sweet fried breads, pastries and candy. The aisles of the Chinese shops are crammed with cookware, rolls of brightly colored cloth, canned goods from New Zealand and the United States, mosquito coils and imports of every variety. You get the feeling that if you poke around long enough, you might discover a preserved 1000-year-old duck egg.

The best time to explore the narrow streets and browse through the stores is in the cool of the morning. Otherwise, fumes from cars and heat from the asphalt can be oppressive. A stroll through Papeete should be done in a leisurely manner, with several rest breaks at any of the many outdoor cafés and snack bars. There you can sit at tables shielded by canopies, sip a local Hinano beer or eat ice cream and watch the procession of tourists and locals go by. On Sunday mornings, activities cease and Papeete becomes a sleepy and provincial town.

Unless you debark from a cruise ship, you will enter Papeete at Faa'a (yes, that is three vowels in row) Airport, 3.1 miles (5 kilometers) west of downtown. There is not much to see in Faa'a or its environs. The area near the airport is slumlike, consisting of ramshackle homes inhabited mostly by the unemployed. There are, however, a few impressive hotels along the waterfront south of the airport, specifically the elegant Beachcomber Parkroyal and the Maeva Beach. Heading south, away from Papeete, the area becomes more suburban in character, especially in the more affluent communities of Punaauia and Paea, which are 15 to 20 minutes by car from town. The stretch of road from Papeete to Punaauia is a freeway, or the closest thing that Tahiti has to a freeway. However, during weekday morning rush hour, after 7 a.m., the two-lane road is typically bumper-to-bumper with BMWs, Renaults and Volkswagens, which, when combined with the local buses or *Le Truck,* can make for a 45-minute commute on the 6.2-mile (10-kilometer) segment of road into town. The same procession begins in the opposite direction after 5 p.m.

The short four-lane "freeway" ends just short of downtown Papeete and drops motorists on the main drag, Boulevard Pomare, which runs along the waterfront. This is the main artery flowing through Papeete. Once an array of clapboard warehouses and rundown shacks, Boulevard Pomare is now dominated by sleek shops. Proceed on it and you'll pass the Tahiti Tourist Board (Fare Manihini) and all the banks, airlines, nightclubs, boutiques and travel agencies that you could ever hope for. Unfortunately, much of the business day this four-lane, tree-lined thoroughfare can be clogged with exhaust-belching traffic.

This doesn't seem to bother the blocks-long row of yachts (mostly from the United States) that are moored in the heart of town. The Tahitian government evidently takes the foreign yachts seriously. The waterfront esplanade directly opposite the yachts has undergone a transformation. The concrete sidewalk has been expanded and modern electrical fixtures have been added to accommodate every yacht mooring.

As you follow Boulevard Pomare north, the harbor will be on your left-hand side. If you bear left on this road you'll follow the contours of the bay, passing the French naval base and eventually crossing a bridge. This will bring you to Fare Ute and Motu Uta, a landfill-created shipyard and dock area where the majority of inter-island vessels are berthed. From the air or on a map this resembles a huge mandible ready to shut its maw on all those expensive yachts and container ships.

Motu Uta was once an island in Papeete Harbor. It is now a mooring spot for copra boats.

When the wind blows from the direction of the docks, Papeete's air is filled with the strong aroma of copra (dried coconut meat), the main export of the islands. You will find the source of the smell in Fare Ute, where the copra boats are moored and where there is a coconut-oil processing plant. Here the vessels unload the crop they have picked up from the outer islands and exchange it for store-bought commodities. Watching the pallets containing beer, rice, drums of kerosene, sacks of flour, cases of canned butter and jugs of wine being loaded onto the rusty steamers gives you a feeling of the old days when all travel and trade were done by these boats.

Beyond the waterfront, Papeete has numerous neighborhoods with names like Patutoa, Orae, Mamao, Puea and other Tahitian monikers. These tend to be quiet, residential areas with perhaps a corner grocery store or a bakery. Located north from town (in the opposite direction from the airport) are the suburbs of Mahina and Arue.

SIGHTS

A good point of reference, and the best place to begin your tour of Papeete, is on Boulevard Pomare at **Fare Manihini**, which is home to the Tahiti Tourist Board. Situated on the waterfront, directly opposite the beginning of Rue Paul Gauguin, it consists of a cluster of brown buildings designed to resemble traditional Tahitian *fares* (homes). As you walk in the entrance there is an interactive map that shows the locations of shops, landmarks, airline offices and the like. Simply press the button on the board and look for the corresponding light of the shop, airline office or landmark to blink. Inside the office is an information desk staffed by sharp, English-speaking *vahines* who will be able to field your questions. The walls are lined with racks containing brochures, lists of hotels and pensions, schedules of ferryboats and other data. There are often art exhibitions showing at Fare Manihini, as well. Note that the bureau is open on weekdays only. (There is also an information office at Faa'a Airport, but it may be staffed by taxi drivers waiting for fares, rather than information officers). ~ Boulevard Pomare; 50-57-00.

In addition to finding general tourism information at Fare Manihini, there is also a small bargelike information office called **Mer et Loisirs** anchored directly across from Le Rétro café, literally on the water. Also affiliated with the tourist board, this office specializes in all things nautical and can help you in any number of ways—from chartering a yacht to organizing a boat trip to Tetiaroa. Unlike the tourist board office in Papeete, Mer et Loisirs will book tours, in addition to providing advice. (However, when I visited they seemed more interested in selling me a ticket to Tetiaroa than offering general information. What's more, no one spoke English.) ~ 43-97-99.

If you walk north along the **waterfront esplanade** you will pass the local fishing fleet, the Moorea-bound ferries that deliver people and goods daily to Tahiti's closest island neighbor, the boats that journey to the outer Society Islands, and maybe a French naval vessel or two. In the late afternoon you may see the fishermen bring their catch ashore here.

In the evenings the parking lot that extends north of Fare Manihini to the Moorea ferry terminal resembles a carnival. Many food vendors have *roulottes* (vans) with fancy neon signs. They gather here to set up their barbecues and stools around their vans and open up their mobile restaurants.

Note that behind the Socredo Bank (also on the waterfront about 50 yards north of the tourist office) is a small booth with a money-changing facility (providing the same exchange rate as a commercial bank). Why would you need a money changer behind a bank? Convenience. It's open seven days a week and is very handy for visitors who happen to be wandering around Papeete on a weekend and are in need of cash.

Walk south from Fare Manihini along the waterfront. You'll see the many aforementioned yachts, as well as *pirogues* (racing canoes) stacked upside down under trees. Cross Boulevard Pomare at Avenue Bruat and you'll find yourself at **Bougainville Park**, which was originally named Albert Park after the Belgian king and World War I hero. The name was later changed to Bougainville Park to honor the French explorer. On sunny days people usually occupy its concrete benches or enjoy the shade of its huge banyan tree. Of the two cannons prominently displayed, the one nearest the post office is off the *Seeadler*, the vessel skippered by the notorious World War

I sea raider Count von Luckner, whose boat ran aground on Mopelia Atoll in the Leeward Islands. The other belonged to the *Zelee*, the French navy boat sunk during a German raid on Papeete in 1914. ~ Boulevard Pomare.

Adjacent to the park is the main **post office** cum telecommunications center, facing the harbor. It's a massive brown, multi-level affair with phones, fax and telegram service. ~ Boulevard Pomare; 41-43-00.

There is also a section for philatelists, a big revenue earner for Tahiti. The **philatelic department** is on the ground level at the Boulevard Pomare entrance. ~ Boulevard Pomare; 41-43-35.

Vaima Center is a modern, four-level, block-square shopping center located directly across from the waterfront, about one block north of the post office. There are boutiques, banks, travel agencies,

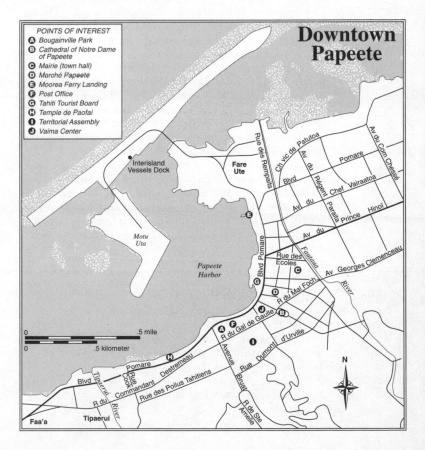

Downtown Papeete

POINTS OF INTEREST
- Ⓐ Bougainville Park
- Ⓑ Cathedral of Notre Dame of Papeete
- Ⓒ Mairie (town hall)
- Ⓓ Marché Papeete
- Ⓔ Moorea Ferry Landing
- Ⓕ Post Office
- Ⓖ Tahiti Tourist Board
- Ⓗ Temple de Paofai
- Ⓘ Territorial Assembly
- Ⓙ Vaima Center

airline bureaus, book stores, restaurants and the like. If you find yourself at Vaima Center, you should not have to walk more than two or three blocks to take care of any of the above activities.

One block north of Vaima Center, and one block from the waterfront, is one of the most famous landmarks in Tahiti, the **Marché Papeete** (municipal market), which covers one square city block between Rue 22 September and Rue Francois Cardella. In 1986, the then 131-year-old market underwent a metamorphosis that changed it from a dark, crowded, seedy Casbah to a modern, well-lit, clean place of business. The old marketplace (a charming labyrinth of shabby, cramped stalls flavored by accumulated tropical filth) was one of the last true old-time South Pacific institutions left in Papeete. The new Marché Papeete is an airy, sunshine-filled, double-decked venue resembling something out of the 19th-century gaslight era in Paris or the French Quarter of New Orleans.

Just south of the Marché Papeete and across the street from the inland side of Vaima Center is the stately **Cathedral of Notre Dame of Papeete** which literally rises above the din of honking automobiles and screeching motorbikes that circle around this imposing structure. Located in the very heart of Papeete, it is painted a genteel gray with a red-tiled spire and a red roof. Consecrated in 1875, the church was completely restored in 1987. The original stained glass dates from 1875 and a modern stained-glass window was added in 1988, designed by Deanna de Marigny.

The other major church in town is the Protestant **Temple de Paofai**, which is located on Boulevard Pomare about three blocks south of Bougainville Park. Constructed in 1873, this large, handsome structure is supported by two rows of six powerful old oak columns. The ceiling, painted sky blue, is adorned with three superb stained-glass windows. You may want to consider spending part of Sunday at a church in Tahiti, listening to the hymns and studying the women's hats. It's preferable to wear white if you do so. ~ Boulevard Pomare.

✔ **CHECK THESE OUT—UNIQUE SIGHTS**

- Peruse the **Musée de Tahiti et des Iles**, where you'll find displays of flora and fauna and Polynesian culture and history. *page 132*
- Wander the reconstructed **Marae Arahurahu**, with its replica of a wooden platform where human offerings were left for the gods. *page 134*
- Take a look through the **Gauguin Museum**, where the artists memorabilia are on display alongside original sketches and prints. *page 142*
- Experience a true traditional Tahitian village in Tahiti Iti's **Tautira Village**. *page 151*

Two blocks south of the cathedral is the **Territorial Assembly**. Constructed in the late 1960s as the chamber of the democratically elected representatives of the French Polynesian government, the modern Territorial Assembly building sits directly over the source of what once was the Papeete River. (The river has since been redirected to nearby Bougainville Park.) In this same area, Queen Pomare once had her home and eventually a royal palace, which, in typical governmental fashion, was not completed until after her death in 1877. Nearby was an exclusive clubhouse for high-ranking military officers and civil servants where Gauguin (while he was still accepted) used to drink absinthe. The clubhouse has long since disappeared. The other important building occupying these grounds is the High Commissioner's residence.

Standing directly in front of the Territorial Assembly on Rue du Général de Gaulle is a monument depicting **Pouvanaa a Oopa**, considered one of the greatest contemporary Tahitian leaders. A decorated World War I hero and a courageous Tahitian nationalist, Pouvanaa served as a deputy in Paris for the Tahitian Territorial Assembly. He was later jailed on what many believe were trumped-up charges by the metropolitan French government and exiled from his beloved Tahiti from 1958 to 1970. After his release (at age 72) he served as an elected official until his death in 1978. (The park where his statue resides has recently been refurbished.)

Five blocks north of Pouvanaa's memorial is the new **Mairie (Town Hall)**, which was inaugurated in May 1990 by the late French President Francois Mitterand. The newest landmark in Papeete, it is a two-story, 19th century–inspired veranda-style civic complex, reminiscent of colonial South Pacific architecture. Painted dark red, it has dormers and a turret on the roof, which add more eclectic features to this French-influenced edifice. There are also several abstract sculptures around the grounds of the *Mairie* done by Petero, an Easter Islander who resides in Tahiti. ~ Rue Paul Gauguin.

LODGING

Generally speaking, you will have little difficulty finding lodging around Papeete. For most visitors, Tahiti is merely a transit zone to the outer islands of French Polynesia. There are vacancies year-round, with one notable exception: During the Heiva celebrations (starting at the end of June and lasting until August) it is virtually impossible to find a hotel room in Papeete. Finding a hotel in late December can also be problematic. If you want to avoid crowds, these periods are not the time to come.

The accommodation possibilities in greater Papeete are divided into two general categories, those in town and those on the beaches of Papeete's suburbs. The major international-class hotels are actually to the east or south of the Papeete city limits.

While finding a room in Papeete may be easy, you won't get much value for your dollar—inexpensive rooms are scarce. They range from converted private homes with makeshift dorm rooms and communal bath/shower arrangements to spartan family-run hotels. None of the budget accommodations are located downtown, but none are more than 10 to 15 minutes by foot from the heart of Papeete. There are also a few individuals with private homes that take in guests. Staying with families can be an inexpensive and often enriching alternative to hotels. Sometimes it affords you a chance to see a side of Tahiti you would otherwise never experience but rates and services listed are more subject to change than are other types of accommodation.

To avoid surprises, travelers should be aware that the prices for backpacker and budget accommodations start at US$15 to US$30. Expect to pay in the neighborhood of US$15 to US$20 for a bed in a shared room and US$30 to US$50 for a private rooms with bath in a budget hotel. The least expensive mid-range hotel room in the Papeete area is around 8000 CFP (just under US$100)—and that will not amount to much in the way of amenities. The average mid-range accommodation in town (for example, the Royal Papeete, which is equivalent to an average motel room in the U.S.) will cost around US$120.

One of the better budget accommodations in town is **Mahina Tea**, a no-frills, family-run hotel. There is no pretense of luxury about this fading two-story, aquamarine-colored concrete structure. It has 16 rooms, all with private bath, as well as six additional studios with bathroom and kitchen. The rooms are clean and very basic. The floors are threadbare linoleum and the bathrooms have aging tile. Some of the second-story units have small balconies. Hot water is available from 6 to 11 p.m. Mahina Tea represents good value for budget travelers and the only downside I've heard is that the local roosters can be aggravatingly noisy in the early morning. It's a family-owned hotel and it shows. The staff is cordial and in the lobby is a collection of photos and memorabilia. Visitors are as likely to be local students as budget tourists. To find it take Avenue Bruat (off of Boulevard Pomare) and bear right at the gendarmerie. ~ Rue de Sainte Amelie; 42-00-97. BUDGET.

Also a good value in the budget category is the aptly named **Tahiti Budget Lodge**. Located next to the College Lamenais, a public school, this lodging is akin to a '50s-style American motel. It's a very clean, whitewashed structure with 11 rooms, a large outdoor dining area, and a communal kitchen for guests. There is also a snack bar on the premises. Rooms are clean, albeit on the minuscule side—they vary in configuration from single rooms to dorm-style accommodations housing up to three people. The staff will meet visitors at the airport on most international flights. Aside from its popularity with backpackers, Tahiti Budget Lodge is also a rooming house for French travelers working in Papeete. It is by no means as inexpensive as some other places, but it is worth the extra dollars for those who wish to avoid the more marginal accommodations. To get there from Boulevard Pomare, walk down Rue du 22 September, cross Rue du Mal Foch and continue down Rue Eduard Ahne. ~ Rue du Frere Alain; 42-66-82. BUDGET.

Around the corner from Tahiti Budget Lodge is **Teamo**, another spot popular with backpackers. It is a large, rambling, home with six rooms, including two shared rooms that can house up to ten people. There are several common eating quarters and a large porch with sitting area. Teamo is not as scrupulously maintained as some of the other hostels and pensions, and it gets decidedly mixed reviews; some feel this is a great bargain while others complain about poor service, noise and cramped quarters. Teamo provides airport transport. ~ Rue du Pont Neuf; 42-00-35. BUDGET.

One of the more reasonable places to stay in Tahiti is the **Territorial Hostel Center** across the street from the OTAC cultural center and sports complex. Resembling a college dormitory, it offers clean, shared accommodation in 14 rooms. There is also a canteen that serves inexpensive meals. The doors are locked at midnight. For reservations, write to Office Territorial d'Action Culturel, BP 1709, Papeete. You must have a student ID or youth hostel card to stay here. Visitors are dealt with on a first-come, first-served basis. ~ Boulevard Pomare; 42-68-02, 42-88-50. BUDGET.

Chez Myrna is a tidy private home on the southern fringes of Papeete very near the Faa'a district border. Owned by Walter and Myrna Dahmmeyer, a friendly middle-aged couple, it is a five-minute walk inland from Rue du Commandant Destremeau and about ten minutes from downtown Papeete. The Dahmmeyers have two clean, airy rooms with shared bathroom. The minimum stay is two nights and a deposit is required. Meals are served on a small picnic table on the outside patio and food is reportedly very good.

✔ CHECK THESE OUT—UNIQUE LODGING

- *Budget:* Rest your backpacks at **Te Miti**, where fruit trees abound and the surf is not far away. *page 136*
- *Moderate:* Treat yourself to the tranquility of **Te Anuanua Hotel**, far from the madding crowd out on Tahiti Iti. *page 153*
- *Moderate to deluxe:* Gaze from the balcony that faces the azure Pacific at the **Hotel Royal Papeete,** in the center of town. *page 106*
- *Ultra-deluxe:* Relax in splendor at **Tahiti Beachcomber Parkroyal,** close enough to enjoy Papeete yet far enough away to avoid the hustle. *page 134*

Budget: under $100 Moderate: $100–$150 Deluxe: $150–$200 Ultra-deluxe: over $200

Chez Myrna comes recommended. ~ Tipaerui Valley; 42-64-11. BUDGET.

Two kilometers south of Papeete is the **Hotel Tahiti**. The hotel occupies a large area on the water and has 92 individual rooms in a two-story pink colonial-style building and, closer to the sea, 18 thatched-roof bungalows. The guest rooms (painted a sickly chartreuse) are clean but have paper-thin walls. The room I saw was rather tired-looking but clean. If you get a room, make sure it faces the sea, not the busy road—traffic noise could be a problem. It is obvious a few generations ago this was one of the best resorts in town. Today the hotel's luster has faded and there is a sad weary feeling about the place. It is one of the least expensive hotels in town but at nearly US$100 it is still overpriced. The staff seemed cordial when I was there but I have heard complaints. The Hotel Tahiti is located on the seaside at the southern end of Rue du Commandant Destremeau, a busy thoroughfare, 15 minutes by foot from town. ~ Auae; 82-95-50, fax 81-31-51, or 800-421-0000 in the U.S. MODERATE TO DELUXE.

Note that all hotels charge an eight percent tourist tax on top of the tariff.

Prince Hinoï, located just off Boulevard Pomare in downtown Papeete, is a fragile boxy-looking building constructed in the late '80s. It has 72 air-conditioned rooms and the requisite cocktail bar. The rooms, done entirely in pastels, are on the small side but come with television and video. Perhaps its biggest plus is its downtown location but traffic noise could be a problem depending on where the room faces. ~ Avenue du Prince Hinoï; 42-32-77, fax 42-33-66. MODERATE.

The **Hotel Royal Papeete** is directly opposite the waterfront in the midst of Papeete's entertainment and shopping district. A long, three-story building that takes up about half a city block, it sports a colonial-style awning. Balconies grace the rooms that face the ocean. In its heyday, the 85-room Royal Papeete was one of the best hotels in town and it still offers a reasonable value for travelers desiring a comfort level a cut or two above the budget category. Rooms are of average size and though not luxurious are reasonably appointed. Oddly enough, the hallways are decorated with Fijian *masi* (tapa cloth) and war clubs. The hotel is the home of La Cave, one of the best nightclubs in town. There's also a good bar, Le Tamure Hut, downstairs. ~ Boulevard Pomare; 42-01-29, fax 43-79-09, or 800-421-0000 in the U.S. MODERATE TO DELUXE.

Hotel Le Mandarin, which opened in 1988, is one of the newer hotels in downtown Papeete. A marble facade is at the entrance. It has 37 air-conditioned rooms, average in size and quality. Among the amenities are television and direct international dialing. It is within walking distance of the Papeete town hall, the waterfront and the business district. Within the hotel complex is the Le Mandarin

Restaurant, one of the better Chinese restaurants in town. ~ Rue
Colette; 42-16-33, fax 42-16-32. MODERATE TO DELUXE.

DINING

Papeete's eateries vary from inexpensive *roulottes* (vans converted
into mini-eateries with collapsible shelves that serve as tables) to
fine restaurants worthy of any Parisian's palette. Note that most
restaurants in town are closed on Sunday.

Among the *roulottes*, I found **Vesuvio** to have excellent thin-
crust pizza. The seafood special was topped with mussels, calamari,
fish, clams and cheese. **Chez Jimmy**, a Chinese food specialist, features chow mein, curry beef, chicken and mixed vegetable dishes.
Carnivores might want to sample **Chez Robert's** steak with herb
butter as well as his own steak sauce. ~ BUDGET.

Perhaps the best *roulotte* in French Polynesia is **Tikipeue**, which
is parked more or less permanently on the waterfront opposite the
Pitate Bar next to the yachts. It has terrific meals including sashimi,
steak and fries, chicken and fish. It is reputedly the only *roulotte*
licensed to serve alcohol. Desserts are also first rate—don't miss the
vanilla pie. Some people actually reserve it upon entering, knowing how fast it disappears. Note that in addition to sitting outside
the truck at a counter and a table, there's actually room for about
six people to sit inside. There is also a tiny bar. ~ BUDGET.

The Vaima Center, the popular downtown shopping center, has
some good reasonably priced outdoor cafés, **Le Rétro** in particular—an extensive and popular open-air brasserie on the Boulevard
Pomare–side of the complex. With two levels, an abundance of
tables and glaring neon, Le Rétro is an eating and meeting place
that includes everything from breakfast right through to a late-
night coffee. It turns out complete meals, sandwiches, salads and
ice cream. It is one of the few Papeete restaurants open seven days
a week and, open past midnight. Le Rétro is probably the only place
to go for a meal after everything else is shut down. ~ Boulevard Pomare; 42-86-83. BUDGET TO MODERATE.

Across the alley from Le Rétro, on the adjacent corner is a brand-
new restaurant, the **Pacific Blue Café**, which falls into the category
of wide-open sidewalk café/restaurant. They have a variety of fancy
daiquiris and mixed drinks (the kind in which you expect to see a
miniature parasol) and a slew of ice cream and sorbet concoctions
served in large goblets. Food includes a variety of salads, *poisson
cru*, sashimi, seafood and meats. The chef told me his favorite dish
was pan-fried fish in coconut cream. Like Le Rétro, its street corner location is a great place to people watch. ~ Boulevard Pomare;
MODERATE TO DELUXE.

On the backside of Vaima Center, opposite the cathedral, you'll
find **L'Oasis**, a sprawling outdoor café with tasty sandwiches, pastry and ice cream. It is considered by locals to be among the best

outdoor cafés in town. In addition to snack-type food, you can also get dishes such as chicken, beef or fish. It's a nice place to sit with a strong coffee or a cold beer and watch the world go by. ~ Rue du Général de Gaulle. BUDGET.

Casse-croute, or French bread sandwiches, are the best local eating bargain and are offered at **Le Motu**, a small takeout sandwich and ice cream eatery also on the side of the Vaima complex. ~ Rue du Général de Gaulle; 41-33-59. BUDGET.

Many of the better value daytime eating places cater particularly to office workers at lunchtime. **Polyself** next to the Bank of Polynesia is a bustling cafeteria with local dishes such as *poisson cru*, sandwiches, soups, salads and various Chinese–Tahitian offerings. This little place has consistently good food. Get there early in the lunch hour or they will have sold out most of their fare. ~ Rue Paul Gauguin; 43-75-32. BUDGET.

Also well-visited by the lunch crowd is **Snack Jimmy** just opposite the town hall. On any given day this neon-lit greasy spoon is filled with locals scarfing up Tahitian and Chinese dishes. Fare includes sweet and sour soup, stir-fried veggies with pork, chicken and shrimp, chop suey, chow mein and other Chinese dishes. Sandwiches are also available. ~ Corner of Rue Colette and Rue des Ecoles; 43-63-32. BUDGET.

The market environs feature some of the least expensive restaurants and cafés in town. The cuisine is Chinese–Tahitian and generally the eateries offer the option of takeout food. These are prototypical blue-collar restaurants with no pretense of catering to the tourist trade. Typical of this category are **Waikiki** on Rue A. Leboucher ~ 42-95-27; **Acajou Marché** on Rue Francois Cardella ~ 43-19-27; **Te Hoa** on Rue du Mal Foch ~ 42-99-27; and **Restaurant Cathay** on Rue du Mal Foch ~ 42-99-67. The best item to order is a local mainstay called *maa tinito*, a mixture of red beans, pork, fresh vegetables and whatever else the chef feels like throwing in. These establishments also have chop suey, Chinese-style soups, and mixed vegetable dishes. ~ BUDGET.

HIDDEN ►

Upstairs at the **Marché Papeete** there are several open-air snackbars that serve hamburgers, sandwiches, *steak frites, poisson cru, maa tinito* and other Tahitian dishes for the budget-priced pocketbook. The eating area is breezy and some of the tables have canopies. Most of the clientele are local and it's an excellent spot for the weary shopper to have a meal. ~ BUDGET.

If you feel that a sandwich will do, one of the better specialists in this category is **Epi D'Or** located right next to Restaurant Cathay. Typical fare is ham or cheese sandwiches on baguettes. ~ Rue du Mal Foch. BUDGET.

If you are in the mood for dessert, **La Marquisienne** is a fine neighborhood patisserie on the same block as the Mandarin Hotel.

It's a good place to stop for a coffee or some pastry when the blood sugar drops. ~ Rue Colette near the corner of Rue Paul Gauguin; 42-83-52. BUDGET.

I have yet to see a tourist in **Kikiriri** located between Rue Paul Gauguin and Rue des Ecoles. Situated on a second-floor walkup, it has a small, unpretentious dining area. Kikiriri combines French and Chinese culinary arts, making the food both excellent and reasonably priced. Seafood is the best part of the menu and dishes include shrimp curry, mahimahi and crab. (The menu lists at least 20 Chinese and seafood dishes). There's also great understated local ambience. ~ Rue Colette; 43-58-64. MODERATE TO DELUXE.   ◄ HIDDEN

Clearly the most popular pizzeria with locals is **Lou Pescadou**   ◄ HIDDEN
located one block from the Vaima Center. It turns out a fine array of Italian food in general, but the speciality is pizza cooked in a wood-fired oven. The four seasons pizza is my favorite. Patrons come here just as much for the atmosphere as for the food. The walls are covered with movie posters and the noise level is a perpetual loud chatter. Definitely check this place out. ~ Rue Anne-Marie Javouhey; 43-74-26. BUDGET TO MODERATE.

A good place to sample French cuisine or simply to have an after-dinner drink is **Morrison's Café** on the top floor of the Vaima Center. Named after Jim Morrison (of the Doors rock band), it's an indoor/outdoor café with a huge wooden terrace surrounding a swimming pool. Patrons dine at marble tables while sitting on plastic chairs. The Continental French menu includes dishes such as escargot, smoked salmon, seafood gratin, a large selection of salads and cold dishes such as carpaccio and sashimi. There is also a Tex-Mex dinner where the menu boasts of the large quantities of meat. The clientele is young and hip and the owner, Pascha Allouch, is a

ROULOTTES—MEALS ON WHEELS

At night along the waterfront parking lot, at the north end of Boulevard Pomare, *roulottes* or vans, some of which are decked out with colorful electrically lit signs, serve the best inexpensive food in town. Even if you are not planning to eat, just walking around these purveyors of meals on wheels is an obligatory part of the Papeete experience. Some of the owners have put a great deal of effort into ornately painting or affixing neon signs to the vans advertising gastronomic themes ranging from pizzerias to crêperies. *Roulottes* dole out grilled chicken, steaks and fish piled high with *pommes frites*, omelettes, pizza and chop suey. There are also vans specializing in ice cream and several that serve crêpes. Most of the *roulottes* are open only in the evenings, although some are open during the lunch hour.

bon vivant who will keep the jokes flowing at your table. There is a full American-style bar that's well stocked with tequila. Seventies-era rock music is played on the weekends—sometimes there is a cover charge. If the music isn't enough to tempt you, Morrison's is the only establishment in French Polynesia that has a "scenic" elevator (built outside the restaurant with a fine view of the waterfront). It operates from the ground floor of the Vaima Center. ~ Vaima Center; 42-78-61. MODERATE TO DELUXE.

La Pizzeria also produces very good pizzas and although it may lack the chic atmosphere of Lou Pescadou, it does have the advantage of an outdoor dining area facing the waterfront. Try the pizza with capers, seafood and black olives. The food is just as good as Lou Pescadou but the ambience is more subdued. There are entrances from Boulevard Pomare and from Rue du Commandant Destremeau. ~ Boulevard Pomare; 42-98-30. MODERATE.

Le Bistrot du Port is a fine outdoor café under shady trees. It turns out tasty seafood, French cuisine and local dishes. The specialty of the house is sashimi prepared from locally caught tuna. Despite the prominent outdoor location on the waterfront, this is generally a local scene. ~ Corner of Avenue Bruat and Boulevard Pomare; 42-55-09. BUDGET TO MODERATE.

Le Snack Paofai near the huge Protestant Church is also a good bet. They have inexpensive snacks and sandwiches—typical fare is *salade russe*, steak and *pomme frites*, fish and chow mein. ~ Corner of Rue Cook and Rue du Commandant Destremeau; 42-95-76. BUDGET.

DELUXE TO ULTRA-DELUXE DINING   For the well-heeled, there is no shortage of expensive restaurants in Papeete. Varieties of cuisine include French, Chinese, Vietnamese and often a French–Tahitian fusion. In general, whatever the cuisine, the visitor will not go wrong ordering seafood in French Polynesia. When you blend French culi-

✔ CHECK THESE OUT—UNIQUE DINING

- *Budget:* Watch the world go by at **L'Oasis**, one of the best outdoor cafés in Papeete. *page 107*
- *Moderate:* Join the local families who dine at the **Hotel Royal Tahitien** on weekends under a canopy of *pandanus* leaves. *page 127*
- *Deluxe to ultra-deluxe:* Get off the tourist track at **L'o a la Bouche**, where nouvelle French cuisine is served amid understated elegance. *page 111*
- *Ultra-deluxe:* Dine where the local elites does at **Moana Iti**, where delicious food has been served for 20 years. *page 111*

Budget: under $12 Moderate: $12–$20 Deluxe: $20–$30 Ultra-deluxe: over $30

nary standards with locally caught seafood, the combination is difficult to improve upon.

Moana Iti, located beneath Club 106, has had the same owner for 20 years and features a traditional French menu. The atmosphere is elegant. The restaurant's reputation is very good and it's not unusual to see high government officials dining there during the lunch hour. Specialties include homemade pâté, duck fillet, rabbit and shellfish dishes such as Coquille St. Jacques. ~ Boulevard Pomare between Avenue Bruat and Rue Zelee; 42-65-24. ULTRA-DELUXE.

The intimate **La Corbeille d'Eau** to the west side of the Vaima Center is considered by many the best French restaurant in Papeete—a restaurant *gastronomique.* The seafood dishes are first-rate, as are the traditional French dishes such as filet mignon and escargot. ~ Boulevard Pomare; 43-77-14. ULTRA-DELUXE.

Mariposa in the Vaima Center can best be described as "old Tahiti." An outside terrace facing the street is great for drinks and people-watching. The cuisine is Continental, ranging from French to Tahitian. Seafood is particularly good and service is excellent. ~ Rue Jeanne d'Arc; 42-02-19. DELUXE TO ULTRA-DELUXE.

Despite the Tahitian name, **Manava** has the typical decor of a French provincial restaurant. Management has revamped the menu and there are a variety of new dishes prepared by a new chef. These include minced tuna or salmon, oysters grilled in cheese, mahimahi with marinated shallots, and pork filet mignon with curry cream and pineapples. Try the lime crêpe for dessert—the specialty of the house. The art on the wall is courtesy of Christian, the owner's son. Manava is located opposite the government buildings complex on Avenue Bruat. ~ Avenue Bruat; 42-02-91. DELUXE TO ULTRA-DELUXE.

One of the newer and better restaurants in Papeete is **L'o a la Bouche,** which roughly translates as "salivating in the mouth"—an apt description for this gem of an establishment. The decor has a tasteful, understated elegance. The nouvelle French cuisine, mostly seafood, is superb. One dish we sampled, the Coquille St. Jacques with shrimp, was an original creation. It was fresh and prepared perfectly. Other dishes tasted were *Feuillete de Saumon des dieux* (fish prepared with a pastry crust) and *Salade de magret de canard* (smoked duck salad). This is a restaurant you do not want to miss. ~ Impasse Cardella; 45-29-76 DELUXE TO ULTRA-DELUXE.

◄ HIDDEN

One of the best Chinese restaurants is **Le Mandarin** at the Mandarin Hotel—one of the few restaurants in town open seven days a week. They have an excellent reputation and specialize in a Hong Kong-style cuisine (which means mostly seafood). The chef, who is from Hong Kong, changes the menu on a weekly basis. ~ Rue des Ecoles; 42-99-03. DELUXE TO ULTRA-DELUXE.

In the same league as the above eateries is **Le Dragon D'Or,** located down the street from Le Mandarin, between Rue Paul Gauguin and Rue des Ecoles. Fine service and Cantonese-style cuisine make it popular with locals and visitors. (Food served at Le Mandarin and Le Dragon D'Or is known locally as *chinoise rafinée*, which differentiates it from ordinary Chinese restaurants). Again, seafood is your best bet, but the menu also features pork, chicken and beef dishes. ~ Rue Colette; 42-96-12. DELUXE TO ULTRA-DELUXE.

If Vietnamese food is in order, **Saigonnaise** (also called Le Baie d'Along) is a reliable choice. The dining area is on the small side, which makes for a cozy atmosphere. If you want to keep the meal light, the seafood combination soup is a good bet. Closed Sunday. ~ Avenue du Prince Hinoï; 42-05-35. BUDGET TO MODERATE.

Likewise, **La Riziere** is a fine choice for Vietnamese food. Decor is fancier and the prices are as well. The five-spice chicken and whole fish platters are excellent. ~ Impasse Cardella; 45-29-76. MODERATE TO DELUXE.

GROCERIES There is no shortage of supermarkets as well as mom-and-pop grocery stores in Papeete to pick up a baguette, a wedge of cheese or a bottle of beer.

However, the mother of all markets in French Polynesia is the **Marché Papeete** (municipal market), which takes up a square block between Rue 22 September and Rue Francois Cardella. There you will find all manner of fresh fruits, vegetables, produce, fish and meat, as well as handicrafts and clothing.

For convenience, a visit to a supermarket or grocery store might make more sense. In Papeete, some of the stores to consider are **Magasin Louise Wong** on Cours de l'Union Sacrée ~ 42-08-98; **Magasin Elastic** on Rue Colette ~ 42-80-44; **Supermarche Liou Fong** on Avenue du Prince Hinoï ~ 42-09-55; and **Supermarche Cecile** in the Fariipiti neighborhood ~ 43-52-67.

SHOPPING Shopping in Papeete is a mixed bag—quality and selection are good but prices are very high. Here it's possible to purchase items from around French Polynesia: tie-dyed pareus from Moorea, wood carvings from Ua Huka, shell hatbands from Rangiroa, fine woven hats from Tubuai, tapa cloth from Fatu Hiva and black pearls from the Tuamotu islands.

For the fashion-conscious, there are a number of boutiques with island-style and French clothing. Perhaps the best indigenous items to purchase are jewelry made from the famous Tahitian black pearl.

The upstairs section at the **Marché Papeete** is a good place to pick up handicrafts costing 2500 to 20,000 CFP. Despite the prices, very few of the carvings are quality items. Prices for typical items range from 1000 to 2000 CFP and up for pareus and starting at 1500 CFP for the least expensive hats. In general, the best time to buy crafts is during fairs or festivals.

Shop 'til
You Drop

The "new and improved" municipal market, completely reorganized from the inside out, is much larger than its predecessor. Whereas in the old days fruit, flowers, watermelons and other produce would be sold on the sidewalk outside the perimeter of the market, today all selling goes on within the market's walls. The ground floor is reserved for flowers, taro, rootstalks and daily catches of fresh seafood. These are sold chiefly by Polynesians—an unwritten law here maintains that Tahitians may sell fish, taro, yams and other Polynesian foods; the Chinese sell vegetables; and Europeans and Chinese are the bakers and butchers. Downstairs, on the sidewalk, fruit and vegetables are displayed in the same traditional manner although the surroundings are aesthetically more sterile (and undoubtedly cleaner). You can still stroll through the aisles and find bananas, pineapples, starfruit, coconuts, oranges, papaya, limes, mangoes, avocados, cassava root, lettuce, tomatoes, onions, carrots, beans, potatoes, cabbage and even flower arrangements. The wary shoppers eyeing, squeezing, touching and scrutinizing the merchandise are still present.

An upstairs section, served by two escalators, is dedicated to handicrafts and is a good place to pick up inexpensive items such as woven pandanus hats, mats, bags, shell necklaces, pareus and other clothing. There are carved goods such as tikis, bowls and ukuleles as well. On the same floor are several small cafés that serve hamburgers, sandwiches, *steak frites*, *poisson cru* and other budget dishes. The upper deck also provides an ideal place to take market photos without intruding on anyone's territory.

You'll find the best time to visit Marché Papeete is early Sunday morning when out-of-towners come to sell their goods, shop and attend church in Papeete. Don't be afraid to sample the exotic-looking fruits, vegetables and fish. The results will be very satisfying.

Unlike Asiatic countries, one does not haggle or bargain when shopping in the public market places in Tahiti. Tahitians, though not so much Chinese merchants, might find it rude to haggle over prices. If you try to dicker with a Polynesian, more than likely the seller will get angry and either inflate the price or decide not to deal with you altogether. The only exception in the "dickering rule" is when you are making a large purchase of black pearl jewelry. The margins on these items are very high and a merchant might well consider knocking off a percentage in order to make a sale.

Although the Marché Papeete is an interesting place to begin looking for souvenirs, quality is generally mediocre. Better to check out **Manuia Curios**, in a row of shops facing the cathedral. It's a source of better-than-average quality carvings as well as shells, bags and other woven goods. This shop is also one of the few places where you can get traditional Tahitian dance costumes. ~ Place Notre Dame; 42-04-94.

Ganesha, located on the second floor of Vaima Center, has a superb selection of South Pacific handicrafts including *masi* (tapa cloth), mats, museum-quality carvings and other items from Fiji, the Solomon Islands and other areas. They also have small vials of sandalwood oil (the real thing) that has a sublime scent. A perfect gift for someone who enjoys fragrances. ~ Vaima Center; 43-04-18.

Aline Tamara Curios is located a block south of Vaima Center in downtown Papeete. One friend described it as a supermarket for tourists. There are T-shirts, *monoi* oil, postcards, key-ring holders and handicrafts. Nothing out of the ordinary, but Aline offers good prices (especially on T-shirts), plenty of selection and a handy location. ~ Centre Commerciale; 42-54-42.

French Polynesia issues beautiful stamps, which are popular with philatelists around the world. Those interested should stop at the special sales area on the ground floor at the main **post office.** Phone cards, known as *telecartes,* adorned with various Tahitian themes and motifs have also become a collectible item and are available in any of the post office branches. ~ Boulevard Pomare; 41-43-00.

Black pearls are a product indigenous to French Polynesia and make a special gift or souvenir. To educate yourself on the origin and development of the black pearl, a good place to start is at the **Tahiti Pearl Center**, also known as the Musée de la Perle Noire in the Paofai section of Papeete. It's actually a store with some museum-quality exhibits rather than a museum that sells black pearls. ~ Boulevard Pomare; 43-85-58.

In general, there are two main types of black pearl retailers: the large shops such as the Tahiti Pearl Center and the small artisans. There are five different classes of black pearls and the question for the consumer boils down to this: *How much are you willing to spend?* Those with plenty of money who are concerned with getting the crème de la crème one might consider **Didier Sibani** at the Vaima Center ~ 45-02-02; **Vaima Perles** also at the Vaima Center ~ 42-55-57; or **Tahiti Perles** on Boulevard Pomare ~ 53-50-10.

These are big operators that sell the very best and demand top dollar. For both quality and price it is a good idea to consider a purchase from smaller artisans who create their own jewelry. They also have good grades of pearls and offer creative designs on a par with the expensive outlets. Artisans cater to a broader market and their prices are more affordable.

Some of the better ones are **Stephane Labaysse** on Rue Jean Gilbert just off Boulevard Pomare ~ 42-70-60; **Moana Pai** at PK 22.5 in Paea ~ 53-37-41; and **Frederic Missir** on Rue du Général de Gaulle at the Vaima Center ~ 43-37-98. Of the three, Labaysse speaks fluent English.

While not exactly your average souvenir, you might want to bring home your own genuine Polynesian **tattoo**. (Polynesian tattoos utilize traditional Polynesian motifs, including geometric patterns and sometimes stylized animals such as birds or turtles.) Expect to pay around 10,000 CFP (around US$120) for a simple wrist or ankle tattoo. There are two popular places, both approved by the local public health authorities. **Jordi's Tattoo Shop** is behind the Prince Hinoï hotel. They promote the fact that they sterilize their equipment with an autoclave and always use new needles. ~ 43 Rue Leboucher; 42-45-00. **Tattoo Maniac,** above Bar Taina, also has a good reputation among tattoo aficionados. ~ Corner of Boulevard Pomare and Rue Clappier.

When buying pearls, if a deal seems too good to be true, hold off on your purchase. There have been reports of merchants who peddle artificially colored pearls, which is *not* what you want. Buyer beware.

If you enjoy browsing the newsstands or bookstores and are interested in a coffee-table book on French Polynesia to bring home, there are plenty to choose from in the shops. **Archipels** has a wide selection of books, principally in French but with a reasonable English section. Maps, however, are scarce here, and prices on some of the travel books were more expensive than at other shops. There is, however, an extensive section on Tahiti and the Pacific in English and French. ~ Rue des Remparts; 42-47-30.

The **Vaima Librairie**, which occupies space on the second and third stories of the Vaima Center, also has books in French and English. It has the best travel section and books on Tahiti and the Pacific in Papeete. ~ Vaima Center; 45-57-44.

Finally, **Polygraph** devotes much of its space to stationery and magazines, as well as having a good selection of books. It's also an excellent source for maps and nautical charts. One store down from Polygraph is a gallery cum bookstore that sells English-language books solely on French Polynesia and the South Pacific. Though associated with Polygraph, it is closely supervised by Gilles Artur, director of the Gauguin Museum. If you have an interest in Pacific literature, this is a mandatory stop. ~ Avenue Bruat; 42-80-47.

OUTDOOR CAFÉS & BARS   There is never a shortage of nightlife in Papeete, one of the liveliest ports in the South Pacific. The capital has a wide assortment of pubs, clubs and bars ranging from posh outdoor cafés and bars to sleazy servicemen's dives. Fortunately, Papeete is a small town, and most places are within several minutes' walking distance of each other, mostly along the waterfront

NIGHTLIFE

or in the Vaima Center area. Wherever you go, be prepared to spend some cash—the cheapest beer in town is at least US$5 (400 CFP) and cocktails range from US$6 to US$8 (500 to 700 CFP). On weekend nights, most clubs have a cover charge of at least US$12 (1000 CFP), which includes a drink.

Le Kiosque, a walk-in kiosk at the waterfront entrance to the Vaima Center, has a good selection of magazines and newspapers (including the *International Herald Tribune*, *USA Today*, *Time* and *Newsweek*).

At the seedy northern end of Boulevard Pomare, opposite the Moorea ferry terminal, are the hangouts of the more colorful denizens of the night—soldiers, sailors, *Légionnaires*, prostitutes, transvestites, transsexuals, travel writers and even the odd tourist. Despite the relative seediness of this two-block area, you will feel safe. These are places for the more adventurous visitor to watch the world go by while sipping an espresso, a glass of wine or perhaps a Hinano. Typical of the bars in this category are **Le Zizou**, a disco bar that has a cover charge during the evenings. At peak hours, it is chock full of French military conscripts and their female and/or transvestite companions. ~ Quai Galliéni; 42-07-55.

In the same vicinity and category within a block radius are **Le Taina Bar** (42-64-40) and the **Calypso** (42-17-53); both are located next to the Kon Tiki Hotel at Quai Galliéni. Depending on entertainment, both may have cover charges on the weekends.

Morrison's Café, located at the top floor of the Vaima Center, is named after Jim Morrison (of the Doors) and decorated with 1960s and 1970s rock posters. A restaurant/outdoor café with a huge wooden terrace surrounding a swimming pool, this is where you can hear live '70s-era rock music on the weekends. There is a full American-style bar well stocked with tequila. Sometimes there is a cover charge. ~ Vaima Center; 42-78-61.

LOCAL BARS Undoubtedly the friendliest spots in town are the rollicking working-class bars where locals come to unwind with conversation and a few beers. They are noisy, crowded, smoke-filled dens that may have a trio or quartet strumming away on ukuleles and guitars. These places seem formidable at first because of the mass of people packed inside. As a visitor, once you're in and flash a few smiles, the locals will be quite amiable.

Typical of this scene is the **Saloon Bar**, two blocks from the waterfront Boulevard Pomare. This is a no-frills Tahitian bar that has no name other than the words "bar" and "saloon" on a street sign decorated with a red star. There's usually someone sitting on a stool, strumming a guitar. ~ Rue Emile Martin.

CLUBS For those interested in meeting locals, the club scene is a great way to make friends—if you know how to dance. Dance is a vital part of local culture and Tahitians appreciate a foreigner with the right moves. The flip side is, if you can't dance too well, don't make these venues a place to learn. A local might suffer through one spin on the dancefloor with a rank amateur, but never a second time. Would-be dancers interested in meeting Tahitians should practice their dips before they get to Papeete.

Of the dance-hall scene, the classiest is **La Cave** at the Royal Papeete Hotel. Keeping with the cave motif, La Cave is dark and often has loud, live music. It has more of a ballroom atmosphere than other dance halls and is popular with *mahus* (transvestites). Cover. ~ Boulevard Pomare; 42-01-29.

While in the building, you may want to peek into **Le Tamure Hut**, also inside the Royal Papeete Hotel. While more of a bar, with little room to dance, it has a live band that plays a range of music from local *kaina* flavor to rock-and-roll. There is a nice mix of Tahitians and tourists. There is a cover charge Wednesday through Saturday evenings, but admission is free if you're a guest at the hotel. It's perhaps a more comfortable place for visitors who just want to sip a beer and meet some locals rather than step out on the dancefloor. Cover. ~ Boulevard Pomare; 42-01-29.

Continuing on the dance-hall circuit, down the socioeconomic ladder from La Cave is **Le Pitate**. Sporting garish red lights and movie posters on the ceiling, the Pitate features dim lights and live, electrifying Tahitian music. It is the most popular club among working-class Tahitians and the more the evening rolls by, the more rough it gets. Fortunately, at the door sits a bouncer with fists the size of hams. There is, as one local put it, "very little pretension" at the Pitate. Though seemingly intimidating, the Pitate welcomes visitors, especially if they join the locals on the dancefloor. Cover on weekends. ~ Corner of Boulevard Pomare and Avenue Bruat; 45-59-00.

DISCOS Papeete's discos have a universal character—flashing lights, a pulsating beat and a high decibel level. In addition to the bars and discos that service the servicemen, there are also several clubs that have performances by transvestites or transsexuals. They are popular with visitors (gay and straight), French servicemen and locals alike.

The best place in town to see a bump-and-grind female impersonator is **Le Piano Bar**. The Piano Bar is the meeting place for *mahus* and features shows at least once an evening. It's a famous institution in Papeete and anyone who wishes to visit should do so. Visitors of any gender are welcome. You can spend the evening dancing or watching the assorted clientele drift in and out of the swinging doors. Cover. ~ Rue des Ecoles; 42-88-24. A few yards away, the **Bounty Club** is a disco frequented by sailors, *mahus* and the same following as the Piano Bar. It also has a female impersonator striptease stage show with a similar ambience. Cover. ~ Rue des Ecoles.

Perhaps the classiest disco in town is the **Rolls Club** on the ground floor of the Vaima Center. It's gone through several incarnations and now has the latest in laser lights, mirrors and shiny black furniture. The crowd is mostly early to mid-20s and 30s and mostly *demi* (Tahitian half-castes) and Chinese. The clientele is always dressed to kill—here's where you'll see the single "beautiful people." Visitors are also welcomed. It's open Friday and Sunday for Tahitian nights mixed with disco; Thursday and Saturday are exclusively disco. Cover. ~ Boulevard Pomare; 43-41-42.

Le Rétro, also in the Vaima Center behind the Rétro brasserie, attracts an older, well-heeled clientele. The decor is elegant and glitzy. Cover. ~ Vaima Center; 42-86-83.

Perhaps the only bar with an Afro–Caribbean flavor is **Le Paradise**, opposite the harbor, across from the *roulottes*. This is the only bar where the deejay plays a combination of zouk, reggae, calypso, Caribbean and African music. It's a bit classier than the average military hangout. The crowd here is older and there can be an interesting mix of French and Caribbean clientele. Once inside, you are required to order a drink. If you enjoy Afro–Caribbean music and a lively crowd sprinkled with servicemen and their Tahitian consorts, this is the place to go. ~ Quai Galliéni; 42-73-05.

CASINOS   Private, 24-hour gambling casinos are now in operation at three hotels in Papeete—the Royal Papeete, Prince Hinoï and the Pacifica. The casinos offer blackjack, roulette, mahjong and poker. Though the hotels are ostensibly for members only, admission cards can be obtained for free at the hotels for nonresidents. For more information on gambling in Tahiti, U.S. residents can call Don Chapman, a Hawaii-based tour wholesaler. ~ 808-396-2225, fax 808-396-0091.

DANCE TO A DIFFERENT BEAT

For the average Tahitian, the dance halls (as opposed to the discos) are the most popular places to go. For the visitor it's a great place to get some exposure to one of the most important elements of Tahitian culture—dance—and possibly rub shoulders with the natives. All the dance halls have amplified sound systems and bands that play Tahitian waltzes, fox trots, rock-and-roll and music for the sensual *tamure*, the hip-shaking dance that has been known to cause palpitations in middle-aged men. In the background the thunder of drumbeats reverberates through the room. Originally an Eastern Polynesian (Tahitian and Cook Island) dance, the *tamure* has become a pan-Polynesian phenomenon and close to the national pastime in French Polynesia.

In order to orient ourselves geographically, imagine
Papeete as the domain of a giant goddess sitting atop
a throne. If she's facing the harbor, her backside would

▼▼▼▼▼▼▼▼▼▼▼▼▼
North of Papeete

be snug against the wall of Mt. Aorai, the highest peak of the verdant mountain range that towers above the city. Fanning out to our
mythical goddess' right (north) would be the districts of Pirae, Arue
and Mahina. Formerly principalities or dominions run by local chiefs,
the districts have evolved into bedroom communities of Papeete.

Over the past few decades, the migration of islanders from other
parts of French Polynesia as well as the metropolitan French has
swelled the population of these communities. Consequently, Pirae,
Arue and Mahina have mushroomed into suburbs complete with
grocery stores, schools, villas, slums, playgrounds and other familiar
urban offerings.

For the visitor, it is now impossible to distinguish where Papeete ends and Greater Papeete begins. The suburb-like nature of these
neighborhoods is clearly evident during rush-hour traffic (8 a.m.
and 5 p.m.) when the coastal road is clogged with BMWs, Peugeots
and Volkswagens creeping slowly, inexorably, to crowded parking
lots in town or returning home.

The word "suburb" should not dissuade the visitor from seeing what lies beyond the city limits or even choosing a slightly
out-of-town hotel or guest house. The ubiquitous *Le Truck* makes
commuting into town for sightseeing or shopping (during non-rush
hours) easy. The quietude of the suburbs is also a welcome relief
from the noise and exhaust fumes of Papeete.

One does not have to travel more than 1.5 kilometers from the edge
of Papeete on Avenue du Prince Hinoï (which becomes Avenue du
Général de Gaulle in Pirae) to enter Pirae, home of Tahiti's current
president, Gaston Flosse, who also serves as Pirae's mayor. Pirae is
headquarters for the infamous **Centre du Expérimentation de la
Pacifique** (CEP), the agency that was responsible for nuclear testing.
The complex of institutional buildings that comprise the CEP is on
your left. This huge bureaucracy, which used to employ thousands
of French Polynesians and metropolitan French, was being down-
sized even prior to the nuclear detonations of 1995. The testing facility has long been a key component of France's independent nuclear arsenal, *force de frappe*, which was developed during the days
of Charles de Gaulle. French Polynesia was chosen as a venue to
test nuclear weapons when Algeria (a former French colony that was
once used as a testing range) became independent. ~ Avenue du
Général de Gaulle.

On a lighter note, if you travel another kilometer east, the road
will cross the **Fautaua River** (PK 2.5, Pirae), which is the source for
Pierre Loti's Pool (Bain Loti). Pierre Loti was the pen name for Julien

SIGHTS

Viaud, the French merchant marine whose book *The Marriage of Loti* describes the love affair of a Frenchman and a native girl. The pool where he first saw the enchanting Rarahu (the novel's heroine) is several kilometers up the Fautaua River Valley. Unfortunately, this romantic spot on the river is now covered with concrete, but is marked by a bust of the author. Bain Loti is also the trailhead for a three-hour hike to the Fautaua Waterfall (see the "Hiking" section at the end of this chapter).

Perhaps the most famous manmade landmark in Tahiti is the **Tomb of King Pomare** V. A sign on the ocean side of the road marks the access road to the tomb. The Pomare line rose to power as a direct consequence of the European discovery of Tahiti. The first of the lineage, Pomare I, used ex-members of the *Bounty* crew, who were armed with guns, to defeat his enemies. His son and successor, Pomare II, was crowned at a temple just a few feet away from the site of the present-day tomb, where the Protestant church now stands. During the ceremony, a *Bounty* crew member, James Morrison, reported that three human sacrifices were made on behalf of the new king. ~ PK 4.7, Arue.

In 1812, Pomare II became the first Tahitian convert to Christianity and after three years managed to convince the populations of Moorea and Tahiti (with the use of arms where necessary) to follow his example. In his religious zeal, Pomare II constructed a temple in the shape of an oval hut. It was larger than King Solomon's temple and constructed from breadfruit tree pillars, palm fronds and other local materials. The Royal Mission Chapel, as it was called, was about 712 feet long (longer than St. Peter's in Rome), 54 feet wide and could hold 6000 people. Pomare II died in 1821 at the age of 40 from the effects of alcohol. Soon afterward, the Royal Mission chapel fell into disrepair. Today, a 12-sided chapel built in 1978 stands where the Royal Mission chapel once did.

The tomb itself was constructed in 1879 for Queen Pomare, who died in 1877 after a reign of 50 years. During this period, the country became a French colony. The Queen's remains were removed a few years later by her son King Pomare V who, feeling that his end was near, apparently wished to occupy the mausoleum by himself. Pomare V lived on a stipend supplied by the French government, and died in 1891 at the age of 52. In true Pomare tradition, he drank himself to death. An account of his funeral is given by Paul Gauguin in *Noa Noa*.

Local tradition has it that the object on the tomb's roof—which misinformed tour guides often say represents a liquor bottle (which would have been a fitting memorial to Pomare)—is actually a replica of a Greek urn.

Among the American literati who made their homes in French Polynesia, none did more to publicize Tahiti in the 20th century than James Norman Hall, whose home is now being turned into a museum. The works of Hall and Charles Nordoff, authors of the *Boun-ty Trilogy, Hurricane* and *The Dark River*, will forever be synony-mous with Tahiti. Hall died at his Arue home in 1951 and is buried on Herai Hill just above. To find the Hall residence from town, pass the primary school on the sea side of the road. Immediately after crossing a small bridge over the Vaipoopo River, look for Hall's green house on the mountain side, which is visible from the road. At the time of writing it is being prepared for public visitation—check with the visitor's bureau to determine if the restoration is com-plete. ~ PK 5.4, Arue.

On the ocean side of the road, the **Hyatt Regency Tahiti**, which sits atop **One Tree Hill** in Mahina, affords a magnificent view of Moorea and Matavai Bay, where captains Samuel Wallis and James Cook once anchored. To get there, look for the hotel sign on the sea side of the road and pull into the parking lot. It's about 100 yards

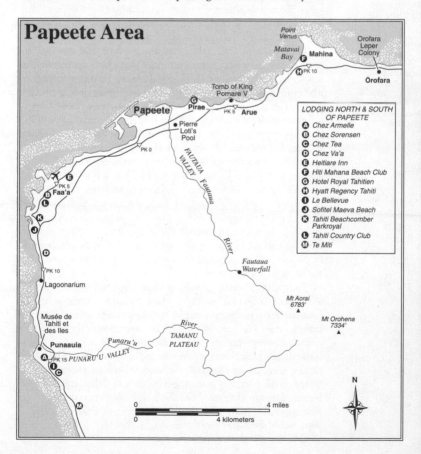

Papeete Area

Point Venus

Matavai Bay

Mahina

Orofara Leper Colony

Ⓕ

Ⓗ PK 10

Orofara

Tomb of King Pomare V

Ⓖ

Pirae

PK 5 Arue

Papeete

Pierre Loti's Pool

PK 0

FAUTAUA VALLEY

Fautaua River

Ⓧ PK 5

Ⓔ

Ⓑ Faa'a

Ⓛ

Ⓚ

Ⓙ

Ⓓ

PK 10

Lagoonarium

Fautaua Waterfall

River

TAMANU PLATEAU

Musée de Tahiti et des Iles

Punaru'u

Punaauia

Ⓐ PK 15 PUNARU'U VALLEY

Ⓘ

Ⓒ

Ⓜ

Mt Aorai 6783' ▲

Mt Orohena 7334' ▲

LODGING NORTH & SOUTH OF PAPEETE
Ⓐ *Chez Armelle*
Ⓑ *Chez Sorensen*
Ⓒ *Chez Tea*
Ⓓ *Chez Va'a*
Ⓔ *Heitiare Inn*
Ⓕ *Hiti Mahana Beach Club*
Ⓖ *Hotel Royal Tahitien*
Ⓗ *Hyatt Regency Tahiti*
Ⓘ *Le Bellevue*
Ⓙ *Sofitel Maeva Beach*
Ⓚ *Tahiti Beachcomber Parkroyal*
Ⓛ *Tahiti Country Club*
Ⓜ *Te Miti*

N

0   4 miles
0   4 kilometers

(90 meters) across a grassy park to the cliff. (There is also access to the beach at the bottom of the hill via the road on the left at the entrance of the parking lot.) Wallis originally called this piece of real estate "Skirmish Hill" because he bombarded the Tahitians gathered here with cannonballs from his ship. Captain Cook eventually changed the name to One Tree Hill because of the solitary *atae* tree that grew here at the time. When the hotel was built in 1968 the owners kept the Tahitian name. The Hyatt Regency clings to the hillside like a scallop to a rock. ~ PK 8.1, Mahina; 48-11-22.

Point Venus and **Matavai Bay** are of great historical significance and a fine place for a rest stop. Several stores at a road junction (including the Venustar) and a *Poste* sign are the clues to the Point Venus turnoff. It's about one kilometer from the coast road to the car park. This area has all the natural amenities—shady trees, a river, beach and exposure to cooling trade winds—that make a wonderful picnic ground. Near the beach area, toward Papeete, note that a local outrigger canoe racing club stores its vessels here. There are also a few souvenir shops near the road.

In the early days of Tahiti, this tiny point of land was used by some of the most important visitors of that era—captains Wallis, Cook and Bligh. Until the 1820s, when Papeete became a more popular port of call, all visiting ships anchored in the area. Although Wallis, Tahiti's European discoverer, landed here in 1767, it was Captain Cook's expedition in 1769 that gave the land its name.

Cook was sent by the Royal Geographical Society of England to record the transit of Venus which, theoretically, would enable scientists to compute the distance between the earth and the sun—a figure that would be an invaluable tool for navigators. On June 3, 1769, the weather was good and the transit was recorded by the best instruments available at the time. Unfortunately, as Cook found out, the edges of Venus could not be seen sharply enough through telescopes to accurately record the transit and his measurements were for naught. However, his journey was still a success, because of the many new species of flora and fauna gathered by the other scientists on the trip.

During the *Bounty* episode in 1788, Captain Bligh also landed at this spot, collecting breadfruit plants to use as a cheap source of food for the slave population in the West Indies. His landing became grist for Hollywood, which has come up with three different cinematic interpretations (1935, 1962 and 1983). According to historian Bengt Danielsson, during the shooting of the 1962 *Bounty* version with Trevor Howard and Marlon Brando, a sequence was filmed on Matavai Bay featuring thousands of Tahitian extras welcoming the visitors ashore. The director, wishing to portray the Tahitians in their former glory, had the Tahitian extras don long-haired wigs and false teeth before the filming to compensate for attributes most of them no longer possessed.

In 1969, captains Samuel Wallis, James Cook and Louis-Antoine de Bougainville were honored by wooden sculptures at Point Venus, but the monuments, along with the quaint Museum of Discovery, were swept away by a storm several years ago. Bligh, the third navigator to visit the area, was not remembered by any monument. Near where the sculptures once stood is an abstract monument, described by Danielsson as a "needle pointing to heaven," to commemorate the arrival of the first Christian missionaries on Point Venus in 1797. Dispatched by the London Missionary Society, they abandoned their mission in 1808 and did not re-establish themselves until 1817. Though they worked actively for the British annexation of the islands, the British missionaries were eased out of Tahiti after the French takeover in 1842. The missionary era came to an end in Tahiti in 1963 when an independent Protestant church run by Polynesians was formed.

> Cook also anchored off Matavai Bay in 1773, 1774 and 1777, during his subsequent voyages of exploration.

About 150 yards (135 meters) northeast of the Missionary Society memorial sits a monument enclosed by an iron railing. According to the text on a bronze plaque (which has now disappeared), the column was erected by none other than Captain Cook in 1769 and refurbished in 1901. However, not only was the monument not built by Cook (it was a product of the local public works department), it is not on the spot where Cook made his astronomical observations (which took place between the river and the beach).

Finally, the most visible (existing) landmark on Point Venus is the **lighthouse**, constructed in 1868 (despite the 1867 date perhaps over-optimistically inscribed on the entrance). ~ PK 10, Mahina.

Though little remains today, the **Orofara Leper Colony** is still a poignant landmark in French Polynesia. Prior to WWI, victims of leprosy, what is now called Hansen's disease, were ostracized and chased into remote areas away from the general population. By government decree, in 1914 the Orofara Valley was set aside as a leper colony for all those in Tahiti who suffered from the disease. Until the development of sulphur drugs, there was little the French Protestant mission treating the patients here could do. Nowadays, it is possible to cure Hansen's disease. ~ PK 13.2, Mahina.

Continuing along the eastern coastal road will bring you to the district of Papenoo and to **Papenoo Village and Valley**. There's a popular surf break just before Papenoo, a typical rural village of the type that has been rapidly disappearing since the end of World War II. Many of its homes are built in the old colonial style, with wide verandas. The Catholic and Protestant churches and *mairie* (town hall) rest along the highway. Past the village, a new bridge (the longest in Tahiti) spans the Papenoo River. The Papenoo Valley, the island's biggest, was formed by an ancient volcanic crater. The river's mouth (where the bridge is located) is the only hole in the crater wall. One can drive up the Papenoo Valley about one kilometer and continue on foot on a trail that leads across the island (see "Outdoor Adventures" section in this chapter). A few residents live at the entrance of the valley. The deeper reaches of this narrow valley are steep and unfit for agriculture or habitation. ~ PK 17.1, Papenoo.

In Tiarei, the next district down the coastal highway, is the ever-popular **Arahoho Blowhole**, one of Tahiti's biggest roadside attractions. It's unmarked, and located at the base of a steep cliff on a narrow shoulder on the mountain side of the road. Over countless years, battering surf has undercut the basalt shoreline and eroded a passage to the surface beneath the road. When waves crash against the rocks, the result is a geyser-like plume of sea water that showers onlookers. It's easy to miss the blowhole when coming from the direction of Papeete, so keep an eye open for the parking lot on the coast side of the road. Be careful crossing the road because the blowhole is on the shoulder of the road, at the crest of a hairpin turn. A few hundred yards from the blowhole, the small, crescent-shaped black-sand beach is a good spot to picnic and swim. There are also several vendors selling coconuts, *mape*, a delicious Tahitian chestnut, and, if it's the right season, *rambutan*, a wonderful lychee-like red-spined fruit native to Asia. ~ PK 22, Tiarei.

Another hundred yards (90 meters) down the coastal road is the entrance to the three **Fa'aurumai Waterfalls**. Take the inland turnoff where the waterfall sign is posted and drive inland 1.3 kilometers. The rainforest on both sides of this small valley is thick, nearly impenetrable and filled with *hutu* and *mape* trees. If you look carefully, you'll notice star fruit, guava and *mape* along the trail. From the parking lot, it's several hundred yards to Vaimahutu, the first fall, which cascades 100 feet to the earth and empties into a pool. Walk another 20 minutes down and you will reach the other two falls, Haamaremare iti and Haamaremare rahi. These are less dramatic but beautiful nonetheless. Bring a swimsuit if you want to stand under the falls and insect repellent to keep the mosquitoes away. A lot of work has gone into the waterfalls park—the access road has been newly paved, new bridges across the creek have been constructed and *Respectez la Nature* signs have been placed in the vicinity. ~ PK 22.3, Tiarei.

LODGING   In the suburb of Pirae, the **Hotel Royal Tahitien** is a sprawling complex of 45 rooms along the shoreline. The ocean view is good and there is a black-sand beach popular with residents, but which is not always clean. The crowd at the hotel is an unusual amalgam of French servicemen, Americans and Europeans. The rooms are fairly large by Tahitian standards, well maintained and clean. The expansive tropical grounds are well manicured. There is a good open-air restaurant on the premises frequented often by locals. To find it,

Romeo & Juliet Tahitian Style

Once a beautiful 17-year-old girl named Fauai lived in Tiarei. Like all island girls, she loved to decorate her hair with flowers. Every morning, accompanied by her friends, she traveled through the nearby valleys gathering blossoms to make crowns of flowers. Her father, Chief Marurai, adored her with an obsession. Jealous and cruel, he wouldn't let any man approach her. As a result, two of his best warriors accompanied her during her strolls. One day, Fauai encountered Tua, a handsome young man. Not aware of the *tabu,* he snatched her crown of flowers, and ran away laughing. Without hesitation the guards chased Tua and killed him. Following the tragedy, Fauai took refuge with her ill mother. She later returned to the valley with her entourage, looking for medicinal plants to treat the old woman. They encountered Ivi, an emaciated boy who was seeking plants to treat his own malady. She pitied him and wanted to help, but there was the problem of the guards. What could she do?

She had an idea. She asked her friends to hide in the bush and begin screaming to distract the guards. Once the screams rang out, Fauai ordered the guards to see what the commotion was all about. She then joined Ivi. When he saw her he turned pale with fright and told Fauai to leave. She told him she wanted to help find herbs that might heal him. She took his hand and led him deeper into the forest. By this time the guards were alerted to her deception and began searching for the princess. They could be heard in the distance yelling her name. Ivi had to rest frequently to catch his breath and the calls from the guards drew closer. Realizing they would be found together, Ivi told the girl to return to her keepers and leave him alone to die. She refused, telling him that if he must die, she would die with him.

Ivi then revealed a secret to the princess. He was not a sick young boy but the forest spirit of the valley. He told her that in a few moments the two of them would be imprisoned forever in a waterfall. As soon as his words were complete both were stuck to the sheer wall of a rock face and Ivi was transformed into a handsome young man. A deafening noise filled the air and from high above the cliff two enormous masses of water poured down, entirely covering the two young people.

When the guards arrived, they discovered two magnificent falls cascading into two pools. From that day on, Ivi and Fauai remained hidden behind the falls. The warriors never returned to the village. On the way back, a third waterfall swallowed them up.

turn off at the *mairie* (town hall) sign approximately three kilometers from town on the ocean side of Avenue du Général de Gaulle. The location is a bit far from Papeete for walkers but *Le Truck* runs along Avenue du Prince Hinoï (which becomes Avenue du Général de Gaulle in Pirae) and it's easy to commute to town in this manner. ~ Pirae; 42-81-13, fax 41-05-35. MODERATE.

Hyatt Regency Tahiti is perched on the summit of "One Tree Hill," a moniker coined by Captain James Cook, who anchored in Matavai Bay below more than 200 years ago. The Hyatt enjoys one of the finest vistas of any hotel in French Polynesia and also offers a picturesque black-sand beach nestled at the base of the cliffs. Adjacent to the hotel is a grassy park with a jogging track (with great views) popular with locals and visitors. Unfortunately, the caliber of the natural environs does not extend to the rooms, which are decidedly average in size and quality of furnishings. The hotel does have four restaurants and an outdoor dining area that takes advantage of the setting, as well as a novel swimming pool ringed with sand, made to look like a tropical beach. The verdict—average, overpriced rooms with stunning views. ~ PK 8.1, Mahina; 48-11-22, fax 48-25-44, or 800-233-1234 in the U.S. ULTRA-DELUXE.

The **Hiti Mahana Beach Club** is on 12 acres adjacent to a black-sand beach in the Mahina district. Operated by Coco Pautu, the beach club is a combination campground and dormitory popular with budget travelers chiefly because it is one of the few inexpensive hostels in the Papeete area. Unfortunately, it is situated in a neighborhood that can only be described as a Tahitian slum. Perhaps because of the neighborhood, there have been many reports of thefts. The dorm building, which sleeps around a dozen, consists of a few cots and mattresses strewn on the floor occupying just about every square inch of the room. The camping area is situated directly in front of the dorm building and can accommodate about ten tents. Regrettably, it is the only place to camp on the island so backpackers who prefer to pitch a tent don't have a choice. Coco speaks excellent English but his attitude, which smacks of don't-bother-me-unless-you-plan-to-spend-money, may not endear him to his guests. If you look closely at the now derelict century-old two-story mansion known as *Maison Blanc* on the beach club property (formerly the club dorm), you will get an idea of how much things have deteriorated over the years from pure neglect. A small restaurant is located on the premises, and banks, grocery stores, inexpensive restaurants and fresh produce are nearby. ~ Mahina; 48-16-13. BUDGET.

DINING   Most of the restaurants on Tahiti are concentrated in Papeete. However, there are a few restaurants in Papeete's bedroom communities worth checking out and rarely will you see a tourist in them.

The **Hotel Royal Tahitien** has a large outdoor restaurant covered with a tightly stitched *pandanus* leaf canopy. The dining area faces the sea (looking out toward Moorea) and is often filled with local families on the weekends. The specialties here are seafood. We found the shrimp curry and the poached parrot fish with vanilla sauce very good. A wide range of salads and meat such as pepper steak and veal cutlets are also available. ~ Pirae; 42-81-13. MODERATE.

> Discount outlets or *hypermarches* are *the* place to go for yachties or those who need to stock up on all manner of consumer items such as shampoo, canned goods, detergent, etc.

The Dahlia is one of the best family-style Chinese restaurants in Tahiti. A cut or two above the neon-lit inexpensive Chinese eateries in town, the Dahlia offers the usual fare of chicken, shrimp and beef dishes, presented in a simple but tasty manner. The soups are particularly good. It's a local favorite and worth the few-minute journey out of town. ~ PK 4.2, Arue; 42-59-87. BUDGET.

Hyatt Regency Tahiti has four restaurants on the premises including a Japanese "Benihana"-style eatery where the chef performs a slice-and-dice routine before your very eyes. The main restaurant is the **Mahana**, whose menu offers seafood specialties. Friday and Saturday evenings, Mahana provides a barbecue seafood buffet; it is also one of the few places in town that has brunch. Some of the better offerings are steamed rock lobster with vegetable couscous, parrot fish filet, duck breast and Thai style-green curry shrimp. One of the best features of the hotel is a spectacular outdoor eating area (with a fish pond) that overlooks Matavai Bay, where Captain Cook once anchored. There's also a buffet dinner during weekend dance shows. If you don't feel like eating, the outdoor restaurant makes a terrific place to sip a beer and watch the sun set. ~ PK 8.1, Mahina; 48-11-22. DELUXE TO ULTRA-DELUXE.

On the water in Mahina, **Mon Fare** serves traditional French cuisine such as filet mignon, escargot and the like. All meals are served à la carte. ~ PK 12, Mahina; 48-22-23. DELUXE TO ULTRA-DELUXE.

GROCERIES

Numerous mom-and-pop local or small grocery stores line the highway and side streets of Pirae, Arue and Mahina. For serious shoppers and long-term residents, it's best to jump in a car or on *Le Truck* and visit one of the larger discount outlets such as **Tropic Import** in Pirae ~ 43-47-70, or **Continent** in Arue ~ 45-42-22 (known as a *hypermarche* or super store), which has outlets in Arue and Punaauia. These merchandisers are the least expensive places in French Polynesia to buy groceries, as well as other consumer goods. This is where the savvy locals go to shop.

Some of the better grocery stores in the area are **Supermarche Hippo** at PK 4 on the corner of Avenue du Général de Gaulle at the

Hippodrome (racetrack) turnoff in Pirae ~ 42-82-01, **Magasin Arue** at PK 6 in Arue ~ 42-71-13, **Supermarche Venustar**, at PK 10 in Mahina ~ 48-10-13, at the Point Venus turnoff.

SHOPPING

On the main road in Pirae there is an open market area three kilometers from town where shell necklaces, jewelry, clothing and other souvenirs are sold at a small **pavilion** just off of Avenue du Général de Gaulle. The easiest way to find it is to pass the mammoth CEP (nuclear energy facility) and look for the *Artisan* sign pointing toward the market a few hundred yards farther down the street on the sea side of the road. *Le Truck* regularly makes stops so it is quite accessible from Papeete.

NIGHTLIFE

Polynesian dance reviews are regularly staged at the **Hyatt Regency Tahiti** on Friday and Saturday evenings. The performers, which may number up to 25 members, usually dance on the lanai overlooking Matavai Bay—a spectacular setting. One need not be a guest of the hotel to watch. (Check with hotel for times.) ~ PK 8.1, Mahina; 48-11-22.

BEACHES & PARKS

One naturally associates Tahiti with beaches, and there is no shortage of sand on this tropical island. Unfortunately, most of it is not the powdery white substance that many people who come to Tahiti expect. There are fine white-sand beaches in French Polynesia but not many on Tahiti. Most of the beaches in the Papeete vicinity are of the brown or black sand variety. They are of volcanic origin and finer in grain than white-sand beaches.

PLAGE TAAONE Located about five kilometers east of Papeete, this black-sand beach fronts the Hotel Royal Tahitien in Pirae and abuts a seawall. Named after the Taaone district, it stretches about a thousand yards. Offshore is a beautiful view of Moorea but the beach itself is not particularly picturesque. *Plage Taaone* is popular with locals and tends to be liberally sprinkled with soda cans and other litter. The amenities at the beach, which include restrooms and a restaurant, belong to the hotel. The Royal Tahitien management prefers that only guests use the restrooms but if you buy a soda or a drink at the bar it's acceptable to use the facilities. I did see swimmers but the water looked murky and uninviting. Most of the Taaone denizens I saw were sun worshiping rather than swimming. Restrooms, restaurant. ~ Take Avenue du Prince Hinoï to Pirae, approximately three kilometers east of Papeete and turn left at the *mairie* (town hall) sign. The hotel and beach that front it are behind the Pirae town hall, just off the main drag.

LAFAYETTE BEACH This long stretch of black sand is in Arue at PK 7. Mostly used by locals, it's easy to get to, as it lies at the edge of the coastal highway. There are shady trees along the periphery of the beach. As local beaches go it's not spectacular, but it is conveniently located. There is one outdoor shower but this is not a great swimming beach. ~ Take an Arue-bound *Le Truck* to PK 7 or pull off the road in your rental car at the small parking lot adjacent to the beach.

TAHARA'A BEACH (HYATT REGENCY) In Mahina at the foot of "One Tree Hill" is a crescent-shaped, black-sand beach, which has a dramatic view of Honu (Turtle) Point to the south. Standing on the beach, which is nestled snugly against the steep hillside, it seems as though you are at the bottom of a deep basin. Numerous shade trees line this beach, which is relatively close to town but feels much more isolated. The beach is public but the amenities are theoretically only for patrons of the hotel. According to the bartender on duty, as long as one purchases something from the snack bar one can use the facilities. I visited the beach on a Sunday and it wasn't very crowded. The swimming is excellent. Toilets, shower, snackbar (which serves beer) and deck with picnic tables. ~ Take the coastal road north to the Hyatt Regency and take the hotel exit. Park outside the hotel lot near the perimeter of the park. The access to the beach is a narrow, black-top road, which is immediately to your left upon entering the hotel grounds. (You must walk down, rather than drive). The trek down the steep winding road to the beach takes about ten minutes. Hotel guests may take a shuttle bus to the beach at frequent intervals. PK 8.1, Mahina.

TAHARA'A (HYATT REGENCY) PARK Atop of One Tree Hill, adjacent to the hotel, is Tahara'a Park, a large expanse of grass that overlooks Matavai Bay. The park has a short jogging trail that skirts the perimeter of the cliff. It may also be filled with soccer players or joggers on the weekend. ~ Take the coastal road north to the Hyatt Regency and take the Hyatt hotel exit. Park in the lot near the perimeter of the park. PK 8.1, Mahina.

◄ *HIDDEN*

POINT VENUS Point Venus has a fine beach, but unlike the narrow crescent of sand at the Hyatt, it is wide open and more easily accessible. It's a good swimming beach and is popular with picnickers because of a shady grove of palm and ironwood trees. Surfers should know there is a hollow right reef break off the end of the point. It's intense—for experts only. A long paddle is required. This is also a choice windsurfing spot. Picnic tables, drinking water, showers and restrooms. ~ To find the turnoff to Point Venus, look for several stores on the ocean side of the road (including the Venustar) and a *Poste* (post office) sign at PK 10. Turn left and go another kilometer to the coast road until you see the parking lot. PK 10.1, Mahina.

ARAHOHO BEACH 🏊 🏃 Across the highway and just a few yards down the road from the Arahoho Blowhole is a small crescent-shaped black-sand beach. It's a terrific spot to picnic and boogie board the beach break. Swimming can be a touch dangerous— the currents are very strong. Take great caution. There is a short beach break that will only be of interest to boogie boarders. Just across the road may be several vendors selling coconuts, *mape*, Tahitian chestnut and, if it's the right season, *rambutan*, a lychee-like red-spined fruit native to Asia. Picnic tables, drinking water, restrooms. ~ Take the east coast road to the Arahoho Blowhole. If you are driving, watch out for blowhole spectators who may be standing on the highway. The blowhole is actually on the mountain side of the road. There is little if any room on the shoulder of the road (on the inside of a hairpin turn) to observe this phenomena so curious visitors may be in harm's way. About 20 yards east of the blowhole on the ocean side of the road is a small parking lot. Pull in there. PK 22, Tiarei.

FA'AURUMAI WATERFALLS This is a series of three easily accessible waterfalls that has been turned into a park of sorts. The lowest fall is a ten-minute walk from the parking lot and plummets about 100 feet into a pool surrounded by boulders. This is an obligatory stop for most visitors to Tahiti and it's worth the effort to see it. Bring a swimsuit if you want to stand under the falls or take a dip in the pool below. (Don't forget insect repellent). Restrooms, drinking water and picnic tables. ~ Just 100 yards or so past the blowhole is the entrance to the 1.3 kilometer-long road leading to the three Fa'aurumai Waterfalls. From the parking lot it's several hundred yards to the first fall. The other falls are separated by 20-minute walks up a winding, but well-maintained path.

PAPENOO 🏊 🏃 There is a long stretch of black-sand beach along the shoreline of Papenoo Village. The beach is well known primarily because it faces one of the best surf breaks on the island. There are no shade trees near the beach but there are some on the shoulder of the road. It's easy to park on the shoulder of the road and watch the action if the surf is "working." This is a very long beach break, and judging by the numbers of surfers out on a day when conditions are right, it's very popular. There's also a right-hand point break. At the Papenoo river mouth (on the east side of the point) are some excellent sandbar breaks—surfing at low tide here is best. If you are going to surf here don't come in large groups—the locals will not like it. When conditions are fine it can get quite crowded. ~ Take the coastal road to Papenoo about three kilometers past the waterfalls. Park along the shoulder of the road. To get to the river-mouth break take the first left (coming from Papeete) after the Papenoo River bridge. PK 25, Papenoo.

Driving toward the airport from town (in a southerly ▼▼▼▼▼▼▼▼▼▼▼▼▼
direction) are the communities of **Faa'a** (where the **South of Papeete**
airport lies), **Punaauia** and **Paea**. These districts have
evolved into bedroom communities of Papeete. During rush-hour
traffic in the morning and evenings, the highway is as clogged as
an L.A. freeway. As a matter of fact, the L.A. freeways at rush hour
might be an easier commute because in Tahiti there is really only
one road. Of the three districts, Punaauia and Paea are the most
prosperous and suburban in nature. Faa'a is a mixed bag—there
are resorts, middle-class housing and slum areas. Faa'a is where
many of the less fortunate islanders from throughout French Polynesia move in order to look for work in the big city. (It was said
that many of the participants who took part in the infamous riot
that resulted in the destruction of half the airport on September
5–8, 1995, were disenfranchised Polynesians living in Faa'a.)

Jumping on the short section of freeway south of Papeete or
using the old coastal road, **Tahiti Faa'a International Airport** is the
first landmark you will encounter. Faa'a Airport is as modern as
any in the world, but still has distinct Tahitian touches such as
barefoot kids, rotund Tahitian women selling leis and perhaps an
unattended dog sleeping near the ticket counter. ~ PK 5.5, Faa'a.

The **Tahiti Beachcomber Parkroyal**, the top hotel on the island, is   **SIGHTS**
situated at **Tata'a Point**. In ancient Tahitian times, it was considered to be a holy place where the souls of the dead were said to depart to the netherworld. There may still be dead souls who inhabit
the corridors of the hotel. ~ PK 7.2, Punaauia; 42-51-10.

The **Sofitel Maeva Beach** is just beyond the highway entrance
and is a popular local beach. The hotel complex includes Tahiti
Aqua Maeva, a great water sports center with scuba diving, snorkeling, glass-bottom boat and harbor cruises. From this point, motorists can either take the four-laned "freeway" and zoom back to
Papeete, or take the old coastal highway north to town. ~ PK 8,
Punaauia; 42-80-42.

Recently reopened, the **Lagoonarium** combines a good restaurant with an equally decent aquarium. There are large tanks with
sharks and other pelagics as well as numerous exhibits of tropical
reef fish. There is an entrance fee to the aquarium, but if you eat
at the restaurant, entry to the aquarium is free. (Of special interest
is the Polynesian dance reviews put on at the Lagoonarium.) Admission. ~ PK 11, Punaauia; 43-62-90.

If you take the road one and a half kilometers farther, you will
see the **2+2=4 Primary School**. A 19th-century French landowner
donated the land for this school and had the above mathematical
equation inscribed at the entrance. According to historian Bengt
Danielsson, the donor, dubious about the propriety of introducing

the French educational system to Tahiti, figured that if nothing else the children would learn at least one thing of value. ~ PK 12.5, Punaauia.

Just south of the school, in an area now subdivided, is the site of a home where **Paul Gauguin** lived from 1897 to 1901 and where he produced about 60 paintings. Among these are *Where Do We Come From* (the Museum of Fine Arts, Boston), *Faa Iheihe* (Tate Gallery, London) and *Two Tahitian Women* (the Metropolitan Museum, New York). Note that this landmark is merely the site of Gauguin's former home—the structure is long gone.

Beyond the bridge at the entrance of the **Punaru'u Valley** was once a fortress built by the French during the Tahitian uprising of 1844 to 1846. The site is now used as a TV relay station. The road up the valley leads to a trail (see "Hiking" in this chapter) to the Tamanu Plateau where oranges grow in profusion. In the 19th century, Tahiti was a large exporter of oranges to New Zealand and—believe it or not—to California. ~ PK 14, Punaauia.

One of the obligatory stops on your visit to Tahiti should be at the **Musée de Tahiti et des Iles**. No visitor to Tahiti with an interest in the island's culture should miss the museum. To get there, head to (PK 15) in Punaauia and turn toward the coast at the *Musée* sign posted and from there it's about one kilometer. Coming from Papeete by public transport, a Punaauia *Le Truck* will take you close to the main road junction. The last truck back to Papeete departs at 4:30 p.m.

Opened in 1978, the museum is an excellent introduction to Tahiti. Exhibits cover the gamut, from flora and fauna to Polynesian culture and history. Though damaged in a cyclone in 1983, it was later revamped and remains perhaps the finest and most modern museum of the South Pacific. Judged by international standards, a museum curator would find the displays lacking in sophisticated museum technology but the material is wonderful. It consists of four sections:

Milieu natural—This area covers flora, fauna, geology and Polynesian migration exhibits. Many of the displays include sophisticated, electrically operated diagrams and instructional aides.

Traditional Polynesian culture—These exhibits examine precontact homes, costumes, religion, games, dances, musical instruments and ornaments.

Post-European era—The exploratory and missionary period are extensively covered. The historical displays include figures illustrating captains James Cook, Louis-Antoine de Bougainville and Samuel Wallis, the Pomare dynasty, the missionary era and the history of the Chinese population.

Outdoor exhibits—A living natural-history section includes a botanical garden consisting of plants that Tahitians brought with them (such as taro, *ava*, yams and medicinal herbs). There is also a

Canoe Room where traditional outrigger and dugout canoes are displayed.

In addition to the museum's exhibits of traditional arts and crafts, there is a wonderful collection of paintings and prints. Most of these are available for viewing in the **Exhibition Building**, which has rotating shows ranging from artists like John Webber (Captain James Cook's artist) to modern-day Tahitian painters, sculptors and potters. Exhibitions are not limited to local art, but show works from throughout the Pacific and the rest of the world. The building is the home of special events programming such as demonstrations of tapa-making, mat-weaving, instrument-making, traditional dances and exhibits illustrating the latest archeological excavations. Admission. Closed Monday. ~ PK 15.1, Punaauia; 58-34-76.

Near the mouth of the **Orofero River** is a popular surf break. Surfing is a sport the Tahitians have practiced since time immemorial and they brought it with them to Hawaii. Surfers practiced their sport in the buff to the horror of missionaries and surfing was prohibited during the missionary years. It wasn't until the 1960s, after Tahitians had visited Hawaii by plane, that the sport made a comeback. The same beach was also the site of a *marae* where in 1777 Captain Cook witnessed a human sacrifice.

This area was also the scene of an important battle in 1815 that pitted Pomare II, by then a Christian convert, against the heathen forces of the *Teva I Uta* clan. Pomare's well-armed Christian soldiers, aided by white mercenaries, overran their adversaries, but with true Christian mercy spared the enemy from unbridled revenge. Pomare spared human life but unfortunately all the artistic treasures—the wooden and stone carvings—were either tossed into the

AFTERMATH OF THE RIOTS OF 1995

You will look in vain for the damage sustained during the demonstrations that were ignited by the underground nuclear detonation in Mururoa on September 5, 1995. The facilities destroyed during the riot (including the arrival section, the boutiques, Air Tahiti office and Socredo bank) were quickly repaired. The airport was actually closed from September 5–8. French authorities responded by bringing in 800 *gendarmes* from France to shore up security throughout the island. When I visited in late 1995, the only trace of damage at the airport were some trees blackened by burning cars torched in the parking lot. Needless to say, security measures had been increased dramatically. *All* baggage coming into Papeete was thoroughly searched, which took an extra two hours. Perhaps the zealous incoming baggage searches will have ceased by the time this book is in print. Either that, or the custom's officials will have seen fit to hire more people.

fire or destroyed, leaving future generations with very little in the way of Tahitian art. One of the results of this episode is that modern-day artisans carve tikis that are copies of works from the Marquesas Islands or those of the New Zealand Maoris. ~ PK 20, Paea.

HIDDEN ▶

A visit to the South of Papeete sites ends at **Marae Arahurahu**. Danielsson writes that this particular *marae* (there's a sign on the main road at the turnoff) had no great historical importance, but it so captured the imagination of Dr. Sinoto of the Bishop Museum in Honolulu that he completely reconstructed the shrine. The rectangular pyramid is about the size of a tennis court and has a flat top with a wooden platform where animal and human offerings were left for the gods. The *marae* is used occasionally during the Tiurai festival in July as a stage for re-enactment of ancient rituals such as the "Crowning of a King" ceremony or similar events. The temple is in a lush valley bordered by steep cliffs. ~ PK 22.5, Paea.

LODGING

The **Heitiare Inn** is directly across the street from the RIMAP military base, two minutes from the airport. It is a clean, wooden structure with six rooms, five of which are air-conditioned. Several of the rooms have a private bath and the rest have communal bath facilities. Communal kitchen facilities are available, as is a nearby swimming pool. The outdoor patio/deck is spacious and tiled. Rooms are clean and of adequate size and management is pleasant but the Heitiare is overpriced. ~ PK 4.3, Faa'a; 83-33-52, 82-77-53. BUDGET TO MODERATE.

Chez Sorensen is also quite near the airport—200 yards to be exact. It's a three-bedroom concrete house with private bath and common kitchen. A large open deck serves as a living room. Breakfast is included and is excellent and meals are available. Given the proximity of the airport, the price and the good will of the proprietress, Chez Sorensen is a smart choice, especially as a transit hotel. ~ PK 5.5, Faa'a; 82-63-30. BUDGET TO MODERATE.

The **Tahiti Beachcomber Parkroyal**, two kilometers beyond Faa'a Airport and eight kilometers from Papeete (15 minutes with cooperative traffic conditions), is a compromise between city and town—close enough to enjoy Papeete but far enough away to avoid the hustle. It is considered by many to be the best large resort hotel on Tahiti. The beachfront hotel has 185 standard rooms and 17 air-conditioned over-the-water bungalows. Its management poured US$5 million over several years into refurbishing the rooms, and the bar/restaurant and conference hall have been totally revamped. The Beachcomber also has extensive water sports and an exotic freshwater pool with sandy bottom that overflows into the sea near the lagoon bungalows. There are three restaurants on the premises, all of which are quite good. A nice touch is that you can also wash your clothes for free at washers and dryers in several locations, a welcome surprise in French Polynesia. ~ PK 7.2, Punaauia; 42-51-10, fax 86-51-30, or 800-835-7742 in the U.S. ULTRA-DELUXE.

The **Sofitel Maeva Beach** was one of the first upscale hotels to be constructed in Tahiti after the jet age allowed for mass tourism to the islands. Though a decent hotel, it is approaching middle age and is clearly second to the Beachcomber in luxury status. The 230-room Sofitel Maeva Beach occupies an expansive beachfront location and has numerous yachts moored just offshore in the bay. It has a curious (now dated) terraced six-story stepped architecture and a huge lobby with white marble-like tiles. Rooms, which have tiled white floors and white walls, are of average size and demeanor. The units facing the sea have balconies. Avoid the bottom-floor rooms, as they can be quite damp. There are two restaurants, the *Bougainville*, which offers French–Tahitian cuisine and a smaller Japanese restaurant, the *Sakura*. There is a large outdoor dining area facing the lagoon and the beach, which makes for a pleasant meal in the evening or an after-dinner drink. Perhaps because of the comparatively large size of the hotel it feels more like a property on the Mediterranean rather than a resort in Polynesia. The beach that fronts the property is a good place to swim when the water quality allows for it. (It is best to check with the tourist office on this.) ~ PK 8, Punaauia; 42-80-42, fax 43-84-70, or 800-221-4542 in the U.S. DELUXE TO ULTRA-DELUXE.

> With 230 guest rooms, the Sofitel Maeva Beach is the largest hotel in French Polynesia.

Chez Va'a is on the mountain side in the Nina Peata neighborhood—far from the main road. The property has an elegant relaxed feel about with touches such as rattan furniture and a cool tile floor in the living room. The owner, Liliane Mataiki, is friendly and her place has a pool and one good-sized room with communal bath (hot water). Tariff includes breakfast. Chez Va'a also provides free airport transfer. ~ PK 8, Punaauia; 42-94-32. BUDGET TO MODERATE.

The **Tahiti Country Club** is on Punaauia Hill, two kilometers from the airport and six kilometers from town. Situated on several acres, the property has 40 rooms in long, block-like units. All rooms have a refrigerator and TV—ground-floor units are air-conditioned and the upper floor rooms have ceiling fans. Rooms have white tile and are larger than average in size. Additional amenities include tennis courts and water sports. The property is decent but not as luxurious as the country club moniker suggests. ~ Punaauia; 42-60-40, fax 41-09-28. MODERATE TO DELUXE.

Chez Armelle is an eight-unit complex on one of the best white-sand beaches on the island. The units are clean, basic and modern—all have private bath, overhead fan and double bed. Armelle is cordial, helpful and has a small budget-priced restaurant/snack bar in the back of her pension. A shaded outdoor patio in the back looks over the sea. One of the best things about Chez Armelle is that it's

◄ HIDDEN

on the beach, yet not so distant from town if you don't mind taking *Le Truck*. Snorkeling gear, surfboards and bicycles can be rented. To find it (coming from town), look for the large Mobil Station in Punaauia and take a right shortly after the *Plage de Toaroto* (Toaroto Beach) sign. There is also a *Chez Armelle* sign posted on the highway. Take the small access road (past the first home) heading toward the beach. Chez Armelle looks like a winner. ~ PK 15.5, Punaauia; 58-42-43. BUDGET TO MODERATE.

Le Bellevue is a well-maintained private home located on the mountain side of the road. It has one very clean studio with a kitchenette and private bath. Minimum stay is three nights. ~ PK 16, Punaauia; 58-47-04. BUDGET TO MODERATE.

Just two and a half kilometers east, **Chez Tea** is a house on a white-sand beach, next to the sign that says *tatouage* (tattooist). The owner, Tea Hirshon, sometimes has long-term tenants so it's suggested that you call her or write to BP 13069, Punaauia, Tahiti, to see what's on the agenda. She has three comfortable, very funky bungalows filled with art. The place has a very bohemian feel and there is a nicely landscaped garden with beach access. ~ PK 17.5, Punaauia; 58-29-27. BUDGET TO MODERATE.

Te Miti is marked by a sign that announces "Bed and Breakfast." Located on the mountain side of the road, it consists of two homes on a quarter-acre of land loaded with banana, mango, breadfruit and papaya trees. There is both dorm-style accommodation with several beds to a room and good-sized private bedrooms—unusual for budget lodging in Tahiti. The rooms have fans and plenty of space for storage of clothing and suitcases. The buildings are modern and have tiled floors, clean showers and toilets. There is also a patio with space to lounge or read. The young managers are friendly and provide breakfast as part of the package. (They will also cook guests lunch and dinner, but that is extra.) The only thing missing that backpackers might conceivably want are cooking facilities. There is, however, a refrigerator where guests can store perishables. This is one of the best, if not *the* best budget lodging on the island. It's also ideal for surfers because of the proximity to breaks on the south side of the island. To get there, take the Paea bound *Le Truck* to PK 18.6 and walk several hundred yards inland, up the street that has the *Te Miti* sign. It will be on your left. Management will provide transportation from the airport if you arrive at night and call them. During the day you must take *Le Truck*. ~ PK 18.6, Punaauia; 58-48-61. BUDGET.

DINING   Coming from town about 1.5 kilometers before the airport on the ocean side, you will find **Le Grand Lac**, which offers good, inexpensive, Hong Kong– and Singapore-style Chinese food. Their specialty is seafood dishes and the menu has a litany of items ranging from a whole fish braised in a spicy black bean sauce to locally caught crabs. ~ PK 4.2, Faa'a; 85-05-53. MODERATE.

Though hotel dining is not always recommended in Tahiti, the two restaurants at the **Tahiti Beachcomber Parkroyal** are reasonably priced and quite good. Next to the pool is the **Lotus Restaurant**, an indoor/outdoor eatery on the patio that serves lunch and dinner (a sumptuous salad bar at a reasonable price or à la carte grilled food). The **Hibiscus**, which has uncharacteristically inexpensive prices (for French Polynesia), is also recommended for breakfast. For example, you can get a great omelette at a budget price. In addition to à la carte items, one can also get a full breakfast—but this is quite a bit more expensive. Fish and grilled steak are available for lunch or dinner. ~ PK 7.2, Punaauia. BUDGET TO DELUXE.

Farther down the road in Punaauia at **L'Auberge du Pacifique**, you can get first-class seafood as well as tourist menus. They also serve excellent drinks distilled from tropical fruit. ~ PK 11.2, Punaauia; 43-98-30. ULTRA-DELUXE.

Just minutes down the road you will find **Coco's** which has a lovely view of the sea, good seafood and an American-style bar. ~ PK 13, Punaauia; 58-21-08. ULTRA-DELUXE.

The **Bougainville Restaurant** at the Sofitel Maeva has long had the reputation of being one of the best on the island. Specialties include both French and Tahitian cuisine. Many of the dishes are a French–Tahitian fusion that utilizes fresh seafood combined with classic Polynesian ingredients such as coconut milk and local herbs served with a French flair. The best time to come is Sunday, when they offer a traditional Tahitian feast. ~ PK 8, Punaauia; 42-80-42. DELUXE TO ULTRA-DELUXE.

LIFE IN A LOCAL BAR

Someone will most likely buy you a beer and ask where you're from and whether you're married. Tahitians are extremely curious about one's marital status. If you have no spouse, they will shake their heads and say, "*Aita maitai* (no good). Maybe you find a nice Tahitian to marry." You might also be questioned about a person they have met from the same area. "You know Jimmy from L.A.? He come here two years ago. He nice man." Expect to be chided a little if you go to working-class bars. Tahitians are generally polite, but often the visitor bears the brunt of their jokes. Laugh along. One evening at a local dive, several Americans were entertained by a drunken Tahitian comedian who told outrageous jokes. He was bringing the house down. The routine was entirely in Tahitian, and the Americans were the butt of every joke.

Chez Armelle is a budget accommodation that also has a small restaurant/snack bar with a shaded, outdoor patio that looks over the sea. Dishes range from sandwiches and hamburgers to steak and *frites*, grilled fish and pasta. The food is tasty and reasonably priced. Ambience on the beach is great. ~ PK 15.5, Punaauia; 58-42-43. BUDGET.

GROCERIES Throughout Tahiti there are the ubiquitous grocery stores to buy bread and other everyday items. Volume shoppers or penny pinchers who don't mind trekking an extra kilometer for a bargain should definitely shop at the discount, warehouse-style outlet (called *hypermarche*) known as **Continent**. It's part of a huge shopping center called Moana Nui located just off the freeway. Though prices still pale in comparison to American-style merchandisers such as Costco or Sam's Club, all manner of food and consumer goods are less expensive at these stores than anywhere else in the country. Prices are such comparative bargains that it is actually less expensive for residents of the outer islands to take a ferry (with car) to Tahiti, stock up on groceries and return to their home island, than to buy from a local grocer. Competition in the retail area did not exist in Tahiti until the *hypermarche* was introduced in the early 1990s. (On the outer islands, especially Bora Bora, the gouging continues unabated). ~ PK 8.3, Punaauia; 43-25-32.

Some good local supermarkets include **Supermarche Faa'a** at PK 4.9 in Faa'a ~ 82-77-19, **Supermarche Marina Lotus** at PK 9.2 in Punaauia ~ 42-99-02 and **Supermarche Paea** at PK 19.5 in Paea ~ 53-26-65.

NIGHTLIFE The big hotels put on island-night dance performances, often combined with a buffet dinner of Tahitian food. One of the best of these performances is the show at the **Beachcomber Parkroyal** on Friday and Sunday evenings. Ringside seats come with the purchase of a buffet dinner, although you can watch the show for the price of a drink at the bar. ~ PK 7.2, Punaauia; 86-51-10.

A Polynesian *spectacle* at the **Sofitel Maeva Beach** takes place in the Admiral de Bougainville restaurant on Friday and Saturday nights at 8 p.m. ~ PK 8, Punaauia; 42-80-42.

The **Lagoonarium** dance performances are more than a cut above the ordinary and worth seeing if dance is an important part of your itinerary. Performances are scheduled Friday and Saturday evenings. Admission. ~ PK 11, Punaauia; 43-62-90.

BEACHES & PARKS   **SOFITEL MAEVA BEACH HOTEL** ⚓ 🐟 ⛴ 🚣 🏊 This is the closest beach to town heading south. The sand is brown in color—a sort of hybrid of the black and white sand varieties. It's popular with locals on the weekends and swimming is very good—with one caveat. The tourist board warned me that due to large amounts of effluent, it is sometimes not advisable to swim in this area. According to the Tahiti Tourist Board, some visitors have experienced rashes after swimming here. Best to check with the tourist office regarding the (health) status of the water if you plan to swim. Midway between the beach and the barrier reef, which is about 200 yards offshore, is a pontoon anchored in nine feet of water. It makes for great sunbathing and a 360° panorama, but keep in mind there's no shade on the pontoon.

> Tahiti Aqua Maeva is the only place on Tahiti that rents kayaks and offers waterskiing.

The beach here is public, but the restrooms and restaurant facilities belong to the hotel. There are a few canopies (no trees) to shade you on the beach and a multitude of beach chairs courtesy of the hotel. On the beach is **Tahiti Aqua Maeva**, an aquatic sports center that caters to divers, kayakers, jet ski enthusiasts and the like. Kayaks are available but the sport is new in Tahiti. Possibly because the traditional *pirogue* is so popular, locals don't seem to be terribly interested in the kayak. Restrooms, restaurants. ~ Take the "freeway" south to the Mavea Beach Hotel and park in the hotel lot. PK 8, Punaauia; 86-51-10, fax 86-51-30.

PLAGE DE TOAROTO (TOAROTO BEACH) Plage de Toaroto is but one entry point to a long, fine-white sand beach in the Punaauia district that runs approximately from PK 15.5 down to PK 19. Even though this is a long stretch of beach front, it lies opposite a residential area and is accessible only at a few points. Usually not more than 50 feet wide, it is generally clean and uncrowded. The water is deep enough in most areas to make it fine for swimming. The snorkeling is also good. There are toilet facilities near the main road and Chez Armelle, a local pension, also has a snack bar open to the public. ~ Take the main highway south to Punaauia. Keep an eye open for the Mobil Station (on the inland side of the road) and perhaps 50 yards after the station note the green *Plage de Toaroto* sign. Take a right and pull into the parking lot. From there, walk down to the easement to the beach.

◄ HIDDEN

HOTEL TAHITI VILLAGE BEACH This is the opposite end of the same long stretch of white-sand beach as Plage de Toaroto. The public access is actually on the former grounds of Hotel Tahiti Village (which has since been torn down). The beach is narrow, clean and generally not too crowded. Swimming is good, particularly if the tide is high. Snorkeling can also be done. There is a large pavilion with toilet and shower facilities (they were under construction when I last visited). ~ To find it, look for the large wooden sign on the ocean side of the road at PK 20 that announces you have just entered the district of Paea. Go through the large green wooden gate, which opens up to a huge parking lot.

▼▼▼▼▼▼▼▼▼▼▼▼▼▼▼▼▼▼▼▼
Outer Districts of Tahiti

Just 12.5 miles (20 kilometers) either side of Papeete takes you far from the center of commerce, beyond the suburbs into what locals call le district—the outer reaches of the island. Here life is generally slower, the population density is lower, and the culture is more traditional. Though the Tahiti of Gauguin and Stevenson are long gone, a visitor may still glimpse something of the way things were. You may pass an old man peddling a bicycle with a fresh baguette tucked under his arm or see the family of a fisherman peddling the day's catch dangling from twine on the shoulder of road. Whatever you do, don't confine yourself to Papeete, thinking that you've seen it all.

Since we have already covered the attractions from Papeete to PK 22.1, in the North of Papeete section, let's begin the round-the-island tour in Tiarei at the next landmark, which is at PK 25, the Gardens and Copra Plantation. Likewise, since we have covered the area from Papeete southward to the Marae Arahurahu, PK 22.5, that is where the tour will end.

SIGHTS

Gardens and Copra Plantation is a private reserve, but you can park and view the lily ponds and accompanying flora that thrive in the area from the main road. The coconut plantation here, one of many on Tahiti and its neighboring islands, was once an important source of cash for the average Tahitian. Although harvesting copra (dried coconut meat) continues to be a vital occupation for islanders outside Tahiti, it is of secondary importance in a Tahitian economy that now relies on tourism, black pearl cultivation and the governmental bureaucracy as sources of jobs. ~ PK 25, Tiarei.

Though nothing more violent than a cockfight occurs here today, in another era this area was a **Battlefield**. The annexation of Tahiti by France in 1843 sparked armed resistance among Tahitians, and guerrilla warfare continued until the rebellion was crushed in 1846. The most important battle of this war was fought at Mahaena on April 17, 1844. The battlefield stretched from the beach southward to the present-day church and city hall. Heeding the advice of British sailors and French army deserters, Tahitians dug three parallel trenches and awaited their French adversaries. Two French warships appeared and a force of 441 men stormed the Tahitian position, which had approximately twice the defenders but lacked modern weapons. When the dust cleared, 102 Tahitians were dead and the French had lost only 15 men. After this blow the natives realized that guerrilla warfare was the only alternative and they continued to operate from bases in the bush until their main stronghold was captured in 1846. ~ PK 32.5, Mahaena.

In April 1768, less than 100 years before the battle, Captain Louis-Antoine de Bougainville anchored here. To find **Bougainville's Anchorage** look out to sea and note the two offshore islets, Variararu and Oputotara. The former has a few trees and the latter just brush. Just off Oputotara is where Bougainville anchored. Although cultured to the bone, Bougainville was not much of a sailor. His choice of this particular anchorage, which lacked the proper shelter and wind conditions, was not the best. He managed to lose six anchors in ten days and nearly lost the ships as well. Soon after this debacle some Tahitians actually salvaged one of the anchors and gave it to the King of Bora Bora as a gift. Captain Cook later took possession of it in 1777. ~ PK 37.6, Hitiaa.

To get a terrific **vista** of the Peninsula, stop here. At this point you have a splendid view of Tahiti Iti, Tahiti's panhandle and the high, verdant peaks that tower over it. From here it's easy to see how Tahiti Iti (little Tahiti) is the smaller loop of this figure eight of an island. ~ PK 39, Hitiaa.

The **Fa'atautia River Bridge** is a good place to stop and view the Vaiharuru Falls in the distance. This site was chosen by U.S. filmmaker John Huston to make a cinematographic version of Herman Melville's *Typee*. Unfortunately, because his first attempt at a Melville movie, *Moby Dick*, was commercially unsuccessful, the scheme was abandoned. ~ PK 41.8, Hitiaa.

The Isthmus of Taravao marks the halfway point of your round-the-island tour. On the outskirts of the community of Taravao note the sentry at the gate marking the entrance to the **Military Base** on your right. Military and police installations have existed here since 1844 when the French guarded the isthmus to prevent marauding guerrillas from filtering down from the peninsula to the main part of the island. The old fort (within the army camp) still stands. Since then, the site has served as a gendarmerie, an internment camp for Germans unfortunate enough to be on the island during WWII and, most recently, a military base. ~ PK 60.5, Taravao.

Past the fort, on your left, is the junction to Tautira, which will take to the north coast of Tahiti Iti. A kilometer down the north coast road is the junction to the inland road that straddles the Taravao Plateau.

Shortly after passing the junction you will see a few buildings and shops scattered alongside the road with little thought to aesthetics or planning. You are now in downtown **Taravao**. Though the backdrop of the community has drop-dead vistas of lush mountains and shoreline (which makes the drive to the island's end worthwhile), the town is not particularly attractive. Other than the military base and a few very good restaurants (worth checking out), there is not much to this community. Recently a massive new dock was built near Taravao with the idea of bringing jobs and commerce to the area, but it has yet to be determined what will be shipped in and who will actually use the facility. At the south end of town on your left is the junction to the southern coast, which will take you to Teahupoo, the village at the end of the line. Note that the coastal roads on the periphery of the peninsula do not meet—rather they terminate before reaching the far end of Tahiti Iti. To circumnavigate the island you must hike.

Continuing on the loop around Tahiti Nui, look carefully among the mango trees on the hill and you will see the former home of English writer **Robert Keable**. Although not a household name today, Keable produced two religious novels, *Simon Called Peter* and *Recompense*, which sold a combined total of 600,000 copies in the 1920s. Obsessed with the question of why Tahiti and Tahitian women held so much attraction for white men, he provided his own answers in two more books: *Tahiti, Isle of Dreams* and *Numerous Treasure*. Keable's well-maintained home is in its original 1920s condition, but it is not open to the public. ~ PK 55.5, Papeari.

The **Debarkation Point of Ancient Tahitians**, according to traditional accounts, was the first place where the ancient Polynesians settled over 1000 years ago. Because of this, families chiefly from this district have always been held in the highest prestige among their counterparts in the other districts of Tahiti. The present-day village is known for its beautiful gardens and roadside produce stands. The Papeari inlet has a number of oyster beds and fish traps. Around this area, and throughout the rural side of the island, you often see fishermen on the side of the road selling their fresh catch dangling from nylon cord strings. ~ PK 52, Papeari.

The **Botanical Gardens of Papeari** were established in 1919 by Harrison Smith, a physics professor who left the Massachusetts Institute of Technology at age 37 to dedicate the rest of his life to botany in Tahiti. He introduced a range of tropical shrubs, trees and flowers to the islands from throughout the world, and some became important local products. My favorite among these is the huge, delectable grapefruit known as the *pamplemousse*, which originated in Borneo. Smith did not merely putter around in his own garden but generously gave seeds and cuttings to Tahitian farmers to help them improve their own crops. After his death in 1947 the garden was willed to another botanist and, through the help of U.S. philanthropist Cornelius Crane, was given to the public.

The massive gardens are laced with footpaths that wend their way through acres of well-tended palms, hibiscus, elephant ears, bamboo, bananas and many other species. There were also several Galapagos tortoises brought to Tahiti in the 1930s, which were given to author Charles Nordhoff's children. At the time of writing, one of the tortoises is still living.

The gardens, which you may find more interesting than the Gauguin Museum, were spruced up in 1990 for the visit of the late French President Francois Mitterand. Admission. ~ PK 51.2, Papeari.

Opposite the garden grounds is a modern, Japanese-style structure—the **Gauguin Museum**, with exhibits chronicling the life of

Tahiti's most famous former resident. The walls are covered with documents and photographs from the Gauguin era, along with reproductions and—for the first time in years—some original Gauguin works, among them sketches, block prints and the original blocks. Though a century has passed since Gauguin put his brush to canvas, the joyous and perplexing moods of Tahitians that he captured are still displayed today on every street corner in Papeete.

Those taking *Le Truck* from Papeete to the Gauguin Museum should start early in the morning. The last *Le Truck* heading to town is at 1 p.m., and it's a long walk back to town.

There are also some original paintings by artist Constance Gibbon Cummings, an Englishwoman who stayed in French Polynesia for six months in 1877. She has left me with some exquisite landscapes of Tahiti and Moorea. For sale at the gift shop are post cards, T-shirts, stationery and excellent reproductions of Gauguin's works, Cummings' paintings and the works of other artists who lived on the island. Bring along some insect repellent when you visit—the mosquitoes can sometimes be a nuisance. Note that there are separate entrances for the museum and the nearby beach park, both of which are open seven days a week. The Botanical Garden has a small and reasonably priced café. Admission. ~ PK 51.2, Papeari; 57-10-58.

The **Vaihiria River** originates from the lake of the same name —Tahiti's only lake. At 1500 feet (450 meters) above sea level, it is bounded on the north by 3000-foot (900-meter) cliffs, which make up the southern wall of the Papenoo crater. The lake is known among locals for its large eels and nearby plantations of *fe'i* (mountain bananas). It is accessible with the aid of a guide (see Four-Wheel-Drive Tours at the end of this chapter), but there are waterfalls visible from the road. ~ PK 48, Mataiea.

After living briefly in Papeete, Paul Gauguin moved to **Mataiea Village** in October 1891, where he lived until May 1893. He rented a bamboo hut, found a *vahine* and painted such masterpieces as *Hina Tefatou* (the Museum of Modern Art, New York), *Ia Orana Maria* (the Metropolitan Museum of Art, New York), *Fatata te Miti* (the National Gallery of Art, Washington, DC), *Manao Tupapau* (Albright-Knox Art Gallery, Buffalo), *Reverie* (the William Rockhill Nelson Gallery of Art, Kansas City) and *Under the Pandanus* (the Minneapolis Institute of Art).

Twenty-three years later, when Somerset Maugham came to the village culling information about Gauguin's life for his novel *The Moon and Sixpence*, he discovered three painted glass doors in the wooden bungalow belonging to Gauguin's landlord. These paintings by the great artist had never been discovered. Most of the paintings had been mutilated by children's play but Maugham picked the best one up for 200 francs and painstakingly shipped it back to Europe. Near the end of his life he sold the forgotten door at Sotheby's for a princely sum. ~ PK 46.5, Mataiea.

Shortly before World War I, poet Rupert Brooke jumped on a boat in San Francisco and headed for Tahiti "to hunt for lost Gauguins." He ended up in Mataiea, where he rented a bungalow, which became **Rupert Brooke's Love Nest**. Instead of discovering lost masterpieces, Brooke found his first and only true love. Mamua inspired one of his best poems, *Tiare Tahiti*. Brooke eventually left Tahiti with a heavy heart and several years later died on a hospital ship off Gallipoli, a casualty of the war. His beloved Mamua fell three years after that, a victim of Spanish influenza. ~ PK 44, Mataiea.

Although the fairways of the **Olivier Breaud International Golf Course** are trim and green now, in former times this area was white with cotton. The plantation that flourished here for a short time had a tremendous impact on Tahiti's population and history. The story begins not in Tahiti but in the United States, during the midst of the Civil War. The war made it impossible for Europeans to import cotton and created a tremendous demand for this commodity. Scottish wine merchant William Stewart, who made a living importing liquor to the South Pacific, responded by setting up a cotton plantation in Tahiti. He acquired land in Atimaono, the only area in Tahiti capable of large-scale agricultural development and, with the help of blackbirders (slave traders), he recruited labor. This did not work too well, so coolie labor from China was used and thus the seeds of the powerful Chinese community in Tahiti were planted. Working conditions were atrocious and violence tempered by the guillotine was the rule of the day. ~ PK 41, Atimaono.

Despite the awful circumstances, by 1867, 2470 acres of high-grade cotton were planted and the harvest lived up to Stewart's dreams. In the meantime, he had built a huge villa and spent his evenings as the king of the roost, entertaining Tahitian high society. However, there was a catch. The Civil War had ended and with it the shortage of cotton from the South. There were also problems with the weather, which was not ideal for cultivation of cotton. Stewart could not compete with his American counterparts, who were geographically much closer to Europe, and he fell into bankruptcy. He died at the young age of 48. A number of the Chinese coolies elected to stay and intermarried with the local population.

The access road to the ruins of **Marae Mahaiatea**, once a great temple, is posted on the highway. Today the *marae* is only a huge pile of boulders but early European visitors like Cook were astounded by its dimensions— 270 feet (81 meters) long, 90 feet (27 meters) wide and 550 feet (165 meters) high—and its architecture. Not only did the builders need a considerable amount of skill to construct the temple, they had to build it without the benefit of iron tools. Danielsson claims it was once the most spectacular monument in Tahiti. The temple's fall into decay is not only the fault of nature—apparently the old temple was used by William Stewart as a source of stones for his building projects at the cotton plantation a few kilometers away. In the words of J.C. Beaglehole, the great biographer of Cook, "Nature and human stupidity combine as usual to wipe out the diverse signs of human glory." ~ PK 39.2, Papara.

In Papara, you will find a beige-colored Protestant church and a seashell museum. In the graveyard of this **Tahitian church** lie the remains of a former United States Consul and Yankee hero of the Civil War, Dorence Atwater. At age 16, Atwater joined the Union Army, was captured by rebel scouts and served time in three Confederate prisons until he was sent to a hospital where he ended up as a clerk recording the deaths of Federal prisoners. Fearing that the Confederates were not keeping accurate records, he copied the lists and escaped, bringing them to the attention of the federal government. In 1875, Atwater wed the beautiful Princess Moetia of the local chief's family, which had ruled the district for generations. (At one point his grave was marked, but it no longer can be identified). ~ PK 36, Papara.

Across the street from the church is the **Musée des Coquillages** (Seashell Museum), housed in a white colonial-style building. The museum has a very extensive shell collection as well some aquarium exhibits. It's also a good place to pick up quality souvenirs such as woven pandanus hats, baskets, and purses, which are sold in the gift shop. Admission. ~ PK 36, Papara; 57-45-22.

The border between the districts of **Papara** and **Paea** have the least amount of rainfall and are among the most desirable areas in Tahiti to live in. Note the fine homes on the coast (owned mostly by Europeans) and the quiet lagoon and beaches, sheltered by a barrier reef. ~ PK 29.

Just before Paea is the **Maraa Fern Grotto**, which always seems to be an obligatory stop on the visitor's itinerary. Actually there are three grottos, which are accessible from a trail that skirts the base of the rock face. The grottos are gaping holes in the cliff with shallow pools of water filled from water constantly seeping from the ceiling. Ferns dangle like stalactites and the vegetation around the grottos is lush. Its main significance is that it is an optical illusion—it seems to be smaller than it is. The area is, however, popular as a stop and has been improved to accommodate more cars and picnickers. It is a cool place to visit on a hot day. ~ PK 28.5, Paea.

LODGING

Almost all of the Tahiti accommodation possibilities are located either in downtown Papeete or close to town along the coast on either side of the city limits. There are a handful of possibilities elsewhere on the island, for those who really want to get away from it all or who want to spend more than one day on an island circuit. They're found farther out around Tahiti Nui (the main part of the island), on Tahiti Iti (the smaller appendage) or up in the central mountains. See the Tahiti Iti section for accommodations on that peninsula.

HIDDEN ▶   **Fare Nana'o** came on the scene several years ago and remains one of the most popular, offbeat pensions in Tahiti. If you are going to stay on the far side of the island, this is *the* place to consider. Located on the water, it has seven very original bungalows constructed from natural materials, mostly wood, stone and pandanus thatch. Rooms are large, airy and, invariably, unconventional. The owners, Monique and Jean-Claude Michel, emphasize that the shape of the walls, the support beams, the doors and windows are determined by the natural shape and contours of the trees and stones. Even the outhouse is unusual—a fine ceramic toilet, complete with houseplant and floor lined with white coral belie the rustic exterior. You pay extra for food and activities such as sightseeing, sea tours, sailing and the like. Transport to and from the airport is extra. Those with a taste for the unusual or the bohemian may find Fare Nana'o to their liking. It seems to be popular with Japanese visitors and comes highly recommended. ~ PK 52, Faaone; 57-18-14, fax 57-76-10. MODERATE TO DELUXE.

Chez Denise Thouvenin is on the east coast of Tahiti Iti. It's on the mountain side of the road, nestled in the shadow of coconut palms near the lagoon and far from the tourist track. The property consists of one very comfortable, well-appointed home, with two bedrooms, common bathroom with hot water and fully equipped kitchen. Price includes airport transfer and meals. Credit cards are not accepted but the hospitality and swimming are terrific and the food is reportedly very good. This is a good deal if you don't mind being in a fairly remote area. If you are planning to stay here, it's best to consider renting a car. ~ PK 15, Tautira; 57-77-60. BUDGET TO MODERATE.

One of the unconventional bungalows featured at Fare Nana'o is actually in a tree!

One would think that the cool highlands of Tahiti would be a perfect place for a hotel and indeed in the pre-airplane era of tourism the mountains and Vaihiria Lake were an obligatory stop. Nowadays **Fare Maroto Relais** is the only mountain lodging in Tahiti. Located in the center of the island, high in the Papenoo Valley where the Vaituoru and Vainavenave rivers converge, it affords a splendid view of the valley and adjacent mountains. Relais, however, was never meant to be an alpine resort, as it was erected as housing for construction workers for a nearby hydroelectric dam. It's fairly basic, as you might expect for construction crews. The sturdy concrete structure has ten rooms with four bunks, a terrace and bathroom with hot water. There are also three concrete bungalows, each with two bedrooms, terrace and private bath. A deposit is required for reservations. One more thing: you need to ride in a helicopter or rent a four-wheel-drive vehicle to get there, unless you wish to hike in. The best thing about the resort is that it makes a great base camp from which to explore the interior of the island. A number of hikes and excursions are available to archeo-logical sites and nature preserves. Call Rosa Lacour (42-94-16) for more information about hikes or using the setting as a venue for groups or seminars. ~ Papenoo Valley; 41-48-60, fax 43-28-78. MODERATE TO DELUXE.

Hiti Moana Villa should not be confused with the budget ac-commodation in Mahina with a similar name—Hiti Mahana. Run by Auguste and Henriette Brotherson, the three well-appointed bungalows might be suitable for surfers or golf fanatics given its close proximity (about a ten-minute drive) from the Papara surf break or the Atimaono Golf course. Minimum stay is three nights. ~ PK 36, Papara; 57-93-93, fax 57-94-44. MODERATE TO DELUXE.

Fare Ratere south from Papeete near Mahaiatea beach is on the sea side in a peaceful locale with two local-style bungalows set in spacious, well-tended grounds. Each bungalow has two rooms, a mezzanine, living room with TV, kitchen and private bath. The maximum capacity of this excellent, classy property is six guests. ~ PK 39.5, Papara; 57-48-29. DELUXE TO ULTRA-DELUXE.

Although most of Tahiti's restaurants are concentrated in Papeete, there are enough places scattered around the island to provide a se-lection of lunch stops for visitors making an island tour. The fol-lowing places are listed district by district in the same sequence as the round-the-island circuit.

DINING

The **Restaurant-Bar Gauguin** is located on the water approxi-mately one kilometer before the Gauguin Museum. There is a wide selection of seafood and the restaurant has a solid reputation. It is a large structure, shaded by a huge tree, and has both indoor and outdoor dining. Next to the restaurant is a pier with several at-tached fish pens where you can gaze at what may be your dinner. Our recommendation is the stuffed mahimahi or the shrimp curry with coconut cream. ~ PK 49.5, Papeari; 57-13-80. MODERATE TO DELUXE.

Snack Musée Gauguin is located at the entrance of the botani-cal gardens. It's an unpretentious outdoor café where you can choose to sit under a pavilion or outside, shaded by trees, only several feet from the lagoon. The rustic surroundings give one the feeling of being on a picnic. What's more, the food is quite good and the ser-vice very cordial. There is a nice selection on the menu including *poisson cru*, sashimi and stuffed mahimahi. ~ PK 50.5, Papeari. BUDGET TO MODERATE.

Snack restaurant **Chez Myriam**, located on the main drag in Taravao, resembles an American fast-food restaurant from the 1950s. It is easily recognizable with a faded red awning. Myriam will take your orders from a counter behind a window. The eatery has outdoor and indoor seating and a fairly extensive menu posted on a chalkboard. Myriam serves basic Tahitian fare such as steak and fries, *poisson cru*, sandwiches and mahimahi. It's also a good place to go for ice cream. If you are there on a Saturday try her couscous, which is reportedly very good. ~ PK 60, Taravao; 57-71-01. BUDGET TO MODERATE.

HIDDEN ▶   L'Escale is also on Taravao's main street. From all accounts, it is the hands-down favorite for French cuisine. Run by an amiable Frenchman by the name of Claude, L'Escale is a fairly large restaurant by Taravao standards, with a total of about a dozen tables on two levels and a bar that seats several patrons. It has a comprehensive Continental menu including many salads (*salade nicoise* and hearts of palm to name a couple) but the real specialty of the house is fish and there is nearly always a reasonably priced seafood *plat du jour*. Claude's recommendation is the mahimahi in coconut cream and marinated tuna. Ice cream is the item to choose for dessert, including a great coconut, Kahlua and vanilla. ~ PK 60, Taravao; 57-07-16. MODERATE TO DELUXE.

HIDDEN ▶   Chez Jeannine in downtown Taravao is a small white storefront that looks like a takeout counter until you walk through the building and see half a dozen tables in a small courtyard in the back. The owner is a petite woman of French and Vietnamese origin and her speciality is Vietnamese cuisine. Chez Jeannine looks deceptively ordinary until you sample the culinary wizardry. The menu features over six different varieties of shrimp dishes alone but Jeannine says her specialty is *fruit de mer* (seafood). Nice, if simple, ambience and, judging by the number of local customers packed into her restaurant on a weekday afternoon, her food is well liked. ~ PK 59.5, Taravao; 57-29-82. MODERATE.

Ah Ky Vairua is a large outdoor pavilion on the main drag in Taravao. It's the kind of extremely rustic establishment you would expect to find in a developing country— simple, no frills and no thought of pretension. It has about half a dozen tables on a bare slab of concrete that screams "budget Chinese food." It is your basic greasy-spoon restaurant featuring chow mein, chop suey and a few mixed vegetable dishes. Strictly for those interested in spending as little money as possible. ~ PK 60, Taravao; 57-20-38. BUDGET.

At the halfway point on the island circuit, the community of Taravao has a number of small snack bars and restaurants. If you're looking for respite and a meal on your way around the island, then you've come to the right place.

Baie Phaeton is an attractive white structure with a red-tile roof. With a balcony overlooking Phaeton Bay, it has a splendid view of the yachts moored just offshore and the rugged heights of Tahiti Iti in the distance. Primarily a Chinese restaurant, it has a rather large selection of seafood but poultry is also available. There are also a number of salads, as well as sashimi and tuna. Specialty is *fruit de mer* and curry shrimp. You can also get the standard Chinese mainstays of chop suey and chow mein, along with friendly service and nice surroundings. ~ PK 58.9, Taravao; 57-08-96. BUDGET TO MODERATE.

Chez Bob Tardieu is a local favorite for French cuisine, specializing in seafood dishes. The small restaurant, run by the owner and his wife, has excellent home-style French cuisine—when you can find the chef in. He is open intermittently, so it's best to call first before you drive all the way to Faaone. ~ PK 51.8, Faaone; 57-14-14. DELUXE TO ULTRA-DELUXE.

The **Nuutere** combines French cuisine with what is available locally. Housed in an attractive white colonial-style building with blue awnings, it has an extensive seafood menu and serves meat dishes as well. Open daily for lunch and dinner. ~ PK 32.5, Papara; 57-14-15. DELUXE TO ULTRA-DELUXE.

GROCERIES

There are markets along the coastal road in every district. Some of the better stores include **Chez Steevie** at PK 42 in Mataiea ~ 57-90-43; **Magasin Alice** at PK 37.5 in Papara ~ 57-42-80; and **Magasin Jissang**, at PK 17.5 in Papenoo ~ 48-16-69.

BEACHES & PARKS

MARAA FERN GROTTO The grotto is a minor roadside attraction that ends up being an obligatory stop for the tour buses. There are actually three grottos, gaping holes in the cliff filled with shallow pools of water that seeps from the top of the caverns. The grottos are accessible from a trail that skirts the base of the rock cliff face. The grottos are a cool respite on a hot day and are a favorite of children who half expect a dinosaur to leap out of the shadows. Picnic tables and fresh water. ~ At PK 28.5, Paea, look for the turnoff on the mountain side of the road that resembles a freeway rest stop. Pull in and park.

PLAGE TAHARUU 🏄 🏃 One of the best surf spots on the south side of the island is the expansive beach break at Papara. The beach in question is of fine black sand and covers a swath of about half a mile. This is a beach break with lefts and rights that surfers and boogie boarders will enjoy. One can swim, but it's definitely a secondary activity on this beach. Some shade is available and there is plenty of parking space. There are a few makeshift shacks on the beach—perhaps club houses of sorts for the surfers. A wave-riding entrepreneur has a small concession (a few surf boats leaning against a tree) that he will rent by the hour or the day. ~ To get there, drive two miles out of Papara to PK 38. Cross the white bridge over the creek and note the sign designating the beach. Pull into the parking lot. Note that the creek bisects the beach and there is another parking lot (with more shade trees) on the opposite side.

MOTU OVINI BEACH PARK This is part of the Botanical Gardens and Gauguin Museum complex and is open seven days a week. The good news is that this is a particularly nice botanical garden—so nice that it has become another obligatory stop for the tour buses. The rocky, black-sand beach that fringes the park is thin and the water seemed murky. The bad news is that you must pay a fairly stiff entrance fee to get into the nearby museum and a separate one to enter the beach park cum botanical garden. It's an expensive proposition to do both, especially with a family in tow. Drinking water, toilets. ~ Simply take the coastal road south to PK 51 in Papeara. The signs for the museum/park complex are on the sea side of the road and are quite prominent.

▼▼▼▼▼▼▼▼▼
Tahiti Iti

Tahiti is like a figure eight on its side with the smaller loop, Tahiti Iti, joined by the narrow isthmus at Taravao to the larger loop, Tahiti Nui. At the isthmus is a junction where two roads branch off and follow the contours down either side of the Tahiti Iti Peninsula. The road, however, does not completely circle Tahiti Iti. The easterly road runs 18 kilometers round the coast from Taravao to Tautira, while the southerly road also runs 18 kilometers along the south coast from Taravao to just beyond Teahupoo. The two roads do not meet. Walking trails continue some distance beyond the end of both roads but even to walk the complete coastline would be difficult. A third road straddles the middle of the Tahiti Iti peninsula to a viewpoint where it dead-ends. Along the two coast roads, the red-and-white kilometrage (PK) markers start at "0" from Taravao.

Tahiti Iti is verdant, wet and rugged. Thick rainforests blanket the mountains, which tower over the coastal roads. The Taravao plateau, which straddles both coasts, is carpeted with grassy meadows akin to an alpine setting sans the pine trees.

The largest community on Tahiti Iti is Tautira, a fishing village on the north coast. It was here in 1773 that Captain Cook's second expedition almost met its doom. One morning, the esteemed navigator awoke to find his two ships drifting perilously close to the reef. (Apparently the crew had been too busy entertaining Tahitian visitors the evening before to notice.) The ships eventually did run aground, but were saved by smaller boats that kedged the larger vessels off the reef. Cook lost several anchors in the confusion. In 1978, by sheer luck, one of the anchors was located and brought to the surface. The event was properly celebrated by locals and the crew of movie producer David Lean, who was on location to promote a new version of the *Bounty* incident. Although the film was never made, the anchor can be seen at the Musée de Tahiti et des Iles.

This serene setting was also the scene of a confrontation between the British and the Spanish over 200 years ago. Angered by the English presence in the Pacific (which the Spanish felt was theirs to plunder), the Viceroy of Peru was ordered by his king to send a

country lane lined with coconut palms—a scene that is repeated throughout French Polynesia.

Top left: Portrait of a Pamotu woman wearing a flower tucked behind her ear in true Polynesian fashion.

Middle right: A mosquito coil that is burned to keep the pesky critters away.

Bottom: Colorful Tahitian fabric decorated with a tapa-style motif.

ship to Tahiti. He promptly sent the *Aguila*, commanded by Boene-cha, which after having the misfortune of striking a reef, anchored in a lagoon about three kilometers from Tautira Village and formally took possession of Tahiti for the King of Spain.

Less than a year later, on his second voyage of discovery, Cook wound up in the same vicinity and soon heard about the landing of the dastardly Spanish. In 1774, Boenecha returned to the area with two Franciscan priests in an effort to give the locals a little religion. The mission failed miserably. Captain Boenecha soon died and the priests, scared witless by the Tahitians, erected a veritable fortress to keep the curious natives away. The *Aguila* returned at the end of 1775 with provisions, but the priests would have none of the missionary life and gladly sailed back to Peru.

Cook came back to Tautira in 1777 on his third voyage and found the padre's quarters still in good condition. The house was fitted with a crucifix, which bore the inscription *Christus vincit Carolus III imperat 1774*. On the reverse side of the cross, Cook ordered his carpenter to carve *Tertius Rex Annis 1767, 69, 73, 74, & 77*. By this time, historian Bengt Danielsson writes, "both England and Spain had realized that Tahiti was an economically as well as strategically worthless island and gave up their costly shows of force."

One hundred years later, Tautira was the temporary abode of Robert Louis Stevenson, who anchored the *Casco* here in 1888. He was taken in by local royalty and stayed for about two months, calling Tahiti a "Garden of Eden." Although on assignment for the *New York Sun* to write about the cruise, he spent his time in Tautira working on *The Master of Ballantrae*, a Scottish horror story. Upon Stevenson's return to England, his mother sent a silver communion service to the local Protestant church, where it is still being used.

TARAVAO TO TAUTIRA   The road winding from Taravao to Tautira often follows the base of steep verdant cliffs. This is, as the locals call it, *le district*—the countryside. About half a kilometer from the junction is a sign that marks the road to the Taravao Plateau, which meanders nine kilometers and dead-ends smack in the interior of Tahiti Iti. Several hundred yards from the road's end will take you to tiny Lake Vaiufaufa.

The coastal road continues to wind eastward, past homes with well-tended gardens. It's not unusual to pass a young man strumming a ukulele as he walks on the shoulder of the road. Near the end of the line, the Vaitepiha River, PK 16.5, empties into Vaitepiha Bay just on the outskirts of **Tautira**.

Tautira really does feel like it's sitting on the edge of the island. Wedged between the towering green mountains of Tahiti Iti and the

SIGHTS

◄ *HIDDEN*

sea, this is as close as you'll get to a traditional village setting in 20th-century Tahiti. Romantics might be disappointed that it is not a fishing village out of *Mutiny on the Bounty* but it is nonetheless a bucolic backwater that merits a visit. There are no thatched-roof bungalows (which is what you will find at the resorts). Rather, Tautira has cars, four-wheel-drive trucks and boat trailers parked in the front yards of comfortable modern homes divided by hedges of hibiscus. Built on a point of land, the village is bisected by a number of lanes that are shaded by breadfruit and mango trees. The paved streets are filled with teenagers on bicycles, children walking hand in hand with adults, and vehicles dodging potholes.

A beachfront road skirts a fringe of grass separating it from the rocky, black-sand beach. Planted firmly on the grassy strip are trees or rough-hewn racks from which blue nylon fishing nets hang limply. On the sandy shore, *pirogues* (outrigger canoes) sit beached. The locals, nearly all Polynesian, are friendly and smile at the occasional visitor as they go about their chores, raking leaves or mending fishing nets. ~ PK 18.

TARAVAO TO TEAHUPOO   About half a kilometer past the junction, there's an atmospheric **research station**, which was constructed during International Geophysical Year (1957–58) to study the ionosphere. ~ PK 0.5, Afaahiti.

Heading east down the coastal road you'll come to the former site of **Zane Grey's Fishing Camp**. Although the author of *Riders of the Purple Sage* and 60 other pulp westerns spent his life cranking out stories about the old American West, his real passion in life was deep-sea fishing. From 1928 to 1930, he spent many months in Tahiti with his cronies catching marlin, mahimahi, sailfish and other sport fish. Like Melville's protagonist in *Moby Dick*, Grey dreamed of landing his own version of the white whale and on May 16, 1930, he finally did—a 12-foot, 1000-pound silver marlin that probably would have weighed 200 pounds more had not the sharks ripped off so much flesh. ~ PK 7.3, Vairao.

Describing this episode in *Tales of Tahitian Waters*, Grey gives one an insight into French colonial mentality. He relates that French officials had the local chief spy on the Americans because they thought the fishermen might actually be surveying the area for the U.S. government, which perhaps had designs on taking over Tahiti as a naval base. Said Grey, "The idea of white men visiting Tahiti for something besides French liquors, the native women, or to paint the tropical scenery had been exceedingly hard to assimilate."

Almost three kilometers farther, you will see several ponds at the CNEXO **Oceanographic Research Station**. They are for breeding shrimp—one of the many ambitious projects of the Centre National pour l'Exploitation des Océans, a French government agency. ~ PK 10.4, Vairao.

The last **Refuge of the Nature Men** was well hidden at the end of the island. Years ago, the "nature men," as Danielsson called them, lived off the land, often as ascetics or beach-combers, and were a common fixture through-out Tahiti. As civilization marched on, this re-mote area became their last refuge. The best-known of these rugged individuals, who bore a strong resemblance to the underground comic-strip character "Mr. Natural," was Ernest Darling. Anticipating an entire generation perhaps half a cen-tury too early, Darling lived stark naked, slept on the ground with his head pointing north, and produced an endless stream of pamphlets extolling the virtues of nudism, vegetarianism, abstinence, pacifism, Christian Socialism and phonetic spelling. ~ PK 18, Teahupoo.

Interested in hiking the coast of Tahiti Iti with a group? Contact any number of pro-fessional guides or ecologi-cal organizations that reg-ularly lead groups into the area (see "Hiking" at the end of the chapter).

VISTA POINT   At **Afaahiti**, PK 0.6, just out of Taravao on the east-coast road, the Taravao Plateau is signposted on your right, just be-fore the school. You will pass pastures with grazing cattle before you reach the dead end seven kilometers later. A short walk takes you a gorgeous panorama of the narrow Isthmus of Taravao with the mountains of Tahiti rising in the distance. The junction for a second, rather rougher and more potholed, road is just before the viewpoint car park, and ends up on the coast road to Tautira at PK 2.5. The two approaches can be combined to make a circuit route. Take care on the less-traveled, second road. During especially rainy weather it may not be passable.

There is simply not much out here in the wilds of eastern Tahiti. If you decide to visit, you will be treated to a great deal of tranquility.

LODGING

In the Tahiti Iti area, the **Te Anuanua Hotel** just off the road is highly recommended, especially for its excellent food, and is con-sidered one of the better small hotels on the island. Located in very rural surroundings just outside of Pueu Village, there are three thatched-roof bungalows with two rooms per bungalow. Amenities include private bathroom and balcony. Activities include bicycle riding, windsurfing, and lagoon and mountain tours. ~ PK 9.8, Pueu; 57-12-54, fax 45-14-39. MODERATE.

When on the north coast, visit **Magasin Nico Star**. ~ Tautira; 57-19-32. On the south coast, there's **Magasin Teahupoo**. ~ PK 16.5, Teahupoo; 57-10-59.

GROCERIES

TAPUAEMAUI BEACH   This is a very slender strip of white sand several hundred yards long at PK 8.5 on the southern shore of Tahiti Iti. It's remarkable only in that it's the sole white-sand beach for perhaps 30 miles (50 kilometers). There are a few shade trees

BEACHES & PARKS

and some canopies to protect you from the sun. It's about a 50- to 75-yard swim from the shore to the reef. The water is very clean here (compared to the opposite side of the island) but not too deep, unless you are lucky enough to be there during high tide. A small store (Magasin Notehei) is on just the other side of the road from the beach and sells a few snack items. The proprietress is friendly and speaks English. Picnic tables, fresh tap water. ~ Take the southern coastal highway at Taravao past the Puunui turnoff in the direction of Teahupoo two kilometers or so past the marina.

TAUTIRA BEACH ~ At the terminus of Tahiti Iti's northern coastal highway is the community of Tautira, where a large black-sand beach fronts the village for about half a mile. It faces Captain Cook's old anchorage and is situated at the mouth of the Vaitepiha River. The primary reason to visit the area is the view from Tautira toward the rainforest-covered highlands of Tahiti Iti. On the shoreline is a grassy strip where the fishermen hang their nets from simple racks or coconut trees. The setting is bucolic and very serene. The swimming is good. ~ You can find the beach by driving to the end of the northern Tahiti Iti Road, PK 18. Bear to your left and follow the road along the shoreline.

▼▼▼▼▼▼▼▼▼▼▼▼▼▼▼
Outdoor Adventures

CAMPING

There is only once campground in Tahiti, the **Hiti Mahana Beach Club**, and it's not a particularly great place. Camping anywhere on the island without permission is strictly taboo. ~ PK 10.8, Mahina; 48-16-13.

DIVING

Tahiti has a variety of sites for all levels of divers and is a good place to get certified. The west coast, in particular, because of its location lee of the prevailing trade winds means often flat-calm conditions on the surface of the lagoon. Given the availability of film processing in Papeete, it's also a good place to check out equipment. If you have any qualms about your gear, shooting a few rolls in the lagoon and getting them quickly developed in town is always an option.

There are a variety of dive sites in Tahiti, with subjects ranging from wrecks to sharks. Some of the better-known ones include:

The **Aquarium**, with a depth ranging from 9 to 36 feet (3 to 10 meters) is where one goes to feed fish by hand. Fish come in such abundance that it's sometimes difficult to see a few yards ahead. It's generally calm here, which makes it easy to shoot still camera or video and ideal for beginners. Just east of the Aquarium are **wrecks** of a *Catalina PBY* seaplane and interisland vessel that one can visit on the same dive. Both the ship and the plane are in a state of sufficient deterioration so that it's easy to dive into the interior of both vessels. It's possible to swim through the engine room of the plane and the cockpit of the aircraft (and even sit in the pilot's seat). The **Tahiti Wall** and **Shark Cave** are located on an outer reef where a sheer drop descends from a plateau of 12 feet (4 meters) to **Blue Infinity**. Along the cliff face are caves and crevices where one can feed white-tip sharks and moray eels. The **Underwater Fresh Water Springs** entails a pinnacle about 90 feet (28.5 meters) off the reef, which is adjacent to a freshwater spring at about 25 feet (7.5 meters). The fresh water, which flows through the coral, is readily visible and resembles heat waves rising from pavement on a hot day. If a diver swims through the mass of fresh water rising to the surface, the image is blurred almost beyond recognition. The **Blue Hole**, located inside the lagoon, has a maximum depth of only 45 feet (16 meters). The site has eagle rays, nurse sharks and sting rays. The Vavi Area is characterized by a number of dropoffs and is rich in coral. There are a variety of soft coral, sea fans, Gorgonias and Alcynaceans. The Vaiau Cove is located about 1200 yards (360 meters) before Vaiau pass. The horseshoe-shaped cove is perhaps the best dive in the Peninsula area. One crosses the reef and enters a huge space full of grottos filled with red mullet and sweepers.

Tahiti Aquatic Maeva is run by American Dick Johnson, a long-time Tahiti resident. Adjacent to the Maeva Beach Hotel, he operates a variety of nautical activities including glass-bottom boat trips, cruises and sailboat rentals. Underwater photography lessons are also available. PADI (Professional Association of Diving Instructors) and CMAS (Confederation Mondiale des Activite's Sub-aquatiques, or World Underwater Federation) certification courses are also available. Full PADI/CMAS certification takes about five days. ~ PK 8, Punaauia; phone/fax 41-08-54.

Tahiti Plongée, located at Marina Lotus nine kilometers from Papeete, is headed by Henri Pouliquen. It is open seven days a week to divers of all levels. First-dive instruction and night diving are available; instruction is available in French or English. CMAS and PADI certification are available. ~ Punaauia; 43-62-51, fax 42-26-06.

Tahiti Yacht Club Diving Center calls itself Tahiti's first diving school and has all equipment available, two dive boats, and a decompression chamber only three minutes by car from the premises. They offer bilingual instruction, night diving and diving outside the reef. CMAS and PADI certification are available. ~ Arue; 42-23-55, fax 42-37-07.

Tahiti Aquatic Beachcomber is a small dive operation equipped with a Boston Whaler. English-speaking instructor and PADI certification available. Contact Joël Jügel. ~ Punaauia; 86-51-10, fax 86-51-30.

Ta'itau Diving Center in Taravao is located at the Pu'unui marina. Contact Joel Roussel. ~ Taravao; 57-77-93, fax 57-77-98.

Cowan Diving Center is found off the road to Pomare's Tomb. Contact Jean Pierre Renaud. ~ Pirae; 446-32-78, fax 42-14-09.

Tahiti Charter Island is located at Hotel Tahiti. Contact Alain Vallant. ~ Papeete; 77-02-33, fax 45-28-12.

SURFING & WIND-SURFING

The north coast of Tahiti offers good surfing—there are both beach breaks and reef breaks. The best time for quality surf is actually in the winter as the big winter storms from Antarctica and New Zealand provide plenty of swells to the Society Islands' southern shores. When the swells come out of deep water and break along the reefs, the result can be very powerful, hollow waves. On the southern coat of the island most of the breaks (with the exception of Papara) tend to be passes in the reef system and a long paddle is obligatory. Some of the popular reef breaks (going from west to east) are at **Taapuna Pass**, PK 10, just off of **Musée de Tahiti et des Iles**, PK 14.5, and off of **Paea** at the mouth of the Orofero River. There are also a number of breaks off of Tahiti Iti including **Tapuaeaha**, PK 9, **Ava iti**, PK 14, **Teahupoo**, PK 14.5 and **Vairao**, which is close to the most easterly tip of the island. All these passes necessitate transport on a boat—otherwise they are 20-minute paddles. Start making friends as soon as you get to the airport! If you are a serious surfer, get a copy of *The Surf Report*, Vol. 6 #4, from Surfer Publications. ~ P.O. Box 1028, Dana Point, CA 92629; 714-496-5922. This is the best information on surfing in French Polynesia.

Windsurfing is also catching on in Tahiti, but is not nearly as popular as surfing. Some of the better breaks are off of Point Venus, Sofitel Maeva Beach, Musée de Tahiti et des Iles, off the Orofero River, and off of Vairao in Tahiti Iti.

Rentals   To rent boards try **Kelly Surf** ~ Centre Fare Tony, Papeete; 45-44-00 or **Local Style** ~ Point Venus; 48-07-16, 48-24-13.

FISHING

Sportfishing inside the reef is not particularly good because of problems with pollution and overfishing. Outside the barrier reef is another matter. There are an abundance of marlin, yellowfin tuna, mahimahi and other pelagics. There are several vessels that cater to deep-sea anglers, but a good place to start is **Polynesian Fishing**, which has charter trips available aboard the *Guymar*. ~ PK 31, Haapiti; 56-30-20, fax 56-32-15. Another source of information on fishing excursions (and all things nautical) is GIE **Mer et Loisirs** in Papeete. Located on a small barge directly opposite Le Rétro, GIE Mer et Loisirs is a government agency affiliated with the Tahiti Tourist Board. They offer unbiased information on charters as well as trips to Tetiaroa and Moorea. (The people manning the desk at GIE Mer et Loisirs may or may not speak English.) ~ Papeete; 43-97-99, 43-33-68.

SAILING

The popularity of bareback charters in Tahiti has grown tremendously over the last five years. This entails renting a fully provisioned boat for several days or, preferably, several weeks. Those who are not up to actually sailing the vessel on their own have the option of "renting" a skipper and even a host or cook, as well. Prices vary from season to season. There are two very fine operations in French Polynesia, both in Raiatea, where you may partake in a bareboat charter. They are **Stardust Marine** in Raiatea ~ 66-23-18, or **The Moorings** in Raiatea ~ 66-35-93. Prices and more details can be found in Chapter Eight.

Another charter company to look at is **Archipels Croisieres**, based in Moorea. It has been active in French Polynesia for many years and features voyages throughout the archipelago. These include an eight-day charter to the Marquesas (Nuku Hiva, Ua Huka, Hiva Oa, Tahuata and Fatu Hiva); a seven-day Society Island trip (Bora Bora, Tahaa, Raiatea and Huahine) or Tuamotu trips to Rangiroa for three and four days. Diving charters with the Manta Ray Club in Rangi are also available. ~ Moorea, 56-36-39.

Yacht charters and bareboat charters are available in Tahiti and the outer islands. GIE **Mer et Loisirs** in Papeete opposite the main post office has information on the spectrum of yachts available. When I was there, no one spoke English and they seemed to be particularly interested in selling trips to Tetiaroa. ~ Papeete, 43-97-99, 43-33-68.

There are a number of local firms to choose from. **Enjoy** has catamarans up to 40 feet. ~ PK 7.2, Punaauia; 86-51-10, fax 42-18-88. **Tahiti Yacht Charter** in Papeete, based in the Vaima Center, moors vessels at the Apooiti Marina on the island of Raiatea. ~ 45-04-00, fax 43-99-31. **Polynesie Yachting Charter** is a Papeete agent for yachts based in Moorea, Tetiaroa and the Society Islands. ~ Papeete; 43-37-52, fax 43-24-28.

GOLF

At Atimaono in the Papara district, the **Olivier Breaud International Golf Course** is a 6944-yard, par 72, and Tahiti's only course. The area was formerly a cotton plantation established during the U.S. Civil War to provide Europe with the fiber, which was then in short supply. The course was designed by Bob Baldock & Son, a Costa Mesa, California, firm that has designed links throughout the United States and Mexico. It features expansive fairways, two artificial lakes and lush greens planted with hybrid Bermuda grass from Hawaii.

The golf course is a 45-minute drive from Papeete and is open daily from 7 a.m. to 6 p.m. year-round. The course has recently undergone a 100-million CFP renovation that includes a new clubhouse, restaurant, pro shop, pool, tennis courts and driving range. Clubs can be rented. To get there, call **Hui Popo**, a tour company that caters to enthusiasts and will pick you up at your hotel Monday through Saturday. (Ask for Titaino). ~ PK 41, Papara; 57-40-32.

TENNIS

Tennis fanatics can play at any number of hotels, as well as nine private clubs. Most will accept guests for a minimal fee. Try the following: **Fautaua Tennis Club** in Pirae ~ 42-00-59; **Fei Pi Sports Association** in Arue ~ 42-40-60; **Excelsior Club** in Papeete ~ 43-91-46; **Chon Wa Tennis Club** in Mamao ~ 42-01-31; **Club A. S. Dragon** in Papeete ~ 43-31-13; and **Club A S Phoenix** in Punaauia ~ 42-35-56.

There are also less-formal local clubs whose facilities are available, including the **Pirae Tennis Club** behind Pater Stadium, **Tamarii Pater Tennis Club** also near the stadium near the Fautaua River, and the **J. T.** (Young Tahitian) **Tennis League** (Pirae; 43-80-83).

RIDING STABLES

Evidently, some residents of Tahiti have a love for horseback riding because there are several first-class facilities available. **Club Equestre de Tahiti** is on the road to the Hippodrome at the foot of the mountains. ~ Pirae; 42-70-41. **L'Eperon de Pirae** is also in Pirae near the Hippodrome and is open every day (except Monday) from 8 a.m. to 7 p.m. ~ Pirae; 42-79-87. **Poney Club de Tahiti** is also at the Hippodrome in Pirae. ~ Pirae; 43-49-29. Fees are the least expensive on the island. **Ranch Tropical** is open every day and has Marquesan and New Zealand horses available. ~ Punaauia; 45-34-34. **Ranch le Centaure** is open every day except Monday, and also has New Zealand and Marquesan horses. ~ Vairao; 57-70-77.

BIKING

It's not recommended that you bring your bike to Tahiti unless you plan to spend most of your time on some of the more remote islands that are not overrun by automobiles. Tahiti is definitely overrun by cars and it does not strike me as a bike-friendly environment. There have been some serious accidents with travelers on bikes in Bora, and Club Med will not even rent bikes to its guests. Note that many of the larger hotels rent bikes. Because of traffic in the Papeete area, it's not recommended that you bicycle in or near

✔ CHECK THESE OUT—UNIQUE OUTDOOR ADVENTURES

- Throw down a towel on **Tahara'a**'s black-sand beach and gaze out at Honu Point. *page 129*
- Hike the fruit-laden trail to **Fa'aurumai Waterfalls**, where 100-foot cascades empty into fresh cool water pools. *page 124*
- Take a guided tour of the **Vaihiria River** area, known for its large eels and mountain banana plantations. *page 143*
- Dive the **Aquarium** where the fish are in such abundance that it's hard to see a few yards in front of you. *page 154*

town. I'm not aware of any bicycle rental agencies in town, but there are several sales and repair shops.

Upon your arrival in Tahiti, the verdant hills beckon, but venturing into the bush can be a dangerous proposition unless you know what you are doing and where you are going. Torrential rain can swell streams into rivers and easy-to-find trails can be overgrown with vegetation in no time. It's always best for the serious hiker to be accompanied by a guide. In many instances, you may even need to rent a four-wheel-drive vehicle to get to the trailhead.

HIKING

Despite the requirements, Tahiti has a variety of excellent trails and guides for hire. Here are six treks of varying difficulty. Most, but not all, require guides. Listed below are several individuals and ecologically oriented organizations (à la the Sierra Club) that organize treks into the bush. Generally these activities are scheduled during the weekends because nearly all the participants are locals.

Mataiea/Vaihiria Lake/Papenoo (18 miles/29 kilometers), a two-day hike across the island via Vaihiria Lake (Tahiti's only lake), begins on the south coast, traverses the island's ancient volcanic crater and ends in Papenoo on the north coast. Allow 45 minutes by four-wheel-drive vehicle to the Mataiea trailhead. Hikers should be in good physical condition and a guide is required.

The **Mt. Aorai** (20 miles/32 kilometers) trek begins at the end of the Belvedere restaurant road (near Papeete). This two-day hike requires a guide. Small *fares* (huts) have been built for hikers along the trail.

The **Fautaua Waterfall** (4 miles/6.4 kilometers) hike is a day trip up the Fautaua Valley. To get there, take an ordinary car to Bain Loti (of Pierre Loti fame) and walk for three hours to the waterfall. A guide is not necessary, but permission is needed from the Service des Eaux et Forets.

The **One Thousand Springs** (4.2 miles/7 kilometers) hike is a comparatively easy jaunt and no guide is required. Take Mahinarama Road (near the Hyatt Regency) to the end (about five kilometers) and walk for two hours to the springs. From this junction, it is possible to climb Mt. Orohena (Tahiti's highest), but a guide is required for such an undertaking. The short hike follows the Mahina Valley rift along the banks of the Tuauru River to the source of the springs. At the height of approximately 2000 feet (650 meters) is a magnificent 180-degree view of Mt. Orohena, Mt. Pito Iti and Mt. Pihaaiateta.

To get to the **Tamanu Plateau** (10 miles/16 kilometers), take a car to Punaauia (about 15 kilometers from Papeete) and enter the Punaru'u Valley road to the trailhead (one to two kilometers by car). Walk to Tamanu Plateau—an eight-hour hike. Trekkers should be in good shape and a guide is required.

The **Lava Tubes hike** (5 miles/8 kilometers) starts at PK 40 on the east coast and involves taking a four-wheel-drive vehicle for about eight kilometers. From there, it's an easy half-hour walk to the first lava tube, an hour to the second, and three hours to the third.

GUIDES   The Tahiti Tourist Board recommends several guides who regularly lead hikes to the hinterlands. Two of these are Zena Angelien and Pierre Florentin. You may contact them by phone.

Zena Angelien leads a variety of different treks on the peninsula separating Tahiti Iti and Tahiti Nui, which she calls Le Circuit Verde (The Green Route). These entail one- to-three day hikes along the *sauvage* coastline of Tahiti Iti, including the mist-shrouded Te Pari Cliffs. You do not have to be a triathlete to participate but hikers should be in good physical condition. Typical excursions include walks through thick jungle, wading waist deep across untrammeled rivers and streams and hiking precipitous bluffs. The scenery is breathtaking and sights include *marae* (ancient temples), burial caves, grottos and petroglyphs. Zena will take a minimum of five and a maximum of ten people. Those feeling a bit insecure will be relieved to know that Zena always takes her two-way radio, is insured and has medical training. Backpacks and tents are available. Zena will provide custom hikes for those with special needs or schedules. ~ Taravao; 57-22-67.

Pierre Florentin runs Tahiti Special Excursions and is reputedly an experienced guide who brings visitors almost exclusively to Tahiti's interior valleys and mountains. He visits seven different locales in Tahiti and his hikes vary in degree of difficulty. Trips are scheduled only on weekends or holidays.

The longest trek is a three-day hike to Mt. Orohena, French Polynesia's highest peak (7334 feet/2236 meters), in the district of Mahina. Vistas include the Papenoo, Punaru'u and Tuaru valleys, Tahiti's north coast and the Tahiti Iti Peninsula. Pierre also has a two-day hike along the Tahiti Iti Peninsula, walking in a northerly

BE PREPARED

If you plan to do extensive hiking, it is suggested that you bring a sleeping bag, backpack, gloves, utensils (bowl, knife, fork and spoon) and food supplies. Recommended food is dried fruit, concentrated milk in a tube, soup, chocolate, etc. Hard-core trekkers may want to pick up an excellent guide (in French) to walks in Tahiti and Moorea called *Randonnées en Montagne* by Paule Laudon, published by Les Editions du Pacifique. It is available in Papeete bookstores.

direction around the Te Pari Cliffs and the Fenua Aihere wilderness to Tautira village.

Another two-day hike, recommended only for those in excellent physical condition, is to the summit of Mt. Aorai (6783 feet/2068 meters). The trek includes a visit to the Fare Ata refuge and a magnificent vista of Papeete and Moorea. Most people do not even know about the Hitiaa Lava Tubes but Pierre will take you there. On Tahiti's southeast coast, the Lava Tubes are underground burrows with streams meandering through them. There are also panoramic views of the peninsula.

For a pleasant day trip, one might consider a visit to the Papenoo Plateau on Tahiti's north coast. The valley has several easy-to-reach plateaus with a plethora of orange, grapefruit and avocado trees. Swimming is at the foot of Topatari Waterfall.

Finally, there are two half-day trips, to the Fautaua Waterfalls near Papeete and to the Plateau of a Thousand Springs. Of the two half-day trips, the hike to the springs is the more difficult. Note that transport is extra, as are rentals for sleeping bags and backpacks. ~ Pirae; 43-72-01.

Te Ro O Nui Te Pari I Honoura Association is another organization that specializes in hiking the Te Pari Cliffs and other Tahiti attractions. Excursions depart weekends (two days and one night) from the Tautira Marina to the Te Pari area. A guide will lead you to various spots such as the Vaipoiri Grotto, where the group will stop to bathe, picnic and set up camp for the night. The next day a boat will pick up visitors from the grotto area and drop them at Tehaupoo, at which point they will return by car to Tautira. A minimum of four participants is needed. Contact Alfred Mervin or ask for Odette. ~ Pirae; 42-80-19, 57-19-56.

Te Fetia O Te Mau Mato, associated with Te Ora Nahi, an environmental protection association, also leads day trips approximately twice a month into Tahiti's interior and the coastal area of Taravao. Excursions include Papenoo Valley, the Taravao plateau and coast, the Fautaua Valley, Mt. Aorai or Mt. Rotui as well as the Te Pari Cliffs. ~ Ask for Mr. Pierre Wrobel for more information. ~ Papeete; 43-04-64, 81-09-19, 42-53-12.

Te Rau Ati Ati Association is another environmental organization dedicated to safeguarding Tahiti's natural beauty. They occasionally lead treks and those wishing to participate should call Marc Allain for information. ~ Mahina; 48-10-59.

Transportation

AIR

Tahiti Faa'a International Airport is perhaps the only international airport in the world with three consecutive vowels. With its collection of pariah dogs, lei stands and blaring Tahitian music, the airport is as distinctly Tahitian as any institution on the island. The airport's runway was originally constructed by filling in a lagoon. Prior to its completion in 1961,

Tahiti was served by a flotilla of passenger vessels and New Zealand TEAL flying boats.

Amenities at the airport include: two banks that open for an hour before international flights depart and for an hour after arrival; a post office that keeps regular business hours; a Tahiti Tourist Board information center that opens for arriving international flights; and a snack bar with restaurant. There is a *consign* (storage area for luggage) and shower facilities for transit passengers; three duty-free shops and a (non-duty-free) boutique, Manureva, which has fashions, souvenirs and a newsstand. The Galerie Leonard da Vinci is an art gallery.

If you decide you can't uproot yourself from Polynesian soil and would like to stay longer, the airport has an office of Police de l'Air et des Frontieres—the place to go to extend your tourist visa.

All incoming international flights to French Polynesia touch down at the Faa'a Airport. Tahiti is generally a stopover destination between Australia or New Zealand and the United States. There are also connections between Tahiti and Chile via Easter Island, as well as connections from other Pacific islands.

Airlines that fly into Tahiti include Air France, Air New Zealand, AOM French Airlines, Corsair, Hawaiian Airlines, Lan Chile, Polynesian Airlines and Qantas.

There are two car rental offices (Hertz and Avis) and offices for Air New Zealand, Qantas, Lan Chile, AOM, Air France, Hawaiian Airlines, Air Moorea and Air Tahiti. In separate buildings are offices for Heli Pacific and Tahiti Conquest Airlines, both charter carriers. Note that the office for Air Moorea is in a separate wing from the international and Air Tahiti offices and is adjacent to Tetiaroa's office.

Faa'a Airport is five-and-a-half kilometers from Papeete and getting there via *Le Truck* takes 15 minutes to town and costs 120 CFP during the day and 200 CFP at night. Le Truck runs to and from the airport until 1 a.m. To get to town from the airport, walk directly across the street and parking lot upon leaving customs, climb two flights of stairs up to road level and cross the road. Look for a good spot to wait for the next Papeete-bound truck. From the city you want one of the numerous *Outumorao Le Trucks*. The last stop that these vehicles make is after the Sofitel Maeva at Punaauia.

CAR RENTALS

For the visitor spending any appreciable time in Tahiti, or wishing to do an around-the-island tour solo, renting a car is a necessity. Although the accident rate statistics are fairly appalling, Tahitian motorists are generally courteous compared with U.S. or Continental drivers. They do have their own idiosyncrasies, such as passing on blind curves, tailgating and turning without signaling. Beware also of children playing in the street, pedestrians who seem oblivious to traffic, as well as drunk drivers and numerous dogs. Be especially careful in rural districts like Tahiti Iti where there is less traffic and pedestrians often take little heed of vehicular traffic. Always drive very defensively. Prepare to pay around 120 CFP per liter of gas.

Car rental agencies in Tahiti are:

Avis ~ Papeete; Rue Charles Vienot; 42-96-49; Beachcomber Hotel ~ 82-84-00; Maeva Beach Hotel ~ 42-09-26; Hyatt Regency ~ 48-12-07; Airport ~ 82-44-23.

Bernard ~ Papeete; 42-01-55

Budget ~ Airport; 83-01-05, PK 5 — Faa'a; 82-30-04

Europcar ~ Fare Ute; 45-24-24

Hertz ~ Papeete, Rue Commandant Destremeau; 42-04-71— Airport; 82-55-86

Pacificar ~ Papeete, Rue des Ramparts; 41-93-93

Robert ~ Papeete, Rue Commandant Destremeau; 42-97-20

The local bus, known as *Le Truck*, is the most practical and widely used form of transport on the island. In the scheme of things, *Le Truck* is somewhere between a jitney and a bus—a small to midsize truck or lorry with wooden benches that run the length of the vehicle. Seating, which is fairly low, is along the perimeter. The vehicles, which come in a variety of lengths and makes, are all noted for their lack of shock absorbers. The entrance/exit is generally, but not always, at the front, behind the driver's cab. The drivers are usually owner-operators who, like all independent truck drivers, must hustle to survive. They are often accompanied by their wives, girlfriends or children, who sit with them in the cab.

PUBLIC TRANSIT

Each vehicle has a route number and an out-of-town destination painted on the front. The trucks have a few official highway stops (with canopies and benches marked by blue signs with a *Le Truck* logo), but will generally pull over along any stretch of the road if you wave them down.

The trucks run on weekdays from the first light of dawn until about 10 p.m. On Saturday, they operate until midnight. Service is quite frequent on the shorter hauls, even on Sundays, whereas service to more-distant destinations drops off sharply on Sundays. Service also drops off sharply after the early evening and there can be long waits after 9 p.m.

Drivers are usually paid after the trip is completed. The fares for adults/children range from 120/60 CFP (if you're going from Papeete to the airport (just under six kilometers) and a few kilometers beyond up to a maximum of 400 CFP to the other side of the island. Unlike taxis, a visitor won't have to fear being overcharged on *Le Truck*. The fare within a 20-kilometer radius of Papeete is 200 CFP or less.

There are four *Le Truck* stations in greater Papeete but the main departure point for passengers headed toward the west coast (toward Faa'a Airport) is the central marketplace in Papeete. Each station (which has its own color code) has a large notice board listing all the bus services from Papeete. As elsewhere in the world, the *Le Truck* for each destination is numbered, i.e., *38 Paea, 31 Punaauia*, etc. Service from the various bus stations is as follows:

Hitchhiking is possible, with varying degrees of difficulty for foreigners. The idea is to be as conspicuously non-French as possible. Although Tahitians enjoy meeting foreigners, hitching isn't as easy in Tahiti as it used to be.

Arret Central du March, the main station at the public market on Rue du Général de Gaulle, is coded red and includes service to bedroom communities such as Faa'a, Punaauia and Paea, as well as the more-distant destinations such as Papara and Taravao. The popular Outumaoro *Le Trucks* to the airport and the west-coast hotels go from here. *Le Truck* numbers from this station include: 30 Outumaoro, 31 Punaauia/Punaruu, 32 Punaauia/Taapuna, 33 Pamatai, 34 Puurai/Oremu, 35 Taravao, 36 St Hilaire, 37 Teroma/Heiri, 38 Paea/Maraa, 39 Papara.

Arret Central du Front de Mer, the second-most important station, coded blue, is on the seafront Boulevard Pomare, opposite Fare Manihini where the Tahiti Tourist Board is housed. Here transportation is available to districts along the east coast such as Pirae, Arue and Mahina as far as Papenoo. Those staying at Hiti Mahana will utilize this station. *Le Truck* numbers from this station include: 60 Mahina, 61 Arue, 62 Erima, 63 Papenoo, 64 Tenaho, 65 Nahoata, 66 Hamuta, 67 Princesse Heiata, 68 CPI.

Embarquements Long Distances, the station for long-haul service to the east coast and Tahiti Iti (taking the easterly route), is also on Boulevard Pomare opposite the Moorea ferry terminal. Destinations include Tautira, Hitiaa/Mahaena and Teahupoo. The color code for this station is yellow. *Le Truck* numbers include: 40 Tevaiuta, 41 Teahupoo, 42 Tautira, 70 Hitiaa/Mahaena.

Gare de l'Hotel de Ville, the fourth station, coded green, is beside the Town Hall or Hotel de Ville. From here, *Le Trucks* run east to Point Venus and beyond. Destinations include some of the more obscure residential areas in Papeete and Pirae such as Mission and Mamao (where a hospital is located). Perhaps the most useful *Le Truck* from this station is Pomare V, which one can take to visit the Pomare V tomb. *Le Truck* numbers include: 1 Titioro, 2 Mission, 3 Motu Uta, 4 Tipaerui, 5 CPS/Mamao, 6 Vairaatoa, 7 Pomare V, 8 Taupeahotu, 9 Culina, 10 Manganui.

TAXIS

Local taxis, compared with cabs in other countries, are very expensive. The government regulates taxi fares, and has established rates from Papeete to virtually every hotel and restaurant. Computerized meters have recently been installed in every taxi. This may cut down on blatant rip-offs but they are still expensive.

Inside the greater Papeete area the taxi fare should not exceed 900 to 1000 CFP, so be suspicious of anything much more than that for a ride within town. The tariff from town to the airport or vice versa is around 1600 CFP, except after 8 p.m. when the price goes up 50 percent to 70 percent. All other fares double from 8 p.m. to 6 a.m., and on holidays and Sundays the minimum rate may go up by 25 percent. Got all that? Quantum mechanics is simple compared with calculating Tahiti taxi fares.

Any complaints should be directed to the Tahiti Tourist office. Although in theory taxi fares are regulated, some drivers may not adhere quite so strictly to the rules—especially if the passenger is a tourist.

AERIAL TOURS

There are two standard helicopter tours above Tahiti. A 40-minute flight cruises over Papeete, the lagoon above Faa'a, the major hotels and Matavai Bay to the north of town. The pilot then heads inland to point out Le Diademe, Mt. Orohena and the rainforests nestled in the deep cleft valleys. A 50-minute tour takes you around the island to the Tahiti Iti Peninsula and the Isthmus of Taravao. For more information, contact **Héli Pacific**. The company also has regularly scheduled tours to Moorea. ~ Faa'a; 85-68-00.

DRIVE TOURS

Tahiti's interior is one of the most beautiful (and seldom seen) attractions, making an inland tour a high priority.

Adventure Eagle Tours, run by William Leteeg, has a total of six tours, two of which are inland excursions—the "Morning Mountain Tour" and the "Mountain & Waterfall Tour." Both visit 4592-foot (1400-meter) Mt. Marau, which entails a climb in a jeep wagon to see what Mr. Leteeg calls "Tahiti's Grand Canyon where no big buses can go." The Mountain & Waterfall Tour also takes in Vaimahutu Falls and is a half-day trip, whereas the Morning Mountain Tour takes only two hours. ~ Papeete; 41-37-63.

Mr. Leteeg's other excursions are variations on circle island tours that read like a menu in a Chinese restaurant. Each tour has a selection of landmarks and you can pick and choose the items you wish to visit. These include the Gauguin Museum, the Vaihpahi garden and waterfall, the Papenoo surfing beach, the Fern Grotto of Maraa, Point Venus, the Arahoho Blowhole and other points of interest. He also has a city tour of Papeete that includes visits to the Black Pearl Museum, Lagoonarium and the Musée de Tahiti et des Iles. Call William for more details.

Ron's Tours has four-wheel-drive tours to Tahiti's interior as well as guided hikes. The "Moroto Safari Adventure" is a full day's journey that follows the coastline to the Papenoo River valley up into the mountainous heart of the island and on to Vaihiria Lake and the Mataiea River valley. Ron's Landrover crosses the rivers on 20 occasions and visits waterfalls, rainforests, and *marae*. Price includes lunch at the Relais del la Maroto. The guided hikes include a half-day Fautaua Waterfall trek that entails a visit to Pierre Loti's pools and a visit to the falls and the Te Faaiti (the little valley) hike to Tahiti's only national park. This is an all-day trek through a tropical rainforest. BYO lunch or you can arrange a picnic. Both treks are of intermediate difficulty. ~ Papeete; 46-60-80, fax 46-60-70.

HIDDEN ▶

Safari Tahiti Expedition also has a variety of land tours to remote sections of the island, including Vaihiria Lake, the Lava Tubes and Tahiti Iti. ~ Contact Patrice Bordes for more information. This come highly recommended. ~ Papeete; 42-14-15.

Billy "Manga" Rotui, a retired Tahitian fisherman, is an engaging character who also gives personalized tours of Tahiti Iti in his World War II–vintage jeep (when it's running). He lives in Taravao but unfortunately, has no phone and speaks very limited English. You can try inquiring at the tourism office, but he is tough to find. Billy evidently does not go out of his way to find clients.

BOAT TOURS

GIE Mer et Loisirs is a government-run office specializing in nautically oriented information for visitors. Through this small office, located on the waterfront barge opposite the post office in Papeete, one can charter trips to Marlon Brando's private island (Tetiaroa), to Moorea or other areas. For those willing to spend the money, Tetiaroa is a nice spot to visit. ~ Papeete; 43-97-99, fax 43-33-99.

▼▼▼▼▼▼▼▼▼▼▼▼▼▼▼▼▼▼▼▼▼▼

Addresses & Phone Numbers

In addition to the full telephone contacts listed below are emergency numbers such as police, fire department, etc., that can be dialed by keying in only two digits.

Fire Department ~ 18

Hospital ~ Mamao Hospital, Mamao, Papeete; 42-01-01

Hospital ~ Taravao Hospital, 57-13-33

Medical Clinic ~ Clinic Cardella, Rue Francois Cardella, Papeete; 42-81-90

Medical Clinic ~ Paofai Clinic, Boulevard Pomare, Papeete; 43-02-02

Pharmacy ~ Pharmacie de la Cathedrale, Place Notre Dame, Papeete; 42-02-24

Police emergency ~ 17

Police Station ~ Gendarmerie, Avenue Bruat, Papeete; 42-02-02

Post Office ~ Main Post Office, Boulevard Pomare, Papeete; 41-43-00

Visitor information ~ Tahiti Tourist Board (Fare Manihini), Boulevard Pomare; Papeete 50-57-00, fax 43-66-19

FIVE

Moorea

After Tahiti, the second-most popular tourist attraction in French Polynesia is Moorea. And no wonder. The island is dramatically beautiful, with sharp serrated peaks that command deep cleft valleys, which were once centers for vanilla cultivation.

Lying 12 miles (19 kilometers) west of Tahiti, Moorea is encircled by a lagoon of translucent green, fringed by an azure sea.

The island is triangular in shape, one side punctuated by two large but shallow bays (Cook's Bay and Opunohu). Covering an area of 51 square miles (132 square kilometers), and it is the only other major island in the Windward group besides Tahiti.

Moorea (which is pronounced MOE-oh-ray-ah, with a pause or glottal stop between the o's) means yellow lizard. The name was taken from a family of chiefs that eventually united with the Pomare dynasty of Tahiti. Archeological evidence in the Opunohu Valley suggests that people were living on the island as early as 1600 A.D., which corresponds with the oral history of the valley. At the time of Cook's return in 1774, there was internecine fighting among the islands' chiefs and warfare with tribes on neighboring Tahiti. The battles continued for many years and the arrival of the missionaries in 1805 actually helped the Pomare dynasty gain power in Tahiti by supplying arms and mercenaries in return for support. After Pomare I conquered Tahiti, Moorea (which had been his refuge) became no more than a province of the Tahitian kingdom. During the latter half of the 19th century, colonists arrived and cotton and coconut plantations began to spring up. Vanilla and coffee cultivation came later, in the 20th century.

Tourism is now by far the largest industry and the island's attraction for visitors is no mystery. The high peaks, the deep green valleys, and the white-sand beaches are generally still pristine. The island and the islanders retain their charm but not without a struggle. Several years ago locals fought off the planned development of a golf course in the verdant heart of the island that would have encroached upon archeological treasures.

Moorea is quick and easy to reach from Tahiti—shuttle flights leave every 30 minutes from Faa'a Airport and ferries depart from Papeete at least six times daily.

Once on Moorea, sightseeing can be easily accomplished via *Le Truck*, rental car or scooter. Naturally, the numerous tour companies, touted at every hotel, will be more than happy to show you around on their private *Le Truck* or minibus.

The complete circuit of the island is 36 miles (59 kilometers) and the coast road is marked by red-and-white PK (kilometer) markers at regular intervals. The highway markers begin at the airport at PK 0, and from there go round to PK 35 in a counterclockwise direction and PK 24 clockwise. (One would think it would be more logical and less confusing to go in one direction and just continue to count kilometerage consecutively until you reach the point where you started. However, this is not the way it works.) If you are confused, consult the map and remember this is not a big island. There is little chance of getting lost unless you hike into the bush.

For ease of visitors who wish to do a circle island tour, our island circuit starts at the airport and proceeds counter-clockwise around the island. The PK marker number is followed by the distance from the starting point. As a common courtesy, visitors should take care not to trespass on private land to take photos.

▼▼▼▼▼▼▼▼▼▼
Vaiare Bay to Opunohu Bay

Visitors arrive on Moorea at the eastern corner of the island either at the airport (near Temae Village) or four kilometers south of the airport, at the ferry terminal at Vaiare Bay. Thus, if you can imagine Moorea as a three-toed hoof print, your point of entry would be on the right toe. From the Hotel Sofitel Ia Ora near the airport, it's easy to get around thanks to a relatively new service that taxi drivers lobbied against for years—a regularly scheduled bus system. The new mini-bus service departs eight times a day from the Sofitel Ia Ora and goes as far as the Linareva Hotel, at the opposite (northwestern) end of the island. Most of the hotels, shops and indeed the majority of the population are concentrated along Moorea's northern coast.

SIGHTS

Cargo boats and daily ferries from Papeete dock in **Vaiare Bay**. A large pier can accommodate two ferries simultaneously, and a parking lot is where drivers of trucks, autos and motorcycles await their turn to drive up the ramp onto the vessels. Ancillary facilities such as warehouses, service stations and the island's largest supermarket are clustered in the area. As always, ubiquitous *roulottes* (food vans) are parked nearby to feed workers and passengers. The ferryboat personnel manning the ramps are quite efficient and perhaps nothing in French Polynesia runs as smoothly as the loading and unloading of vehicles and cargo at the terminal. ~ PK 4.

The luxurious **Hotel Sofitel Ia Ora** is a good place to begin exploring the island. Located about a kilometer south of the airport, its numerous thatched-roof bungalows are dispersed over a quarter-mile-long strip of beach front. The hotel property basks in the shade of coconut trees that line the shore on the southern end of

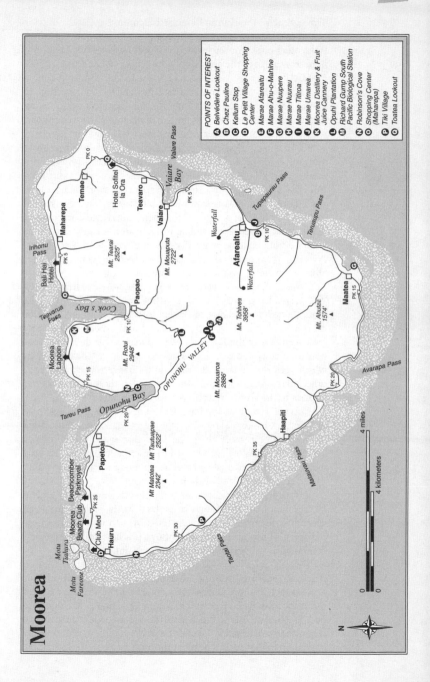

Moorea

POINTS OF INTEREST

- **A** Belvédère Lookout
- **B** Chez Pauline
- **C** Kellum Stop
- **D** Le Petit Village Shopping Center
- **E** Marae Afareaitu
- **F** Marae Ahu-o-Mahine
- **G** Marae Nuupere
- **H** Marae Nuurau
- **I** Marae Titiroa
- **J** Marae Umarea
- **K** Moorea Distillery & Fruit Juice Cannery
- **L** Opuhi Plantation
- **M** Richard Gump South Pacific Biological Station
- **N** Robinson's Cove
- **O** Shopping Center (Maharepa)
- **P** Tiki Village
- **Q** Toatea Lookout

Motu Tiahura
Motu Fareone

Beachcomber Parkroyal
Moorea Beach Club
Club Med

Hauru
PK 25
PK 30

Papetoai

Mt Matotea 2342'
Mt Tautuapae 2522'

Tareu Pass
Opunohu Bay
PK 20

Moorea Lagoon
PK 15

Teavarua Pass
Cook's Bay

Bali Hai Hotel
Irihonu Pass
PK 5

Maharepa
Temae

Hotel Sofitel Ia Ora
PK 0

Teavaro
Vaiare
Vaiare Bay
Vaiare Pass

Mt Tearai 2525'

Paopao
PK 10

Mt Rotui 2948'

OPUNOHU VALLEY

Mt Mouaputa 2722'

Mt Mouaroa 2886'

Mt Tohivea 3958'

Waterfall

Afareaitu
PK 10

Tupapaurau Pass

Waterfall

Mt Ahutea 1574'

Maatea
PK 15

Teruaupu Pass

Avarapa Pass

Haapiti
PK 35

Matauvau Pass

Taotai Pass

4 miles
4 kilometers

N

Temae Beach—the best and longest beach on the island. Sofitel is one of two luxury resorts on Moorea (the Beachcomber Parkroyal is the other one). You can get to the beach from the hotel but public access (north of the hotel) is a better idea. ~ PK 1; 52-86-72, fax 56-12-91.

Passing the Sofitel entrance and heading in the direction of Cook's Bay, the coastal road climbs the only significant grade along the perimeter of the island. At the top of the hill is **Toatea Lookout**, which offers a magnificent view down the coastline and across to Tahiti. Leaving the lookout point, at the bottom of the hill just past a bridge is the public access to **Temae Beach**. The sign is clearly marked and it's about one kilometer to the beach via a dirt road from the coastal highway. Temae is perfect for swimming. A long white-sand beach edging translucent blue water, Temae is shaded by great numbers of coconut palms. There's almost no coral around, which makes it ideal for wading in the water. It's generally clean except during holidays when I've seen it littered with beer bottles. If you continue west, along the beach access road, you will eventually end up alongside the airport runway. ~ PK 0.

Temae Village was where, tradition has it, novelist Herman Melville persuaded the chief to have the *vahines* perform for him the erotic *Lory-Lory*, a dance forbidden by the missionaries. Melville came here after his release from jail in Tahiti, where he and other crew members of the *Lucy Ann* were punished for their participation in a mutiny. Temae Village is still famous for its dancing troupes, which perform regularly for the island's dance revues. However, other than a few shops and some residences, there is nothing that imparts to the visitor that this is a formal "village." ~ PK 1.

You will recognize you have arrived in **Maharepa Village** (pronounced MA-ha-ray-pa) by noting the brightly colored pareus strung between coconut trees along the road that mark the Lili Shop. Though the term "village" is used to describe Maharepa, it's little more than a cluster of shops and hotels along the roadside rather than a community or township.

A little less than a kilometer from the Lili Shop is the **Bali Hai Hotel**, one of the first hotels to be built at the start of jet plane tourism in French Polynesia. Operated by a trio of American entrepreneurs known as the Bali Hai Boys, it is now one of the oldest continuously run establishments on the island. ~ PK 5.5.

Directly across the road from the Bali Hai Hotel is **Maison Blanc**, a renovated turn-of-the-century plantation house that is now a souvenir shop. During the vanilla boom in the latter part of the 19th and early 20th centuries, a number of homes like this were built in Moorea, but no other plantation house that I am aware of is in such excellent shape. (With a careful eye, you can still see other plantation houses tucked away in the bush or along the side of the road.) The style consists of clapboard construction, iron roofing and a veranda with white wooden fretwork. ~ PK 5.5.

Almost one kilometer past Maison Blanc (still in Maharepa Village) you will find a **shopping center** that has a post office, bank, patisserie, boutiques, a stationery store, and several other shops. It's oriented both for locals and visitors. ~ PK 6.3; Maharepa.

Paopao Village marks the beginning of **Cook's Bay**, one of the most photographed landmarks in French Polynesia. It also has the obligatory trinket shops, car and bike rental outlets and a wharf. Movie buffs might note that this was one of the sites for production of *Return of the Bounty*, although most of the scenes were shot in Opunohu Bay. ~ PK 7.

Another place to stop on Cook's Bay is the **Moorea Aquarium** (which is part of the **Moorea Pearls Center**). The brain child of Teva, a local jeweler, this establishment is actually a combination aquarium and jewelry store that specializes in black pearls. The aquarium consists of 40 well-maintained tanks with approximately 1500 species of marine flora and fauna. At the back of the building is a garden where, beneath a shade tree, Teva's assistants give a short discourse on black pearl cultivation. Admission. ~ PK 8; 56-30-00.

Paopao Village is the central community in the Cook's Bay area and is an important junction for the road leading to the island's interior. Paopao also has an important dock used by trading vessels and an array of services including a pharmacy, grocery stores, bank and doctor's office. In the evenings, it's worth a walk or drive to see whether the mobile food stalls, known as *roulottes*, are parked on the wharf. If so, be sure and stop. The food is reasonably priced and very good. Paopao also has a small open-air **public market**, which is best visited early in the day. Finally, Paopao is where you turn off to get to the Belvédère Lookout and interior valleys and/or the Paopao-to-Vaiare walk. ~ PK 9.

A half-mile west of Paopao is a **Catholic church** worth visiting. Here you'll find an altar inlaid with mother-of-pearl and a mural

✔ CHECK THESE OUT—UNIQUE SIGHTS

- Drop by the **Kellum Stop** for a peak into the history of a homestead established by an American family in 1925. *page 172*
- Go back in time and explore the archeological treasures of **Opunohu Valley**. *page 174*
- Visit the **octagonal church** in Papetoai Village, built by the London Missionary Society in 1822. *page 183*
- Take the **ferry** from Tahiti to Moorea and perhaps spot a flying fish or dolphin as you rub shoulders with the locals. *page 205*

featuring brown-skinned Polynesian versions of St. Joseph, the Virgin Mary, the Archangel Gabriel and the infant Jesus. The landscape painted in the background depicts Moorea. ~ PK 10.

The **Richard Gump South Pacific Biological Research Station** was constructed on land donated by San Francisco jewelry magnate Richard Gump, in cooperation with the University of California at Berkeley. Here UC Berkeley has established a biological research facility for terrestrial and marine life. The station consists of two buildings, a dormitory, a lab and several boats. It is open to researchers from around the world, whose interests may range from insects to dolphins. The facility welcomes guests, but you should correspond with the University of California ahead of time rather than simply show up. Michael Poole, the director of the biological research station, has a Ph.D. in marine biology. Dr. Poole has established a **dolphin tour**, which takes visitors out in the lagoon to observe these fascinating creatures. The tour is highly recommended. (Book it through your hotel tour desk—there is no direct phone to the Biological Research Station). There is a fee for the tour, but no admission fee to the research station. ~ PK 10.9.

Several hundred yards off the main highway (on the mountain side of the road) is the **Moorea Distillery and Fruit Juice Cannery**, which specializes in the island's agricultural products—pineapple, grapefruit, *pamplemousse* and papaya. A local greets you and gives a well-rehearsed monologue describing the various stages of the canning process. On the grounds is a small kiosk where visitors are served shots of *Eau de Vie* ("life water"), an excellent fruit liqueur derived from local produce. Tasty *pamplemousse* fruit juice is available in liter cartons at any grocery store in French Polynesia, but freshly squeezed at a café or restaurant is even better. Oddly enough, you can taste samples of the *Eau de Vie* but samples of the fruit juice (sans alcohol) are not available. The cannery is open weekdays—only in the morning hours. ~ PK 11; 56-11-33.

Continuing west you will come to **Opunohu Bay**, Moorea's second dramatic inlet. Opunohu is less developed and therefore less "touristy" than Cook's Bay. It also has good snorkeling, but crown-of-thorns starfish and stonefish can pose a danger, so take heed. ~ PK 14.

HIDDEN ►

While in the neighborhood, you would be remiss not to spend a hour or two at **Kellum Stop**. (See "Kellum's Legacy" in this chapter.) The Kellum home, which looks like a large farmhouse, is tucked among the coconut palms and mango trees. The Kellum Stop is open mornings—only from 8 a.m. to 12 noon Tuesday to Saturday. Please respect Marimari Kellum's privacy and do not ask for a tour during off-hours. Admission. ~ PK 17.5, midway between the Club Med and Club Bali Hai. Look for a small wooden sign on the mountain side of the road that marks the driveway to

Kellum's Legacy

On a magnificent stretch of Opunohu Bay, in the shadow of Mt. Rotui, rests the Kellum Estate—a solid, weatherworn bit of Americana nearly lost in the vastness of the South Seas. The small, hand-lettered sign that marks the Kellum Stop on PK 17.5 belies the impact that the Kellum clan had on Moorea.

The saga began in 1924 when Medford Kellum Sr., a wealthy Miami businessman, and his family set out from Hawaii on the *Kaimiloa*, a four-masted schooner, to survey the lesser-visited islands of the South Pacific. Along with his crew, various members of the scientific community were invited to participate. Included were botanist Gerrit P. Wilder and Kenneth P. Emory, the most famous ethnologist and specialist in Polynesian studies of his time. (The story of Emory's life and ground-breaking studies on Polynesian culture and society are recounted in the book *Keneti*, by Bob Krauss, published by the University of Hawaii Press in 1988.)

When the *Kaimiloa* arrived in Moorea in January 1925, an enormous tract of land, some 3500 acres of lush tropical splendor held by a German company, was up for auction. The property comprised nearly the entire Opunohu Valley, including numerous archeological sites, verdant meadows, streams and rugged cliffs. The Kellums purchased the land and Medford Kellum Jr., along with his American wife started a cattle, copra and vanilla plantation.

In 1962, the French government purchased most of the land from the Kellum clan with the proviso that they build an agricultural research facility, which still exists. Kellum, a sturdy Yankee with a down-to-earth demeanor, died in 1992 at the age of 90. With his passing, an enormous part of the island's recent history went with him. The Kellum home, however, remains the way Medford Kellum kept it, due largely to the efforts of his daughter, Marimari.

An accomplished archeologist who studied in the U.S., Marimari has graciously opened the doors to the Kellums' Eden by giving private tours (in English or French) of the grounds. The one-hour tour includes a walk through the splendid garden where over 50 varieties of herbs and flowers grow. Here she explains how the local flora was used medicinally, cosmetically and in the construction of homes and utensils by the Polynesians of old. Of special note is a magnificent 65-year-old *tipanier* (plumeria) that was brought from Hawaii as a seedling. Also described in the tour is the Kellum's colonial-style home. Local artifacts are also on display, including the fabled tiki which Hugh Kelley (of Bali Hai fame) tracked down.

the estate. Park, walk to the gate on the opposite side of the road and ring the cowbell attached to it.

Drive west of the Kellum Stop and you'll come to the Opunohu Valley Road, which is the second access to the island's interior. The road eventually links up with the Paopao Valley Road and comes to a dead end at the Belvédère Lookout. (Along the Paopao Valley Road look for vanilla plantations, which are readily identifiable by the vanilla vines that wind around posts.) Just prior to the road's junction on the main highway are several prawn ponds. ~ PK 18.

PAOPAO AND OPUNOHU VALLEYS   The Opunohu Valley, with its reconstructed *marae* (temples), fine vistas and lush green meadows, is well worth a detour off the perimeter road. A round trip can be made by leaving the coast road at Paopao at the top of Cook's Bay and climbing up into the Paopao Valley to join the Opunohu Valley Road and return to the top of Opunohu Bay. Prior to European contact, these central valleys were teeming with people. Now they are largely deserted and devoted to agriculture.

The Opunohu Valley population declined in the early 19th century, soon after the abandonment of the traditional religion. Over 500 ancient structures have been identified here, including religious and secular stone buildings as well as agricultural terraces. The complexity of the remains indicates a highly developed social system. The chief remnants of these buildings are six marae, reconstructed in 1967 by Y. H. Sinoto of the Bishop Museum in Honolulu. A council platform and two archery platforms have also been rebuilt. From the junction at Paopao, PK 9, it is several winding kilometers to the *marae*. All are an easy walk from the road. Before reaching the *marae*, you will drive through a pineapple plantation. Stop at the first hill, turn to the left and park. Walk across the road for a spectacular view of both Cook's and Opunohu bays.

The **Opuhi Plantation**, located on the Paopao Valley Road, two kilometers south of the junction at Paopao, is a small boutique and botanical garden owned by an old Tahiti hand and member of the local literati, Alex Du Prel. Du Prel formerly managed the Brando property on Tetiaroa and is a great raconteur. (He is also editor of *Tahiti Pacifique*, a local literary magazine.) The planation is open to the public and has a fine collection of local flora including *opuhi* (ginger), guava, mango, breadfruit, vanilla, various varieties of ferns and other species of fruit trees. ~ Paopao Valley, 56-28-94.

The large **Marae Titiroa** is right by the car park and information board. This large temple complex was restored by Y. H. Sinoto in 1969. The platform area or *ahu* is strictly reserved for the gods while the tablet-like stones protruding from the earth were backrests for chiefs or priests. This particular temple was used for animal sacrifices, which were placed here as offerings to the gods. A clear trail runs into the woods from here to the Council Platform, a smaller *marae* and the impressive Marae Ahu-o-Mahine. Another *marae* can easily be reached by rock hopping across the river from Marae Titiroa but the woods in the valley hide countless other traditional structures.

The **Marae Ahu-o-Mahine** has the most elaborate form and features a three-stepped *ahu* (platform). It was once the community *marae* for the Opunohu Valley and was built some time after 1780 A.D. Note that it is constructed with handcrafted, round dressed stones, similar to those of Marae Arahurahu in Paea, Tahiti. The intricacy of this particular temple is evidence of the highly developed society that existed in pre-contact times.

> When touring the *marae*, be sure and bring along plenty of mosquito repellent.

Archery was a sacred sport in ancient Tahiti, practiced only by people of high rank—chiefs' families and warriors. As is clearly visible from the map, **archery platforms** have distinct crescent forms at one end. Archers balanced on one knee to draw their bows and aimed for distance rather than accuracy. Of the three archery platforms in the Opunohu Valley, two have been restored. As in other parts of Polynesia, bows and arrows were not used as weapons of war. The tracks to the two archery platforms and the connecting Marae Afareaitu from Marae Titiroa are not easy to follow, and it's easier to drive around by road. Look for any small parting of the scrub between Marae Titiroa and the nearby parking area, and the Belvédère Lookout.

Between the two restored archery platforms is **Marae Afareaitu**, similar to Marae Titiroa farther down the trail. A small *ahu* near one end is the principal structure of the *marae*, which was reserved for the gods. On the perimeter of the *marae* are two small shrines, one attached and one detached from the main temple. Some of these independent shrines are associated with agricultural terraces and suggest that crop-fertility ceremonies were held there.

A few more kilometers up the road is **Belvédère Lookout**, the finest vista of the valley. Standing on the ridge of the caldera (crater), the lookout point affords a great vista of Opunohu and Cook's bays. Belvédère Lookout was part of the setting for the latest film version of the *Bounty* story (*Return of the Bounty*) with Anthony Hopkins and Mel Gibson (which gave much-needed temporary employment to the locals). Continue back down the road, this time taking a left toward Opunohu Bay. On this route you will pass scenery that but for the coconut trees might belong to a Swiss valley—you'll see verdant pastures with fat, contented cattle grazing. Continue along and you are once more on the perimeter road that circles the island.

On a white-sand beach facing Tahiti, two kilometers south of the airport, the **Hotel Sofitel Ia Ora** is one of two luxury hotels on

LODGING

Moorea. There are three bars, two restaurants (one of them an exceptional gourmet establishment) and all the amenities you could want: boutique, outrigger canoes, tennis, and water sports. Facing an expansive stretch of beach, the grounds are so big that when you check in, a vahine must drive you to your room in a golf cart. The bungalows are quaint and far enough apart to afford plenty of privacy. Each bungalow has its own view of the sea. For the price, these accommodations are on the average side. ~ PK 1; 52-86-72, fax 56-12-91, or 800-221-4542 in the U.S. ULTRA-DELUXE.

Located at the entrance to Cook's Bay, about five kilometers from the airport, the **Bali Hai Moorea** was established by three Americans who came before the Tahiti tourist boom to run a vanilla plantation and wound up as hotel magnates. The hotel consists mainly of thatched-roof bungalows that spread over a long narrow swath of land wedged between the main road and the lagoon. The garden bungalows are split level—bedroom on top and bathroom below. The bathroom is akin to an indoor arboretum with a profusion of plants. Due to fierce competition on Moorea, the Bali Hai lowered its prices and the over-the-water bungalows are probably the least expensive in French Polynesia. These charming accommodations have steps that lead into the water so you can swim or snorkel in your front yard. The hotel also has a huge thatched-roof restaurant, a little patch of beach, tennis and pool. On Wednesdays there is an excellent dance review open to all. In the evenings one is treated to a parade of tupa (land crabs) that stroll through the hotel lobby in search of food. Avoid the bungalows located near the road because of the loud traffic noise at night. The hotel is still American-run and North Americans will feel quite comfortable here. ~ PK 5, 56-13-59, fax 56-19-22, or 800-282-1401 in the U.S. MODERATE TO DELUXE.

The **Cook's Bay Resort Hotel** is a contemporary hotel built in a turn-of-the-century style with gingerbread trim. The resort is U-shaped, cupping in its confines a pool, a pool bar and small beach. A boardwalk joins the pool area over the water to a restaurant/bar and dock. Cook's Bay Resort is a good bargain in the mid-price range. Its 76 rooms and 24 individual bungalows make it one of the largest operations on the island. The smallish standard rooms, done in pastels, are modern affairs, almost incongruous with the colonial exterior. They are clean, basic and have overhead fans, as well as a view of the sea. The bungalows are also well-appointed, but rather small. There are two restaurants and a pizzeria (under separate management) that is excellent. The hotel provides complimentary masks, snorkels and *pirogues* (outrigger canoes). Excursions such as picnics and canoe trips are available and bikes can also be rented. The hotel frequently has specials. Before you book, check to see if they are offering any special tariffs. The American-born hotel manager, Donny, is friendly and accessible if you need to speak to him. ~ PK 7, 56-10-50, fax 56-29-18. MODERATE.

Club Bali Hai primarily has time-share units but they also rent to walk-in guests. Fronting a small beach, Club Bali Hai is a more intimate property than its sister property, the Bali Hai Moorea. Also located on Cook's Bay, the bungalows are surrounded by well-tended gardens and there is a dramatic view of Mt. Rotui. More than 39 rooms are available; they come in three configurations—over-the-water bungalows, garden bungalows and motel-like units (part of a large building). Even the most basic rooms (which go for less than US$100) have tiled floors, plenty of space, a small refrigerator, and large bathrooms. The garden bungalows each have small mezzanines that will sleep an extra person—a good deal for families. Kids are welcomed here. ~ PK 8.5; 56-13-68, fax 56-19-22, or 800-282-1401 in the U.S. MODERATE TO DELUXE.

Chez Albert is on the inland side of the road about eight kilometers from the airport, across from Club Bali Hai. Along with a terrific views of Mt. Rotui and Cook's Bay, it is one of the best, if not *the* best accommodation in the budget category. Nestled at the base of the mountains, it's a small, family-run affair with 18 clean (albeit sterile-looking) cabin-like units, equipped with kitchenettes and small balconies. All have hot water. Stores and restaurants and even a beach are within easy walking distance. The grounds at Chez Albert are very spacious and well manicured, and Albert's staff will give you *pamplemousse* (grapefruit) or other edibles that fall from the trees when available. The two-person units at Chez Albert are of higher quality than the other units—they include tiled floors, nice bathrooms with more than adequate kitchenettes but no ceiling fans. Perhaps you can ask management if portable fans are available. Guests must stay for a minimum of two nights to get the least expensive rates. ~ PK 8.5; phone/fax 56-12-76. BUDGET.

✔ CHECK THESE OUT—UNIQUE LODGING

- *Budget:* Get cozy at the foot of the mountains at **Chez Albert**, the top choice for those on a shoestring budget. *page 177*
- *Moderate to deluxe:* Revel in the Polynesian hospitality at **Village Faimano**, amid shady trees and ocean breezes. *page 178*
- *Moderate to deluxe:* Steal away at **Linareva**, where lovely thatched-roof *fares* provide all the seclusion you could ever want. *page 193*
- *Ultra-deluxe:* Check in to the posh, friendly **Beachcomber Parkroyal**, and swim in the manmade lagoon with its underwater coral garden. *page 184*

Budget: under $100 Moderate: $100–$150 Deluxe: $150–$200 Ultra-deluxe: over $200

The **MUST Lodging** is exclusively for divers using MUST. Located off a back road, it's not easy to find. It's a better idea to look for MUST's headquarters on the jetty near Cook's Bay Resort and have them take you there. Accommodations are in a simple, two-room home on a banana plantation. The house has one communal bathroom with hot water. Tariff includes three meals. ~ Call Philippe Molle for more information. Paopao Valley, 56-17-32, 56-15-83. BUDGET.

HIDDEN ▶

Perhaps the best example of a family-run lodging can be found midway between Paopao and Papetoai, at the top of the point between Cook's Bay and Opunohu Bay. **Village Faimano** has six airy, thatched-roof bungalows, each with kitchen facilities. The setting is very Polynesian and there is nothing presumptuous about Faimano, which makes it one of my favorite places to stay. There are lots of shady trees and fresh ocean breezes. The management is very laid back (what else would you expect?) and leaves you to your own devices. Another plus is the proximity to a white-sand beach/swimming area on the property. All of the units have private bath, some with hot water. Garden bungalows sleep three or four, while the larger units sleep four to six. No credit cards are accepted, so don't forget to bring cash and be prepared to pay one night's deposit for a reservation. No towels are provided. The proprietress, Hinano Feildel, offers discounts for longer stays. Activities include canoeing, snorkeling gear and fishing in the lagoon. ~ PK 14; 56-10-20, fax 56-36-47. MODERATE TO DELUXE.

Moorea Lagoon has a friendly, very local atmosphere. During the holiday periods and sometimes on weekends, much of the clientele is from Papeete, which says a lot about the property. The hotel has been completely renovated and there are 45 rooms and four bungalows, 12 acres of gardens, a pool, bicycles, a bar/restaurant and boutique. The units are spacious and well-appointed with polished wood floors. There is a full array of water sports and a fire-dancing show every Saturday night. ~ PK 14.5; 56-14-68, fax 56-26-25. MODERATE TO DELUXE.

Few yachts are anchored in Opunohu Bay. Robinson's Cove, three kilometers down the road, is the more popular anchorage. ~ PK 17.

Chez Nani is located about 50 yards from Hotel Moorea Lagoon. It has three thatched-roof bungalows with wide trap-door windows that let the breeze waft through. There's a kitchen and cold-water bath. The setup is similar to Village Faimano, though slightly less traditional. The beach area (shared with Village Faimano) is just a few steps from the bungalows and the gardens shaded by coconut palms are exquisite. You must provide your own towels. ~ PK 14; 56-19-99, 82-79-37, 82-90-19. MODERATE TO DELUXE.

Close by, **Chez Francine** is a single home with two bedrooms and private bath with hot water. Rooms are spacious and have woven bamboo walls—a nice touch. One room has a kitchenette.

Discounts are provided for long-term renters. The only problem with Chez Francine is its proximity to the main road, which makes things a bit noisy. ~ PK 14.5; 56-13-24. BUDGET TO MODERATE.

As on Tahiti, in the evenings be sure and check out the **roulottes** (restaurants on wheels) that park near the ferry stop in Vaiare, the wharf at Paopao at the head of Cook's Bay and at various other places on the island. The food at these mobile eateries is economically priced and generally quite good. The outdoor setting, on the waterfront beneath the stars, is wonderful. Expect to pay around 900 CFP (US$10) or less for a meal at a roulette. The average entrée at a restaurant will be 1400 to 1800 CFP (US$16 to US$20).

DINING

Mahogany, located next to Magasin Remy between the Temae Beach and the airport, is the first eatery you will pass driving along the north coast from the airport or the ferry terminal. It is a large wooden structure akin to an old roadhouse. Mahogany offers reasonably priced Polynesian dishes including poisson cru, sandwiches and steak and *pommes frites*. The atmosphere is local, as is most of the clientele. It's the only restaurant I've been to on the island that offers fresh fruit. ~ PK 4.3; 56-39-73. BUDGET.

Just west of the Bali Hai is a shopping center where you will find **Patisserie Sylesie**, a small café in an outdoor setting that serves Continental and American-style breakfasts. It has good pastries, ice cream, coffee and croissants, as well as more substantial fare such as pizza, crêpes and even hamburgers. If you are staying at the nearby Bali Hai or Cook's Bay Hotel, it's a good place to pop in for breakfast. ~ PK 4.5; 56-15-88. BUDGET.

Le Pêcheur or "The Fisherman" is a small roadside restaurant with indoor/outdoor seating and an attractive awning. On the menu you will find *poisson cru*, mahimahi, mussels, curried shrimp, marinated tuna with fresh veggies and coconut milk and non-seafood items such as pepper steak and escargot. There is also a selection of salads and soups. It's as good an inexpensive eatery as you'll find on the island. ~ PK 6.2; 56-36-12. BUDGET TO MODERATE.

Also in Cook's Bay, **Le Cocotier** is another good, inexpensive restaurant. The food is tasty and moderately priced by Tahitian standards. With about six small tables, the atmosphere is intimate. Fare includes *poisson cru*, sashimi, mahimahi and marinated tuna slices. Cocotier does a lively lunch trade and one can have a steak and *pommes frites*, cheese platter, a few glasses of wine and a coffee for the equivalent US$25 per person. Originally a private home, the restaurant is one of the more friendly establishments on the island. ~ Maharepa; 56-12-10. BUDGET TO MODERATE.

At the Cook's Bay Resort Hotel, **Cook's Pizza** is very popular with both visitors and locals. The seafood special is a favorite and features mussels, shrimp, calamari and olives. Spaghetti and other pasta are also available. One of the best things about the restaurant is its waterfront setting that overlooks Cook's Bay and Mt. Rotui. Service is rather slow, but there's always the view to keep you occupied. ~ PK 7; 56-10-50. BUDGET TO MODERATE.

La Crêperie, owned by a young Parisian couple, is an indoor/outdoor restaurant with a spacious dining area on the balcony. Breakfast is available from 8 to 10 a.m. and a full complement of crêpes —jam, ice cream, sugar, chestnut cream, hazelnut cream and whipped cream—is offered. Savory *crêpes salée* include fried eggs, bacon and eggs, omelettes, ham and cheese and chicken/curry rice. *Cidre Brut*—partially fermented (dry) apple cider served in an ice-cold champagne bottle is traditionally consumed with *crêpes salée*. ~ Paopao; 56-12-06. BUDGET.

Alfredo's is a large, whitewashed, colonial-style building with green trim located just west of Club Bali Hai in Paopao. It has indoor/outdoor dining on a balcony with a view of the many yachts moored in Cook's Bay and a mango tree in the front yard. On the menu are a wide variety of salads and appetizers such as carpaccio, sushi and stuffed mussels. The specialties of the house are filet of tuna tartar, grilled fresh tuna in mustard sauce, mahimahi sautéed with lemon and shrimp curry with coconut milk. Items such as steak, pizza and pasta are also available. Unlike most restaurants on the island, Alfredo's has a full bar. Most everything I've heard about this establishment has been positive. ~ Paopao; 56-36-43. BUDGET TO MODERATE.

Club Bali Hai serves a breakfast buffet with coffee, baguettes, juices and fruit, as well as a regular breakfast menu. I'm told they have the best hot dog in the world, served for lunch at the outdoor bar. The *poisson cru* is tasty and reasonably priced. ~ PK 8.5; 56-13-68, fax 56-19-22. BUDGET TO MODERATE.

HIDDEN ▶   Don't let the modest trappings of **Te Honu-Iti**, which means small turtle in Tahitian, mislead you into thinking this is another

✔ CHECK THESE OUT—UNIQUE DINING

- *Budget:* Join local diners at **Mahogany**, a wooden eatery reminiscent of an old roadhouse, where tasty Polynesian dishes are served up. *page 179*
- *Budget to moderate:* Dine on some of Polynesia's best pizza at **Le Sunset Restaurant Pizzeria** while enjoying the view of the lagoon. *page 189*
- *Moderate to deluxe:* Feast on seafood as you waft the evening away on **Le Bateau**, the only floating restaurant on Moorea. *page 194*
- *Ultra-deluxe:* Stop by for the sumptuous brunch or extravagant buffet at **Beachcomber Parkroyal**, where the setting parallels the cuisine. *page 189*

Budget: under $12 Moderate: $12–$20 Deluxe: $20–$30 Ultra-deluxe: over $30

greasy spoon. This cozy, unassuming seafront restaurant is owned by a gourmet chef and locals reckon that it is one of the best French/seafood restaurants on the island. Dishes include grilled mahimahi, shrimp curry and *fruit de mer*. Besides seafood, chicken and steak are also on the menu. Entrées range from 1200 CFP to 1600 CFP (US$14 to US$18). In addition to scrumptious food, there are outdoor tables and a nice waterfront view of Cook's Bay. ~ Paopao; 56-19-84. MODERATE TO DELUXE.

Near Te Honu-Iti is **Snack Rotui**. With the usual array of French bread sandwiches and soft drinks, it's little more than a few stools surrounding a fast food–style service counter. Snack Rotui is a good place to sit and meditate on the view of Cook's Bay. ~ Paopao. BUDGET.

Starting from the direction of the airport and heading west, you will find **Magasin Remy** at PK 4.5 ~ 56-32-27, **Libre Service Maharepa** at PK 5.8 ~ 56-35-90, and **Magasin Lee Hen Soi Louk** in Paopao ~ 56-15-02. Paopao Village also has a small open-air public market, selling mostly produce, which is best visited early in the day.

GROCERIES

An art gallery at the **Hotel Sofitel Ia Ora** has a fairly good selection of carvings and paintings from local artists. ~ PK 1; 56-17-61.

SHOPPING

In Maharepa, the shopping possibilities include **Maison Blanc**, a renovated turn-of-the-century plantation house that is now a souvenir shop. They stock quality jewelry, pareus and other souvenirs. It's located directly across the road from the Bali Hai Hotel. ~ PK 5.5. Maharepa; 56-13-59. The **Golden Nugget Art Gallery** has paintings by A. J. Kerebel for sale. ~ Maharepa; 56-38-22.

In Paopao, **Galerie Baie de Cook** have a variety of paintings, pottery and carvings from local artists. ~ 56-25-67.

Galerie Van Der Heyde has been on the island for years and has a selection of paintings and primitive art. They also have museum artifacts on display. ~ PK 7; 56-14-22.

If you're looking for jewelry, consider visiting Ron Hall's **Island Fashions** near Cook's Bay. Hall came to Tahiti on a yacht 20 years ago with none other than actor Peter Fonda and never looked back. ~ PK 6.9; 56-11-06.

The **Moorea Aquarium**, despite its name, is really a jewelry store next to a building with 40 fish tanks. The store is run by Teva, a long-time resident and well-known jeweler specializing in black pearls. Teva (one of those people who uses one name) is a large, blond-haired *demi* (part Tahitian) whose countenance always seems to bear a look of indifference. Admission. ~ Paopao; 56-24-00.

On Moorea it's best either to not expect too much nightlife or, better yet, bring your own. The **Bali Hai** has a quite popular Wednesday night island dance show and buffet. ~ PK 5; 56-13-59.

NIGHTLIFE

The **Cook's Bay Resort** also has regular island-night dance shows featuring the lively *tamure* on Tuesday, Thursday and Saturday. ~ PK 7, Maharepa; 56-10-50. Meanwhile, **Club Bali Hai** has happy hour twice weekly. It's probably the best place on the island to meet locals (especially Americans who live on Moorea) and watch the sunset. ~ PK 8.5; 56-13-68.

BEACHES & PARKS

Beaches are all public property in French Polynesia, but getting to the beach may entail passing through a residence or hotel property. Fortunately, most of the hotels along the north coast do not mind you walking through their grounds.

TEMAE BEACH There are numerous small beaches along the northern coast of Moorea but Temae is clearly the longest and the best. This white-sand beach begins near the Hotel Sofitel Ia Ora and stretches about a mile north to the airport. The water is clear and calm, which makes it popular for swimming and snorkeling. Unlike other beaches, it's easy to wade into deeper water without stepping on rocks or coral. The only downside here is the occasional sea urchin in the shallow areas. These are creatures you don't want to step on. If in doubt, watch where the locals swim so as to avoid these spiny animals. There are plenty of coconut palms and shade trees, which makes it popular with picnickers. Locals often go topless so it's a good place for visitors to do likewise if they are so inclined. The beach tends to be crowded on weekends and, on occasion, (especially during holiday weekends) strewn with trash. Toilets, shower facilities. Though you could enter from the Sofitel Ia Ora, the public access at the northern end of the beach is better. ~ To find this, look for the *Plage* (beach) sign just south of the airport. Take the rutted dirt road about one kilometer to the water and park in the small lot on your left. The shower and toilet areas will be on your right-hand side.

Keep an eye out for sea urchins at Temae Beach! Their spines are hard to remove from your feet!

VILLAGE FAIMANO/MOOREA LAGOON BEACH Village Faimano, Moorea Lagoon Hotel and several other pensions share this thin strip of white-sand beach located at the very center of the north coast between Cook's and Opunohu bays. Shaded by trees and off the beaten track, this tranquil stretch of sand about half a mile in length is not generally visited by tourists. Swimming is excellent, it's easy to wade out without stepping on coral or rocks, and the water is deep. The facilities there belong to the hotels. If you are going to use the toilets or showers, you should ask permission. There is a restaurant/bar at the Hotel Moorea Lagoon. Some of the best snorkeling on Moorea is just offshore. ~ Take the coast road to PK 14.5 between Cook's and Opunohu Bay. Look for the sign denoting the Moorea Lagoon Hotel and park in the lot.

This section of the north coast road runs about nine kilometers from Papetoia Village at PK 22 to the Hauru Point area at PK 31.

▼▼▼▼▼▼▼▼▼▼▼▼▼▼▼▼▼▼▼

Papetoai to Hauru Point

Here you'll find a high concentration of hotels, restaurants, shops and other attractions. Among the more well-known properties in this area are the huge Club Med complex and Beachcomber Parkroyal. In addition to the high-end accommodations, backpackers will be happy to know that some of the best campgrounds in French Polynesia are located on this short length of coastline.

Papetoai Village was the seat of the Pomare I government and the scene of his conversion to Christianity. An **octagonal church** built by the London Missionary Society in 1822 (and reconstructed on several occasions) still stands and is the oldest European building in use in the South Pacific. In 1811, years before Moorea's importance as a vanilla-growing region was established, the island was the London Missionary Society's center for evangelical work for the entire Pacific. The church is built on the site of a former Polynesian shrine, but all that remains of the Polynesian temple is a slim monolith outside the octagonal church. Tall and austere, the church faces the lagoon and is surrounded by a thick, whitewashed concrete wall. The black gate entrance is only ceremonial—if you want a closer look, it's easy to hop the retaining wall. Each side of the sanctuary has three large stained-glass windows. Behind the church is a cemetery and a solar energy panel. In front of the church is a large breadfruit tree and a detached bell tower resembling a fireman's ladder. (A century-late afterthought?) To find this edifice, look for the post office (the sign that says *Poste*) on the ocean side and turn inland about 100 yards (90 meters). ~ PK 22.

Hauru Village is the focal point of Moorea's hotel properties, including the huge Club Méditeranée and the Moorea Beachcomber Parkroyal Hotel. Another noticeable landmark on the strip is Le Petit Village, which bills itself as "The Biggest Colonial-Style Shopping Center in Moorea." Quite a claim. It's a collection of shops, boutiques and restaurants catering to the numerous hotels in the area. (Note that there are several public phone booths in the shopping center, which are handy for international calls).

An excellent place to garner information on any activities on the island is the **Moorea Tourist Bureau**, which is located in a kiosk at Le Petit Village. Hours are 9 a.m. to 6 p.m. daily, except Sundays and holidays. They have a collection of brochures and a very helpful staff. At most hotels you can obtain a one-page map/brochure of Moorea that also provides useful numbers of hotels, banks, ferries, and other essentials on the back. There is also a tourist desk at the airport that is open 6 a.m. to 11 a.m. daily except Thursday and Sunday. Tours can be booked from this office, and chances are

SIGHTS

the advice you will receive will be accurate. (Hostesses from the tourist board also distribute maps and brochures down at the dock at Vaiare every morning at 9:30 a.m. except Sunday.) ~ PK 28; 56-29-09, 56-26-48.

Hauru marks the beginning of a three-mile stretch of sandy beach although finding your way to the *plage* is not always easy.

Varari is where the once *sauvage* side of Moorea emerges, with fewer people and a taste of what life is like on the outer islands of French Polynesia. Until just a few years ago, the paved surface ended on the main road. There are scattered copra plantations and the feeling is more rural. Driving on the road you may see locals on bicycles returning from the market cradling a fresh baguette, or along the shore at low tide, women on the reef searching for shellfish. ~ PK 28.

Varari is also the site of **Marae Nuurau**, a Polynesian temple used by the Marana royal family from which the Pomare dynasty originated. The *marae* is in a coconut grove at the mouth of a small creek and covers several acres. The surrounding walls of the temple and the *ahu* or central platform are made of coral. Much of the structure is intact, but restoration is needed.

A giant Polynesian figure standing like a guardian at the entrance to **Tiki Village** (a quasi-amusement park that purports to be a replica of a pre-European–contact Tahitian village). In actuality, Tiki Village is the home of a very accomplished dance troupe, which performs four times a week. This dance troupe has a dramatic, show-biz flair that differentiates them from other performers and are worth the price of admission. (Recently Dustin Hoffman and his wife "re-married" at Tiki Village in a traditional Polynesian ceremony that is part of the troupe's repertoire.) You can also get a tattoo at Tiki Village from the resident artist if you are so inclined. There is a beach on the premises, though not particularly good for swimming. Admission. ~ PK 31; 56-10-86, fax 43-20-06.

LODGING   For backpackers, some of the best camping and low-budget lodgings can be found in the Hauru Village area of Moorea. Camping prices are subject to change more than other types of accommodation because of the occasional price wars that break out between the owners of the two rival campgrounds. In addition to budget lodging there is a fine selection of mid-range and upscale properties in this area.

The newest and most luxurious hotel on Moorea is the 150-room **Beachcomber Parkroyal**. Originally a deserted, swampy backwater, after 16 months of dredging and bulldozing the site became a sort of ecological purgatory—scoured of plants on the surface and dead below the sea. To remedy things, sand was brought in from

Offshore from Hauru are Motu Tiahura and Motu Fareone, two islets that offer good snorkeling. (Note that all the hotels in the area have snorkeling trips to the *motus*.)

elsewhere to create a beach where there had been none. In the nearly dead lagoon, live coral was transplanted from an underwater nursery where it was incubated for 18 months. On the scarred face of the land, shrubs and coconut palms were planted. Shortly, like a fairy tale, life took root above and below the lagoon. Today, all the shrubs have filled in the once-desolate surface, and the grounds are superbly maintained. As a result, the Parkroyal management received a special PATA (Pacific Asia Travel Association) environmental excellence award for its good deeds. Swimming in the manmade lagoon is very good. The reception area is covered by a huge thatched-roof canopy. The exterior of the reception area and bungalows are painted in warm earth tones. The bungalows, which also have thatched roofs, are airy and posh, and the interiors are painted in bright colors such as turquoise. The bathrooms are large and well appointed. From all reports, the food is excellent, the staff is friendly, and I've heard nothing but praise for the service. In this instance, you get what you pay for. ~ PK 24, Haapiti; 56-19-19, fax 56-18-88, or 800-835-7742 in the U.S. ULTRA-DELUXE.

Unarguably the top mid-range hotel on the island is **Les Tipaniers**, near Club Med. Shaded by a number of trees, there are 21 *fares* on a wide grassy area facing the lagoon. Some are brown with gingerbread trim, others have thatched roofs with woven bamboo walls. Many are equipped with kitchenettes that include refrigerators and four-burner stoves. Rooms are smallish, but units are modern and well appointed with tile floors, overhead fan, spacious bathrooms and phones. In addition to the restaurant (a fixture on the island for years), a new Tahitian-style thatched-roof eatery has been built on the property (next to the lagoon) that serves breakfast and lunch. The Scubapiti dive center is located on the hotel grounds, as are a full array of other nautical activities. (Tipaniers also has an annex, about four kilometers east of the main hotel, consisting of five self-contained thatched-roof bungalows on the water.) All things considered, Les Tipaniers is a terrific value for the price. ~ PK 25; 56-12-67, fax 56-29-25, or 800-521-7242 in the U.S. MODERATE TO DELUXE.

Moorea Beach Club is a 40-room, 46-bungalow lodging on the beach. It has modest bungalow-style accommodations, as well as a two-story row of units that are spartan, tacky and overpriced. Amenities include a restaurant, bar, windsurfing, snorkeling, a swimming pool and tennis. There are better, less expensive properties than Moorea Beach Club. ~ PK 25.5; 56-15-48, fax 41-09-28. DELUXE.

The **Hibiscus** has 29 thatched-roof bungalows, packed rather closely together in a grassy, well-manicured garden. About half of the units have kitchenettes. The bungalows are on the small side, but all come equipped with private bath and hot water. During my last visit, management was in the process of renovating the place, which seemed a bit drab, but as the French would say, *correct* (which roughly translates as "OK but nothing special"). The property has a restaurant, snack bar, pool and beach. On the grounds of the hotel is Le Sunset Pizzeria, which has a outstanding outdoor setting and fine food. (Tariffs rise during holidays.) ~ PK 27; 56-12-20, fax 56-20-69. MODERATE.

Nelson and Josianne sits on a broad swath of land, shaded by coconut trees and fringed by a thin strand of white-sand beach. One of two places on the island to camp, the facilities are clean and well appointed, including a new and very much improved cooking/dining area. Covered by a thatched roof, the cooking/dining area is large, airy, clean, and has eight picnic tables, two refrigerators, two sets of burners and two sinks that can accommodate the large number of backpackers staying here. The common bathing area/toilets were clean, but there have been complaints that there aren't enough of these facilities for the guests. There is also a new snack bar in a structure near the water. Travelers can set up their tents, or stay in one of the barracks-like dorms or several spartan bungalows. There are also three first-rate bungalows with two bedrooms (a hundred yards along the road from the campsite), with kitchenette and private bath with hot water. On weekends, the better units are generally occupied by local tourists from Papeete. There are free boats every day to the nearby *motu* for snorkeling, a service to the guests. Josianne, the proprietress, can sometimes be short-tempered but is generally civil. There is a two-day minimum stay in any of the accommodations. ~ PK 27; 56-15-18. BUDGET TO MODERATE.

Moorea Camping, located about a half-kilometer west of Nelson and Josianne, is also on the beach. The facilities at this campground/budget lodging are quite respectable. The shower and baths were the cleanest I've seen in any campground in the islands. The cooking facilities are clean and adequate, but not in the same league as the other campground. The cooking area is practically on the water and has picnic tables that face the sea. Lights at the communal area go off at 10 p.m. sharp. Although Moorea Camping is half the size of Nelson and Josianne, there is still room for 30 tents. The large, clean dorm unit has six small rooms, each with four bunks. There are several other thatched-roof bungalows with a variety of sleeping configurations. These larger units are clean, well ventilated and some come with small refrigerators. The dorm rooms are small, rather cramped, and stuffy. Snorkeling trips to the *motu* across from Club Med are offered. Another activity to consider while staying here is the shark-feeding tour, which is operated by the campground management and is reputed to be the best on the island. ~ PK 27.5; 56-14-47. BUDGET TO MODERATE.

Just down the road from Moorea Camping is **Moorea Village**, also known as *Fare Gendron*. Facing a fine white-sand beach, Moorea Village has 50 very basic Tahitian-style bungalows (15 with kitchenettes), bar, restaurant, tennis and volleyball facilities. There is also a large swimming pool on the premises. The self-contained bungalows represent good value, especially for families. All bungalows have been redecorated and a new refrigerator and extra cots have been added to each unit. Fairly large in scale compared with other properties on the island, the grounds are clean and well tended. Avoid the *fares* near the road as they tend be noisy. The noise from the disco at nearby Club Med on the weekends also can be bothersome. ~ PK 27.8; 56-10-02, fax 56-22-11. MODERATE TO DELUXE.

If you come looking for Billy, owner of **Chez Billy Ruta**, chances are you will find him underneath the chassis of a truck or some other vehicle. A genial guy, he is not only a full-time mechanic, but a tour guide, dance impresario and hotelier. Billy's 12 A-frame–style bungalows are on the water but are small, spartan and unappealing—perhaps taking a back seat to the vehicles, tours and dance shows that occupy much of his time. Accommodations are adequate but overpriced. ~ PK 28; 56-12-54. BUDGET TO MODERATE.

The **Club Med Moorea** is a focal point for the young, the hip, and, possibly, the restless. It's not everybody's cup of tea, but it fulfills a need for people who like to choose from readily available activities—and activity is what Club Med is all about. The organization has expanded its demographic base to include families as well as its traditional singles market. As in all Club Meds, there are enough planned activities for a lifetime. In Moorea, in addition to the usual diversions, there are more tours available than on any other property. For example, there are boat/snorkeling trips to the

HOME VISITS

Some of the best values on the island are in the guesthouse category. These are run by entrepreneurial islanders who rent out rooms or homes, often with self-contained kitchen facilities. Neither hotels nor pensions, the great advantage of these properties is privacy. They are generally less expensive than hotels, but don't confuse less expensive with cheap. The style of accommodations range from comfortable to spartan. For visitors who like the feel of staying in someone's home rather than being another anonymous guest in a hotel, this might be the ticket. Many guesthouses require minimum stays of several days. They almost always provide bed linen, but no towels. It's advisable to check out a property personally before you plunk down your bags.

lagoons and the usual circle-island tours, scuba lessons, day trips to Tahiti, and deep-sea fishing. It also is the only spot on the island with regular entertainment. Accommodations here are average and somewhat tired. Dining facilities are enormous and reminiscent of a college-dorm cafeteria. Food is generally acceptable—never bad, but not particularly scintillating. The tariff includes three meals per day, all the wine and beer you wish to consume and a number of activities. Club Med Moorea is the larger of the two French Polynesian Club Meds (the other is on Bora Bora) and has a capacity of 700 people. Club Med Moorea is also much less expensive than its counterpart on Bora Bora. ~ PK 28, Hauru Point; 56-13-68, or 800-824-4844 in the U.S. DELUXE.

On the water with plenty of beach front, **Fare Matotea** has spacious, well-manicured grounds. There are eight thatched-roof bungalows with kitchen and bath with hot water. Rooms are large and well maintained—some sleep up to six. The management is pleasant enough, but sometimes seem indifferent to the needs of guests. Renting a bungalow at Matotea would be good for a family or a group of friends, but it's almost mandatory to speak French if you want to communicate with the owners. Two nights is the minimum stay required and credit cards are not accepted. Canoes are free of charge for guests. ~ PK 28.7; 56-14-36. MODERATE TO DELUXE.

Jeanne Salmon's **Fare Manuia**, located on Hauru Point, has six well-appointed and maintained thatched-roof bungalows in a wide grassy area near a fine beach. All are self-contained, with kitchens and private bath with hot water. Fare Manuia is a good bet for families or couples. There is plenty of room for families in the units, a grassy area for kids to play and a beach nearby. Extra mattresses are available. The minimum stay is two nights, you must provide your own towels, and no credit cards are accepted. A *pirogue* (canoe) is available free of charge and a three-person jet-ski can be rented on the premises. Ms. Salmon speaks excellent English. ~ PK 30; 56-26-17. MODERATE TO DELUXE.

Tahiti Village Polynesian Bungalows, which is directly across from the Tahiti Village theme park, is one of the newer places on the Moorea scene. Squeezed rather closely together over an expanse of grass are ten thatched-roof bungalows of various configurations. The units appear to be well constructed, with tile floors, overhead fans, modern kitchenettes and small bathrooms (with hot water). There is a double bed downstairs and mezzanine sleeping area above. You'll find Polynesian Bungalows modern (if a bit claustrophobic) and, given the competition, overpriced, especially if you are sleeping five or more. Beach access is only 100 yards away. There are mountain-bike rentals. ~ PK 31; 56-30-20, 56-30-77, fax 56-32-15. MODERATE TO DELUXE.

Overlooking the sea, the restaurant at the **Beachcomber Parkroyal**
is noted for its brunches and buffets. The tables are overloaded
with fresh fruit, fish, cold cuts and desserts. The dinner menu is
eclectic and has a large variety of meat and poultry, as well as
seafood dishes—the chef's specialty. The hotel's style is simple yet
elegant. Cuisine here is very good, considering that it is "hotel
fare," but it is generally more expensive than you'd pay in a good
local restaurant. ~ PK 27; 56-19-19. ULTRA-DELUXE.

DINING

Les Tipaniers, near Club Med, is a local institution serving
French, Italian and Tahitian specialties, including pizza. Their reputation for good food, especially the Italian cuisine, is well de-
served. There are actually two restaurants on the property—the
original building near the main road and a new thatched-roof bungalow with an open-air dining room facing the lagoon. The new
restaurant serves breakfast, lunch and evening drinks. The cuisine
is lighter and somewhat less expensive than the other, older restaurant. Continental, Tahitian and American breakfast is served, and
for lunch there are a large variety of salads, burgers, sandwiches,
poisson cru and lasagna. The prices don't range beyond 1650 CFP,
about US$18. BUDGET TO MODERATE.

◄ HIDDEN

The older restaurant is *gastronomique* and has a larger menu.
A large selection of salads are available as well as sashimi, tuna
tartare, fish soup, pizza, pasta, mahimahi with vanilla sauce and
broiled tuna. Try the duck, or, if you are a meat lover, the lamb sir-
loin with goat cheese is a favorite. ~ PK 25; 56-12-67. MODERATE
TO DELUXE.

Attached to Magasin Réne (a grocery store) in between the
campgrounds, is **Snack Michel**, an inexpensive café with hamburgers and other basic fare in the budget range. ~ Haapiti. BUDGET.

Almost next door is **Rest Stop**, a tiny establishment serving
snacks, salads, pizza and juice. It's a pleasant, shaded stand with
several tables. ~ Haapiti. BUDGET.

Le Sylesie II patisserie, adjacent to the Carol Boutique (near the
Hibiscus Hotel), is a good place for a coffee, cold drink or ice
cream or for breakfast and other light meals. ~ Haapiti; 56-20-45.
BUDGET.

The open-air **Le Sunset Restaurant Pizzeria** resides on the
grounds of the Hotel Hibiscus. Covered by a pavilion, it's a pleasant, breezy place, providing a terrific vista of the lagoon. In particular, the pizzas are worth trying. Salads, desserts, wine and espresso are also served. ~ PK 27; 56-26-00. BUDGET TO MODERATE.

◄ HIDDEN

Across the road, at Le Petit Village shopping center, is the
Chinese Café Restaurant, a small, attractive open-air restaurant
overlooking a garden. They serve stir-fry dishes, including mahimahi with a delicious black-bean sauce, chicken, duck and beef

with vegetables. Prices do not range past the 1500 CFP (US$17) level for entrées. Sashimi, *poisson cru* and an array of local fresh fruit are also available. ~ PK 28; 56-39-41. BUDGET TO MODERATE.

With a fine reputation for simple, reasonably priced cuisine, **Tropical Iceberg** serves light, healthy dishes. Located at Le Petit Village in a large white structure with an open-air deck, the house specialty is Italian fare (including wonderful pizza). There is also a fine selection of seafood such as tuna and mahimahi, as well as a wide array of salads and desserts. It's a good place to stop on a hot afternoon for an ice cream or a light snack. ~ PK 28; 56-29-53. BUDGET TO MODERATE.

GROCERIES   **Keck Alexandre** has a general selection of groceries and canned goods. ~ Papetoai; 56-10-03. **Magasin Ami Réne** is a small store near the two Hauru Point campgrounds, which makes it convenient for backpackers. ~ PK 21, Papetoia; 56-12-56. There is also a grocery store in the **Le Petit Village Shopping Center**, opposite the Club Med, that is small and overpriced, but conveniently located near the hotels. ~ PK 28.

SHOPPING   **Woody Sculpture**, just before the Hauru Point enclave, has wood carvings of bowls and abstract creations from artists on the island. ~ PK 24; 56-17-73. The art selection at **Gallery Api**, next to Club Med, is tasteful and includes a fine array of carvings, sculptures and paintings. ~ PK 28; 56-13-57. **Galerie d'Art**, across from Club Med, features stone sculptures as well as works done in wood and on canvas by Guy Tihoti, a Tahitian artist. ~ PK 28; 56-30-30.

NIGHTLIFE   For a sunset or after-dinner drink, the new bar/restaurant on the lagoon at **Les Tipaniers** offers pleasant surroundings and a remarkable view. ~ PK 25; 56-12-67. At **Club Med**, there's nightly entertainment and a cabaret on the weekends, but you must register with security before entering the property. ~ PK 28; 56-15-00.

Tiki Village on the west side of the island has dance performances on Tuesday, Thursday, Friday and Saturday evenings at 6 p.m. For those desiring a special moment, Tiki Village will arrange feasts for your wedding, anniversary or honeymoon. ~ PK 31; 56-10-86, 56-18-97.

BEACHES & PARKS   The hotel strip that runs from Les Tipaniers at PK 25 all the way down to Tiki Village at PK 30 sits on one almost continuous stretch of sand. (That's why the hotels were built there!) The only issue is beach access. There is no public easement or road to any of the beaches. One must either pass through a private residence (not a good idea) or through a private road running through a hotel property. My advice is to do the latter. Once at a beach adjacent to a

The Tale
of Bali Hai

It is impossible to write about tourism on Moorea without mentioning the Bali Hai Boys: Jay Carlisle, Muk McCallum and Hugh Kelley. After arriving in Moorea in 1961, the three invested in a rundown vanilla plantation and inadvertently became owners of a ramshackle hotel. Their timing was impeccable. Airlines were just beginning to land in Tahiti and, when a journalist discovered their dumpy but charming hotel, success was just around the next coconut tree. Since then, the "boys" have established hotels on Raiatea and Huahine (the latter has since closed) and turned the original plantation into a successful experimental farm and egg-laying facility. The Bali Hai Boys are known to be free-spending good-timers who have left their mark on the island in many ways.

Lumbering Hugh Kelley is fond of telling the story of the return of Moorea's missing tikis. The two stone reliefs were in an ancient religious shrine on the vanilla plantation and were left undisturbed by the three Americans. A week after Kelley showed them to a wealthy Honolulu businessman, the tikis disappeared. Kelley denied rumors that he had sold the priceless artifacts and vowed to get them back somehow. Several years passed with no trace of the relics, until an American woman approached Kelley with some startling news. She had seen the tikis at the Honolulu home of the same businessman who was the last person to see them in Moorea. Apparently this man was an avid collector of Polynesian artifacts.

Kelley decided to take the matter into his own hands and flew to Honolulu to question the teenage son of the businessman about the tikis. The son insisted he knew nothing until Kelley blurted out a heart-rending tale of a dying Tahitian woman who supposedly owned the tikis. With mock anguish, Kelley claimed the woman was shivering on her deathbed because she thought the tikis were in a cold place. The boy broke down and assured Kelley the tikis were in a warm place—on the balcony of his father's apartment. That was all the wily Kelley had to know. He confronted the businessman and threatened to spread the word to the Honolulu papers if the man didn't return the tikis. Faced with an embarrassing situation, the businessman consented. Several months later, amid pomp, press coverage from Tahiti and Hawaii, and incantations by Moorea's *tahua* (shaman), the sacred tikis were returned to the island. (One of the tikis can now be found at the Kellum Stop in Moorea. If you take the tour, ask Marimari to show it to you.)

hotel, please respect the fact that the amenities belong to the hotel and are not for the general public. Ask permission to use the facilities (toilet, changing room, etc.) if you need to do so. Most likely your requests will be granted.

BEACHCOMBER PARKROYAL Located opposite the hotel grounds, this is actually an "artificial" beach. All that white sand was brought in and a beach was created where none existed before. Artificial or not, the swimming is excellent. Unlike most of the lagoon beaches, the swimming area is deep (having been dredged out during the construction of the hotel). All the amenities that you would expect of a luxury hotel can be found at this superb strand—a first-class restaurant, bar and a full array of nautical activities. Some of the activities are for guests only, whereas others, such as diving or parasailing, are open to visitors. Coming from the direction of the airport, go two kilometers past Papetoai Village and look for the Beachcomber Parkroyal sign on the road and pull in the parking lot.

MOOREA BEACH CLUB The Moorea Beach Club is not my favorite hotel on the island but the beach is generally underutilized and very clean. There is a nice stretch of white sand here along with some shade trees. A restaurant and toilets are available. ~ Look for the sign on the road at PK 25.5 and pull into the lot.

▼▼▼▼▼▼▼▼▼▼▼▼▼▼
Haapiti to Afareaitu

The 12-mile length of road from Haapiti to the Ferry Terminal at Vaiare is sparsely populated and was the last section of the coastal road to be paved. If you are going to experience the "real" Moorea anywhere, it's going to be here, where the traffic is less frequent, the pace is slower and the landscape is less shaped by commercial interests.

SIGHTS

Haapiti Village is one of the villages least influenced by tourism or commercial interests on the island. There are approximately 1000 people living in the vicinity of the village—a collection of humble wooden homes dispersed along the side of the road. Many of the homes are surrounded by neatly trimmed hibiscus hedges that enclose front yards brimming with flowers. Haapiti boasts a soccer field, a Chinese store and two churches. The small gray-trimmed church in the center of the village is dwarfed by the huge, twin-towered Eglise de la Sainte Famille on the south side. The latter was formerly the center of the island's Catholic mission. ~ PK 24.

Along the roadside at **Atiha Bay**, one sees *pirogues* (canoes) set on blocks beneath the shade of ironwood trees. Fishing nets hang from poles. This bay has a double reef and sometimes young boys can be seen surfing from the inner reef on homemade plywood boards. One gets the reassuring feeling that traditional life for the

Polynesian goes undisturbed in this nook of the island. A glance across the lagoon reveals a fine view of Tahiti. ~ PK 20.

Another six kilometers down the road is **Maatea Village**. Perhaps because of its rural setting, Maatea is a close-knit, friendly village with charming homes draped in flowers. To catch a glimpse of island life in one of the few traditional communities left on the island, turn inland from the coastal road at the center of the village. Meander down the shaded dirt road and soon you'll be in the Toto Valley. Among the breadfruit and mango trees you'll see modest homes and people going about their daily tasks— raking leaves, gathering fruit or perhaps hanging the wash. At the entrance of Maatea is a Chinese store, a school and one of the few movie houses on the island.

> Adjacent to Marae Umarea is a lovely coral garden ideal for snorkeling.

Maatea is the site of **Marae Nuupere**, an ancient Polynesian temple that is on private land but is accessible from the beach. The shrine is on a small coral hillock constructed on the shore. ~ PK 14.

Continuing along the road you will reach **Afareaitu Village**. This is Moorea's administrative center. A tranquil village nestled along the coastal road, it has the typical jumble of small grocery stores, a few churches, and a long yellow barrack-like hospital. Like the other Moorean communities of Papetoai, Haapiti and Maharepa, Afareaitu Village was built around ancient temples and chiefs' dwellings. ~ PK 10.

Chez Pauline, a family-style guesthouse, is worth stopping at. They have a wonderful collection of prehistoric stone tikis, no doubt imbued with ample *mana* (spirit). There are also other artifacts such as adzes and grinding stones and several wooden relics. All have been collected from around the village. ~ PK 9; 56-11-26.

Down the road toward Maatea you'll come upon **Marae Umarea**, the oldest (900 A.D.) in Moorea. At the other end of Afareaitu, at PK 9, is an unpaved track leading to a waterfall (see the Afareaitu Waterfall Hike in "Hiking" later in this chapter).

The village of Haapiti is just beyond PK 35 where the road markers recommence and start counting down in the opposite direction. Just before the village is **Linareva**, one of the most impressive lodgings in all of French Polynesia. The grounds are immaculate and the classic, thatched-roof *fares* are truly elegant. Each one has a kitchenette (with a full complement of utensils), rattan furnishings, polished wooden floors and TVs. Linareva provides seclusion attractive to those seeking privacy. There are 12 units ranging from garden and ocean-shore bungalows to a large villa that sleeps up to seven. Occupants may use the canoes, bicycles, masks/snorkels, barbecue and raft free of charge. One of Moorea's finest restaurants is found here as well. Linareva offers first-class quality at a reason-

LODGING

◄ HIDDEN

able price—a rarity in French Polynesia. ~ PK 35; 56-15-35, fax 56-25-25. MODERATE TO DELUXE.

One of the few accommodations on the south coast of Moorea, **Chez Pauline** is about eight kilometers south of the airport. A quaint, colonial-style home surrounded by lush vegetation, it is the oldest family-run lodging on the island. Rooms are of average size and quality, but very clean. Chez Pauline could use some renovation, but despite this, it is still one of the few places on the island where you can get an authentic local ambience and a home-cooked meal. Nonguests can also dine at Chez Pauline if they make a reservation. ~ PK 9; 56-11-26. BUDGET TO MODERATE.

Fare Manu is just north of Afareaitu, about four kilometers from the ferry dock at Vaiare. Best described as neo-Polynesian, it is built like a traditional *fare* with no walls, constructed almost completely from local materials such as ironwood, coconut wood and *pandanus*-thatch. In a charming way, Fare Manu is reminiscent of a tree house, utilizing sturdy ironwood limbs to support a roof and upper story (for sleeping). There are no right angles except a V-shaped, pitched roof. The floor is concrete, embedded with seashells and paved with ironwood flagstones. The unit is self-contained, with a shower/bath separate from the main building, and there are two rooms that sleep up to six. Located near shops, just a few yards from the shore, directly opposite a *motu*, Fare Manu is surrounded by a fragrant garden of *Tiare Tahiti* flowers. This place has a special, funky, Bohemian feel about it that appeals to grownups and kids alike. Fare Manu is a bit difficult to find: Look for it on the seaside, adjacent to two white A-frame homes. Directly opposite the driveway is a large boulder. Call Ms. Heipua Bordes for more information. ~ PK 8.2; 57-26-54. MODERATE TO DELUXE.

> Pineapple has replaced vanilla as the biggest cash crop (although economically it is not as significant, by a long shot, as tourism).

DINING

Moored directly off the Linareva Hotel grounds at PK 34.5 is a floating bar/restaurant known appropriately enough as **Le Bateau**. It is considered by locals to be one of the finest, if not *the* top eating establishment in town. The interior of the vessel, formerly an inter-island boat, is all hardwood embellished with plenty of brass nautical antiques. A panoramic view of the reefs and the high peaks nearby add to your enjoyment. The best dishes to order are the seafood plates such as the shrimp or mahimahi. ~ PK 35; 56-15-35. MODERATE TO DELUXE.

HIDDEN ►

Two kilometers south of Linareva, **Tubb's Pub Restaurant and Jewelry Store** is a nondescript shack on the side of the road that proclaims on its shingle: "Everything you always wanted to know about Paradise but were afraid to ask." Despite the overconfident claim, no one would ever call this establishment pretentious. Run by expat American Bob Parks (who calls himself the Recreation and Park Department), Tubb's Pub is the ultimate local hamburger joint. With an exposed concrete floor, fishing nets draped from the ceiling and coconut tree stumps serving as bar stools, the decor is, shall we say, bare bones. If you get tired of the bar stools, you can stroll to the back yard and sit at a picnic table facing the famous Haapiti Surf Break and watch the water acrobatics. Typical fare includes hamburgers, chicken teriyaki, and the least expensive beer on the island. (In case you are wondering, Tubb's Pub also has a modest selection of very reasonably priced black pearls, hence the jewelry store part of the name. ~ PK 37; 56-38-98. BUDGET.

At the end of the Hauru Point strip, about one kilometer south of Tubb's Pub, is **Daniel's Pizza**, which has a wood-fired oven in the garden. Daniel's is not a restaurant but will take your orders for pizza over the phone and deliver. However, if you drop by his home/pizza kitchen, he may serve you—his pizzas are apparently very good. ~ Haapiti; 56-39-95. BUDGET TO MODERATE.

Chez Pauline is affiliated with the small, family-run hotel of the same name in the village of Afareaitu. You must call Pauline to reserve a place. Although she is getting along in years, her place still has the old-fashioned hospitality and home-style cooking. There is no regular menu—you simply get what she happens to be serving, whether it's seafood, chicken or beef. ~ PK 9, Afareaitu; 56-11-26. BUDGET TO MODERATE.

There are several basic local markets on the coastal road from Haapiti to Afareaitu. They include **Magasin Varari**, Haapiti; 56-15-54, **Magasin Loto Haapiti**, PK 23; 56-3712, and **Magasin Ivon**, Afareaitu; 56-11-54. **Toa Moorea Supermarket** has the largest selection of groceries and canned goods on the island. It's located opposite the ferry terminal. ~ Vaiare; 56-18-89.

GROCERIES

Tubb's Pub sells a limited selection of black pearls (without settings) at very reasonable prices. ~ PK 37; 56-38-98.

SHOPPING

This is definitely the quiet end of the island. The only thing remotely resembling nightlife takes place at **Le Bateau** on the grounds of the Hotel Linareva where weekday happy hours are from 12 noon to 2 p.m. and 4 to 6 p.m. ~ PK 35; 56-15-35. An inexpensive beer can also be had at **Tubb's Pub Restaurant and Jewelry Store**, which has a small bar adorned with coconut-log bar stools. ~ PK 37; 56-38-98.

NIGHTLIFE

HAAPITI BEACH 🏊 ⛵ 🏄 There is a short stretch of sand opposite the village of Haapiti. Since this is the least-visited side of the island, the beach denizens will most likely be locals and chances

BEACHES & PARKS

are, it will not be crowded. This a good spot for a picnic, but shade is scarce. Swimming is fair, as the lagoon in this area tends to be shallow. Snorkeling is average. Being that this is the remote side of Moorea, there are no facilities here. ~ To get there, look for the fire station at PK 25 in Haapiti on the inland side of the road. The doors are generally open and you'll see the trucks parked inside. Access to the beach is across the road, opposite the fire station.

▼▼▼▼▼▼▼▼▼▼▼▼▼▼

Outdoor Adventures

There are two campgrounds on Moorea—both located in the Hauru Point area on the northwest side of the island. There are **Nelson and Josianne**, PK 27, Haapiti; 56-15-18, and a few hundred yards to the west, **Moorea Camping**, PK 27.5; 56-14-47. (See "Lodging" in the "Papetoai to Hauru Point" section for more information.)

CAMPING

DIVING

According to local expert Bernard Begliomini, proprietor of Bathy's Club, Moorea has a variety of underwater attractions that will satisfy the veteran diver. It also is a good place for beginners because of the lack of strong currents. The most popular underwater activities are fish and shark feeding. Hereabouts, lemon sharks, Napoleon fish and moray eels are the primary species you'll encounter. A 10- or 20-minute boat ride provides the opportunity to see white tip sharks, gray reef sharks, lemon sharks, nurse sharks and black tips. Some of the better-known dive sites include: **Le Tiki**, a 75-foot dive where you can feed lemon sharks, schools of perch and Napoleon fish; **Taota Pass**, a drift dive where one can find schools of jackfish, leopard rays and nurse sharks; **Ray Corridor**, a site where it's possible to observe and swim with several species of rays including manta and leopard rays; **Napoleon Plateau**, the home of friendly 60-pound Napoleon fish; and the **Shark Dining Room**, a site dedicated to feeding both sharks and eels.

There are three major scuba operators on the island. MUST, or **Moorea Underwater Scuba Diving Tahiti**, run by Philippe Molle, has exploratory dives for experienced divers, night diving as well as facilities for teaching novices. The tariff includes equipment. Open-water certification is also available. They are located adjacent to the Cook's Bay Hotel. ~ Maharepa; 56-17-32, fax 56-29-18. **Scubapiti**, run by Marc Quatrini, operates out of Les Tipaniers. He also teaches beginners the basics as well as taking out the experts. The price of a dive includes equipment and transportation to and from your resort. ~ Haapiti; 56-20-38, fax 56-29-25. **Bathy's Club Moorea**, based at the Beachcomber Parkroyal, also has a variety of dive trips that visit sites throughout the lagoon and beyond. They specialize in underwater photography and are fully equipped with photo gear, video cameras and underwater scooters. They also have a video center that allows you to edit your adventure. ~ Haapiti; 56-19-19, 56-21-07.

Surfing on Moorea, while not "world-class," has some very consistent breaks. The best on the island is at **Haapiti**, a left hander
that averages a six- to ten-foot face but can churn up 20-foot monster waves under the right circumstances. It's best to be taken there
by boat. Otherwise, it's a half-hour, half-mile paddle. If you can
find transportation, a local boat will cost you about 800 CFP
(US$10) round-trip. There are no board rentals on Moorea, so
come prepared if you plan to surf.

SURFING & WIND-SURFING

Other breaks on the island, starting from the airport area and
going counterclockwise, include **Airport** (midway between Faaupo
Point and Aroa Point), **Teavarua Pass** (outside of Cook's Bay),
Tareu Pass (outside of Opunohu Bay), **Taota Pass** (outside the reef
at the Hotel Beachcomber Parkroyal), **Haapiti** (mentioned above),
Avarapa Pass (outside of Atiha Bay on the southernmost point of
Moorea) and **Tupapaurau Pass** (off of Afareaitu). Without exception, all of these spots are reef breaks that entail 10 to 30 minutes
of paddling or, better yet, transportation via boat. If you're in the
vicinity of Haapiti, contact Bob Parks at Tubb's Pub for information on surf shuttles. ~ 56-38-98.

A discussion of the surfing scene on Moorea would not be complete without examining the state of affairs between local surfers
and visitors. To be candid, as elsewhere in French Polynesia, Moorean surfers are not overjoyed at the sight of *popa'a* (foreigners)
cavorting on their waves. Still, they are more tolerant than their
counterparts on Huahine. Visitors to Moorea should be sensitive to
this and make an effort to befriend their Polynesian brethren before
getting wet. My impression is that a well-mannered, outgoing visitor will probably not have difficulties. But while an individual will
generally be tolerated, a group of strangers is definitely problematic.

Sailboarding is practiced to some degree on Moorea but it's not
as popular as surfing. The main reason is the cost of gear and transportation. Some of the best spots to windsurf, starting from the
western side of the island and going counterclockwise, are just in-

✔ CHECK THESE OUT—UNIQUE OUTDOOR ADVENTURES

- Sail into Moorea's lagoon on a **Dolphin Tour**, a program that teaches
  human mammals about these incredible creatures. *page 172*
- Explore the rainforest and the inner reaches of the **Opunohu Valley** on
  a four-wheel-drive tour. *page 174*
- Feed lemon sharks and schools of perch as you dive **Le Tiki**, a
  75-foot dive off the outside reef-slope near Hauru Point. *page 196*
- Paddle out to catch a wave at **Haapiti Beach**, a left-hander that
  averages a six- to ten-foot face. *page 195*

side of **Motu Tiahura**, off of **Haapiti** (inside the lagoon), and the midpoint between Maatea and Haumi on the southeast side of the island, known as **Culina Point**. All of these sites are in the medium to expert range.

FISHING

Fishing in Moorea, outside the lagoon, can be excellent. A variety of pelagics such as tuna, mahimahi, marlin and other species are snagged on a regular basis. Inside the lagoon, fish are not as plentiful due to overfishing and the hotel and population pressures on the environment.

Half-day and full-day fishing trips are available with **Te Nui Charters**, which has the 31-foot Bertram and is based in Cook's Bay. ~ 42-75-42 or 56-15-08. You can also charter the **Heitana**, another Bertram, moored at the Beachcomber Parkroyal. ~ 56-16-42.

SAILING

A day trip outside the lagoon is one of the best ways to appreciate Moorea. In fact, the island is best admired from afar, particularly from the deck of a sailboat. Vessels can be chartered for day sails, sunset cruises or longer excursions to the outer islands. Contact **David Parkin**, owner of the *Esprit*, a 50-foot trimaran. ~ Afareaitu; 56-17-90. **Bernard Calvet** is the skipper of the *Manu*, a 38-foot catamaran moored off the Beachcomber Parkroyal. ~ Haapiti; 56-19-19.

OTHER WATER SPORTS

Virtually all of the hotels, as well as the Moorea Visitors Bureau, book nautical day trips and other ocean sports activities. These include snorkeling trips to *motus*, day-long tours around the island via boat (that usually include a picnic), and the obligatory "sunset cruise." The companies vary in quality and style.

In addition, many of the hotels have expanded their nautical activities from merely offering snorkeling, diving or canoeing to include a whole new range of possibilities. Those interested in waterskiing, jet skiing and aqua six (a sort of surface submarine used for viewing underwater life without getting wet) activities can contact the **Hotel Sofitel Ia Ora**, Temae; 56-16-41, or the **Beachcomber Parkroyal**, Haapiti; 56-12-90, for information.

One the best purveyors of nautical excursions is Hiro Kelley who runs **Lagoon Excursions**. Hiro, the son of "Bali Hai Boy" Hugh Kelley, has a variety of tours including glass-bottom boat rides, *motu* picnic and snorkeling trips, sunset cruises, and moonlight champagne rides. Though Hiro is half-Tahitian, he seems to have inherited his father's Irish charm and talent for putting his clients at ease. He will pick clients up at any hotel in Moorea. Boat tours are once daily and snorkeling tours leave twice daily. Kelley's prices are fair and competitive with other operations. ~ Maharepa; 56-13-59.

Dolphins—
Up Close
and Personal

The Beachcomber Parkroyal is home to **Dolphin Quest**, an attraction that calls itself an interactive program. You begin with a dockside orientation where trainers feed the animals. Then there's a lecture on the natural history and biology of the species. Next you are invited to go to the shallow end of the lagoon to meet the dolphins up close and personal.

Though this type of attraction has many animal activists up in arms, Dolphin Quest stresses that the animals are given a chance to frolic outside their pens during the day. This is the only place in French Polynesia that allows human interaction with dolphins—for a cool 7000 CFP (US$80). ~ Haapiti; 56-19-19.

If you prefer meeting your dolphins in the wild, the most unusual excursion is the **Dolphin Tour** established by Dr. Michael Poole. He takes you outside Moorea's lagoon to observe these fascinating creatures. Though a fee is charged, this is not a commercial venture. Dr. Poole runs the Richard Gump South Pacific Biological Research Station, which is affiliated with the University of California at Berkeley.

You accompany Dr. Poole on a speedy vessel that seeks dolphins in the lagoon and observes their playful behavior. There is no comparable tour like this in the South Pacific and it comes very highly recommended. Cost is 4000 CFP (US$50). Book it through your hotel tour desk—there is no direct phone to the Biological Research Station.

Albert Family Enterprises is also a Moorea institution that operates a budget hotel, a rental car agency and nautical tour activities, as well. They offer a daily Moana Lagoon Safari Picnic that entails visits to Cook's and Opunohu bays via outrigger canoe, snorkeling at one of the *motus*, and a barbecue. Hotel pickup is available. ~ Paopao; 56-13-53.

One of the most popular activities on the island is fish and shark feeding. This is offered by **Lagoon Excursions, Moorea Camping,** and just about every tour operator. Moorea Camping has reputedly the best shark feed on the island but they will not pick visitors up from other hotels. ~ PK 27.5; 56-14-47.

Polynesian Parasail operates out of the Beachcomber Parkroyal. For those who have always wanted to try parasailing (but were a bit intimidated), this is the place to do it. One is lifted from the deck of a boat like a feather and dropped gently back down on the deck when the tour is complete. The operation struck me as quite professional. The chute, which is launched from the boat like a kite, provides you with a spectacular view from as high as 450 feet above sea level. The experience is silent to the point of being eerie, yet thoroughly enjoyable. The vessel used is the *U'u'pa*, an immaculate, high-tech speedboat. Polynesian Parasail also provides one-and-a-half-hour island tours, which include background information on the history, geology and culture of French Polynesia. You're apt to see fish, sea turtles and, if you're lucky, dolphins. Check it out. ~ Haapiti; 56-19-19.

RIDING STABLES

Horseback riding on Moorea is a pleasure. The trails are uncrowded and there is a variety of terrain ranging from beaches to rainforests. **Rupe Rupe Ranch** is on the inland side of the road about a kilometer west of the airport. The ranch is owned and operated by Rene Denis, an enthusiastic Connecticut Yankee and 20-year veteran of Moorea. She knows and loves her horses and they show it. Rides are scheduled twice daily, in the morning and afternoons. ~ PK 2, Teavaro; 56-26-52.

Nearby in Temae, **Ranch Pegase** also provides regularly scheduled trail and beach rides. ~ Temae; 56-34-11.

On the other side of the island, **Tiahura Ranch** is located near Moorea Village on the inland side of the road. They also offer daily rides in the hills and on the beach. ~ Papetoai; 56-28-55.

BIKING

Bicycling is a better proposition on Moorea than on neighboring Tahiti, mostly because there is a lot less vehicular traffic. That does not mean you should relax about safety. There are still more cars, often speeding dangerously, than you'd want, but if you drive defensively, bicycling is still safe. It is possible to see the entire island by bike; however, it's a long haul—especially if your bike is sub-standard. Going up to Belvédère would be especially taxing, even with a mountain bike.

Another issue: Keep a very sharp lookout for dump trucks and other vehicles associated with construction work. They stop for no one. A friend of mine was run off the road and nearly met her maker recently thanks to one of these vehicles. If you do decide to take your bike inland to the Opunohu Valley, be careful riding down the hills on the steep grades that are unpaved. Better yet, on dirt or gravel roads, dismount and walk your bike down.

Renting a bicycle is a good idea if you want to tour the portion of the coastal road that *Le Truck* does not service. Some of the properties (such as Bali Hai and Cook's Bay Resort) provide free bikes or you can rent bikes from **Albert's Rentals**, a family-owned business that has an outlet across the street from the Bali Hai on Cook's Bay. 56-13-53, 56-19-28. **Poissonaire Friedmen**, a fish market, also rents bikes. ~ Maharepa; 56-18-68.

Ron's Services is the only local company that organizes bike tours, *Mountain Bike Adventures*. These are three- to four-hour tours of Moorea's interior and coast. Excursions visit the old church at Papetoai, shrimp ponds at Opunohu, the beach at Opunohu Bay and pineapple plantations. Bikes have 21 speeds, comfortable seats and good brakes. After completing the tour, you can keep the bike until 5 p.m. Be sure and bring along plenty of water. ~ Haapiti; 56-10-29.

Moorea has ample trekking possibilities if you are so inclined. In addition to going it alone, there is at least one organized tour. Below are some suggestions for those interested in making their way *a pied*:

HIKING

Le Col des Trois Cocotiers or the Pass of the Three Coconut Trees (4 miles/6.4 kilometers) This is a fairly easy hike that takes in the amphitheater of Moorea's caldera (volcanic crater) and a thick rainforest, and penetrates to the bottom of a silent valley beneath a canopy of tropical vegetation. The goal of the hike is the "Three Coconut Trees Pass," a locally famous landmark.

Soon after the trailhead begins one starts a descent toward a stream. Cross the stream and continue on the path on the opposite side. After about 250 yards, after the path has taken a second curve, take the cutoff on the right, which should be marked. From this path you should be able to see the rim of the caldera along with *Mouaroa* (known as the "cathedral") on the right. The Three Coconut Tree Pass is also visible, as well as *le Tamarutofa*, the big tooth, on the left.

The path should be cleared and is marked with orange paint. It descends to the river and passes through a *mape* (Tahitian chestnut) grove. (If you are not sure what a *mape* tree is, look on the

ground for the flat, brown, oblong nut. Though it bears little resemblance to the European chestnut, there is a similarity in flavor.)
The path soon crosses a stream. Take the trail that continues on
the other side, which should be marked with orange arrows painted
on the trees. Follow the riverbank and cross the small tributary.
Continue along the path through vegetation and the *mape* trees
grove on toward the rim of the caldera through a forest of *pandanus* trees. At the top of the pass, 1262 feet (385 meters), you
should see the trunk of a fallen coconut tree. Take the trail along
the rim on the right for a few meters. Keep an eye open for a
barbed-wire fence. Continue climbing toward Mouaraoa to the
foot of the "Three Coconut Trees" at about 1312 feet (400 meters).
There is a terrific view of Opunohu Valley, Belvédère and the crest
of the volcano, known as *le Rotui,* which was "Bali Hai," the mountain featured in *South Pacific.*

To find the trailhead you should have an automobile or a
scooter. Take the Belvédère inland road from the Opunohu Valley
at PK 18.1. At the junction of the Belvédère road and the Paopao
route (at 1.8 kilometers from Opunohu Bay) take the first road on
the right which leads to the buildings at the agriculture station.
From this point you should be able to see the "Three Coconut Tree
Pass" on your right in between Mt. Mouaraoa, at a height of 2886
feet (880 meters) to the west and Tamarutofa and Tohivea rising
3958 feet (1207 meters) east of the caldera. Facing the buildings,
turn to the left, continue straight ahead through the parking lot.
Pass the new buildings and park your vehicle.

Afareaitu Waterfall Hike (5 miles/8 kilometers) is a popular
trek to the Afareaitu Waterfall that begins in a small, *sauvage* valley
and ends where the Tevaiatiraa River falls from
a sheer cliff. The trailhead is located at the turnoff just outside of Afareaitu Village. Several hundred yards inland you will come to a Vanilla Cooperative (where you can see how this valuable crop is
cultivated and can purchase vanilla extract). Continue
walking inland beneath a variety of trees including
mango, *miro, tou* and past a host of flowers of every
description such as orchids, Tahitian basil, and vanilla
plants. Cross the wooden bridge and soon you'll reach a large
open area filled with mango trees and a vista of the mountains.
Continue straight ahead on the path staying on the left bank of the
river. You should be able to see the waterfall from here. Note the
well-preserved *marae* on your right. (At the end of the wall at the
archeological site is a foot path on the left that descends to the river
and dead ends.) Instead of taking that path, continue on the main
one where again you will pass *mape* trees. Cross the small tributary.

The dense foliage around
Afareaitu Waterfall, which
includes numerous ferns
and broad *mape* leaves,
makes this a stunning
setting.

Shortly you will arrive at the falls. The falls, or *cascade* in French, is about 60 feet high and, depending on the time of year, the volume of the water will vary. Likewise, depending on the volume of water, the pool at the bottom may or may not be deep enough to swim in.

To find the turnoff to the falls road, go to PK 8, look for the hospital in Afareaitu, and then head about 200 yards in the direction of the airport. Take a dirt road inland that begins opposite an A-frame house. You'll know it's the right road if after several hundred yards you run into the Vanilla Growing Coop building. A 200 CFP admission fee will be charged by the owner of the land. (Don't worry about finding him—he'll find you.)

Traversing **Vaiare to Paopao** (5 miles/8 kilometers) is a short and easy hike. Between Tearai, 2525 feet (770 meters), and Mouaputa, 2722 feet (830 meters), the ridge descends to a pass that is used to travel from the Vaiare Valley to the northeast section of the crater. Ascending the trail, the route passes through groves of *mape* and, on the way down, through a rugged basalt formation into a bamboo forest.

At the very beginning of the trailhead, look on your right for a large boulder, **ofai Tahinu**. Note the large cavity in the stone which in the old days was used to make *monoi* oil for the queen. Five or six yards before the stone look for a track that leads from the left-hand side of the road and, within a few steps, look for a large, blocklike stone known as **ofai pahu** or drum stone. (It is partially hollowed out and when hit with a piece of wood has a deep resonant sound). Continuing on the trail, take a left-hand cutoff that follows the riverbank.

Stick with this for another ten minutes and take a cutoff to the left, which climbs toward the pass. The trail should be marked by a sign that says *Paopao*. However, sometimes the sign is taken down or purposefully turned around to point in the wrong direction. To make sure you are headed the right way, look for the opening of the trail among the mango trees and for red marks on trees or on rocks. (If you miss the correct cutoff, you will come to a river. You may note other trails that ascend toward the ridge but none of them will actually reach it. Therefore, you should turn back.)

Continuing on the track, you'll note that as you go through the mango grove the tree trunks are marked with red splotches of paint. This will continue up to the pass. As long as you see these, you are on the right trail. The track follows the right-hand side of the riverbank, climbing through an area dotted with coffee plants and *mape* groves. After about 45 minutes of walking, you should come upon a huge boulder on your right. About 15 minutes later you will reach the pass and will find a sign that reads *Oaa*. The view at this point is blocked, but if you follow the sign with an arrow pointing to the left and climb the ridge along the crater to the high point, you will find a wonderful vista of the valley below. In contrast to the somber forests you have passed through to reach this point, you will be able to hear the sounds of civilization, including tractor motors and other engines emanating from the agriculturally rich Opunohu and Paopao valleys.

Moorea has a population of 11,000 people.

You will then descend from the pass through a *mape* forest where you will see a jumble of basalt rocks and a bamboo grove. The track eventually reaches a dirt road that you can take past a home and then across a river. At the fork in the road, take a left leading toward the school and eventually to Paopao.

To get to the trailhead go to PK 4.5 in Vaiare, then take the road that leads to the Capo homestead (Mr. Capo is a horticulturist), climbing past the bridge along the Mouaputa River. At the fork of the road, take a right that leads you to the CJA youth center (*Centre pour Jeune Adolescent*). Park the car before the center, about 800 yards from a peripheral road.

Mt. Rotui from the north (5 miles/8 kilometers) Mt. Rotui, one of the most distinctive peaks on Moorea, has been compared to a fortress or castle, with its ramparts and gothic windows. In Polynesian mythology, it is traditionally known as a purgatory, where dead souls awaited their ascension to heaven at Mt. Temehani on Raiatea. In either case, the view at the summit that takes in the entire amphitheater of the ancient volcano may not be celestial, but is certainly remarkable. (In modern mythology, Rotui was the fabled Bali Hai mountain in the movie *South Pacific*.)

To get to the top it's a much easier proposition to approach Rotui from the north. The trek starts opposite the Village Faimano Hotel. Look for a path on the right that heads directly toward the north face of Rotui. It's about a 45-minute walk to the top. On the way you'll pass through a quiet grove of guava trees. However, there are a few wasps' nests in the grove so keep an eye out. Once you reach the ridge, hike along the crest until you mount the summit. At the top is a marvelous view of the caldera. On the way down, make sure you bear to the right in order to stay on the correct path.

Coming from Paopao, go to PK 14.2, after the Moorea Lagoon. Park opposite the Village Faimano Hotel and ask the charming proprietress (Hinano Feildel) for permission to use the trail (the beginning of which crosses her property).

ORGANIZED HIKES   Ron's Services offers organized hikes to the interior. There are three different hikes: the "Three Coconut Pass" trek to Mouaroa (for beginner or intermediate hikers); the Vaiare to Paopao Trail (for beginner or intermediate level) that traverses the mountains from the ferry dock area to the island's interior; and the Mouaputa hike (intermediate level), which entails a trek from the waterfalls of Afareaitu to the summit of Mouaputa, the fabled Pierced Mountain. The latter hike is fairly arduous and is a full day's activity. The two others are not particularly strenuous and are half-day outings. ~ Haapiti; 56-10-29.

▼▼▼▼▼▼▼▼▼▼

Transportation

Moorea Airport has direct service from Moorea to the outer islands via Air Tahiti. ~ 56-31-13.

AIR

There are regular connections between Moorea and Bora Bora, Huahine, Manihi, Maupiti, Raiatea and Rangiroa. There is also helicopter service between Moorea and Tahiti's Faa'a Airport with **Héli Pacific**. ~ 85-68-00.

FERRY

There are at least three vessels available from Papeete for the 12 mile (20-kilometer) journey to Moorea. In Papeete, they dock on the quay several hundred yards north of the tourism office, Fare Manihini. I found taking the ferry preferable (as well as more economical) than the airplane. The short journey provides an opportunity to meet locals, see a slice of Tahitian life, and (if the seas are calm) a pleasurable travel experience. While on the water it's possible to see flying fish propelling themselves off the crests of the waves and dolphins swimming up to the bow. The ferries are crammed to the scuppers with men, women, children, animals, cars, cases of Hinano beer and every other provision imaginable.

All ferries stop at the terminal in Vaiare, four kilometers south of the airport.

The ships that ply the waters between Moorea and Tahiti are the *Tamarii Moorea*, a traditional ferry that transports both passengers and automobiles, and the sleek, high-speed catamarans *Aremiti* and *Tamahine IIB* that only carry people. The crossing takes about one hour on the *Tamarii Moorea* and 35 minutes on the *Aremiti* and *Tamahine IIB*. Because of the frequency of service you need not worry about reservations. Tariff for either boat costs 800 CFP for adults or 400 CFP for children one-way. (Note that the *Le Truck* service is coordinated with the arrival and departure of boats so you must tack on another 200 CFP for transportation to or from the dock at Vaiare to your hotel.)

Schedules are available at the Tahiti Tourist Board office in Papeete or the Moorea pier. For more information, call the **Ferry Services** in Moorea. ~ 56-31-10.

CAR RENTALS

It is very difficult (if not impossible) to see the entire island on your own without a motorized vehicle. If you rent a car or scooter, be sure to check for such minor details as properly inflated tires and brakes that work.

Pacificar is the largest car-rental agency on the island and has seven locations on Moorea including the airport, ferry dock, Hotel Sofitel Ia Ora, Bali Hai Club, Bali Hai Hotel, Club Med and Beachcomber Parkroyal. They provide cars, scooters and bicycles. ~ 56-11-03.

Europcar a newcomer on the scene, has locations at the airport, ferry dock, Club Med, Beachcomber Parkroyal and Sofitel Ia Ora. ~ 56-34-00.

Albert's Rentals, a much smaller, family-owned business, also has three locations—next to the **Bali Hai** ~ 56-30-58, on **Cook's Bay** ~ 56-19-28, and by Club Med in **Haapiti** ~ 56-33-75.

MOTOR SCOOTERS & CYCLES

Albert's Rentals has motor scooters and motorcycles at its location across from the Bali Hai Hotel Cook's Bay. ~ Maharepa; 56-13-53. **Pacificar**, primarily an auto rental agency, also has motor scooters at some of its locations. ~ 56-11-03.

PUBLIC TRANSIT

If you arrive via ferry, there will be a *Le Truck* at the dock ready to pick up hotel-bound passengers and transport them for 200 CFP, seven days a week. In addition to the *Le Trucks* that operate in conjunction with the ferries, there is a new transportation service that runs independently from the north coast of the island between the Hotel Sofitel Ia Ora near the airport and the Hotel Linareva on the opposite end of the island.

These minibuses run Mondays through Saturdays with the same departure times from the Linareva and the Ia Ora terminals: 8 a.m., 9 a.m., 11 a.m., 1 p.m., 3 p.m., 5 p.m., 7 p.m. and 9.30 p.m. The fare is 200 CFP (for adults) and 100 CFP (for children under 16) to any point on the line. This new service is something that has been needed on the island for years and breaks the monopoly that the taxis and car-rental agencies enjoyed. The new operation also makes it much easier for visitors to eat out in the evenings, rather than feeling like they are trapped in their hotels after a certain hour.

If you arrive at the airport, and want to avoid the exorbitant taxi ride to your hotel, an option is to take a short cab ride from the airport (where there is no bus stop) to the Hotel Sofitel Ia Ora. From there you can take *Transport Publique* to your hotel.

TAXIS

Taxis are inordinately expensive here. Even before you move a yard, the cab's meter is set at 800 CFP (about US$10). The 16-mile (25-kilometer), 20-minute trip from the airport to the Hauru Point hotel enclave can cost 5000 CFP (US$60) or more. If you really *do* need a taxi, phone 56-10-18.

*bove: This coconut cart being pulled by a motor scooter is typical of islander
igenuity.*

elow: Children playing on the dock in Rangiroa.

This whitewashed church is typical of those found in every island community in French Polynesia.

Hitching is possible, but not easy on Moorea. Perhaps because of   **HITCHING**
the vast number of tourists, locals are less apt to pick up hitchhikers. With the new minibus service on the north coast of the island,
the need to hitchhike has been greatly reduced.

One way to explore Moorea is to take one of the four-wheel-drive   **DRIVE**
tours. Four outfits offer expeditions into the island's interior to see   **TOURS**
a number of archeological sites, pineapple plantations, and stunning views. Each tour company essentially visits the same sightseeing places and one would be hard-pressed to say that one is better
than another.

Moorea Safari Tours, run by veteran tour operator Ron Sage,
specializes in four-wheel-drive off-road visits in a sturdy Land
rover to the island's inaccessible interior. Called the Painapo Safari
Adventure Tour, the itinerary includes a visit to various Polynesian
archeological sites, a swim in a river, a visit to a bamboo forest,
and pineapple, vanilla and coffee plantations deep in the highlands.
The trip is well worth it for those who wish to see beyond the
fringes of Moorea. In addition to the standard tour, Sage offers a
variation on the safari theme—an excursion to view the jungle by
the light of the full moon, while sipping champagne. ~ Haapiti; 56-
35-80, fax 56-10-66.

In a similar vein, **Inner Island Photo Tours** has excursions twice
daily (mornings and afternoons) aboard an air-conditioned Toyota
to the inner reaches of Moorea. Call Alex Roo Haamataerii for details. ~ Temae; 56-20-09.

Also visiting Moorea's interior is **Tefaarahi Adventure Tours**,
which operates a See Everything Tour. Their tour departs twice
daily (in the morning and the afternoon) and can be booked either
at the Moorea tourism office or from hotel tour desks. ~ Haapiti;
56-41-24.

Albert Family Enterprises has a three-hour overland Jeep Safari
Excursion. Albert's, like all the four-wheel-drive operations, visits
the inland pineapple plantations, archeological sites and vista points.
Paopao; 56-13-53.

Albert Family Enterprises opposite the Club Bali Hai has a
plethora of tours and photo safari expeditions. One combines an
interior island tour with a circle island tour, another an interior island tour with shopping. ~ Paopao; 56-19-28.

Circle island tours, which can be booked at any of the island's
hotel, are usually conducted in vans or buses. They are a standard
fixture on Moorea and take about four hours. In addition to the
obligatory stops at Cook's Bay and Opunohu Bay, they generally
include a visit to the archeological sites at Le Belvédère. I can't recommend one tour company over another—they all seem pretty
much the same.

▼▼▼▼▼▼▼▼▼▼▼▼▼▼▼▼▼▼▼▼▼▼▼▼

Addresses & Phone Numbers

Bank ~ Banque de Polynesie Maharepa; 56-14-59

Bank ~ Banque Socredo Teavaro; 56-13-06

Bank ~ Bank of Tahiti Maharepa; 56-13-29

Bank ~ Westpac Bank Tiahura; 56-12-02

Dentist ~ Jean Marc Thurillet, PK 5.5, Maharepa; 56-32-44 (speaks very little English)

Ferry Boat Information ~ 56-30-16

Hospital ~ 56-24-24, 56-23-23

Pharmacy ~ 56-12-03 in Paopao or 56-38-37 in Haapiti

Police Station ~ 56-13-44

Post Office ~ Maharepa PK 6.3; 56-10-12 and Papetoia 56-13-15

Town Hall ~ 56-10-36

Visitor information ~ Moorea Tourist Bureau, PK 28, Haapiti; 56-29-09, 56-26-48

SIX

Bora Bora

Perhaps no island in the world, except Tahiti, is as synonymous with South Pacific paradise as is Bora Bora, located some 165 miles (264 kilometers) northwest of Tahiti. The popular myth of Bora Bora was primarily fueled by the writings of James Michener, who called it the most beautiful island in the world. Michener may well be correct. Bora Bora possesses a captivating beauty. The center of the island is dominated by Pahia and Otemanu, two towering volcanic peaks of shear black rock that look down on you wherever you are on the island. Sloping down from these peaks to the beaches and boat-filled bays are hillsides of lush tropical foliage.

However, Bora Bora's most alluring attractions start where the island stops. First there is a translucent lagoon tinged with myriad hues of blue. Open to the ocean by only one pass, the lagoon is enclosed to the east by *motus* and to the west by a reef. It is so well-protected from the open ocean that swimming in its clear, calm water is like swimming in a resort pool. In fact, almost without exception, the hotels on Bora Bora—even the most upscale ones—don't have swimming pools. It would simply be redundant.

Bora Bora's lagoon offers everyone who visits the island, regardless of budget, something the best resort pools in the world can't offer at any price—the living ocean. Within the lagoon, and easily accessible to novice scuba divers and snorkelers, are all varieties of sea life: corals, tropical reef fish, clams, eels, rays of all types, barracuda, octopuses and, most popular of all, sharks.

The *motus* that protect and create Bora Bora's amazing lagoon are something to experience in and of themselves. No journey to paradise is complete until you escape to a *motu*. These miniature palm-covered islands take you away from the distractions of civilization. You won't find roads or cars and there isn't any shopping nor are there restaurants, but isn't that the whole idea? You can climb a stone stairway through the overgrown jungle to a sacred Polynesian site on Motu Toopua, or rest on a secluded stretch of beach on Motu Piti Aau. Most hotels will arrange a day trip to a *motu* for you. If you want to escape civilization for longer than a day, there are also a small number of hotels that are located right on Bora Bora's *motus*.

Known in ancient times as Vavau, Bora Bora was a haunt of Hiro, one of the most powerful gods in the Polynesian pantheon. Hiro's son, Ohatatamu, was supposed to have been the first king of the island.

The first European to visit the island was Captain James Cook, who came in 1777 after having previously sighted the island in 1769. Bora Bora remained with its own sovereign until 1888 when it was annexed by France. The last queen, Terii-Maevarua II, granddaughter of Queen Pomare IV of Tahiti, died in Tahiti in 1932.

In recent years Bora Bora has evolved into a mecca for well-heeled American and European tourists. Much of her population of 5500 are dependent upon tourism for their livelihood and have learned a thing or two about capitalism.

Bora Bora is a microcosm of the extremes that French Polynesia has to offer. No superlatives can adequately describe its spectacular beauty and no value can be placed on the opportunity of experiencing this for yourself. However, you should prepare to pay a premium, even by Tahitian standards, for this privilege. At the same time, you may find that many of the locals have a certain ambivalence toward tourists, no doubt because they have seen too many.

At the risk of dating myself, Bora Bora is no longer the sleepy community that it was in the 1970s and 1980s. The island has undergone a great deal of tourism development over the past decade, even after I had assumed it had reached the saturation level. Not only are hotels growing in size and number, traffic, especially between Vaitape and Matira, is quite heavy when the island is at full capacity. The good news is that Bora Bora now offers a better selection of hotels in all price ranges and a good selection of more reasonably priced restaurants. Attitudes may be changing as well. The precipitous drop in tourism due to the negative publicity from the nuclear tests severely impacted the residents of Bora Bora. Hotel and tourism-related jobs disappeared and for the first time in many years, locals understood that they could not take visitors for granted. This caused many locals to make more of an effort to be hospitable. Whether this change of heart will persist remains to be seen.

Though the drop in tourism was jarring for the younger generation of Bora Borans, when seen from a historical perspective the ebb and flow of foreigners to the island is nothing new. During World War II, 4500 U.S. troops were stationed on the island. In 1977 the island was again occupied, this time by an army of Italian filmmakers shooting Dino De Laurentis' production of *Hurricane*. Again the economy boomed—local merchants turned a handsome profit and many of those hired by the moviemakers were riding new motorbikes or playing new cassette decks. When the Italians left, business as usual became the order of the day. Women returned to work in the hotels and men returned to their fishing boats. The islanders' flexibility is both admirable and a matter of survival.

So much of what you will discover on Bora Bora involves unusual twists on the traditional way of doing things. Even the process of flying to Bora Bora is unique. If you are arriving on an interisland flight from Tahiti, try to get a seat on the left-hand side of the plane so that you can see the breathtaking views of the island, lagoons and reefs of Moorea, Huahine, Raiatea, Tahaa and Bora Bora itself. When your plane lands at Bora Bora's airport, you will not walk down the steps onto the island of Bora Bora, but rather onto one of its many *motus*—Motu Mute. However, this is not an inconvenience; it's a free boat tour of Bora Bora's beautiful northeast

Bora Bora

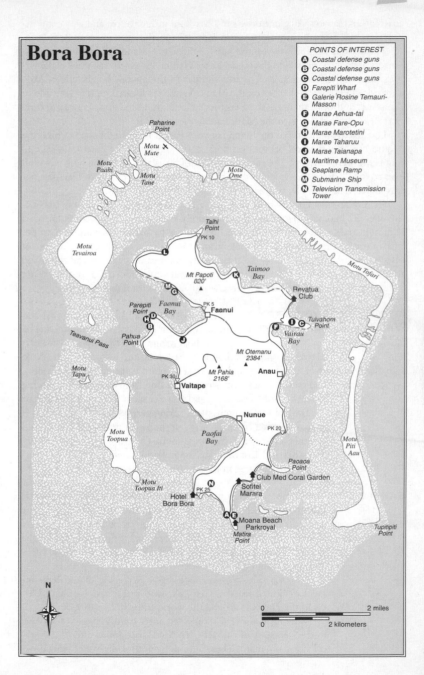

Paharine Point

Motu Mute

Motu Paahi

Motu Tane

Motu Ome

Motu Tevairoa

Taihi Point

PK 10

Motu Tofari

Ⓛ

Mt Papoti 820'

Ⓚ

Taimoo Bay

Ⓜ

Faanui Bay

PK 5

Faanui

Revatua Club

Parepiti Point

Ⓓ
Ⓖ
Ⓑ

Ⓕ Ⓘ Ⓒ

Tuivahora Point

Pahua Point

Ⓙ

Vairau Bay

Teavanui Pass

Mt Otemanu 2384'

Motu Tapu

Mt Pahia 2168'

Anau

PK 30

Vaitape

Nunue

PK 20

Motu Toopua

Paofai Bay

Motu Piti Aau

Paoaoa Point

Motu Toopua Iti

PK 25

Ⓝ

Club Med Coral Garden

Sofitel Marara

Hotel Bora Bora

Ⓐ Ⓔ

Moana Beach Parkroyal

Matira Point

Tupitipiti Point

N

0   2 miles

0   2 kilometers

coastline and lagoon. All plane tickets to Bora Bora include a free and very comfortable ferry ride from the airport to the dock at Vaitape, the main town on Bora Bora.

The dock at Vaitape is the central hub for the whole island. All supplies and passengers arriving at the island disembark here. Waiting for you at the dock is the visitors information center as well as free shuttles to the upscale hotels, and reasonably priced buses to all locales on the island. Vaitape is located on the west side of the island, and while there are some visitors facilities there, the vast majority of travelers head straight down to the Matira area.

Located at south end of the island between Raititi Point and Paoaoa Point, the Matira area has the best beaches on Bora Bora, almost all the hotels and a good number of its restaurants. The entire north half of the island, including both west and east coasts, is pretty much ignored by travelers and is void of visitor facilities, but it is a nice area for a day trip when you want to escape the crowds.

Getting around Bora Bora is fairly easy. The coastal road around the island is 20 miles (32 kilometers) long and almost entirely level, with only one short unpaved section near Marae Aehua-tai. It's ideal to explore by bicycle, but do keep an eye out for traffic, especially between Vaitape and Matira. (Cars and motor scooters can also be rented.) Depending on the form of conveyance used, the round-the-island tour can take anywhere from 90 minutes to several hours. Along the route there are a number of ancient *marae* and several World War II coastal defense guns.

▼▼▼▼▼▼▼▼▼▼▼▼▼▼▼▼
Vaitape & Nunue Area

Vaitape is Bora Bora's main community, and the arrival point for passengers transferring by shuttle boat to and from the airport. The heart of town is only a few hundred yards long and is studded with shade trees. It's pleasant and easy to get around Vaitape. The pulse is slow, and groups of locals cluster around storefronts gossiping or trading jokes. Even the few autos and bicycles seem to pass languidly by.

Despite the leisurely pace, taking care of chores in town is a snap. There is a complete array of shops in town, a gas station and several good, inexpensive restaurants. There are not, however, very many hotels. Most of the accommodations and more formal eateries are concentrated in the Matira Beach area.

SIGHTS   The newest structure in town is the modest **Centre Artisanal de Bora Bora**, which also houses a **tourist office** directly opposite the wharf. It's a good place to window-shop or purchase inexpensive souvenirs. If the tourism office is open, as it usually is during the arrival of passengers from the airstrip, it's a good source of information. ~ Vaitape, 67-76-36.

Near the tourism office, opposite the pier, is a granite slab **monument** dedicated to Alan Gerbault, who single-handedly sailed his yacht the *Firecrest* around the world from 1923 to 1929.

Walking a mile (1.6 kilometers) north from Vaitape you'll come to the remnants of the old **Club Med**, abandoned after one tropical storm too many. These once-popular over-the-water bungalows now lie undisturbed, rotting away in the humid air while the Club Med crowd enjoys the new Coral Village on the other side of the island. Just past the Club Med ruins is **Pahua Point**. Keep an eye out for a marked path on the hillside that leads up the hill to what once was a battery of Mark II coastal defense guns constructed by the Seabees. It's a 10- to 15-minute walk up the steep hill to the **coastal defense gun emplacements** overlooking Teavanui Pass. From here you have a bird's-eye view of the boats coming and going through the island's only access to the open ocean.

◀ HIDDEN

Changing your orientation 180 degrees, heading south of Vaitape you pass through the village of **Nunue**, a spread-out collection of houses, shops and restaurants that edge Paofai Bay.

The first sight you come across while circling the bay will be the remnants of **Tautu's Museum**. A collection of anchors, a Mark II coastal defense gun, the carcasses of various vehicles and other objects strewn around make up what was informally known as Tautu's Museum. Tautu used to live in the A-frame behind the medley of material that made up his front yard. Tautu's aim was to convert a few defunct interisland ships into a floating bar/museum some day, but to no one's surprise, it didn't quite happen.

Just beyond Tautu's Museum keep an eye out on the mountain side of the road for a turnoff that begins next to a double-columned telephone pole. (Near the area is a cluster of boutiques and shops so it is difficult to miss.) This cutoff will take you up to a **television transmission tower**, and eventually across the island. Atop the crest of the steep hill there is a magnificent panoramic view of Vaitape to the west, and of Motu Pitiaau and distant vistas of Raiatea and Tahaa to the east.

Near the cluster of shops, boutiques and the inland road leading to the TV tower you will see the intriguing-looking **Bamboo House Restaurant**. ~ Nunue; 67-76-24.

✔ **CHECK THESE OUT—UNIQUE SIGHTS**

- Inspect one of the remaining **coastal defense gun emplacements** established during World War II. *pages 213, 218, 229*
  - Browse the selection of **black pearls** at a shop selling these marvels of Mother Nature, but if you plan to buy, prepare to reach deep into your pockets. *pages 217, 227*
    - Gaze from Club Med's **belvédère** for a view of Bora Bora's blue lagoon and string of *motus*, as well as distant Tahaa and Raiatea. *page 228*
      - Join the locals at Matira's **public beach** on Saturday or Sunday for swimming and beach fun, Tahitian-style. *page 228*

Almost immediately beyond the turnoff from the main road is **Bloody Mary's**, a Bora Bora institution. Outside is a huge double-boomed canoe with one boom longer than the other, for tacking against the wind. A prominent sign lists the varied celebrities who have darkened the doorway of this establishment over the years. In addition to its fame as a watering hole, Bloody Mary's also serves fine seafood. ~ Nunue; 67-72-76.

Continuing a bit farther south on the coastal road you will come to the Hotel Bora Bora and the beginning of the Matira Beach area.

LODGING   There are no accommodations in Vaitape itself. Most affordable lodging lies just outside of town and south in Nunue.

Three kilometers north of Vaitape is the **Bora Bora Yacht Club**, which has aesthetically pleasing but overpriced accommodations. There are six bungalows—three over the water and three in the garden. All are painted turquoise and sport thatched roofs. All the rooms have hardwood floors, four-poster beds (with mosquito nets), batten-style windows and step-down bathrooms. The views of the lagoon are wonderful. The Yacht Club also has French Polynesia's only floating bungalows, which are actually catamaran units. They are equipped with kitchenette, bathroom and solar electricity and can accommodate four people. There are also moorings for 17 yachts, as well as laundry and bathing facilities for yachties. Other amenities include water-sport activities and boat rentals. ~ Vaitape; 67-70-69, 67-71-34. MODERATE TO DELUXE.

Le Recif is an inexpensive hotel with a disco that goes into full swing on weekends. At the back of the property is a pleasant garden with three bungalows, one with a kitchen. Two of the lodgings can take three people and the larger unit can handle up to six. The place is clean and the rooms are of average size, but are rather run-down and on the threadbare side. The other issue is noise. If you

---

✔ CHECK THESE OUT—UNIQUE LODGING

- *Budget:* Escape to paradise with a stay at **Chez Maeva Masson**, the former home of one of French Polynesia's most famous painters. *page 224*
- *Budget to moderate:* Slip away from the international crowd at **Chez Nono Leverd**, a favorite stopover for visiting Tahitian nationals. *page 224*
- *Moderate to deluxe:* Journey to the **Revatua Club** for the atmosphere that best defines Tahiti's unique culture—barefoot, relaxed, Polynesian yet somehow also French. *page 232*
- *Ultra-deluxe:* Watch fish swim beneath your over-the-water bungalow as you relax in the lap of luxury at the **Moana Beach Parkroyal**. *page 221*

Budget: under $100   Moderate: $100–$150   Deluxe: $150–$200   Ultra-deluxe: over $200

stay over the weekend you had better like the loud music that emanates from the disco. Le Recif is located two kilometers north of town. ~ Vaitape; 63-73-87. BUDGET.

Chez Ato et Sylvain is the closest thing to Shangri-la that exists in Bora Bora—at least when you're talking about altitude. Cooled by the trade winds, Chez Ato is in an Eden-like setting on the mountainside, splashed with hibiscus, frangipani and other flora. The structure is hexagonal, with an open courtyard that consists mostly of a pond with an enormous boulder in it. There are five small, spartan rooms with plenty of light, two communal showers and one toilet. A sturdily built Bora Boran, Ato was always a gracious host who would ply you with the abundant fruit that grows on his estate. Unfortunately, he is seldom on the property nowadays, and has delegated his job to others. Evidently his associates have not done a good job. From reports I have received, the rooms have not been maintained and the tariff for a room (about 4000 CFP per night) is way overpriced. The property lies in the shadow of Mt. Otemanu, on a verdant hillside about a half-kilometer from the main road, about two kilometers south of Vaitape. ~ Nunue; 67-77-27. MODERATE.

Chez Rosina is a local-style home with four rooms, each with private bathroom. There is also a communal kitchen and a living room. Rooms are of average size, but are clean and well appointed, especially considering the low price. The house has a warm atmosphere thanks to Rosina, who is a convivial Tahitian. The private bathrooms, with hot water, make this one of the best values on the island. Tariff includes breakfast plus lunch or dinner. The only feature the property is missing is a nearby beach. Excursions are available. Payment is by cash only. Round-trip transfers to the airport are provided. Chez Rosina is located four kilometers south of Vaitape on Paofai Bay. ~ Nunue; 67-70-91. BUDGET.

◄ HIDDEN

North of town, the **Bora Bora Yacht Club** is a popular restaurant and watering hole. If you try to visualize what a restaurant in Tahiti should look like it would most likely resemble the Yacht Club. The bar is made of rough-hewn hardwood, and there's ample decking around the restaurant, much of it over the water. Part of the aqua-deck has been cut away to expose the reef below. This open area has been turned into an aqua-pen, where all manner of creatures—turtles, surgeon fish, sharks and the like—swim about. It's definitely worth a look if you're in the neighborhood. The menu includes salads, appetizers, mixed seafood, shrimp and *poisson cru*—all well prepared. The food is tasty, if overpriced. ~ Vaitape; 67-70-69. DELUXE TO ULTRA-DELUXE.

DINING

The **Restaurant Vaitape** is an inexpensive café that doubles as a bakery. It features the usual—coffee, croissants, buns and other pastries. It is good for breakfast and is open on Sundays. You can find it in the center of town, across from the Bank of Polynesia and the post office. ~ Vaitape. BUDGET.

HIDDEN ► **Snack Michel** is about 100 yards (90 meters) from the Commercial Center (a collection of shops and offices) in town, toward the Faanui area. Possibly the best budget eatery on the island, it's a local, indoor/outdoor affair with four or five tables. Fare includes *ma'a tinito*, the traditional Tahitian dish that includes red beans, pork and veggies. Other dishes such as chow mein or steak and fries are available. ~ Vaitape; 67-71-42. BUDGET.

At the Commercial Center is the air-conditioned **L'Appetisserie**, a cozy little café that offers terrific cakes, ice cream and sherbets (all homemade) as well as croissants, quiche, pizza and a *plat du jour* that is usually a bargain. ~ Vaitape; 67-75-43. BUDGET.

HIDDEN ► **Snack Au Cocotier**, featuring basic Chinese food, is the newest eatery in the neighborhood. The specialty of the house is *poisson cru*, which is reportedly the best on the island and is reasonably priced. Snack Au Cocotier is located on the mountain side of the road between Chin Lee's market and the pharmacy. ~ Vaitape; 67-74-18. BUDGET.

One of the most promising new additions to the restaurant scene is the **Bamboo House**, three kilometers south of Vaitape. Looking like a cross between a Philippine *nipa* hut and a Tahitian *fare*, it has small bar and outdoor terrace that looks quite inviting. Not only is the food good, but the menu has items for every pocketbook. The lunch menu has such offerings as hamburgers, steak or shrimp fettucine. Dinner is much more expensive. Reports from locals I've spoken to is that the cuisine comes highly recommended. Entrées include pasta, stuffed jackfish, grilled salmon and lobster fricassee. Along with a tasty menu, the wine list has excellent selections from Bordeaux, Alsace and Beaujolais. As one local told me, "Service takes forever, it's very expensive, but the food is very good." ~ Nunue; 67-76-24. MODERATE TO ULTRA-DELUXE.

✔ CHECK THESE OUT—UNIQUE DINING

- *Budget:* Experience relaxed island atmosphere at **Mahana View**, a "grass shack" restaurant overlooking Bora Bora's serene lagoon. *page 226*
- *Moderate to deluxe:* Discover a rarity hereabouts at **Le Tiare**—authentic, *affordable* French cuisine prepared by a renowned chef. *page 227*
- *Moderate to ultra-deluxe:* Select a table on the **Bamboo House**'s breeze-cooled terrace or inside its magnificent bamboo structure. *page 216*
- *Moderate to ultra-deluxe:* Witness the formula for a perfect tropical island restaurant at the long-standing Tahitian-American favorite, **Bloody Mary's**. *page 217*

Budget: under $12 Moderate: $12–$20 Deluxe: $20–$30 Ultra-deluxe: over $30

An institution on the island, **Bloody Mary's** near Hotel Bora Bora, is decidedly rustic. The sand floor, thatched roof and coconut-tree-stump bar stools are reminiscent of a stage set from the television show *Gilligan's Island*. And, the seafood couldn't be fresher. Diners choose their own fresh fish (on ice) and the chef slaps them on the grill. Or maybe you would prefer lobster? For turf lovers, the menu includes barbecued chicken and T-bone steak. At lunchtime, Bloody Mary's features reasonably priced pizza, and it's a good place to sip draft beer. As a testimony to its celebrity appeal, the management has placed a wooden sign at the entrance with a list of names of the famous, and not so famous, luminaries who have crossed the threshold. Closed Sunday. ~ Nunue; 67-72-86. MODERATE TO ULTRA-DELUXE.

GROCERIES

When shopping for a quantity of groceries or any other major purchases, Vaitape is clearly the place to go. A good general store to start at is **Chin Lee**, the largest market on the island. They have recently revamped the store. ~ Vaitape; 67-73-86. **Magasin Nunue** also has a good selection of groceries. ~ Nunue; 67-70-02. **Establissements Loussan** is the best place to purchase meat and produce in town. ~ Nunue; 67-70-59.

SHOPPING

Vaitape does not have much in the way of serious shopping. The best boutiques, jewelry and gift shops are located along the road to Matira. However, for small-ticket items such as T-shirts and pareus a good selection can be found at a boutique called **Pakalola**, in the heart of town. It also has good maps of Bora Bora. ~ Vaitape; 67-71-82.

Several Vaitape general stores such as **Magazin Roger** and **Chin Lee** also stock inexpensive T-shirts and pareus. ~ Vaitape; Chin Lee: 67-73-86.

About three kilometers from Vaitape, heading toward Matira, one can find a cluster of shops near the Bamboo Restaurant including **Boutique Gauguin,** which has a fine selection of expensive gifts. ~ Nunue, 67-76-67.

Next door to Boutique Gauguin is OPEC, a new upscale black pearl boutique that also carries carvings from the Marquesas. ~ Nunue.

Located in the same vicinity, the **Honeymoon Boutique** is a fine place to shop. They offer a nice collection of pareus and other clothing. The owners usually stock items of high quality and price them fairly. ~ Nunue; 67-78-19.

NIGHTLIFE

Bora Bora is a fairly quiet place. When you come here it's best to be prepared to entertain yourself. In the Vaitape area the only nightclub (on weekends) is **Le Recif**, Bora Bora's only disco and after-hours club. It is a working-class Tahitian nightclub—crowded, noisy, dark and smoke-filled. Toward the end of the evening, a number of the patrons may be drunk. It's best to go when accompanied by a local. ~ Vaitape; 67-73-87.

Bloody Mary's is always a good place to stop for a beer or two. Tap beer is reasonably priced and there may be an informal Tahitian combo strumming away on guitars and ukuleles. ~ Nunue; 67-72-86.

▼▼▼▼▼▼▼▼▼▼▼▼▼
Matira Beach Area

The Matira Beach area, which stretches from the end of Nunue Village to the area around the south tip of the island, is the focal point for tourism on Bora Bora. Most of the accommodations, as well as boutiques and restaurants, are clustered near Matira Beach—clearly the best and largest beach.

The beginning of the Matira Beach area brings you to the luxurious Hotel Bora Bora, at Raititi Point. The Hotel Bora Bora is characterized by the over-the-water bungalows so often depicted as the epitome of elegance and beauty in Tahiti travel brochures.

SIGHTS

Matira Point, a pin-shaped spit of land with an access road bisecting it, is the site of several hotels and the best public beach on Bora Bora. The beach is popular with locals on the weekends. Matira takes its name from the 490-ton British ship *Mathilda* wrecked on Moruroa Atoll in the Tuamotus in 1792. The crew managed to get back to Tahiti where they were robbed. King Pomare I of Tahiti responded by offering his protection to the seamen and punishing the thieves. Three of the survivors decided to remain in Tahiti and one, a Mr. O'Connor, married Pomare's cousin. Years later his granddaughter (named Mathilda, after the ship) settled in Bora Bora and married a local chief. They named their property "Matira," which is the Tahitian pronunciation of Mathilda.

The most accessible World War II **coastal defense guns** can be found in the Matira area. They are on an elevation that overlooks the southern most point of the island. They can be reached by a path that runs up the hill from the mountain side of the Hotel Matira. It took 400 G.I.s to literally drag the two 13-ton guns up the hill. Even with the aid of blocks and tackle, it couldn't have been an easy task. The whole gun assembly weighed 51,000 pounds (38,100 kilograms) and the weight of each piece of the gun assembly is stamped upon it. Note the graffiti inscribed on the cement: "Battleing (sic) Battery B-276C." If you have any trouble finding the trail, use the Hotel Matira as a landmark. The southernmost bungalow on the lagoon side the property is directly across from the trailhead. (If in doubt ask at the hotel.)

Just after rounding Matira Point you might consider a stop at

HIDDEN ▶   **Galerie Rosine Temauri-Masson,** a boutique that is more like a

Bora Bora and World War II

In January 1942 America was still shaken by the Japanese raid on Pearl Harbor. With much of its Pacific fleet out of commission, the Pentagon had to reappraise the perimeter that could be defended until a counteroffensive against Japan could be mounted. The arc 1987 miles south from Hawaii to the Free French Society Islands (now French Polynesia) and westward through Samoa and Fiji to New Zealand was believed to be defensible in those somber, early days of the war. Bora Bora, 3975 miles along the direct route from Panama to New Caledonia and Australia, was selected to be the first of a chain of refueling bases across the South Pacific. It was code-named Bobcat.

By January 21, 1942, the Bobcat convoy—four cargo vessels and two recently converted passenger ships—was being filled with disassembled sea-planes, spare parts, bombs, ammunition, trucks, bulldozers, pontoon barge sections, landing craft and prefab buildings, as well as military personnel. The six-ship convoy arrived in Bora Bora on February 17 without incident.

According to an article by Jack Roudebush and Donald I. Thomas, both U.S. Navy captains who were there: "The island was virtually unspoiled by civilization; no vehicles; no roads except coral paths for bicycles and pedestrians and coconut log bridges across streams; and no utilities except a minimal water supply. . . ."

Paradise was soon filled with some 4500 U.S. servicemen, a seaplane squadron, coast and anti-aircraft defense artillery, trucks, bulldozers, tents, prefab buildings and thousands of tons of other equipment and supplies.

The face of Bora Bora quickly changed. According to Roudebush and Thomas, "the din created by heavy trucks and bulldozers shattered its tranquillity, to the delight of the young natives who had never seen these mechanical monsters." All footpaths and bridges were destroyed by the vehicles and the Seabees set about construction of heavy-duty "American" roads.

As part of the island's defense, seven-inch guns were painstakingly unloaded and hauled up the hills. Three of the four original batteries can still be seen today, as can the remains of many of the other military paraphernalia. The guns were never fired in anger—the Battle of Midway eliminated any threat of hostility. In any case, they were of little military value—their range hardly went beyond the outer reef, and the considerable recoil from any prolonged use would literally have knocked the big guns off their bases!

By 1943, the Seabees had constructed an airstrip on the northern side of the island. This now serves as Bora Bora's commercial airport. The island was handed back to the French in June 1946.

museum. This was once the home of painter Jean Masson, a pro-lific French artist who lived and worked for many years on Bora Bora. His lithographs and other works are available at the gallery. Some of his paintings, characterized by their striking colors, still hang in his former home, now the Maeva Masson pension behind the shop. ~ Matira; 67-72-04.

The next several kilometers beyond the point are peppered with hotels, restaurants and local homes. The most significant property in this area is the **Sofitel Marara,** which was built in 1977 by film-maker Dino De Laurentis to house his film crew during the filming of *Hurricane* (which, by the way, bombed). ~ Matira; 67-70-46.

The coastal road climbs up as it passes Club Med and then drops down (past the Club Med tennis courts) to the coast again before arriving in the village of Anau.

LODGING

Travelers seeking lodging have a lot to choose from in the Matira area when it comes to price categories. In addition to the more pedestrian bungalows, virtually all of the high-end hotels have over-the-water bungalows, a style of lodging pioneered in Bora Bora. The majority of the posh hotels are located within several minutes' walk of each other, making the Matira Point area truly a "Gold Coast."

Starting at Raititi Point, about five kilometers east of Vaitape, **Hotel Bora Bora** has one of the best locations on the island, with splendid views, a fine white-sand beach and excellent snorkeling. The feeling at Hotel Bora Bora is of a country club—quiet, reserved and one of the best honeymoon getaways in Tahiti. There are 55 impeccable *fares*, including 15 over-the-water units and several *fares* with private swimming pools. Even the most basic bungalows have separate bedroom and living room areas and an outside ter-race. Rooms are exquisite, and the hotel is overflowing with amen-ities. In addition to a restaurant, there are two bars that overlook the sea, a boutique and, of course, a complete array of water ac-

FEEDING THE FISH

If you think you've done everything there is to do on the island, what about feeding the fish? Grab a stale loaf of French bread and walk out on the dock at the Hotel Bora Bora. Casting your bread anywhere will result in a feeding frenzy that will roil the waters. This is *the* place to cast your bread because it is a marine park and no fishing is allowed. Bring the kids and they will never stop talking about it. Note: Be sure to ask the hotel's permission before you embark on this fish-feeding expedition.

tivities. (The diving concession is run by the Bora Bora Diving Center—a topnotch operation.) The management, to its credit, has created a nature preserve around both the hotel grounds and the waters surrounding the property that is rigorously maintained. For over 20 years, guests have fed fish by hand so the creatures are quite tame. In the early evening, it's not unusual to see huge manta rays gliding gracefully around the pier under the lights. ~ Matira; 60-44-60, fax 60-44-66, or 800-421-1490 in the U.S. ULTRA-DELUXE.

Proceeding south around Rafau Bay on the coastal road you will come to the newest budget accommodation on the island, **Pension Reva**. Located on the mountain side of the road near Ben's Place, it has several very basic rooms in a home. Reports are that budget travelers are quite satisfied. ~ Matira; 67-78-09. BUDGET.

Continuing south on the coastal road is the **Hotel Matira**, which is located on a fine white-sand beach. It has 28 bungalows, some with kitchenettes. There is also a good, moderately priced Chinese restaurant on the premises. The thatched-roof bungalows are well constructed and of average size, but are overpriced. The owners have recently built four new beach bungalows adjacent to the road, with an ugly concrete wall protecting them from the traffic, and perhaps the din. Transfers to Vaitape (which is about seven kilometers away) are not included. ~ Matira; 67-70-51, fax 67-77-02. DELUXE.

Off the main road, on the smaller dead-end access road that leads down to Matira Point, you will find the **Bora Bora Motel** on your right. This new mid-range lodging is a small property managed by the affable and loquacious Mike Henry. The attractive, modern and well-appointed thatched-roof units are all cooled by overhead fans. There are four cozy studios decorated with white tile that accommodate up to three adults. Each has private bath, double bed, living room, dining area, terrace and kitchen with large refrigerator. There are also three apartments that will sleep up to four adults that come with a double bed, living room with sofa bed, dining room, terrace, kitchen and private bath. The beach is excellent for swimming. The management is friendly and accommodating, but I think it is a bit overpriced. The motel offers discounts to airline employees. ~ Matira; 67-78-21, fax 67-77-52. DELUXE.

On the east side of Matira Point, literally across the road from the Bora Bora Motel, is the elegant **Moana Beach Parkroyal**. Smaller and more intimate than the Hotel Bora Bora, it is just as luxurious. It is also recognized as a perfect honeymoon hotel. In fact, some people prefer it to any other hotel on the island. The hotel's 30 over-the-water bungalows put you in the lap of luxury: woven *pandanus* mats and tapa cloth adorn the walls, rattan furniture and glass coffee tables allow you to peer directly into the lagoon below. There is even transportation (by speedboat) directly from the airport to your very own bungalow. Activities include the

Text continued on page 224.

Motu
Getaways

In addition to the lodging found on the main island of Bora Bora, there are also accommodations on the outlying *motus* worth considering. These range from moderate to ultra-deluxe, and are one of the best ways to enjoy a holiday in French Polynesia, particularly if privacy is high on your list. Another upside of staying on a *motu* is that you will usually receive very personalized service (the smaller ones are usually run by families) and tranquility. The downside is that to shop, send a telegram, sightsee, check out a restaurant or do anything connected with the outside world means jumping on a boat and going to the main island.

Constructed of white coral, **Fare Corail** is a house belonging to the French explorer Emile Victor. Located on Motu Tane (a private island), five minutes by boat from the Bora Bora airport, it is relatively isolated. Fare Corail has a superb white-sand beach and the swimming conditions are excellent. The house consists of a living room, bedroom, dining room, kitchen, terrace and bath. Activities include outrigger canoeing and visits to Vaitape. A three-day minimum stay is required and a 20 percent deposit is mandatory for reservations. A round-trip transfer to and from the island is provided. ~ Motu Tane; 67-74-50. MODERATE.

Oasis du Lagoon is on the east coast of Motu Roa. The private-island resort has received good reviews. There are five units amid a grove of coconut palms and papaya trees. The villa (which sleeps up to eight) has three bedrooms, a mezzanine, a kitchen and a living room with a view of the lagoon. There are four other bungalows, all with self-contained kitchen facilities and private bath. The units are clean, attractive and occupy well-manicured grounds a few yards from the beach. I have had reports that the couple who manage the small resort are friendly and helpful. Cash is king here, no credit cards are accepted. ~ Vaitape; phone/fax 67-73-38. DELUXE TO ULTRA-DELUXE.

With its gorgeous white-sand beach and splendid view of Bora Bora, **Miri Miri** is a fine place to unwind. Situated on the private Motu Paahi, the property has received kudos from guests for the service and quality of the accommodations. Miri Miri has four bungalows, each with private bath and terrace.

Bedrooms are simple but elegant, with woven bamboo walls that allow fresh air to circulate. Water activities are available, as are motorboat rentals. Rates include breakfast. Lunch and dinner are also available. This is a cash-only facility. It's located ten minutes by boat from the airport. ~ Motu Paahi; 67-71-39, fax 67-72-00. DELUXE.

Mai Moana is a private island aimed at the well-to-do traveler who desires the seclusion of a small offshore resort but doesn't want to share it with a hundred other guests. There are three *fare*-style bungalows near a white-sand beach. The *fares* are well appointed, and come with a double bed, private bath and dressing room, not to mention a television, video and phone. Windsurfing and other nautical activities are there for the sporting set. Unlike less expensive offshore operations, Mai Moana has a small restaurant/bar on the premises. Located on Motu Iti, Mai Moana is five minutes by boat from the airport or ten minutes from the ferry dock. Round-trip transfers are included in the tariff. ~ Motu Iti; 67-70-69. ULTRA-DELUXE.

Located on Motu Toopua, a small islet inside Bora Bora's lagoon, **Bora Bora Lagoon Resort** is unlike the other offshore accommodations. It is a large luxury resort, with 30 beach bungalows, 50 over-the-water bungalows, including two suites and two handicap units. To call the units well-appointed would be something of an understatement—they are posh. Features include wood floors, private lanais, television and phones. A lot of attention has been paid to detail. For example, all guests are greeted by a private boat at the airport but when you're shelling out close to the GNP of a developing country to stay at a hotel you would expect the very best. In addition to the bungalows, there are three restaurants on the property as well as a full complement of activities including tennis, volleyball, windsurfing, diving and other nautical activities. ~ 60-40-00, fax 60-40-01, or 800-432-2672 in the U.S. ULTRA-DELUXE.

usual water sports and sunset cruises. The food at the resort is *nouvelle cuisine*—the chef is imported from the Bel Air Hotel in Los Angeles. There are ten beachside bungalows in addition to the over-the-water bungalows. ~ Matira; 67-73-73, fax 67-71-41, or 800-835-7742 in the U.S. ULTRA-DELUXE.

Farther down the road, on the west side of Matira Point, is **Chez Nono Leverd**. It is perhaps the nicest mid-range accommodation on the island. A good sign is its popularity with local tourists as well as overseas visitors. Not only are the units clean and well appointed, but they are on the beach. There's a family atmosphere at Chez Nono. The property has six units: a house with six rooms (that can be rented out individually) with shared kitchen and bath (all with hot water); and self-contained Polynesian-style *fares* with kitchenettes and bathrooms. The house also has a large sitting room with television. Bicycles are available for rent and excursions can be arranged, including canoe trips that feature picnics and snorkeling. Breakfast is available, but you're on your own for dinner. (There are plenty of inexpensive eateries nearby.) A deposit is needed to reserve a room. The proprietors are congenial, but in the past were not apt to go out of their way for you. Perhaps the decrease in visitors to the island has changed their attitude. ~ Matira; 67-71-38, fax 67-74-27. BUDGET TO MODERATE.

Chez Robert and Tina rests at the tail end of Matira Point, a minute's stroll down the road from Chez Nono Leverd. Robert has two units: a house with three bedrooms, living room, kitchen, terrace and common bath; and a second house with five bedrooms, kitchen and bath. Both places are clean, but the rooms are small, spartan and dreary. Circle-island tours via outrigger or picnics on the beach are available on request. The location is good, but Robert's moodiness is often a bit much to deal with. Round-trip transfers from the dock are provided. ~ Matira; 67-72-92. BUDGET.

Back on the main coastal road, **Chez Maeva Masson** can be found directly behind the Galleries Rosine Temauri-Masson. The pension was the former abode of artist Jean Masson and his works (some of them very good) still line the walls of his funky, slightly off-center, Bohemian home. Chez Maeva Masson still feels like a home, rather than the typical, nondescript, thrown-together-for-the-tourists shack that sometimes passes for low-end lodging in Tahiti. Chez Masson is a two-story wooden structure with a large and well-equipped communal kitchen. It's clean and airy with a large dining room/salon area and a single (cold water) bath and shower that may not be enough for a full house. Rooms range from a loft-like sleeping area (known as the dorm) that accommodates up to four or five people, to separate rooms for individuals or couples. There are several canoes and a small boat that can hired. Aesthetically, Chez Maeva Masson is very hip, but slightly overpriced for the backpacking crowd. ~ Matira; 67-72-04. BUDGET.

Just before La Bounty Restaurant, on the mountain side of the road, you will come upon **Chez Léon**, a new lodging with several *fare*-style bungalows clustered close together. Local and friendly in character, it has garnered very good reviews. From all reports this modest accommodation has clean rooms and *sympathique* management. Evidently the rooms here are less expensive than Village Pauline, the other popular low-cost lodging. ~ Matira. BUDGET TO MODERATE.

◄ *HIDDEN*

Just down the road, **Bora Bora Beach Club** has friendly employees and a good beachside location. It's a fairly new hotel with basic amenities. The 36 rooms are of average size and quality. All have a refrigerator, ceiling fan and private terrace, but the walls are thin enough to make you hope you don't get a nightowl as a neighbor. Free activities include windsurfing, canoe paddling and volleyball. There is also a restaurant, bar, pool and excursions. ~ Matira; 67-71-16. DELUXE.

Next door to the Beach Club is the **Sofitel Marara**, which was originally constructed by Italian film producer Dino De Laurentis to house his staff during the production of *Hurricane*. Although the movie bombed, the hotel was a better investment. It has 64 bungalows, a restaurant, bar, boutique, an excellent array of water activities, tennis and excursions. If you think of the Hotel Bora Bora as first-class seating on an airplane, Hotel Marara might be considered business class. The atmosphere is a bit more relaxed, the staff friendly and the prices lower— although it's not inexpensive by any means. Rooms are spacious and well appointed, but not ostentatious. ~ Matira; 67-70-46, fax 67-74-03, or 800-221-4542 in the U.S. ULTRA-DELUXE.

The Sofitel Marara has consistently good Tahitian dance revues that begin at 8 p.m. daily. No cover.

Down the road a bit, **Village Pauline** is situated on a white-sand beach shaded by lovely coconut palms. Amenities include a quality shower/bathing area, clean toilets and kitchen facilities and an infrastructure on par with any camping facility in French Polynesia. Pauline has added a nice touch—several picnic tables covered with *palapa*-style thatched roofs facing the sea. These make a nice common eating and reading area. There are also eight small but clean bungalows or beach cabins suitable for a single traveler or a couple. There are also six larger *fares* with double beds, kitchenette and private bath. The property has expanded across the road, with four new rooms constructed in a row—a motel-like arrangement. They are minuscule boxes surrounded by a pleasant garden area with a communal shower/bath. The camping area is also on the mountain side of the road and will accommodate up to 30 people. (Note that the facilities close to the road might be noisy.) Transportation is available on a daily basis for shopping trips or to catch your boat or plane—for a fee. Pauline is notorious for changing prices during July and August when demand increases. For many years she enjoyed a virtual monopoly on quality low-end lodging facilities, but with the introduction of several new places you now have a choice. ~ Matira; 67-72-16. BUDGET.

DINING

The biggest change in the restaurant scene on Bora Bora has been the sprouting up of decent budget-priced eateries, especially in the Matira area.

Along Rofau Bay, just beyond the Hotel Bora Bora, you will come to **Snack Matira**, opposite the Chez Helene boutique. It has very basic fare including hamburgers, pizza, chicken and soft drinks. ~ Matira; 67-77-32. BUDGET.

Continuing down the road is **Ben's Place,** an open-air café on the island side of the road. Ben's has a wider (and more expensive) range of food than Snack Matira. Ben Teraitepo, an engaging native Bora Boran, and his American-born wife, Robin, enjoy shooting the breeze with their guests. They have the only menu I've seen in French Polynesia that is completely in English. In fact, there is no hint of a French influence here. Ben's has pizza, lasagna, steak (including salad and fries) or tuna steak. This is the kind of place that may be too expensive for the average backpacker, but provides an off-beat alternative to hotel cuisine. Open daily except Thursdays. ~ Matira; 67-74-54. BUDGET TO MODERATE.

Turtles were sacred to the ancient Polynesians, and were only consumed by chiefs and priests.

Directly opposite Ben's Place is a small stand called **Snack Julie** that offers good *poisson cru* and other local fare. ~ Matira. BUDGET.

A few steps past Ben's is the **Restaurant Matira**, which offers basic stir-fried Chinese fare. The food is average, but the restaurant is in a nice locale, on a patio overlooking the lagoon. The menu includes chop suey, seafood, fish and lobster. This is also a great place to take a break on your stroll around the point. ~ In the Hotel Matira, Matira; 67-70-51. BUDGET TO MODERATE.

As you turn the corner, just prior to arriving at the Moana Beach Hotel, look for the **Mahana View**, a new eatery operated by a Tahitian and his American-born wife. On the beach and adorned with bamboo cane on the exterior, it has a wonderful view of the lagoon, tasty food and a friendly ambience. The dining room serves seafood and—and it's probably the only place on the island where you can dine on Mexican cuisine. ~ Matira. BUDGET.

HIDDEN ►

If you take the access road to the Moana Beach Hotel, keep an eye open for **Temarama**, another new restaurant that has received kudos from locals. The chef is reportedly first class. He specializes in Chinese, French and seafood dishes. The *poisson cru* and shrimp dishes are worth a try. ~ Matira; 67-75-61. BUDGET TO MODERATE.

Snack La Bounty, near the Bora Bora Motel, is a modest thatched-roof bungalow-style affair with an outdoor patio sporting white plastic dining tables. It has French/Tahitian cuisine. Other dishes include fish, sashimi, shrimp, salads and the best pizza on the island. Snack La Bounty is popular with French visitors. ~ Matira; 67-70-43. BUDGET TO MODERATE.

Opposite the Bora Bora Beach Club is Le Tiare, a fine new addition to the restaurant scene. From reports I've received, this is one of the best moderately priced restaurants on the island. Le Tiare specializes in French cuisine. The chef was formerly at the Bora Bora Beach Club. ~ Matira; 67-61-39. MODERATE TO DELUXE.

◄ HIDDEN

The Le Tiare market is a tidy shop located directly in front of the Bora Bora Beach Club. It has a comprehensive selection and is the only market on this side of town. Matira; 67-61-39.

GROCERIES

For those who don't fish, bonito can be purchased at roadside stands for about US$1 per pound.

There is no shortage of souvenir shopping possibilities on Bora Bora. Note that many of the items on sale come from Southeast Asia or China, however. Balinese woodcarvers are obviously adept at adding "Bora Bora" to their handicrafts.

SHOPPING

Located a short distance north of Raititi Point is Moana Arts, an establishment run by Erwin Christian, a famous Tahitian photographer. There is a superb selection of cards, posters and fashions shot by Mr. Christian, a descendent of the famous Bounty mutineer, Fletcher Christian. ~ Matira; 67-70-33.

A few hundred yards north of the Hotel Bora Bora is Martine's Creations, a small boutique that began as a roadside stand and is now a chic shop selling black pearls and tie-dyed and air-brushed T-shirts that are her own creation. It's a good place to start looking for souvenirs and is less expensive than hotel gift shops. Martine's is one of Bora Bora's many boutiques and family-run craft stands, an important cottage industry on the island. ~ Matira; 67-70-69.

Along Rofau Bay look for a small vendor named Chez Helene, opposite Snack Matira. Helene has good quality pareus, that you can see her making. They're sold at competitive prices.

Across the road from Chez Helene is Galerie Rosine Temauri-Masson, run by the widow of French artist Jean Masson. Masson, a prolific painter, lived and worked for many years on Bora Bora. His paintings are characterized by striking colors. Masson was one of the first painters to take an interest in the hand-colored, decorative cloth typical of the region. Lithographs of his work are available in the gallery at reasonable prices. ~ Matira; 67-72-04.

Approximately six kilometers from Vaitape is Matira Point, most of which is a white-sand beach. Unfortunately, it is occupied by a number of hotel properties. But, as in all of French Polynesia, all beaches have a public access.

BEACHES

HIDDEN ▶   **MATIRA BEACH** 🐚 Perhaps the best-kept secret on the island is the sole public beach on Matira Point, a hidden local favorite. This long stretch of white sand is great for swimming or picnics and the crowd is almost always Tahitian. There is not much in the way of facilities but there are several mushroom-like canopies for shade, and a toilet. A note of caution: It's not prudent to leave any valuables on the beach unattended. ~ The beach is located on Matira Point. To find it, look for the sign for Moana Beach Parkroyal. This marks the small road that bisects Matira Point. Walk to the end of the road; the beach will be on your right-hand side.

▼▼▼▼▼▼▼▼▼▼▼▼▼▼▼

Anau Village to Faanui

The beginning of Anau Village starts at Chez Stellio, a backpacker campground located just over the hill from the new Club Med, which sits on its own bay. The old Club Med on the other side of the island was smaller and prone to storm damage. The new Club Med is a much more ambitious development both in size and quality.

SIGHTS   The first stop in the area is Club Med's own **belvédère** (lookout) atop the ridge above Mataorio Bay. The path to the lookout is accessed by Club Med's private tunnel under the road, but if you go just beyond the Hibiscus Boutique toward Anau you can see where the steps emerge from under the road and make your way up to the path. ~ Anau; 60-46-04, or 800-824-4844 in the U.S.

Anau extends another one kilometer along the shoreline. Anau is the least adulterated, most typical Polynesian village on Bora Bora. This is because it is the most isolated settlement on the island. Until the construction of the new Club Med, there has never been a major hotel in the vicinity. Anau is strung out along a rocky stretch of coastline. It has churches, a school, a general store and rambling, tin-roofed homes with well-kept gardens. But despite the bucolic setting, it is not a terribly friendly place.

Across from Chez Stellio is the terminus for a dirt road that traverses the island. The short, steep pathway to the television tower and the other side of the island starts beside a truck maintenance shop. The trek, about a half-mile (two kilometers) in length, follows the saddle of the island. The track is easily negotiable. Some of it is paved but most of it is dirt. At the **summit** is an outstanding view of the Motu Piti Au.

If you instead continue just past Anau, you are in the shadow of 2384-foot (727-meter) **Mt. Otemanu**, the highest point on the island. It has been said that the mountain has never been climbed because of the crumbling nature of the sheer rock walls below the summit. At the base of these walls, and not easily accessible, is the **Otemanu Cave,** formerly a burial site. Rumor has it that G.I.s added that well-known World War II graffiti "Kilroy was here" to the cave walls, but I haven't been able to verify that as the ascent to the cave is steep and dangerous. I don't recommend you try it either.

Four kilometers past Anau the road climbs the coastline as it crosses **Tuivahora Point**, then drops and rises again like a roller coaster. In between dips, on the sea side, is **Marae Aehua-tai**, one of several ancient Polynesian temples on Bora Bora. This *marae* is one of the best preserved on the island and appears to be a wall of black basalt slabs propped upright like giant tombstones. From the *marae* site there are fine views across the lagoon as you stand nearly in the shadow of Mt. Otemanu.

At Tuivahora Point the road bends sharply and there is an off-shoot of a trail that descends to a private home. The trail continues behind the house out along the point to **Marae Taharuu**, a tall, natural obelisk that appears to still be used by Tahitians. The black thumb-like boulder juts up from the earth. There are marvelous views in both directions from this vantage point. If you do take the small trail to the *marae*, be respectful of the proprietor.

The Tuivahora Point area is also the locale for the most spectacular **coastal defense gun emplacements** on the island. To get there, take the first right at the bottom of the hill, a rutted jeep track that follows the contours of the shoreline. Continue along this lonely road past a concrete platform that looks like a foundation for a home. Carry on to the second platform down the road, and after a few steps, stop. At this point, backtrack a few yards and follow the jeep track that goes straight up the hill. There's an outstanding view, but a newly created open-pit garbage dump makes

RESPECT THE MARAE

Stories abound of those who purposefully or inadvertently defiled sacred shrines and suffered grave consequences. One such story is about a laborer working near Marae Marotetini in 1973. He discovered a rusted biscuit tin containing what were believed to be the charred remnants of clothing worn by the last queen of Bora Bora. The tin was accidentally destroyed and not long afterward, despite the efforts of modern medicine, the worker died of a mysterious malady. According to author Milas Hinshaw's account of the incident in *Bora Bora E*, the worker's dead body "turned black—resembling a corpse that had been consumed by fire." Hinshaw and his son claim to have been cursed by this same *marae* when they picked up several human bones there and took them home as souvenirs. Not until five years later, after returning the bones to their resting place, did the author's spate of bad luck stop. Why it took him five years to figure this out, I do not know.

visiting the guns hard on the nose. When the dump is not burning and smoke is not an issue, flies and the odor can be offensive.

Considering that this is one of the most beautiful views on the island, it was a rather unenlightened choice for a garbage dump. But according to the mayor, this was the only public land available to build it.

From Tuivahora Point, for the next few kilometers the coast is virtually uninhabited, sprinkled only with a few houses and banana groves, coconut palms and taro patches.

As you continue along the road look for the Colonial-style **Revatua Club** facing Taimoo Bay. This club has a beautiful swimming pool and clear ocean water for snorkeling. Revatua is the only accommodation on this side of the island and the hotel's **L'Espadon Restaurant** is a superb place to sit on the veranda and quench your thirst. Just a few steps past the hotel is a small stand selling souvenirs and coconuts for drinking. ~ Anau; 67-71-67.

Two kilometers past Taimoo Bay is the minuscule **Maritime Museum**, run by Betrand Derasse, an architect who has constructed a number of traditional Polynesian boat models and models of European ships with a historic connection to French Polynesia, such as Captain Cook's *Endeavour*. ~ Faanui; 67-75-24.

Another two kilometers brings you to **Taihi Point**, the northernmost spot on the island. From here you can trek up the hill to the top of Popoti Ridge, the site of a former U.S. Navy radar installation. (See "Hiking" later in this chapter.)

Just past the point are the remnants of a Hyatt Hotel. It was to be built on the hillside and over the lagoon. But when it was close to completion the developer ran out of money. The incomplete hotel is now slowly deteriorating under the tropical sun. Beyond the hotel site are the **Bora Bora Condos**, a collection of houses perched on stilts on the hillside. Some of them are owned by Jack Nicholson and Marlon Brando, but don't look too hard—chances are the stars are in Hollywood or some other sybaritic locale. ~ Faanui; 67-71-33.

Strewn along the next five kilometers, which includes the Faanui Bay area, are a collection of relics and artifacts from both ancient Polynesians and the U.S. government. At the 25-kilometer point you can see a **boat pier** and **seaplane ramp**. The pier, still used today, was a World War II addition to the island. The concrete ramp sloping gently into the lagoon was used as a seaplane base. It was here that up to 12 OS2U single-engine float seaplanes could tie up. Just another kilometer down the road is an old **submarine slip**. Resembling a giant concrete vat, it was built to accommodate submarines, but over the years has seen more action as a swimming hole for village children.

You are now on the fringes of **Faanui Village**. Look for a *40 kilometer per hour* speed limit sign and you'll see **Marae Fare-Opu**, an ancient Polynesian temple on the sea side, squeezed between the road and the water's edge. Two of the slabs are clearly marked with turtle petroglyphs.

The Faanui Bay and Village section are where most of the U.S. servicemen were stationed during Operation Bobcat during World War II. Faanui Bay was chosen by the U.S. Navy as the most strategic place for a base. The location was protected on all sides by land, was directly opposite a *motu* and could only be seen from the air. The bay had to be extensively dredged to accommodate submarines and other vessels, and to this day it remains environmentally damaged from this endeavor. Visible in the area are pilings from a dock and several Quonset huts nestled in the bushes. They are found mostly along the mountain side of the road. Also visible is a massive ammunition bunker on the hillside.

From the Faanui church at the head of the bay, a road runs directly inland. It can be taken to the ridge above and then down to the other side of the island to Vairau Bay. (See "Hiking" later in this chapter.)

Situated in a coconut plantation that overlooks a small field on the inland side of the road is **Marae Taianapa**. Associated with Mt. Pahia, the 2168-foot (661-meter) peak that towers over Vaitape, this *marae* is a fairly large temple with two small petroglyphs. (You've overshot the temple if you come to the Hinano Beer and Coca Cola depot, about 100 yards beyond the temple.) Right behind this depot is the Faanui Power Station, a steam generator powered by burning coconut husks.

Various landmarks on Bora Bora carry the god Hiro's name, including the bell of Hiro on the very southern tip of Motu Toopua. It's actually a rock that when struck, produces a bell-like ring.

Bora Bora's major freight unloading facility, **Farepiti Wharf**, is a sturdy dock built by the Seabees during the war. Interisland ships from Tahiti still dock here. Walk along the shoreline for about 100 yards beyond the dock and at the tip of the point lies **Marae Marotetini**, which historically was the most important temple on Bora Bora. It was restored in 1968 by Dr. Y. H. Sinoto, head archeologist of Honolulu's Bishop Museum. According to the old religion, the *marae* is associated with Mt. Otemanu. Near the *marae* are two tombs built for the Bora Bora royal family during the last century.

LODGING

Inaugurated in December 1993, the **Club Med Coral Garden** is located on a nice beach about 12 kilometers from Vaitape. Relocated from its previous site, it now sits at the foot of Paopao Point. There are 150 twin-share bungalows. Unlike the larger Club Med on Moorea, there is nothing rundown or chintzy about this new Club Med. It comes highly recommended as a honeymoon or dream-vacation getaway. Bungalows are well spaced throughout the "village," and each one has a view of the sea. The interiors are modern and very comfortable, as are the posh bathrooms. All are cooled by overhead fans, which are quite adequate, and come with many amenities. An aesthetically debatable choice was made by the designer to paint the facility in pastel shades of yellow, mauve and chartreuse—hence the name Coral Garden. Some of the locals have complained that the pastel motif clashes with the traditional Polynesian-style thatched bungalows. The Club Med machine is in full force here. Club Med Coral Garden offers the usual battery of activities such as snorkeling, windsurfing, volleyball, tennis, a so-so driving range, archery, aerobics classes, basketball, outrigger canoe rides, visits to a neighboring *motu*, and excursions of every kind. *And* the service and food are excellent. A full array of quality salads, seafood, meat dishes and desserts are available buffet-style. If you like the Club Med environment and the all-inclusive Club Med program, then Club Med Coral Garden is a bargain for top-end visitors. For more information on Club Med, it's best to contact your travel agent. ~ Anau; 60-46-04, or 800-824-4844 in the U.S. ULTRA-DELUXE.

On the fringes of Anau Village is **Chez Stellio**, just beyond Club Med. Chez Stellio abuts a seawall but lacks a beach. This is clearly a backpacker's facility. There is a more-than-adequate communal kitchen. The facilities are clean and acceptable, but it doesn't have the same flair as Chez Pauline. There is a dorm unit that sleeps ten, as well as a house with five rooms and cooking facilities. Two rooms in the home have double beds, while the other three have two singles each. Prices for long stays are negotiable. All in all it's a bit rough around the edges, and far from town but satisfactory. ~ Anau; 67-71-32. BUDGET.

Also set far away from the teeming crowds is **Revatua Club**, on the eastern side of Bora Bora. Reopened under new management, it has been completely renovated. There are 16 rooms. A boutique and bar/restaurant are built on stilts over the water. There is also a pontoon into the lagoon that leads to a huge seawater swimming pool. The atmosphere is definitely barefoot, local and French, which I found comfortable. L'Espadon, the hotel restaurant, serves excellent French and Tahitian food—among the best on the island. The friendly bar is a good spot to meet local folks. There is excellent snorkeling nearby, and I'm sure they have the only glass-bottomed double canoe with a stereo. Tours are also available. Located 12 kilometers from Vaitape, on the leeward side of the island. ~ Anau; 67-71-67, 67-73-31, fax 67-76-59. MODERATE TO DELUXE.

Near the decaying Hyatt Hotel at the north end of the island in Faanui you'll find **Bora Bora Condos**. There are 11 bungalows on the mountain side and three over the water. Each bungalow has two bedrooms, a living room, dining room, bathroom and terrace, and accommodate five people. Though the bungalows are well maintained, the crumbling remnants of the old hotel nearby makes

Shark
Feeding

Shark feeding on Bora Bora was originated by photographer Erwin Christian, a descendent of Fletcher Christian of HMS *Bounty* fame. A tour leader takes you, snorkel and flippers in hand, to an area of the lagoon that has been roped off. Your guide stands in the roped-off section throwing bait in the water while a dozen or so black-tip reef sharks go into their patented feeding frenzy. The audience stands a safe distance away.

Is shark feeding necessarily a "good" thing to do? The jury is still out. From what I can determine, feeding sharks inside the lagoon is somewhat innocuous—the sharks are fed daily, and the participants are small reef sharks. There are some divers who feed sharks outside the reef and this can be dangerous if not properly handled. You not only attract larger, more aggressive species (i.e., hammerheads, grays and tiger sharks), but if these creatures get used to being fed on a regular basis and you don't happen to have food when you run into them, they instinctively look to your hands for something to eat. If you don't happen to have anything for them . . . well, you get the picture. Michel Condesse, the capable owner of the Bora Bora Diving Center, assured me he has not had problems with sharks biting divers. However, snorkelers or divers feeding moray eels have run into problems; morays are less circumspect about what they latch onto.

If you're interested in participating in this spectacle there are two outfitters to contact:

Franck Sachs of **Moana Adventure Tours** has come recommended as a shark-feeding specialist inside the lagoon. ~ Matira; 67-70-33.

Nono Leverd has a popular shark feed. Nono will actually pick small reef sharks, show them to tourists and then let the sharks go. It's not a recommended practice for visitors. ~ Matira; 67-71-38.

the area seem rather eerie and deserted. Not only is it far from any dining or tourist area, there is simply no compelling reason to stay here. ~ Faanui; 67-71-33. DELUXE.

DINING

You don't have much choice out this way. There is only one eatery—**L'Espadon**, the restaurant at the Revatua Club. Specialties of the house are grilled seafood and *fruit du mer*. A pleasurable spot to dine is the outdoor restaurant that overlooks the lagoon. ~ Anau; 67-71-67. MODERATE TO DELUXE.

GROCERIES

There is a small market in the village of Anau. You can purchase soft drinks and other small grocery items. The selection isn't as good as the bigger markets in Vaitape, but if you're staying on this side of the island and need just a few small things it's a lot more convenient.

SHOPPING

Occasionally a small vendor sets up a stand selling green (drinking) coconuts and shell leis a hundred yards or so past the Revatua Club.

NIGHTLIFE

Club Med has a daily variety show that is always good for a few chuckles. This is usually followed by dancing or some other activity. The Club is primarily restricted to guests, but with permission, outsiders can usually come in. ~ Anau; 60-46-04.

▼▼▼▼▼▼▼▼▼▼▼▼▼▼

Outdoor Adventures

CAMPING

There is only one campground on Bora Bora, **Village Pauline**. A common cooking area and shower/toilet facilities are provided for campers and guests who occupy the *fares* and other accommodations. The camping area is located on the mountain side of the road, not on the beach. Bring your own tent. ~ Matira; 67-72-16.

DIVING

There are popular dive sites both inside and outside the lagoon. Since there's only one pass, Teavanui, it can be a long trip to some of the outer reef dive sites. Sites closer to the pass are well visited. Manta rays are often seen in the lagoon's shallow waters. Calypso Club does a manta ray dive daily in the waters between Anau Village and Motu Pitiaau, an area nicknamed **Manta Bay** or **Manta's Reef**. Manta rays are harmless plankton feeders. Their impressive size (up to 18 feet in length and weighing up to two tons!) and graceful appearance make them favorites with divers. Moray eels and turtles are also spotted, but it's the rays that are the big attraction. **Manta Ray Channel** or **Manta Ray Pit** is another lagoon dive site where the magnificent rays are regularly encountered. It's just south of Motu Toopua Iti, the smaller *motu* to the south of Motu Toopua. Eagle rays are also encountered in the lagoon, particularly in **Eagle Ray Channel** between Motu Toopua and the main island.

The **Aquarium** is a popular diving and snorkeling site. It's located between Motu Piti Aau and the inner edge of the outer reef near Tupitipiti Point, immediately offshore from Club Med, just south of their *motu* beach.

Outside the reef the **Tapu Dive** is popular, both for its proximity to Teavanui Pass and for the large numbers of moray eels that are seen. It's also a good spot to observe giant Napoleon fish and jackfish. The dive starts at about 75 feet, makes its way up almost to the surface as it approaches the outer edge of the reef, then turns and descends back to the dive boat's anchor line. Moray eels are encountered along the way. They have become so familiar with divers that they often come up and make close-up, face-to-mask inspections. The **Teavanui Pass Entrance**, right at the mouth of the pass, is another popular outer-reef dive.

White Valley Dive, also known as **Muri Muri**, is a curving sandbar off Paharire Point, off Motu Mute, where the airport is located. Larger species, in particular large shoals of barracuda, are often encountered here. It's not unusual to see up to 30 gray sharks, turtles and dolphins. Outside the reef at **Tupitipiti Point**, just the other side of the reef from the Aquarium lagoon dive, is an excellent dive site. The one drawback is the time it takes to get there. According to Michel Condesse of Bora Bora Divers, it has the best coral wall in all of Polynesia as well as numerous caves. **South Point Dive** on the outer reef directly south of Matira Point, also a long haul to get to, is an above-average dive destination, with an emphasis on pelagics rather than the reef system. The lack of rich reef life here can be traced to the damage caused by dredging the lagoon during World War II and overfishing inside the lagoon.

The two dive operators on Bora Bora are the Calypso Club and the Bora Bora Diving Center. **Bora Bora Diving Center** is run by an engaging French couple, Michel and Anne Condesse. Located in a tidy green bungalow just past the Bora Bora Hotel (coming from town), they serve both the general public and Hotel Bora Bora, Hotel Bora Lagoon Resort and Club Med. Their staff consists of five bilingual instructors and they have four dive boats, four air compressors and dive gear for more than 30 people. Their equipment appears to be well maintained. They dive at over ten different sites, primarily outside the lagoon. They will take you to see a variety of undersea flora and fauna, including manta and eagle rays, turtles, Napoleon fish, shark, barracudas, dolphins and moray eels. Introductory dives are performed just off the pier at the Hotel Bora Bora. Bora Bora Diving Center is a PADI certified facility and a Three Star CMAS operation. ~ Matira; 67-71-84.

The Calypso Club, near the Bora Bora Beach Club, is run by Claude Sibani. They have three instructors and a full complement of dives both in the lagoon and outside the reef. Sibani offers open-water certification and introductory dives. I have received some complaints about the safety of the equipment from at least one reader. ~ Matira; 67-77-85.

SNORKELING Alas, snorkeling is not particularly good along the shore of Bora Bora, except for the areas around the Hotel Bora Bora and the Revatua Club. The reason given is that the island has been overfished. The waters around the Hotel Bora Bora are teeming with fish because the hotel has established an underwater "park" where fishing is strictly forbidden. The hotel grounds are not generally open to the public, but if you obtain permission it's okay to snorkel. The Bora Bora site is the most accessible site. A more difficult area to reach, but an excellent spot, is known as the **Coral Garden**, located offshore from the Sofitel on the south tip of Motu Roa. Many of the hotels and pensions feature this as part of their excursion program and will drop you off at the *motu.*

SAILING One can see Bora Bora by hiring a boat on the island or chartering a vessel from another point, such as Tahiti or Raiatea, and seeing Bora Bora as part of a larger island tour. For those interested in the latter, see sailing sections on Tahiti, Moorea and Raiatea. Most of the skippers on Bora Bora will do day trips or will be amenable to extended charters.

If you are interested in hiring a vessel on Bora Bora contact **Thierry or Luisa Jubin,** who conduct tours on the *Coup de Coeur,* a 40-foot Jeannot Sun Fizz that operates out of the Bora Bora and Moana Beach hotels. ~ Matira; 67-76 08. **Steeve Walker** skippers a 62-foot ketch based at Club Med. ~ Nunue; 67-72-37.

A catamaran can be hired through long-time French Polynesian resident **Rich Postma**, the dean of the cruise scene. His vessel, the *Taravana,* is affiliated with the Hotel Bora Bora but he will take anyone who wishes to come along. Rich has a knack for making

✔ CHECK THESE OUT—UNIQUE OUTDOOR ADVENTURES

- Go where few have gone before—the narrow, steep trail that cuts through dense jungle as it climbs 2000 feet up **Mt. Pahia.** *page 238*
- Scuba dive the calm waters of Bora Bora's **lagoon;** you are almost guaranteed to see elusive giant manta rays. *page 234*
- Snorkel a few feet away from the most feared and misunderstood creatures in the ocean on a **Shark Feeding,** where you can watch the frenzy unfold. *page 233*
- Skip across the gentle waves as you take a **catamaran cruise** around the lagoon in search of the best *motu* for a secluded picnic lunch. *page 236*

everyone feel very special on his cruises. He once took Raquel Welch for a spin around the lagoon. He has a variety of trips, including sunset cruises, deep-sea fishing, or six-hour barbecue picnics that feature snorkeling and beachcombing on an isolated *motu*. His pride and joy is a Hobie Cat 21, *Wet and Wild*, that can take up to four passengers plus the captain for light fishing or sailing around the lagoon. The vessel is comfortable, very fast and inexpensive to charter for a couple. ~ Matira; 67-70-79, 67-76-62.

Another cruise company, calling itself **Bora Bora Fun**, has similar day trips aboard their cat, the *Taaroa Catamaran*. The tour includes snorkeling and reef walking, or simply lounging on the beach of a *motu*. They are moored at the Bora Bora Beach Club. Charters can also be arranged. ~ Matira; 67-61-55.

Like his enterprising brother Dany, who runs Tupuna Mountain Expeditions, Nono Leverd has a day trip that has received good recommendations from visitors. **Teremoana Tours** provides motorized canoe trips that include shark feeding, snorkeling, a visit to the den of the leopard rays and a picnic on a *motu*. Teremoana, by the way, is the name of Nono's *pirogue*. ~ Matira; 67-71-38.

The **Nautical Center** at the Bora Bora Beach Club provides water-skiing, parasailing, outrigger tours, jet skis, motorboat rentals, Hobie Cats, windsurfing, glass-bottomed boat tours and pedal cars. It is open to the general public. ~ Matira; 67-71-16.

OTHER WATER SPORTS

FISHING

Sportfishing is quite good just outside Bora Bora's reef, where you can hook blue marlin, yellow fin tuna, sailfish, wahoo and mahi-mahi as well as bottom fish such as snapper and grouper. Inside the lagoon it is possible to snag some of the smaller reef fish, but because of *ciguatera* (a type of food poisoning), it's probably not a good idea to eat your catch.

Perhaps the premier charter boat skipper on Bora Bora is **Keith "Taaroa" Olson**. Keith, who first tuned into the Tahitian way of life while visiting French Polynesia with his parents in the 1960s, later dropped out of American society and has made Bora Bora his home for the past two decades. His vessel, the *Te Aratai II*, is a 26-foot (8-meter) Farallon. Keith speaks fluent Tahitian and is well versed in the local culture. He's a good source of information about French Polynesia. He is amenable to short trips for neophytes who would rather not to spend five hours at sea. ~ Matira; 67-71-96, 67-72-86.

Some of the other vessels available are the *Jessie L*, a 35-foot Luhrs, skippered by **Alain Loussan**. ~ Nunue; 67-70-59. The *Lady C* is a 29-foot Phoenix, captained by **Steeve Ellacott**. ~ Tiipoto; 67-72-12. The *Mokalei* is a 37-foot Stryker under the command of **Kirk Pearson**. ~ Matira; 60-44-60.

BIKING

At one time the larger hotels provided free bicycles for their guests, but this practice has stopped. A bicycle is ideal for shopping or sightseeing and it's worth renting a bike for a round-the-island tour. One word of caution—traffic on the island, especially the corridor from Vaitape to the Matira area, has gotten quite heavy. A number of accidents involving tourists on bicycles have occurred. You should always ride defensively, and avoid riding at night.

Bicycles can be rented at **Bora Bora Rent-A-Car**, located 200 yards past the post office in the Matira direction. ~ Vaitape; 67-70-03. **The Hibiscus Boutique** rents bikes as well. ~ Nunue; 67-72-43.

HIKING

VAITAPE AREA The **Nunue to Anau** (1.5 miles/2 kilometers) hike will take you across the lower spine of Bora Bora. It can be easily traversed along a 20-minute track beginning at the **Television Transmission Tower**. The hike starts in the Nunue area, 1.5 miles (2 kilometers) from town heading toward Matira. Atop the crest of the steep hill, there is a magnificent panoramic view of Vaitape to the west and Motu Pitiaau and Raiatea and Tahaa to the east. (You will get into trouble if you're caught climbing the TV tower so suppress that urge.) At the top of the trail, turn left toward the TV tower (instead of to the right toward a private home). The overgrown footpath down the hill will take you to the village of Anau. Across the island it's only ten minutes up and ten minutes down, but it can be hot so bring water. If you are doing this on a bike, be sure to walk the bike down the hill. The terminus on the Anau side is at a truck maintenance shop—directly across the road from Chez Stellio. To find the trailhead on the Nunue side, look for a road that begins next to a double-columned telephone pole. (Near the area is a cluster of boutiques and shops so it is difficult to miss.)

The trek to 2168-foot (661-meter) high **Mt. Pahia** (5 miles/9 kilometers) can be climbed with the aid of a guide or independently in half a day. The trail itself is very narrow and steep, but can be negotiated by individuals in good shape. You should budget three hours up the mountain and three hours down. The vista at the top is well worth the hike, which passes through dense jungle. The trailhead is in downtown Vaitape. Just across the main street, opposite the pier, look for the basketball court that is adjacent to the *gendarmerie*. The road going toward the mountain that passes the court and Socredo Bank leads to the trail. Take three or four quarts of water per person for the hike and bring good shoes. (Be sure and tell someone of your plans lest you get lost!) If you want the guided tour, contact Ato, the proprietor of Chez Ato. ~ Nunue; 67-77-27.

ANAU VILLAGE TO VAITAPE Another way to traverse the spine of Bora Bora can be accomplished by taking the track from **Faanui to Vairau Bay** (3 miles/6.4 kilometers) in 40 to 50 minutes. The scenery is spectacular and the trek can be done by people in average physical condition. I recommend that you start on the Faanui side as the trailhead is easier to find at the Faanui church. The easiest thing to do is follow the tire tracks made by the vehicles using the road. To find the trailhead on the Vairau side, look for the power line that crosses the island. Where the sealed road bends to the right take the unsealed fork to the left. As it climbs up toward the ridge, more forks are encountered—continue to take the left fork. Eventually, the track comes to the ridge top and drops down the other side to Vairau Bay just south of Tuivahora Point. Don't forget to bring water and mosquito repellent.

A short but steep hike to 820-feet (249-meter) **Papoti Ridge** (1 mile/1.6 kilometers) will take you to the old U.S. military radar installation. The 20- to 30-minute trek to the top of the ridge affords a magnificent view of the island's northern end. This is the same horizon the U.S. Navy personnel scanned in search of enemy ships over 50 years ago. To get there, you must go to Taihi Point, the northernmost tip of the island. Look for the trailhead at the point where the coastal road winds up the hill.

Transportation

AIR

The airstrip on Bora Bora is located on the northernmost offshore islet, Motu Mute. The field was constructed by the American military during World War II and necessitates taking a shuttle boat from the airport. There are **Air Tahiti** flights to Bora Bora from Papeete four to six times daily and once daily from Moorea. The flight time is about 50 minutes. Flights also connect Bora Bora with Raiatea, Huahine, Manihi, Maupiti and Rangiroa. There is a free boat service between the airport and the main dock in Vaitape. ~ Vaitape; 67-70-35.

A small charter carrier, **Air Alizé**, also has service to Bora Bora four times a week out of Raiatea on a nine-passenger Piper Chieftain. Prices are generally lower than Air Tahiti, but the service is much less frequent. ~ Vaitape; 67-74-34.

SEA

Bora Bora is accessible from Papeete via the interisland vessels— *Taporo IV*, Papeete, 42-63-93; the *Vaeanu* ~ Papeete, 41-25-35; the *Ono Ono* ~ Vaitape, 67-78-00; and the *Raromatai Ferry* ~ Papeete, 43-19-88. The journey on a conventional vessel takes half a day from Papeete.

CAR RENTALS

All major hotels can arrange rentals; if you aren't staying at a large hotel, try **Bora Bora Rent-A-Car** (67-70-03), **Maeva Rent-A-Car** (67-76-78) or **Mataura Rent-A-Car** (67-73-16), all in Vaitape.

MOTOR SCOOTERS

Scooters are available in Vaitape at **Bora Bora Rent-A-Car** (67-70-03) or **Maeva Rent-A-Car** (67-76-78).

TAXIS

All the hotels have some form of airport transfer service. A general **taxi** service is also available. ~ Vaitape; 67-72-25.

AERIAL TOURS   Flightseeing over Bora Bora is possible via **Héli Inter.** They will fly you to the top of Mt. Pahia and provide you with the option of hiking back down on foot or returning back on the chopper. Héli Inter can also be chartered to fly you to other islands, transfer you to the airport or take you most anywhere else. For more information, call Philippe Morin. ~ Vaitape; 67-62-59.

Aerial tours can also be arranged with **Tahiti Conquest Airline.** ~ Faa'a, 85-55-54, fax 85-55-56.

JEEP TOURS   **Tupuna Mountain Expeditions** offers four-wheel-drive Land Rover tours of the island. It is owned and operated by Dany Leverd, a likeable local fellow who brings to his tour the personal view of a Bora Bora native. As a government surveyor for several years, he possesses an intimate knowledge of the flora and fauna as well as the culture and history of the island. The local angle makes a real difference. Another nice touch is a stopover at his family's estate, which was once a village with a population of 2000. Like Bora Bora Jeep Safari, Dany's tour also takes in the old coastal defense gun emplacements, bunkers and other vestiges of the U.S. presence. The tour takes approximately three hours and is conducted both in the morning and afternoon. Definitely worthwhile. ~ Matira; 67-75-06.

Bora Bora Jeep Safari, operated by a charming Frenchman by the name of Sebastien, is a four-wheel-drive, two-hour, circle-island tour of Bora Bora, taking in the rugged and seldom seen interior of the island. Stops along the way include the scenic World War II gun emplacement and the radar station atop Popoti Ridge, which is otherwise inaccessible, ancient Polynesian temples, Quonset huts, former ammo dumps and sensational vistas. A four-wheel-drive tour is one of the best things to happen to Bora Bora and should be on your must-do list, especially if you are a World War II buff. Call Sebastien and he'll pick you up at your hotel, or ask at the tour desk. You may be able to negotiate a special price for groups or individuals by calling him directly. ~ Nunue; 67-70-34.

It's possible to hitch-hike on Bora Bora—not easy, but possible.

Addresses & Phone Numbers

Doctors ~ Dr. Juen: 67-70-62, speaks English; Dr. Martina Roussanaly: 67-70-92

Hospital ~ 67-70-77

Pharmacy ~ 67-70-30

Police Station ~ 67-70-41, 67-70-03

Post Office ~ 67-70-74

Town Hall ~ 67-70-41

Visitor information ~ Bora Bora Visitors Bureau, Vaitape wharf; 67-76-36

SEVEN

Huahine

One of the most picturesque and geographically diverse islands in the Society Group, Huahine has deep cleft bays, rugged mountains and long white-sand beaches. Huahine is actually two islands: Huahine Iti and Huahine Nui (Little Huahine and Big Huahine). They are part of the same land mass and are connected by an underwater isthmus. (For the convenience of motorists, there's a bridge.)

The islands, located 109 miles northwest of Papeete, are verdant, rugged and scenic enough to make renting a car well worth the expense. The coastal road follows the terrain's steep contours providing breathtaking views of Bourayne and Maroe bays. Maroe Bay, which is particularly spectacular, was once a volcanic basin and the high mountains framing it are remnants of the caldera wall.

The 4500 residents of Huahine have a long tradition of independence and pride in their Polynesian heritage. According to a Tahitian proverb, "Obstinacy is their diversion." To this day, their sense of dignity, and perhaps a bit of arrogance, is still manifest. Not surprisingly, you will hear more Tahitian than French spoken on Huahine.

Perhaps this is why the island seems to entice the visitor who is more interested in absorbing culture than a tan. Huahine has also attracted about 30 long-term American residents, more per capita than anywhere else in French Polynesia.

Huahine is also a magnet for surfers. Although it does not have the type of waves that bring people to Hawaii or Australia, it does have some of the best and most consistent breaks in French Polynesia.

Most of the island's accommodations and rich archeological sites are clustered at the north end of Huahine Nui in the Fare and Maeva area. If you are staying at a Fare accommodation, it's easy to see the old Polynesian temples in the Maeva region on foot or by bicycle.

In June and July you may experience the *mara'amu*, a trade wind that blows with tremendous force, bringing downpours and gusts that can wash the sea over the road. During this time long-sleeve shirts or jackets may be necessary in the evenings. With this in mind, I recommend staying in Fare and its environs during these months because it is sheltered from the stormy weather.

Perhaps the biggest inconvenience on Huahine, from the visitor's standpoint, is the overall lack of public transportation. Occasional *Le Truck* service is available to far-flung communities such as Parea at the opposite end of the island. There are also taxis, but they are very expensive. The only other option for travelers lacking an automobile is to stand on the side of the road with their thumbs out. Fortunately, hitchhikers are frequently picked up.

▼▼▼▼▼▼▼▼ Huahine Nui

Huahine's administrative center, maritime hub and largest settlement is Fare, pronounced "Far-ay." The pre-colonial name was *Fare nui atoa* (the great house far away). Fare has been a port of call for Europeans since the 1830s when whaling ships stopped here following the northward whale migrations in May and June. Whalers regularly exchanged guns for pigs or perhaps traded a few yards of cloth for bananas, yams and sweet potatoes.

In the late 19th century, Fare was a temporary residence for the ruling Pomare family and was later settled by white traders who took Polynesian wives. In the 1920s, Chinese merchants established stores in the area and have remained a fixture ever since. Fronting the shoreline, Fare's main street has a number of clapboard storefronts and retains a Wild West character. It has the usual complement of Chinese shops and a quay to accommodate copra boats and ferries. There are several pension-style hotels shaded by huge trees and a number of excellent budget restaurants. It is a slow-moving town in the heat of the day, disturbed only by an occasional auto kicking up dust or the sounds of giggling schoolchildren.

SIGHTS

A good place to begin your visit of the island is at the main **tourist office** on the south side of the dock in Fare. ~ 68-86-34.

If the tourist office isn't open (which is often the case), tourist information is also available at the airport. You may also want to pay a visit to Heidi Lemaire, an American who runs the **Pacific Blue Adventure** dive shop on the main street. She likes to provide information to visitors. ~ 68-87-21.

Another landmark is the **post office**, a bright white, colonial-style edifice on the road heading out of Fare on the north end. ~ 68-82-70.

Fare is separated from **Maeva**, the other major community on Huahine Nui, by about six kilometers of road tracing the northern coast of the island. The road faces a bay known as **Lac Fauna Nui**, which is enclosed by a huge *motu* the shape of a upside-down salad bowl. Though Fauna Nui is called a lake, it's actually a bay with an inlet so narrow you can toss a stone across it. (The mouth of this inlet is opposite the Hotel Sofitel Heiva.)

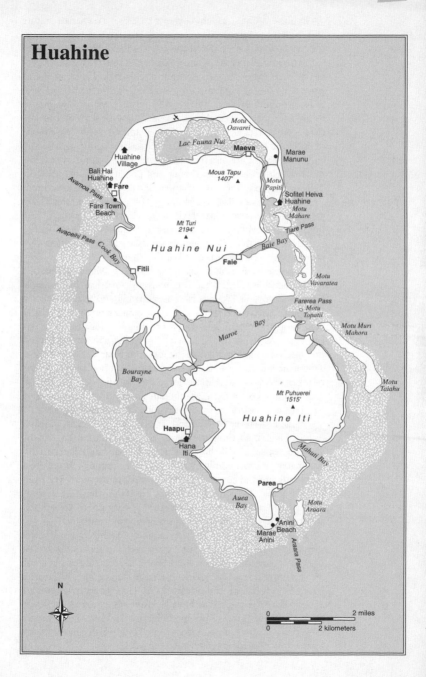

Huahine

Motu
Oavarei

Lac Fauna Nui

Huahine
Village

Maeva

Marae
Manunu

Bali Hai
Huahine

Avamoa Pass

Fare

Fare Town
Beach

Moua Tapu
1407'

Motu
Papiti

Sofitel Heiva
Huahine

Motu
Mahare

Avapeihi Pass

Cook Bay

Mt Turi
2194'

Huahine Nui

Tiare Pass

Baie Bay

Fitii

Faie

Motu
Vavaratea

Farerea Pass

Motu
Topatii

Maroe
Bay

Motu Muri
Mahora

Bourayne
Bay

Mt Puhuerei
1515'

Motu
Taiahu

Huahine Iti

Haapu

Hana
Iti

Mahuti Bay

Parea

Auea
Bay

Motu
Araara

Anini
Beach

Marae
Anini

Araara Pass

N

0   2 miles

0   2 kilometers

In ancient times, Huahine was a center of Polynesian culture and ruled by a centralized government. This differed from the warring tribes found on most of the other islands. Huahine is laden with archeological artifacts and is sometimes referred to as an open-air museum. Most of the important archeological sites on the island are no more than five kilometers from Fare in the Maeva area. In that community alone there are 16 restored *marae*. The majority are ancestral shrines of local chiefs. The stone slabs of these ancient temples jut out on the landscape, and are eerily reminiscent of the Druid ruins of Stonehenge. In the nearby lagoon, rich in crab and other sea life, are nine ancient fish traps constructed from stone, some of which have been rebuilt and are in use today. (See the "Hiking" section later in this chapter for a description of these sites.)

HIDDEN ▶   Above Maeva village on Matairea Hill is **Matairea-rahi**. This is the second most important temple in French Polynesia. Here you can find foundations of priests' and chiefs' homes and a huge fortification wall guarding the mountain sanctuary from sea raiders. (See the "Hiking" section at the end of this chapter.)

Opposite Maeva, just across the bridge, is **Marae Manunu**, a classic *marae* reconstructed originally by American archeologist Kenneth Emory in 1933. It is approximately 100 feet (30 meters) in length, constructed in a rectangular manner resembling a shoe box. Around the perimeter of the structure are huge basalt tablets approximately eight feet (2.5 meters) tall and up to six feet (almost two meters) wide looking like gravestones. Near the old temple is a **monument** to the 1846 Battle of Maeva. The monument is marked by seven cannons and commemorates the unequivocal French rule over Eastern Polynesia, even though constitutionally the region was only a protectorate until formal annexation in 1880.

While in Maeva, be sure and stop at **Fare Pote'e,** an old-style meetinghouse built along the coastal road opposite Lac Fauna Nui. The 100-year-old, oval-shaped structure, which had fallen into disrepair until it was rebuilt in 1972, is being restored. It will be a small museum and cultural center. Craft demonstrations and tours by local guides to archeological sites are also planned. A new organization, Opu Nui, has been formed specifically to protect this structure and other ancient monuments from disturbance.

In the Fare Pote'e area are numerous 16th-century **lakeside marae**. Here the individual chiefs worshiped their ancestors at their respective temples. Heading south along the coastal road you will see stones piled in a "V" shape inside the lagoon, an area particularly rich in fish, crab and other sea life. These stone structures are ancient **fish weir traps** that have been rebuilt by archeologist Dr. Sinoto from the Bishop Museum in Honolulu, Hawaii. They work as well now as they did hundreds of years ago. Fish enter the traps by the flow of incoming and outgoing tides.

This archeological complex is the core of a planned historical/ecological "living" museum being organized by Dr. Sinoto, along with the French Polynesian government and the people of Huahine. With the cooperation of the local population, scientists and the local government, a master plan will eventually be created to ensure the integrity and maintenance of the archeological treasures. The master plan will also provide zoning recommendations for restaurants, hotels and commercial buildings.

Dr. Sinoto believes that agriculture can be revived by practicing age-old Polynesian ecology methodologies (such as taboos against overfishing) in combination with modern agricultural and aquacultural techniques. He would also like to rebuild the chiefs' and priests' houses near the *marae* and have families and caretakers occupy them on a full-time basis.

An obligatory stop on Huahine is a working **farm** owned by a Frenchman and his Tahitian wife. Here you can see local crops

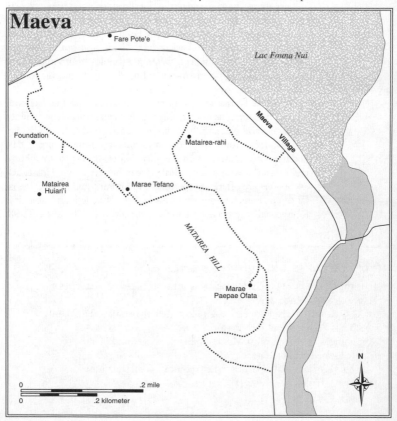

such as taro and banana under cultivation as well as the preparation of dried bananas, their main business. The owners also operate a small eatery with fresh fruit juices and light snacks. The farm is near the Hotel Bellevue and is marked by a number of signs. Admission. ~ Fare; 68-86-58.

LODGING

HIDDEN ▶

Huahine Village is the island's newest hotel. Located on the northwest corner of the island, it is situated on a white-sand beach. The garden and the beach bungalows are fashioned in classic *fare* style with thatched roofs and are spacious—a single and double bed in each. A covered terrace faces the lagoon. All of the public facilities—the reception area, the bar and restaurant (which can accommodate up to 120 people) are located next to the lagoon beneath a high peaked canopy thatched with *pandanus* fronds. From the exterior this property resembles other resort clones, but it differs in spirit because it is run by Tahitians. Locals feel comfortable here and are more apt to frequent the restaurant on their time off, play their guitars and hang out. The staff is helpful, friendly and provides visitors with a local experience. The hotel offers a variety of tours, picnics on a *motu*, horseback riding, diving and other activities. Weekends occasionally bring *pétanque* (boules) tournaments and there is usually music and dancing. Located off the airport road. ~ Fare; 68-86-99, fax 68-86-99. MODERATE TO DELUXE.

Le Petite Ferme, known primarily as a riding stable, has budget accommodations in a friendly family-farm setting. The facilities are simple and pleasant. In addition to basic rooms, dorm beds are also available. Rates are reduced if you stay more than one day, and breakfast is included in the price. Naturally, if you are a horse enthusiast this would be an ideal place to hunker down. Horseback excursions are offered to the beach, mountains and around the island. The French family that runs Le Petite Ferme is amicable. It is located halfway between Fare and the airport. ~ Fare; 68-92-98. BUDGET.

✔ CHECK THESE OUT—UNIQUE SIGHTS

- Tour the **marae** in Maeva, where ancient stone slabs bear an eerie resemblance to Stonehenge. *page 244*
- Make your way to the **Fare Pote'e**, an old-style Polynesian meetinghouse, which has been painstakingly restored. *page 244*
- Commune with the spirits at **Marae Anini**, an important Polynesian temple located on Huahine Iti. *page 257*
- Worship the sun at **Anini Beach**, where you can luxuriate in the translucent blue water. *pages 257, 259*

On the fringes of the "wilds," you'll find **Chez Lovina**. Starting from the bottom of the budget scale is a dorm with 15 bunks and a camping area for up to 20 tents. Moving up the ladder are several small bungalows that are equipped with televisions and fans. (The kitchen and bathrooms for these units are in a separate *fare*). There are also larger bungalows that have a mezzanine, sofa, television, living room, kitchenette and private (cold water) bath. In some units the proprietors will allow you to cram twelve people into one structure. A small restaurant/bar is also on the property. There is a beach about 150 yards away. Chez Lovina is about one kilometer, or a 15-minute walk, north of Fare in a rather flat and mosquito-ridden part of the island. Transportation to the airport and the docks is available from the owners for a fee. There are good specials in the low season. Take your mosquito repellent! ~ Fare; 68-88-06, fax 68-82-64. BUDGET.

Chez Marie-Louise, a campground with a few tentlike houses, has received mixed reviews. There are four units with various configurations, some with kitchen and private (cold water) bath, others with communally shared bath and toilet. Some visitors recommend this pension highly, especially for the food. In one instance, Marie-Louise taught some of her guests how to make *poisson cru*. However, I've received other comments that the atmosphere was rather strange. Chez Marie-Louise is located in the flatlands about one kilometer north of the dock. ~ Fare; 68-81-10. BUDGET.

Situated on a fine white-sand beach, the **Bali Hai Huahine** is the largest hotel on the island. It has 43 units, including over-the-water bungalows, lakeside units and beachfront *fares*. The hotel environs, which were originally swampland, consist of a series of tiny lakes filled with lilies. The grounds are attractively landscaped with rows of hibiscus, frangipani and other tropical flowers. The lobby is aesthetically pleasing and has a wonderful collection of artifacts that were unearthed when the hotel was constructed. Recently reopened after a long hiatus, the hotel has been completely revamped and is under new management. All of the units have new beds, the floors have been retiled and the rooms redecorated. Rooms are spacious and many of the units have verandas fronting the sea or one of the tiny lakes. A large dining area faces the lagoon, offering a splendid view of Tahaa, Raiatea and Bora Bora. The location is ideal, about five minutes from town and a ten-minute drive from the airport. The Bali Hai is located close to the foot of the new pier in Fare. ~ Fare; 68-84-77, 68-82-77, or 800-282-1401 in the U.S. DELUXE TO ULTRA-DELUXE.

Hotel Te Moana is a family-run, local-style pension with six bungalows. Each of the *fares* is slightly different but all combine traditional building materials with an artistic sense of charm and elegance. The units have floors of coral pebbles, and the walls, which are constructed of local materials, allow air and light to enter the structures. A nice touch is that each unit has an enclosed sink and shower area that is open to the sky under a canopy of coconut palms. There is a restaurant on the premises. A two-day minimum stay is required and you must pay in advance. Return transfers to and from the airport or dock are available for a fee. Hotel Te Moana has a great location on a beach, a five-minute walk to Fare along the water or ten minutes on the road. I have received complaints, however, that the service has deteriorated. Hotel Te Moana is next door to the Bali Hai, which can be an advantage if you want to catch their dance show or have a drink at their bar. ~ Fare; 68-88-63. BUDGET TO MODERATE.

Known for its fine cooking, **Pension Enite** has eight clean rooms surrounded by well-kept gardens. Rooms have fans, a common bathroom and hot water. There is also a living room with a television. Meals are served in an open-air restaurant/bar directly on the beach. The minimum stay is two nights. Guests must have a *demi-pension*—tariff includes breakfast and dinner. Discounted rates are offered for children. Be forewarned: the owners can be moody. Pension Enite is a few steps east of the dock in Fare on the sea side. ~ Fare; 68-82-37. DELUXE.

The accommodation of choice for surfers is the **Hotel Huahine**, a three-story building at the northern edge of Fare across from the dock. It has ten rooms, a restaurant, a bar and more often than not seems to be full of activity, with people hanging around watching television in the main room, playing Ping-Pong or just sitting around drinking and smoking. In fact, it always seems to be noisy. The building is adequate but not impressive. Each room has an individual toilet and shower but you cannot lock the door. Supposedly the owners are going to make improvements. As it is now, however, the place looks rundown, with paint peeling from the walls and springs popping through the couch cushions. We were told that it is the only hotel in town that will barter in exchange for a room. It is characterized by anarchy or at the least a lack of any rules. One night's deposit is required to stay here. Food is available but you must inform the proprietor if you plan to dine there ahead of time. ~ Fare; 68-82-69. BUDGET.

Highly recommended for the backpacker and budget traveler, and also popular with locals, is **Chez Guynette**. The proprietors, Alain and Helene Guerineau—he's French, she's Canadian—urge prospective visitors to reserve ahead. Chez Guynette, otherwise known as Chez Bed, has seven guest rooms, each with electric fan, private (cold water) bath, and a dorm with eight cots and a communal bath. Each dorm guest gets a lower bunk for sleeping and an upper bunk for storing belongings. There is a strict lights-off policy (the lights are on a timer) at 10 p.m. in the dorm and common areas. Screens on the bedroom windows translate into mosquito-free sleep. If you need anything that is not standard, such as a reading lamp, just ask the owners and they will provide it. If you stay more than one night, the rates go down. (BYO towels, but Chez Guynette provides sheets.) The owners have put a lot into renovations and the pension is impeccably clean, quiet and pleasant. Their thoughtfulness and orderliness show in many ways. For example, no shoes are allowed in the house and there is always a bucket of water at the front door for travelers to wash their sandy feet. In the communal kitchen each room has its own plastic tub for its food, and every few days the food is moved from one refrigerator to another so that the first one can be thoroughly cleaned. There is also a neatly arranged bulletin board with every possible item a tourist could want to know. The inexpensive restaurant the owners run is also first rate. You won't go wrong staying here. Chez Guynette is located on the waterfront in downtown Fare, just a few yards from the Hotel Huahine. ~ Fare; 68-83-75. BUDGET.

One of the main shops in Fare, **Taahitini**, has six rooms for rent above the store. Each has a private (cold water) bath and the rooms are unusually spacious. All have a balcony and those facing north have a terrific view of the Fare waterfront. Although the rooms are large and the location is good, the price is a bit steep for what you get. ~ Fare; 68-89-42. BUDGET TO MODERATE.

Chez Henriette, situated on a pebble-strewn beach, is a family-run business that has grown slowly and steadily. There are currently six bungalows, with more under construction. The row of bungalows on the beach creates a picture of a small local business success. Each unit was built in consecutive order and the newest ones are bigger and more substantial than the previously built ones. They are also the best, though they are located behind the older

----

✔ CHECK THESE OUT—UNIQUE LODGING

- *Budget:* Put down your backpacks for the night at **Chez Guynette** in downtown Fare, and join the local clientele at this special spot. *page 248*
  - *Moderate to deluxe:* Check into a *fare* at **Huahine Village** and revel in the hotel's traditional Polynesian hospitality. *page 246*
    - *Deluxe to ultra-deluxe:* Spend time on the beach at the **Bali Hai Huahine**, where the tropical landscape takes you away from it all. *page 247*
      - *Ultra-deluxe:* Slip into your over-the-water bungalow and marvel at one of the most spectacular settings in French Polynesia at the **Sofitel Heiva Huahine**. *page 251*

Budget: under $100 Moderate: $100–$150 Deluxe: $150–$200 Ultra-deluxe: over $200

ones and are closer to the road. The older units, closer to the beach, are already patched with pieces of cardboard. The bungalows with thatched roofs are rustic, and the interiors are lovingly decorated with fabric curtains and Tahitian quilts on the beds. There are basic cooking facilities and private baths as well. The owners are friendly, and will be even more so if you make an effort to speak Tahitian. Paddle canoes are available for guests. Chez Henriette is about four kilometers (a 20-minute walk) from Fare on the opposite side of the bay from town. ~ Fare; 68-83-71. BUDGET.

Pension Poetaina is a clean, outrageously ornate, three-story pension. There are verandas on every floor of this bright, white edifice, and cement replicas of Greek urns adorn the ground floor. (The family that owns the property lives next door in a very modest Tahitian home.) The rooms are spacious and clean. Each floor has a large sitting area and a separate modern kitchen. All amenities in the kitchen and bathrooms feel Western. My take is that the price seems a bit on the high side for what you get. Some rooms include private (hot water) bath, while smaller rooms share a communal bath. However, if you want to be close to Fare, with all your creature comforts, it's an acceptable choice. Tours, picnics, fishing and other activities are available. A deposit is necessary for a reservation. Children under 12 years are half price. Pension Poetaina is located in the Fare district, one kilometer from the dock and three kilometers from the airport. ~ Fare; 68-89-49. MODERATE.

Pension Meri is a concrete house, something akin to a condo in Hawaii or Florida. The pension includes a living room, television, kitchen, private (hot water) bath and a terrace. A washing machine is at your disposal, as are several canoes. With all the amenities, it is perhaps better suited for long-term guests. Pension Meri is also rather close to the road, which may make it noisy. There is a three-day minimum stay required. I found it hard to find. It is located on the outskirts of Fare, near the sea, about two kilometers south of town. ~ Fare; 68-82-44. MODERATE.

The **Hotel Bellevue**, situated on a bluff with a gorgeous view of the surrounding bays and hills, is one of the better mid-range hotels on the island. It makes a good family-oriented retreat for those interested in the mountains rather than the beach. The main drawback is that it is isolated and not easy to get to without a car. The hotel itself is not fancy, but it does have all the amenities, including solar-heated hot water, steam bath, freshwater swimming pool, horseback riding and fishing. The 15 bungalows are spacious and clean, and have screened windows. Unfortunately, when I was there the rooms were quite stuffy and lacked reading lights and fans. The bungalows farthest from the main house have the best views and provide the best sense of privacy. Each bungalow has a double bed, bathroom, terrace and private parking. There are also eight rooms

with private baths and balconies located upstairs in a large building. The hotel offers a number of day trips throughout the island
as well as fishing expeditions. There are numerous facilities such as
swimming pool, Ping-Pong, basketball and volleyball that provide
plenty of distractions for a family on holiday. If you stay for two
nights the rates are discounted. The food is reportedly excellent but
more expensive than other mid-range accommodations. The staff
here is quite friendly—the clientele consists mostly of French families from Papeete. A one-night deposit is required, and transfer to
the airport is extra. The Hotel Bellevue is located five kilometers
south of Fare. ~ Fare; 68-82-76, fax 68-85-35. MODERATE.

The **Sofitel Heiva Huahine** is not far from Maeva on the tip of
Motu Papiti on the northeast corner of the island. This luxurious
resort has one of the most spectacular settings in
the Society Islands—surrounded by a white-sand
beach with gorgeous views of the mountains and
the lagoon. The property, which has a swimming
pool, occupies several acres of manicured grounds
filled with flowering plants and towering coconut
palms. There are over-the-water bungalows, which
command stunning vistas of the lagoon, and a number
of equally well-maintained thatched-roof beachfront bungalows. Rooms are spacious and well appointed, with verandas facing the sea. The staff is friendly and colorful. Snorkeling
offshore is good, but be careful—there is a plethora of sea urchins
and the current is oftentimes strong. Activities arranged through
the hotel often involve a hefty commission that is tacked on to your
charges. For example, a two-hour horseback ride will cost you 30
percent more if you have the hotel arrange it for you. Unfortunately, the hotel is isolated, making it difficult and expensive to get
about. Round-trip airport transfers are also pricey—something
that isn't discussed before you step in the van. It's almost cheaper
to rent a car. ~ Maeva; 68-86-86, fax 68-85-25. ULTRA-DELUXE.

If you have a rental car
and would like to use
the beach at the Sofitel
Heiva Huahine but are
not a guest, park in
the lot next to bun-
galow number 37.

The restaurant situation in Fare is very good indeed. There's a profusion of excellent inexpensive and mid-range eateries, and good
food can be found in most of the hotels as well.

DINING

Consider stopping along the dock at one of the many **roulottes**
that appear at regular hours as well as when boats come in. Some
of these eateries on wheels are better than others. You can usually
tell which is the right one for you by sniffing the aromas as you
pass by. Two *roulottes* are usually on the wharf every night until
about 10 p.m. The white pastry truck that parks at the wharf every
morning serves tasty bakery items as well as delicious burgers and
a potent espresso. (If you don't like egg salad on your burger, tell
them to hold the egg.) They also serve homemade ice cream. **Café**

Titi'a is on the wharf every day for the lunch hour with hamburgers, cheeseburgers and fish burgers worth stopping by for. There is also a *roulotte* that sells crêpes, waffles and mouth-watering ice cream at the wharf every afternoon until sundown.

HIDDEN ►   Located on the northern end of Fare is **Restaurant Tiare Tipanier**, which has fine food, an extensive menu and good service. Americans will be happy to see that hamburgers and pizza are on the menu. Dinners include fish (considered their house specialty), chicken and beef. There is a fixed-price dinner (appetizer, entrée, wine, dessert and coffee) at a reasonable price. Ice cream and pastries are also served. The setting is pleasant—there are some tables outside—but unlike the other Fare eateries it is not on the water. ~ Fare; 68-80-52. MODERATE.

Though not strictly a restaurant, **Pension Enite** will serve dinner *sur command*, even when you are not a guest. The home-style cuisine is a French/Tahitian blend that usually includes seafood. The food is first rate, though a bit on the pricey side. ~ Fare; 68-82-37. DELUXE.

Just down the street from Enite is **Snack Bar Temarara**. Here you'll find tasty food, fine service and a cozy setting. Its seafood dishes (including lobster) and Chinese meals are consistently good. My favorites are the grilled tuna Creole with coconut sauce and the prawn curry. The homemade coconut ice cream is also worth saving room for. Carnivores will be happy to know that steak and hamburgers are also served. The food is reasonably priced and the mix of tourists and locals provides an interesting ambience. ~ Fare; 68-89-31. BUDGET.

Chez Guynette is both good and inexpensive. Here you'll be offered items such as sandwiches and a wonderful chef's salad. (Full dinners are not served.) Drinks in the afternoon are accompanied by free popcorn. Along with the copious and inexpensive food, one of the best things about Chez Guynette is the camaraderie among the guests. This is no doubt fostered by the environment that the proprietors have created. The location, particularly the front terrace that faces the dock and sea, provides a leisurely atmosphere for guests and locals to sit and chat. What more can you ask for? ~ Fare; 68-83-75. BUDGET.

HIDDEN ►   **Restaurant Bar Orio** is located on the south end of Fare directly over the water. It has a comprehensive menu and excellent service—locals consider it one of the best low-end eateries on the island. There are plenty of choices on the menu—from local entrées to Chinese food, including chicken, fish and meat dishes. ~ Fare; 68-83-03. BUDGET TO MODERATE.

The **Sofitel Heiva Huahine** on the tip of Motu Papiti offers a luxurious setting for their fine cuisine. The hotel has hired a new chef who specializes in seafood and the cuisine is a great improvement over its previous fare. The lobby restaurant/bar utilizes local building materials and mimics traditional Polynesian motifs with ample displays of tapa cloth and sennit (coconut fiber), which is wrapped around beams and support structures. The restaurant area is a cavernous open-air structure. Its focal point, a central podium for dance performances, is surrounded by restaurant tables. Tropical flowers such as bird of paradise, ginger and hibiscus fill the restaurant with a sweet fragrance. The food is first class and I would highly recommend the seafood buffet. Be sure and try *tuai*, a small clam found in the immediate vicinity and prepared in broth. ~ Maeva; 68-86-86. DELUXE TO ULTRA-DELUXE.

Chez Piera, operated by a friendly local family, is located opposite Marae Manunu in Maeva. A small eatery with a delicious plate lunch, they serve *poulet citron* (lemon chicken), chow mein and *maa tinito* (a local concoction of beans, meat and vegetables) along with fresh cooled coconut juice as a beverage. You have the option of eating at nearby tables or taking the food to the beach. It's open daily for lunch and dinner except Sunday. ~ Maeva. BUDGET.

Also in Maeva, just east of Chez Piera in the direction of the Sofitel Hotel is **Snack Vanaa**, which also serves basic Chinese and Tahitian cuisine. Operated by a local family, fare includes chow mein, steak and fries, chicken and fish. The food is tasty and the quantities copious. ~ Maeva. BUDGET.

Faie Glaces, located several kilometers outside of Faie Village on the mountain side of the road, is marked by a sign. Here they serve wonderful homemade ice cream in a parlor setting. Many of the icy-sweet concoctions incorporate local fruit —banana, mango, soursop and coconut. Faie Glaces is an obligatory stop after feeding the eels or on a round-the-island car trip. Their ice cream is also available in the Super Fare Nui market in town. ~ Faie; 68-87-95. BUDGET.

◄ HIDDEN

✔ **CHECK THESE OUT—UNIQUE DINING**

- *Budget to moderate:* Enjoy the breeze of the tradewinds at the lagoon's edge at **Restaurant Bar Orio** as you feast on the local fare. *page 252*
- *Moderate:* Contemplate the extensive menu at **Restaurant Tiare Tipanier**, and gaze out over the waterfront setting. *page 252*
- *Deluxe:* Experience true Tahitian-French cuisine at **Pension Enite**, where you will be guaranteed a memorable evening. *page 252*
- *Deluxe to ultra-deluxe:* Line up for the scrumptious seafood buffet at **Sofitel Heiva Huahine**, and dine amid tropical splendor. *page 252*

Budget: under $12 Moderate: $12–$20 Deluxe: $20–$30 Ultra-deluxe: over $30

GROCERIES   Bread is baked daily behind the Wing Kong Store on the water-front—but don't go in there to purchase bread because it's strictly where bread is made—not sold. Fresh bread is available at virtually all the grocery stores in town seven days a week. (In Fare you can buy bread at 6 a.m.) If you visit the markets early enough you'll also be able to pick up *pain au chocolat* and croissants.

Food shopping is best done at **Super Fare Nui**, located in the center of town. Super Fare Nui runs out of bread by 7 a.m., so get up early if you want fresh bread for breakfast. The store is open until about 10 a.m. on Sunday, which comes in handy because other stores on the island are closed. ~ Fare; 68-84-68.

The other large store in Fare, **Taahitini**, south of the main center of town just past the police station, has a friendly staff, but is slightly more expensive. They also do not stock fresh meats or cold cuts. It's open until 7 p.m. each evening, and on Sunday morning until noon—when other stores in Fare are closed. ~ Fare; 68-89-42.

SHOPPING   I believe Huahine's adherence to Polynesian culture has attracted some of the best artists in French Polynesia. I would even venture to say there are more talented artists on this island than anywhere else in the South Pacific. This is obviously a good thing for those seeking gifts and souvenirs in the island's art galleries. The latest phenomenon in Fare are the **thatched-roof stalls** (usually open daily) where vendors sell fruit, vegetables and handicrafts. One stall is set up near the dive shop and has an excellent selection of shell jewelry, baskets and other souvenirs.

Boutique Blanche Bellais in Maeva has quality clothing and locally made *tifaifai*-style quilts at reasonable prices. Across the street from the shop is the studio where the *tifaifai* are made. ~ Maeva; 68-83-97.

Vanilla and locally made *monoi* oil scented with *ylang-ylang*, a fragrant flower, are sold informally at **small stands** along the road or in the front yards of homes in the Maeva area.

HIDDEN ►   **Galerie Te Mana** is a Polynesian art gallery run by Dorothy Levy and is laden with creations made by local artists. Here you will find the art and music of Bobby Holcomb, Dorothy's long-time friend and companion. Holcomb's art and music made an indelible impression on Huahine, and all of French Polynesia. (His music is still aired on Tahiti's radio waves and in Hawaii as well.) Those interested in Holcomb's life may want to chat with Dorothy or purchase a book at the gallery that features reproductions of his paintings. He was a prolific painter, and the neo-Polynesian school he developed had quite an influence on the local art scene and the *Maohi* (Polynesian) cultural revival. The gallery also sells beautiful pottery fashioned by Peter Owens, as well as jewelry, books, clothing, tapes and CDs. (Dorothy Levy is the president of Opu Nui, which supports and encourages the restoration of the *marae*.) Hospitable and outgoing, she is an important source of information about Huahine and its culture. Galerie Te Mana is located at the junction where the road turns off to the airport, a 30-minute walk from the center of town. ~ Fare; 68-81-56.

If you need to launder clothing, a cleaners is located near the post office. A single item of clothing costs anywhere from 200 CFP to 600 CFP to clean.

Gallery Puvaivai, run by Joe and Frederique Perrone, is located on the road to the airport, a 20-minute walk from the center of Fare. The gallery is adorned with original paintings and one-of-a-kind, hand-printed pareus on the walls. The owners also stock locally cultivated black pearls at bargain prices. Other interesting items are the fishhooks made by local craftsmen. Although Joe and Frederique are from the U.S. and France, their art reflects the many years they have lived on Huahine, and the love and appreciation they have for Polynesian culture. They are exceptionally friendly and knowledgeable. ~ Fare; 68-78-09.

Across from the wharf, **Boutique Roti** has a beautiful selection of local crafts, pottery, textiles and clothing all at reasonable prices. ~ Fare; 68 85-59.

Next door to the Banque de Tahiti is **Aux Trois Bonheur**, a clothing and fabric store with a wonderful section of pareus at good prices.

Souvenirs, postcards, film and the like can be purchased at **Jojo's**, next door to Chez Guynette on the waterfront. ~ Fare; 68-89-16.

Super Fare Nui, a grocery store, also sells the New Zealand edition of *Time* magazine. ~ Fare; 68-84-68.

Across the street from Super Fare Nui are several thatched-roof **stalls** selling produce and souvenirs. One merchant has a terrific selection of crafts including shell jewelry, baskets and *tifaifai*.

Sofitel Heiva Huahine has regular happy hours from 5 to 6 p.m. and 9 to 10 p.m. ~ Maeva; 68-86-86.

NIGHTLIFE

Huahine Village usually has a string band performing *kaina* music on weekends and is open to nonguests. You'll find local color here and few tourists. ~ Fare; 68-86-99.

Dance revues are performed regularly at the Sofitel and the Bali Hai Hotels on weekend evenings. ~ Maeva; 68-86-86.

FARE TOWN BEACH In Fare you can find a white-sand beach literally after stepping off the tarmac or dock. The shoreline near the pier is an excellent beach shared both by the pension Te Moana and the Bali Hai Hotel. There is adequate shade here and facilities are available through the nearby hotel properties. The beach is a five-minute walk north of town along the shore, or ten minutes on the main road.

BEACHES & PARKS

MOTU PAPITI BEACH On Motu Papiti, in the archeological zone, is a long white-sand beach extending from Marae Manunu down to Hotel Sofitel Heiva. Shaded by coconut palms, it's perfect for a stroll and for beachcombing. However, the coral and shallow water make swimming or snorkeling iffy. Note that the farther you walk from the hotel the less people you will find. ~ Located five kilometers east of Fare.

Need some reading material? There is a lending library at the Bali Hai Hotel. Trade books you have read for another. Inquire at the gift shop.

SOFITEL BEACH The long stretch of white-sand beach at the Sofitel Huahine is one of the choice spots on the island. The beach slopes gently into clear turquoise waters and is superb for swimming. It's open to the public, but don't use the hotel's beach chairs or other furniture. You can snorkel offshore but there are quite a few sea urchins in the area. ~ To get there simply walk or drive to Maeva, and cross the bridge that connects the *motu* with the mainland and continue south.

MOTU TOPATI'I With an archetypal South Pacific setting of fine white-sand and coconut palms, Motu Topati'i is a wonderful place to laze the day away. Located at the foot of Maroe Bay, the swimming is wonderful. Bring your snorkeling equipment, for the water is clear and there are a number of reef fish to be spotted. The area is used by the Sofitel hotel for their *motu* excursions so you might not be alone. ~ To get there you'll have to hire a local boat crew or go as part of an organized excursion with a hotel.

Huahine Iti

Huahine Iti lies to the south of Huahine Nui and is connected by an underwater isthmus (as well as a manmade bridge). Like the northern portion of the island (Huahine Nui), the southern (Huahine Iti) side is verdant and rugged. On the western side of the isthmus is Bourayne Bay. On the opposite side, you'll find Maroe Bay, which dominates the north coast. Both bays are spectacular dark blue bodies of water that shimmer in the tropical sun. Along the shoreline, where the sea is shallow, the color of water is light turquoise. These inlets are popular with sailboats and they can often be seen anchored offshore. Along the coastline there are also several striking inlets—Teapoa and Haapu on the western coast and Mahuti Bay on the southeast corner of Huahine Iti. Shallower than the other bays, they cleave deeply into the island and are surrounded by steep precipitous coastline. Vistas of the coastline are accessible from the road.

SIGHTS

On the perimeter of Huahine Iti is a dirt road that may not always be in the best state of repair, but is generally accessible with a standard automobile. The southern side of the island lacks the number of Polynesian temples found on Huahine Nui, but there is at least one major archeological site to visit, **Marae Anini**. Located on the southernmost tip of Huahine Iti, it once served the community as a place of worship of the deities Oro and Hiro. In 1818, the last priest of the temple told Reverend Ellis, an early missionary, that he was aware of 14 cases of human sacrifice at this shrine.

The principal feature of the *marae* is its **ahu** (platform). Sometimes they are compared to altars, which is not correct. They are set aside for the gods Oro and Hiro. The **upright stones** are backrests for priests and chiefs, or memorials for deceased chiefs. A small *marae* was built when a royal family adopted a child of lower rank. A platform far out on the perimeter of the *marae* was where the house of Oro stood. Under each post of the house a human sacrifice was rendered.

After visiting Marae Anini you might want to take a picnic lunch, towel and good book and set yourself up on the lovely white-sand **Anini Beach** nearby. Shaded by ample coconut palms, its generally calm waters make it an enjoyable place for a swim.

Most (but not all) of the hotels that occupy Huahine Iti are upscale properties. Because you are more isolated here, it is best to rent a car to tour the island.

LODGING

The 26-unit **Hana Iti** occupies 54 acres on the west coast of Huahine Iti. It has been called outlandish, and is, perhaps, American owner Tom Kurth's vision of paradise. Rumor has it that upon seeing the property, Kurth immediately purchased it from the Spanish superstar Julio Iglesias. The brochure describes it as "cliff-hanging thatched villas camouflaging great space, privacy and comfort" that are constructed from natural materials of the region. Native hardwoods, bamboo, stone and shell are combined in each villa's interior to create a natural, roughhewn, yet harmonious environment. They have blended natural elements—such as living trees growing in, through and around the structures, and a waterfall that cascades into an outdoor swimming pool—into the decor. With rates reaching the stars, the hotel attracts a discriminating clientele. Diana Ross once rented the entire hotel for several days for a few of her close friends. ~ 68-85-05, 68-87-41. ULTRA-DELUXE.

While I was last in Huahine, *fares* were under construction at the restaurant **Fare Mauarii** on Auea Bay. On the northeast coast of Huahine Iti, located on a beautiful white-sand beach, the property is lined with coconut palms and looks enticing. The planned structures, thatched-roof *fares*, will be completed soon. ~ Parea; 68-86-49. BUDGET TO MODERATE.

The **Relais Mahana** is on the southern tip of Huahine Iti in a deafeningly quiet spot with a wonderful white-sand beach. That's as much as I know. The owner would not allow me to look at the property and refused to provide any information, perhaps thinking

I was a spy or saboteur. He emphasized that he would choose what guidebooks he would appear in. So, I have no first-hand impressions, other than what appeared to be a great deal of pretentiousness. Feedback from visitors I spoke to was mixed. Along with the lovely beach, you'll apparently find first-class (and free) activities—a swimming pool, tennis, Ping-Pong, kayaking and bike riding. Someone remarked that sometimes it was difficult to truly relax because the hotel was run in an almost "military" fashion. Activity notices are posted and if the appropriate rules are not followed, the "chief" will let you know. ~ Parea; 68-81-54, fax 68-85-08. DELUXE.

HIDDEN ►   **Aruua Camping** is the newest campground on the island. There are six structures on the property resembling mini-tepees. There are no doors—and no security. There is a kitchen for those who want to prepare their own meals and a good snack bar. You'll need transportation to get there—or you can take the truck from Fare to Parea. The property is located off the road just before a monument to Gaston Flosse, near the *marae* at Parea. A sign on the road marks the property. ~ Parea. BUDGET.

The **Huahine Beach Club**, as one letter-writer dryly put it, "is part of the chain of Tahiti hotels sharing the word beach" in their name. It certainly resembles the others: thatched bungalows, a lobby decorated with wicker chairs, revolving ceiling fans, potted palms and even a canoe hanging from the ceiling. The one culturally out-of-place decorative piece in the lobby is a Balinese urn, complete with bamboo pipe in a pool of water. If you are sensitive to this style of decor, it will jar your sense of place. Located near the village of Parea, not far from the Relais Mahana, the Beach Club has 16 bungalows that accommodate up to four people. The beach is small and the views, at least toward Parea, are not particularly attractive. The day I was there the hotel and the grounds looked

ARCHEOLOGICAL SLEUTHS

Those interested in following up on the research in Huahine conducted by the venerable Yosihiko H. Sinoto of the Bishop Museum should look for:
• *Report on the Preliminary Excavation of an Early Habitation Site on Huahine, Society Islands* in Journal de la Société des Oceanistes XXXI (1974): 143-86.
• *Excavations on Huahine, French Polynesia* in Pacific Studies 3 (1979): 1.
• *The Huahine Excavation: Discovery of an Ancient Polynesian Canoe* in Archeology 36/2 (1983): 10-15.
• *Archeological Excavations of the Vaito'otia and Fa'ahia Sites on Huahine Island, French Polynesia* in National Geographic Society Research Reports 15 (1983): 583-99.

neglected. Debris from the trees littered the beach, the activities board was not up to date, and ashtrays in the lobby were stuffed with French cigarettes. No one in management could be found. The guests we spoke to were not happy campers. They were disappointed, especially with the beach and the poor snorkeling in the lagoon. ~ Parea; 68-81-46, fax 68-85-86. DELUXE.

Fare Mauarii, located just west of Parea on the beach, is a small **DINING** restaurant that offers French and Tahitian dishes. Open daily, it is a pleasant respite for hungry visitors making their way around the island. The menu is limited, and the prices are not as inexpensive as they are in town, but the peaceful setting and views of the sandy beach make it worth a stop. ~ Parea; 68-86-49. BUDGET TO MODERATE.

There is a small store on the premises of **Fare Mauarii** on the south- **GROCERIES** ern end of the island, where drinks and snacks can be purchased. ~ Parea; 68-86-49.

There are also small stores in Haapu and Parea. The one in Haapu is off the road and hard to see, and the store in Parea is open at odd hours. If they're open they're great places to buy drinks after visiting the archeological area at Marae Anini. There are a few drinks-only roadside stands outside of the main population centers. These are marked by Hinano, Coca Cola or Fanta signs.

The **gift shop** in Hana Iti has superb pottery produced by a tall, **SHOPPING** lanky American transplant by the name of Peter Owens who lives on a *motu* near Maeva. Check it out. ~ 68-85-05.

From Point Tereva on the southwest coast to the Huahine Beach **BEACHES** Club on the southeast side is a stretch of white sand beach that **& PARKS** fringes the southern tip of the island. This stretch of beach is unequaled in the Society Islands, except perhaps for the Matira area of Bora Bora. You can park virtually anywhere along this coastline. Be respectful of private property, however.

ANINI BEACH 🏊 Anini Beach is a long strand of white sand ◄ *HIDDEN* bound by clear turquoise waters. Swimming here is good. There are two surf breaks close to the beach off a small *motu*—a clean righthander and a sloppier left on the other side of the channel. If you are going to surf, it's best to go in the morning before the trades start blowing. Be sure and lock your car—unfortunately, the surfing crowd attracts people who rip off visitors. No facilities. ~ To get there look for the Marae Anini sign and park near the archeological site that is in walking distance of the beach.

RELAIS MAHANA 🐟 The Relais Mahana hotel on the southwest tip of Huahine Iti has some of the best snorkeling on the island. The reason—the hotel regularly feeds fish off the dock. ~ To get there take the coastal road and park at the hotel, which is clearly marked.

Outdoor Adventures

CAMPING

Chez Lovina is a budget accommodation on the fringes of Fare, about a 15-minute walk north of town. There is room for about 20 tents on the property. Communal toilet/bath facilities are available. ~ Fare; 68-88-06, fax 68-82-64.

I've also heard good reports about the Aruua Campground in the Parea area. They are said to have excellent amenities, including a snack bar. A good beach is located nearby.

DIVING

Huahine has a variety of sites for divers of all levels. The island is still fairly unknown as a dive destination, which means the sites you visit will not be overrun by humankind. Aquatic life is rich and includes the larger pelagics as well as standard reef fish. It's not unusual to see eagle rays, sharks, Napoleon fish, tuna, barracuda and turtles.

Dive sites of note include **Avapeihi Pass**, known for its shark feeding and large schools of jack, barracuda and spade fish; **Sea Anemone Reef**, a large seabed laden with blue, violet, yellow and green coral as well as a rich variety of sea anemones; and **Bullfish Drop-off**, which has schools of bullfish, blood sea bass, unicorn fish, and white-spotted pufferfish.

Dive Operators   **Pacific Blue Adventure** is located on the quay in Fare next to the tourist office. It has operated on the island for more than five years and has the reputation of being a well-run shop. They offer diving in the passes and outside the lagoon. There are two vessels, one of which holds up to 15 divers. There are two dives daily, at 9:15 a.m. and 2:15 p.m., supervised by English-speaking PADI instructors. Open-water and resort courses are available for beginners and there are a variety of dives for advanced aficionados. (They offer a 10 percent discount to guests at Chez Guynette.) If you are on a yacht and are willing to moor at their pier, Pacific Blue Adventure will fill up your water tanks. Contact Heidi Lemaire for details. ~ Fare; 68-87-21, fax 68-80-71.

SURFING

There are excellent reef breaks throughout the Society Islands, but surfing seems to be the most popular with American and Australian visitors in Huahine. It's not the size of the waves that draws surfers, but their consistency and perfect shape. Of the four major breaks on the island, three are in the Fare area. They include **Fitii**, which has a good right peak on south-southwest swells; **Fare**, which has an excellent left reef break and a long wall; and **Bali Hai**, which walls up on north-northwest swells. Getting to the action on most

Pouvanaa a Oopa— Modern Tahitian Hero

Huahine is the birthplace of Pouvanaa a Oopa, the greatest 20th-century French Polynesian leader. A decorated World War I veteran, Pouvanaa was the son of a Danish sailor and a Polynesian woman. In 1947, he was jailed by the French for advocating Polynesian veterans' rights, and became the spokesperson for the Tahitian independence movement. Blessed with charismatic oratorical skills, and well-versed in the Bible, Pouvanaa established himself as the most powerful politician in the French Polynesian Territorial Assembly. Known as Metua— "beloved father to the Tahitians"—he lambasted the colonial system for its treatment of Polynesians as second-class citizens and fought for legislative reforms that would grant Polynesians greater autonomy.

At the zenith of his power, Pouvanaa was convicted of conspiracy in a plot to burn down Papeete and was sent to the notorious Baumette Prison in Marseilles. At the age of 64 he was sentenced to eight years of solitary confinement and banished from Polynesia for another 15 years. Ten years later he was pardoned for the crime many felt he did not commit, and he returned to Tahiti. Eventually he went back into politics and again served in the Territorial Assembly. He died in 1976.

of these breaks involves long paddles. The fourth site in **Parea** has a fairly clean right on southeast swells, but it's the last resort and is probably the least consistent. It's also rather a long drive to get there.

One caveat about the surf scene on Huahine: Locals are not enthusiastic about visiting surfers. If you feel bad vibes, or at the very least indifference, it's probably not your imagination. The best way around this is to befriend a local and have him or her introduce you to the gang. For more detailed information on Huahine (and all the Society Islands), get a reprint of the *Surf Report*, which costs US$6. ~ P.O. Box 1028, Dana Point, CA 92629; 714-496-5922.

FISHING

Fishing in Huahine is above average. A variety of pelagics such as tuna, mahimahi, marlin and other species can be snagged outside the reef on charter boats. Surf casting on Huahine is nonexistent because of the barrier reef that surrounds the islands.

Moana Tropical can arrange fishing charters in the lagoon or in the open sea on a Riviera 35 motorboat. ~ Fare; 68-87-05, fax 68-88-10.

Visitors curious about how local bonito fishermen operate might be able to talk their way aboard a fishing vessel by donating a case of beer to the cause. This would be looked upon rather favorably by the captain.

SAILING

Sailing charters are not available on Huahine. You must charter a vessel from Raiatea or another one of the Society Islands if you wish to see Huahine by sailboat. However, the island is popular with private yachts. Yachties should always contact the harbor master, Mathias, for any questions about anchorage, water and the like. Fare's harbor is generally a popular place to moor because of the availability of water and provisions. Yachties should note that because of the establishment of new pearl farms in the Huahine area, finding proper anchorage is no longer simply a matter of dropping an anchor. A vessel in the wrong place may inadvertently damage a pearl farm.

✔ CHECK THESE OUT—UNIQUE OUTDOOR ADVENTURES

- Walk **Motu Papiti** at **Marae Manunu** and relish the isolation. *page 256*
- Hike the trail along the **archeological zone** that takes in old temples, vanilla plantations and a magnificent banyan tree. *page 264*
- Dive **Avapeihi Pass**, known for its shark feeding and large schools of jack, barracuda and spade fish. *page 260*
- Surf any of the four major breaks in the **Fare area,** with their perfectly shaped waves. *page 260*

Above: A throne styled as an armchair is part of an old Polynesian temple called Marae Papiro, located in Mataiva.

Above: A heliconia flower.

Above: A plumeria blossom.

Left: Plantains, fruits that resemble bananas, are boiled or cooked in an underground oven and are eaten as a side dish.

Right: Colorful clusters of bananas meet the eye everywhere in French Polynesia.

Left: Ripening breadfruit, a yellowish fruit rich in carbohydrates, is a staple on the outer islands.

Matairea Cruise is a family-run business that takes visitors on a seven-hour boat tour around the island with numerous stops for snorkeling, shell gathering and fish observation. Price includes a picnic lunch on the beach with Tahitian food and demonstrations on how to prepare it. ~ Fare; 68-89-16.

Vaipua Cruise is another seven-hour cruise around Huahine with similar stops. Their picnic lunch is a barbecue that includes wine and beer. Children are half-price, and there is a minimum of four people. Contact Colette or Henri. ~ Fare; 68-86-42.

Moana Tropical has a plethora of motorboat tours around the island, including picnics, visits to Raiatea and a *motu*. ~ Fare; 68-87-05, fax 68-88-10.

BOAT TOURS

Le Petite Ferme Stable, located halfway between the airport and Fare, has 12 Marquesan horses trained in Western style. Able wranglers can take group camping tours of two days or more as well as shorter rides. There are a variety of excursions, including a one-hour beach ride and visit to a coconut grove, or a two-hour ride to Lac Fauna Nui and the beach. All-day rides plus picnics at the sea can be arranged. The operation offers a variety of rides and will cater to your individual skills and needs. ~ Fare; 68-82-98.

RIDING STABLES

Biking around Huahine is a good option, especially if it means short trips from Fare to the market or short-distance sightseeing. Unlike Moorea or Tahiti, traffic is by no means overwhelming. Roads near the villages are generally in good shape, but in the outlying areas, especially on the periphery of Tahiti Iti, the roads are not paved and in some instances not well maintained. A special caution when going to Maroe Bay—after Faie Village the road is unpaved and has a treacherous uphill grade. Don't even try it on a rental bike. Unless you have a mountain bike, it's not advisable to see the entire island in a day. If you do attempt to see the whole island by bike, you'd better be in good shape. Naturally you should bring plenty of water.
Bike Rentals **Europcar**, located in town near the entrance to the Bali Hai, has bike rentals. ~ Fare; 68-82-59, fax 68-80-59.

Pacificar, with an office in town near the dock, also has bikes. ~ Fare; 68-81-10.

If all else fails, there is also a small bike rental agency located near Snack Te Marara.

BIKING

Huahine is akin to a giant outdoor museum. In many instances, the old temples and other archeological remnants have been painstakingly restored. In conjunction with the restoration project, a series of trails have been constructed and are maintained for the benefit of the visitor. Those with an interest in the old relics will find delight in hiking these tracks that criss-cross the old village complex. Throughout the archeological region were vanilla plantations,

HIKING

marked by posts, and covered with twisting vines. Most of these plantations now go largely untended.

Fare Pote'e to Marae Paepae Ofata (1.5 miles/2 kilometers): A few minutes' walk south of Fare Pote'e, along the coast road (opposite the Protestant church), is one of the trailheads for the many reconstructed *marae* on Matairea Hill. The trailhead is not obvious—it is set behind a house—so ask a local to show you. Keep in mind that the beginning of the trail is on private land, so be respectful of the plants growing on it. The ten-minute hike to the main section of the trail is a bit steep at the beginning. At the summit, the trail opens up and the area is covered with ferns and manioc patches. (At this point the mosquitoes begin to attack, so bring repellent along.) In former times, this was a vanilla plantation and you can still see the vines spiraling up the trees and bushes. It's worth taking the 25-minute hike to the top of the trail for a spectacular view from Marae Paepae Ofata overlooking the fish traps, the Sofitel Heiva and the narrow inlet that marks Faie Bay.

Beginning in 1984, excavators found that Matairea Hill was occupied from 1450 to 1700 A.D. In efforts to uncover the past, they revealed a new historical trail that begins at the shore and goes to Marae Tefano, the **Shoreline to Matairea Temple Complex trail** (1.5 miles/2 kilometers). The trail begins at the fortification wall built in 1846, when the French marines attacked Maeva, and continues up Te Ana hill. The trailhead is located a few minutes' walk west of Fare Pote'e in the direction of Fare. Just a few steps after the trail begins is a large stone-paved area that was part of a round-ended house **foundation** that most likely belonged to a supreme chief. Interestingly, the front terrace with the large paved area is oriented inland, facing the sacred mountain of Moua Tapu. The trail goes through the old fortification wall that protected residents from invaders from Bora Bora. Just up the trail, the **Matairea Huiari'i complex** was created by families who occupied the entire inland slope of the hill. Each residential unit had one or more *marae*.

EEL-WATCHING

Along with archeological sites at Maeva the giant eels at Faie are the biggest attraction on Huahine. The creatures have grown three to four feet (over a meter) long from the food, mostly canned fish, tossed at them by villagers and visitors alike. Mornings are best for eel watching and visitors can piggyback onto the Sofitel Heiva feeding tours that leave the hotel at 9:15 a.m. (Call to find out which days the tours operate.) Charlie, one of the local guides, speaks English and doesn't mind if you are not a guest at the hotel. All of the guides handle and hand-feed the eels.

To have a density of so many chiefly families in one place was very unusual.

The most significant marae on the hill is **Matairea-rahi**. It was the most important temple in the Society Islands prior to the building of Taputapuatea in Raiatea. According to oral tradition, when Taputapuatea was about to be built, stones from Matairea-rahi were transported to the building site to ensure that the new temple would retain the old temple's *mana* (power). Matairea-rahi consists of two structures: in the first, nine upright stones represent ten districts—the tenth stone is missing. There are also stone posts that serve as intermediaries to the gods. In the rear is an **ahu** (raised platform), which was a throne for the gods. Below the *ahu* is a lower platform where sacrifices—some human—were placed. On the other structure stood a house built on posts where the images of the gods were kept. The house was actually seen in 1818 by Reverend William Ellis, a missionary who saw a building perched on stilts guarded day and night by men to protect the holy images inside.

Just a few minutes' walk from Matairea is **Marae Tefano**, also an impressive sight. Its *ahu* is huge and the temple basks in the shade of a huge banyan tree, probably planted there around the time that the *marae* was constructed.

Walk ten minutes south of Fare Pote'e, cross the small bridge and continue to your left on the *motu* to another very impressive temple, **Marae Manunu**. This became the *marae* for the community of Huahine Nui after Matairea-rahi. Next to the low offering platform is the **grave** of Raiti, the last high priest of Maeva. When he died in 1915, one of the huge *marae* slabs fell. He was buried at the *marae* at his request.

A thorough tour of the *marae* near Maeva takes several hours and a bit of walking, so it is suggested you do it in the early morning. In the late afternoon you will have to deal with the mosquito population. Bring plenty of repellent whenever you go.

Moua Tapu Trail (3 miles/4.8 kilometers) leads to Moua Tapu, which towers above the northeast corner of the Huahine Nui. At 1407 feet (429 meters), it is not the highest peak, but it does offer a spectacular view of the Maeva environs. The summit affords a stunning vista of the coastline. ~ To get there take the road to the microwave tower that is accessible just west of Fare Pote'e and is distinguished by a barrier that crosses the entrance. Once at the tower, start climbing upwards following the ridgeline. It takes about one hour for the hike each way.

Transportation

AIR

There are air connections between Huahine and Tahiti, Bora Bora, Moorea and Raiatea. **Air Tahiti** has service from Papeete two to four times daily. Flight time is about 35 minutes. Most flights connect with Bora Bora and Raiatea as well. ~ Fare; 68-82-65.

There is also an air connection between Huahine and Raiatea four times a week and to a lesser extent Bora Bora, Maupiti and Papeete on **Air Alizé**, a new charter carrier based in Raiatea. Fares are less expensive than Air Tahiti, but the service is much less frequent. ~ Fare; 68-82-59.

SEA

The *Temehani II* ~ 42-98-83; *Taporo IV* ~ 42-63-93; and the *Raromatai Ferry* ~ 43-19-88 all sail to Huahine regularly out of Papeete.

Of all the boat services, the *Ono Ono* is the fastest, taking slightly less than three hours to sail from Papeete to Huahine. ~ Fare, 68-85-85; Papeete, 45-35-35.

CAR, JEEP & MOTOR SCOOTER RENTALS

There are two rental agencies, **Pacificar** and **Europcar**. Both have offices in the center of Fare as well as desks at the airport and at the Sofitel Heiva Hotel and the Relais Mahana Hotel. The rates for both agencies differ ever so slightly, but Pacificar seems to have a wider selection of vehicles, especially when it comes to the larger cars. You can usually get a good deal on the weekend rate (three days for the price of two). Pacificar offers a weekend rate for rentals beginning Thursday or Friday. Guests at the local pensions receive discounts of 10 percent from both agencies. Be sure to ask for the discount. Gasoline can be bought at the Faremiti or Mobil stations in Fare.

I've received positive reports about the service at Pacificar. In addition to cars, Pacificar rents motor scooters. ~ Fare; 68-81-10.

Europcar has vehicles that range from a minuscule Fiat Panda to jeeps as well as motor scooters. ~ Fare; 68-82-59, fax 68-80-59.

PUBLIC TRANSIT

One of the biggest problems about visiting Huahine is the dearth of public transportation. Each district on the island has its own *Le Truck* that leaves the villages in the morning to take locals into Fare. By 9 or 9:30 a.m. all *Le Trucks* have left Fare again to return to the villages for the day, where they stay until the next morning. Thus, the only solution (other than hitching) is to rent a car or scooter. The island is simply too big to use a bicycle—don't even consider it.

TAXIS

Taxi service is provided by **Pension Enite**, with a mini-bus stationed at the airport for the arrival of each flight. ~ Fare; 68-82-37.

HITCHING

Hitching around the island is quite good. Huahine is still enough off the beaten track that hitchhikers are somewhat of a novelty and locals will generally pick them up.

TOURS

Huahine Land Tours is the Huahine version of the overland four-wheel-drive tours that have become so popular on Bora Bora, Moorea and Tahiti over the last few years. They have departures twice daily for sites that include a vanilla plantation, *marae* and the eels. Children under 12 are half price. The brochure says "Let yourself be seduced by famous sunset trips and other ones on request." Why not? ~ Fare; 68-89-21.

Felix Tours provides archeological bus tours daily (except Sunday). Stops include Marae Manunu, a fish trap, the Maeva and Fare Pote'e area, the eels of Faie, a vanilla plantation, the town of Fare, a French military cemetery, Maroe, Mahuti and Auea bays, as well as panoramic views. Tours leave at 9 a.m. and return at noon. ~ Fare; 68-81-89.

▼▼▼▼▼▼▼▼▼▼▼▼▼▼▼▼▼▼▼▼▼▼
Addresses & Phone Numbers

Doctor ~ Dr. Le Chat; 68-88-33
Hospital ~ 68-82-48
Police Station ~ 68-82-61
Visitor information ~ tourist office; 68-86-34

EIGHT

Raiatea and Tahaa

As legend has it, Raiatea and Tahaa were originally one island until a giant eel swallowed a young girl. Possessed by her spirit, the enraged creature broke through the surface of the earth, causing the sea to gush. The impact of the water cut the island in two and Raiatea and Tahaa were created.

Raiatea is the bigger of the two islands, has a greater population and a well-developed infrastructure. These sister islands sit 122 miles (192 kilometers) northwest of Papeete, and 25 miles (40 kilometers) west of Huahine. The two islands share a common coral foundation and protected lagoon. Tahaa is slightly less than two miles northwest of Raiatea—about a 20-minute boat trip.

Raiatea, the largest of the Leeward Islands, was of seminal importance to Polynesian culture as a religious and cultural center. This was chiefly because the island was home to Marae Taputapuatea, the largest and most significant shrine in eastern Polynesia. Polynesians from as far away as New Zealand came to worship at the temple and tradition has it that any new temple constructed on neighboring islands had to include a stone from Taputapuatea. In addition, scientists have unearthed evidence pinpointing Raiatea as a jumping off point for the ancient Polynesian mariners who populated other islands.

It was at Taputapuatea that Captain Cook first had a glimpse of Polynesian navigational acumen. In front of a *marae* dedicated to navigation, a local named Tupai drew a map of the neighbor islands in the dirt for the English explorer's benefit and gave him a discourse on navigational theory. Amazingly, Tupai knew the navigational specifics without ever having left Raiatea. Cook was impressed.

With an area of 105 square miles (170 square kilometers), the highest point on Raiatea is 3335-foot (1017-meter) Mount Tefatua. The island is totally surrounded by a reef, with several navigable passes. There are about 10,000 residents on the island.

Raiatea has the only navigable river in French Polynesia—the Faaroa. Considered the original source of migration by the Maori (or *Maohi*, as the Tahitians call themselves) to the far reaches of Polynesia—Hawaii and New Zealand—the Faaroa has great historical significance to the Polynesians. Upon his arrival in Raiatea, Captain Cook noted that logs were floated down the river to build the numerous ships that were under construction.

Mount Temahani, another famous landmark, is supposedly the birthplace of Oro, one of the principal Polynesian gods. Mount Temahani is an extinct volcano that is also home to the *tiare apetahi*, a white gardenia indigenous to the mountain ecosystem. Legend has it that the blossom's five petals represent the five fingers of a young Tahitian maiden who fell in love with a Tahitian prince but was prohibited from marrying him because she was a commoner.

Raiatea receives plenty of rainfall to irrigate its fertile soil, and has a lagoon rich in sea life. Its main products are copra, vanilla and, in recent years, a burgeoning black pearl industry.

Raiatea

As a tourist destination, Raiatea hasn't changed dramatically over the last decade. The chief settlement, Uturoa, is still the sleepy provincial capital it always was, but it now has excellent markets in which to purchase provisions. Raiatea has never been much of a conventional tourist draw because of the absence of beaches on the main island. (Locals will emphatically point out to you that the beaches on the outlying *motus* are quite nice.) There are a number of excellent mid-range hotels catering to divers and those interested in the cultural aspects of the island, chiefly the Taputapuatuea archeological site. What *has* changed is the island's reputation as a yacht charter center.

Raiatea has just the right mix of modern conveniences and traditions to make it an excellent destination for the visitor who wants to see something of an unspoiled French Polynesia. One of the nicest things about the island is that it remains undiscovered. From the visitor's standpoint this is good because Raiateans are not inundated by tourists and are still relatively friendly.

SIGHTS

Uturoa, which translates from Tahitian as "long jaw," is the island's capital and only port. It is both a commercial hub and the administrative headquarters for the Leeward Islands.

The second-largest town in French Polynesia, Uturoa consists of one main street, flanked by two-story cement structures interspersed with a few old-style clapboard buildings. The government administrative complex, **Tavana Hau**, is a row of *fare*-shaped buildings. Beginning with the mayor's office on the north side, the order of rank descends until you reach the lowly cesspool inspector's office.

One block from main street is a quay lined with fishing boats. Though hardly a metropolis, Uturoa does have an electrical power station, a hospital, *gendarmerie*, courthouse, supermarkets, restaurants and other amenities. There is also an ice plant whose purpose is to provide refrigeration for fish shipments to Papeete.

The **public market**, in the heart of town, comes alive at the crack of dawn every day. Though not as large in scale as Papeete's *marché*, vendors sell all the produce, fish and necessities you could ever want. If you are inside the public market early in the day you can get bread and pastries from several vendors.

Along the **waterfront** area (Fisherman's Wharf) are several outdoor cafés that still evoke the old South Seas ambience. And, along with the traditional old businesses, a new block of stores has been constructed that includes everything from a travel agency to an electronic shop to an immaculate French-owned grocery store.

The local **tourism office**, adjacent to a small crafts market, is a good source of information. Unfortunately, it is only open intermittently. Visitor information is also available at the **airport tourist office**. ~ Uturoa; 66-23-33.

One of the newer attractions on the island is the modern **Apooiti Marina complex**. The marina is home to the largest restaurant on the island, The Clubhouse, which has a large veranda that is a superb spot for sipping a beer on a balmy evening. It is also the base for Moorings Yacht Charters. The Apooiti Marina should not be confused with what is known locally as the *Nouveau Marina*, located about one kilometer from town. (Evidently the city of Uturoa owns this mostly empty but modern marina and is looking for a private party to take it over.) ~ Uturoa; 66-35-93.

HIDDEN ▶

The small but fascinating **Na Te Ara Museum** is also located at the Apooiti Marina complex. The creation of Patrick Festou, a native of New Caledonia, the museum has an excellent collection of preserved flora and fauna indigenous to French Polynesia. Specimens from other regions in the South Pacific and Asia are also included. There are more than 25,000 items in the exhibit, including shells, turtles, butterflies, coral, beetles, birds and some mammals. Of special interest is the collection of crabs—the largest in French Polynesia. It includes rare specimens from as deep as 2200 feet (671 meters) beneath the sea. A major addition was added in 1995 that includes 16 new aquariums for coral-reef sea life as well as species from fresh-water habitats. Hours are 9 a.m. to noon and 2 to 5:30 p.m. Closed Sunday. Admission. ~ Uturoa; 66-27-00, fax 66-20-94.

Though Uturoa is the island's focal point, you will eventually want to visit some of the outlying communities. Getting around town with public transportation is not a problem but it can be problematic in the outlying areas. Roads are well maintained but *Le Truck* tends to run infrequently to the far reaches of the island. Hitchhiking, however, is easily accomplished.

One of the best ways to explore Raiatea is to rent a vehicle and drive the 60-mile (96-kilometer) circumference of the island. Many

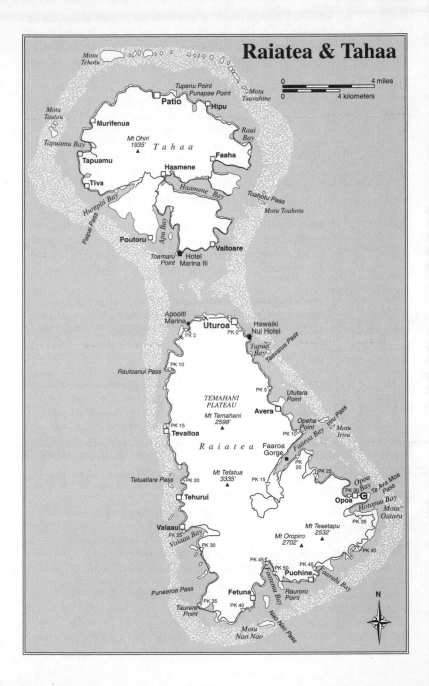

Raiatea & Tahaa

Motu
Tehotu

Motu
Tautau

Tupenu Point
Punapae Point
Patio
Hipu
Motu
Tuuvahine

Murifenua

Raai
Bay

Mt Ohiri
1935'
T a h a a
Faaha

Tapuamu Bay

Tapuamu

Haamene

Tiva

Haamene Bay

Toahotu Pass

Hurepiti Bay

Apu Bay

Motu Toahotu

Paipai Pass

Poutoru

Vaitoare

Toamaru
Point
Hotel
Marina Iti

Apooiti
Marina
Uturoa
Hawaiki
Nui Hotel

PK 5
PK 0

Tupua
Bay

Teavarua Pass

PK 10

Rautoanui Pass

*TEMAHANI
PLATEAU*

PK 5
Utufara
Point

Mt Temahani
2598'
Avera

Opeha
Point
Iriru Pass

PK 15
Tevaitoa

PK 10
Faaroa Bay
Motu
Iriru

R a i a t e a
Faaroa
Gorge

Mt Tefatua
3335'
PK 15

PK 20

PK 25

Tetuatiare Pass
PK 20

Opoa
Bay
Te Ava Moa
Pass

PK 30
Opoa

Tehurui

Hotopuu Bay
Motu
Oatara

PK 35

Vaiaau
PK 25
Vaiaau Bay

Mt Teaetapu
2532'

PK 40

PK 30
Mt Oropiro
2702'

PK 45
PK 50
PK 45
Puohine

Punaeroa Pass

Faaruhi Bay

Fetuna
Rauroro
Point

Faaemu Bay

Taurere
Point
PK 35
PK 40

Motu
Nao Nao

Nao Nao Pass

N

0   4 miles
0   4 kilometers

of the rural roads vary in quality from fair to poor, depending on the weather. On the west side of the island the paved road ends just after Tevaitoa (although there is a short stretch again in Vaiaau). The road is also paved along the island's northeastern edge between Uturoa and Faaroa Bay. From Faaroa Bay there is a paved road that climbs over the saddle to Faatemu Bay where it joins the (unpaved) coastal road and provides access to the communities of Fetuna and Puohine. On the southerly road to Fetuna (about 45 kilometers from Uturoa) you can see gorgeous landscapes during the entire length of the journey. Give yourself an entire day to circumnavigate the island. (Note: There is no gasoline outside of Uturoa.)

HIDDEN ▶   Most of the lodging facilities organize excursions up the **Faaroa River**. The journey begins at the mouth of the river, a fjordlike inlet with steep, verdant cliffs on either side. As the boat travels up the tiny passage the valley becomes a narrow gorge, passing through a rainforest thick with foliage. The trip continues until the course becomes too shallow to navigate. Gliding up the river you can easily imagine the ancient throngs of *va'a* (canoes) dwarfed by the steep walls of **Faaroa Gorge** heading westward into the great Pacific expanse.

TAPUTAPUATEA ARCHEOLOGICAL AREA   Along with Huahine, Raiatea is an archeologist's delight. Scientists have unearthed artifacts that have linked the island to Hawaii, corroborating the locally held belief that Raiatea was a staging area for ancient Polynesian mariners. (If you look at a map you will note that the island's position is directly at the center of the Polynesian triangle.) An additional link to Hawaii is Raiatea's original name—Havai'i.

There are a number of *marae* on Raiatea, including **Marae Taputapuatea**, considered to be one of the most significant temples in all of Polynesia. A national monument, it encompasses a large area on the flat, wide promontory named **Matahiraterai**, situated between Opoa and Hotopuu bays. Besides Marae Taputapuatea,

RAIATEA AND TAHAA EXPERIENCES

- Explore the most sacred temple in eastern Polynesia—**Taputapuatea**, now a national monument. *page 272*
- Stay at one of the finest small hotels in all of French Polynesia, **Hotel Vahine Island**, an offshore beach resort on a tiny *motu*. *page 285*
- Absorb the stunning views of Faaroa Gorge while you dine on seafood at the elegant **Le Fetia**. *page 279*
- Night dive in the Raiatea–Tahaa lagoon for a view of the **Three Masted Wreck**. *page 287*

there are five or six other shrines in the vicinity. They are found on
a flat, sandy point, isolated by a ridge to the east called Matarepeta
Hill, and a smaller hillock approaching the shore on the west.

According to Kenneth P. Emory, an American archeologist, the
depression between the hills was sacred to the god Oro. It was
called Te Po (the Night), while the rest of Raiatea was referred to
as Te Ao (the Day). The exact boundaries of Te Po were marked in
the west by a dikelike structure, Tuiamarafea, and in the east by a
small basalt boulder in the water, Tupi-ofai. (Tupi-ofai also marks
the boundary between the Opoa and Hotopuu districts.) Marae
Taputapuatea occupies the central position in Te Po, and its *ahu*
(altar) lies due north and south.

Marae Taputapuatea held great importance to ancient Polynesians. When constructing new *marae* on neighboring islands, a
stone from Taputapuatea had to be used in the making of the new
temple. Within the Taputapuatea area there are 19 *marae* as well
as one main oblong shrine that is 142 feet (43 meters) in length.
This large temple is considered the home of Oro, the god of war
and an important deity in the Polynesian pantheon. According to
local lore, four men were buried alive in an upright position in the
temple to guard Oro and keep him from straying. Unlike any other
marae, Taputapuatea has a catacomb-like room (not accessible to
the public). A great number of human sacrifices were performed at
Taputapuatea. In 1969, approximately 5000 skulls were discovered on the temple site. To get there take the Opoa-bound truck
from town. Only one truck per day visits the site and leaves Uturoa
in the morning. ~ Faaroa; 66-23-64.

Also look for an obelisk-like basalt slab that stands about ten
yards (nine meters) from the main temple. Known as **ofa'i tapu
taata** (the sacrifice stone), this is where unfortunate victims met
their fate in a particularly bloody ceremony. Here the right eye of
the victim was removed for the priest, and the left eye was taken
for Oro. If the priest deemed the ceremony unworthy, the poor victim was taken to a large upright slab of limestone (resembling an
oversized gravestone) and was scraped against the rough surface of
the stone until what was left of his body dripped with blood.

There was a sacrifice held in Captain Cook's honor. Legend has
it he was offered an eye to eat which he summarily swallowed. The
last significant sacrifice was held in 1853 when 100 men were killed.

If you want to get the full story on Taputapuatea, consider Bill
Kolan's **Almost Paradise Tours**. ~ Faaroa; 66-23-64.

LODGING

Only one hotel, the Hinano, is located within Uturoa's city limits.
Most of the accommodations are clustered within an eight-mile
(12-kilometer) radius of town. It does have a good selection of
small mid-range hotels and budget guesthouses. Raiatea is more

akin to a provincial capital, and does not have the stereotypical luxury beach hotels one might associate with Tahiti.

HIDDEN ► Located in a tranquil setting adjacent to the lagoon, the **Sunset Beach Motel Apooiti** has 16 modern, self-contained bungalows with wooden floors. They are comfortable, clean and well maintained. Each bungalow comes with a picnic table, living room, TV and complete kitchen with large refrigerator and stove. Situated in an expansive grassy area that was formerly a copra plantation, the large, American-style cabins afford a great deal of privacy. The motel is ideal for families or couples who might want to cook for themselves. There are also excellent camping facilities on the property. The office/reception area has a sitting room with a deck overlooking the sea with a view of Bora Bora and Tahaa. Contrary to the name of the property, there is no beach but the grounds are on the waterfront. Guests can swim off the pier. The English-speaking manager, Moana Boubee is friendly, and often provides seasonal fruit to guests. Tours are available and the motel also provides free transportation for guests to and from town once a day for shopping. They also offer free airport transfer. For those who need nocturnal action, The Clubhouse restaurant/bar is only one kilometer away. The Sunset Beach Motel Apooiti is located two kilometers from the airport and five kilometers west of town. ~ Uturoa; 66-33-47. BUDGET TO MODERATE.

In the heart of town, across from the public market, is the **Hinano Hotel**. Recently completed, it looks clean and new but strangely lacks windows. (Maybe to keep out the noise?) My guess is that it was built to appeal to local business travelers. Who else would want to stay in downtown Uturoa? There are ten average-sized rooms, half with overhead fans and half with air-conditioning. Contact Augustine Moulon for more information. ~ Uturoa; 66-13-13, fax 66-14-14. MODERATE.

HIDDEN ► The largest and one of the newest lodgings on the island is the 32-room **Hawaiki Nui Hotel**. Completed in 1995, it is the most luxurious accommodation on the island. Among the amenities are nine over-the-water bungalows—the only property on Raiatea with this type of room. The quarters are spacious and well appointed. Each has a color television, a small safe, hair dryers, mini-bar and direct-dial telephones. The staff is reportedly very friendly and attentive. A full array of nautical activities and tours are provided. The cuisine, with an emphasis on seafood dishes, is quite good. The Hawaiki Nui is located at the site of the Old Bali Hai Hotel, one kilometer southeast of Uturoa. ~ Uturoa; 66-20-23, fax 66-20-20. DELUXE TO ULTRA-DELUXE.

One of the few hotels with a marina, **Chez Marie-France** is a perfectly adequate mid-range accommodation that also provides budget-priced rooms and dorm facilities. Its slogan, "Warmth and comfort of a family pension with the advantages of being a motel," loses something in the translation. Chez Marie-France has four modern, spacious, well-appointed bungalows with tile floors, kitchenettes, phones, TVs, overhead fans, modern bathroom and a mezzanine or loft that sleeps up to six. What the bungalows do lack is a refrigerator, but free ice is available. The entire complex has room for 40 guests. There is also a small house with two communal bathrooms (with solar-heated water), a dorm area with 12 bunks and a communal kitchen with a two-burner stove and a sink. Chez Marie-France also has a fine restaurant on the premises that is open to the public. This is a good place for families. A wide variety of tours are available through the pension. Located 2.5 kilometers southwest from the ferry dock in Uturoa (directly on Tupua Bay). ~ Uturoa; 66-37-10, fax 66-26-25. BUDGET TO MODERATE.

Pension Manava has three bungalows with rooms overlooking a garden. Two of the bungalows come without a kitchen; one self-contained unit has cooking facilities. Each has clean tile floors and airy bathrooms decorated with plants that give them a pleasant greenhouse feel. Two additional bungalows are under construction as we go to press. There are also three dormitory rooms—two with two bunk beds and one with four bunk beds. In addition, there is a small, clean common kitchen with a refrigerator and sink. There's also a common shower and toilet. Proprietress Roselyne Brotherson is helpful and friendly. Excursions are available to Mt. Temehani, Tahaa and various *motus*. The pension is situated in Avera, six kilometers south of Uturoa. ~ Avera; 66-28-26. BUDGET.

Facing the sea, **Peter Brotherson's Camping** (aka Peter's Place) is a combination dormitory and campground. There is a single-row, dormitory-style barracks with seven spartan rooms that sleep two, a communal kitchen with three burners, refrigerator, a small area to store food and two picnic tables. The two communal toilets and showers are fairly clean. The camping area is grassy and large enough to make you feel comfortable. Many backpackers have found Peter's Place to their liking. Excursions are available at competitive rates. Located next door to Pension Manava, about six kilometers south of Uturoa. ~ Avera; 66-20-01. BUDGET.

THE SPANISH CLAN

In 1863, a Chilean slave ship was wrecked near the village of Tiva. Before a rescue party arrived, several of the crew members disappeared. They hid in the village, married islanders and became the ancestors of Tahaa's Feti Panior—the Spanish clan. To this day their descendants live in Tiva and are renowned for their beauty.

Also located in the Avera area is the **Kaoha Nui Ranch**, a pension that doubles as a riding stable. A local home, it has one room with a private bath, which can handle up to three individuals. There are an additional four rooms with two single beds each and communal bath facilities. There are also kitchen facilities so that you may prepare your own food. ~ Avera; 66-25-46. BUDGET.

Only the more upscale properties accept credit cards, so bring traveler's checks to Raiatea.

A largely Tahitian clientele checks into **Pension Yolande Roopinia**, a basic local-style guesthouse that appeals to backpackers as well. Yolande doesn't speak much English but that has not proven to be an impediment. She is quite friendly and will go out of her way to be helpful. The pension consists of one long barracks-like building with four self-contained units, all of which have been recently painted and repaneled. Each unit has a kitchenette and private bath. The facilities are quite adequate. There is a common salon for guests that faces the sea, as well as a common cooking area. Meal plans are available. Airport transfer is extra. It's located in Avera, seven kilometers south of Uturoa on the water next to Raiatea Village Hotel. ~ Avera; 66-35-28. BUDGET TO MODERATE.

Hotel Raiatea Village has six seaside bungalows and six garden bungalows, all with kitchenettes. The atmosphere is pleasant, but the accommodations are overpriced, especially when compared with Pension Greenhill, one kilometer down the road. Although the hotel is located on the water, I do not advise swimming here because of the presence of a particular type of algae that causes extreme itching. (The owners shrugged off the danger, which made me uneasy.) Bicycle, canoe and car rentals are available. The 12 seaside bungalows all have private bathrooms with hot water. The hotel offers a full battery of excursions. Located near the Avera area at the foot of Faaroa Bay, a ten-minute auto ride from town. ~ 66-31-62, fax 66-10-65. MODERATE.

HIDDEN ▶   **Pension Greenhill** offers outstanding views, good food, a comfortable atmosphere and modest prices. Perched on the side of a ridge overlooking Faaroa Bay, the view is superb. The pension is run by the charming but sometimes irascible Marie-Isabelle and her amicable husband, Jason. Accommodations include one large family villa, one apartment, a double bungalow and a honeymoon suite. All have clean private baths with hot water. New on the premises are a swimming pool, a deck overlooking the bay and a jacuzzi. (If you prefer to swim in the bay, it's easy to cross the road to the marina and jump off the dock.) Dining is at a common table. Marie-Isabelle is an entertaining host who has lived throughout the world and is definitely an attraction in her own right. What is unusual about Greenhill is that all excursions, including airport transfer, are included in the tariff. They request that you make reserva-

Polynesian Navigators Revive Ancient Skills

The skills and heroic feats of ancient Polynesian navigators have not been lost on their modern-day descendants. In 1992, dubbed unofficially as the "Year of the Polynesian Canoe," Taputapuatea became the site of a graduation ceremony for traditional navigators from throughout the Pacific who are relearning the art of steering by the stars and swells. The event attracted over 100 participants, including Hawaiians, Tahitians, Cook Islanders and New Zealand Maoris. It was reportedly the first time in 800 years that Polynesian navigators had come to one of the most sacred religious sites in eastern Polynesia.

On March 18, 1995, the shrine was again the venue for a Pan-Pacific gathering. A convocation of traditional double-hulled sailing canoes from Hawaii, the Cook Islands, New Zealand and Tahiti converged at Taputapuatea. In addition to the canoes, a reed raft constructed by Easter Islanders (living in Tahiti) was also there. The assembly not only revitalized ties between Polynesians from the three corners of the Polynesian triangle, but revived the importance of Taputapuatea as a Polynesian cultural center. The crews were welcomed with elaborate rituals, chants and speeches that brought new life to what many had thought was a dying culture.

Participating in this voyage of rediscovery were eight Polynesian canoes. They all retraced the 1500-year-old route from Tahiti to the Marquesas, and from the Marquesas to Hawaii.

tions at least two days prior to arrival; a minimum two-day stay is required. Be forewarned: This place is not for everyone. Marie-Isabelle has a strong personality. Her style may not be to your liking and you might feel uncomfortable staying here. Complaints have been received. ~ Twelve kilometers south of Uturoa on Faaroa Bay, Faaroa; 66-37-64. BUDGET TO MODERATE.

The 15-room **Hotel Tenape** was under construction as this book went to press. Located near the airport and built on a five-acre parcel of land, it is the first hotel situated on the west coast of Raiatea. It is a two-story Polynesian-style building with public facilities on the ground floor and air-conditioned rooms with terraces on the first floor. It will have a restaurant, pool and dive center round out the facilities. As of now there is no telephone number or address for the hotel. ~ Ten kilometers west of Uturoa.

DINING

Starting from the northern tip of the island is **The Clubhouse**, facing the Apooiti Yacht Harbor. It is the largest restaurant in Raiatea. With a bamboo motif, The Clubhouse is shaded by a massive thatched-roof canopy. The menu is reasonably priced and quite comprehensive. Some of the better dishes include *poisson cru*, chicken curry, mahimahi, grilled lobster and spaghetti with crab. The restaurant has a long bar and indoor/outdoor seating with a capacity of up to 200 guests. In addition to the food service, The Clubhouse is a fine place for a sunset cocktail or to catch the regular entertainment on the weekends. ~ Apooiti Marina, Uturoa; 66-11-66. BUDGET TO MODERATE.

There are several local bars and restaurants in Uturoa where you can take in the local scene and the gastronomical flavors of the island. A good place to begin is **Moana**, a Chinese restaurant in "downtown" that shares the same building as the Zenith disco. I recommend you try the house special, the Moana chow mein. ~ Uturoa; 66-27-49. BUDGET TO MODERATE.

The **Jade Garden** is a more basic Chinese eatery on the main street. It has the standard litany of dishes, including chow mein, chop suey and a variety of soups. ~ Uturoa; 66-34-40. BUDGET.

Restaurant Michele at the Hinano Hotel is an inexpensive indoor restaurant that serves generous portions of French and Tahitian food such as fish, steak and pastries. It's popular with locals. ~ Uturoa; 66-14-66. BUDGET.

HIDDEN ►

My favorite restaurant in town is **Quai des Pêcheurs** (Fisherman's Wharf). As you might guess, it is located on the waterfront in downtown Uturoa. The sign on the door says Disco Quai Dep because it doubles as a nightclub on weekends. It's cozy, comfortable and has a small outdoor patio that offers a 180-degree view of the bay. Sometimes a nice tradewind blows, which does wonders for the comfort level. Dishes include steak, mahimahi, crab or shrimp. The proprietress, incidentally, is a former Miss Tahiti. ~ Uturoa; 66-36-83. BUDGET TO MODERATE.

A block from the waterfront, **Snack Chez Remy** is recognizable by its turquoise paint job and the Hinano Beer logo. It has good French/Tahitian food such as *maa tinito*. You can sip a local beer with the locals and drink in the terrific local color. Open only for breakfast and lunch. ~ Uturoa. BUDGET.

Snack Moemoea, an outdoor café with a distinctive blue awning, is located on the waterfront. Here you'll find the best hamburgers in town. ~ Uturoa; 66-39-84. BUDGET.

For a croissant or a cup of coffee, visit **Le Traiteur**, a patisserie on the main street in town in the same building as the Westpac Bank. ~ Uturoa. BUDGET.

Chez Marie-France, a popular small hotel, also has a fine family-style restaurant. Cooled by overhead fans, it serves American and continental breakfast as well as lunch and dinner. The specialty of the house is seafood. *Poisson du jour* (fish of the day) is always a good choice. The small bar, which seats about six, has a regular happy hour in the evenings. Closed Monday. ~ Uturoa; 66-37-10. BUDGET TO MODERATE.

When you are tired of slumming it, check out **Le Fetia** at the Stardust Marine marina. Situated on the water in a very attractive Colonial-style setting, the restaurant features fish, duck, chicken—and a fabulous view of Faaroa Bay. Call before you go down there, the restaurant has gone through quite a few chefs lately and is often inexplicably closed. Located directly across from Pension Greenhill. ~ Faaroa; 66-10-71. MODERATE.

◄ HIDDEN

There are a host of markets and general stores in Uturoa. For volume shoppers or yachters the best bet for local produce, fish or poultry is the municipal market in town that opens at dawn every day. The savvy traveler should occasionally skip restaurant food and head here for a picnic of pâté, fresh fruit and wine.

GROCERIES

For bulk goods, pharmacy items and the like, be sure to check out Uturoa's **Champion Store** downtown. Part of a European discount chain with outlets in Papeete, it also has a variety of everyday products as well as gourmet items such as exotic goat cheeses,

DINE AROUND

There are several small no-name budget eateries across from the market as you walk toward the water in Uturoa. From the outside they look like stalls, but once inside you can sit down and order local fare such as *maa tinito*, *poisson cru*, steak and fries or chicken and fries.

pâté and duck confit. The prices are generally better than at the two main Chinese stores.

For a more conventional supermarket, check out **Supermarche Leogite.** ~ Uturoa; 66-35-33. Likewise, **Supermarche Liaut** has all the basics including a nice array of wine, beer, pâté, cheese and other items for a picnic lunch. ~ Uturoa; 66-21-09.

SHOPPING

If you're looking for good quality souvenirs, the **Arii Boutique** in town has handpainted T-shirts and pareus with Tahitian motifs. ~ Uturoa; 66-35-54.

Adjacent to the tourist office on the waterfront are several stalls operated by *mamas* (the Tahitian equivalent of the Russian *babushka*)—older local women clad in muumuus who sell pareus, shells and other inexpensive souvenirs. The crafts stall directly in front of the airport terminal also sells crafts and souvenirs.

A new commercial center has been built in downtown Uturoa that will have a variety of shops.

NIGHTLIFE

The **Zenith** is a rollicking local disco, appealing to the younger crowd. It is located in the same building as the Moana restaurant. ~ Uturoa; 66-27-49.

From what I gather, the best scene for singles or couples in their 20s and 30s on the weekend is the **Quai des Pêcheurs.** By day it's a tame waterfront restaurant, but on Friday night a live local band plays, and on Saturday there's a disco. During the week, Quai des Pêcheurs is the perfect spot for an early evening cocktail. ~ Uturoa; 66-36-83.

Although Raiatea is the last bastion of fire walking in French Polynesia, you'll rarely see it performed here. Raiatean fire walkers are generally seen in Tahiti during the Tiurai (or *Heiva*) festival.

Another fine venue for a sunset drink is **The Clubhouse,** located at the Apooiti Marina. It's a nice place to sit outdoors and watch the sailboats come in. ~ Uturoa; 66-11-66.

Chez Marie France, a small hotel, offers a daily happy hour. ~ Uturoa; 66-37-10.

BEACHES

Alas, Raiatea is bereft of beaches on the main island. There are, however, a number of excellent beaches on the *motus* that dot the fringing reefs. You'll have to rent or hire a boat to get there. Most of the tour operators and hotels have picnic-at-the-beach options.

MOTU NAO NAO   At the southern end of the island, just across from the village of Fetuna, is a large *motu* called Nao Nao that has a beautiful stretch of white sand and is good for picnics.

OPEHA POINT   Another *motu* worth considering is located off Opeha Point, near the mouth of Faaroa Bay. It has a fine white-sand beach and good snorkeling.

Omai,
Friend of
Captain Cook

Raiatea is the birthplace of Omai, the first Polynesian to visit Europe. The nephew of the king of Raiatea, Omai became an attendant to Huahine's king, Oree. When Captain James Cook arrived in Huahine on his second voyage in 1773, Omai made himself indispensable by procuring food for the crew, protecting the sailors from theft and threats of harm by a jealous chief.

Captain Furneaux, second in command in Captain Cook's party invited Omai to accompany him on the return trip to England. So in 1774 the Polynesian set sail for England.

Omai soon became the darling of English society. Friendly and charming, he was dressed by his benefactors in velvet jackets and other finery. Over the next two years he dined in London's best homes, met the king, learned to shoot and skate and was a favorite with the ladies.

En route back to Tahiti, he served Captain Cook as a translator in the Society Islands and Tonga. He returned to Tahiti in 1776, bearing gifts of firearms, wine, tin soldiers, kitchenware and a globe of the world. But the hapless Omai was soon cheated out of many of his treasures by Tahitians.

Cook saw to it that Omai was moved to Huahine, where Cook's carpenters built him a house and supplied him with pigs, chickens and tools. Not long after the return home Omai died. Some of his souvenirs and artifacts from England were still around when the first missionaries arrived in 1797.

Tahaa

Only 20 minutes from Raiatea by boat is Tahaa, a dryer, less fertile sister island sharing the same lagoon. Approximately 55 square miles (90 square kilometers) in area, Tahaa has nine villages and a population numbering around 4000. The island is surrounded by a reef with two passes. Long a poor relation to the more economically developed Raiatea, Tahaa offers the visitor an even more tranquil place to stop over—off the beaten track and friendlier than its neighbor.

Tourism is not Tahaa's mainstay. Most people here live by subsistence farming, although vanilla and copra are produced commercially. In fact, Tahaa is the leading producer of vanilla in the Society Islands. Livestock and chicken ranches are also important to the island's economy. Local crafts such as handwoven hats, baskets, place mats, bedspreads, shell necklaces and wood sculpture are cottage industries.

SIGHTS

The largest community on Tahaa is **Patio** on the north coast. Patio has a lazy, backwater ambience, and is little more than a collection of concrete structures that include a *gendarmerie*, infirmary, post office and school.

Tahaa's road system is less developed than Raiatea's, making it a challenge to get around. Because there is no public transportation available, you will have to rent a car or walk if you want to explore the island on your own.

Tahaa is not stunning in the manner of Bora Bora or Huahine. It lacks the dramatic land- and seascapes of those islands. There isn't a major population center on Tahaa—rather, the island's inhabitants are scattered in a number of villages. There aren't any conspicuous gathering places in those communities, making it difficult for you to observe daily life. This characteristic, combined with a virtual absence of transportation, makes Tahaa difficult to get to know.

But its strength is as a port-of-call for yachts. Splendid sailing in the lagoon, the ease of finding protected moorage and lots of *motus* to explore make it an ideal setting for a sailboat. In addition, several hotels go out of their way to cater to the yachting trade.

If you are not a yachtie or a diver, the only other major activity on Tahaa is hiking. There are a number of trails and a coastal road that allow you to see most of the island by foot. If you have a mountain bike at your disposal, all the better.

Tahaa's terrain is rugged and rocky, covered with vegetation adapted to its relatively dry, tropical climate. There are coconut palms and much of the same flora that inhabit the rest of the Society Group, but Tahaa does not have Tahiti's lush cover of rainforest. There are, however, several strikingly beautiful bays on the island, the most attractive being **Haamene** and **Hurepiti**. Both are narrow, fjordlike passages that furrow deep into the body of the island. They are easily accessible on foot and offer stunning views.

Excursions to points of interest can be arranged with local guides, including visits to sites where the mythical Polynesian hero, appropriately named Hiro, left his mark. These **landmarks** include Hiro's bowl, left footprint, crest and boat. All of them are rather subtle and difficult to ferret out if you don't know what to look for. For example, Hiro's footprint is little more than an indentation on a rock. All of the sites are located on private property so it's best to go on a guided tour if you wish to see them.

Despite the fact that the framework for tourism is in an embryonic stage on Tahaa, there is a good selection of accommodations in the mid-range area. As in other isolated French Polynesian destinations, you should expect to pay with traveler's checks—only a few resorts accept plastic.

LODGING

Chez Pascal is clearly the budget traveler's choice for Tahaa. The house is very clean and brightly decorated with colorful fabrics and the rooms are large and simply furnished. There are two private baths as well as cooking facilities. The electricity is solar powered. The tariff includes breakfast and dinner, or *pension complete* if you don't feel like cooking. A range of activities are offered at reasonable prices, including a trip to Motu Tautau, where the *Pêche aux Cailloux* (fishing festival) is held. The management is extremely friendly and generous—they also enjoy dining with guests. Chez Pascal is a good value compared to other accommodations in a similar price range. It is located in Tapuamu close to the quay. ~ Tapuamu; 65-60-42. BUDGET TO MODERATE.

◄ *HIDDEN*

Chez Murielle is a pension situated on the mouth of Hurepiti Bay, with lovely views over the lagoon toward Bora Bora. Operated by Teagai Shan-Soi and Murielle Hitimaueit, it is constructed in the traditional manner, with a *pandanus* thatch–roof and woven coconut front walls. Decorated in a Tahitian motif with bright fabrics and bric-a-brac scattered about, the rooms are good sized with high ceilings, a double bed and a cold-water bathroom. There is a comfortable sitting area in front of the *fare*, and a small restaurant in a thatched-roof pavilion. When I visited in the early afternoon, the clientele was exclusively Tahitian and they were either playing pool or watching the game in progress. Of all the mid-range or budget properties on Tahaa, Chez Murielle had the most appeal. It is very relaxing and Polynesian in flavor, and provides an opportunity to get to know the local people. Teagai speaks some English. Transfers can be arranged from the quay at Tapuamu, about five kilometers away. ~ Hurepiti Bay; 65-67-29. BUDGET TO MODERATE.

Hibiscus Tahaa Lagoon is run by Leo and Tearere Morou (aka Lolita). Located on the shore of Haamene Bay, they have a large dock and other facilities for yachts. There are also three small bungalows, two family bungalows and a large *fare* converted into a dorm. The bungalows have mosquito nets over the beds, are spacious, comfortable and have a sitting area out front. The bathroom is small but satisfactory. The hotel consists of a large structure housing a dining terrace, dining room, bar and salon. The grounds at the hotel are well landscaped and tidy. The dorm seemed adequate and clean. Yachts are a very important source of their income so Leo and Lolita cater to them by offering free services in exchange for their patronage at the restaurant. The hotel is festively decorated, with flags and nautical pennants providing a charming and welcoming ambience. The evening I was there Leo functioned as the host of a large dinner party, mixing like a skilled politician among the guests. Hibiscus Tahaa Lagoon offers excursions and a land tour at a reasonable price but the guide doesn't speak English. I would recommend Hibiscus for someone who likes a boisterous and social crowd, as yachties tend to be when they hit shore. Leo speaks English and will arrange for transfers from Raiatea. ~ Haamene Bay; 65-61-06, fax 65-65-65. BUDGET TO MODERATE.

Chez Perrette is a clean, tidy pension, redolent with local flavor. Decorated with bright fabrics and a variety of knickknacks, it has one large thatched-roof bungalow with a kitchen and bath. The bungalow is older and not particularly appealing. There are also two rooms in a main house that are charming and, I think, more desirable than the bungalow. However, they offer less privacy. Each of the guest rooms is fair sized and has a free-standing closet. There is a large common bathroom. Rates are rather steep considering what you get. Breakfast is the only meal covered in the fare. (Other meals are available at extra charge.) Activities can be arranged. While Chez Perrette is attractive, the setting is not particularly scenic. The high price and remote location—ten kilometers from Haamene on the east coast—earn a guarded recommendation. ~ Haamene; 65-65-78. MODERATE.

Mareva Village, owned and managed by Yannick and Mareva Ebb, was opened in 1994. The "village" consists of six bungalows lined up like soldiers on the beachless shore. However, the quality of the accommodation is first rate: New Zealand lumber and fixtures were used in building the facility. Each bungalow is identical—a living room with a television and a couch that converts to a bed, a ceiling fan, a kitchen with refrigerator and a well-appointed bathroom with a hot-water shower. A deck, large enough to dine on, at the front of each bungalow overlooks the lagoon toward Raiatea. The "village" has a restaurant with a deck that commands a stunning view of the lagoon, Raiatea and the open ocean. They serve a mix of French, Tahitian and Chinese cuisine. My guess is that the bungalows might be attractive for families. A variety of excursions are offered, including deep-sea fishing, snorkeling trips, a *motu* excursion and land safari. Transfers are provided from Raiatea at an additional cost. Mareva Village is located in Poutoru on the south coast of the island. ~ Poutoru; 65-61-61. MODERATE.

Hotel Marina Iti combines a nautical atmosphere with first-rate accommodations that have a decidedly European flavor. There are seven nicely appointed bungalows, including a honeymoon suite. With privacy in mind, this unit is located at the end of the row of lagoonside bungalows, and has a lovely view of the lagoon and Raiatea. All units have private baths and small outdoor terraces. The restaurant has a chef from France and the cuisine is decidedly French. There is a beach, but it has a rather shallow shelf with a depth up to about three feet until you reach the reef edge—good for kids perhaps. Marina Iti is an excellent, well-run hotel that might appeal to someone who is interested in the conventional rather than the exotic. The hotel provides rental cars and transfers to Raiatea. Various nautical activities are also offered, including boat trips to Bora Bora or Huahine and excursions to Marae Taputapuatea and other attractions on Raiatea. Located on the southernmost tip of Tahaa in the midst of a well-tended coconut plantation, the Marina Iti is just a ten-minute boat trip from Raiatea. ~ Toamaru Point; 65-61-01, fax 65-63-87. MODERATE TO DELUXE.

> Except for a Bank of Socredo Agency in the village of Tapuamu, there is no banking on Tahaa. ~ Patio; 65-63-00.

Bounded by long stretches of white-sand beach, **Hotel Vahine Island** is tucked away on an eight-acre *motu* off the northeastern shore of Tahaa. Run by Luis and Laura Barroco, a hospitable Portuguese couple, the minuscule island resort is among the best small island getaways in French Polynesia. Along with a small but splendid beach, there are coral gardens for reef-walking or snorkeling. The grounds are well maintained and the eight seafront bungalows and three over-the-water units reflect the quality that one would expect at an ultra-deluxe resort. The bungalows are dispersed over the landscape to maximize privacy and to provide nice views of the sunset. The seafront bungalows are small, with only room for the bed and closet, but there is room for a child to sleep in a loft. The nicely appointed over-the-water units are larger and include a salon—equal to anything I saw on Bora Bora or Huahine. To help wile the hours away, the lounge has plenty of books in English and French as well as a nice assortment of CDs and videotapes. The food, included in the tariff, is reportedly very good. A full battery of nautical activities and a host of tours are also available. Transfers are provided by the hotel from the airport in Uturoa. If you have the means, this is the place to stay not only on Tahaa but perhaps in all of French Polynesia. ~ Motu Tuuvahine; 65-67-38, fax 65-67-70. ULTRA-DELUXE.

◄ HIDDEN

DINING   The restaurant scene is primarily confined to the hotels. In fact, there is only one restaurant/bar that isn't affiliated with a lodging facility. Not to worry—given the difficulty of getting around the island—you tend to eat where you reside.

Outside of the hotel scene the only place you'll find is **Restaurant/Bar Tissan** in Patio. Open for lunch and dinner on Friday and Saturday, it offers Chinese and Tahitian fare including *poisson cru* and chow mein. This is the place to go for local ambience. ~ Patio. BUDGET

Restaurant Ti'a Mahana at Chez Murielle offers a mix of French, Tahitian and Chinese food. The owner made a special point of informing me that he offered crab, lobster, shrimp, and either lagoon or ocean fish. ~ Hurepiti Bay; 65-67-29. BUDGET TO MODERATE.

The sunsets and views of Bora Bora are stupendous from Tapuamu Bay.

Hibiscus Tahaa Lagoon has good cuisine, including baked mahimahi, leg of lamb, calamari, salad and fresh fruit for dessert. Continental breakfast is offered in the morning—coffee, tea, hot chocolate, bread, butter and jam. You can probably get something more substantial if you ask for it. ~ Haamene Bay; 65-61-06. BUDGET TO MODERATE.

Hotel Marina Iti has a French chef who generally cooks French cuisine. The ambience is enhanced by the fine lagoon views. Seafood is always a good bet; the restaurant will prepare a traditional feast, *tamaara'a*, baked in an underground oven upon request. ~ Toamaru Point; 65-61-01, fax 65-63-87. MODERATE TO DELUXE.

GROCERIES   There are small stores in Patio, Poutoru, Tapuamu, Faaha and Haamene that have soft drinks, snacks and other basics. However, most locals rely on day trips to Uturoa on Raiatea to take care of serious grocery shopping.

SHOPPING   In Hurepiti, **Sophie Boutique** has a selection of pareus and shirts, as well as a limited selection of crafts. ~ Hurepiti; 65-62-56.

NIGHTLIFE   Nightlife is minimal indeed, but the **Hibiscus Tahaa Lagoon** is often a meetingplace for yachts. When yachts are in town, the owners provide a wonderful evening's entertainment with good dining accompanied by local music. ~ Haamene Bay; 65-61-06.

BEACHES   Without exception, the best beaches are on the *motus* that fringe the barrier reef. Except for Vahine Island, a private resort, the beaches on the *motus* don't have any facilities. A boat ride to any of the *motus* can be arranged through the various resorts.

MOTU TAUTAU AND MOTU TEHOTU   Motus Tautau and Tehotu are small offshore islets accessible only by boat. Both have fine white-sand beaches and offer better than average snorkeling.

Sunset Beach Motel Apooiti is situated on the edge of the lagoon. Here they have a spacious camping area for about 30 people. The management is quite hospitable. There are also excellent communal shower/bath facilities and a lounge area. It's two kilometers from the airport and five kilometers west of town. ~ Avera; 66-33-47. BUDGET.

CAMPING

Peter Brotherson's Camping (aka Peter's Place) is a combination dorm and campground facing the sea. There is a huge camping area set up for up to 30 tents; a large communal kitchen with two sinks, small stove, tile floor and plenty of storage space; and clean, communal bathrooms/showers. It's located six kilometers from Uturoa. ~ Avera; 66-20-01. BUDGET.

Located on Hotopuu Bay, **Havai'i Camping** is a place for hardcore backpackers. It is far away from anything except the spirits that haunt the nearby Marae Taputapuatea. Located near the shore, it is reached by descending a steep hill that can be treacherously muddy and slippery when it rains. It did not look like a whole lot of fun the day I was there. Some food is available on the site, but it's best to bring your own. Transfers from Uturoa cost 2000 CFP. ~ Taputapuatea; 66-32-33. BUDGET.

There are no campgrounds on Tahaa.

The Raiatea–Tahaa lagoon offers excellent diving. There are a wide variety of both reef fish and pelagics. An unusual blue-and-purple colored coral can be found on the reef. Lagoon dive sites are numerous, and many are within a 10- to 20-minute range by boat from port. Fish feeding is practiced, attracting schools of Napoleon Wrasses, brown and white eels, Picasso triggerfish, yellow perches, red snappers, rainbow runners, silver jacks and plenty of white-tip, black-tip and grey sharks. Pelagic species include barracuda, surgeon fish, tuna and rays.

DIVING

Some of the more interesting dive sites include **Avera Pass**, which has abundant coral, including black varieties; the **Coral Garden**, which has some terrific specimens of *agaricia* and *montipora*; and **Coral Caves**, where there are—you guessed it—coral caves.

There are several wreck dives in Avera Pass, including Coaler Wreck (an interisland vessel) and a Catalina seaplane. **Coaler Wreck** is at about 100 feet (30 meters) just off the Hawaiki Nui Hotel. The vessel is an old German coaler that went down just before the turn of the century. The bridge has since disappeared and it's easy to access the rather large hold. Inside is great deal of immobile marine life, including sponges, gorgonians and black coral. When diving the wreck it's also possible to see alevins, shrimp and an old solitary barracuda who has established this as his hunting ground.

The **Three Masted Wreck** is one of the best wreck dives in French Polynesia and is great for night diving. **Japanese Garden**, which at a depth of ten feet (three meters), is perfect for beginners and has a plethora of triggerfish, sharks, Napoleon Wrasses, moray eels as well as coral. Other sites worth visiting are **Paipai Pass**, which offers cave dives; **Perch Ballet**, which often has schools of snappers, Napoleon Wrasses and black-tip sharks; **Toahotu Pass**, which is known for barracudas and platax; and **Octopus Grotto**, a deep dive renowned for legions of octopuses.

The **Catalina** belonged to an interisland airline company. It went down in February of 1958 about two kilometers southeast of Teavarua Pass on a beautiful day. Evidently in making a turn over the lagoon the plane's right wing clipped the water causing the fuselage to split in half before sinking. Miraculously, all 11 passengers survived. The boat now rests at a depth of 100 feet (about 30 meters) in a sandbank and is remarkably intact. The plane is now home to thousands of striped sea bass, yellow-finned surgeon fish, one-spot sea bass, soldier fish and immobile marine life such as sponges and black coral.

Hemisphere Sub, operated by Hubert Clot and Floriane Voisin, provides equipment rentals, transportation and lessons for diving enthusiasts. Hemisphere Sub is a new operation but the owners are quite experienced, having operated the Manta Raie Club in Rangiroa. There are two instructors and the dive boat handles up to ten people inside or outside the lagoon. They provide open-water certification courses and two daily dives. Hemisphere Sub has some unusual excursions, including drift dives, shark feeding and Napoleon feeding. When I was there the Scuba Pro gear seemed to be well maintained. In addition to transporting you on their boat, for an extra charge they will bring your gear and rendezvous with your yacht at sea. A minimum of three people is needed for the special rendezvous service. ~ Uturoa; 66-14-19.

FISHING

Fishing is a way of life in the islands and the low population density in the area combined with a rich reef system makes it good sport. With a little luck it's possible to hook mahimahi, marlin, sailfish, jack and tuna.

The Sakario, a Bertram 28 with a capacity for four passengers, is one of the better local fishing boats available for half- or full-day charters. ~ Uturoa; 66-35-54, fax 66-24-77. Fishing expeditions can be inexpensively arranged though **Mareva Village**. ~ 65-61-61. **Hotel Marina Iti** also charters vessels. ~ 65-61-01.

SAILING

Cruising is definitely the best way to see Raiatea and Tahaa. Public transportation and often, road conditions, leave a lot to be desired on these islands. Consequently, if you have the time and money, touring Raiatea and Tahaa from the deck of a sailboat is the best way to explore the area. There are many good anchorages, plenty of fresh water is available and there are several uninhabited off-shore *motus* accessible only by boat.

Among the yacht harbors on Raiatea, the **Apooiti Marina** is the premier facility. Constructed several years ago by the Moorings Ltd., an internationally known purveyor of sailing vacations, it's one of the more exciting recent developments on the island. Apooiti has moorings for private vessels, as well as 30 of their own yachts that range in length from 38 to 52 feet (11.5 to 15.5 meters).

The Moorings offers two options for nautical adventurers: bareboating, for those who already have the skill to sail a yacht, and crewed yachts where experienced sailors are provided (at a much greater cost, of course). In either case, the staff supplies all provisions from bread to drinks. Because of Raiatea's geographical position in the Society Islands, cruising to Bora Bora, Huahine and Maupiti is easy. Prices start at approximately US$490 per day or US$3430 per week for a Moorings 35, the least expensive yacht. Note that these prices are for high season, July 1–September 1. ~ Uturoa; 66-35-93, fax 66-20-94, or 800-535-7289 in the U.S.

Stardust Marine South Pacific is in Faaroa Bay, directly below Pension Greenhill. Stardust Marine has a flotilla of 25 boats of all types, including catamarans. They will provide transportation from the airport and, like the Moorings, can outfit you for just about anything. Stardust also provides the option of bareboating or hiring a crew. Rates start at US$3300 per week for a Sun Dance 36 Jenneau (in low season). Vessels of up to 52 feet (15.5 meters) are also available. All Stardust boats have a minimum three-day hire. ~ Faaroa; 66-23-18, or 800-634-8822 in the U.S.

Danae III, IV & V are cruising yachts located in Apooiti Harbor. They provide charters ranging from 3 to 18 days. ~ For more information, contact Claude Goche, BP 251, Uturoa; 66-12-50, fax 66-39-37.

Coco Charter Polynesie has a 47-foot (14 meter) sloop that charters tours throughout the Society Islands. The vessel has a full complement of amenities, including TV and stereo, as well as snorkeling and fishing gear. ~ Uturoa; 66-10-21, 65-61-01.

◆◆◆

PÊCHE AUX CAILLOUX

Pêche aux Cailloux is a local fishing festival held every year in October or November. It's a dramatic spectacle, involving the coordinated action of men in boats who drive fish into the lagoon toward the beach by pounding the water with stones attached to cords. On shore a large number of people wait with their nets. Call the Comité de Fetes de Tahaa at the Mairie (Town Hall) for information. ~ Patio; 65-63-00.

WIND-SURFING   Windsurfing in the Raiatea–Tahaa lagoon is quite good and it's possible to rent gear at the Hotel Marina Iti. ~ 65-61-01. Sailboarding gear is also available at the remote **Hotel Vahine Island.** ~ 65-67-38.

RIDING STABLES   If you prefer seeing Raiatea from the back of a horse, a visit to **Kaoha Nui Ranch** is in order. Located in Avera, the ranch offers a variety of trips ranging from a few hours to four-day camping trips. The rides traverse vanilla and pineapple plantations, bamboo forests, archeological sites and other attractions. ~ Avera; 66-25-46.

BIKING   Biking in and around Raiatea is a possibility, although a serious trip, such as from Uturoa to Taputapuatea, would necessitate a mountain bike and take a full day to complete. Traffic is not terribly heavy on this island, but the roads in the peripheral areas are unpaved, dusty and often in poor condition.

Tahaa is a good island to explore by bike because there is so little traffic. On the other hand, the roads are usually in need of repair. It's possible to ride around the island by bike, but keep in mind the coastal road does not completely circle Tahaa. Do not attempt a long ride unless you have a sturdy mountain bike. Give yourself the whole day to do an extensive ride and check with a local who knows his or her way around before attempting to do so. **Bike Rentals**   Bikes can be rented at **Hotel Raiatea Village** ~ Uturoa; 66-31-62, **Hotel Marina Iti** ~ Toamaru Point; 65-61-01, or **Pension Hibiscus** ~ Haamene; 65-61-06.

HIKING   Walking is still the basic form of transportation on these islands, and paths are well maintained.

Mt. Temehani and the Temehani Plateau (2 miles/3.2 kilometers) affords marvelous views of the northern end of the island and the outlying *motus*. There are two access trails, both taking about two hours. On the eastern side of the island, the trailhead begins several hundred yards south of the Hawaiki Nui Hotel. The trail follows a westerly direction for about one mile (1.6 kilometers)

RESCUE THE TURTLES

Leo Morou, the manager of Hibiscus Tahaa, is the founder of Foundation Hibiscus, which is dedicated to saving the local turtle population. To date, they have placed over 100 turtles on nearby Scilly Island. There is a holding pen at the resort where Leo keeps the turtles brought to him by local fishermen until the animals can be transferred. To support his efforts he offers high-quality T-shirts for sale.

and then jogs south to the plateau. It is quite manageable in dry weather but after a rain it may be slick. On the west coast you can pick up the trail a few hundred yards south of the PK 10 marker. (See Chapter Four for an explanation of the PK system.) It follows a southeasterly course and is slightly shorter and more direct than the eastern track. The peak and plateau area is home to the indigenous *tiare apetahi*, an endangered species of gardenia that is celebrated in local myth.

Haamene to Hurepiti Bays (2.5 miles/4 kilometers): The saddle trail between Haamene and Hurepiti bays is a fairly easy trek that offers one of the most dramatic views on the island. The hike begins in the village of Haamene on the small main street and proceeds over the "hump," the geographic center of the island, in an westerly direction to Hurepiti Bay. At the summit you can see Bora Bora to the west and a magnificent view of Haamene Bay to the east. The trek can be done in a leisurely two hours. The track is quite good over the entire route and is not strenuous.

The walk between **Patio and Hipu** (1.5 miles/2 kilometers) is a leisurely stroll along several kilometers of the northern coast. It's not hard to find the right track. Basically the island has only one main road and it follows the coastline. Starting from Patio, walk east along the perimeter road and follow it until you reach the community of Hipu. The entire walk is only 45 minutes.

▼▼▼▼▼▼▼▼▼▼

Transportation

AIR

Flights with **Air Tahiti** from Papeete to Raiatea are available seven days a week (at least three times daily). Flying time is 35 minutes. There are also regular flights to and from Bora Bora, Huahine, Maupiti, Moorea (through Papeete) and Rangiroa (from Bora). ~ Uturoa; 66-32-50.

Air Alizé has flights out of Huahine three times a week and Bora Bora five times a week to Raiatea. ~ Uturoa; 66-10-00.

There are no direct flights to Tahaa.

SEA

Raiatea and Tahaa can be reached by interisland steamer from Papeete. The *Vaeanu* (41-25-35) and the *Taporo VI* (42-63-93) take about nine hours. The *Raromatai Ferry* also sails regularly from Papeete. ~ 43-19-88.

The speedy new *Ono Ono* will get you from Papeete to Raiatea in under four hours. ~ Uturoa; 66-35-35.

Getting from Raiatea to Tahaa and back is easy and can be a good way to meet locals. Generally, you can be assured of catching a ride with one of the established shuttles known as *navettes* that carry interisland commuters. Or, as a last-ditch effort, you can ride on the schoolchildren's boat at 3 p.m. The shuttle boats leave Tahaa at around 5 a.m. and return from Uturoa at around 11 a.m. Most of Tahaa's far-flung communities are served by the *navettes*.

The *Uporu*, a speedy new transport boat with a capacity of 57 passengers, has recently inaugurated service between Raiatea and Tahaa. This appears to be the best way to get from one island to the other. It departs four times daily from the airport, stopping at Marina Iti on the southern tip of Tahaa. ~ Uturoa; 65-67-10.

CAR & JEEP RENTALS

RAIATEA There are four car rental agencies in the Uturoa area, two of which have airport offices—Pacificar and Europcar.

Pacificar had the most reasonable rates when I was last there. Tariff includes insurance and mileage (but no gas). It is part of a large local chain of rental agencies and has locations both at the airport and the Apooiti Marina. ~ Uturoa; 66-11-66. **Europcar** is also part of a large chain. It has bureaus in town, at the Hawaiki Nui Hotel and at the airport. One reader suggested that dealing with Europcar can be problematic. ~ Uturoa; 66-34-06. **Location Guirouard** is located at the Motu Tapu Garage. ~ Uturoa; 66-33-09. **Tahiti Voyage** is situated right in the center of town. ~ Uturoa; 66-35-35.

TAHAA The **Hotel Marina Iti** has some Fiat Clios and two four-door pickup trucks for rent. The rates include fuel and 100 free kilometers (just enough to circle the island). The pickup trucks are an economical way for a large group to see the island. Reservations are essential. ~ Toamaru Point; 65-61-01, fax 65-63-87. **Europcar**, open seven days a week, has vehicles at the service station at Tapuamu dock. ~ Tapuamu; 65-67-00, fax 65-68-08. **Tahaa Transport** Services has autos and a minibus for rent. ~ Patio; 65-67-10. **Hibiscus Tahaa Lagoon** has both cars and trucks. ~ Haamene Bay; 65-61-06.

Pacificar has a Jeep Wrangler available. ~ Uturoa; 66-11-66.

PUBLIC TRANSIT

Le Truck service is available to Raiatea's outlying districts between 5 a.m. and 6 p.m. Trucks regularly travel from Uturoa to Fetuna on the far end of the island at 9 a.m. daily. The trip takes about two hours and turns around at 12:30 p.m. for the return leg, arriving at Uturoa at 2:30 p.m. (The last truck to Fetuna departs at 3:30 p.m. from town, but does not return until the next morning.) The price is 250 CFP one way, and it's well worth taking the trip for the scenery and the local color.

All trucks are color-coded, depending on the destination (and owners). The Fetuna bus is turquoise, Vaiaau is red and Opoa is blue. Those wishing to visit Taputapuatea should take the Opoa bus. Figure that the ride from Uturoa to the archeological site will take from one to one-and-a-half hours. From the bus stop it's an easy walk to the temple. The truck to Taputapuatea leaves from town Monday through Friday at 10 a.m. The round-trip fare is 500 CFP. Check with the driver regarding the return leg so that you do not get stuck in Opoa for the evening. The bus terminal is located in downtown Uturoa, adjacent to the public market.

As throughout the rest of French Polynesia, taxis are very expensive in Raiatea. For instance, a taxi ride from Uturoa to Raiatea Village costs 2000 CFP and a one-way ride from town to a distant part of the island can be as much as 6000 CFP.

TAXIS

RAIATEA Perhaps because of the dearth of tourists, hitchhiking is quite acceptable on the island. In other words, if you stick your thumb out, chances are someone will pick you up.

HITCHING

TAHAA Hitching is possible, but given the scarcity of automobile traffic it's tough to find rides. Since there is no major commercial center, Tahaa is a pretty quiet place. I would be careful about heading to Marina Iti by boat and then trying to hitch from there as it is located in a very isolated part of the island.

For the adventurous, **Air Nao Nao** has one ultralight airplane piloted by Jean-Louis Cochet, who will fly visitors over the Raiatea–Tahaa lagoon. He calls his flights "photo-video safaris" and claims you can often see sharks and manta rays from the air. ~ Uturoa; 66-25-73, 66-35-93.

AERIAL TOURS

Raiatea also has its own **Aeoroclub**, a flying school that offers charter flights and aerial tours of the Society Islands. ~ Uturoa; 66-28-88.

Almost Paradise Tours is run by Bill Kolans, a straight-shooting retired U.S. Marine Corps colonel. Bill sailed to Raiatea in 1979 from his native Hawaii and has remained a fixture here ever since. He is an amateur archeologist, well-versed in the history and culture of Polynesia. He is also the only English-speaking guide on the island. His tour to Marae Taputapuatea is quite popular with Americans and well worth the price. Bill's tour runs about two-and-a-half hours, and includes transportation to Taputapuatea. Bill will also pick you up from your lodging. You can write to him at BP 290, Uturoa, Raiatea. ~ Faaroa; 66-23-64.

WALKING TOURS

◄ *HIDDEN*

Havai'i Tours has excursions to Marae Taputapuatea and circle island tours that visit other *marae*, vanilla plantations and other areas. Picnics on *motus* can also be arranged. ~ Uturoa; 66-27-98.

For those who want a guide, **Andre Lemoine** offers mountain walks around the island. ~ Hurepiti; 65-62-56.

Vanilla Tours, located in Hurepiti, is owned and operated by Alain and Cristina Plantier. They can accommodate four to eight people seated in the back of a covered pick-up truck. Although I did not go on this land safari, it has received good reviews from several dif-

JEEP TOURS

ferent sources. Vanilla Tours will meet visitors at Marina Iti, making a day trip possible from Raiatea. The tour focuses on the different aspects of local agriculture, including a stop at a taro garden. The Plantiers have their own vanilla plantation and bring the tour there for about 45 minutes for a demonstration of the "marrying of the male and female" vanilla plant. They provide descriptions of the economic and medicinal use of plants, as well as the obligatory scenic stops. The tour finishes at the Plantiers homestead, where guests are given a tour of the grounds and their traditional Colonial-style home. ~ Haamene; 65-62-46, fax 65-68-97.

In addition to Vanilla Tours, **Tivini Tours**, operated by the Hibiscus Hotel, offers jeep safaris on the backroads of Tahaa. ~ Hurepiti; 65-61-06.

▼▼▼▼▼▼▼▼▼▼▼▼▼▼▼▼▼▼▼▼▼▼▼

Addresses & Phone Numbers

RAIATEA
Ferry ~ Uporu; 65-67-10
Hospital ~ Uturoa Hospital; 66-35-03
Navettes (Water Taxis) ~ 65-61-01
Pharmacy ~ Uturoa Pharmacy; 66-34-44
Police ~ 66-38-97
Taxi Service ~ Municipal Market; 66-20-60
Visitor information ~ Raiatea Tourism Office; 66-23-33

TAHAA
Doctor ~ Dr. Marc Charbonne; 65-60-60
Police ~ Gendarmerie, Patio; 65-64-07
Visitor information ~ Tahaa Visitors Bureau, Patio; 65-63-00

NINE

Maupiti

Maupiti is still the unexploited gem of the Society Islands, despite its increasing popularity with travelers. Surrounded by small coral islets on the fringing reef, Maupiti is covered with lush vegetation. A variety of fruits, including mangoes, breadfruits and bananas, grow in profusion. In two hours or less, you can hike the five and one-half miles (nine kilometers) around the island without seeing another soul.

With an area of 15 square miles (25 square kilometers), Maupiti is the smallest and most isolated island of the Leeward Group. It lies 23 miles (37 kilometers) west of Bora Bora and has a population of about 1200. There is only one pass—Onoiau—that leads into Maupiti and it is so narrow that the government boat that calls once a month can only enter the pass diagonally, and then only if the sea is calm.

The island is strikingly different from the other Leeward Islands because of its minuscule size, its isolation and the comparatively dense population of the villages. The population has doubled in the past decade or so and there are countless children and dogs running about. The three contiguous villages of **Farauru**, **Vai'ea** and **Pauma** together fill one long crowded strip along the eastern side of the island. Perhaps because of the population density, there seems to be never-ending, frenetic activity in the community.

If you stay at any of the pensions on the main island, you will be awakened at 5 a.m. by motor scooters en route to the bakery. The supply of bread usually runs out by 6 or 7 a.m. and people adjust their schedules around the opening of the bakery. Evenings in the village are also a beehive of activity. Walking from one end of the string of villages to the other end you will see people sitting, talking or occasionally strumming guitars and singing. The villagers with televisions tend to place them in the house near the door so that when something of interest is on (like the World Cup), neighbors can gather around the front porch and watch from there.

People here have a disarming friendliness that matches the lush beauty of their island. They are perhaps the most hospitable islanders in the Society Islands. Here, unlike some other islands, the children in the streets might take your hand with a smile and say a *Bonjour!*

Water is a significant problem on Maupiti, although it became considerably less so with the 1994 installation of a pipe that brought potable water into the homes.

Maupitans also appear to be a fairly industrious lot. They work hard at farming a variety of cash crops such as watermelon (*pastèque*), which is grown on the *motus*. The work is labor intensive as soil must be transported from the main island and each plant must be watered by hand. There is also a growing pearl industry here. About 50 people from Maupiti have temporary dwellings on the island of Mopelia (approximately 400 kilometers west of Tahiti), where they occasionally make trips to cultivate oysters. Copra, which is heavily subsidized by the government, is another source of income, and government boats are always filled with pungent brown sacks of the product.

Perhaps because of their isolation and their independent streak, Maupitans have adopted a "no hotel" policy in order to preserve the island as it is. They have had several offers to build large, modern hotels, but the village elders have refused. Maupitans are well aware of the changes that have occurred on Bora Bora due to tourism and they don't like what they see.

Other than a post office (near the mayor's office) and a few tiny markets that are primarily adjuncts to people's homes, there is little in the way of amenities on the island. Banking is done whenever the bank representative flies into town for a couple of days. For visitors who expect to be entertained or need Club Med–style activities to keep them occupied, Maupiti is not an appropriate destination. As one travel writer, James Kay, described Maupiti two decades ago:

"There are no hotels, just a few no-star–rated boarding houses, no rental cars, bikes or motor scooters, no taxis or buses, no bars or restaurants, no bank, no credit cards, and nothing in the way of planned activities. I mean nothing."

I wouldn't agree that there is "nothing" on the island, although it is true that after 20 years, there still hasn't been a lot of development. In my opinion, this is not a bad thing. However, activities are left to the individual, and the only tours that pensions undertake are day trips to nearby *motus*.

SIGHTS

HIDDEN ►

Maupiti is full of *marae* (about 60 in all) and one of the best is **Marae Vaiahu**, just beyond the south end of the village. According to the man who guided me around, Marae Vaiahu is the most important *marae* because of its historical significance. (It seems to be a standard comment that every island has *the* most important *marae*.) I was told that all of the kings from across Polynesia (including Hawaii) had to come to this particular *marae* to be crowned. Maupitans say that Marae Taputapuatea on Raiatea got its name from a place on Maupiti called Taputapuatea. (On Raiatea I was told that Taputapuatea means "very taboo far away place." On Maupiti the term refers to the cutting of the brother's umbilical cord and sending it far away. *Tapu* in Tahitian means taboo, but it also means "to cut").

At Marae Vaiahu, look for two large **stone chairs** used by the kings. One is the old original chair and one is newer, constructed at the time of the missionaries. It was the king who presided over the people of the island and made all of the political decisions.

Also look for a rectangular pit in the ground with some magical stones in it. (These are not the original stones.) The pit was used

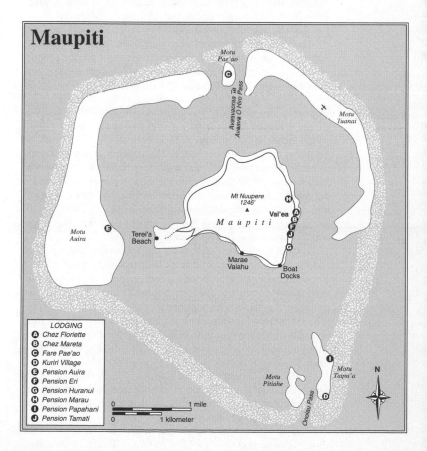

Maupiti

Motu
Pae'ao

Avaavaoraa ia
Avaava O Hiro Pass

Motu
Tuanai

Mt Nuupere
1246'

Maupiti

Vai'ea

Motu
Auira

Terei'a
Beach

Marae
Vaiahu

Boat
Docks

Motu
Tiapa'a

Motu
Pitiahe

Onoiau Pass

Motu
Papahani

N

LODGING
- Ⓐ *Chez Floriette*
- Ⓑ *Chez Mareta*
- Ⓒ *Fare Pae'ao*
- Ⓓ *Kuriri Village*
- Ⓔ *Pension Auira*
- Ⓕ *Pension Eri*
- Ⓖ *Pension Huranui*
- Ⓗ *Pension Marau*
- Ⓘ *Pension Papahani*
- Ⓙ *Pension Tamati*

0   1 mile

0   1 kilometer

with special stone charms to attract fish. In the old days, a woman (perhaps a priestess?) would take the stones (which were thought to be fish) and put them in the pit with their heads facing the mountain. The fish would respond by swimming in the lagoon from the sea toward the mountains. When enough fish were caught, the woman would turn the stones around, with the heads facing the sea, and the fish would swim out of the lagoon into the ocean.

Maupiti used to have two main villages, one on either side of the island, that fought each other. The one on the eastern side of the island was once adjacent to Marae Vaiahu. The original wharf was also at the site of the *marae* as well, and you can still see the large stone that held up the pier.

Another interesting archeological site on the island is the **Hara-nae Valley**, just north of the village, where wonderful petroglyphs of turtles and other figures can easily be seen if you walk about a half-kilometer up the dry stream bed. (Asking a local child to show you the way might be a good idea.)

There are also 16 ancient **graves** on Motu Pae'ao and several 9th-century graves on Motu Tuanai. To get there ask the proprietor at your lodging to arrange for a local boatman to take you there and point out the location of the graves.

LODGING   In general, Maupiti offers two categories of accommodation: in the village, which are in the midst of things and tend to be noisy; and on the *motus*, which are more isolated but where it is difficult to get transportation into the village. The choice is a matter of taste and style. Those who know a smattering of Tahitian and enjoy the local foods might prefer to stay in the thick of things *en ville*, sharing daily life with Maupitans who will respond warmly to anyone who makes an attempt at speaking Tahitian. Once a connection is made, English speakers will hear a lot more English in the village and communication becomes easier.

Visitors to the outer islands should realize that accommodations at budget and even moderate resorts tend to be rustic. For example, in most of the pensions, especially on the *motus*, you will need to use a bucket to flush the toilet. Chances are you will be sharing the pension with a plethora of animals (dogs, chickens, etc.). Along with the animals are the insects. Many of the lodgings are riddled with mosquitos, so be sure to take your repellent along. Mosquito coils, which can be purchased anywhere in French Polynesia, are also an option.

Visitors on the *motus* should also note that the physical isolation of the *motu* (and high cost of gasoline) means that, except for the occasional shopping trip, *motu* dwellers will be less apt to visit the village with great regularity.

Pension Marau is a relatively new undertaking. It consists of a three-bedroom home with a large terrace, a dining room, a self-contained kitchen and a communal (cold water) bath. Only one of the bedrooms has a great view, although it is also the room with the least amount of privacy because the window opens onto the shared veranda. There is a bathroom with a sink inside the house while the shower and toilet are outside. The price for lodging also includes excursions, which makes it an even better deal. Children under 12 are half price. Pension Marau, located in the center of Vai'ea village close to the schoolboat dock, is set on a hillside with a fine view of the lagoon and a *motu*. (To get there you must climb some cement steps.) ~ Vai'ea; 67-81-19, or 53-29-03 in Tahiti. MODERATE.

Chez Floriette is one of the older pensions on the island and has a good reputation. It's a pleasant, clean and spacious four-room house, each room having a double bed. There is also a bungalow with one double and one single bed. Visitors share communal baths (with cold water) and Floriette assures me that there are no problems with her water. Floriette is irrepressibly cheerful, an engaging host who runs a clean, quiet place—and who speaks better English than she thinks. Activities include *motu* picnic excursions and long walks. Tariff includes three meals and airport transport. The only downside is the racket caused by the marathon basketball games that go on directly outside the pension. Next door to both Chez Floriette and Chez Mareta is a hall where locals practice their church songs. "It's lovely," as a friend of mine explained, "but practice can last a long time. . . ." Chez Floriette is not far from the old boat dock near the school. Children under six stay free. ~ Vai'ea; 67-80-85. MODERATE.

Next door to Chez Floriette you'll find **Chez Mareta**. This pension is getting a bit haggard and is not the cleanest in town. For example, when I inspected the bathroom, the toilet had no seat. It is, however, inexpensive. There are three rooms on the mezzanine floor, each with a double bed, and three rooms on the ground floor, each with two double beds. You will eat well here, but chances are you will eat the same thing until the food runs out.

MAUPITI EXPERIENCES

- Explore **Marae Vaiahu**, a temple of great significance in the Polynesian pantheon. *page 296*
- Soak up the sunshine and village ambience at **Pension Eri**. *page 300*
- Enjoy the isolation and tranquility of your private beach at **Kuriri Village,** where the food and hospitality are Polynesia at its finest. *page 301*
- Hike around the island to pristine **Terei'a Beach**, one of the most stunning strands in all the islands. *page 302*

There is also a salon, terrace, kitchenette and common bath. Activities include trips to the *motus* and picnics. Children are 1000 CFP unless they don't eat much, in which case they stay free. Mareta only speaks Tahitian, but her daughter-in-law speaks French and some English. ~ Vai'ea; 67-80-25. BUDGET TO MODERATE.

> One thing that anyone in town can do is to wander down to the mayor's complex around noon for the daily spirited game of *boule*.

The bluish house with white latticework along the porch is **Pension Huranui**, a three-bedroom home. Each room has a double bed. There is also a living room, a large terrace and two communal bathrooms with cold water. The pension is located north of the old boat dock, on the left. Transfers to and from the airport are 1000 CFP. Contact Mr. and Mrs. Hura Temataru, Farauru District, Maupiti. ~ Vai'ea; 67-81-07. MODERATE.

Pension Eri is a new house with four clean rooms, each containing a double bed. It also has a salon, kitchen, terrace with a *motu* view, and communal baths with cold water. Eri also offers airport transfers, *motu* picnics and auto tours of the island. The management is very hospitable. It's located one kilometer from the old boat dock. ~ Vai'ea; 67-81-29 (between noon and 1 p.m. and after 6 p.m.). MODERATE.

Pension Tamati is fairly new. Here you'll find a large building with nine rooms that include five doubles and four singles. All have private baths with cold water. This property is not well maintained and there are better places to go. Children under 12 are half price. Pension Tamati is just north of the old dock. Contact Mr. Ferdinand Tapuhiro. ~ Vai'ea; 67-80-10. MODERATE.

LODGING ON THE MOTUS   Staying on a *motu* is a wonderful alternative to the typical "mainland"-style pensions. *Motus* are generally quiet, isolated and have a beachfront. Keep in mind that most of your time will be spent on a very small islet and getting off the island involves hiring a boat or perhaps hitching a ride with your hosts. All your meals will most likely be consumed at the pension where you reside.

HIDDEN ►

Located on a white-sand beach that's a 20-minute boat ride from the airport is **Pension Papahani**. Situated on Motu Tiapa'a close to the pass, this renovated lodging has had some very good recommendations. The owner, Mlle. Vilna Tuheiava (who has the most delightful giggle), is quite hospitable. There are two large, traditional *fares* with a double bed in each of the four rooms. One of the bungalows is on the beach, the other is in a well-tended garden. The bathroom, showers and dining room are communal. In fact, the bathroom facilities are fairly primitive—a hose embedded in an open-air concrete slab serves as a shower, the sink is in another concrete cubby, and there are two adjoining toilets in a wooden outhouse. The meals are good, abundant and attractively presented with flowers on the plate. In the evening, dinner is served as the sun sets. Visitors may also be entertained by Vilna's brother, Tehu, who sings, plays the guitar and has a surprisingly good knowledge of U.S. geography. (At least, he seems to know most of the U.S. state capitals.) Vilna's son, Rudy, serves as a guide for boat tours of the lagoon or a hike up the mountain for 2000 CFP per person. Excursions and other activities are available. Swimming is excellent here. ~ Motu Tiapa'a; 67-81-58. MODERATE.

Kuriri Village, which shares the same *motu* with Pension Papahani, has a white-sand beach with excellent swimming in a clear lagoon, amidst an undersea tropical garden. Reports have been very positive regarding the food, the setting and the kindness of the owner, Gérard Bede. There are three bungalows set on the ocean side of the *motu* that afford a panoramic view of Bora Bora. The bungalows are constructed in traditional Polynesian style, each with a double bed and mosquito net. There are two communal (cold water) bathrooms. Activities include canoeing, kayaking, snorkeling, fishing and guided hikes on the main island. Children under 12 are half price. Kuriri Village is situated on Motu Tiapa'a, a 20-minute boat ride from the airport, near the pass. ~ Motu Tiapa'a; 67-82-00. DELUXE.

Pension Auira (also called Chez/Pension Edna) is a rustic accommodation that has had good reviews. The people I spoke to raved about the food and the hospitality of the owners, but I have heard other reports that the property was a bit overpriced. There are seven bungalows—three are on the beach. Two have one room with a double and single bed and a bath; the other is a family unit with one double bed and three single beds, plus bath. There are four garden bungalows that share a communal bath. Each has a double bed and single beds. At low tide you can walk directly across to Terei'a Beach on the main island. There is a restaurant/bar, washing machine, fishing trips and tours of Maupiti. (And the tap water is potable.) This lodging is charming, but may not be for everyone. There are numerous dogs living on the *motu* that tend to cluster around the bungalows and they bark and draw flies. The beach is fine, but garbage occasionally washes up. There are no planned activities. Tariff includes all meals. Airport transfer is 2000 CFP. Located 15 minutes by boat from the airport on isolated Motu Auira. Write to Mme. Edna Terai on Motu Auira, Maupiti for reservations. ~ Motu Auira; 67-80-26. MODERATE TO DELUXE.

Another top-rated pension is **Fare Pae'ao** on tiny Motu Pae'ao, located on the northern side of the lagoon. There are three traditional *fares*, each with a double bed and private (cold water) bath. The maximum capacity of each unit is four people. The food is reportedly very good, as is the hospitality. Children under 12 years old are half price. Not only is the swimming great, the beach is lovely and there are a host of activities including windsurfing, snorkeling, beachcombing and fishing. Fare Pae'ao is only ten minutes by boat from the airport and transfer is 1000 CFP per person. Write to Jeannine Tavaearii, Motu Pae'ao, Maupiti. ~ Motu Pae'ao; 67-81-01. MODERATE.

DINING   You are on your own when it comes to eating. There are no restaurants in the villages. You will have to have all your meals in the facilities where you are staying, or when possible use the kitchens available. However, the markets on the island do not have ample quantities of food, so you will have to bring your supplies from home or from one of the larger islands you visit.

GROCERIES   The are several tiny markets that are part of people's homes and provide basic items such as kerosene, mosquito coils, soap and the like. If you need these types of items, the best thing to do is ask somebody where to shop.

BEACHES   **TEREI'A BEACH**   There is only one beach on this small island but it is pristine, perhaps one of the most beautiful small white-sand beaches in all of French Polynesia. Located on the western side of the island, it is a crescent-shaped expanse of coral sand shaded by coconut palms. Snorkeling is good nearby. ~ If you are staying in the village, it is about a 45-minute walk to the beach. If you are staying on Motu Auira, you can walk the half-kilometer or so across the reef at low tide to the beach, but the water is waist-high. This can be a long walk so think twice before doing it.

BURNING THE MIDNIGHT OIL

On Maupiti, as in many isolated communities, the residents have the curious habit of burning their lanterns all night. If you ask them why, they may or may not tell you that this is done to keep the *tupa'pau* (ghosts) away. According to the Maupitans, this island is a haven for every type of ghost, spirit and supernatural creature imaginable. There is even a semiannual beach party strictly for ghosts; every so often someone from the village passes the beach while these exclusive affairs happen to be going on. Maupitans say that from the empty beach—once the site of a village—the sounds of musical instruments and laughter are quite audible.

Snorkeling is particularly good in Maupiti. The ecosystem has not been adulterated or overfished the way it has been in Tahiti, Bora Bora and some of the other islands. Snorkeling is best off the *motus* or near Terei'a Beach. The coral formations are typical of the Society Islands—acpopora, pocillopora and fungia coral are common. The reef fish you will see include parrot fish, unicorn fish, labrida, triggerfish, red mullet and groupers.

Outdoor Adventures

DIVING

You can hike around the island in an hour or two, depending on your mood. The main road basically circles the island. You can walk to the beach (where the road becomes a path) or better yet, take the route that bypasses the beach from the back side of the island and follow it over the mountain and into town. At the high point of the road, you'll come to a spot where the view of the surrounding lagoon will inspire most any photographer. Cars seem ill-adapted for the island and the road through the village functions as a children's playground as well as a resting spot for the numerous canine inhabitants.

HIKING

If you can find a child to accompany you, ask him or her to show you the trail to the 400-foot cliffs that tower over the village. It's only a 10- to 15-minute hike and is not too strenuous, but local knowledge of the path is essential. Once on top, you are directly above the village. From this vantage point you can see the *motus*, the pass, and the church below.

Flights are available from **Air Tahiti** or **Air Alizé**. Because of the limited number of flights to Maupiti, Air Tahiti is usually booked a month or so in advance. Air Alizé is an excellent alternative. The eight-seat aircraft makes you feel like you have your own plane, and the pilot may even circle the island if you ask. Air Tahiti has four flights a week, arriving from Papeete, Raiatea and Bora Bora. Air Alizé also has four flights a week, all originating in Raiatea.

Transportation

AIR

Air Tahiti has a bureau next to the post office in the mayor's complex in the center of the village in Maupiti. Hours are Monday and Thursday from 8 to 11 a.m., and Friday 9:30 to 11 a.m.

The airport is located on a *motu* so regardless of the carrier that gets you to Maupiti, you'll need to get from the *motu* to the mainland. All hotels and pensions pick up their guests; some do it for free and others charge as much as 2000 CFP. A launch from Vaie'a also meets each flight. Fares are 400 CFP for passengers and 200 CFP for large items like coolers and cartons. The launch will also take you to the *motu* to meet your departing flight. The launch's timetable is set up to coincide with Air Tahiti's schedule, allowing you to check in one hour and 45 minutes prior to departure.

Air Alizé on the other hand has no such requirement and, in fact, will wait for you if you are not yet at the airstrip when they are scheduled to depart.

SEA   The dangerous pass makes boat travel to Maupiti an unreliable but nonetheless interesting way of getting there. The regular interisland vessels that stop at the other Society Islands do not go to Maupiti because they are not heavy enough to negotiate the pass. Thus, you are limited to government cargo boats, either the *Meherio II* or *Te Aratai*. Both leave from Raiatea, occasionally stopping in Bora Bora. If you inquire at the local tourist office in Uturoa, you will be told that the boat leaves every two weeks from Papeete, stopping at Raiatea on the way. During June, July and early August, when the *mara'amu* (a tradewind that brings downpours and gusts with tremendous force) blows, this schedule is frequently not met, so anyone who wishes to travel by boat at this time must keep in contact with the boat agents in Papeete. (Note that there are now two docks on Maupiti, the old one behind the school and the new one on the southern end of the village that's used by larger vessels.)

TEN

The Tuamotu Islands

According to Polynesian mythology, the Tuamotu Islands were formed when Tukerai, a Polynesian cross between Neptune and Hercules, tried to shake the sea one day. The result was a storm of biblical proportions from which chunks of earth were tossed to the surface, creating the land that became known as the Tuamotu chain.

Encompassing an area larger than western Europe, the Tuamotu Islands (sometimes called the Paumotu Group) consist of two parallel chains running northwest to southeast. Numbering 78 islands (only 41 of which are inhabited), they comprise the largest chain of atolls in the world. Despite the numerous islands and the vast area they cover, the total land mass of this group is only 1500 square miles (3885 square kilometers). And the entire population consists of a mere 12,000 souls.

The climate in these islands is generally hot year-round, but the period between May and October is the coolest and driest. Most of the rain falls during the hot season—stretching from December to February. Since the elevation of the islands ranges only from 6 to 20 feet, they are prone to severe damage from cyclones. In 1991 and 1993, the area was racked by devastating storms that destroyed the entire economy of several of the atolls.

Designated the "Dangerous Archipelago" by Louis-Antoine de Bougainville, who sailed through in 1768, the Tuamotu Group has also been called "Labyrinth." There is no mystery to these grim monikers—the razor-sharp coral reefs are littered with the wrecks of many a vessel.

The first European to sail through these shores was Ferdinand Magellan, who came in 1521 but only sighted one island—Pukapuka. Dutchmen Jacob Lemaire and Wilem Cornelisz van Schouten dubbed them the "Green Islands" when they sailed through in 1616. Captain James Cook briefly visited in 1767, while the early 19th century brought the missionaries.

No part of French Polynesia has undergone as radical an economic change as the Tuamotus. Agriculture (primarily the harvesting of coconuts) and fishing have been the mainstay of the area for generations. This has fundamentally changed in the last decade as the black pearl industry and, to some degree, tourism have expanded in these far-flung atolls. For all practical purposes, today copra is dead as a cash crop in the Tuamotu Islands. Perhaps this is an example of free-market economics in action. The copra farmers had been kept afloat only because of artificially high subsidies paid by the government to keep the population on the farm rather than crowding into Papeete looking for work. The emergence of pearl cultivation has not only provided work, but has also given locals an incentive to stay on the islands.

Even commercial fishing, a seemingly logical business to undertake on an island, has taken a back seat to pearl cultivation. Commercial fishing is primarily confined to Arutua and Kaukura because of their proximity to Tahiti. (Given the great distances between many of the Tuamotu islands and Tahiti, the cost of shipping fresh fish is simply not viable.)

These traditional forms of employment have slowed down or died a natural death as pearl farming, a much more lucrative enterprise, has taken hold. Pearl farming has spread like wildfire throughout the archipelago, with about 30 islands involved. And for good reason. It has made a lot of Paumotu people better off economically.

Nowhere is this more evident than on Manihi, where the French Polynesian black pearl industry was born. Visit Manihi's main village of Turipaoa and you will find a supermarket (where a one-room market once stood) and stores stocked with any number of consumer goods. You will also see shiny new Nissan Pathfinders, Yamaha motorcycles and numerous scooters vying for space on the one kilometer or so of road. Even the residents of nearby Ahe, an island once considered the poor relative of Manihi, are now much better off materially than they ever were because of black pearl–related businesses on the island.

Along with the march toward progress and materialism, budget and mid-range lodgings have sprung up on some of the outer Tuamotu islands that are not as caught up in the pearl industry. Some offer better bargains than the Society Islands, and they come with true Paumotu hospitality. A visitor in search of a genuine island

SAFE PASSAGE

Visiting an atoll by yacht or small boat is no mean feat. Many of these islands, which consist of rings of coral, have only one boat passage into the lagoon. When the tide changes, the passes can become treacherous slip streams where currents run as fast as seven knots or more. These fast currents make navigating a boat through a narrow passage lined with razor-sharp reefs extremely difficult at best. According to Rodo Williams, one of the last old-time Polynesian navigators, a simple way to approximate when the water is slack is "when the moon is directly overhead, or directly beneath, the current should not be dangerous."

experience should consider going directly to one of the more remote pensions. If you have a deserted island fantasy, the Tuamotus are the place to live it out. The primal sounds and colors of these atolls cast an unforgettable spell. However, be prepared to live on quantities of fish, rice, corned beef, stale French bread, *ipo* (a Tuamotan dumpling) and perhaps some turtle.

The actual settlements consist of little more than a church, a grocery store, a pier, a water tower or cistern and several rows of clapboard or fired-limestone homes with tin roofs. In the evening, the major pastime is playing guitar, listening to Radio Tahiti and watching television, which broadcasts news, music and messages to the outer islands. For young people, time is spent cooking, fishing, harvesting copra and planning liaisons with girlfriends or boyfriends.

Despite the higher standards of living, the trading schooners are the most important link with the outside world. When a boat arrives, the entire village flocks to watch the vessel being unloaded with staples from the mainland. Onboard there may be a store, run by the supercargo, that sells staples and luxury items such as cigarettes, hard liquor, chocolate and coffee.

There's an eerie solitude on these atolls that's not found on high islands. You notice it almost immediately. There is something elementally different, something you feel but is difficult to articulate. Perhaps it is because you are forced to look inward. There are no caves to hide in, no mountains to climb, no valleys to explore and nowhere to escape to. You become aware that you are on an insignificant speck of coral in the middle of an immense ocean. You feel stripped of all the familiar trappings of civilization while the mercilessly brilliant sun beats down upon you and the air is thick with humidity. There is only the endless chorus of lapping waves on the reef and the rustle of ceaseless trade winds through the palm fronds.

Rangiroa

Of all the Tuamotu islands, Rangiroa is the most popular with visitors—primarily divers and travelers seeking an atoll experience. Located 200 miles (322 kilometers) northwest of Papeete, Rangiroa is actually a series of islands around a lagoon, making it the largest atoll in the Tuamotus, and the second largest in the world. Indeed, it's 393-square-mile (1020-square-kilometer) lagoon is the star attraction. Marine life of every size and description, including sharks, manta rays, jack, surgeon fish, mullet, pompano, parrot fish, grouper, puffer fish, butterfly fish, trumpet fish and eels, live in its waters.

Most of the water flowing into and out of the immense lagoon is carried through two passes, which provide the only access for boats venturing in and out. The two towns, Avatoru and Tiputa, each sit on the eastern shore of a pass. The extraordinary tidal flow through the passes allows for exceptional scuba diving and snorkeling. Divers can observe a virtual freeway-traffic stream of marine life zipping by.

This huge atoll has miles of empty white-sand beaches and silent groves of coconut palms. Rangiroa's lagoon is so wide that it is impossible to see the opposite shore when standing on one side

Text continued on page 310.

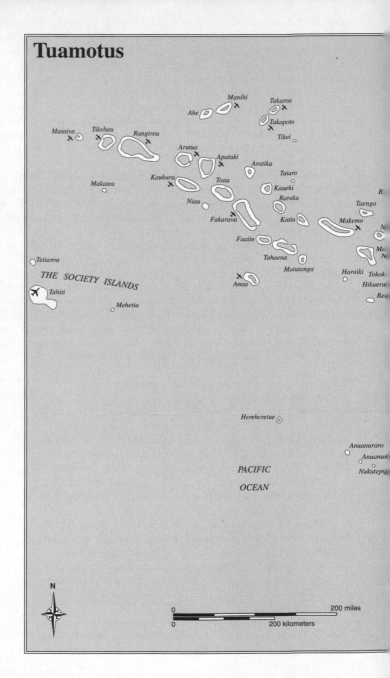

Tuamotus

Manihi

Ahe

Takaroa

Takapoto

Tikei

Mataiva   Tikehau   Rangiroa

Arutua

Apataki   Aratika

Taiaro

Makatea   Kaukura

Toau   Kauehi

Niau   Raraka

Taenga

Fakarava   Katiu   Makemo

Faaite

Tahaena

Motutonga   Haraiki   Tokok

Anaa   Hikuero

Ree

Tetiaroa

THE SOCIETY ISLANDS

Tahiti

Mehetia

PACIFIC

OCEAN

Hereheretue

Anuanuraro

Anuanu

Nukutepi

N

0   200 miles

0   200 kilometers

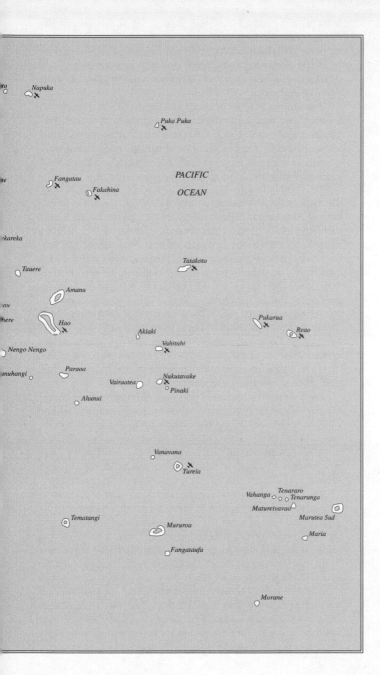

to
Napuka

Puka Puka

ne
Fangatau
Fakahina

PACIFIC

OCEAN

kareka

Tauere

Amanu

Tatakoto

au
here
Hao
Akiaki
Vahitahi

Pukarua

Reao

Nengo Nengo

nuhangi
Paraoa
Vairaatea
Nukutavake
Pinaki

Ahunui

Vanavana
Tureia

Tenararo
Vahanga
Tenarunga
Matureivavao

Tematangi
Marutea Sud

Mururoa
Maria

Fangataufa

Morane

looking for the other. I highly recommend you hire a boat and play Robinson Crusoe for a day.

Some of the local hotels specialize in diving, snorkeling and glass-bottomed boat excursions. From port it is possible to see local divers spear fish and then feed the unfortunate, wriggling creatures to the nearest shark.

Tourism has been an important factor in the island's economy for about two decades. In the days before tourism, Rangiroans depended mainly upon copra, fishing and the mother-of-pearl trade for their income. The mother-of-pearl industry disappeared when plastic buttons replaced pearl shell, but tourism, and lately black pearl cultivation, has reinvigorated the island economy.

SIGHTS   The bulk of the island's approximately 2000 people live in the villages of **Avatoru** and **Tiputa**, which are a 45-minute boatride from each other on different *motus*. Avatoru is at the western end of a string of connected islands, separated only by channels. The Avatoru Pass separates this island chain from the next island to the west. Most of the hotels and pensions, the Rangiroa Visitors' Bureau, shops, banks, the major resort hotel Kia Ora Rangiroa and the airport are on the Avatoru side.

Directly across the pass at the eastern end of the Avatoru chain, Tiputa separates the Avatoru chain from the next island. Various amenities and government agencies are more or less equally divided between Avatoru and Tiputa. However, of the two communities, Tiputa is the main administrative community, and has a town hall, post office, *gendarmerie* and infirmary.

You'll see many trees, stately walkways and even manicured lawns in the towns—a rarity on islands where fresh water and soil are precious commodities. During the island's heyday, soil was actually brought in by those who could afford it. Both towns have Mormon and Catholic churches that are worth visiting. (If you visit the cemetery in either community, note that the real estate is divided into two sections.)

The old **Catholic church** in the center of Tiputa is particularly attractive, as are the facades of many homes that hark back to a grander era. One of these old colonial homes has a dome-shaped **shrine** or chapel constructed of concrete. The structure is inlaid with stones, shells, and has a statue of the Virgin Mary. It's hard to miss.

In Avatoru it seems there's always a crowd hanging around the docks. (Perhaps there is not much else to do.) A boat crosses with reasonable frequency between the dock by Chez Glorine on the Avatoru side of Tiputa Pass to Tiputa Village. You can transfer via Kia Ora, which allows you a one-hour layover, for about 1000 CFP, or ask over at Chez Glorine for someone to suggest an impromptu water taxi that will take you across the pass for half the price.

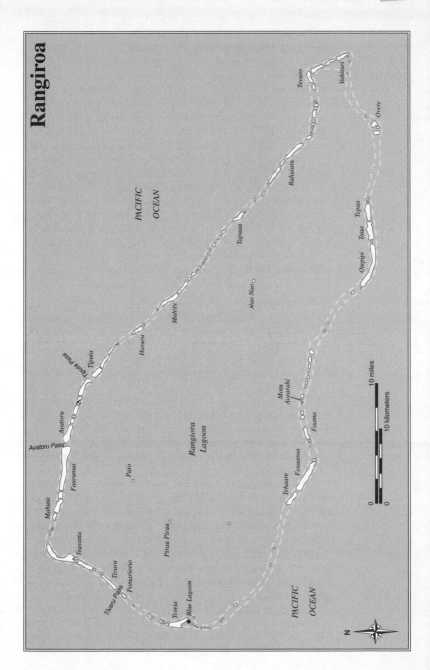

Rangiroa

PACIFIC
OCEAN

Tevaro

Vahituri

Ovete

Rahuiatu

Tepau

Tuputa

Tiaua

Nao Nao

Otepipi

Mahetu

Haruru

Tipuia Pass

Tipuia

Motu
Aveavohi

Avatoru

Faama

Avatoru Pass

Faurumai

Tehaare

Fenuaroa

Mahuta

Paio

Teavatia

Tivaru

Pirau Pirau

Pomarionio

Tiaru Pass

Toreia

Blue Lagoon

Rangiroa
Lagoon

PACIFIC
OCEAN

N

10 miles

10 kilometers

0

0

There are several tiny islands within the lagoon that are important bird sanctuaries. **Paio** is the best-known. Local boats will take you there for a minimal fee.

LODGING   For those visitors needing creature comforts, life on a remote atoll can seem spartan. Rangiroa is an exception—here you can check into a luxury hotel and enjoy life on a faraway island at the same time. Apart from a couple of pensions in Tiputa, all of the local accommodations are on the Avatoru segment of the island. The following four Avatoru pensions—Rangiroa Lodge, Pension Henriette, Pension Herenui and Pension Hinanui—occupy a narrow piece of *motu* real estate. This puts them on the beach, but they are also adjacent to the road, which means more exposure to foot and vehicular traffic. For those who really want to get away from it all, there are lodging possibilities on the outer atolls. Almost all of the lodging facilities will organize bicycle rentals, picnic excursions to other *motus*, pearl-farm tours, glass-bottom boat trips and fishing or snorkeling expeditions. The pensions and small hotels usually offer meal programs with the room tariff. These are referred to as *demi-pension* (two meals) or *pension complete* (three meals).

AVATORU AREA   Avatoru's hotels and pensions are scattered along the lagoon side of the island. The descriptions that follow start at the western end at Avatoru Pass and move east along the island, past the airport to Tiputa Pass at the eastern end.

Starting at the west end of Avatoru you'll find **Pension Henriette**. The main building has an attractive, colonial-style veranda with "Pension Henriette" written in large letters on the awning. It has four bungalows of various configurations, all with a private bath. The largest unit has a living room with television, dining room and communal bath. The meals are very good—Henriette's dessert specialty is banana crêpes—and they come highly recommended. Located about five kilometers from the airport. ~ Avatoru; 96-04-68, 96-05-65. BUDGET.

Chez Punua has a total of four thatched-roof bungalows, two of which are rather tattered-looking beachside *fares*. Each one comes with one double bed and a communal bath. Punua also has two bungalows with one double and one single bed and private bathroom. They also share six spartan bungalows listed with Chez Nanua's that are located 45 minutes by boat across the lagoon. Punua's address is the same as Nanua's. It is located across the road from Chez Henriette on the western end of Avatoru. ~ Avatoru; 96-04-73. BUDGET.

Next up is **Rangiroa Lodge**, which has six spartan cabin-like units beside the lagoon. They are rather plain—no thatched roof here! The bathroom facilities are shared. There are picnic tables and a terrace. Meals can be purchased. Children under 12 years are half price and *pension complete* and *demi-pension* are available. ~ Avatoru; 96-02-13. BUDGET TO MODERATE.

A short distance to the east is friendly **Pension Herenui**, which has five thatched-roof bungalows—all with private bath and terrace. The bungalows are practically sitting on the white-sand beach very close to the shore, and are shaded by coconut palms. The rates include all meals. Quite a few activities are offered here, including bicycling, drift snorkeling and waterskiing. Herenui is located about four kilometers from the airport. Contact Mme. Victorine Sanford. ~ Avatoru; 96-04-71. BUDGET TO MODERATE.

Continuing east you'll come to **Pension Hinanui**. It has two well-constructed, white-washed, red-roof bungalows, each with private (cold water) bath and terrace. Tariff with two meals or *pension complete* is available. Good wine, fine food, nice management and excellent service distinguish Hinanui from many other pensions. The small shop on the premises is also handy. Children under 12 are half price. ~ Avatoru; 96-04-61. BUDGET TO MODERATE.

Rangiroa Village, not to be confused with Rangiroa Beach Club or Rangiroa Lodge, has small cottages lined up neatly in a row along the beach like playhouses on a Monopoly board. On closer inspection, some of the structures could use a facelift, which management says is in the works (including the restaurant). All cottages are spacious and have private bath (with hot water!) and a covered deck. There are four family bungalows, each with a mezzanine level. Family units house a maximum of six people. There is a restaurant/bar, a sparkling white-sand beach and plenty of activities. The resort is close to the western end of the island, one kilometer from Avatoru Village. ~ Avatoru; 96-03-83. MODERATE TO DELUXE.

Continuing toward the airport, past Rangiroa Village is **Chez Nanua**, which has four small, turquoise-colored bungalows with

---

✔ **CHECK THESE OUT—UNIQUE LODGING**

- *Budget to moderate:* Set up a hammock at **Chez Eugenie Ennemoser** in Takaroa as trade winds rustle through the coconut palms. *page 335*
- *Moderate:* Enjoy a genuine Paumotu experience at **Kiritia Village** on Fakarava. *page 336*
- *Ultra-deluxe:* Fulfill your Robinson Crusoe fantasy at Rangiroa's "ultra-deluxe primitive" **Kia Ora Sauvage**, located on a remote atoll. *page 318*
- *Ultra-deluxe:* View the technicolor underwater world from an over-the-water bungalow at **Manihi Pearl Beach Resort** on Manihi. *page 323*

Budget: under $100   Moderate: $100–$150   Deluxe: $150–$200   Ultra-deluxe: over $200

thatched roofs. There is also space for camping—the only place on the island that I'm aware of that has this amenity. The *fares* offer various sleeping arrangements, but toilets and showers are communal. Some of the *fares* are located very near the shore of the lagoon so that the small ladder needed to get inside your unit is practically in the water. It's about as barebones as you can get, but the place does have a Polynesian spirit. And the meals are quite nice—copious and family-style. ~ Avatoru; 96-03-88. BUDGET.

Pension Cécile has four slender thatched-roof bungalows, resembling an A-frame. Each has an attached bathroom with cold water and a small porch. The units are spotlessly clean, well maintained and the food is very good. This is clearly one of the best quality pensions on the island. Cécile speaks good English and both she and her husband, Alban, couldn't be more welcoming. (You have the option of getting a room or *pension complete*). It's located about midway between the Avatoru Pass end of the island and the airport (about five kilometers west of the airport). Transportation to the airport is free. ~ Avatoru; 96-05-06. BUDGET TO MODERATE.

Pension Tuanake is owned and operated by Roger and Iris Terorotua. Three bungalow units resemble slim Swiss chalets, not exactly the thatched-roof *fares* you might expect to see in the South Seas. However, don't hold this against them! Pension Tuanake is one of the best bargains on Rangiroa. It is located just a few hundred yards east of Pension Cécile. ~ Avatoru; 96-04-45, fax 96-03-29. MODERATE.

HIDDEN ▶ **Pension Raira Lagoon** has garnered kudos from many travelers. The owners, Bruno and Hinano, are industrious—they aim to please their guests. They also speak English. Nine traditional-style bungalows are offered, each with sun deck and private bath. The bungalows, which have ceiling fans, have recently been upgraded. The property has been landscaped, food has been improved and the service is excellent. The premises are regularly sprayed and, unlike other properties in the islands, are comparatively mosquito-free. There is a restaurant on the grounds that serves excellent, attractively presented food. *Pension complete* is available. Snorkeling is fairly good in the lagoon right off Raira Beach. Credit cards are accepted. Pension Raira Lagoon is located about two kilometers from the airport, near the Rangiroa Beach Club. ~ Avatoru; 96-04-23, fax 96-05-86. BUDGET TO MODERATE.

The **Rangiroa Beach Club** is placed more or less in the center of Avatoru next to Raira Lagoon. The hotel is under new management, which has upgraded 20 *fares* with thatched roofs, ceiling fans and mini-refrigerators. The bathrooms have hot and cold water and are quite clean. The food is reportedly good, as are bartender Lionel's mai tais. I'm told the manager will give guests a free tour of the island and can arrange additional tours. ~ Avatoru; 96-03-34. MODERATE TO DELUXE.

Paumotan
Practicalities

Virtually all the lodgings in the Tuamotos offer a *pension-complete* plan, which means you pay an extra 2000 to 3000 CFP for three meals a day. This is usually advisable even when there are cooking facilities because on the remote islands there are few, if any, markets and no restaurants, except on Rangiroa.

Most guesthouses located more than ten minutes by boat from the airport will charge a transfer fee from 500 to 2000 CFP per person to pay for gasoline. And most of the pension-style accommodations in the Tuamotus discount their tariffs by 500 CFP per person per day for those staying more than three days.

Many of the pensions offer excursions (sometimes free) to a *motu* where you can swim, picnic and perhaps snorkel. You may be dropped off by a small boat while the owner is on the way to work. Be sure to bring your sunblock, a hat and a good book.

While in the Tuamotus, be prepared to conserve water, which is always a scarce commodity. At times it may be so scarce that people bathe in the sea rather than showering with fresh water. At a small pension you should not expect warm-water showers. Any water at all is a blessing and, besides, it's so hot a cold shower is refreshing.

Likewise, do not expect the electricity (if there is any at all) to be on more than a few hours a day. Many, but not all, of the pensions have generators, but fuel is expensive. All guests are provided with kerosene lamps, which work quite well and will add a romantic touch to your stay.

If you bring your American Express Card, don't expect to use it (or any other credit card) in the Tuamotus except at large resorts such as the Kia Ora Rangiroa or Manihi Pearl Beach Resort. And except for Rangiroa, there are no banks, so bring cash.

It goes without saying that the most visited islands in the Tuamotu Group, Rangiroa and Manihi, have the most amenities. The other islands have only started to develop tourism. Except for an airstrip, a few lodgings, and perhaps a basic shop or two, there's little else on a typical atoll.

Finally, given the isolation of these islands, it's not a bad idea to call, write or fax before you drop in. A letter addressed to the pension, in care of the village and the name of the island, will get there. The postman will not have to ring twice.

HIDDEN ►   A good value, **Chez Felix and Judith** offers six traditional-style bungalows. Painted a distinctive chartreuse, the *fares* have thatched roofs and small porches. The two family bungalows have two (cold water) private baths; the others have one private bath. The bungalows are clean and many are shaded from the sun by nearby trees. The management is helpful and friendly and the pension is clean. Visa cards are accepted. Chez Felix and Judith is situated between Kia Ora Hotel and Chez Martine on the western side of Avatoru. ~ Avatoru; 96-04-41. BUDGET TO MODERATE.

Pension Martine is a new accommodation offering three bungalows—two with one double bed, and a family bungalow with one double and one single bed. Each bungalow comes with private (cold water) bath. Pension Martine is located directly across from the airport terminal. ~ Avatoru; 96-02-53. BUDGET TO MODERATE.

Over-the-water bungalows are the main attraction at **Kia Ora Rangiroa**, one of the best high-end accommodations on this beautifully forlorn atoll. It's the largest hotel on the island, with 30 bungalows, 5 suites, 10 over-the-water bungalows, a restaurant and an over-the-water bar. The over-the-water bungalows come with glass-top coffee tables that allow you to watch the underwater life while relaxing in your own *fare*. And you have your own water-side deck besides. Rooms are spacious and nicely appointed, and the hotel appears to be well looked after. Nautical activities include snorkeling, windsurfing, sailing, parasailing and fishing. Diving facilities at the Kia Ora are first class and the equipment is well maintained. You can find the hotel close to the eastern end of the island, about three kilometers from the airport. ~ Avatoru; 96-03-84, fax 96-02-20. ULTRA-DELUXE.

TIPUTA AREA   There are several accommodations in the Tiputa area, on either side of Tiputa Pass.

Chez Glorine is one of the better pensions on Rangiroa for several reasons: the food is good; the hospitality is generous; the service is above average; and the location is stunning. There are six bungalows with various sleeping configurations, all with private bath. Unlike most accommodations, Glorine has a restaurant/bar facing the pass. Chez Glorine is adjacent to the dock, directly across from Tiputa Village on the Avatoru side (the eastern side) of Tiputa Pass. ~ Tiputa; 96-03-58. BUDGET TO MODERATE.

Pension Marie has seven thatched-roof bungalows, each with private bath. There are also three private rooms with double beds and private baths located in a concrete house above the restaurant/bar. I have had reports that the food was not good, and in at least one of the *fares* it is impossible to lock the door. Pension Marie is located near Chez Glorine toward the tip of the pass. ~ Tiputa; 96-03-92, 96-03-94, fax 96-04-44. BUDGET TO MODERATE.

Crossing Tiputa Pass, **Chez Lucien** has three bungalows shaded by several trees. Looking more like cottages with shake roofs and large porches than Polynesian *fares*, the bungalows have varied sleeping configurations, and all come with private baths. Chez Lucien's rooms are more spacious than the average accommodation and are well maintained. A deposit equaling one night's stay is required to secure reservations. It's located about a half-kilometer from the boat dock. ~ Tiputa; 96-03-55. BUDGET TO MODERATE.

One of the best bargains on the island, **Pension Estall** has four simple thatched-roof bungalows, each with one room and private bath. There is also a large three-bedroom concrete house that sleeps up to 12 people. Estall has been in the hospitality business for a long time and her pension is a perennial favorite. A combination of comfortable accommodations, good food and nice management has earned high recommendations for Pension Estall. A deposit equaling one night's stay is required for reservations. Estall can be found a half-kilometer from the boat dock in Tiputa, situated between the ocean and the lagoon. ~ Tiputa; 96-04-16, 96-03-16. BUDGET TO MODERATE.

The setting for **Relais Mihiroa** is an old coconut plantation on the far east side of Tiputa village next to the lagoon. It consists of four attractive one-bedroom bungalows with private bath and a small porch overlooking the lagoon. Rattan furniture gives the place a Polynesian feel. The bungalows will accommodate a maximum of eight people. (Additional bunks are available upon request.) There is a restaurant/bar on the premises. Relais Mihiroa is more expensive than other pensions, but the price is commensurate with the quality. ~ Tiputa; 96-02-14. BUDGET TO MODERATE.

> Punua runs Sharky Parc excursions. He will take you fishing, snorkeling or on a picnic to one of the uninhabited *motus*.

OUTSIDE OF TIPUTA AND AVATORU   In addition to the hotels and pensions clustered around the communities of Avatoru and Tiputa, there are accommodations on *motus* located in other areas of this enormous atoll. Due to their extreme isolation, these places do not have phones.

Two Avatoru pensions, Chez Punua and Chez Nanua, share six very small and spartan thatched-roof bungalows with communal baths on **Motu Teavatia**, a privately owned *motu* 45 minutes by boat from Avatoru. This is one possible place for a Robinson Crusoe–style trip—they'll take you out and leave you alone, literally, on the *motu*, and pick you up later. ~ Avatoru; 96-04-73. BUDGET.

Travelers have found **Village Sans Souci** to be a friendly yet extremely isolated place. Here you'll find 14 bungalows, with showers and toilets in a separate building. This is a do-it-yourself resort: sheets are provided, but you have to make the beds and look after the rooms yourself. There's a restaurant on the premises, and the daily rate includes breakfast, lunch and dinner. Many of the usual nautical activities are available, and you'll find plenty of opportunity to take long, solitary walks along the fringes of the atoll. If the tide is right, it's possible to take a four-hour trek to Avatoru. There's an extra charge for airport transfer. Credit cards are accepted. The resort is located an hour's boat ride from Avatoru on Motu Tivaru, adjacent to Tivaru Pass. ~ 96-03-72 in Papeete. MODERATE TO DELUXE.

HIDDEN ►

If you want to fulfill your Robinson Crusoe fantasy in luxury, consider **Kia Ora Sauvage**, located on Motu Avearahi 30 kilometers and a one-hour boat ride from Avatoru on the opposite side of the lagoon. A sister property to Hotel Kia Ora Rangiroa, one might classify Kia Ora Sauvage as "ultra-deluxe primitive." The five bungalows have been completely reconstructed with local materials such as native woods and *pandanus* fronds from nearby trees. Comfortable and civilized, the *fares* have nifty, semi-outdoor bathrooms. Despite the rustic nature, there is a restaurant and bar on the grounds. Prices, on the other hand, are not primitive—they are identical to those at the Kia Ora Rangiroa. There is a two-night minimum stay and space permitting, guests at Kia Ora Rangiroa can switch over to the remote offshoot. Round-trip transfers to the *motu* cost US$70. ~ Papeete; 96-02-22, fax 96-02-20. ULTRA-DELUXE.

DINING

There is a dearth of restaurants on Rangiroa. One reason is that most visitors get meal plans with their lodging and don't venture out to explore the culinary arts of other facilities. Another reason is that the population of this island is too small to sustain a large number of eateries.

Patisserie Afaro is a good bet for coffee, juice and French pastries. ~ Avatoru; 96-04-91. BUDGET.

You can find sandwiches and inexpensive dishes at **Chez Henriette** (96-04-68) and **Chez Mareta** in Avatoru. BOTH BUDGET.

If you have a chance, try the yellow and purple ice cream served in pink cones at Daniel's store in Avatoru.

Raira Lagoon offers home cooking in a simple, village-style outdoor setting that overlooks the sea. Traditional dishes such as *poisson cru* (marinated fish) and *ipo* (Tuamotu-style dumplings) are sometimes served. ~ Avatoru; 96-04-23. BUDGET TO MODERATE.

Kia Ora Village is clearly the best (and most expensive) restaurant on the island. Come for the very fresh—some come straight from the lagoon—seafood dishes such as tempting seafood brochettes and mahimahi. The restaurant bar is on the water, which makes for a very pleasant setting. For those who care, it's the only place on the island where you can get espresso. ~ Avatoru; 96-03-34. DELUXE TO ULTRA-DELUXE.

Copra (dried coconut meat) is the most important cash

Above: A coconut tree–studded motu, often found off larger high islands or in the Tuamotu archipelago.

Below: Sunset over Maupiti is a scene that you might encounter on any of French Polynesia's high islands.

Chez Glorine is an excellent local-style eatery that overlooks the sea. Traditional dishes such as *poisson cru*, grilled or fried fish, and *ipo* are often served, but Glorine's specialty is *langouste* (lobster). ~ Tiputa; 96-03-58. BUDGET.

There are several small markets in Avatoru and Tiputa that stock a few basic items. If you are going to need anything more than simple items (such as instant coffee, milk or cookies), purchase them in Papeete. **GROCERIES**

Carole Pareo boutique sells pareus and handpainted T-shirts with fish motifs. (It also doubles as a bike/scooter rental agency.) ~ Avatoru; 96-02-45. **Ocean Passion** sells locally painted pareus and other souvenirs. ~ Avatoru. **SHOPPING**

In Tiputa, local arts and crafts such as shell leis, seashells and small carvings can be purchased at the **artisan house** in the main square.

If you consider that almost the entire island is fringed by white sand, you'll understand why it's difficult to recommend a single beach. It seems just about every pension or hotel claims to have *the* beach in its front yard. In addition to the local beaches, there are day trips to *motus* around the lagoon provided by tour operators or various guest facilities. **BEACHES**

L'ILE AUX RÉCIFS L'Ile aux Récifs, or Reef Island, is a *motu* on the south side of the lagoon noted for its fossilized coral formations. Snorkeling here is excellent—perhaps the best accessible site in all of Rangiroa. ~ To get there you must take a boat. Any hotel or guesthouse can arrange a visit.

BLUE LAGOON MOTU A popular trip to this *motu* is the Blue Lagoon cruise, a half-day affair offered by several tour operators. It includes a boat trip to a scenic *motu* area and a picnic. Also included in the excursion is a shark feeding, probably the high point of the Blue Lagoon experience, which is otherwise a bit overhyped. Facilities exist, but they could use upgrading. For example, the docks are poorly maintained, and the kitschy little *fares* on shore were dilapidated and full of garbage when I was last there. ~ There are several tour companies that visit the lagoon. It's best to go in a covered boat such as Kia Ora's vessel because you will get soaked if the weather is not accommodating and a squall passes through. In fact, it's a good idea to take motion sickness tablets and a cushion—the slightest breeze rocks the boat exponentially.

TIPUTA VISTA POINT If you are in the Tiputa area, one of the best things to do is check out the vista point that also serves as a modest picnic area on the Avatoru side of Tiputa Pass. An informal park, there are several circular benches with canopies where you can relax and watch the dolphins jumping in the pass or see the sun set. ~ It's located just as the road makes a right fork at the Paradive (scuba) shop. If in doubt, ask at Paradive.

MOTU NUHI-NUHI In the Tiputa area there's good snorkeling and shallow diving at Motu Nuhi-Nuhi. You'll find a rich variety of marine life in the Nuhi-Nuhi Valley to the south of the *motu*. If you have the inclination, take a walk to the edge of the pass between 4 p.m. and dusk. With a little luck and a sharp eye you may see dolphins surfing the waves. ~ During low tide you can walk along the reef (with your reef shoes) or better yet, take a local boat. Walk to the edge of the pass from either the Tiputa or Avatoru side of the atoll. The *motu* is on the inner side of the pass. It's impossible to miss, it's the only small islet in the area.

Outdoor Adventures

CAMPING

Chez Nanua has the only camping facilities on the island, and perhaps in the entire Tuamotu Group. Space is limited. It's advisable to bring your own tent. ~ Avatoru; 96-03-88.

DIVING

Divers from the world over come to Rangiroa for a unique diving experience. Only two passes carry water into and out of Rangiroa's remarkable lagoon. As a result, the incoming and outgoing tides swirl through the passes at a phenomenal rate, carrying an amazing variety of marine life—and intrepid divers—with them. Dives through the passes are almost all drift dives, where you drop into the pass and let the tide sweep you through. The Rangiroa dive operators are experts at handling this—it is impossible to anchor a dive boat and divers have to be carefully followed to their pick-up point. A wide array of large species are encountered in the passes, but Rangiroa is particularly renowned for its large population of sharks. Gray sharks, black-tip sharks and white-tip reef sharks are regularly seen; hammerheads are less frequently viewed.

Motu Fara, the small *motu* at the southern end of the Avatoru Pass, divides the pass into two smaller channels. At average depths of less than 50 feet, **Tiny Pass** on the west side of the *motu* is a dramatic dive site, with its colorful coral and a countless assortment of smaller reef fish and larger species. The **Avatoru Pass Caves** are located on the wider and deeper pass that runs down to the east side of the *motu*. There are also superb dives, particularly for sharks and other pelagics, on the outer edge of the reef at the east and west side of the pass portal.

South of Avatoru Pass, beyond Motu Fara, the area known as **Mahuta** has coral formations and a rich variety of both lagoon and ocean fish, which meet in this intermediate zone. The area from here back to Motu Fara is also excellent snorkeling territory. **Papiro**

Point, south of Tiny Pass and farther into the lagoon, is also a prime snorkeling site.

Caves are found on the west side of the entrance to Tiputa Pass and in the center of the pass, before the area known as **The Valley.** The **Tiputa Caves** are also known as the **Shark Caves** or **Shark Point,** with good reason—large numbers of sharks can be observed here. Shark-feeding trips add to the excitement, but there are often so many sharks that any extra encouragement is scarcely necessary!

Large swells sometimes run through the channel and dolphins are often seen playing in the waves or jumping the bows of passing ships in Tiputa Pass.

All three Rangiroa dive operators are located on Avatoru. They offer lessons and lead dives to the lagoon, the passes and the open sea. Night dives are also possible.

Hotel Kia Ora dives are run by Yves Lefevre. ~ Avatoru; 96-03-84. Lefevre also operates the **Raie Manta Club.** ~ Avatoru; 96-04-80.

The third outfit, **Rangiroa Paradive,** is located next door to Chez Glorine and is operated by Bernard Blanc. Bernard is a charming, obliging chap. (If you want to see what a stonefish looks like, there's a preserved specimen in his office.) ~ Avatoru; 96-05-55.

Even though Rangiroa has one of the largest lagoons in the world, fishing is not a big draw. With a little luck, however, you can hook a marlin or a mahimahi. The vessels available for charter work out of the **Kia Ora Hotel** and include the *Heikura Iti*, the *Parata*, the *Tutuke* and the *Ava*. ~ Avatoru; 96-03-34.

FISHING

Although snorkeling with the current through the pass is an easy activity, even for novices, you also have the option of viewing the colorful underwater spectacle from the comfort of a glass-bottomed boat. Local operators are available for independent or group excursions. If you wish to sail in the Blue Lagoon or to the bird sanctuary on Motu Paio, or want to check out the dolphins frolicking at Tiputa Pass or Site Ohutu in late afternoon, contact the following operators.

BOAT TOURS

Tane Tamaehu offers tours with a glass-bottomed boat. ~ 96-04-68. **Tixier Tevaea** runs a 26-foot vessel and offers many different excursions. ~ 96-04-50. **Punua Tamaehu** of Chez Punua also has a tour boat. ~ 96-04-73.

Te Ono Ono is the tour boat that operates out of Kia Ora Rangiroa. It takes in both passes, with a pause for snorkeling at one of them and dolphin chasing in late afternoon. ~ Avatoru; 96-03-34.

Rangiroa Parasailing is a fairly new operation run out of the Kia Ora Hotel. The 20-minute flight takes place in the lagoon in front of the hotel. ~ Avatoru; 96-02-22.

PARA-SAILING

BIKING   If you are not into water sports, there's not a lot to do on an atoll. Landlubbers, or those just wishing to explore the island, might consider renting a bike at the concession in front of **Chez Nanua**. ~ Avatoru; 96-03-88.

Raira Lagoon also has a fleet of aging bikes—they would do well to replace them with newer models. ~ Avatoru; 96-04-23.

If you just want to cycle or scoot around, Carole Plovier at **Pareo Carole** has bikes. ~ Avatoru; 96-02-45.

Kia Ora Rangiroa has bicycles that they rent to their guests. ~ Avatoru; 96-03-84. **Rangi Atelier** rents bicycles to the public. ~ Tiputa; 96-04-92.

Some of the other accommodations on the island also have bikes for rent. Check with the management.

▼▼▼▼▼▼▼▼

Manihi

Enclosing a magnificent clear blue lagoon teeming with fish, Manihi is another classic atoll made up of an oblong string of flat *motus*. The population numbers approximately 600, most of them living in the village of Turipaoa. Like many of the other Tuamotu islands, commercial fishing takes a distant second to the cultured pearl business. Visitors with an interest in the cultivation of black pearls will definitely find Manihi of interest. And those pursuing underwater adventures will find diving conditions ideal. The plush Manihi Pearl Beach Resort features first-class diving.

When I first came to Manihi in the late 1970s, I found the inhabitants to be friendlier than those of Rangiroa, which at that time was the only other major tourism center in the Tuamotus. The current 600 or so inhabitants are still friendly, but tourism has declined with the growth of the black pearl industry.

In the late 1970s, the presence of the hotel and the nascent cultured pearl industry made the island a relatively prosperous community. (In those days prosperity meant owning Mercury outboards, Sony tape decks and clothing without holes.) What a difference a couple of decades make! Nowadays wealth on the island is not simply defined by who owns the newest outboard motor. Pearl farming has turned islanders into a Polynesian version of the Beverly Hillbillies. They drive up and down the half-mile or so of road on shiny new Toyota trucks while their children whiz along the atoll on motorcycles. The truth is, Manihi today is a far cry from the little fishing community it once was. However, it's still humble in its own Paumotu way.

SIGHTS   Entertainment in Manihi consists of watching Sunday soccer games, shooting pool, playing the local version of bocce ball and catching sharks off the pier. The latter is done at night with a handline attached to a giant hook baited with a chunk of moray eel.

When participants land a shark, they slash its spinal cord with a machete and extract the shark's jaw for a souvenir. Considering the ecological implications of this practice, I would discourage it.

Manihi's villagers take pride in their limestone and clapboard homes, which line the two main streets. Most homes have attractive front and back yards arranged with shells, shrubs and flowers. They are either fenced in or surrounded by curbs to discourage the bands of scrawny, marauding dogs that populate Polynesian villages. The village boasts one main concrete dock, a flagpole and a square where old people gossip under the shade of a huge tree.

Located in the main village of Turipaoa, **Chez Teiva** has a house with three rooms, private bath and kitchen. There are also four *fares*, each with double and single beds, kitchen and communal bath. From all reports, the proprietress is an excellent cook. Write or call Mme. Puahea Teiva at Turipaoa Village, Manihi for reservations. ~ Turipaoa; 96-42-45. BUDGET TO MODERATE.

LODGING

Set on a white-sand beach, **Manihi Pearl Beach Resort** is the newest incarnation of Kaina Village, a hotel that sustained serious damage in a 1993 cyclone. The former 16-bungalow resort has been expanded and upgraded to 30 rooms. The hotel is strictly a top-of-the-line property, with 22 over-the-water bungalows and 8 beach bungalows. The over-the-water units are spacious, approximately 376 square feet and feature king-sized beds and glass-bottom tables for viewing the lagoon waters below. The beach bungalows are equally spacious and have terraces that overlook the lagoon. All units have telephones, overhead fans, small refrigerators and a mini-bar. The channel near the hotel has been dredged to allow small boats to enter the marina, and a saltwater pool has been constructed at the edge of the lagoon. Nearly every type of water sport is offered, from windsurfing to deep-sea fishing, and the property has one of the better dive operations, Manihi Blue Nui, based there. ~ Manihi; 96-42-73, fax 96-42-72. ULTRA-DELUXE.

Manihi is 322 miles (520 kilometers) northeast of Papeete.

For a mid-range lodgings with a restaurant and swimming pool on the premises, try **Le Keishi**. There are seven bungalows (two facing the lagoon), each with mosquito netting, private bath (cold water) and tiled floors. There is also a single over-the-water bungalow that has one bedroom with double and single beds. Le Keishi is remote and excursions are expensive. One reader commented that the owners are not particularly enamored with visitors. Le Keishi is on Motu Taugaraufara, a 20-minute boat ride from the airport, on the northern side of the lagoon. Children under 12 are half price. *Pension completes* are available. Visa cards are accepted. Contact M. Meurisse, Motu Taugaraufara. ~ Turipaoa; 96-43-13. DELUXE.

DINING   Dining out will not require a big decision-making process. There's only one restaurant on the island, **Manihi Pearl Beach Resort**. The restaurant has a terrace that faces the beach and the new pool. While generally catering to their own guests, they do accept visitors from other pensions. French cuisine and seafood are served, and considering the quality and quantity of fresh fish available, it's safe to say seafood is your best bet. However, what is served depends on what the fishermen have brought in. *Poisson cru* is consistently good and snapper is generally on the menu. ~ Manihi; 96-42-73. ULTRA-DELUXE.

GROCERIES   There is a market in the village that sells bread, tin fish, bottled water and other basics.

SHOPPING   Black pearls are the only conceivable item you would want to pick up on this island. Word has it that Petero, a well-known local entrepreneur, sells good quality pearls at his boutique in the village for much less than what you'd find in Papeete.

BEACHES   The entire island is fringed by white-sand beaches, interspersed with coral.

MANIHI PEARL BEACH RESORT Far from the village, the white-sand beach at Manihi Pearl Beach Resort provides excellent opportunities for swimming and snorkeling. For visitors staying at lodging on other parts of the atoll, it's not practical to use the facilities here on a regular basis, but if you are fortunate enough to stay at the resort, all manner of nautical and beach activities are available through the hotel. Nonguests can use the facilities with permission, but if you are staying elsewhere it's a long haul by watertaxi.

▼▼▼▼▼▼▼▼▼▼▼▼▼

Outdoor Adventures

DIVING

Manihi's weather patterns are consistently dry and the area has a large variety of species concentrated in shallow waters. This makes for good diving conditions. Unlike Rangiroa, the main passes in the Manihi area have milder currents, which make them less demanding for inexperienced divers.

Dive sites are numerous. **Tairapa Pass** is a drift dive through the pass where you'll see plenty of pelagics, including schools of barracuda and tuna. Sometimes you'll even spot a turtle, eagle ray or manta ray, or you can visit with white tip and nurse sharks in their **Shark Caves**.

The **Drop Off** is just that, a sheer wall just outside the reef that descends over 5900 feet (1800 meters). Undersea life includes gray sharks, Napoleon fish, giant jack fish, schools of snappers and sea pike barracuda, tuna, marlin and other pelagics. Once a year thou-

Manihi's Pearl Industry

The island's 20-year-old cultured pearl industry provides the fuel that powers Manihi's economy. Throughout the lagoon are buoys that mark the roughly 200-yard-long stations, with rows of pearl oysters dangling from lines stretched above the surface of the lagoon. Depending on the weather, water temperature or other conditions in the lagoon, these lines can be raised or lowered to provide optimal growth for the oysters. Lustrous black pearls with a silver sheen unique to French Polynesia are the result.

Every year tiny spheres of Mississippi River mussel shell (or a similar species) are implanted in the black pearl oysters collected from the lagoon by local divers. After three years, the oysters are harvested. Out of every 100 oysters, only seven will eventually yield commercially acceptable pearls.

Most of the hotels or pensions provide tours of the pearl facilities, which are ubiquitous on this island. Tours generally include a boat ride in the lagoon where a diver is sent to retrieve an oyster. The mature oyster is opened and the pearl is extracted and passed around the boat for inspection by the guests. Of course, there are no free samples.

The local hero who showed other Polynesians that they could succeed in the pearl farming business is known simply as Petero. When pearl farming was in its inception, the entrepreneurs were Japanese, Chinese or European businessmen. Polynesians did benefit from employment, but they were not the actual farmers or producers who profited directly. Petero showed them that it didn't have to be that way. He became the first Polynesian grafter (the technician who actually implants the seed within the oyster). Petero eventually started his own pearl farm and has prospered. His empire has grown from a pearl farm to a pool hall, curio shop/boutique that can be found on the ocean side of the atoll. (He reportedly sells good quality pearls at a substantially lower price than the pearls sold in Tahiti.) There are now approximately 30 pearl farms in Manihi alone. Most are family owned, and many are found on the more isolated *motu*.

sands of groupers gather in this area to breed, which, according to local dive operator Gilles Petre, is an amazing sight.

The Circus, situated between the pass and the lagoon, is populated with Napoleon fish and black-tip reef sharks. It's also a favorite refuge of manta and eagle rays, which can be observed year-round, alone or in groups, at an average depth of 30 feet (9 meters). The rays have become used to divers and are approachable.

Sailboards, paddling canoes, waterskis, and jet skis are available for rent at Manihi Pearl Beach Resort. ~ Manihi; 96-42-73.

West Point is on the ocean side of the reef and offers a magnificent coral garden that begins at a depth of 5 feet (1.5 meters) and descends another 90 feet (27 meters). Here you can find table coral, fire coral, antler coral and flower petal coral. On good days visibility is up to 200 feet (60 meters).

Manihi Blue Nui is a diving operation run by Gilles Petre who has four instructors on staff. Dive sites, most of which are outside the reef, are generally close to shore so drive time on the dive boats is minimal. ~ Manihi; 96-42-73, fax 96-42-72.

FISHING   Fishing trips where you can snag some tuna, mahimahi and jack can be arranged through **Manihi Pearl Beach Resort**. ~ Manihi; 96-42-73. Other pensions will arrange trips as well.

BIKING   There are unpaved roads and paths located around the atoll that make for interesting bike rides. A typical bike ride might take you along a lane pockmarked by land crab burrows and through shady groves of coconut palms. Bikes can be rented at **Manihi Pearl Beach Resort**. You might want to check with other lodging facilities as well. ~ Manihi; 96-42-73.

Tikehau

Tikehau comes close to the picture-postcard version of what paradise should look like. There is still quite a *sauvage*, or wild, quality to the place. You can walk along the beach or snorkel across the channels separating the *motus* without encountering another soul.

Just over 350 people inhabit Tikehau, which has a near-circular shape and a diameter of 16 miles (26 kilometers).

SIGHTS   The main village of **Tuterahera** is a tidy little island village. The streets are laid out in an orderly fashion and rubbish is less apt to be tossed about than in other Tuamotu communities. According to Arai, the proprietor of Panau Lagoon, the clean streets are due to his vigilance as the local *gendarme*. Another reason may be that the village was completely rebuilt after a devastating cyclone in 1983. There are four stores in town, but only one is obvious—the others are part of people's homes.

When Jacques Cousteau's research group made a study of the Tuamotus in 1987, they found that Tikehau's lagoon contained one of the largest concentrations of fish in the entire archipelago, many of which are found in a number of fish parks. In actuality, these parks are nothing more than a bunch of poles connected with chicken wire that trap the fish. After being caught they are then air-freighted to Tahiti.

Among the points of interest on Tikehau is the deteriorating hull of an old wooden **shipwreck**, the *Mihimani*, which is lodged on the shore and lays keeled over to one side. Nearby, located very near the pass on the same side of the lagoon, is the fishing village of **Tuheiava**. (Note: The village has no store or food available.)

At the far east end of the atoll, away from the village, is a settlement called **Eden**. Founded by the Taiwanese New Testament Church religious organization, the residents of this group support themselves by growing fruit and vegetables. They also recently started a pearl farm and have an aquarium. Visitors are welcomed.

On a *motu* south of Eden are the **ruins** of an unfinished five-star Italian hotel that went bankrupt.

Typical activities on Tikehau include visits to the fishing village, picnicking on a *motu* or a visit to the bird sanctuary, a minuscule island (about 18 kilometers from the village) that you can circumnavigate in minutes.

LODGING

Large by Tuamotu standards, **Tikehau Village** offers six bungalows (and is classified by the tourist board as a small hotel rather than a pension). Each bungalow has a private (cold water) bath. There is a small restaurant/bar on the premises. Excursions are available to a *motu* (including free use of snorkeling gear) and to a fish reserve. The proprietors also offer an automobile tour of the island and visits to the village. Tikehau Village looked to be rather run-down and in need of repair, but if you can put that aside, it has a wonderful location on the beach with a view of the lagoon. The small resort is situated one kilometer from the center of Tuterahera Village. ~ Tuterahera Village; 96-22-91, 96-22-86. MODERATE.

Panau Lagon features six bungalows—four with private bath and terrace; one bungalow with communal bath; and an over-the-water bungalow with private bath. The A-frame-style bungalows (built in a mediocre fashion) are located on a broad beach with a splendid view of the lagoon. The owner, Arai, is amiable and will loan you the use of his bikes. The multitude of pigs and children contribute to an authentic Polynesian atmosphere here and his two teenage sons will take you on excursions in the boat, including visits to the fish park, pearl farm and picnics on a *motu*. The downside is the swampy ditch across from the facility, which seems to contribute to the mosquito problem. The accommodation here is comfortable, fairly priced and on the beach. Children under 12 are half price. ~ Tuterahera; 96-22-34, 96-22-99. MODERATE.

HIDDEN ▶

A ranch-style home with a large shaded porch and three bedrooms is what you'll find at **Chez Habanita**, run by Roland and Habanita Terriateatoofa. There is a kitchen and common bath on the premises as well. Activities include visits to outlying *motus* with a picnic lunch, fishing and—you guessed it—trips to the fish park. Roland and Habanita are wonderful hosts. They speak English and provide decent food. Habanita also doubles as the local Air Tahiti representative and is a good source of information. Chez Habanita is perhaps the best low-budget accommodation on Tikehau and comes highly recommended. ~ Tuterahera; 96-22-48. BUDGET.

Chez Colette Huri, located in Tuterahera Village, consists of two houses. The buildings are modern concrete structures with tile floors, surrounded by manicured gardens. One has three bedrooms and the other comes with two bedrooms. A communal bath, living room with television, and kitchen are available in both homes. Day trips to the fish reserve, fishing excursions and picnics are offered. Chez Colette Huri is fairly priced and comfortable, but nothing out of the ordinary. ~ Tuterahera; 96-22-47. MODERATE.

Tikehau's long, narrow islets are lined with paths that lead from one end to the other. A bike ride will take you through shady coconut groves to the edge of the reef. Some accommodations also offer bike rentals.

A three-bedroom home is what **Chez Isidore et Nini** offers. Each room has a double bed. Communal bath facilities, a kitchen and dining room are also available. There are the usual activities, including the well-known visit to the fish park. Located in Tuterahera Village, the main disadvantage of this pension is its relatively long distance (several hundred yards) from the beach. ~ Tuterahera; 96-22-38. BUDGET TO MODERATE.

New and attractive, **Chez Justine** is located near the air strip in Tikehau. Though it is near a white-sand beach, it suffers from the same drainage ditch problem as Panau Lagon. However, the windows are screened, cutting down on the mosquito problem. Justine has two family-style bungalows, each with two double bedrooms, private bath, terrace and fan. A third, smaller, self-contained bungalow is also available. A small restaurant is on the premises. The total capacity for all three units is ten people. All the usual activities are provided. Contact M. Tetua Laroche or Mlle. Teiva Justine for more information. ~ Tikehau; 96-22-88 or 96-22-37 mornings. BUDGET TO MODERATE.

In the center of Tuterahera Village is **Chez Maxime**, with nearby access to the beach. Maxime has a five-bedroom home, each room containing a double and single bed. There is also a living room, dining room and communal (cold water) bath. A fully equipped kitchen is available for use by guests. ~ Tuterahera; 96-22-38. BUDGET.

Mataiva

Located at the extreme northwest end of the Tuamotus, Mataiva is a perfect place to experience the slow-moving life in a remote corner of the Tuamotus. You can hang out at the old wooden bridge, watch people fish and chat with the giggling village children. People here are patient, friendly and, like most Polynesians, somewhat shy.

However, Mataiva may not meet everyone's expectation of paradise. There is a somewhat brackish look about the island that one notices almost immediately upon landing. Mataiva is a rich source of phosphate. The atoll has within its lagoon about 70 phosphate-rich pools that were at one time commercially exploited.

There is only one, rather difficult, pass into the ten-square-mile (25-square-kilometer) lagoon, along with nine shallow channels or *hoas*. Mataiva is also a rich fishing ground, and the shallow lagoon has many fish traps, marked by vertical wooden poles that protrude in a number of areas.

There are enormous amounts of dark, almost black, coral (no doubt resulting from the phosphate) that give the land a surrealistic, moonscape quality. Some of the landscape is stained yellow, perhaps another legacy of the mining operation. Debris from a major cyclone that struck in the early 1980s may still be visible in some of the more isolated areas.

SIGHTS

Pahua is the main village. (The village's name refers to a large mollusk or clam found in the reefs of Mataiva and throughout the South Pacific.) Almost all of the Mataiva's population of about 200 live in Pahua, which is separated by a pass connected by a long, narrow, wooden-plank bridge. Despite the separation of the village by a body of water, locals still refer to both sides as Pahua. The village has a church on either side, but only one store (on the south side of the pass) with a narrow selection of items.

Sometimes it seems like the only thing that moves on Mataiva are the land crabs, which seem to be in plentiful supply. If you stand still and listen, there seems to be a constant rustling of these creatures in the brush. Mosquitos, too, are plentiful (which makes it hard to understand why some of the pensions don't have mosquito screens).

As one might expect, there isn't a lot to do on an atoll in the middle of nowhere. Riding a bike along the coconut-palm–lined roads of Mataiva, however, is a must. The road goes most of the way around the island—about 20 miles (33 kilometers)—and is connected by narrow concrete bridges. One note: Apart from mosquitoes and crabs, dogs also abound here, creating a potential problem for bicyclists. Riding a bike inevitably attracts these canine creatures and you don't want to be on a bicycle in the middle of a territorial dog fight. Cycle with caution.

In addition to bike rides, excursions to the **swimming hole** at Ponahara (actually an inlet with a series of pools that connect the lagoon and the sea) and the coral beaches of **Pofai-Tounoa** and **Tenupa** are also worth your time.

Teaku is a bird sanctuary located inside the lagoon. It can be visited by boat for picnics or birdwatching.

A *marae* at **Papiro**, on the opposite side of the atoll from Pahua, is constructed from stone slabs. The *marae* is shaped in the form of an armchair, designed purportedly for King Tu, a legendary figure of Polynesia. It actually resembles a sofa, complete with backrest and armrests, and was rebuilt after the original was destroyed by a cyclone.

Mataiva is located 186 miles or 310 kilometers north of Papeete and 24 miles or 80 kilometers west of Rangiroa.

Another, perhaps more prosaic, attraction, located 100 yards (90 meters) behind the pension Mataiva Cool, is the fiberglass **wreck** of the *Cayuse*, an American boat that washed ashore in 1982. This was evidently the second American boat to meet its demise upon the shores of this phosphate atoll. The first belonged to the now-deceased author Jack Ferguson, who spent nine years in the Pacific and wrote a book about Mataiva entitled *Island of Nine Eyes*, which takes its name from the nine channels.

Local-style fishing (usually with hand lines) can be arranged with guesthouses. This means jumping on a *pirogue* (canoe) with the village children, baiting a hook with a live hermit crab and trying your luck on the reef. (Be sure and bring a hat and your sun block).

You can bike most of the way around the atoll, which is approximately 20 miles (33 kilometers) in circumference. Bikes are available at Mataiva Cool. ~ Pahua; 96-32-53.

LODGING

HIDDEN ▶

Mataiva Cool may sound a bit presumptuous or even preposterous given how intense the sun gets in the Tuamotu Group, but one would be hard-pressed to improve on it. For starters, it's on a white-sand beach, with a magnificent view of the lagoon. The property consists of eight bungalows, each with private (cold water) bath, terrace and fan; and five small *fares* with kitchen and communal bath. The bungalows are clean, fairly new and offer relative comfort. The electricity usually stays on until about midnight (which means you can run your fan until then). A modest restaurant/bar is on the premises, and the food is very good. The owner, Aroma Huri, speaks a few words of English and does his best to make you feel at home. His daughter, Diana, helps to organize excursions and looks after guests. Boat trips to the surrounding *motus*, with picnic lunch, are available and there is a boat and several bicycles in fairly good shape for hire. Children under 12 are half price. Mataiva

Cool is situated on the south side of the pass in Pahua. ~ Pahua; 96-32-53 in Tahiti; 43-18-84. BUDGET TO MODERATE.

On Pahua's north side, closer to the lagoon, is **Mataiva Village**. The property has a manicured, orderly appearance and a better beach than Mataiva Cool. It consists of six attractive bungalows lined up along the shore. Small coconut trees have been planted in between the shoreline and the units, creating a pleasant shady front yard. Each of the bungalows has one bedroom with double bed, a small terrace and private bath. In addition, there are two concrete houses, each with three bedrooms with double beds. The bathrooms in the houses are communal and the water is refreshingly cold. Some bungalows lack proper ventilation and mosquito screens. The food, on the other hand, is good. ~ Pahua; 96-32-48, 96-32-42. BUDGET TO MODERATE.

GROCERIES

There is one modest store (on the south side of the pass) stocked with basics—mosquito coils, instant coffee and the like. (Like most stores on most of the atolls in French Polynesia, there's no fresh fruit or vegetables.)

BEACHES

PONAHARA This swimming hole is actually an inlet between the ocean and the lagoon. (If it were larger and deeper, it would be a pass.) However, unlike a pass that can be filled with rushing water, Ponahara is shallow and calm. It's also filled with nooks and crannies, and pools of various depths that allow swimming and bathing. Facilities are minimal. There are a few simple benches and a dilapidated shack sits near the swimming area. Paper from yesterday's picnic may litter the area. ~ Ponahara is located on the inside of the lagoon, approximately one quarter of the way around the island, about seven kilometers from the village heading south and then looping east. To get there, you could either ride a bike or hitch a ride.

POFAI-TOUNOA BEACHES A classic white-sand (coral) beach shaded by coconut palms, Pofai-Tounoa is a perfect place to kick back. Swimming is good here. There are no facilities available. ~ It's about two to three kilometers from the village heading north. You can easily walk or bike it from the village.

TENUPA BEACH Tenupa is also a lovely white-sand beach on the ocean side of the island. There are no facilities here and only limited shade. ~ Located on the eastern end of the island, the opposite side from the village, about 15 kilometers away. It's possible to get there by bicycle, but it is much better to organize a boat trip with your pension and take in the nearby bird sanctuary at Teaku, a tiny island inside the lagoon, at the same time.

▼▼▼▼▼▼▼▼▼▼▼▼
**Other Northern
Tuamotu Islands**

The Northern Tuamotus are among the least-visited islands of French Polynesia. Windblown atolls, with coral beaches parched white by the sun, they offer the visitor an opportunity to bask in a warm hospitality seldom experienced in the well-trodden Society Islands.

SIGHTS

TAKAPOTO Takapoto is a ten-mile-long island retreat. Come here to get away from any semblance of Western civilization and bask in Tuamotan hospitality. What you'll find in plenitude is solitude, beautiful white-sand beaches and plenty of fish to watch while snorkeling. What Takapoto doesn't have is a pass into the lagoon, but villagers get around this by landing whaleboats near the reef. It is said that when residents of the island return by boat, a double rainbow appears over the island.

Located 386 miles (624 kilometers) northeast of Papeete, there are about 465 people living here. Most dwell in the community of **Fakatopatere**, which is about one kilometer from the airport.

Takapoto, and its neighbor Takaroa, were hammered by two very destructive cyclones in 1991 and 1993, which proved to be an unmitigated disaster for the island's nascent black pearl industry. But over the past few years several small pensions have sprouted up on this distant atoll. There's nothing in the way of luxury accommodations and amenities out this way, so bring a suitcase brimming with unread novels and leave your wristwatch at home.

TAKAROA Resembling a giant protozoan, this oblong atoll is about 14 miles long (24 kilometers) and 1 mile wide. The island is separated from Takapoto by only a little over eight kilometers of ocean and is home to about 400 people. Takaroa is one of the few remaining Tuamotu atolls with an existing *marae*.

The pass here is nine feet deep and anchorages are good in all parts of the lagoon. Like nearby Takapoto, Takaroa suffered extensively from cyclones in 1991 and 1993, which destroyed the local black pearl industry.

Takaroa more than any of the outer Tuamotus gives you the opportunity to experience Polynesian life with a local family. You will be able to share daily routines and learn something about life on an isolated atoll.

FAKARAVA The second-largest atoll in French Polynesia, Fakarava has an unusual rectangular shape measuring 37 miles by 15 miles (60 kilometers by 25 kilometers).

Rotoava Village, located near **Garve Pass** (which measures three quarters of a mile wide), is home to most of the atoll's 248 inhabitants. There is also a small settlement in **Tetamanu Village** on the southern end of the atoll.

Local fishermen traditionally work Garve Pass by placing bottom lines, each attached to a buoy. When a fish strikes, the buoys bob furiously, attracting thousands of sea birds. The sight and sound of the birds circling overhead and squawking incessantly is a memorable spectacle.

Fakarava is the site of the oldest **Catholic mission** in the Tuamotus. The coral-fired limestone church was built by the followers of Pere Laval in the early 1850s. Laval was in the Gambiers 20 years earlier and had constructed the same type of buildings in Rikitea (in the Gambiers) during that period. The church is still in use today.

Black pearl cultivation has become an important source of income on Fakarava. The island hosts one of the business centers of black pearl king Robert Wan. It is not open to the public, but the numerous grids marking black pearl stations throughout the lagoon are visible to all.

KAUKURA   There's not much to say about the oval-shaped Kaukura. Situated 201 miles (325 kilometers) northeast of Tahiti, it is 24 miles (40 kilometers) long and has a shallow lagoon with a narrow pass. The population numbers around 300, all of whom live in the village of **Raitahiti**. Local income is derived from pearl nursery production and fishing. One reason to venture here is to stay at the **Pension Rekareka** for a true cross-cultural experience.

> The island of Fakarava is approximately 248 miles (400 kilometers) northeast of Tahiti.

ARUTUA   Known for its abundance of fish and its talented musicians, the tiny island of Arutua is almost circular, with a circumference of approximately 17 miles. The abundance of fish can be be attributed to a system of fish parks and pearl farms. Most of the nearly 300 inhabitants live in the village of **Rautini**. Pearl farming, pearl nurseries and fishing are the most important income earners, but tourism, in the form of small pensions, also exists.

AHE   Ahe, the most popular of the Tuamotus with the yachting community, can only be reached by launch from neighboring Manihi. In the old days, Ahe never reaped the benefits of the tourist trade and consequently it was isolated and poor. Whereas on Manihi even two decades ago most residents had modern water cisterns, slept on beds and washed their dishes under a freshwater tap, life on Ahe presented a different scenario. A cistern was apt to have been a rusty oil drum, children slept on a mat on the floor and the dishes were likely to be washed in the waters of the lagoon.

Thankfully, with the growth of the pearl industry, this way of life has become history. No longer the poor relative, Ahe has become immersed in the pearl business by acting as a shell nursery for Manihi's pearl farms. Money has also come to this once poor island community, but not in quite the same materialistic or organized fashion that is seen on Manihi.

Even with the change in lifestyles, residents haven't lost their friendliness toward yachters. The playful rivalry between Manihi and Ahe (where many families are related) is also still evident. Ahe residents would like the visitor to believe that wealth, which they say has changed Manihi residents, has left Ahe inhabitants unfazed.

MAKATEA   Flying between Tahiti and Rangiroa you may spot the island of Makatea, about 124 miles (200 kilometers) northeast of Tahiti. It was first sighted in 1722 by the Dutch navigator Jacob Roggeveen, best known for having named Easter Island after he paused there on Easter Sunday earlier the same year.

Makatea takes its name from its geological formation—a *makatea* is an upthrust coral reef that dies and then fossilizes after it is raised above sea level. Although part of the atoll-dominated Tuamotus, Makatea is a high island with steep cliffs dropping over 150 feet (45 meters) into the sea. These forbidding cliffs would have dissuaded settlement of the 8-square-mile (21-square-kilometer) island if it had not been a rich source of phosphate.

In 1908, British and French commercial interests managed to build a dock at the port of **Temao**, and exploitation of the island commenced. Between World War I and World War II, a yearly average of 115,000 tons of phosphate were mined, using imported Asian labor. The phosphate was exported principally to New Zealand and Japan, and for 50 years Makatea remained an important part of the French Polynesian economy.

After World War II, the Asian labor force was replaced by a working population of around 700 Polynesians. In the 1960s, the annual phosphate production climbed to 300,000 tons a year. The island was finally worked out and mining was abandoned in 1966, although about 60 people have remained. Temao still has its deep-water docking facilities and a short stretch of railway line.

LODGING   **TAKAPOTO**   All four pensions listed here provide transportation to and from the airport and are located near the airport, in the village of Fakatopatere. In addition, they will all discount their tariffs by 500 CFP per person per day for guests staying more than three days. Electricity is available from 7 a.m. to 10 p.m. Since there are

---

✔ CHECK THESE OUT—UNIQUE OUTDOOR ADVENTURES

- Dive **Tiny Pass** in Rangiroa's lagoon and try to count the myriad reef fish that swim by. *page 320*
- Snag a tuna or jack on a fishing trip arranged through **Manihi Pearl Beach Resort**. *page 326*
- Motor along the gentle waters of **Tikehau's lagoon** and birdwatch at one of the *motu* sanctuaries. *page 327*
- Snorkel at **L'ile aux Récifs**, the best accessible site in Rangiroa, where fossilized coral formations are the star attractions. *page 319*

no restaurants on the island, the pensions provide *pension complete*—three meals a day—as part of the tariff.

Chez Lea Teahu has one large bungalow home, with a tin roof and old-fashioned shuttered windows that open and close like venetian blinds. There are four bedrooms, and a dorm with four double and four single beds. There is a communal bath and kitchen. Visits to a nearby *motu* are offered. ~ Fakatopatere; 98-65-56. BUDGET.

Smaller in size, **Chez Emile Taraihau** consists of one bungalow with a double bed, outside bath, kitchenette and terrace. ~ Fakatopatere; 98-65-25. BUDGET.

Chez Cathy Ruamotu has one house with two bedrooms, each with a double bed, living room, fully equipped kitchen and common bathroom. Trips to remote *motus* are available. ~ Fakatopatere; 98-65-68. BUDGET.

Chez Terai Mahaeahea has one house with one bedroom furnished with a double bed, and another room outfitted with a double and single bed. ~ Fakatopatere; 98-65-54. BUDGET.

TAKAROA   Accommodations on Takaroa are in or near the village of Teavaroa, which is located two kilometers from the airstrip. All guesthouses have electricity, and provide round-trip transfers to and from the airport. As in most pensions on the outer islands, after the third day the price drops by 500 CFP per person.

Located just a few yards from the beach, **Chez Eugenie Ennemoser** is a modern five-bedroom house with a living room, fully equipped kitchen, huge terrace, communal (cold water) bath and probably the only jacuzzi within 500 nautical miles. The Ennemosers, who hail from Germany, provide trips to a *motu* as well as other excursions for an additional fee. French, German and English are spoken at Chez Eugenie, and it's cash only, please. Though the Ennemosers have been on the island for a while, their pension is new. The management is friendly and quite helpful. ~ Teavaroa; 98-22-36. BUDGET TO MODERATE.   ◄ *HIDDEN*

In a wonderful classic South Seas setting on the private *motu* of Tikagagie you will find **Tikagagie Village**. The "village" is made up of a house and six bungalows. The beachside bungalows are A-frame structures raised above the ground by metal pipes. They have thatched roofs and plaited palm-frond walls that keep them cool. The house has seven rooms, each with a double bed, along with a kitchen, living room, communal (cold water) bath and terrace. Activities at Tikagagie Village include picnics on a *motu* and a visit to the old family pearl farm. Teariki and Maroaitiare Noho, the owners, take good care of their guests, *and* the food is good! The complex is located about ten kilometers from the airstrip. (It takes 20 minutes to get there by boat). (One night's deposit is necessary to make a reservation.) A minimum two-night stay is mandatory. ~ Call Voyagence Tahiti travel agency in Papeete; 43-72-13, fax 43-21-84. BUDGET TO MODERATE.   ◄ *HIDDEN*

On the more basic side, **Chez Vahinerii Temanaha** is a concrete house with two rooms, each with a double bed. There is also a kitchen, living room and communal bath. Visits to a *motu* are provided. If you ask, other excursions, such as fishing trips, can be arranged. The scoop on Chez Vahinerii is that it's basically a nice place to stay, but leaves much to be desired in the way of service. A Tahitian friend told me that the owner, Vahinerii, pretty much abandons guests, and regards cooking for them an onerous chore. Chez Vahinerii Temanaha is located near a beach close to the airstrip. ~ Teavaroa; 98-22-10. BUDGET.

> Nearly all the housing on Arutua was seriously damaged or destroyed in 1983 when a cyclone ravaged the atoll.

FAKARAVA   Situated on a spit of land shaded by coconut palms, **Tetamanu Village** has four small bungalows perched on the edge of the lagoon, each with two single beds and two common baths. A small dock juts out from the land, making this a good spot for swimmers to jump in the lagoon. Tetamanu Village is a three-hour boat ride from the airport to the interior of Fakarava's lagoon. Write to BP 9364, Motu Uta, Tahiti for information. ~ In Tahiti: 45-20-30, 43-91-82. MODERATE.

For the more adventurous, the **Sea Bell**, a 60-foot (18-meter) vessel with four cabins, will take the intrepid traveler on a seven-day fishing, swimming, snorkeling and eating odyssey in the waters of the lagoon. The owner/operator, Sunny Richmond, provides return transport to and from Fakarava's airport. I believe Sunny's excursions are fine, but overpriced. A deposit is required for reservations. This trip is connected with Tetamanu Village. ~ For information, call Jean-Pierre. In Tahiti, 45-20-30, 43-91-82. DELUXE.

HIDDEN ►   One of the best bargains in the Tuamotus, **Kiritia Village** has three thatched-roof bungalows by the sea, each with a bedroom, terrace, living room and a communal bath shared by all guests. There is also a house on the property that has three bedrooms, each with double and single beds and a living room. One of the highlights of Kiritia Village are the excursions to a *motu*— complete with picnic, deep-sea fishing and net fishing. Or try the nighttime guided adventure to catch lobsters that ends with a traditional Polynesian feast. Mme. Kachler, who runs the property, is an entertaining and informative host. Kiritia Village combines tasty food and local hospitality with a marvelous price. Mme. Kachler, by the way, speaks English. Kiritia Village is four kilometers from the airport. ~ Rotoava; 98-42-37. MODERATE.

HIDDEN ►   At **Openu Island**, you will find a traditional Tahitian *fare* built alongside the lagoon. Simple, it has one room with a double bed (perhaps it would be better to call it a mattress), and toilet facilities outside. But the setting is exquisite. Activities include spear fishing, snorkeling, line fishing, excursions to the reefs and picnics to

The
Outer
Limits

The Moruroa and Fangataufa atolls are not open to visitors but are well known as nuclear testing sites. Testing began above ground in 1966, but was moved underground in 1975 and restricted to Moruroa. Total tests exceed 165 to date, including neutron tests, the publicly acknowledged hydrogen series and the well-publicized 1995 series. Although the base at Hao was built to provide logistic assistance for the military, it is also an airfield used by civilian (Air Tahiti) flights, and visitors to some Tuamotu destinations may find themselves landing there.

From what has been written in the world press, after the experiments ended in 1996 Moruroa ceased to function as a test site. Presumably the military will either destroy or put much of the infrastructure in mothballs. The once-large civilian workforce, which numbered several thousand during Moruroa's heyday in the 1960s and 1970s, will never return.

These employees, mostly Tahitian, were paid well and pumped billions of francs into the economy. This supported a sizable portion of the population, but with the end of the Cold War, and the tests, this workforce had to be let go. This has created unemployment and some of the social problems associated with joblessness.

Today only the military caretakers remain on the island. According to the local press, the atoll will most likely never be reactivated as a test site because of the emergence of electronic simulation as an alternative to nuclear detonations. The end of the cold war and the anti-nuclear passions of other regional governments may also have had something to do with the cessation of testing. It is said that Hao will most likely be turned into a commercial deep-sea fishing port.

the *motus*. Here you'll find true Polynesian flavor and traditional hospitality. The owner will even teach you how to weave mats from coconut fronds or give you lessons on how to cook Paumotu style. Guests are well looked after and well fed with Paumotu specialties. Round-trip transfer from the airport to the pension is 15,000 CFP. There is a minimum stay of seven nights, and a deposit is required for reservations. The resort is located on Motu Openu, an islet situated in the pass opposite Tetamanu Village. It is about three hours from the airstrip by boat. ~ Tetamanu; 82-90-54, 58-35-26. BUDGET TO MODERATE.

HIDDEN ►   **KAUKURA**   **Pension Rekareka** has two locations. The village setting consists of a large home with six rooms located upstairs. Each room has a double bed and there is a spacious living room with television, a dining room and communal bath. Rekarkea "annex" has four small thatched-roof *fares* on the private Motu Tahunapona, a 15-minute boat ride from the village. On the *motu* each bungalow (better described as a tiny cabin with a peaked roof) has one small room. There are also communal bath facilities. Mme. Claire Parker, the proprietor, takes care of her patrons by providing good food and clean accommodations at a fair price. She is also helpful and friendly. The pension is about two kilometers from the airstrip. ~ Raitahiti; 96-62-40, 96-62-39. MODERATE.

ARUTUA   All lodging on Arutua is found in or near the village of Rautini, which is a 30-minute boat ride from the airstrip.

Surrounded by a white picket fence and shaded by palm trees, **Pension Mairava** is located in a classic island setting. In the midst of Rautini Village, it has one house with six rooms and a communal bath. Rooms are of average size, and like most accommodations in the Tuamotu Islands, they are simple. The proprietor, Edouard Charles, a broad-shouldered Paumotu fisherman, will take you fishing or to visit the pearl farm in the lagoon. Write to the Charles

LOCAL HERO

The most famous man on Arutua is Arii Parker, who made a fortune as a pearl farmer. However, he will always be remembered more as a local hero rather than as a successful businessman. One windy day in 1993 a boatload of young French marines was crossing Arutua's pass. Inexperienced in handling the boat in a treacherous stretch of water, they capsized. Without a moment to spare, Parker sprang into action and single-handedly saved the lives of all 15 marines. For his valor and bravery, he was awarded the French Legion of Honor.

family, c/o Rautini Village, Arutua, French Polynesia for reservations. ~ Rautini; 96-52-37. BUDGET TO MODERATE.

Also in the village, **Pension Pikui** is a house with communal bath and three rooms—two with double beds and one with three singles. The proprietors, the Tuteina family, also have a house on Motu Mutukiore, with two bedrooms. Activities here include picnics, trolling in the lagoon or fishing off the reef for lobsters. The cost for these excursions varies according to how much gasoline is consumed by the boats. ~ Rautini; 96-52-34. BUDGET TO MODERATE.

Another home to unpack your bags in is **Chez Nerii**. Here you will have one room with a double bed, living room, dining room and communal (cold water) bathroom. Excursions are provided to the fish park and a family-owned black pearl farm. ~ Rautini; 96-52-55. MODERATE.

AHE There is no official pension in Ahe, but arrangements can (and must) be made at private homes from any of the pensions in Manihi.

I use the term "Eastern" Tuamotus loosely to place the islands in a geographical setting. Two islands, Anaa and Nukutavake, offer accommodations. The military island of Hao, and the atolls used in nuclear tests, Moruroa and Fangataufu are also in this area.

Eastern Tuamotu Islands

ANAA Anaa could be considered a model of the prototypical sun- and wind-scarred atoll. Located 271 miles (437 kilometers) east of Tahiti, it is an oval-shaped island comprised of 11 islets that enclose a shallow lagoon. Once the most populous atoll in the Tuamotu Group, it is now a quiet backwater of 700 inhabitants that sees few visitors.

There is no pass through the coral reef, but landing is easy on the lee side, where the reef slopes up to the shore. Several years ago the island was devastated by a cyclone, but has since been rebuilt. **Tuuhora** is the most important of the five villages.

NUKUTAVAKE Nukutavake is located in the eastern region of the Tuamotu Archipelago, 675 miles (1125 kilometers) northeast of Tahiti. The atoll is oblong in shape, almost two miles long and 500 yards wide. There is a lagoon, but no navigable pass. The majority of the island's 142 residents live in the villages of **Mohitu** and **Terau**, at the northeast end of the island. Nukutavake is new to tourism and visitors are still a novelty.

ANAA Sitting right beside the lagoon, **Te Maui Nui** is located in Anaa's Tuuhora Village, near the airstrip. Operated by the charming Francois Mo'o, it has two very clean thatched-roof bungalows—one with three bedrooms and the other with one bedroom.

LODGING

Both accommodations have communal (cold water) bath. They also have outdoor terraces for dining, covered with a thatched roof. Francois formerly lived in Papeete where he ran a snack bar and his years of working in the restaurant business are evident in the professional manner in which he runs the property. He decided to go back to his roots as good luck would have it and run the Te Maui Nui. Francois is helpful, speaks some English and serves good food. Te Maui Nui is one of the better deals in the archipelago. ~ Tuuhora; 98-32-75. BUDGET TO MODERATE.

NUKUTAVAKE There is only one place to stay on Nukutavake, but fortunately it is one of the better pensions in the Tuamotu Group. On the lagoon side of the atoll, **Pension Afou** is close to the docks on the sea side near a white-sand beach. There are three local-style bungalows, each with a double bed. The site has a dining room and shared bath facilities. The proprietors, the Teavai family, are pleasant and helpful hosts. The food is good, and the atmosphere is typically Paumotu. Pension Afou is located one kilometer from Tavavanui Village. Transportation to and from the airport is provided. ~ Tavavanui; 98-72-53. MODERATE.

HIDDEN ►

Transportation

AIR

RANGIROA There is no shortage of flights to Rangiroa. Air Tahiti services the island every day of the week from Papeete—the flight time is 60 minutes. The airport in Rangiroa is near Avatoru. There are also flights between Rangi and Bora Bora and from Rangi to Manihi three times a week.

MANIHI There are **Air Tahiti** flights to Manihi from Papeete five times a week. The direct flight time from Papeete takes one hour and 25 minutes, or one hour and 50 minutes with a stopover in Rangiroa. Rangiroa to Manihi flight time is 40 minutes. Flights to Manihi are also available Kaukura and Takaroa.

TIKEHAU Air service via **Air Tahiti** between Tikehau and Papeete is three times weekly. Flying time is 55 minutes direct from Papeete or one hour 30 minutes via Rangiroa.

MATAIVA Flying time via **Air Tahiti** direct from Papeete is 55 minutes or 1 hour 35 minutes via Rangiroa. Service and to and from Papeete is twice weekly.

TAKAPOTO Air transportation is provided by **Air Tahiti**. There are flights from Papeete twice a week, with connections to Kaukura and Apataki. Flying time is one hour 30 minutes direct from Papeete.

TAKAROA Service via **Air Tahiti** from Papeete to Takaroa is three times weekly. Flight time from Papeete is two hours and ten minutes via Manihi or Takapoto.

FAKARAVA Service via **Air Tahiti** from Papeete is twice weekly and flying time direct from the capital is 1 hour 20 minutes (or 2 hours and 30 minutes via Rangiroa).

KAUKURA   Flying time from Papeete via **Air Tahiti** is one hour direct or one hour 40 minutes via Rangiroa. Service (also on Air Tahiti) to and from the island is twice weekly from Papeete.

ARUTUA   Service to and from Arutua via **Air Tahiti** is twice weekly from Papeete. Flying time is one hour 15 minutes.

EASTERN TUAMOTUS   Flying time to Anaa direct from the capital via **Air Tahiti** is one hour ten minutes and service is twice weekly. Nukutavake has weekly air service with **Air Tahiti** but the price is steep—around US$800. Flying time from Papeete is a mere eight hours and 40 minutes! It is an island-hopping flight with five stops.

SEA

RANGIROA   Interisland vessels frequently visit Rangiroa. At least four different vessels visit the island regularly from Papeete. The *Rairoa Nui* (42-91-69) and *Dory* (42-88-88) arrive weekly. The *Manava II* (43-83-84) and *St. Xavier Maris Stella* (Papeete; 42-23-58) come at least once a month.

MANIHI   There are several interisland vessels sailing to Manihi regularly from Papeete including the *St. Xavier Maris Stella* (42-23-58), which departs every two weeks, and the *Manava II* (43-83-84), which departs monthly.

TIKEHAU   At least four different vessels visit the island regularly from Papeete, including the *Rairoa Nui* (42-91-69) and *Dory* (42-88-88), which arrive weekly. The *Manava II* (43-83-84) and *St. Xavier Maris Stella* (42-23-58) come at least once a month.

MATAIVA   Interisland vessels that visit Mataiva from Papeete include the *Dory* (42-88-88) on a weekly basis, the *St. Xavier Maris Stella* (42-23-58) bi-weekly, and the *Manava II* (43-83-84) monthly.

TAKAPOTO   Interisland vessels that visit Takapoto from Papeete include the *Ruahatu* (43-32-65) every fortnight and the *Manava II* (43-83-84) monthly.

TAKAROA   Interisland vessels that visit the island from Papeete are the *Ruahatu* (43-32-65) every fortnight and the *Manava II* (43-83-84) on a monthly schedule.

◆◆

SHIPWRECKED ON RAROIA

It was on the reef of Raroia that Thor Heyerdahl's raft *Kon Tiki* was wrecked in 1947, and his crew of five Scandinavians were washed ashore. They were en route to Mangareva in the Gambier Islands to test Heyerdahl's theory based on an Inca legend that it was possible to sail from South America to Polynesia.

FAKARAVA   Fakarava is visited by the *Manava II* on a monthly basis. ~ Papeete; 43-83-84.

KAUKURA   Interisland vessels that call on the island from Papeete include *Cobia II* (42-88-88) and *Dory* (42-88-88) on a weekly basis.

ARUTUA   Interisland vessels that visit the island from Papeete include the *Dory* (42-88-88) on a weekly basis, the *St. Xavier Maris Stella* (42-23-58) bi-weekly, and the *Manava II* (43-83-84) monthly.

AHE   There is a daily skiff from Manihi to Ahe. The island is also visited by the *St. Xavier Maris Stella* (Papeete; 42-23-58) bi-weekly or the *Manava II* (Papeete; 43-83-84) monthly.

EASTERN TUAMOTUS   To visit Anaa or Nukutavake by interisland vessel you can take the *Ruahatu* every fortnight. ~ Papeete; 43-32-65.

PUBLIC TRANSIT

RANGIROA   All transportation to and from the airport can be arranged through your hotel or guesthouse. Given the small area of land, there is no need for buses or taxis. Getting around the atoll by boat is easy.

A small watertaxi crosses frequently between the dock by Chez Glorine (on the Avatoru side of Tiputa Pass) to Tiputa Village. The best thing to do is ask at Chez Glorine for a recommendation for someone who will be able to take you across the pass. (Their prices will be less than what you would pay for transportation at the Kia Ora.)

MOTOR SCOOTER RENTALS

RANGIROA   There's only one road around the main atoll and you can ride all the way to one end of the island and back again, a round trip of about 12.5 miles (20 kilometers), in a couple of hours. **Rangi Atelier** rents motor scooters. ~ Tiputa; 96-04-92.

ELEVEN

The Marquesas Islands

Whether seen from a sailing vessel or from the air, few sights are as dramatic as landfall in the Marquesas Islands. They rise like jagged spires from the sea. Yet, because of their isolation, few travelers have ever experienced the pleasure.

Volcanic in origin and geologically precocious, the Marquesas are rocky and precipitous. They have no coastal plains, but are veined with deep, lush, trenchlike valleys. The water surrounding the islands is indigo blue and there are few reefs.

The Marquesas are comprised of ten main islands (six of which are inhabited) and are located 875 miles (1400 kilometers) northeast of Tahiti. They are divided into two groups: To the north is Nuku Hiva, Ua Huka and Ua Pou and in the south is Hiva Oa, Tahuata and Fatu Hiva.

The climate in the Marquesas is, on average, similar to the rest of French Polynesia, but the seasons are reversed. The islands lie in the midst of a trade-wind belt from the northern latitudes, bringing northeasterly winds most of the year. There is no real rainy season, but rainfall is heavier in June and July. The mean year-round temperature is a balmy 79°F (28°C).

Because of their proximity to the equator, the islands have been a backwater of the Pacific, and even in this day of air travel, still remain secluded.

According to a theory held by University of California anthropologist Pat Kirch, the six major islands of the Marquesas were settled around 2500 years ago by Polynesian mariners from Samoa or Tonga. In 1595, the first European, Spanish explorer Alvaro de Mendaña, "discovered" the Marquesas en route to establishing a new colony in the Solomon Islands. Mendaña was a politically savvy man who called them "Las Marquesas de Mendoza" in honor of his patron, the Marquis de Mendoza y Cañete. After Mendaña's landing (in which natives in Fatu Hiva and Tahuata were massacred), the islands remained undisturbed for almost 200 years until Captain James Cook arrived. Cook's appearance was followed first by whalers, and then, by 1862, slave ships.

Contact with the white man brought enslavement to some and disease to others. The slavers, known as "blackbirders," needed laborers for guano mining and South American plantations. Making promises of a better life, the blackbirders picked up their unfortunate victims, often with the help of other islanders, and sold them to the highest bidder. They plied their trade on most of the Marquesas, but principally sought their prey on the north coasts of Nuku Hiva and Hiva Oa.

While relatively few Marquesans ended up as slaves, the repercussions of this nefarious activity were enormous. When the French heard of the abductions, they took diplomatic action to secure the return of the Polynesians. However, before this could take place, a smallpox epidemic broke out in South America's coastal cities, and the repatriated Marquesans brought back the deadly virus with them to Nuku Hiva. This decimated the population and nearly destroyed Marquesan civilization.

When Cook first visited the islands, the inhabitants numbered at least 50,000. Some believe that the total population was as high as 100,000 before contact with outsiders. Regardless of what the pre-contact population was, 50 years after Cook visited the number of inhabitants was down to about 30,000 and fell to 2000 before the numbers started to increase again. Today it stands at about 8000.

The first missionaries arrived on the scene in 1797, and in the following half-century various evangelistic sects zealously competed for the souls of the Marquesans. During this period of intense missionary activity, the American writer Herman Melville jumped ship from a whaler here. He later wrote *Typee*, based loosely on his experiences in the Marquesas. This rather embellished autobiographical account was the first South Seas romance, the earliest of a genre that brought many a white man to the shores of the Pacific islands.

In 1804, a Russian exploratory mission commanded by Admiral de Krusenstern arrived at Nuku Hiva for ten very productive days. Aside from collecting ethnographic items (still in Russian collections), the voyage was illustrated and documented by scholars and artists. The Russian visit was also documented by two beachcombers living in the Marquesas. One was a Scotsman by the name of Edward Robarts, who lived on Tahuata, Hiva Oa and Nuku Hiva. (His journal has recently been published.) The other, Joseph Cabri, a Frenchman, lived on Nuku Hiva and published a short romantic narrative. Both men introduced the Russians to the tribes with whom they were allied.

In 1842, the French sent Admiral Dupetit-Thouars to colonize the Marquesas in order to establish a naval base, but the French found relatively little use for the islands. The French set themselves up on Tahuata, ostensibly to protect the local population from other European invaders. However, fighting soon broke out and the French carried out a successful war against the Marquesans on the island. Still, their presence was not seen as beneficial to either the locals or the Europeans, and after two years they withdrew their garrison to Nuku Hiva.

From the late 18th century through the 19th century, whalers from throughout the world converged here. The best sperm whale grounds ran along the equator, and the Marquesas were ideally positioned as "R&R" stops for whalers who plied the equatorial seas. In fact, it was the whaling trade that led to the discovery of the northern group of the Marquesas Islands. And it was this discovery that ultimately contributed to the depopulation of the archipelago—and the near destruction of the

Marquesan culture. In all, the late 19th century was a time of darkness and death for the Marquesan people, marked by periods of savagery, killings and cannibalism. The French administration could do little more than preside over the death of a people.

Today, the islands remain an economic and social backwater. The main commercial product is copra, although the government is now encouraging the cultivation of vanilla. (They attempted to cultivate coffee in the 1920s but it never took off as a cash crop.)

The fishing grounds surrounding the Marquesas are rich with tuna and are fished by locals as well as large Taiwanese and Japanese vessels that pay the French Polynesian government a fee for the privilege of fishing in territorial waters. Much to their consternation, the Marquesans are not direct beneficiaries of these monies, and, lacking modern fishing vessels, it is difficult for Marquesan fishermen to capitalize on their rich offshore resources. Local commercial fishing is also hampered by the expense of shipping fresh seafood to Papeete and beyond because of the great distances involved.

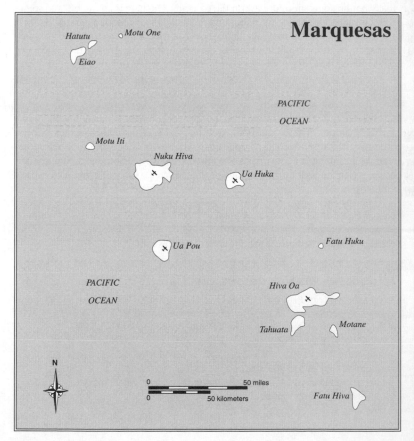

In an effort to open up the islands, the French Polynesian government has approved the construction of an international airport on Nuku Hiva, which is slated to open in 1998. If it is completed it will give quite a boost to the local economy.

Communications in and around the Marquesas Islands are extremely rudimentary. Getting from island to island takes planning, and usually a fist full of bank notes. There is airline service between some of the Marquesas Group, but there are few regularly scheduled boats. To get from one island to another often requires chartering a boat—and that can be very costly.

Getting around an island can also be a chore. Even though maps depict "roads," they are rocky and generally not well maintained. During rainy days they may turn into rutted, muddy jeep trails. Roads are passable year-round, but tourist excursions may be limited if rainfall is unduly heavy. Driving the few roads that do exist requires a great deal of skill, especially during inclement weather. The plethora of precipices (roads are often cut from the sides of mountains) make driving potentially hazardous to newcomers. There are few rental cars and travelers will most likely not be doing much driving on these islands. Hitching is an option, and sometimes it's possible to pick up rides in workers trucks or carriers operated by local communities. (Women traveling alone should opt for a different method of transportation because of cultural mores.) Figure on spending 12,000 to 15,000 CFP (US$140 to US$170) per day for either rental vehicles or to hire a car with driver. If you don't want to spend the money don't expect to do much sightseeing—unless you plan to walk a lot.

Like the cost of transportation, imported food is dear. Fortunately, Marquesans rely on traditional staples—breadfruit, taro, sweet potatoes, bananas and seafood—for the majority of their nutrition. Archeological evidence indicates that this has long been the case. Ancient Marquesans consumed a wide variety of marine resources, including sting ray, porpoises and turtles. They also hunted land and sea birds, which resulted in the extermination of several species of birds such as rails and parrots.

The ancient Marquesans were a warlike lot who practiced human sacrifice as well as cannibalism. Various undertakings required victims to ensure the continued blessings of the gods. These practices had a specific place in their ceremonial life and warfare. Human flesh was generally eaten by males only.

MARQUESAS ISLANDS UNIQUE EXPERIENCES

- Visit the grave of Paul Gauguin at Hiva Oa's **Calvary Cemetery**, where a small stone marker and statue of Ovira commemorate his life. *page 368*
- Perch yourself on the hilltop at **Keikahanui Inn** on Nuku Hiva, and enjoy the view of Taioha'e Bay. *page 352*
- Join Nuku Hiva locals and visitors alike at **Hotel Moana Nui's restaurant,** and dine in a Colonial atmosphere. *page 355*
- Hike from **Hanavave Village to Omoa** on Fatu Hiva, where dizzying views and gorgeous waterfalls will enthrall you. *page 379*

Thankfully, these practices did not survive into the 20th century. However, Marquesans were also well known for their skills as tattoo artists and carvers of wood and stone, a tradition that has continued to this day. Local artisans carry on these traditions in their woodcarvings and hand-crafted ukuleles. Complex traditional design motifs are now imitated and applied in an almost cursive short-hand fashion. There are also ample remains of ancient temples and imposing stone *tiki* throughout the islands that illustrate the once-prolific talents of the ancient Marquesans.

The culinary spectrum of the Marquesas includes *ika te'e* (raw fish) as well as pork, goat and broiled lobster, which is in danger of being overharvested because of its popularity as fare for the few tourists that visit these remote islands. Baked breadfruit, as well as several varieties of fresh and fermented breadfruit pastes and puddings, are common. Taro, *manioc* (the starchy tapioca root) and bananas are also prevalent. While in the Marquesas you'll probably be offered *popoi*, Marquesan-style *poi* made from breadfruit, which has a slightly sour, fermented taste. For dessert you'll no doubt try *poke*, a sweet, gelatinous mixture of pumpkin, banana or papaya and *amidon*. Naturally, there is always French bread, a variety of locally baked breads and a tasty biscuit-like treat, *kato*, made with coconut milk.

▼▼▼▼▼▼▼▼▼▼ Nuku Hiva

Nuku Hiva is the most important and largest island in the Marquesas—being the economic and governmental hub of the archipelago. One hundred and twenty-seven square miles (330 square kilometers) in area with a population of about 2100, its position as a center of civilization is nothing new. There are numerous vestiges of life before European contact. Here you'll find *paepae*—the stone foundations on which the Marquesans constructed their homes, *pa*—fortifications, and *me'ae*—temples that testify to the once large population that the island supported.

Nuku Hiva was the center of ancient stone architecture in the Marquesas and has the largest number of them remaining, particularly the large rectangular *tohua* (ceremonial complexes). These often extended for 100 yards (90 meters) and were surrounded by huge stone platforms.

The manmade symmetry of Marquesan architecture is superseded only by the land's stunning majesty. Nuku Hiva is dramatically beautiful, with three major bays along the southern coast and equally breathtaking inlets on the northern coast. Taioha'e Bay, a cul de sac bounded by precipitous mountains, is located on the island's southern half and is the major port for the entire archipelago.

SIGHTS

Nuku Ataha, the Nuku Hiva airport, is located a few kilometers inland from the northwest coast. To reach the main settlement of Taioha'e you can either go overland by car, which takes about two hours, or via helicopter, which involves a seven- or eight-minute vault over some incredible scenery. One of my friends described the helicopter flight as "seven or eight terror-filled minutes"—but I rather enjoyed it.

Coming from the airport you can also travel east, along the north coast past the village of Pua. There the road becomes an impassible track until the village of A'akapa, where once again a four-wheel-drive vehicle can negotiate the terrain. (Local government authorities told me that the impassible segment between A'akapa and Pua may be finished sometime in the near future, which would make life much easier for residents of the northeast side of the island who must drive a circuitous route to reach the airport. However, this may or may not occur.)

HIDDEN ▶

Driving northeast from Taioha'e, you can travel overland by car to **Hatiheu** then to A'akapa and beyond. The road ends after another five kilometers or so. Motoring east and north from Taioha'e, you can travel to Taipivai and Ho'oumi. All the roads are unpaved and extremely rough and/or muddy during the rainy season.

TOOVII PLATEAU AREA   The central portion of the island is dominated by the **Toovii Plateau**, an alpine-like setting that you first glimpse on your drive in from the airport. Fertile and verdant, the hills above the plateau have been planted with Norfolk Pine. The tree-planting scheme is part of a government-established agricultural station.

Crossing Toovii Plateau in a southerly direction toward Taioha'e necessitates negotiating **Muake Pass**. From the summit there is a spectacular 360-degree view. The vista takes in the rugged coastline and Taioha'e Bay. On the distant horizon the island of Ua Pou rises like an apparition. A short taxi ride will take you to the overlook at 2830 feet (864 meters) above the bay.

In 1813, Muake Pass was the site of a major **fortification** of the Tei'i (Taioha'e) tribe when Commodore David Porter arrived. The entire ridgetop was enclosed by a log palisade. Trenches cut through the ridge, still visible today, were made by the Tei'i to prevent the neighboring Taipi warriors from reaching the fort along the crest. Although the area was greatly disturbed by reforestation projects, road construction and the erection of a radio tower, the remains of the fort can still be seen.

TAIOHA'E AREA   **Taioha'e**, the administrative center of Nuku Hiva and the entire Marquesan archipelago, sits on the shores of **Taioha'e Bay**, the central bay on the southern coast. Bounded by high peaks, its calm, deep anchorage is a refuge for boats from the hurricane-prone southern reaches of French Polynesia. The main frontage road, studded here and there with shade trees, is lined with the requisite bank (Socredo), shops, post office, bakeries and government facilities.

Taioha'e is the undisputed shipping center for the Marquesan Group. On the *quai* a freezer stores the catch of the local fishing co-op. Port facilities have been vastly improved in the past few years and a wharf has been constructed on the east side of the harbor.

An **old fort** and **jail** built for local troublemakers and political exiles stands just a stone's throw east of the Taioha'e town hall. Constructed in 1842, this relic is the oldest original European structure in French Polynesia. The old fort is the site of Commodore David Porter's Fort Madison, built by the American Navy in 1813. In 1814, the British took the fort over and by 1842 the same real estate was occupied by the French under Commandant Collet. It was eventually renamed Fort Collet, the name that stands today.

Today, the jailhouse doubles as an urban planning office cum **tourist bureau**. The bureau is run by the very capable Deborah Kimitete. She knows everything that is going on in town (it helps when your husband is the mayor) and she is proficient in English. She also sells a variety of maps of the Marquesas. You can write to her at BP 38, Taioha'e, Nuku Hiva, Marquesas or give her a call. ~ Taioha'e; 92-02-02.

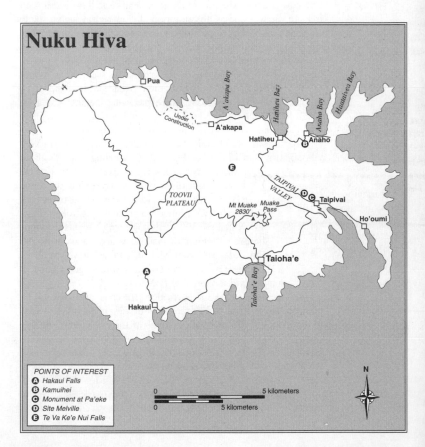

Nuku Hiva

POINTS OF INTEREST
Ⓐ Hakaui Falls
Ⓑ Kamuihei
Ⓒ Monument at Pa'eke
Ⓓ Site Melville
Ⓔ Te Va Ke'e Nui Falls

0   5 kilometers

0   5 kilometers

You might want to stop and see the **Cathedral of Notre Dame,** which was constructed in 1974 and is the largest church in the Marquesas. The interior boasts locally carved wood sculptures. Be sure to take a look at the handsomely carved lectern with the figure of Mary. Mass is held every Sunday.

TAIPIVAI VALLEY AND THE NORTHEAST COAST The east coast of Nuku Hiva is high, rocky and dry. In parts, it is a formidable line of sheer cliffs. Tucked away in the Taipivai Valley, just inland from the coast, are many old temples, or *paepae* (pronounced "pie-pie"), and large *tiki*.

HIDDEN ► Some of the most fascinating archeological sites in all of French Polynesia are found in this region, including the **monument at Pa'eke.** Here you'll find 11 *tiki*, probably representing the ancestral gods of the Taipi sub-tribes. Constructed around 1700 A.D., they still stand at a ceremonial site located in what now appears to be a cow pasture. The trail to the ruins leads uphill (as it seems all treks in the Marquesas do) about one kilometer through a shady coconut plantation. Exotic birdsongs are heard in the distance. The site is surrounded by lush palms, banana plants and a plethora of *nonos* and mosquitos. (Don't forget your repellent!) You'll probably see a few horses grazing on the grounds as well. ~ The monument at Pa'eke is located high on the northern wall of the valley (about four kilometers from where the valley begins). It's a bit tough to find the trailhead (it's not marked) so have a local guide you. (You can ask for Pukiki in Taipivai ~ 91-01-26.)

The famous **Site Melville** (Cite Melville) is where Herman Melville sojourned in 1842 after deserting his whaling ship. It's about two kilometers past the Pa'eke monument on the lefthand side of the road. **Te Ivi o Hou,** the *tohua* or ceremonial site, is located in a remote part of the valley. In 1957, American archeologist Robert Suggs excavated the 300-yard-long area (274 meters) while sharing a house with Heiku'a Clarck, a woman who claimed descent from Melville's fabled Fayoway Peue. (Those interested in more details should get a copy of Suggs' *Hidden Worlds of Polynesia*.)

The monument at Pa'eke was first reported and photographed by the German ethnographer Karl von den Steinen in 1896.

The various bays and coves along the coast are accessible by boat, and, in some cases, by four-wheel-drive vehicle. It's fairly easy to get from the Taipivai Valley to one of the nicest bays, **Anaho,** simply by continuing up the Taipivai Valley floor over the pass to Hatiheu. Anaho Bay, with coconut palms edging its shoreline and white-sand beach, is tucked between two rather high rocky promontories. (Note: Swimmers should keep an eye out for sharks.)

On the way up (before getting to the pass), ask the driver to point out **Te Va K'ee Nui Falls** on your left. The source of the water is a large dam, which provides the electricity for much of the island. (There is a good vista point near the top of the pass where you can see the distant falls.) It's possible to drive nearly all the way to the falls at the end of the valley by taking a new road that runs parallel to the old Taipivai–Hatiheu road.

The village of **Hatiheu**, also located on a sheltered bay, rests in the shadow of some spectacular peaks that tower over the landscape. The village has a secluded, restful feel to it, and there is a fine pension (Chez Yvonne) where you can base your explorations of the region. The area is a mother lode of archeological ruins. Of note are the **petroglyphs** and a well-restored ceremonial plaza, **Tohua Hikokua**, that displays both ancient and modern Marquesan sculpture. This site was reconstructed through the efforts of mayor Yvonne Katupa, the same disarmingly nice woman who runs the pension. A local dance troupe took its name from the Tohua Hikokua site, and they often perform for visitors on the actual plaza.

Continuing inland from Hatiheu, about 500 yards (450 meters) from the restored *tohua*, is an even larger ancient temple complex known as **Kamuihei**. This incredible jumble of ruins, including a *tohua* and petroglyphs, sits amidst a somber, dark jungle. It looks like a movie set from *Raiders of the Lost Ark*. Petroglyphs are relatively common in Hatiheu and A'akapa on the northern coast of Nuku Hiva. The Kamuihei and Hikokua archeological complexes are not far from the main road, but it's a good idea to have someone show you where to find both sites as they entail a short walk in the bush. (Someone you might consult is Alphonse, who works at Chez Yvonne.)

◄ *HIDDEN*

From the village it's a relatively easy hike to **Anaho Beach**. Many Marquesans regard Anaho Bay as the most picturesque in the Marquesas. The snorkeling is also good, but watch out for *moko*, white-tip sharks. Also, be prepared to lather yourself with *monoi* oil or insect repellent. *Nonos* can be a problem in many of the low-lying areas—even on the beach.

Along the northern stretch of coast between Anaho Bay and Pua, 20 kilometers east of the airport, is a journey worth taking. The scenery, which consists of a number of finger-like promontories jutting out to the sea, is spectacular. There are several white-sand beaches tucked along the shoreline, and you will be in the shadow of Nuku Hiva's highest mountains. However, the road stops shortly after the village of A'akapa and the best way to see this section of the coast is by boat. (The Pua area itself is still often regarded as *tapu*, off limits.)

As you near the airport area, the landscape sloping down from the plateau is volcanic and almost lunar in nature.

LODGING   **TOOVII PLATEAU AREA**   If you are stranded on this side of the island without transportation after deplaning at Nuku Ataha, head over to **Moetai Village**. There are five bungalows here, four with three twin beds and a bath, one with four twin beds. The atmosphere is rather dark and eerie—the place has a no-man's-land feel about it, and Moetai Village is definitely a transit accommodation. Rooms are satisfactory, but the meals could be improved upon. (Tariff includes breakfast.) Located about 500 yards (450 meters) from the airport and 32 kilometers from Taioha'e. ~ Moetai; 92-04-91. BUDGET.

TAIOHA'E   **Chez Fetu** is smack-dab in the center of Taioha'e village, west of the bakery and just inland from the waterfront road. It consists of one house with four rooms—two rooms have one double bed each, and two come with two single beds each. Bathrooms are communal and there is also a sitting room, a front porch and a nice kitchen with stove and refrigerator. Also available is one self-contained bungalow with two single beds. The accommodations are very basic, but clean, airy and a good bet for travelers watching their pocketbooks. There are no mosquito screens on the windows so purchase some coils at the store. Fetu and his family are personable and a pleasure to deal with, but the numerous children in the area can be noisy. ~ Taioha'e; 92-03-66. BUDGET.

Facing the sea, **Hotel Moana Nui** is a white, two-story building with a large veranda for its restaurant patrons. It has seven rooms, four of which have double beds and three with two single beds. The average-size rooms are clean and have private baths. The tariff includes breakfast. The hotel operates a restaurant downstairs that is *the* informal gathering place in town. Hotel Moana Nui is located midway between the east and west ends of Taioha'e Bay. ~ Taioha'e; 92-03-30, fax 92-00-02. BUDGET TO MODERATE.

At the western side of the bay you will find what is considered the premier hotel on the island—the **Keikahanui Inn**. Perched on a hill, the inn offers lovely views from all of its five bungalows. Rooms are very clean, freshly painted and well maintained. Each bungalow has a large and small bed, shower (hot water), bathroom and veranda. There are also two larger "beach house" units that come with a double bed, a sofabed, two cots, a kitchen and a bath. The inn is the de facto yacht club for the island and you will nearly always see American yachts moored offshore. The proprietress, Rose Corser, a native Oklahoman, handles mail, laundry, packages and general information for this part of the island. She also monitors Channel 68, the emergency channel, on the radio. Activities include sunbathing on the nearby beach, diving, snorkeling, hiking, tennis, horseback riding, village tours (including visits to local wood sculptors) and excursions to other bays. Ms. Corser is also

The Reality of
Travel in the
Marquesas

Visitors to the Marquesas Islands need to be independent, patient and able to rough it. Overland travel is nearly always by four-wheel drive. In some cases, boat, and even horseback, are used to get from one point to another.

Air service is not frequent and flights may be booked up weeks in advance during school holidays. The flight from Papeete is over three hours and the journey by copra boat may take a week or more depending on the schedule.

Getting to the Marquesas from Papeete is generally not cheap. Round-trip air fare costs around $US800, which can be more than an air ticket from the West Coast of the U.S. to Tahiti.

Another option to get to the Marquesas is via the *Aranui*, a comfortable, regularly scheduled interisland vessel. This is the most intriguing option, but it comes at a price. The cost for the two-and-a-half week cruise runs around US$3000. There are less expensive vessels, but their standards in areas of personnel, maintenance and accommodations are not high. Their schedules are also somewhat erratic.

One other note on things erratic. Prices in the Marquesas are subject to change. It's a good idea to get agreed-upon prices in writing.

the only native-English-speaking hotelier in the Marquesas. Unlike the majority of properties, Keikahanui Inn accepts VISA or Master-Card. ~ Taioha'e; 92-03-82, fax 92-00-74. MODERATE TO DELUXE.

TAIPIVAI VALLEY AND NORTHEAST COAST   Chez Martine Haiti is in Taipivai valley, just inside the village. Her two A-frame-style bungalows are situated next to a stream, across the road from her restaurant/store. Each has one room with a double bed, salon and bathroom (with cold water only). Activities include visits to local archeological sites, excursions on the bay by *pirogue* (including a picnic) as well as visits to the nearby villages of Ho'oumi, Hatiheu or A'akapa. The small restaurant here has excellent food. One-way transfer to and from Taioha'e to the pension is 8000 CFP for as many as eight people. ~ Taipivai; 92-01-19. BUDGET TO MODERATE.

HIDDEN ▶   **Chez Pukiki Vaia'anui** consists of a large home with two bedrooms with double bed, private bath, large living room and kitchen area. This is a roomy, comfortable place located about one kilometer from the main road into the valley. You can cook your own food or the management will provide meals. Your host, Pukiki, is a large, good-natured man who happens to be the local cop. A former French marine, he has traveled quite a bit overseas and has a cosmopolitan outlook. A fine source of information, he provides tours to the various archeological sites as well as visits to Hatiheu. Non-French speaking visitors should make their reservations at Chez Pukiki through Rose Corser at the Keikahanui, Taioha'e; 92-03-82, or call Pukiki in Taipivai. ~ Taipivai; 92-01-26, 92-04-28. BUDGET TO MODERATE.

HIDDEN ▶   **Chez Yvonne** is located right on the waterfront road facing the bay in downtown Hatiheu, approximately a two-hour drive from Taioha'e. Any way you look at it, you're in a remote corner of the universe. The accommodation consists of five spartan but clean bungalows—all equipped with double beds—set in a grassy field shaded by huge *pandanus* trees. The bungalows are a two-minute walk along the beachfront road from Yvonne's small restaurant. If you plan to stay in just one place in the Marquesas, this is a good property to consider. Just take plenty of insect repellent! ~ Hatiheu; 92-02-97. BUDGET.

HIDDEN ▶   **Pension Anaho** is the only place to stay in the village of Anaho. The owners, Leopold and Louise Vaianui, have a home with three rooms, two of which have a double bed and a single. The third room has a double bed with two single beds. The home has a self-contained kitchen, common bathroom and a washroom for laundry. There are also two bungalows on the premises, each with two single beds, a double bed and washroom for laundry. There is a minuscule restaurant/bar on the premises. Children under 12 may stay for half price. ~ Anaho; 92-04-25. BUDGET.

TAIOHA'E Facing Taioha'e Bay is **Kovivi's Restaurant,** located several minutes by foot east of the town hall. It is a brown chalet-type structure with a small veranda. Chinese, Marquesan and French cuisine are served with a flair. Dishes are generally tasty, but especially so when Bernard, the owner, cooks. Business hours are sometimes irregular and reservations are needed. Closed on Saturday morning and Sunday. ~ Taioha'e; 92-03-85. MODERATE TO DELUXE.

DINING

◄ *HIDDEN*

The restaurant at the **Hotel Moana Nui** has a veranda facing the sea where locals and visitors alike gather. They offer a wide-ranging menu that includes fish, chicken and several varieties of pizza. The pizza is made precisely as described in the menu—don't even think about holding the anchovies or adding extra olives. Changes are not permitted! The best way to order is to ask what the cook would like to fix for you rather than what you want. The atmosphere is quite pleasant and there is a Colonial feel to the place. Hotel Moana Nui is centrally located along the main street. ~ Taioha'e; 92-03-30. BUDGET TO MODERATE.

◄ *HIDDEN*

There are two **roulottes** (they don't have names) in town that serve inexpensive local fare along the beach road during the day.

A small, whitewashed, cube-shaped eatery, **Te Ha'e Ma'ona,** is run by Michelin, the wife of the local dive operator. There are several benches with thatched canopies, and Michelin serves steak and fries, *poisson cru* and other local dishes. Located just off the main street on the western end of town. ~ Taioha'e; BUDGET.

Snack Celine, located near the Catholic Mission, serves inexpensive local dishes. Snack Celine is the closest thing to a local fast-food restaurant. Fare includes such standards as hamburgers, steak and fries. ~ Taioha'e; 92-01-60. BUDGET.

The best budget restaurant in town is the small **eatery** tucked in the back of the waterfront *marché.* (It's so off-the-beaten-path it doesn't even have a name.) This is not only the least expensive restaurant in Taioha'e, it's perhaps the only place to get Marquesan dishes. To say the ambience is unpretentious is an understatement. Ripening banana bunches hang from the ceiling above the mismatched tables and chairs. Dishes include sashimi, *poisson cru,* steak and fish served with plantains. The sashimi is good, but the sauce served with it is a variation on a "thousand island" theme. (Don't expect wasabi or soy sauce here.) A nice local touch is the cold, green coconuts served as a beverage. ~ Taioha'e. BUDGET.

◄ *HIDDEN*

The chef at the **Keikahanui Inn** prepares French and seafood dishes. His finest dish is the fresh fish cooked in vanilla sauce. A happy-hour menu includes hamburgers with fries, mini-pizza and smoked fish. Entrées include fish and chicken dishes, steak filet and lobster. French pastries are also prepared. ~ Taioha'e; 92-03-82. BUDGET TO MODERATE.

TAIPIVAI AND HATIHEU **Chez Martine Haiti** has a small restaurant on the terrace of her home in the midst of the village of Taipivai. She often has a catch-of-the-day as well as simple Chinese fare—chop suey and stir-fry vegetables. The only caveat: visitors must make reservations. ~ Taipivai; 92-01-19. BUDGET.

If you're interested in collectibles, the best articles are wooden bowls, small wooden statues and the expensive but exquisitely carved coconut shells made in Fatu Hiva.

In the heart of Hatiheu, **Chez Yvonne** offers mouthwatering, inexpensive lunches and dinners. I sampled the freshwater-shrimp curry cooked in coconut milk and found it to be very tasty. The cuisine, combined with the homey ambience and Yvonne's pleasant disposition, makes it an obligatory stop. It's on the waterfront road facing the bay. ~ Hatiheu; 92-02-97. BUDGET.

Pension Anaho has a minuscule restaurant/bar on the premises where fish with coconut milk, as well as other basic local fare, is served. The food is appetizing, but you must call ahead to let the manager know you're dropping in unless you are staying there. ~ Anaho; 92-04-25. BUDGET.

GROCERIES **TAIOHA'E** Fresh bread is baked daily and is available at any of the general stores in Taioha'e. The stores are located on or near the beachfront road and have a good selection of canned food, fish, cheese and sundries. They include **Magasin Kamake** ~ 92-03-22 and **Magasin Maurice** ~ 92-03-91.

TAIPIVAI **Chez Martine Haiti** has a few basic items such as mosquito coils and soap in her pension. ~ 92-01-19.

SHOPPING **TAIOHA'E** Carvings are one of the best things to bring back from the Marquesas. Good quality items can be purchased in Taioha'e because it is the commercial center where visitors are likely to congregate. Expect to pay 5000 CFP and up for a good carving. **Maison Verde**, a small wooden shack on the west side of Taioha'e Bay, is a good place to start your window shopping.

You can also visit carvers behind the Te Ha'e Ma'ona or check with **Teiki Puketini**. ~ Taioha'e; 92-03-47.

Also check out the family of **sculptors** who live behind the bakery, just off the frontage road.

Dried local bananas, a Marquesan specialty, are a lovely treat, but you'll have to ask around to find them. They are generally not sold in stores.

TAIPIVAI If you are interested in purchasing carvings in the Taipivai area contact **Pukiki**, the local policeman, and he'll put you in contact with a craftsman. ~ Taipivai; 92-01-26, 92-04-28.

NIGHTLIFE Offering a splendid view, the Keikahanui Inn is a good place to imbibe in the evening, particularly during happy hour from 4 to 6 p.m.

When yachts are in town, the bar/restaurant is filled with Americans. On Fridays, it's the only place in town with live music. The rest of the time Keikahanaui is pretty quiet. ~ Taioha'e; 92-03-82.

The **Hotel Moana Nui** is *the* place in town to sip coffee or a beer and watch the world go by. It's also a good spot to meet locals or other travelers. ~ Taioha'e; 92-03-30.

TAIOHA'E   Taioha'e Beach ⤳ Taioha'e Beach, fronting the eastern side of the village, is a long stretch of golden sand. On shore there are plenty of shade trees, while offshore the water is often abob with yachts. The beach is usually clean and is popular with locals, especially on weekends. However, if there are yachts around, keep an eye out for raw sewage and skip the swimming. ~ To find Taioha'e Beach, walk to the west end of town along the frontage road.

BEACHES

TAIPIVAI AND NORTHEAST COAST   Anaho Beach ⤳ This white-sand beach is one of the best in the Marquesas. Protected from the wind and offering plenty of shade, it is a crescent-shaped strand, approximately two kilometers long. Swimming is excellent. Snorkelers can take advantage of the coral reef, and with a bit of luck, spot a turtle or white-tip reef shark (*moko*). Be prepared to cover up or protect yourself from *nonos*, which can be a problem. A freshwater tap is available here and it's possible to purchase beer or soft drinks at nearby Pension Anaho. ~ The access trail is an easy, two-kilometer trek over a 1700-foot (500-meter) pass from the village of Hatiheu.

◄ HIDDEN

Xavier, the local dive operator, reckons that diving in the Marquesas is altogether an entirely different experience than you'll find elsewhere in French Polynesia. You don't have to dive as deeply—40 to 60 feet (12 to 18 meters) is the maximum you need to go—to see a multitude of undersea life, including such pelagics as pygmy orcas and tuna. Xavier also does quite a bit of cave diving, including a visit to a particular cave that is packed with lobsters. Few people dive these waters, so the sealife is generally not frightened of humans.

Outdoor Adventures

DIVING

At **Sentinelle Aux Marteaux** (Sentinel of the Hammerheads) you can see spotted leopard rays, lion fish, groupers and black-tipped reef sharks. (The best time to see hammerheads is January through July.)

Scuba diving in Taioha'e is available through **Centre Plongee Marquises**, which opened in 1993 and is the only dive operation in the Marquesas. Operated by Xavier Curvat (known locally as Pipapo) and Thierry Sicard, it offers dives to about 20 sites near Taioha'e. Xavier speaks English and has lived in the Marquesas for a number of years. He offers packaged trips that include accommodation in Taioha'e as well as trips to Ua Pou. ~ Taioha'e; 92-00-88.

HIKING   **Hatiheu to Anaho** (1.25 miles/2 kilometers) is one of the nicest short hikes on the island. You can easily do a day hike over to Anaho, enjoy the beach, then hike back. It only takes about an hour to 90 minutes (round-trip). The Hatiheu side is steep, slippery and potentially muddy, so wear good hiking shoes or sandals. Along the way you'll see spectacular views of Anaho Bay and neighboring Haatuatua Bay. As you continue along the trail, the views only get better. One panorama offers a scene of Haatuatua and Anaho bays. If you are fortunate, a nice easterly breeze will cool you off. ~ To find the trailhead in Hatiheu, take the first road to the left of Yvonne's restaurant (where the town hall is located). This leads uphill and eventually becomes the trail to Anaho Bay. Keep going straight uphill (don't take the right turn).

Tohua Hikokua (1 mile/1.6 kilometers). There are two archeological ruin sites near Hatiheu. One of them, a huge rock face with petroglyphs, is one of the best in the islands. Tohua Hikokua resembles a soccer field with stone bleachers. There are three ornate *tiki*, but they're new. Although they look weathered, they are not the authentic old stone variety. If you look closely, you'll note there are three old *tiki* in the wall of the platform. The *tohua* is still used by traditional dancers, who often perform for visitors. As you approach the *tohua* from the road, look for the large phallus sculpture on your left near the corner of the platform. It's at least 150 years old and is about three feet (one meter) in height. It is believed that if an infertile woman touches this rock it will help her become pregnant. ~ To get there, begin by facing the church. Take the beachfront road to the right. Continue along the road, which winds uphill to the left. From town, it's about a 15- to 20-minute walk up to Tohua Hikokua.

To reach **Kamuihei** (.75 mile/1 kilometer), a massive *tohua* site in the Hatiheu area, continue up the main road toward Taipivai about one kilometer and look for a massive banyan tree on your left-hand side. The tree is sacred and marks the trail to the petroglyphs. (Ask a local to take you because the petroglyphs are not easy to spot.) The track is not clearly marked (there are several paths that meander back and forth across each other) and is covered with wet leaves and large mossy rocks. It can be quite slippery so take care. Streams trickle down alongside the trail and there are more banyan trees with long tangled roots along the way. The scene is quite eerie, in a beautiful way—exactly what a movie producer might come up with when filming Melville's *Typee*. The trail wanders past the banyans to a small grove. (It takes about ten minutes). At this point look for a large rock (about six feet/two meters high) with petroglyphs of turtles and fish. A rock cairn marks the site—the petroglyphs are on the other side of the rock from the trail. Although the age of the petroglyphs is unknown, they are thought to be much older than most of the *tiki* in the Marquesas.

Just beyond the petroglyph site at Kamuihei is a **tohua complex**, approximately 300 yards long. Located in the midst of dark jungle filled with the sounds of strange birds, it is a massive jumble of boulders and stone platforms. The site is slated to be restored at some point, but even in its present state it gives you a clear idea of the enormity of the construction projects that took place in ancient times. One should not miss Kamuihei if you are in the neighborhood. ~ To find the Kamuihei tohua complex, walk up the main road from Hatiheu in the direction of Taipivai, about one kilometer, and look for the massive banyan tree on your left-hand side.

A visit to the **Hakaui Falls** (4 miles/6.4 kilometers) can be done two ways, one quite simple, the other rather arduous. The recommended method is to charter a boat from Taioha'e for a 20-minute ride around the coast. You will then be let off at the trailhead to the falls. From there it's a two-hour walk (one-way) through the jungle to the magnificent, 1148-foot (350-meter) falls, the highest in the Pacific islands, and among the highest in the world. Someone from the boat will accompany you to the spot. The other way to reach Hakaui Falls is to trek from Taioha'e overland. It takes about four hours along precipitous coastal ridges to get to the falls' cut off. After reaching the Hakaui trail, it's another two hours to reach the falls. The coastal trail has recently been improved by the government and although a guide is not necessary, it is recommended to hire one. The round-trip walk takes about 12 hours, not including a lunch break. That's a lot of walking for one day! If you simply want to see some of the coastline, it might be better to walk part of the coastal trail and leave the falls for another time. Naturally, you will want to take a picnic lunch and plenty of water. ~ To get there by boat costs about 12,000 CFP for the charter. Check with Rose Corser for charter information. 92-03-82. It is probably a good idea to check with Deborah Kimitete at the Urban Planning/Tourism office at the old jailhouse to find out what condition the trail is in before you set off. Taioha'e; 92-02-02.

◄ **HIDDEN**

The waters off Nuku Hiva are rich in sealife and it's possible to hook mahimahi, tuna and other large fish. There are, however, no regular charter vessels that specialize in deep-sea fishing here. If you are interested in trying your luck call **Rose Corser** at the Kekahanui and she can arrange a boat charter. ~ Taioha'e; 92-03-82.

FISHING

For those of you with several weeks of traveling time on your hands, a sailboat is the best way to truly see the Marquesas. Well-heeled visitors can charter a yacht from **Archipels Croisiers Polynesiennes** in Papeete. They also have a yacht in Nuku Hiva that visits Ua Pou, Hiva Oa, Tahuata and Ua Huka. It's possible to fly directly into Nuku Hiva, and transfer immediately to the yacht. ~ Papeete; 56-36-39, fax 56-35-87.

SAILING

ISLAND TOURS

Most tours in Nuku Hiva originate in Taioha'e. However, the term "tour" is misleading. If you don't speak French, a tour will be little more than a taxi ride to an archeological site with no understandable commentary.

From Taioha'e there are three day trips that you should not miss: the Taipivi Valley and various archeological sites; the village of Hatiheu and nearby Anaho; and Hakaui Falls.

Taipivai and its environs (including Hatiheu and Anaho) can be done in one day, but it will be a long day if you are to see everything. My advice would be to start early. Taipivai (sometimes referred to as Taipi) is a one-and-a-half hour drive from Taioha'e over Muake Pass, past a commercial teak grove and into Taipivai Valley. (Upon your descent into the valley, apply insect repellent.) Cost for the tour (to hire the four-wheel-drive vehicle) is 12,000 CFP if you just go to Taipivai Valley or 15,000 CFP if you go on to Hatiheu, which is another half-hour or so down the rocky road. There are two major archeological sites to visit in the narrow Taipivai Valley, including Site Melville, where author Herman Melville spent several months, and the Pa'eke area.

In order to truly see Taipivai you should stay at a local pension such as Chez Pukiki. Pukiki can organize tours to archeological sites and make sure that you get back to Taioha'e and/or the airport. (The perennial problem in the Marquesas is getting from Point A to Point B when you want to.) ~ Taipivai; 92-01-26.

A visit to Hatiheu with lunch at Chez Yvonne Katupa should be on your agenda. She is the mayor of Hatiheu and quite helpful at organizing local tours to the various archeological sites—especially if you plan to stay at her pension. If you plan to have lunch with her in Hatiheu on a day trip, make a reservation. Be sure to stop by her office in the village to see artifacts from the famous Ha'atuatua archeological digs. From Hatiheu you can take a 50-minute trek over the hill to Anaho Bay. Hatiheu also has three wonderful archeological sites a short distance from the village that should be on your agenda. ~ Hatiheu; 92-02-97.

Nuku Hiva **Heli Pacific** provides helicopter tours around Nuku Hiva and neighboring islands. (One-way helicopter fare is 6900 CFP.) ~ The office is in downtown Taioha'e, east of the town hall. Taioha'e; 92-05-21.

▼▼▼▼▼▼▼▼▼
Ua Huka

Ua Huka, 897 miles (1448 kilometers) northeast of Papeete, is around 50 square miles (129 square kilometers) in area and has a population of about 600. Much of inland and upland Ua Huka is arid, rocky grassland sprinkled with shrubs. The desiccated nature of much of the island most likely has to do with the overgrazing caused by the ubiquitous wild horses and goats that roam the land. There is, however, dense vegetation in the Vaipae'e,

Hane and Hokatu areas. The inland valleys are deep, well-watered and bounded by steep cliffs. Off Ua Huka's southwest coast are small islands with extensive bird colonies.

Ua Huka is the flattest and driest of the Marquesas. The island was never popular with early traders because it lacked sandalwood and a protected anchorage, but today its tiny airstrip, located between Vaipae'e and Hane, is serviced once a week by connections to other Marquesas islands and Tahiti.

Most early Polynesians steered clear of Ua Huka because of the scarcity of water. However, those who did set down roots found large quantities of nesting birds and manta rays, both good food sources. Today, people live in three friendly villages scattered along the southern coast. The tiny villages cling to the valley floors and feature tidy little homes. One small road connects the villages.

SIGHTS

The Vaiape'e museum, **Community Museum of Ua Huka**, is a must-see for visitors. It was designed and produced by Marquesan artisans along with cultural authorities and displays a collection of very unusual artifacts. They are grouped by specific areas within the workings of the ancient culture: food preparation, fishing, carving and handicrafts and funeral rites. The museum also contains some material excavated in the 1960s from the Hane Valley beach dune site. Joseph Vaatete, the curator of the museum and resident stone- and woodcarver, is a distinguished artist in his own right. Admission is free to the museum. ~ A 20-minute walk inland from the boat landing, it is located in the town's center.

Over the years, Ua Huka has been deforested by wild horses and goats. In an attempt to "re-vegetate" the island, the mayor has created a **botanical and plant nursery**, which makes an interesting stop. The nursery features more than 400 species of flora, including 120 varieties of citrus plants, the largest collection in the Pacific. There is no admission; the arboretum is open to the general public from 6:30 a.m. to 2:30 p.m. Monday through Friday. ~ It's located between the villages of Vaipae'e and Hane on Ua Huka's main road.

Other sightseeing attractions on Ua Huka are the ruins located high in the Hane Valley, several with

Ua Huka

N

Haunanu
Point

Mt Hitikau
2903'
▲

Hane

Vaipae'e   Hokatu

Haavai   Vaipae'e   Taoho Ote
Bay   Bay   Papa Point
          Tekaho
Hemeni   Point
Island   0   3 miles

              0   3 kilometers

HIDDEN ► ancient tiki. This area is known as a *me'ae*, a sacred place where ancestors are buried. Among the more interesting artifacts here is a replica of the famous "pregnant woman" tiki from Puamau on Hiva Oa. ~ The ruins are located about 30 minutes by car from the airstrip. Ask a guide to take you; they are off the road and involve a short hike.

The vista from the high plateau, excursions to Vaikivi Valley and the Bird Islands near Haavai Bay on the southern coast are also worth checking out. It is possible to reach the **Bird Islands**, which are rocky outcroppings, by boat. Once there, at a prudent distance, it's possible to observe the thousands of birds nesting on the stony surface. (Warning: Climbing on these rocks can be very dangerous.)

The highest point on the island, at 2903 feet (885 meters), is **Mt. Hitikau**, which overlooks Vaipae'e. For an eye-popping panorama, climb the mountain to see the *Aranui* as it snakes its way into Vaipae'e Bay and turns around, with literally inches to spare.

Ua Huka is the home of the blue lorikeet, a gorgeous bird called *pihiti* by locals.

Exploring the plateaus of Ua Huka on the back of a horse is a wonderful way to see this compact island. **Joseph Lichtle** provides mountain and seashore rides. ~ Haavai; 92-60-72. **Alexis Fournier** also offers horseback rides. ~ Vaipae'e; 92-60-05.

Local vessels, with captains, can be hired for sightseeing or fishing trips (about 2000 CFP an hour) weather permitting. In Vaipae'e try **Hubert Fournier** ~ 92-61-24 or **Alexis Fournier** ~ 92-60-05.

LODGING **Chez Alexis Scallamera** is a four-room house. Guest rooms are large, airy and colorfully decorated with floral print carpet and curtains; each has one double bed and one single. There are two communal bathrooms. *Pension complete* is available. Alexis is an excellent English-speaking guide who provides excursions around the island and round-trip transfers from the airport. The pension is located seven kilometers east of the airport and two kilometers west of the dock. ~ Vaipae'e; 92-60-19, 92-61-16. BUDGET.

Hubert Fournier has a large house with several guest rooms. He also offers *pension complete*. I've received good reviews about his lodging and tours. ~ Vaipae'e; 92-61-24. BUDGET.

Auberge Hitikau is an inn-style accommodation consisting of a duplex home with four rooms, each with a double bed. There's a communal bath, a restaurant/bar and excellent excursions to the valleys and to the Bird Islands off Haavai Bay. The Hane Valley *tiki* are a humid 25-minute uphill climb from here. The one report I have had about this lodging was not glowing. Located seven kilometers from the airport. ~ Hane; 92-60-68. BUDGET TO MODERATE.

Chez Maurice et Delphine offers a house with two rooms, each with a double bed. There is an equipped kitchen and two bathrooms with hot water, a salon with sofas and a terrace with mountain and ocean views. *Pension complete* is available. Round-trip transfer to the airport is 4000 CFP. It's 12 kilometers from the airport. ~ Hokatu; 92-60-55. BUDGET.

Chez Joseph Lichtle is close to the sea, with a backdrop of rocky brown hillsides reminiscent of the Baja California desert. You'll find two bungalows, each with a double bed, private bathroom, electricity and an oceanview terrace. There are also two houses, each with three rooms (with double beds), common kitchens and bathrooms. Located in remote Haavai Valley on the western side of Ua Huka, this accommodation is 12 kilometers from the airport and 25 kilometers from the dock. I've been told that this is perhaps the island's best lodging facility. Joseph is a very self-sufficient fellow and raises fresh vegetables and fruit as well as cattle, pigs, chickens and ducks. An amateur archaeologist, he has a small display of Marquesan artifacts and offers excursions to archeological sites as well as the Bird Islands. Transfers from the *quai* at Vaipae'e to the pension is 2500 CFP one-way. ~ Haavai; 92-60-72. BUDGET.

◄ HIDDEN

GROCERIES Several small markets in Vaipae'e stock essentials like matches, cigarettes and mosquito coils; sometimes fresh vegetables are available.

SHOPPING Woodcarving is still practiced in Ua Huka; each of the three main valleys has a carving exposition or display area with works from island artisans. If you plan to purchase carvings in the Marquesas, these outlets are worth checking out. The quality is often excellent and prices are reasonable. Expect to pay around 5000 CFP on up for a good-quality bowl. ~ The expositions are in Vaipae'e (near the museum), Hane (near the post office) and Hokatu (near the beach).

Carvings may also be purchased from individual craftspeople. Ask at the small museum in Vaipae'e for names of artists.

BEACHES There are many small beaches reachable by horse or on foot. But be warned, they're infested with *nonos*, making them quite unpleasant.

Ua Pou

Ua Pou means "Two Posts" or "Two Peaks," which refers to the two massive volcanic spires—Pou Maka at 3264 feet (1043 meters) and Pou Te Tai Nui at 4040 feet (1232 meters—that seem to brush the clouds. The two peaks accentuate the island's jagged, scarplike relief. Both mountains are plugs extruded from the throats of extinct volcanoes. There are six main valleys, most with lush green vegetation, bounded by exceedingly steep cliffs.

Where you arrive on Ua Pou will depend on your mode of transportation. The *Aranui* stops at Hakahau and Hakahetau. Vessels from Nuku Hiva stop in Hakahau as do the taxi services from the airfield (which is located between Hakahau and Hakahetau). If you have a vehicle and a driver, it's possible to get just about anywhere. There's a dirt road that circles the perimeter of the island.

SIGHTS   **Hakahau,** the principle village on the island, sits on the shore of a
crescent beach. The community extends onto a large valley floor.
While in the village you feel like you are in a natural cathedral—
two tall spired peaks tower magnificently overhead.

A manmade cathedral, the local **Catholic church,** lies in the
shadow of nature's sanctuary. Of particular interest in the church
are the exquisite carvings decorating the interior. This is in keeping
with island tradition—residents often fashion stone and wood carvings and weave hats and mats. The church is open to the public.

Hakahau has a small administrative complex near the airport
and the requisite shops, bank, hospital and post office.

HIDDEN ►   The holiest ancient temple on Ua Pou is **Te Menaha Taka'oa.**
The monument was sacred to the local god Te Atua Heato, who was
said to be "white" (i.e., not tattooed). The site was considered quite
tapu (forbidden) up to the late 1800s when it was visited by the
German ethnologist Karl von den Steinen. You will need a guide to
take you there. ~ Contact Georges Toti Teikiehuupoko; 92-53-21.

Ua Pou is the only place in the world, other than Brazil, where
"flower stones" are found. Volcanic in origin, these curiosities are
dark brown stones with yellow flower-like patterns. Ua Pou was
also the source of gray-green *phonelite*, which was traded in pre-
contact days throughout the Marquesas and was used to make
flake tools for woodworking, for butchering animals and as weapons. Called *Klinksteine* in German, the moniker accurately refers
to the sound when the stone is struck—a bell-like ring. You can
find these stones all over Ua Pou.

Also of interest, just off the southern shore, is the islet **Motu
Oa,** which is a sanctuary for thousands of nesting terns. This area
is fragile ecologically, so visiting from a distance by boat is urged.
Bring your binoculars. ~ Contact your pension for more information on transportation.

LODGING   Looking anything but Polynesian, **Chez Marguerite Dordillon** consists of a tidy two-bedroom home with a brown-shingle roof. It has
a double bed in one room and two singles in the other. There is a
large living room and communal bath. No food is available. To get
there it's a two-minute walk from the dock and ten kilometers from
the airport. ~ Hakahau; 92-53-15. BUDGET.

To experience genuine Marquesan hospitality, stay at **Chez
Samuel and Jeanne-Marie.** This lodging consists of two structures,
each with a kitchen and two bedrooms with double beds. The bath
arrangement is communal, and in typical Marquesan style, cold
water is the rule. The pension is one kilometer from the dock, eight
kilometers from the airport. Marquesan cuisine is served at breakfast, lunch and dinner. ~ Hakahau; 92-53-16. MODERATE.

Pension Vaikaka is a large, airy A-frame–shaped structure with
bamboo wall. A basic, no-frills place with two single bunks with

private bath, it is a good bargain for wallet watchers. Vaikaka is located two kilometers from the dock, 13 kilometers from the airport. Contact Valja Klima. ~ Hakahau; 92-53-37. BUDGET.

In a very remote location offering little diversion is **Pension Paeaka**. It consists of a house with a room with a single and double bed, a salon, bath and a kitchen. The pension is in the village of Haakuti, about one kilometer from Haakuti Bay. Contact Marie-Augustine Aniamioi. ~ Haakuti; 92-53-96. BUDGET.

DINING

Chez Adrienne has Marquesan, Chinese and French dishes. Her speciality is seafood. ~ Hakahau; 92-52-16. BUDGET TO MODERATE.

Snack Vehine at Hakahau is worth checking out, but not just for the Marquesan and French cuisine. The owner, Georges Toti Teikiehuupoko, is the president of Motu Haka (the Society for the Preservation of Marquesan Culture) and is well-versed in local lore. ~ Hakahau; 92-53-21. BUDGET TO MODERATE.

GROCERIES

There are several grocery stores in Hakahau. Most are attached to homes. I liked shopping at **Rosalie Tata's**, where you can purchase limited groceries and other items. Basics items can also be found at **Magasin Haeapa** ~ 92-51-77 and **Magasin Mokohe** ~ 92-52-08.

SHOPPING

Kanahau Boutique sells postcards, photos, Marquesan music tapes and clothing, and cold soft drinks. ~ Hakahau; 92-53-41.

Ua Pou islanders are talented woodcarvers and weavers. Sales of their crafts are usually made at the individual's home. To locate a woodcarver or weaver, ask around.

BEACHES

ANAHOA BEACH ~ This fine strand of white sand on Anahoa Bay occupies the equivalent of several city blocks. In the distance are sloping hills and close by you'll find shade trees. The beach is regularly treated with insecticide so *nonos* shouldn't be a problem. The big waves are tempting to bodysurf, but there is an undertow—swim with caution! There are no facilities. ~ The beach is a 40-minute walk north of Hakahau.

HOHOI BEACH ~ The small beach at Hohoi is famous for its "flower stones." They are volcanic in origin and colored dark brown with yellow, flower-like patterns. Unfortunately, they are becoming more difficult to find because locals pick them to sell to tourists. ~ The beach is located about 12 kilometers south of the airport on the southeast coast of the island. You can walk, but it is easier to catch a ride with a local resident.

Outdoor Adventures

FISHING

Fishing for pelagics off the island is very good and one can hook tuna, mahimahi, or even marlin and sailfish. Expect to pay around US$350 for half a day. It is possible to charter boats from any of the captains listed. For charters in Hakatao Village, contact: **Alain Ah Lo** ~ 92-52-80, **Etienne Kohumoetini** ~ 92-53-17/24, **Felix Tata** ~ 92-53-39 and **Ruka Kaiha** ~ 92-53-30.

RIDING STABLES

Horseback riding is a great way to get around the island and guided tours can be organized. Horses and tours are available in Hakahau from **Albert and Atere Kohumoetini** ~ 92-52-28, **Francis Aka** ~ 92-51-83 and **Jules Hituputoka** ~ 92-53-32.

HIKING

Hakahau Vista (1.5 miles/2 kilometers). For one of the island's most spectacular views, follow the track to the cross on top of the hill overlooking the village. Here you'll have a crow's nest view of the Hakahau Bay and Anahoa Beach, which fringes a secluded cove on the other side of the mountain.

For the adventurous, there is the **Hakahetau to Hakahau** (5 miles/9 kilometers) hike. Little shade is provided so it can be brutally hot in the mid-day sun. There is only one track— basically follow the road north, past the airport, up and down the ridge from Hakahetau to Hakahau along the coast. It takes three hours and offers some dramatic vistas.

GUIDED HIKING TOURS Christian Kervella speaks English fluently and operates **Excursions Guides**, offering motorized tours and treks. He has a number of selections, including an eight-day trek for US$840, with meals and all equipment included. Day trips to archeological sites and other points of interest are also available. ~ Hakahau; 92-53-89.

Georges Toti Teikiehuupoko is a school teacher and president of Motu Haka, the Society for the Preservation of Marquesan Culture. He arranges trips to the most sacred temple on Ua Pou, Te Menaha Taka'oa. Georges imparts something of the old culture to visitors. ~ Hakahau; 92-53-21.

Hiva Oa

Hiva Oa is perhaps best known as the burial place of Paul Gauguin. The island was originally named *La Dominica* by Alvaro de Mendaña when he discovered it on a Sunday in 1595. Almost 300 years later, Robert Louis Stevenson said of the island, "I thought it the loveliest, and by far the most ominous spot

To Swim or Not to Swim in the Marquesas

Going to the beach is not generally an option in the Marquesas Islands. I do not encourage you to swim there unless you are accompanied by a local resident. And you will rarely see a local swimming in the water. (This should tell you something!) Swimming is possible, but you need to be aware of the following:

Pollution

Swimming near a village or area where yachts are moored is definitely not a good idea. Cesspools empty into the sea and yachts release their effluents in the open water.

Currents

If the beach is not too infested with *nonos* and is swimmable, the currents and rip tides can be very dangerous. Exercise caution.

Marine life

The waters off of the Marquesas are renowned for the variety (and number) of sharks—hammerhead, tiger, blue-, black- and white-tip, bronze whalers—and rays. You may also find jellyfish and possibly stone fish (extremely toxic) lurking about. I recommend that only experienced divers attempt to explore these waters.

on earth." To this day it still retains a paradox of wild beauty and somber bearing.

Very little of the island's 200 square miles (518 square kilometers) is flat. There are rocky, unpaved roads to most of the island's communities. Major routes run east to west along the spine of the island and also along the southern coast. The airstrip, which was built at the geographic center of Hiva Oa, is about five kilometers north of Atuona. Dirt tracks and horse trails provide access to the spectacular north coast.

SIGHTS   The main settlement on the island is **Atuona**, the second-largest town in the Marquesas. Towering 3903 feet (1190 meters) above Atuona is **Mt. Temetiu**, the island's highest peak. Atuona sits on the shores of **Traitors Bay**, which was created when the sea flooded a tremendous crater eons ago. The village is constructed on a slope at the base of a large valley. To the east, it is bounded by a very precipitous cliff—the highest on the island.

The largest building in town is the boarding school for girls, run by the sisters of St. Joseph of Cluny. There are about half a dozen stores, a hospital and dentist's office, one bank (Socredo), two restaurants and a variety of lodging possibilities.

The population of Atuona is about 1700, only a vestige of the large population the island once had. Many homes are built on the foundations of *paepae* (ancient stone platforms). At one time there were many large *tiki* on the island, but most have now been scattered to museums around the world.

The final resting place of Paul Gauguin and Jacques Brel, the well-known Belgian singer, are in the **Calvary Cemetery**. Brel spent his last years on Hiva Oa and died in 1978. Gauguin's monument is a simple stone marker and a small statue of a Polynesian woman known as "Ovira." Brel's tomb has a bas-relief of him, along with his female companion. ~ To get to their graves, take the uphill road that begins at the Gendarmerie. It's a ten-minute walk.

HIDDEN ►   Another landmark to visit is Brel's **Belvédère**, the site of Brel's home perched above the east side of the valley above Tahauku. The view of town and the bay is stunning from this vantage point. ~ To get there take the road to the airport. The path begins behind the Hotel Hanakee. If in doubt, ask for directions at the hotel.

To further explore the life of Paul Gauguin, visit the **Gauguin Museum**. Both attractive and well designed, it focuses, of course, on Paul Gauguin, who lived very close to the present museum building, and also on Victor Segalen, a French official who resided in the islands after Gauguin's death and wrote extensively about the painter. The museum documents Gauguin's work in French Polynesia and blends aspects of Marquesan culture with the Gauguin material. ~ Atuona.

Right next door is a reproduction of Gauguin's residence, **La Maison du Jouir** (The House of Pleasure), a two-story affair with woven bamboo walls, thatched roof and a carved doorway and trim.

TAAOA VALLEY ARCHEOLOGICAL SITES The most interesting archeological site to visit on the south central coast of Hiva Oa is the immense restored **ceremonial center** at the head of **Taaoa Valley**, west of Atuona. The name of the Taaoa site is unknown, but it includes a large Nuku Hiva–style rectangular ceremonial plaza, or *tohua*, with many cut-stone facings. This type of fully enclosed *tohua*, constructed with extremely large stones, is very rare on Hiva Oa. Extending up the hill above the plaza, you'll find a series of temples with sacred banyan trees, and at least one **mortuary platform**, where the dead were exposed for preparation for burial. On one of the uppermost platforms stands a basalt column

◄ *HIDDEN*

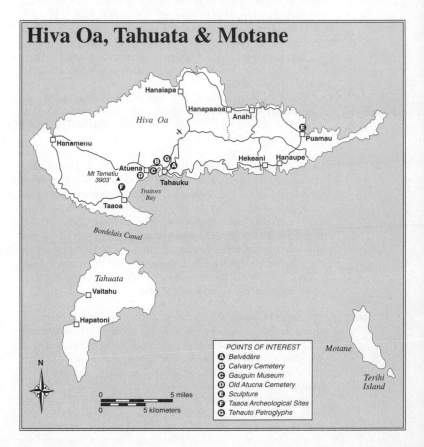

Hiva Oa, Tahuata & Motane

Hanaiapa

Hiva Oa

Hanapaaoa   Anahi

Hanamenu

Puamau

E

Atuena   B G
       D C   A
       Tahauku

Hekeani   Hanaupe

Mt Temetiu
3903' ▲
       F
       Taaoa

Traitors Bay

Bordelais Canal

Tahuata

Vaitahu

Hapatoni

POINTS OF INTEREST
Ⓐ *Belvédère*
Ⓑ *Calvary Cemetery*
Ⓒ *Gauguin Museum*
Ⓓ *Old Atucna Cemetery*
Ⓔ *Sculpture*
Ⓕ *Taaoa Archeological Sites*
Ⓖ *Teheuto Petroglyphs*

Motane

Terihi Island

N

0   5 miles
0   5 kilometers

with traditional *tiki* features carved in low relief. This is said to represent the god Hu'upeke. According to legend, human sacrifices were killed on the *tohua* at the lower end of the complex and carried up and placed on top of this image. Another unusual feature of the complex is the wall that divides the site into units, each containing several structures. These were said to have marked the limits to which different castes were admitted during ritual ceremonies. Make sure you take your mosquito repellent while admiring these Marquesan handiworks. ~ To get there you must take a car or truck about ten kilometers west of Atuona on the coastal road. When you arrive at the phone booth follow the trailhead inland to the archeological sites.

Hiva Oa is one of the few places in the Marquesas where you can rent a car and make your own way around.

PUAMAU The precipitous coastal road (heading west) between **Puamau** and the village of **Anahi** offers panoramas of an absolutely stunning coastline, akin to the rugged, fiordlike coast of Norway or Scotland. It consists of a series of fingerlike promontories jutting into the sea, all carpeted with lush green vegetation.

Just west of Anahi is the village of Hanapaaoa another of those subtly eye-catching little Marquesan hamlets tucked beneath the island's craggy reaches.

HIDDEN ►

On the northeast coast, near the village of Puamau, are the largest **stone sculptures** in the Marquesas. These measure close to seven feet (two meters). The **tiki** of Puamau, at Me'ae Te I'i Pona, are very late in origin, most likely 1700–1750 A.D. Some anthropologists consider them to be archeological links to the *tiki* on Easter Island and those of Necker Island near Hawaii. The detached stone heads at Puamau are said to be representations of victims offered by leaders of the Naiki tribe, which formerly inhabited Puamau. Legend has it that the prone figure is that of Maki'i Tau'a Pepe, a priestess who died in childbirth in great agony. (Maki'i means "death agony.") (Ancient Marquesans believed that women who died in childbirth became malevolent spirits that had to be appeased through worship.) Admission. ~ To get there, hire a guide or get directions in Puamau village. The site is at the base of a large promontory on the east side of the valley.

LODGING

The **Atuona Commune Bungalows** consist of three small units each with a double bed, shower, bathroom, electricity, refrigerator and hot plate. In addition, there are two larger double bungalows, each with two rooms, two double beds, shower, bathroom, gas stove and a veranda. These units, which are owned and managed by the local government, are very well equipped and are a good bargain. There is no meal program, so be prepared to cook your own food or patronize the local restaurants. Bring your mosquito net with you, as there will be plenty of these pests to greet you in the rooms. A room must be booked at the *mairie* (city hall) during office hours. Atuona Commune Bungalows are located in "downtown" Atuona. ~ Atuona; 92-73-37, fax 92-74-95. BUDGET.

Offering a good value, **Temetiu Village** has three bungalows—two of which have a single room with a double bed. The third bungalow has two rooms with three single beds each. There is also a living room with a small library, television and video. All of the units have private baths. There is a good restaurant on the premises. Activities include visits to archeological sites, snorkeling trips and picnics. They do accept MasterCard and Eurocard. Transfer from the airport and back is 2000 CFP. Temetiu Village is one kilometer from Atuona on the main road. ~ Atuona; 92-73-02. MODERATE.

Pension Gauguin is a modest two-story building with four clean rooms, each with a double bed. There are two communal baths with hot water, a salon and a large terrace upstairs with an ocean view. The owner, Andre Tessier, is a pleasant, well-informed guide and provides excursions around Hiva Oa and Tahuata, as well as visits to archeological sites and fishing trips. The food served here is very good also. The house is on the main road, a five-minute walk east of Atuona. ~ Atuona; 92-73-51. MODERATE.

◄ HIDDEN

In Puamau, **Chez Bernard Heita'a** is a house with two rooms, each with a double bed. There's electricity, a common bathroom and kitchen. The advantage of staying at Chez Bernard is its proximity to the *tiki*, which are within easy walking distance. (It's also advantageous because Bernard is the mayor of Puamau.) On the downside, Chez Bernard is extremely isolated, especially if you need to get to Atuona. Transfers from the airport to the pension are a stiff 15,000 CFP. ~ Puamau; 92-72-27. BUDGET TO MODERATE.

Restaurant Hoa Nui (translated means "big friend") blends Chinese and Marquesan cuisines. It is clearly the best eatery in town. Their specialty is freshwater shrimp, which is very good, as is the deep-fried breadfruit. ~ Atuona; 92-73-63. BUDGET TO MODERATE.

DINING

At the hotel **Temetiu Village** you'll find a seafood restaurant that specializes in lobster and shrimp. ~ Atuona; 92-73-02. MODERATE.

Several snack shops dot the town of Atuona. **Snack Atuona** is located across the street from the post office and has basic local fare. **Snack Maire** serves Marquesan and Chinese dishes. **Snack MakeMake** specializes in Chinese food. Here you'll find both good quality and generous portions. ~ 92-74-26. ALL BUDGET.

Snack Tahauku is a beer/snack stand in Tahauku, located in a nearby bay about one and a half kilometers east of Atuona. Spare but friendly, it's the kind of place you go to meet the local population. ~ Tahauku; 92-75-06. BUDGET.

There are several markets in Atuona where groceries and other necessities can be purchased. These include **Magasin Mowsang** ~ 92-73-49 and **Magasin Pierre Shan** ~ 92-73-47.

GROCERIES

SHOPPING   Those interested in purchasing sculptures or precious woods from Marquesan forests such as *tou*, sandalwood and *mi'o iu* (rosewood) can contact **Guy Huhina** by asking for him at the Gauguin Museum.

Gauguin T-shirts are available at several of the shops on Atuona's main street. Next door to the general store is a **handicrafts shop** with fine wood carvings and reproductions of various Marquesan artifacts.

The **Gauguin Museum** has great postcards. ~ Atuona.

See **Jeanine Moreau** at the Gauguin Museum for woven baskets. ~ Atuona; 92-74-22.

BEACHES   **PUAMAU BEACH**   Just east of Puamau village is a long white-sand beach with shade trees that fringes the shores of Puamau Bay. The backdrop is the gently sloping hillside that frames a wide, expansive valley. Swimming here is terrific, but near the church is best. There is no undertow and you can bodysurf when the conditions are right. However, the pounding waves can be very strong so use caution. Fresh water is available and you can buy provisions in the nearby village, a 15-minute walk away. ~ The beach is located just off the road between the dock and Puamau village.

▼▼▼▼▼▼▼▼▼▼▼▼▼▼▼
Outdoor Adventures

As in all of the islands in the Marquesas Group, fishing is quite good. A variety of pelagic fish such as tuna and mahimahi can be snagged. Those interested should call **Andre Tessier** of Pension Gauguin. ~ Atuona; 92-73-51.

FISHING

HIKING   For a short excursion, take the **Old Atuona Cemetery and beyond** (1.5 miles/2 kilometers) hike. It is an older graveyard than the Calvary Cemetery where Gauguin is buried and is located on the west end of the village. There's a wonderful view of the village below and the rugged coastline. If you continue walking for several more minutes you'll reach an ancient *paepae* (stone platform). ~ To get there walk to the bridge past the public school at the end of Atuona and take the road to the right. After about a ten-minute walk take the road to the left—there's no sign pointing to the cemetery—for another 30 minutes, until you reach the site.

The Marquesas kingfisher, found only on Hiva Oa, is in imminent danger of extinction.

It is possible to visit the various archeological sites around the island by foot on the **Atuona to Hanapaaoa** (10 miles/16 kilometers) trek. Some locations require guides and some don't. The trek from Atuona to Hanapaaoa through the center of the island is of medium difficulty, but I highly recommend that you take a guide. The length of the trek is about four hours (one way). ~ The trailhead is on the outskirts of Atuona, but it is best to ask a local for directions. Better yet, take a guide with you.

Paradise
Nearly Lost

Resting midway between Australia and South America, the Marquesas are isolated as is no other landfall on earth. Given their detachment, one would think the ecosystems found on the islands have remained intact and un-blemished. Not so. Over the years, horses and goats have rapidly chewed up native vegetation like hoofed locusts. Birds brought in to combat vermin now edge out rare native species. On every island, rats and cats introduced by Europeans have attacked indigenous birds, and have had few prey to control their own populations.

The onslaught of introduced flora and fauna started long ago when the original Polynesian settlers arrived bringing yams, taro, pigs and even their own species of rats to the islands. The "Polynesian" rat inevitably upset the indigenous ecosystem but probably did less damage than the smaller, common European or Norwegian rat that arrived on European ships. The more aggressive European species preys on young birds and eggs and has been quite injurious to indigenous bird populations. Rats are the biggest threat to the beautiful ultramarine lorikeet found only in the Marquesas. Today, fortunately, on Fatu Hiva the lorikeet is being saved from extinction.

Unfortunately, things are not going as well for the Marquesas kingfisher, which is found only on Hiva Oa. The kingfishers' difficulties started when the great horned owl was introduced to combat the rat population. The owls developed a taste for the kingfishers as well as the rats. Consequently, the kingfisher is slowly dying out.

Europeans were not the only people to introduce predators of rare native flora and fauna. Polynesians bear just as much blame. On Nuku Hiva, the biggest threat to the indigenous Nuku Hiva pigeon is man. Once found in abundance, it has been hunted to near extinction by locals for food. Today, only about 100 pair exist and there is no legal protection for these birds. A similar threat stalks the spectacled gray-backed terns, found only in the tropical Pacific. On two tiny uninhabited islands, jointly known as Bird Island, thousands of sooty and spectacled gray-backed terns use the land to breed and can still be seen taking to the air in great numbers as boats pass. However, this sight may soon become just a memory. Over the last decade, the tern population has decreased from 80,000 to 20,000. Why? Locals scale Bird Islands cliffs to collect eggs by the bucketful. Naturalists tell us this represents a clear danger for the spectacled gray-backed tern, and at present nothing is being done to remedy the situation.

It's possible to see the archeological sites near Taaoa on the **Taaoa Archeological Sites** (1 mile/1.6 kilometers) hike. Taaoa is about five kilometers southeast of Atuona. However, in order to get there from Atuona, you must catch a ride about ten kilometers west, along the coastal road to the phone booth near Taaoa, which marks the beginning of the trailhead. The trail leads inland up the hill. After about one and a half kilometers you'll start seeing *tohua* and other ancient remains.

You can visit the **Teheuto Petroglyphs** (2 miles/3.2 kilometers one way) in the Tahauku Valley with relative ease. It's about a 40-minute walk. Take the airport road 50 yards (45 meters) to the left and look for the sign to the petroglyph site. Follow the road and after 20 minutes take the intersecting road to the left. Five minutes later you will cross an ankle-deep river. Continue to follow the road up the hill. You'll soon reach a small clearing, at which point you need to follow the small trail straight ahead and downhill until you reach the petroglyph. Here you'll find a series of double-outlined stick figures on a massive boulder. Backtrack to the clearing and continue on the trail to the right, uphill for another five minutes, traversing a banana and papaya plantation. Continue up the hill a bit more and look for a *tohua*. It has a paved dance floor, and on the rear wall you'll see two *tiki* heads. This is a gorgeous spot that is worth spending some time in. ~ The trailhead begins near Snack Tahauku in Tahauku, near the intersection of the airport and dock roads. (Ask at the eatery for directions to the trailhead.)

Puamau Hike (1.5 miles/2 kilometers). The *tiki* in Puamau are a sweaty 40-minute walk inland from the small Puamau dock. From the dock, take the road to the left after passing the soccer field and then veer to the right. (When the paved road begins you are now on the property of the village mayor.) One of the graves

THE *NONO*—SCOURGE OF THE MARQUESAS

The visitor's true initiation to the Marquesas is marked by the first brush with the *nono*. These nearly invisible creatures inhabit the seashore, valleys, streams and humid low-lying areas. Resembling a gnat, they are silent and insidious, attacking without the warning buzz of a mosquito. The tiny *nono* draws blood with the aid of an anticoagulant—the result being a red welt, localized swelling and acute itching. Scratching often introduces a staph infection. There are two species of *nono*: the black variety found in marshy areas and the white *nono*, found primarily on beaches. There are a few ways to deal with this minuscule pest— long sleeves and pants and/or copious amounts of *monoi* oil and insect repellent.

is decorated with *tiki*. Some say that this is the final resting place of Te Hu Moena, one of the last chieftesses in the Marquesas, who, legend has it, was buried here with her bicycle. However, just exactly who is buried here is a controversy among many Marquesans. Other locals swear the individual in the grave was a chief. Despite the arguments about the person in the grave, there seems to be universal agreement about the presence of the bicycle. After your sweaty hike, take a swim at Puamau's golden-sand beach. There are no *nonos*, great body surfing and no undertow. (There is an entrance fee of 300 CFP to see the *tiki*.)

Ozanne Rohi has island tours as well as interisland transfers. ~ Atuona; 92-73-43, 92-74-65. Other boat tours in Atuona and transfers are available from **Jean Pierre Moreau** ~ 92-74-22 and **Jo Gramont** ~ 92-72-69.

BOAT TOURS

▼▼▼▼▼▼▼▼▼▼
Tahuata

Only 21 square miles (55 square kilometers) in area, Tahuata is positioned south of the Bordelais Canal, opposite Hiva Oa. The 550 people on the island live in the village of Vaitahu or in smaller villages scattered over the island. Like all the Marquesas, Tahuata is a craggy, precipitous volcanic island. The highest point on the island is the summit of Tumu Maea Ufu, at 1548 feet (472 meters). The inland valleys are covered with scrub and grassy vegetation. A number of pocket beaches dot the perimeter of the island. Many look appealing, but are usually infested with *nonos*.

Tahuata is popular mainly with visiting yachts. (Boats provide the sole source of transportation to the island.) There are no true roads on Tahuata, making getting around problematic.

SIGHTS

The main village is **Vaitahu**, which is backdropped by a massive, verdant cliff. A church, museum, post office, store and handful of wooden dwellings are all that make up the village. On the south side of Vaitahu beach is a small hill where a French fort was once located. On the north side of the valley is a sheer wall. A small river bisects the village.

The **Catholic church** in Vaitahu is a relatively new affair, built in 1988 with funds from the Vatican. Made of round stones, it incorporates gracious carvings and an impressive stained-glass window depicting a brown-skinned Marquesan Madonna into its framework. Set against the rich green hillsides and towering peaks, this spectacular edifice is an aesthetic treat.

The tiny **Vaitahu Museum** in the town hall is also of interest. It contains a great deal of information about a local archeological site excavated in Hanamiai by professor Barry Rollet of the University of Hawaii. Rollet set up the first archeological exhibit with Marquesan titles in the office of the mayor. There is a good illustration, accompanied by photos, of the layers of excavations showing the history of the island with artifacts such as shellfish hooks, soil samples and pork bones.

Vaitahu is the site of Spanish explorer Alvaro de Mendaña's only actual landing in the Marquesas. It was here that he came ashore, said Mass, raised crosses, planted a garden and allowed his soldiers to kill over 200 Marquesans. When Cook called at Vaitahu, nearly two centuries later, another Marquesan was killed. The village was also the site of much European-caused violence in the early 1800s. Home to many deserters, Vaitahu was frequently visited by Westerners who took advantage of Marquesan hospitality.

> Several locals provide horseback riding tours to the Hanatu'una Valley and to other archaeological sites around Tahuata. Contact Naani Barsinas for information. ~ Vaitahu; 92-92-26.

Monuments marking the fighting between the French and Marquesans are still visible in Vaihatu. They consist of the **ruins of the fort** on the hill overlooking the beach, and the **graves** of Frigate Captain Halley and Lieutenant Ladebat, who were killed when the Marquesans ambushed a French column moving up the valley at the start of the French-Marquesan war of 1842. ~ To see the ruins of the fort and a marvelous view as well, hike up the hill behind the cemetery, which takes about 20 minutes. To find the two graves, hike up the main valley road about one kilometer and look for an inconspicuous concrete terrace on the slope. This is the grave site. It was near here where Halley and Ladebat were ambushed.

Petroglyphs can be found in the Hanatu'una Valley, which can be reached by the *Tamanu*, a boat that sails from Vaitahu. Another adventurous method of reaching them is on horseback from Hapatoni. Several locals provide horseback riding tours to the Hanatu'una Valley and to other archeological sites around the island. Contact **Naani Barsinas** for information. ~ Vaitahu; 92-92-26.

Hapatoni is a picturesque and friendly village by the sea, and is only 15 minutes by boat from Vaitahu. The seafront road in Hapatoni is made almost entirely from ancient paved stones. The road is shaded by *temanu* trees, which are often used in woodcarving. There are also **monuments** here to the 1842 battle between the French and the Marquesans.

LODGING   The only place to stay here is **Chez Naani Barsinas,** a house with four rooms. Two rooms have a double and a single bed while the other two have two single beds. *Pension complete* is available. I have had reports that have not been particularly glowing, but there isn't an alternative. ~ Vaitahu; 92-92-26. BUDGET TO MODERATE.

SHOPPING   There is a **handicrafts center** with first-rate woodcarvings in Vaitahu. It's open intermittently and the best thing to do is call Liliane

Teileipupuni Hapatoni if you are looking to buy something. ~ Vaitahu; 92-92-46.

Other local sculptors in Vaitahu include **Edwin Fii** ~ 92-92-68 and **Sebastien Barsinas** (aka Kehu).

TAHUATA BEACHES ~ The north side of the island has several white-sand beaches. All have ample shade trees, but *nonos* may be a problem so come prepared with *monoi* or repellent. Swimming is quite good from the reports I've had. ~ Because the beaches are so remote, they necessitate hiring a driver with a four-wheel-drive vehicle.

BEACHES

Fatu Hiva

Fatu Hiva, the most remote island of the inhabited Marquesas Group, and only 80 square miles (130 square kilometers) in size, was the first island in the Marquesas to be discovered by Europeans. In July 1595, the Spanish, led by Don Alvaro Mendaña, wasted no time in showing their true colors. Apparently the Marquesans had come aboard the Spaniard's galleon and, perhaps, became too bold for the Europeans' sensibilities. The Marquesans were warned off by a few shots. They fled, but returned a barrage of rocks. The Spanish then opened fire on the canoes, killing several people, including a chief. To commemorate their visit, the Spanish left behind three large crucifixes, along with the date carved in a tree.

In the mid-19th century, the island was popular with whalers, despite the lack of good anchorages. This was most likely because it was well away from the authorities' eyes, and the seamen could raise Cain without paying a penalty.

Fatu Hiva was once famous for its talented tattoo artists. During the pre-contact days, an islander's body might have been completely covered by tattoos by the time he died. Unfortunately, the artwork went to the grave with the individual. (The only remnants of these artworks are now displayed in books or in museum archives.) Today, Marquesan tattooing is enjoying a renaissance and is exceedingly popular with most Marquesan men, and to a lesser extent, Marquesan women.

Fatu Hiva

Teaite Hoe Point

Tevaii Point

Bay of Virgins

Hanavave

Cape Matautu

Matakoo Point

Mt Touaouoho 3149'

Omoa

N

0   20 miles
0   20 kilometers

Teae Point

Fatu Hiva, also known as Fatu Iva, shares similar physical characteristics with the rest of the Marquesas Group. It is high, sheer, very rocky and carpeted with lush vegetation. Part of the island is the remnant of a volcanic rim. The highest point on Fatu Hiva is Mt. Touaouoho, at 3149 feet (960 meters).

Thor Heyerdahl (of *Kon Tiki* fame) spent most of 1936 on Fatu Hiva with his first wife and wrote a largely fictional book, *Fatu Hiva*, about his time here.

Today, Fatu Hiva is the only island in the Marquesas where *tapa* cloth, produced from the bark of mulberry, breadfruit or *hiapo* banyan trees, is made. Local artisans also carve wooden *tiki* and manufacture a local style of *monoi*, a perfumed coconut oil with fragrances derived from *tiare* blossoms and sandalwood. (The Marquesan word for coconut oil is *pani*.) The fragrant oil is used as a perfume for massages, to ward off mosquitoes or to attract a lover. *Pani* is a reasonable anti-*nono* protection (you drown them in it instead of killing them with poison), but it doesn't really stop the pests. You may also see local women wearing *umuhei*, a fragrant blend of herbs and flowers contained in a small packet suspended around the neck like a pendant.

SIGHTS

There are two principal valleys—**Hanavave** and **Omoa**—on the western coast of Fatu Hiva, each with several **archeological sites**. According to Marquesan legend, the cliffs of Hanavave are the remnants of a giant eel that came from Nuku Hiva. It visited the island at the request of a Fatu Hiva eel.

The stone structures in Fatu Hiva are not as large, nor are the complexes as extensive as those seen in Hiva Oa or in the northern group. There are still many sites to visit, however, and some interesting **petroglyphs** in Omoa feature huge fish and stick figures. It's possible to walk to these sites, but it's best to ask a local for directions and receive permission from the landowners.

Another island locale to see is the **Bay of Virgins**, formed by two walls, one from the north and the other from the south, that nearly meet at the entrance of the bay. They form a gateway that towers over the bay with massive stone spires. While on Fatu Hiva keep an eye out for the beautiful aquamarine lorikeet, which is making a comeback after near extinction.

LODGING

Nearly every lodging on Fatu Hiva is spartan—don't expect a lot of creature comforts.

What you'll get at **Chez Joseph Tetuanui** is a house with two rooms, a kitchen and a communal bath. The owner also offers tours in his four-wheel-drive truck. ~ Omoa; 92-80-09. BUDGET.

A four-person bungalow with a kitchenette and private bathroom is what you'll find at **Chez Lionel Cantois**. The owner of the property also hires himself and his land rover out for tours. ~ Omoa; 92-80-04, 92-80-05. BUDGET.

Chez Marie-Claire Ehueiana is a house with two rooms, each with double bed, and there's a common bath. ~ Omoa; 92-80-16. BUDGET.

The lodgings at **Chez Cecile Gilmore** are in a two-room home. The rooms have double beds and there's a common bath. At least one traveler I spoke to had a less than sanguine experience with Cecile so it might be best to look elsewhere. Round-trip transfers are available from the dock. ~ Omoa; 92-80-54. BUDGET.

Chez Norma Ropati features a two-bedroom house. Each room comes with a double bed. There is also a kitchen and the bath is communal. *Pension complete* is offered. Round-trip transfers are available from the dock. ~ Omoa; 92-80-13. BUDGET TO MODERATE.

Hanavave is beautiful, but the people are another story. Overnight stays and/or shopping are not a good idea here. However, if you do choose to stay, there are a couple of options. A house with two very basic rooms is what **Chez Veronique Kami** provides. Meals are also available. ~ Hanavave; 92-80-56. BUDGET.

Tapa cloth and sandalwood oil processing can be observed by visitors at **Chez Jacques Tevenino**. There's only one room here, but it is nearby to orange, grapefruit, banana and coffee plants. ~ Hanavave; 92-80-72. BUDGET.

DINING

In Omoa, **Restaurant Ropati** serves breakfast, lunch and dinner. The modest restaurant offers up seafood, when it is available, as well as chicken and pork dishes. ~ Omoa; 92-80-13. BUDGET.

Chez Mme. Bernadette Cantois has a snack bar that offers beef, chicken and seafood cuisine. ~ Omoa; BUDGET.

GROCERIES

There are several minuscule markets in Omoa and Hanavave that sell the bare essentials.

SHOPPING

The unique item indigenous to Fatu Hiva is *tapa* cloth. Prices range from 500 to 5000 CFP depending on the size. The fabric is generally sold by individuals rather than purchased in stores, so ask around if you care to bring some home.

BEACHES

The beach situation in Fatu Hiva is pretty dismal. In Hanavave or Omoa you can swim from rocks along the shore. But always keep an eye out for sharks.

Outdoor Adventures

HIKING

Hanavave Village to Omoa (10 miles/16 kilometers). Hanavave Village, located on the Bay of Virgins, is the starting point for a wonderful trek to Omoa Village. This serpentine hike offers dizzying views and a majestic waterfall visible from the path deep inside Vaie'enui Valley. Take water and give yourself four or more hours for the journey.

Better yet, plan a couple of days if you go into the valley. You'll fall in love with it and want to stay. As you climb out of Hanavave, note the stone *tiki*-like formations and the intriguing "hole" in the top of the bluffs.

Once in Hanavave you can take a small trek that leads to a wonderful cool, deep, freshwater pool in the river. Look for the beginning of the trail off the main road on the left-hand side near a utility pole, about a three-minute walk from the bridge. The trail to the pool is a 15-minute walk from the dock and is well worth the effort. Nature has blessed Fatu Hiva with more rain than any other island in the Marquesas, giving it a verdant landscape.

TOURS

If you plan to spend time on Fatu Hiva you can go horseback riding, hunt wild pig and visit the archeological sites in Omoa and Hanavave. ~ Contact the Marie (Town Hall) for information.

Horses are available in Omoa Village for tours around the island. For more information, contact **Roberto Maraetaata**. ~ Omoa; 92-80-52.

Motorized outrigger tours are available in Omoa from **Xavier Gilmore**. ~ Omoa; 92-80-54.

There are two four-wheel-drive tour operators in Omoa: **Roger Kamia** ~ 92-80-07 and **Chez Joseph Tetuanui** ~ 92-80-09.

▼▼▼▼▼▼▼▼▼▼
Transportation

Always reconfirm your tickets prior to the plane's departure. Bumping of (foreign) passengers is all too common in the Marquesas.

AIR

NUKU HIVA　Air Tahiti has a regularly scheduled service five to six days a week from Papeete to Nuku Hiva. Flying time between Papeete and Nuku Hiva is about three and a half hours. From Nuku Hiva, which essentially is the hub for the other islands in the archipelago, there are flights to Hiva Oa, Ua Huka and Ua Pou. Flights are also possible late in the week from Nuku Hiva to Rangiroa, Manihi and Napuka. ~ Taioha'e; 92-03-41.

UA HUKA　Air Tahiti connects Ua Huka from Nuku Hiva once a week. ~ Vaipae'e; 92-53-41.

UA POU　Air Tahiti has service from Nuku Hiva once a week. ~ Hakahau; 92-53-41.

HIVA OA　Air Tahiti has regularly scheduled service, three times a week to Hiva Oa from Papeete. Flying time between Papeete and Hiva Oa is about three and a half hours. ~ Atuona; 92-73-41.

SEA

The administration boat *Ka'oha Nui* travels on an irregular schedule between the islands. It's usually possible to secure a berth on this modern, well-maintained vessel by inquiring at the local city hall.

NUKA HIVA   Interisland vessels servicing Nuku Hiva include the *Taporo IV* ~ Papeete, 42-63-93; the *Tamarii Tuamotu* ~ Papeete, 42-95-07; and the *Aranui* ~ Papeete, 42-62-40. Of all the vessels, the *Aranui* is the only ship that specifically caters to foreign visitors. The alternatives are the irregularly scheduled boats, which may not be as "user friendly" and may take up to 25 days at sea.

UA HUKA   Boats (with captains) are available for interisland transportation to Ua Huka. The voyage to Ua Huka takes two and a half hours from Ua Pou.

UA POU   Paul Teatiu offers interisland transportation between Nuku Hiva and Ua Pou. ~ Vaipae'e; 92-60-54.

Alain Ah Lo, in Hakatao Village, offers interisland transportation. Hakatao's community boat can also be hired for tours of the island or interisland jaunts at cheaper prices. ~ Hakatao; 92-52-80.

HIVA OA   Hiva Oa is served by the *Taporo IV* ~ Papeete, 42-63-93; the *Tamarii Tuamotu* ~ Papeete, 42-95-87; and the *Aranui* ~ Papeete, 42-62-40.

Anchorage for yachts is far from ideal on Hiva Oa because the southeast tradewinds cause boats to roll during the April to October tradewind season. Yachts generally moor at nearby Tahauku Bay, which has a fair yacht anchorage thanks to a recently built breakwater.

FATU HIVA   Fatu Hiva is accessible by regular boat service from Hiva Oa. The trip takes about three and a half hours. The boat leaves on Tuesday mornings at around 4 a.m. and is supposed to return from Hiva Oa at 3 p.m. the following day.

Fuel for yachties is available from **Maria Seigel**. ~ Omoa; 92-80-10.

NUKA HIVA   The only way to see Nuka Hiva is to hire a car and driver. The main issue for non-French speakers is that the drivers do not speak fluent English. **Jean-Pierre,** who can be hired through Rose Corser, speaks a smattering of English. ~ Taioha'e; 92-03-82.

My first choice would be **Marie Therese Bruneau.** ~ Taioha'e; 92-04-68. Some of the other drivers in Taioha'e include **Richard Teote** ~ 92-00-91, **Georges Taupotini** ~ 92-02-94 and **Teiki Puhetini** ~ 92-03-47.

All of the guides will take visitors to the airport. Standard airport fare is 3000 CFP per person and it's a two-hour drive under optimal conditions.

UA HUKA   When you rent an auto in Ua Huka to sightsee you are, in effect, "renting" a driver along with the car. In other words, visitors don't generally take rental cars out by themselves. Car (or truck) and driver in Vaipae'e can be hired from: **Marcel Paro** ~ 92-

CAR RENTALS & TAXIS

60-24, **Etienne Brown** ~ 92-60-14, **Hubert Fournier** ~ 92-61-24, **Alexis Fournier** ~ 92-60-05, **Joseph Vaatete** ~ 92-61-29, **Alexis Scallamara** ~ 92-60-19 and **Matiki Teatiu** ~ 92-60-06. In Haavai, contact **Joseph Lichtle** ~ 92-60-72.

UA POU   There is now no shortage of transportation on Ua Pou. Road conditions necessitate a local driver and prices (which include driver and fuel) start at US$20 per person, US$100 for the vehicle, for the shortest trip offered. Four-wheel-drive vehicles in Hakahau are available from **Edouard Bruneau** ~ 92-53-51, **Gerard Hapipi** ~ 92-53-22, **Joseph Tamarii** ~ 92-52-14 and **Julien Tissot** ~ 92-50-22.

HIVA OA   As far as I know, Hiva Oa is the only island in the Marquesas where it's possible to rent an automobile without the obligatory chauffeur. (Drivers *are* available if you want one though.)

David's Rent-a-Car is located several hundred yards beyond the cluster of buildings that include the Atuona post office. There are cars and two four-wheel-drive vehicles available for hire. ~ Atuona; 92-72-87.

Romeo Ciantar, located south of Atuona, has a wide selection of Suzuki Samurais and double-cabin four-wheel-drive vehicles for hire. ~ Atuona; 92-74-55.

Ida Clark has a four-wheel-drive Toyota available. ~ Atuona; 92-71-33.

HITCHING   Hitching in the Marquesas can be problematic. Many Marquesans derive their income by hiring themselves out as taxi drivers for tourists, making them reluctant to provide free transportation, especially if they have paying passengers on board.

Also note: Women should never hitchhike without a male escort. Because of cultural differences, it will be misunderstood by the male Marquesan.

For the budget-minded, hitchhiking in Hiva Oa is an option, especially between Atuona and Taaoa because of the comparatively large amount of traffic between the two villages. However, hitching anywhere else on the island can be problematic.

TWELVE

The Australs

Located about 372 miles (600 kilometers) south of Tahiti, the Austral Islands make up the southernmost chain of French Polynesia. Spanning a distance of 831 miles (1330 kilometers), the Australs are geologically part of the Austral Seamount Chain, which ranges from the Cook Islands in the northwest to the Australs in the southeast.

The Australs are made up of the uninhabited coral atoll Ile Maria (or Hull Island) and five high volcanic islands—Rimatara, Rurutu, Tubuai, Raivavae and Rapa. The elevations of the high volcanic islands escalate from northwest to southeast, culminating in the sharp peaks of Rapa. Not surprisingly, there are islands in both the Austral and Cook Island groups that share physical similarities. For example, both Tubuai in the Australs and Rarotonga in the Cooks have a fringing white-sand beach (an unusual feature for high islands in the other archipelagos of French Polynesia). Likewise, Mangaia in the Cooks and Rurutu and Rimatara in the Australs are all extremely rugged upthrust islands with limestone topography.

The climate in the Australs is decidedly more temperate and less rainy than Tahiti and the other islands of the Society and Tuamotu groups. The temperature is warm—the low average can dip to 64 degrees Fahrenheit (18 degrees Celsius)—and the seasons are well defined. The islands lie at the southern boundary of the southeast trade winds, which blow from November to March. In the cold season, from May to September, the winds are more variable and generally westerly, especially in Rapa.

Rurutu has the only modern hotel in the entire region, but a number of pensions and small lodgings have opened up on Tubuai, as well as on the far-flung islands of Rapa, Rimatara and Raivavae.

▼▼▼▼▼▼▼▼
Tubuai

At the core of the Austral Group is the high island of Tubuai, which is composed of two submerged inactive volcanic mountains that create a landmass of 19 square miles (48 square kilometers). The largest of the Austral islands, Tubuai is about three and a half miles (five and a half kilometers) wide and five and a half miles (nine kilometers) long. Most of the population of approximately 1400 live in the two major villages of Mataura and Taahueia, both of which are located on the north coast.

Getting around the island is easy. One road circles Tubuai and another bisects it. In some sections, the road is paved, but for the most part it is gravel or sand. Over the last two decades the roads have become filled with cars, trucks and motorcycles. It seems nowadays only children and visitors ride bicycles.

Physically, Tubuai is comprised of three major features: two distinct clusters of mountains, their valleys and a littoral, or broad swath of land, which runs entirely around the island. The two groups of mountains, of which Taitaa (1308 feet/399 meters) and Tonorutu (1023 feet/312 meters) are the tallest, are joined by a low, broad plain. The high bluffs and broken terrain give way to the softer contours of hillocks, which are covered with tough grass and fern known as *anuhe*. The littoral is sandy, flat and sometimes swampy.

Tubuai is surrounded by a barrier reef and seven *motus*, some of which have excellent white-sand beaches. In addition to several shallow passes where small boats may enter or exit the lagoon, there are three main passes on the reef.

As in all the Australs, the weather on Tubuai is cool and mild compared to the Society Islands to the north. Tubuai lies near the limit of the Southeast trades winds and on occasion is hit by cyclones. The island was severely pummeled by Cyclone William in 1995, with damage estimated at US$1.5 million. To date, rebuilding is still going on.

Though there never has been extensive archeological work done on Tubuai, excavations on the nearby island of Rurutu point to settlement in the year 1050 A.D. Legend has it that there were three settlements on Tubuai, all founded by Polynesians whose canoes were blown off course. Later migrants sailing westward from Raivavae settled on the south side of the island.

The first written records pertaining to Tubuai were made by Captain James Cook, who sighted the island on August 8, 1777, during his third voyage in the Pacific en route to Tahiti from Tonga. Anchored offshore, Cook attempted to convince the crew of two Tubuain canoes to come aboard while the locals did their best to persuade the English sailor to come ashore. Cook stayed put and the Tubuains did not come aboard the boat. In 1789, Fletcher Christian and 24 crewmen took part in the famous mutiny on the HMS *Bounty* in the waters off Tonga. He then sailed to Tubuai in-tent on settling on the island that had been sighted but not yet explored by Europeans.

Their initial encounter with the natives was not promising. An offshore skirmish left 12 locals dead; the crew then sailed for Tahiti, where they loaded the vessel with livestock, food and companions. On June 23rd, the *Bounty* returned with their stores, and 28 companions. This time the Tubuain welcoming committee was more congenial. Christian organized trading with the local chiefs and began work on what was to be known as Fort George. Despite the initial warm reception, the presence of the *Bounty* crew exacerbated already existing rivalries between the islanders while at the same time alienating the local priests. These problems, along with dissension among the ranks of the *Bounty* crew, led to the eventual downfall of the settlers. Today, all that remains of Fort George is a rectangular ditch where the walls of the stockade used to be.

A few months after arriving on the island a second skirmish flared up, resulting in the death of 66 Tubuains. Following the battle, the *Bounty* crew took a vote and decided to return to Tahiti. Accompanied by a local chief and two commoners, the crew set sail for Tahiti after staying less than three months on Tubuai. Upon arrival, 16 crew members opted to settle in Tahiti while the rest, led by Fletcher Christian, ended up on Pitcairn Island. In 1842, the island became a French protectorate, and in 1880 was formally annexed by France.

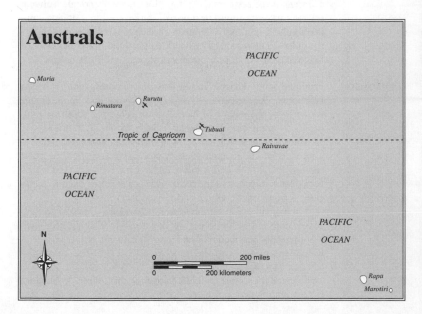

Australs

SIGHTS   Currently, Tubuai is the administrative center for the Austral Group. Despite this, it is still a quiet tropical backwater. The two main villages on the island are **Mataura** and **Taahuaia**. There is very little, though, in the way of commercial development. Locals make a living fishing or as subsistence farmers raising such crops as taro and cassava. Over one-half of the families have at least one adult member working for the government in jobs such as administrative positions and schoolteachers.

Tubuains are generally friendly to strangers but not effusive in their reception. Tourists are a rarity and somewhat of a curiosity. Though amiable, locals are relatively shy. It's up to you to make an effort to get acquainted with your hosts. The good news is that Tubuains do not look at visitors in terms of dollar signs. The bad news is that islanders are not anxious to take you on excursions to outlying *motus*, horseback riding or to participate in formal guided tours of the island. What's more, few people speak English. If you really want to get to know the people, and to have them show you around, have patience—plan to stick around for several weeks.

Bikes can be rented from **Pension Manu Patia**. Bicycling is possible on the perimeter road that circles the island. ~ Taahuaia; 95-03-27.

Tubuai is probably best known for the inhabitants' special manner of singing religious hymns, which is purposefully atonal. This haunting style of singing, which sounds strange to Western ears, is a vestige of the pre-contact culture. Interestingly enough, Tubuain singing must also sound strange to Tahitian ears. In a singing competition held in Tahiti a Tubuain choir was nearly disqualified by the judges. The reason? The Papeete judges did not know what to make of their Polynesian brethren's seemingly off-key singing.

LODGING   **Ermitage Sainte Helene Tubuai** has three houses, each with two bedrooms, a kitchen and a bathroom with hot water. The Ermitage is owned by the widow of Noel Iliari. It is located about six kilometers from the airport. ~ Mahu Village; 95-04-79. BUDGET.

Chez Karine et Tale is run by an American woman married to a local man. The lodging consists of a bungalow with one guest room with a double bed, a salon, kitchen and bath with hot water. Breakfast is included in the tariff. This is a nice but overpriced facility. ~ Mataura; 95-04-52. MODERATE TO DELUXE.

On a small beach by the lagoon, **Chez Taro Tanepau** consists of two units in one home, each with a double and single bed. Each has a private bath facility. The service is friendly, but inconsistent. Round-trip transfers to the ferry are 1000 CFP. Chez Taro is located in Mataura Village. ~ Mataura; 95-03-82. BUDGET.

Located on school grounds, **Bungalow du College de Mataura** is well maintained and clean. Here you'll find a bungalow that houses up to four people. There's also a two-bedroom house with an equipped kitchen, communal bath (with hot water) and a living room. One bedroom has a double bed while the other has two singles. Meals are available from the nearby school-operated kitchen (except during school holidays). Bungalow du College de Mataura is located in Taahuaia Village on the school grounds. ~ Taahuaia; 95-03-32, fax 95-05-58. BUDGET.

Manu Patia consists of two self-contained apartments—one with two bedrooms (each with a double and two single beds) and the other with a double bed. Both have kitchens. You also have the option of pension complete here. Manu Patia is about three and a half kilometers east of the dock and faces the lagoon. The main disadvantage is that it's about six kilometers from Mataura, the main village. ~ Taahuaia; 95-03-27. BUDGET TO MODERATE.

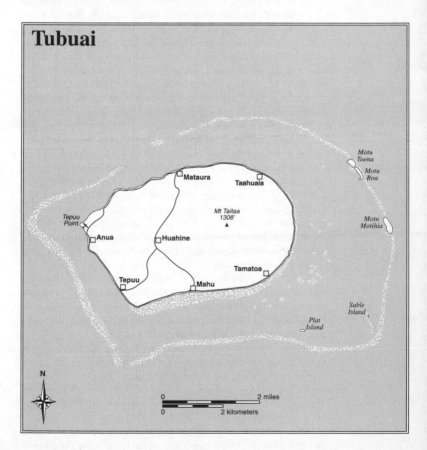

GROCERIES   There are several minuscule grocery stores in Mataura where the most basic items, such as canned milk, mosquito coils and bread, may be purchased.

SHOPPING   For those in search of that special handmade souvenir—a woven mat or hat—you should seek out an individual artisan. Inquire at your pension for information.

BEACHES   A barrier reef surrounds the island of Tubuai and the entire island is fringed by a white-sand beach. There are also beaches that line the outlying *motus* off the east coast of Tubuai that are accessible by small boats.

▼▼▼▼▼▼▼▼▼▼
Rurutu

About 355 miles (572 kilometers) south of Tahiti, Rurutu, with a circumference of about 19 miles (30 kilometers), is an upthrust limestone island with steep cliffs that jut vertically into the sea. The highest peak on the island is Manureva, which reaches an elevation of 1263 feet (385 meters). The island is in the process of being pushed upward by geologic forces. What was once the outer lagoon is now a swamp well inside the perimeter of the island. In the same vein, the coral reefs that once surrounded the island are now sharp 300-foot (90-meter) bluffs that overlook the sea. Polynesians call these raised cliffs—or more precisely, raised-reef features—*makatea*.

Archeological finds on Rurutu suggest that the island was settled from the Society Islands in about 1050 A.D. It was in 1769 that Captain James Cook and his navigator Eric de Bishop landed on Rurutu. (De Bishop spent the last years of his life on the island.) In 1821, a large Rurutuan canoe inadvertently drifted to Raiatea and London Missionary Society representatives provided the travelers transportation to return to their island. Seizing the opportunity to spread their gospel, the representatives also sent two Polynesian missionaries back home with the Rurutuans. Christianity was adopted soon afterward.

In 1828, an English visitor to the island reported that a strange malady had ravaged the population, killing about 2500 residents, leaving only 350 inhabitants. It was said that only two people over the age of 25 survived the epidemic. The French established Rurutu as a protectorate in 1889 and annexed it in 1900.

Rurutu's interior is mountainous while the coastal strip is protected by a continuous coral reef that hugs the shoreline. The upper reaches of the island are carpeted with grass and fern, with dense vegetation, including hibiscus and casuarina, covering the ravines. The soil is not particularly fertile but islanders are able to grow taro, the preferred staple.

The island has a dry and temperate climate, especially in June, July and August. The outstanding physical features are the massive

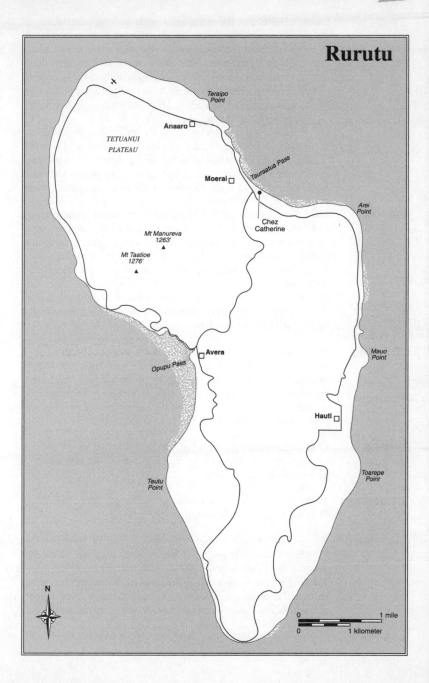

Rurutu

Teraipo
Point

Anaaro

TETUANUI
PLATEAU

Tauraatua Pass

Moerai

Arei
Point

Chez
Catherine

Mt Manureva
1263'

Mt Taatioe
1276'

Mauo
Point

Avera

Opupu Pass

Hauti

Teutu
Point

Toarepe
Point

N

0   1 mile
0   1 kilometer

limestone cliffs and the many caves with grottos, stalactites and stalagmites. (Some of the caves are accessible—with a proper guide. Ask your host to provide a guide. If they can't do it themselves, they will find you one.) Rurutu does not have a lagoon like the islands of the Society Group. However, there are several white-sand beaches that invite swimming and snorkeling. Horseback rides or hikes to inland waterfalls are additional lures.

On Rurutu, the locals use bamboo poles to fish at the edge of the shore.

Rurutu is also known for a custom practiced twice a year (in January and July) called *amoraa ofai*. Young men and women from each village prove themselves with a show of strength. The object is to lift huge volcanic stones on their shoulders. The contest is followed by a traditional feast and dance celebration.

SIGHTS Most of the island's 2000 inhabitants are clustered in the villages of Moerai, Avera and Hauti. **Moerai**, situated at the shore of a small bay on the northeast coast, is the principal settlement. **Hauti** is south of Moerai and **Avera** lies on the west coast of the island. Moerai and Avera are about five kilometers apart and it's easy to walk from one to the other on a well-trodden path that cuts through the center of the island. It is possible to circumnavigate the island's rutted peripheral road via four-wheel-drive vehicle, though such vehicles are not available to rent.

LODGING **Chez Catherine** is a ten-room motel in the village of Moerai, situated on the ocean front. Five guest rooms each have one double bed and the remaining five come with two single beds. Each unit has a terrace facing the sea and a private bath (with hot water). A restaurant/bar is on the premises of the motel. Located near the airport. ~ Moerai; 94-02-43. BUDGET TO MODERATE.

DINING **Chez Catherine** serves breakfast, lunch and dinner at her restaurant/bar on the premises of the motel. The meals are very basic. ~ Moerai; 94-02-43. BUDGET.

GROCERIES There are several small local markets in Moerai, the main village. Only the basics are sold here.

SHOPPING Natives of Rurutu are known throughout French Polynesia for their fine woven hats and mats. Much of the exquisite plaitwork available in Tahiti is made by natives of Rurutu now living in Tahiti. However, it is possible to purchase mats, hats and fans from individual craftspeople on Rurutu. There is one shop at the airport that sells handicrafts—but it's only open when a plane arrives.

BEACHES There are several white-sand beaches on the island. Swimming and snorkeling are possible.

There are excursions via horseback into the rugged interior of the island. Those interested in riding tours will want to contact **Nicodem Atai**. ~ Moerai; 94-03-05.

Outdoor Adventures

RIDING STABLES

Another option is to call **M. and Mme. Iareta**. They have a variety of horseback tours to the interior as well. ~ Moerai; 94-03-92.

Those needing oceangoing transportation can call **Haelemu Poetai**. His vessel accommodates up to ten people and his services as a skipper will cost you 60,000 CFP per day. ~ Moerai; 94-04-31, 94-03-58.

BOAT CHARTERS

M. and Mme. Iareta and **Madeline Moeau** have a Nissan vehicle with capacity for seven passengers for round-the-island tours. ~ Moerai; 94-03-92. Likewise, **Raymond Toomaru** has a Land Rover available for tours. ~ Moerai; 94-02-43.

TOURS

Rimatara

One of the most isolated spots on the planet, Rimatara is the westernmost of the inhabited islands in the Australs. It lacks an airport and a sheltered harbor and is truly off the beaten path. Its three square miles (eight square kilometers) of land make it the smallest of the Australs. The only way to get there is by boat.

The island is primarily of volcanic origin, and rises to a height of only 272 feet (83 meters) at a hill known as Oromana. From the central slopes small brooks trickle into a series of swamps. The water eventually empties beneath an ancient elevated reef that occupies much of the island's fringe. This "reef" has formed a cliff 20 to 30 feet (8 to 12 meters) high surrounding the island in many places. Created from hard, white limestone, the formation has been eroded in many places and extends inland for several hundred yards. The island is also encircled by a coral reef that borders the shore, forming a lagoon near the village of Mutuaura. Here a 500-yard-long (480-meter) islet extends seaward from the main island. The lagoon has a curving, white-sand beach fringed by casuarina trees. The reef has three passes, two on the northern side and one on the east side.

The main village is **Amaru**, which is composed of a few shops, a post office, a gendarmerie, a town hall, an infirmary and a school. **Anapoto** and **Mutuaura** villages are connected by a few rutted dirt roads. Of interest to the visitor is an **old cemetery** near the dock. For its minuscule size, Rimatara has a rather large area of arable land with fertile soil that is used to grow taro, oranges, bananas and breadfruit.

SIGHTS

Although the island has electricity, there are few diversions. There are no car, bicycle, or boat rentals. There aren't any restaurants or bars. (I was told that alcohol is not sold on the island.) Frankly, there is not a lot for the visitor to do here. Walking is the only activity that comes to mind.

LODGING   **Chez William Tematahotoa** is in the main village of Amaru. This white wooden cottage with brown trim and a terrace has three rooms, two with double beds and one with two singles. The guest rooms have private bathrooms with hot water. You must bring your own food if you want to eat. It is located about 200 yards from the sea. ~ Amaru; 94-43-06. BUDGET.

Chez Paulette Tematahotoa is a two-bedroom home in the village of Mutuaura, located two kilometers west of the dock, just a few yards from the sea. Each of the bedrooms has a double bed. Other amenities include a kitchen, living room and a communal bath. Chez Paulette will rent you a room on a daily or monthly basis. The accommodation is acceptable, but food is not provided. Bring your own provisions. ~ Mutuaura; 94-42-27. BUDGET.

Chez Rita is the better place to stay in Mutuaura. It is located about 500 yards from the dock and is a short walk from the beach. The accommodation has three guest rooms, each with a double bed. There is also a cozy salon, kitchen and individual (cold water) baths. The proprietor, Rita, will cook for you. ~ Mutuaura; 94-43-09. BUDGET.

GROCERIES   There are several tiny markets in the villages of Mutuaura and Amaru. Keep in mind that only the basic necessities are available.

SHOPPING   Local artisans produce finely woven hats, mats and fans. Crafts may be purchased from individual craftspeople. Inquire at your pension for information.

BEACHES   There are several white-sand beaches on the island, including one near the village of Mutuaura.

▼▼▼▼▼▼▼▼▼▼
Raivavae
Like Rimatara, Raivavae can only be reached by boat. It sits 395 miles (692 kilometers) southeast of Tahiti—very, very far from the madding crowd. The island is roughly double the size of Rimatara, six square miles, (16 square kilometers) and has a rugged, verdant topography that is said to be one of the most beautiful in the Eastern Pacific. Consisting of craggy, tree-lined hills, its highest peak is 1442-feet (437-meter) Mt. Hiro. The island is completely encircled by a barrier reef on which there are about two dozen wooded *motus*.

Raivavae was noted for its archeological treasures, particularly large stone statues akin to those of Easter Island, though different in appearance. Two of these can be seen at the Gauguin Museum

The Illari Era

Expatriates have always been attracted to Tubuai. One of the best known was the Frenchman Noel Illari, the former president of the French Polynesian Territorial Assembly. In 1947, Illari sided with the Tahitian leader Pouvanaa and a group of Tahitian veterans protesting the hiring of French civil servants to fill jobs the veterans felt they were entitled to. Illari was sentenced to five months in prison by the French government.

Illari never forgave his homeland. He exiled himself on Tubuai and established the Ermitage St. Helene, named after Napoleon's place of asylum. He spent his time writing antigovernment newspaper articles and helped the local population fight monopolistic business practices of local merchants. In the early 1970s, Illari developed lip cancer and, feeling close to death, constructed his own tomb—a ten-foot-tall granite monument on his front lawn. He died several years *after* the tomb was constructed. The inscription reads:

In memory of Noel Illari
Born in Rennese, France 11 September, 1897
died faithful to his God to family and to
his ideals to his grateful country after long
years of moral suffering within isolation
and solitude at this place. Passersby, think
and pray for him.

Next to the tomb is a sign that says:

Interdite aux Chiens et aux Gaullists
(Dogs and Gaullists forbidden)

in Tahiti. (Unfortunately, most of the stone *tikis* have been taken from the island.) There are also several *marae* and the remnants of hill terraces on Raivavae.

Raivavae is said to have been discovered by Captain Cook in 1777. However, Captain Thomas Gayangos of the Spanish frigate *Aguila* was the first European to set foot on the island, in 1775. In the early 19th century, several European ships called on Raivavae, seeking sandalwood. In 1819, Pomare II of Tahiti visited the island and the local chiefs formally ceded it to him. This led to Raivavae becoming a protectorate of Tahiti in 1842 when Tahiti and the other islands under its control came under French jurisdiction. The island was formally ceded to France in 1880 by Pomare V.

SIGHTS   There are five villages on Raivavae, which are home to about 1200 inhabitants. The most important settlement is **Rairua**, located on the western side of the island. Three of the other villages (**Matotea, Mahanatoa** and **Anatonu**) lie on the north or west coasts, with the remaining community, **Vaiuru**, on the southern shore. The various settlements are linked by a coastal road that circles the island. There is also an overland track that connects Vaiuru with Mahanatoa and the northern communities.

Raivavae's cool climate and fertile soil are perfect for growing cabbage, carrots and potatoes as well as more tropical crops such as coffee and oranges. Despite the rich array of vegetables grown on the island, you should bring all the essentials you have room for, even a bicycle if you plan to stay a while. Plan a visit to Raivavae to enjoy its tranquility and bucolic landscape, which is unrivaled in this part of the Pacific.

LODGING   **Chez Annie Flores** is conveniently located near the boat landing for the *Tuhaa Pae II*, which is the only way (unless you have a yacht) that you will ever get to this island. The home has two guest bedrooms, each with a double bed, private bath and kitchenette. It's

THE AUSTRALS UNIQUE EXPERIENCES

- Hire a guide and explore Rurutu's massive **limestone caves**, with their stalactites and stalagmites. *page 390*
- Unpack your suitcases at **Ermitage Sainte Helene Tubuai**, named for Napoleon's place of asylum. *page 386*
- Kickback in the bucolic tranquility of **Raivavae**, and forget the madcap pace of "civilization." *page 392*
- Join the Rapans as they eat mussels, oysters, crabs and lobsters on their isolated and rarely visited isle. *page 395*

easy to meet Mme. Flores. When the ship arrives she'll be selling fruit, fish and vegetables at her stand on the wharf. ~ Rairua; 95-43-28. BUDGET.

There is a small Chinese store in Rairua, the main village. Only the basics are sold here.   **GROCERIES**

▼▼▼▼▼▼▼▼

Rapa

With its nearest neighbor some 360 miles (600 kilometers) away, Rapa is one of the most isolated islands in French Polynesia and not easily visited. The island's terrain is rugged and barren, its most distinctive features are the massive 1000-foot gray cliffs that tower over the sparsely covered landscape. The island is home to about 500-plus people and a plethora of goats.

Unlike other Polynesian islands, it is necessary to obtain permission to stay on Rapa. To do so contact the Subdivision Administration des Îles Australes. Visitors planning to travel to Rapa should keep in mind that there is no airport here and interisland vessels only visit this lonely destination every four to six weeks. So, if you plan to come, your stay will be at least one month in duration. ~ BP 847, Papeete, Tahiti; 42-20-20.

There are six peaks on the island—Mt. Perehau is the tallest, reaching over 2100 feet (650 meters). Rapa once had a volcano, but it collapsed at its center. The resulting bay is now home to the island's harbor. Rapa has many deep caves and valleys, some of which open to the sea and are, in effect, also bays. There is no fringing reef to protect the coastline.

Historically, Rapa has had a connection to Easter Island. The island has strong **fortifications** known as *pa*—dozens of terraces on steep cliffs supported by walls built with basalt blocks piled on top of each other constructed by its ancient Polynesian residents. Discovered (but not claimed for Britain) in 1791 by explorer George Vancouver, carbon-14 dating indicates that there were approximately 2000 to 3000 inhabitants in the 18th century. Subsequent epidemics from the first European ships quickly decimated the local population.

France established Rapa as a protectorate in 1867 and annexed the island in 1881. Lengthy negotiations with Britain were inconclusive in resolving the issue of ownership, though New Zealand hoped that France would cede Rapa to Britain so that it could become an entrepôt between New Zealand and Panama.

These days international powers are not battling to control Rapa. In fact, its remote location makes it difficult to reach, and few boats call on the island.

With its southerly location, the mid-winter climate is freezing by Polynesian standards, with temperatures dropping to 41°F (5°C). The soil is comparatively poor on Rapa, but a variety of produce is grown, including taro (the staple), peaches, pears, passion fruit, figs and superb coffee. (Despite the homegrown coffee, the islanders seem to prefer Nescafé—they ship their beans to Tahiti.)

There is abundant seafood in the waters and on the shoreline. The Rapans eat a lot of mussels, oysters, crab, shrimp, sea urchin and lobster. Goat rounds out their menu.

LODGING   If you get to Rapa, **Chez Tinirau Faraire** is the only show in town. Located near the beach, it consists of one large home with three guest rooms, each with two single beds, a communal kitchen and bath with hot water. It's an acceptable accommodation, but, shall we say, quiet. Prepare to do your own cooking and bring your own food. It would be advisable to write to M. Tinirau Faraire at Haurei Village well in advance to let him know of your plans. ~ Haurei; 95-72-37, 95-72-66. BUDGET.

▼▼▼▼▼▼▼▼▼▼▼▼▼
Transportation

AIR

TUBUAI   Air Tahiti serves the island twice weekly from Papeete, Raiatea and Moorea. Flight time is 1 hour 40 minutes from Papeete to Tubuai. ~ 95-04-76.

RURUTU   Air Tahiti operates twice weekly to Rurutu from Papeete, Raiatea and Moorea. The flight time is 2 hours and 40 minutes from Papeete to Rurutu (via Tubuai). ~ 94-03-57.

SEA   The Austral Islands are served by the 196-foot (60-meter) *Tuhaa Pae II* (Papeete; 42-93-67). The itinerary is Rimatara/Rurutu/Tubuai/Raivavae and also Rapa (occasionally).

The best anchorage is in Avera Bay, which is quite safe during the prevailing easterly winds. Moerai Bay, however, is *not* safe when there are strong trade winds. There are several passes for landing boats on the northeast, west and southeast sides.

There are two passes on the northern coast of Raivavae. Yachting enthusiasts should note that there are anchorages off the village of Mahanatoa (except during north or northwest winds) and at Rairua Bay, at the west end of the island. Rairua Bay has a jetty and offers safe mooring at all times.

THIRTEEN

The Gambier Islands

The distant Gambier Islands (also known as the Mangareva Group) are located 1116 miles (1800 kilometers) southeast of Tahiti. They are comprised of a few atolls and four inhabited high islands—Aukena, Akamaru, Taravai and Mangareva—all formed from rims of extinct volcanic craters.

The islands are small and narrow, the largest being Mangareva with a length of four miles and a maximum width of one mile. The highest point in the group, Mt. Duff (1447 feet/441 meters), is also on Mangareva. The other high islands range form three-mile long Taravai to one-mile-long uninhabited Makaroa.

A principle feature of the group is a barrier reef that encircles the islands. The reef lies several miles off the coast of the main islands, protecting them from the fury of the Pacific. Above water from the north to the southwest and about 19 miles long and 15 miles wide, the reef is dotted with coconut palm-covered *motus*. To the west and southwest the submerged reef completes a circle.

Located just north of the Tropic of Capricorn, you'll find the climate of the Gambiers in this southern latitude is much cooler than Tahiti and the Society Islands. The prevailing winds are easterly trades, which increase in velocity from March to August. The hottest season is from December to March, when the temperature ranges between 73° and 90°F (24° to 33°C). In June and July, by contrast, the temperature only climbs to 78° F (26°C) and can drop as low as 65°F (19°C). The dry and rainy seasons are not well defined—be prepared for rain anytime.

Though the land is not particularly fertile, crops such as cantaloupe, watermelon, lettuce, eggplant, oranges and coffee are cultivated. The grapefruit, in particular, is exquisite. Black pearls are also farmed on Aukena, providing jobs and income for those residents fortunate enough to be involved in the trade.

The Gambier Group was once an independent entity within French Polynesia, with its own flag. This independent status no longer exists. The population of the Gambiers once numbered as many as 5000, but over the past 60 years, many of the inhabitants have migrated to Tahiti. Today, except for Mangareva, with a population of about 625, the Gambier Islands are virtually uninhabited. Only a handful of people live on the outer islands, following agricultural and aquacultural pursuits.

Mangareva

Mangareva, the main island in the Gambier Group, is surrounded by small rocky islets. Like the other high islands in the archipelago, it is characterized by a high, razor-backed ridge, with tertiary ridges running from the spine to the coast and which end in steep promontories. In between are bays and flat land. There are several beaches (not particularly good for bathing) composed of gray sand bespeckled with black grains formed from seaworn lava.

The higher elevations have little vegetation, except for a thick growth of cane grass, which in the drier months can be swept by fires. There is little ecological diversity, but on some of the slopes you can find dense thickets of oranges, *hau*, breadfruit, mango and other tropical trees. Despite the paucity of natural life, the island is aesthetically pleasing, with gentle rolling hills and a Mediterranean climate and feel.

There are three passes through the barrier reef into the outer lagoon. The main port is Rikitea, which provides good shelter from the sea. It is the only port open to commerce in the Mangareva Group. However, anchorage is vulnerable to the southeast trade winds. Rikitea is a small settlement with five shops, a post office, a dispensary and gendarmerie. Perhaps the most incongruous structure in this South Sea backwater is the huge covered sports stadium, and the large athletic field next to it.

The first settlers of Mangareva apparently drifted in small numbers from the Tuamotu Islands. Organized settlement, it is believed, began in the 14th century by people from the higher islands in the northwest. Rarotonga (part of the Cook Islands) is mentioned in the ancient traditions as the origin for some of the settlers, but local culture also shows an affinity to the Marquesans, who may also have been a colonizing source. In housing, clothing and general customs, Mangareva has much in common with Tahiti. (The dialect spoken in Mangareva resembles that of the Maori of New Zealand, the Cook Islands and the Tuamotu Archipelago.)

Though the islands may have been sighted as early as 1687, credit for the European discovery of the Mangareva Group is given to Captain James Wilson of the *Duff* in 1797, who may sighted Mangareva. In 1827, and in subsequent years, several vessels visited the group to obtain pearl shells.

In 1834, the Picpus fathers of France settled on Mangareva, and by 1836 the entire archipelago had been converted to Catholicism. Under the tyrannical leadership of Father Honoré Laval, a Belgian priest, the docile converts were taught to spin, weave, print, construct boats and above all, erect buildings. Laval organized a native police force, ordered women to become nuns and men to become monks. He forced the islanders to work relentlessly to construct a city of coral and stone.

The centerpiece of this city was the largest cathedral in French Polynesia—accommodating 2000 worshippers. In a similar neo-Gothic style, a school, triumphal arches, chapels, a convent, a monastery and a number of stone houses were also built at the behest of Laval. The massive construction projects took their toll on the health of the Mangarevans. A number of people suffered under the conditions of forced labor and servitude and in 1864 the new governor of Tahiti, Comte Emile de la Ronciere, visited the Gambiers to investigate the reports of this reign of terror, as well as Laval's purported trafficking in pearls and shell. When de la Ronciere ordered the prisons opened, he found two young boys in a dungeon

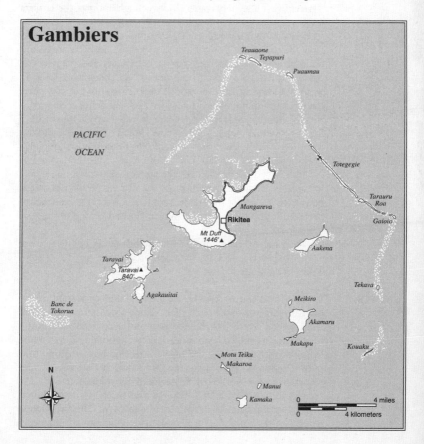

Gambiers

Teauaone
Tepapuri

Puaumau

PACIFIC

OCEAN

Totegegie

Tarauru
Roa

Mangareva

Gaioio

Rikitea

Mt Duff
1446'▲

Aukena

Taravai

Taravai▲
840'

Tekava

Agakauitai

Banc de
Tokorua

Meikiro

Akamaru

Makapu

Kouaku

Motu Teiku
Makaroa

N

Manui

Kamaka

0   4 miles

0   4 kilometers

(which was a large hole in the prison grounds, still visible today)—their cardinal sin had been to laugh during a mass. Laval's reign was finally brought to an end in 1871. You can read about Father Honoré Laval's strange saga in James Michener's collection of stories, *Return to Paradise*.

A testament to Laval's obsession with building are the more than 116 structures that still remain in the Gambiers. (A counterpoint to the injustices perpetrated by Laval is a development center to train youths in mechanics and carpentry that was opened in 1982 by the Freres of the Sacred Heart of Quebec.)

Today, Mangareva's main industry is the cultivation of black pearls, and to some degree, jewelry making, which involves cutting and grinding items out of mother-of-pearl. Robert Wan, the "Pearl King" of French Polynesia, has invested extensively on nearby Aukena, which today produces a number of high-quality pearls. Agriculture is also important. Oddly enough, most of the farmers are Europeans.

Mangareva is tranquil, another South Sea island so far removed from the rest of the world that you sometimes feel you are on another planet. You come here for the tranquility and the undeveloped nature of the island. Locals are shy, and like their cousins in the Austral Group, seldom see visitors. Perhaps it is the slow pace, but residents do not appear interested in going out of their way to show visitors around, even if you are willing to spend money for a tour. It's not that they are inhospitable, but as a friend of mine who recently visited noted, "They have no idea that tourists are interested in seeing the island." Locals also tend to be unreliable. For example, when asking directions for a particular guest house, five individuals will most likely give you five different responses, and if you are lucky, one of the answers may be correct. This could happen even if you speak perfect French. (Virtually none of the residents speak English.)

There are no restrictions on visiting the islands, but flying there is very expensive, perhaps as much as a round-trip ticket from Tahiti to the United States.

SIGHTS   In the main village of **Rikitea** you'll find a number of **ruins**, seemingly from a lost civilization, that include a convent, a triumphal arch, several watch towers, a prison and a court. These mostly tumble-down ruins have an eerie, dark feel about them, even in the light of day. Dominating the village is the **tomb** of Gregorio Maputeoa, the last king of Mangareva, who died in 1868 after having requested status as a French Protectorate for the island.

Not to be missed is **St. Michel of Rikitea**, the Catholic church built under the auspices of Father Honoré Laval. This neo-Gothic wonder of the South Seas was built of fired limestone, and incorporated mother-of-pearl inlay in its interior. (Though in need of repair, it is still in use.) Across the path from the church is the well-maintained 140-year-old **rectory**, occupied by the parish priest.

Chez Pierre and Mariette Paeamara consists of a three-bedroom concrete home, complete with living room, dining room, kitchen, and (cold water) bath facilities. The hosts, Pierre and Mariette, are extremely hospitable. They have a slew of activities available—a visit to a *motu* by outrigger speed canoe, fishing expeditions, or a tour of the family-owned pearl farm. They also provide auto tours around the island as well as visits to historical sites or treks up to Mt. Duff. The food at Chez Pierre and Mariette Paeamara is quite good. In fact, the only problem you might encounter here are occasional water shortages. ~ Rikitea; 97-82-87. MODERATE.

LODGING

Chez Terii and Hélène Paeamara is a two-bedroom home with living room, dining room, kitchen and (cold water) bath. Terii and Hélène are also as hospitable as their kin down the street, Pierre and Mariette. The cuisine they provide is very tasty. Not surprisingly, Terii and Hélène have a similar list of excursions as Pierre and Mariette. They, too, make excellent guides. Water shortages are the only problems you might have to deal with. You can't go wrong staying with either family. ~ Rikitea; 97-82-80. MODERATE.

The latest pension to sprout up on Mangareva is **Chez Linda**. Operated by the gracious Henri Jacquot, it consists of one very comfortable bungalow located on the edge of the lagoon in Rikitea. For the price of a night's lodging, Henri provides breakfast as well as free bicycles for his guests. If you stay a week, he will give you a free boat trip to the *motu* that fringes the lagoon. ~ Rikitea; 97-82-47. MODERATE TO DELUXE.

There are no restaurants on Mangareva, but there is one minuscule **snack bar** that theoretically opens for lunch. The snack bar is nameless, and while a colleague of mine was there recently, she saw

DINING

THE GAMBIERS UNIQUE EXPERIENCES

- Visit **St. Michel of Rikitea**, a neo-Gothic church from the reign of Father Honoré Laval, and still in use today. *page 400*
- Spend some time at one of the **pensions** and avail yourself of the activities they have to offer. *page 401*
- Follow the **goat trail** to the top of Mt. Duff for otherworldly views. *page 402*
- Spot tropical fish as you **snorkel** the blue waters off Akamaru. *page 402*

neither proprietor nor customer during her entire stay of several weeks. In other words, don't count on it being open!

GROCERIES There are five markets on the island and their stock gradually decreases until the arrival of the next interisland freighter. Unfortunately, there's no bakery. Bread is brought in from Tahiti twice a month. So, unless you like stale bread, you are better off acquiring a taste for banana tarts, which are great, and are stocked in some of the shops. Oddly enough, despite the isolation, prices are more reasonable than on Bora Bora or Moorea.

SHOPPING A few local artisans (who can be located via the management of your lodging facility) sell carved mother-of-pearl items. There are no other souvenirs to speak of, except a postcard of Mt. Duff.

BEACHES **AKAMARU AND TORTEGEGIE** There are white-sand beaches on the outlying *motus* that fringe the lagoon. Coconut palms provide shade on both Akamaru and Tortegegie, but there are no facilities. The swimming and snorkeling are quite good. Snorkeling is best on Akamaru. Here you'll find plenty of fish and coral gardens close the the shore. ~ The local pensions will provide transportation and picnic lunches to the beaches and *motus*.

▼▼▼▼▼▼▼▼▼▼▼▼▼
Outdoor Adventures

The trek up Mt. Duff is hard work. The mountainside is filled with scrubby, overgrown vegetation and tall grass that may hide the goat trails

HIKING that meander up to the ridge. You often have to get down on all fours to clamber through the bush (and sometimes mud) to navigate the hill. Getting to the base of Mt. Duff is easy—it is located directly behind the village of Rikitea. You simply follow the goat tracks that seem to dead-end every few feet. It is then up to you to decide which is the correct route to follow. The hike takes about three hours to the peak, but the view of the island and lagoon is worth the effort.

▼▼▼▼▼▼▼▼▼▼
Transportation

The airport is built on the *motu* of Totegegie, across the lagoon from Rikitea, Mangareva's principal village. **Air Tahiti** visits Mangareva twice a month from Tahiti (more

AIR often during school holidays). Flights are scheduled in such a way that you can stay one or three (or more) weeks. The flight time is five hours, sometimes with a stop at Hao. Upon arrival in the Gambiers, sea-shuttle service is provided between Totegegie (where the airport is located) and Rikitea, the main town on Mangareva. The crossing time is 30 minutes.

SEA The **Ruahutu** and the **Manava III** also visit the Gambiers. ~ Papeete; 43-32-65.

Recommended Reading

A formidable number of books have been written about French Polynesia, some of them only readily available in the islands themselves.

CULTURE, ARCHEOLOGY AND NATURAL HISTORY

The Art of Tahiti (Thames & Hudson, 1979) by Terence Barrow gives an overview of Polynesian art before European contact, with an emphasis on Tahiti.

Coral Kingdoms (New York, Abradale Press, 1990) by Carl Roessler is a survey of the world's popular dive sites. Carl Roessler is a dive travel pioneer and a respected underwater photographer.

Diving in Tahiti—a Divers' Guide to French Polynesia (Les Editions du Pacifique, 1991) by Thierry Zysman has an introduction to diving in French Polynesia plus a great many detailed descriptions of specific dive sites in Tahiti, Moorea, Huahine, Raiatea, Tahaa, Bora Bora, Rangiroa and Manihi. Well illustrated and full of color photos.

Exploring Tropical Islands and Seas—An Introduction for the Traveler and Amateur Naturalist (Prentice Hall, 1984) by Frederic Martini is not specifically on French Polynesia but is nonetheless a fine primer on the natural history of tropical islands. The title explains it all. Subjects covered include general island environment, coral reefs, marine life, geology and sharks.

A Fragile Paradise: Nature and Man in the Pacific (Collins, London, 1989) by Andrew Mitchell is for anyone interested in the natural history of the South Pacific, especially the interplay between man and nature. An important and fascinating work, it is both scholarly and yet eminently readable. *A Fragile Paradise* provides a comprehensive background on how the flora and fauna found their way to the Pacific Islands and how the presence of man has altered the ecological equation. A number of fine color prints are also included.

Hidden Worlds of Polynesia (Harcourt, Brace and World, New York, 1963) is by Robert Suggs, an American archeologist who did seminal work in the Marquesas group during the 1950s and 1960s in the areas of archeology and anthropology. Probably the most popular of Suggs' works, *Hidden Worlds* is a narrative that chronicles the year the anthropologist spent on Nuku Hiva excavating for the American Museum of Natural History of New York. It is as much about the problems of living in Marquesan culture as it is about Marquesan archeology. A must for would-be visitors and students of contemporary French Polynesia.

Hiva Oa, Glimpses of an Oceanic Memory (Departement Archeologie, 1991) by Pierre Ottino and Marie-Noele de Berge-Ottino is another fine book on the Marquesas. Both Ottinos are archeologists and their scholarly 50-page booklet is packed with fascinating historical information and maps on the region. For visitors to the Marquesas or armchair archeologists, this is a must-read. Unfortunately, it is only available in Tahiti.

The Island Civilizations of Polynesia (New American Library, Mentor Books, New York, 1960) by Robert C. Suggs, was an attempt to summarize the results of stratigraphic excavations and other approaches to Polynesian pre-history. The book is dated now but is useful as a period piece representative of a certain stage in the development of thought on the topic of Polynesian pre-history.

Islands of Tahiti (Kea Editions, 1991) by Raymond Bagnis, with photos by Erwin Christian, is a coffee-table book on French Polynesia with some evocative images.

Keneti, South Seas Adventures of Kenneth Emory (University of Hawaii Press, 1988) by Bob Krauss is the fascinating biography of Kenneth P. Emory, perhaps the most influential 20th-century archeologist to work in French Polynesia. Emory, a contemporary of Margaret Mead, inspired a generation of archeologists. Bob Krauss refers to Emory as the "father" of dirt archeology in Polynesia. Emory pioneered the study of Polynesian migration and was the first archeologist in Polynesia to carbon date artifacts.

L' Archipel des Marquises (Les Editions Le Motu, Boulogne, 1994) by Paule Laudon, Franck Brouillet, Emmanuel Deschamps and Christian Ruhle, covers the Marquesas region.

Les Atolls des Tuamotu (Editions de l'Orstrom, 1994) by Jacques Bonuallot, Pierre Laboute, Francis Rougerie and Emmanuel Vigneron, is a wonderful source of photographs featuring the atolls of the Tuamotu archipelago.

Les Editions du Pacifique series (available in English) has a number of books on natural history that cover a wide variety of local flora and fauna. Typical titles include *Birds of Tahiti* by Jean-Claude Thibault and Claude Rivers, *Sharks of Polynesia* by R. H. Johnson, *Shells of Tahiti*, *Living Corals*, and other titles.

Little Worlds of the Pacific: An Essay on Pacific Basin Biogeography (University of Hawaii, 1980) by E. Alison Kay, is a 39-page academically oriented book that details the distribution of flora and fauna in the Pacific.

Man's Conquest of the Pacific (Oxford University Press, 1979) by Peter Bellwood and *The Prehistory of Polynesia* (Harvard University, 1979) edited by J.D. Jennings, are for readers interested in more hard-core Polynesian archeology.

Marquesan Sexual Behavior (Harcourt, Brace and World, New York, 1966) by Robert C. Suggs is the result of joint research between Suggs and his wife. It is an attempt, in his words, "to correct some of the wacko psychoanalytic fantasies on this topic published in the late 1930s by Ralph Linton and Abram Kardiner." As a registered nurse, Suggs' wife worked almost exclusively with women while he interviewed men. Good bedside reading from one of the more knowledgeable people on Marquesan society.

Noa Noa by Paul Gauguin is an autobiographical account of his life in Tahiti.

The Snorkeller's Guide to the Coral Reef From the Red Sea to the Pacific Ocean (Exile Publishing, 1994) by Paddy Ryan is both a primer for neophytes that covers every conceivable aspect of snorkeling and a wonderful introduction to the flora and fauna of the coral reef. The book is tightly written and illustrated with glorious color photos of the creatures that inhabit the reef system and the aqueous environs of a tropical island. Paddy, a well-known New Zealand underwater photographer and naturalist, begins by covering the basics, such as what type of gear to buy and tips on first aid. He then looks at the marine flora and fauna found in the reefs. It is a valuable resource both for the serious snorkeler or the armchair traveler who has no intention of ever dipping a toe in the warm waters of a Tahitian lagoon.

The Société des Océanistes publishes a range of small booklets on specific subjects such as aviation in Tahiti, sacred sites, Pomare, Bougainville, etc., etc.

Tahiti from the Air (Les Editions du Pacifique, 1985) by Erwin Christian and Emmanuel Vigneron has wonderful aerial photos of French Polynesia, although the construction of new hotels has already made some of the shots look out of date.

The Tahiti Handbook (Editions Avant et Après, 1993) by Jean-Louis Saquet covers French Polynesia's geography, history and natural history with general information on marine life, plant life, canoe design, arts and crafts plus a great deal more. There are plenty of illustrations and it's very comprehensive, but a bit on the superficial side. (Available in English and French editions.)

Tahiti Romance & Reality (Millwood Press, Wellington, 1982) is a coffee-table book by the prolific James Siers, who specializes in South Pacific photography.

Tahiti, The Magic of the Black Pearl (Tahiti, 1986) by Paule Solomon is informative and has beautiful photographs. *Black Pearls of Tahiti* (Tahiti, 1987) by Jean Paul Lintilhac, is less glitzy than the Paule Solomon book but is more authoritative and factual. The photographs are also very good. Recommended for those with an interest in black pearls.

Tahitians—Mind & Experience in the Society Islands (1973) by Robert I. Levy is a tome-like work written by an anthropologist for anthropologists. It's a bit unwieldy but packed with all kinds of cultural information—a good reference book.

Tatau—Maohi Tattoo (Tupuna Productions, 1993) by Dominique Morvan, photographs by Claude Corault and Marie-Hélène Villierme, is a fascinating account of the resurgence of traditional tattooing in French Polynesia. Terrific black-and-white photos of all the tattoos anyone could hope to see.

Tuamotu (Les Editions du Pacifique, Papeete, 1986), a coffee-table book by Erwin Christian and Dominique Charnay, is a photo essay on the people, as well as the flora and fauna of the Tuamotus.

HISTORY

The Fatal Impact by Alan Moorehead along with David Howarth's book is the best available historical account of early Tahiti. It centers mainly around the three voyages of Captain Cook, portraying him as a humane commander but offering the premise that contact with white civilization in general was to have horrible repercussions. Moorehead points out that within 80 years of Cook's visit to Tahiti the population on French Polynesia decreased from 40,000 to 9000, and the culture deteriorated because of disuse by the end of the 19th century.

Mutiny and Romance in the South Seas: A Companion to the Bounty Adventure (1989) by Sven Wahlroos is a must for *Bounty* enthusiasts. Wahlroos, a Finnish-born psychologist who practices in southern California, describes his book as one that "sets forth the known facts of the story and also points to those circumstances of which we cannot be sure." He feels strongly that Ian Ball's *Pitcairn: Children of Mutiny* is not an entirely reliable source on the subject.

Tahiti: a Paradise Lost (1984) by David Howarth is the best book I've encountered on the experience of the early explorers of French Polynesia—Wallis, Cook, Bougainville and company. It's fascinating and reads almost like a novel. A must for South Pacific addicts.

The Voyages of the Endeavour, 1768-1771 (1955) by Captain James Cook, is the classic edition of Cook's logbooks, edited by J.C. Beaglehole, four volumes.

MODERN ACCOUNTS

France and the South Pacific: A Contemporary History (University of Hawaii Press, 1992) by Stephen Hennigham is a comprehensive work that covers French Polynesia as well as other areas of French influence in the Pacific such as Vanuatu, Wallis and Futuna and New Caledonia. It is probably the most serious contemporary history of the region available in English. For students of issues such as nuclear testing, the Tahitian independence movement and the genesis of the current Tahitian political scene, this is the book to purchase.

The Happy Isles of Oceania (1992) by Paul Theroux is a chronicle of the kayaking adventures of one of America's best writers through the South Pacific. The ever-acerbic but oh-so-astute Theroux is a pleasure to read. The chapters devoted to French Polynesia recount his experiences on Tahiti and Moorea as well as a voyage to the Marquesas. His descriptions of the dysfunctional world of neocolonialism, *Heiva* in Papeete, and his search for a long-lost cousin are entertaining and insightful.

Home & Away (1994) by Ron Wright, is a collection of essays by a man who has been called Canada's most renowned travel writer. And with good reason. Although the book covers a wide swath of turf (other than French Polynesia), Wright unerringly hones in on the Marquesas Islands, where he spent several weeks on the *Aranui*. Very few writers juggle and juxtapose travel, history and life in the late 20th century better than Ron Wright. Leave it to Mr. Wright to turn his vacation into a search for the literary ghost of Herman Melville. What's not surprising is that he tracks Melville down in the deepest jungles of Nuku Hiva. The book may only be available in Canada.

Kon-Tiki is a nonfiction classic describing the 1948 voyage of Thor Heyerdahl's crew of Europeans aboard a Polynesian-style raft sailing from the coast of South America to French Polynesia. The purpose of the voyage was to "prove" Heyerdahl's theory that Polynesians may have migrated from the South American continent instead of Asia. Whether or not you subscribe to Heyerdahl's theories, the book is a great adventure story.

Moruroa Mon Amour—the French Nuclear Tests in the Pacific (1977), by Bengt & Marie-Therese Danielsson, traces the history of the atomic bomb in French Polynesia and the socioeconomic effects it has had on Tahiti. Danielsson, who originally came to French Polynesia aboard the *Kon-Tiki*, has been the leading spokesperson against the nuclear testing program and at times a lonely voice of conscience.

Tahiti Blue and Other Modern Tales of the South Pacific (Les Editions de Tahiti, Tahiti, 1990) by Alex du Prel is a collection of short stories reflecting the modern reality of French Polynesia as interpreted by Tahiti's number-one raconteur. Du Prel, who formerly managed Brando's resort, has been in the South Pacific for many years and is a veritable institution.

Tahiti, Forlorn Paradise (1978) by K.K. Stewart, is a thinly veiled autobiographical novel by a former Oakland, California, writer. The plot centers around an expat writer who has become disenchanted with life in the U.S. Like his spiritual mentor (also from Oakland) Jack London, he seeks to find himself in the balmy South Seas. The not-so-hidden agenda of the protagonist and his equally randy sidekick, Chico Kidd, is to find the mythical little brown girl in the little grass shack. Both set sail for Tahiti full of great expectations. Written in the form of diary, the work chronicles their misadventures.

Tahiti, Island of Love by Robert Langdon is, as one of my esteemed colleagues says, one of the more popular accounts of Tahiti's history. Though most likely out of print, it's worth looking for.

Tin Roofs & Palm Trees (1977) by Robert Trumbull is a serious socioeconomic/political overview of the South Pacific nations with particular emphasis on their emergence into the 20th century. Trumbull is a former *New York Times* correspondent and writes with authority on the subject. This is a good primer on the background of the modern-day South Pacific.

A Writer's Notebook (1984) by W. Somerset Maugham is a well-known collection of notes, journals and character sketches, some of which Maugham later used in his short stories and novels. The collection covers the period 1892 to 1944, with 40 pages devoted to his travels in the Pacific including Tahiti, Samoa, Fiji and Hawaii. For Maugham lovers, the reading is fascinating.

NOVELS AND ISLAND TALES

The Blue of Capricorn (1977) is Eugene Burdick's delightful collection of short stories and nonfiction essays about the South Pacific. Burdick, a master of the craft and coauthor of *The Ugly American*, explores white people's fascination with the tropics. It's one of the best collections of the South Pacific genre available.

South Seas Tales by Jack London is not London's most famous work but has a few good tales including *The House of Mapuhi*, the slanderous story of an avaricious pearl buyer. It's based on a real-life character with whom London had an axe to grind.

Typee: a Real Romance of the South Seas; *Omoo: a Narrative of Adventures in the South Seas, a Sequel to Typee* and *Marquesas Islands* by Herman Melville are all based on Melville's experiences on the islands.

Tahiti's Literati

Ever since its depiction as a Garden of Eden by 19th-century romantics, Tahiti has attracted not only missionaries and vagabonds, but artists and writers as well.

PAUL GAUGUIN AND TAHITI

"The reason why I am leaving is that I wish to live in peace and to avoid being influenced by our civilization. I only desire to create simple art. In order to achieve this, it is necessary for me to steep myself in virgin nature, to see no one but savages, to share their life and have as my sole occupation to render, just as children would do, the images of my own brain, using exclusively the means offered by primitive art, which are the only true and valid ones."

On April 1, 1891, Gauguin left Europe and 69 days later arrived in Papeete. No earthly paradise, Papeete in the late 19th century was a ramshackle, administrative center of a third-rate colony—a collection of brick buildings and clapboard houses with tin roofs. The local populace was equally disappointing. The noble savages he had envisioned were clothed in sarongs, white shirts and straw hats, while their female counterparts wore missionary-inspired ankle-length Mother Hubbard dresses. Local society, composed of French officials and their French or native wives, entertained each other with gossip and endless dinner parties.

Gauguin decided it would be better to spend his time with Tahitians and moved into a Tahitian-style hut. He worked feverishly and by 1893 sailed back to France with 66 paintings and a dozen wooden sculptures. There were numerous landscapes, portraits and scenes that depicted contemporary life in French Polynesia. These included Tahitians bathing in a stream, men inspecting their fishing nets, women weaving hats and the like. Examples of these are *Under the Pandanus*, *The Burao Tree* and *Parau parau*. While the details are realistic and historically correct, as photos of the time confirm, Gauguin's eye is discriminating. He chose the most idyllic and aesthetically pleasing aspects of life on the island as his subjects. Other paintings were taken from themes found in Tahitian myth or religion.

With much fanfare, Gauguin organized a Paris exhibition on November 9, 1893. Unfortunately, no one in France seemed to recognize his genius, and his exhibition failed miserably. Although unsuccessful at selling his art, Gauguin did receive a small inheritance from an uncle, which provided enough money for him to carry on. He returned to Tahiti. So despondent was he that he even told a friend that he was giving up painting "apart from what I may do for my own amusement." In short, this was to be a voyage of no return. On September 9, 1895, he was back in Papeete.

Shortly after his return he sought a proper home. His declining health made him more dependent on being near a hospital, so he moved only eight miles from Papeete, in the Punaauia district. He decided to purchase his own plot, where he constructed a small plank house and studio. (The site is currently marked by a sign adjacent to a school in Punaauia.)

Even though Gauguin no longer had to pay rent, his cash-flow problems continued. He sold few paintings and lived almost solely on the credit granted to him by the local Chinese merchant. Ill health continued to plague him and at the end of 1897 he suffered from fainting fits and long bouts of insomnia, and was coughing up blood. He was ready to take his own life but before doing so he had to paint one last picture. Taking burlap used to make bags for copra as a canvas, Gauguin created his masterpiece: *Where do we come from? What are we? Where are we going?* He then swallowed an enormous dose of arsenic, but vomited up the poison and miraculously recovered.

In 1901, Gauguin received an unexpected offer from a Paris art dealer who agreed to pay him a salary for every picture he produced. With his chronic money problems out of the way, Gauguin, still in search of paradise or at least a primitive culture, decided to move to the isolated Marquesan island of Hiva Oa. His decision to move to the Marquesas was dictated primarily by the fine carvings he had seen in the Tahitian homes of civil servants who had been posted to those remote islands. Despite the exquisite bowls and other artifacts he had seen, Gauguin soon discovered the sad state of the Marquesan population, which had been decimated by disease, liquor and other endowments of Western civilization.

He settled in Atuona, the village and administrative center of Hiva Oa, which had a population of about 500 locals, a dozen European settlers and Chinese shopkeepers, a Protestant missionary and a small Catholic enclave. Gauguin found a vacant lot where he built himself a two-story structure that was the finest home in the Marquesas. Above the door in large letters a sign read *Maison du Jouir (House of Pleasure)*. He soon acquired a companion, Marie-Rose, a 14-year-old *vahine*, who until then had been a resident of the Catholic mission school. She soon became pregnant, returned to her parents and gave birth to a daughter on September 14, 1902.

With plenty of money to spend, Gauguin became well known for his wild parties and quickly incurred the wrath of the local clergy and police. But, with some financial security, two servants, a home and Marie-Rose, he had the wherewithal to produce in just a few months over 20 splendid works. These included *Horsemen on the Beach*, *Et l'or or de leurs Corps* and *The Call*.

In the final months of 1902 the artist's life came to a sad ending. His health declined, new enemies in the tiny community objected to his parties, his near abduction of Marie-Rose and his lifestyle.

On the morning of May 8, Gauguin sent for the Protestant pastor, with whom he shared some interests. He complained of pains and fainting spells. Later that morning a Marquesan neighbor found the artist lying on his bed with one leg hanging over the edge. The visitor was not certain that the painter was alive, so he resorted to a tried and true Marquesan tradition—a bite on the head—to determine Gauguin's state. He then sang an ancient death chant.

Gauguin lies buried in a cemetery on a hill above the village of Atuona. His "House of Pleasure" has been restored near its original location, next to a museum dedicated to the painter and Marquesan culture. (See Chapter Eleven for more information.)

HERMAN MELVILLE

In June 1842, the *Acushnet*, a Yankee whaler, dropped anchor off Nuku Hiva in the Marquesas. Aboard the vessel, 22-year-old Herman Melville couldn't wait to step ashore. He had already faced one and a half years of deprivation at sea and knew he wouldn't be returning home until all the whale oil barrels were filled, perhaps two, three or even four years later. He and a friend named Toby stuffed a few biscuits beneath their clothing and jumped ship. They hid in the deep, forested recesses of the island's interior, safe from the ship's crew that would surely come looking for them. They hiked for days on end with little food and no shelter. The fact that Melville's leg was burning with infection made the trek even more excruciating. The two young men found their way to the Typee Valley, home of a tribe known for its ferocity.

Toby disappeared looking for medical aid for his friend and Melville was to spend the next four months with the Typees, an experience that would be the basis for his first book, *Typee*. He was treated well by the Marquesans, who gave him a servant and royal attention from Mehevi, the chief. However, Melville was never sure of the natives' intentions. Was he being treated as a distinguished visitor or simply being fattened for the kill? After all, these people were cannibals.

Fortunately for world literature, Melville survived his sojourn with the Typee, during which he was held in a sort of protective custody. He dwelt with the Marquesans neither in bliss nor in terror. He observed closely and made some startling revelations. "There were," said Melville, "none of the thousand sources of irritation that the ingenuity of civilized man has created to mar his own felicity." He noted that there were no debtors, no orphans, no destitute, no lovesick maidens, no grumpy bachelors, no melancholy youth, no spoiled brats and none of the root of all evil—money.

Melville adapted well, enjoying the company of a *vahine* named Fayaway and the companionship of the men. His foot, however, was still inflamed and spiritually he was isolated. He needed medical care but the Typees were unwilling to let him go. His situation was well known on the island and with the help of sympathetic natives and a captain who was hard up for crew members, he escaped by joining up with the Sydney whaler *Lucy Ann*, which sailed to Tahiti.

Apparently the conditions on the *Lucy Ann*—inedible food, cockroach and rat infestation and rotten rigging—were so god-awful that upon reaching Tahiti, Melville decided to join the crew members in a mutiny rather than continue. His fellow travelers—with such romantic names as Doctor Long Ghost (the ship's surgeon!), Bembo (a tattooed Maori harpooner), Jingling Joe, Long Jim, Black Dan, Bungs, Blunt Bill and Flash Jack—didn't need much persuading. When they refused to sail and complained to British Consul Charles Wilson in Papeete, Wilson decided against the mutineers and with the support of the French Admiral Dupetit Thouars, had them locked up. Melville was imprisoned in the *Calabooza Beretanee*, the local jail. After his release six weeks later, he went to the remote village of Temae on Moorea (now near the airport) and talked the chief into allowing the women to dance the *Lory-Lory* (the precursor of the *Tamure*), an erotic, passionate performance that the missionaries had forbidden, naturally.

Four years later Melville laboriously put together *Typee: a Peep at Polynesian Life*, which received immediate attention in America and Europe. Some critics hailed it, some doubted its authenticity, and others called it racy. The missionaries (who weren't treated too kindly in the book) found it appalling. Both *Typee* and *Omoo* were outspoken tirades against the ruination of the Pacific by Western civilization. Why, Melville asked, should the natives be forced to participate in an alien church, to kowtow to a foreign government, and to adopt strange and harmful ways of living? In *The Fatal Impact*, Alan Moorehead writes that although Melville was "possibly libelous and certainly scandalous in much that he wrote," his account of the "sleaziness and inertia that had overtaken life" in Papeete in 1842 is remarkably vivid. Perhaps Melville was accurate as well. Moorehead says that many of the Tahitians—by this time caught between the missionaries, the whalers and finally the French—had "lost the will to survive—the effort to adjust to the outside world had been too much."

PIERRE LOTI

Midshipman Louis Marie Julien Viaud, who later became known to the world as Pierre Loti, first came to Tahiti in the 1880s aboard a French naval vessel. His largely autobiographical book, *The Marriage of Loti*, brought him fame and is credited with influencing Paul Gauguin to come to Tahiti. In the book he describes his friendship with Queen Pomare IV and his all-consuming love affair with Rarahu, a young girl from Bora Bora.

Loti's book tells how he came upon Rarahu bathing in a pool (which still can be visited today) in the Fautaua Valley near Papeete. There he witnessed the girl accepting a length of red ribbon from an elderly Chinese man as payment for a kiss. Rarahu was poor and this type of behavior was not unusual for a girl of little means. Nevertheless, as a result of what the incensed Frenchman saw, the Chinese in Tahiti suffered for years following the 1881 publication of *The Marriage of Loti*. Despite Loti's virulently anti-Chinese propaganda, the book gave an accurate account of life in Tahiti during the late 19th century.

ROBERT LOUIS STEVENSON

Robert Louis Stevenson arrived in the Marquesas with his wife and mother in 1888, marking the first leg of his six-year voyage to the South Seas aboard the *Casco*. The South Pacific held him spellbound. In the Marquesas the health of the frail writer improved dramatically. He spent his days wading in the lagoon, searching for shells, or riding horses. The Stevenson clan was impressed by the generosity and kindness of the locals, so much, that even Stevenson's mother, a staunch supporter of the missionaries, began to question whether forcing religion on the natives was actually beneficial.

From the Marquesas the *Casco* set sail for the Tuamotu atoll of Fakareva, where the Stevensons spent the balmy evenings trading tales with Donat Rimareau, the half-caste French governor of the island. The author's *The Isle of Voices* incorporated Rimareau's tales into his story.

Tahiti was the next stop on the *Casco's* itinerary. The travelers found Papeete to have a "half and halfness" between Western and Tahitian culture, which they disliked and they soon set sail for the other side of the island. There the Stevensons befriended a Tahitian princess (whom Pierre Loti had much admired) and a chief, who helped them. By this time Stevenson had become very ill, the family was short of money and the *Casco* needed extensive repairs. The generous Tahitians, who offered the wayfarers food, shelter and moral support, were a godsend. The long stopover allowed Stevenson time to work and recuperate. Stevenson's wife wrote that the clan sailed from Tahiti for Honolulu on Christmas Day of 1888 "in a very thankful frame of mind."

JACK LONDON

Perhaps the most controversial American writer of his day, Jack London first came to French Polynesia in 1906 on the ill-fated voyage of the *Snark*. He and his wife arrived in the Marquesas after nearly dying of thirst at sea because one of the crew members had inadvertently left the water tap open during a storm. The Londons stayed on Nuku Hiva for several weeks, renting the house where Robert Louis Stevenson had stayed. They also visited the Typee Valley, immortalized in Melville's *Typee*, one of London's favorite childhood books. London was, however, disappointed by what he saw. Melville's vision of 19th-century French Polynesia no longer existed, and London referred to the natives as "half-breeds," blaming the whites for the corrupting influence that decimated the Marquesan race both physically and spiritually. He spent his days feasting on tropical fruit, relaxing in the sun, collecting curios and trying to ward off huge wasps and *no-nos*, vicious flies that inflict a nasty bite.

The next stop for the *Snark* was Tahiti, where London was greeted with the news that back home his checks had bounced. To make matters worse, he did not get along with some of the French officials, and thieves stole many items from his boat. Perhaps this is why the writer did not write about Tahiti in more flattering terms. In *The Cruise of the Snark* he wrote: "Tahiti is one of the most beautiful spots in the world," but for the most part was inhabited by "human vermin." He took a dislike to a well-known pearl buyer, Emile Levy, and in *South Sea Tales* unfairly depicted the Frenchman as an avaricious businessman who cheated a native out of a huge pearl and who met a horrible death. London did not bother to change Levy's name or physical description in the story, and the pearl buyer was furious. Even the other residents of Tahiti, who were not terribly fond of the hard-driving businessman, thought London had gone too far. In the end, Levy successfully sued London, who had long since returned to the United States, but who paid dearly in the end for his outpouring of venom.

RUPERT BROOKE

While visiting the west coast of the United States in 1913, Rupert Brooke, the great soldier/poet of the Edwardian age, suddenly decided to tour the South Seas. He came to Tahiti in January 1914, where he lingered until April, nursing an injury caused by bumping against coral. During this time he fell in love with a beautiful Tahitian woman named *Taata* (who he called *Mamua*). It was here that he composed perhaps his three best poems, *The Great Lover*, *Retrospect* and *Tiare Tahiti*. According to biographer John Lehman, it was with Mamua that Brooke had the only "perfect and surely consummated love-affair of his life." Wrote Brooke in *Tiare Tahiti*:

> "Mamua when our laughter ends,
> And hearts and bodies, brown as white,
> Are dust about the doors of friends,
> Or scent a-blowing down the night,
> Then, oh! then the wise agree, Comes our immortality..."

On returning to San Francisco, Brooke's thoughts returned to Tahiti and his lover continued to haunt him. In 1915, on a hospital ship off Skyros, Brooke died of food poisoning at the tender age of 28. On his deathbed in the Aegean, he wrote these instructions to a friend: "Try to inform Taata of my death. Mlle. Taata, Hotel Tiare, Papeete, Tahiti. It might find her. Give her my love." Several years later, when Somerset Maugham came to Tahiti to research a book on Gauguin, Brooke's old friends still wept uncontrollably at the mention of his native name, *Purpure*, the only name they knew him by.

SOMERSET MAUGHAM

Among the works of the English writer Somerset Maugham is *The Moon and Sixpence*, a novel based on the life of Paul Gauguin. During World War I, when, according to Maugham, "the old South Seas characters were by necessity confined to the islands," he visited Tahiti to research the book. There he not only culled reminiscences of the painter from people who knew him, but also learned more of writers like Loti, Brooke, Robert Louis Stevenson and Jack London. Like those writers before him, Maugham was entranced by the magic of the South Seas. He spent his time interviewing everyone who knew Gauguin, including businessmen, a sea captain and a hotel proprietress. In Maugham's words, he wanted to make the protagonist of his novel as "credible as possible."

Despite Maugham's enchantment with Tahiti, most of his short stories about the South Pacific—including *Rain*, which immortalized the prostitute Sadie Thompson—took place in Samoa. Of this the author commented, "The really significant fiction of the world today involves a husband and wife relationship, the problems that lovers encounter and overcome, a cuckolded man, a jilted woman, an unrequited or pretended love for the other. From sexual conflicts we have our revenge and homicidal motives." However, Maugham observed that in a place like Tahiti, "where there are sexual licenses, excesses, the condoning attitude on infidelity, a tolerance of promiscuity, and an absence of sexual possessiveness, there does not exist the emotional tension that precipitates human drama. . . ." In addition, Maugham asserted "that Tahiti is a French possession, and the French with their *laissez faire* and *mènage-a-trois* tolerance of sexual philandering and indulgences don't really provide believable fictional protagonists for any human-triangle, story or play unless you want to make a comedy or farce out of the situation."

Paul Gauguin's case, however, falls into a different category. When the artist came to Tahiti, "the languor of this island, the Polynesian playfulness, the castrative sexuality that abounded there, could not save him from his ultimate and wretched fate. That of course was Gauguin's predetermined course of tragedy," Maugham said.

NORDHOFF AND HALL

James Norman Hall and Charles Nordhoff first met in the military service at the end of World War I when they were commissioned to write a history of the Lafayette Flying Corps. They were vastly different in temperament: Hall was shy, optimistic and romantic. Nordhoff, outwardly more confident, was pessimistic and skeptical. Hall was a native of Iowa. Nordoff had been raised in California. They distrusted each other at first, but their opposite natures were complementary and they eventually became the best of friends. Nordhoff convinced Hall that Tahiti was the place to go and write. When the *Atlantic* assigned them a piece on Tahiti and gave them an advance, they were on their way to the South Seas.

Years later, Tahiti had become their home. An outpouring of articles and books by the two ensued. They wrote some works separately, but continued to work well as a team, and after they collaborated on a boy's adventure, Nordhoff proposed doing another book in the same vein. Hall refused, but instead suggested an idea that was to become the most famous seagoing novel written in the 20th century— *Mutiny on the Bounty*.

During their initial research Nordhoff and Hall could scarcely believe that the most recent book on the *Bounty* incident had been published in 1831! No one had ventured to write a fictionalized account of the event even though it was the kind of story that begs to be transformed into literature. Based at the Aina Parè hotel in Papeete, the two writers plunged into their work. From the British Museum they procured accounts of the voyage, the mutiny, Bligh's open-sea voyage and the bloody Pitcairn experience, along with copies of the court martial proceedings and the Admiralty blueprints of the *Bounty*. Both immersed themselves in 19th-century prose, which helped to set a common style. The resulting narrative was divided into three sections: the *Mutiny On the Bounty*, *Men Against the Sea* (Bligh's open-sea voyage) and *Pitcairn Island* (the adventures of Fletcher Christian, his mutineer cohorts and the Tahitians who accompanied them). The trilogy was completed in 1934, after five years of work. Fifty years and three cinematic versions later, the story still hasn't lost its charm and fascination.

Hall is buried facing Matavai Bay where the *Bounty* dropped anchor and where he and Nordhoff used to sit discussing their work. A bronze plaque on the grave is inscribed with a poem he wrote as a young boy:

> "Look to the Northward, stranger
> Just over the hillside, there
> Have you in your travels seen
> A land more passing fair?"

Lodging Index

Dining Index

Index

HIDDEN GUIDES

Adventure travel or a relaxing vacation?—"Hidden" guidebooks are the only travel books in the business to provide detailed information on both. Aimed at environmentally aware travelers, our motto is "Adventure Travel Plus." These books combine details on unique hotels, restaurants and sightseeing with information on camping, sports and hiking for the outdoor enthusiast.

THE NEW KEY GUIDES

Based on the concept of ecotourism, The New Key Guides are dedicated to the preservation of Central America's rare and endangered species, architecture and archaeology. Filled with helpful tips, they give travelers everything they need to know about these exotic destinations.

ULTIMATE FAMILY GUIDES

These innovative guides present the best and most unique features of a family destination. Quality is the keynote. In addition to thoroughly covering each destination, they feature short articles and one-line "teasers" that are both fun and informative.

Order Form

Ulysses Press books are available at bookstores everywhere. If any of the following titles are unavailable at your local bookstore, ask the bookseller to order them. Or you can order them directly from Ulysses Press (P.O. Box 3440, Berkeley, CA 94703; 510-601-8301, 800-377-2542, fax: 510-601-8307).

HIDDEN GUIDEBOOKS

____ Hidden Boston and Cape Cod, $9.95

____ Hidden Carolinas, $15.95

____ Hidden Coast of California, $15.95

____ Hidden Colorado, $13.95

____ Hidden Florida, $15.95

____ Hidden Florida Keys and Everglades, $9.95

____ Hidden Hawaii, $16.95

____ Hidden Idaho, $13.95

____ Hidden Maui, $12.95

____ Hidden Montana, $12.95

____ Hidden New England, $16.95

____ Hidden Oregon, $12.95

____ Hidden Pacific Northwest, $16.95

____ Hidden Rockies, $16.95

____ Hidden San Francisco and Northern California, $15.95

____ Hidden Southern California, $16.95

____ Hidden Southwest, $16.95

____ Hidden Tahiti $16.95

____ Hidden Wyoming $12.95

THE NEW KEY GUIDEBOOKS

____ The New Key to Belize, $14.95

____ The New Key to Cancún and the Yucatán, $14.95

____ The New Key to Costa Rica, $16.95

____ The New Key to Ecuador and the Galápagos, $15.95

____ The New Key to Guatemala, $14.95

ULTIMATE FAMILY GUIDEBOOKS

____ Disneyland and Beyond, $12.95

____ Disney World and Beyond, $12.95

Mark the book(s) you're ordering and enter the total cost here ⇨ [   ]

California residents add 8% sales tax here ⇨ [   ]

Shipping, check box for your preferred method and enter cost here ⇨ [   ]

❑ Book Rate   **FREE! FREE! FREE!**

❑ Priority Mail $3.00 First book, $1.00/each additional book

❑ UPS 2-Day Air $7.00 First book, $1.00/each additional book

[   ]

Billing, enter total amount due here and check method of payment ⇨

❑ Check   ❑ Money Order

❑ VISA/MasterCard _____Exp. Date _____

Name _____Phone _____

Address _____

_____

City_____ State _____ Zip _____

Money-back guarantee on direct orders placed through Ulysses Press.

ABOUT THE AUTHOR

ROB KAY, a native Californian, lived in Tahiti where he covered French Polynesia for *Pacific News Service*, NBC radio, *New Pacific* and the *San Francisco Chronicle*. Wishing to see more of the Pacific, he signed on as a tour guide for French Polynesia, Fiji, Tonga, American Samoa and Western Samoa. His feature articles on the region have appeared in *Newsday*, the *Los Angeles Times*, the *Arizona Republic*, the *Philadelphia Inquirer*, the *San Diego Tribune* and *Islands* magazine. Rob continues to travel frequently in the Pacific from a home-base in Honolulu, Hawaii.

ABOUT THE PHOTOGRAPHER

ANDI MARTIN and her photographer husband Butch Martin have traveled extensively in pursuit of their freelance careers. As bona fide island lovers, the couple have long been attracted to the lure of the South Pacific. They have visited Fiji and the islands of French Polynesia. They were drawn to the remote Tuamotus for a more traditional glimpse into Tahitian life. The photo team resides and works in New York City.